# MEASURES
## OF LEADERSHIP

# Measures
# of Leadership

*Edited by*

## Kenneth E. Clark & Miriam B. Clark

*with the collaboration of*

Robert R. Albright II
Herbert F. Barber
Bernard M. Bass
V. Jon Bentz
Douglas W. Bray
W. Warner Burke
David P. Campbell
William H. Clover
Robert A. Cooke
Dan Fazzini
Harrison G. Gough
Peter Gratzinger
Hal W. Hendrick
Robert Hogan
Edwin P. Hollander
Ann Howard
T. Owen Jacobs
Elliott Jaques
Frances A. Karnes
James M. Kouzes
Richard Lepsinger
Michael M. Lombardo
Karen S. Lyness
Cynthia D. McCauley
Mary H. McCaulley

Ira J. Morrow
Joseph L. Moses
Robert Most
Lynn R. Offermann
Donal O'Hare
Patricia J. Ohlott
Diana B. Osborn
T. Noel Osborn
Barry Z. Posner
Earl H. Potter III
Robert Raskin
Marian N. Ruderman
Marshall Sashkin
Frank Shipper
C. Paul Sparks
Mel Stern
Robert J. Sternberg
Anna Marie Valerio
Ellen Van Velsor
Steve Wall
Ronald A. Warren
Richard K. Wagner
Clark L. Wilson
Francis J. Yammarino
Gary Yukl

A CENTER FOR CREATIVE LEADERSHIP BOOK
*Greensboro, North Carolina*

*Published by*
LEADERSHIP LIBRARY OF AMERICA, INC.
*West Orange, New Jersey*

**Library of Congress Cataloging-in-Publication Data**

Measures of leadership / edited by Kenneth E. Clark, Miriam B. Clark.

    Papers presented at a conference held at San Antonio, Tex., Oct. 1988, sponsored by the Center for Creative Leadership and the Psychological Corp.

    "A Center for Creative Leadership book."

    ISBN 1-878435-00-0 : $59.50

    1. Leadership—Congresses. I. Clark, Kenneth E. II. Clark, Miriam B. III. Center for Creative Leadership. IV. Psychological Corporation.

BF637.L4m43   1990

158'.4—dc20                             90-32042

                                               CIP

© Copyright 1990 by  **CENTER FOR CREATIVE LEADERSHIP**
                          5000 Laurinda Drive
                          Post Office Box P-1
                          Greensboro, North Carolina 27402-1660

ISBN 1-878435-00-0

Project directed by    **Judy Rock Allen**

Designed by    **Susan S. Lampton**

Typesetting by    **Rossel Computer Consulting, Inc.**
                          Dallas, Texas

Published by    **LEADERSHIP LIBRARY OF AMERICA, INC.**
                          235 Watchung Avenue
                          West Orange, New Jersey 07052

This book is dedicated to

**H. Smith Richardson, Jr.**

without whose leadership and determination
neither the Center for Creative Leadership
nor this volume would exist today.

# Foreword

Two organizations, founded on the belief that empirical research can separate fact from fiction in the field of leadership, are the Center for Creative Leadership and the Psychological Corporation. Their presidents join in introducing this volume.

## Center for Creative Leadership

The Center for Creative Leadership and the Psychological Corporation sponsored in October 1988 a conference that brought together a critical mass of leading theoreticians and practitioners in the behavioral science and related fields. These were strong personalities made stronger by a lifetime of labor within their disciplines. This gathering in San Antonio addressed the subject of leadership in a wonderfully broad yet rigorous context. This book, *Measures of Leadership*, edited with great diligence, creativity, and clear mastery of the subject matter by Kenneth and Miriam Clark and made rich and robust with original papers and candid commentary by participants is one specific outcome of that conference. You will find here a diverse menu that will appeal to a wide range of appetites.

As we enter the 21st century our fascination with leaders and leadership continues. More and more during the last decade we have been rediscovering the enormous power of motivation and reexamining the role and mode of leaders in stimulating and focusing human potential. Although our attention to environments and methods which nourish individual and team productivity in organizations derives in part from an accelerated academic and popular interest in human behavior, part of the outpouring of treatises on leadership and management is simply a pragmatic response to demand. Of late our productivity has slipped and we need an injection to stimulate efficiency.

From the papers and people assembled in San Antonio came a flood of best practice ideas and arguments. The topics reached across a wide band: The essential purpose of leadership. The role of leaders in society. Nature and nurture. Style, learned behaviors, patterns of success and failure within organizations—and the definitions of "success." The nature and environments for learning. The difficulty of establishing criteria for effectiveness. The importance of intelligence and the continuing quest to capture the essence of the processes and abilities which might constitute "intelligence." An early identification of talent. The importance of "personality," the double-edged sword of charisma. The creation and use of survey instruments to determine preferences and tendencies. Social and professional responsibility. Probes, data analyses, excursions, comparisons, doubts, models, revisions, and inspirations!

Within this volume there is fertile ground for the apprentice to explore and the knowledgeable scholar to critique and nourish. The studies in the later chapters will be exciting for students, senior scientists, and human resources specialists, as well as those practicing managers who are amenable to honing their skills on the solid foundation of reputable works. There is here both an introduction and review of behavioral science methodology as well as cutting edge adventures into practice. The editors and contributors have produced a rare public integration and examination of a contemporary, scientific activity. This is an "insiders' " look, designed for all of us, pulling no punches, making no false promises.

The linkages between theory and practice portrayed here, this bridge between conceptual launchings and useful tools, represent a main theme of both the Center for Creative Leadership and the Psychological Corporation: translating and making learnings accessible and comprehensible. And, hopefully, in a digestible—if challenging—format.

This book and others of its type—products of lengthy study, vigorous debate, considerable hard work, and a lot of heart—are intended as meaningful contributions toward the attainment of the noblest goals of our society. One small step in a world that needs all the best each of us can deliver.

**Walter F. Ulmer, Jr.**
President, Center for Creative Leadership
September 1989

*The Center for Creative Leadership is a nonprofit educational institution founded in 1970 in Greensboro, North Carolina. Its mission is to encourage and develop creative leadership and effective management for the good of society overall.*

*The mission is accomplished through research, training, and publication—with emphasis on the widespread, innovative application of the behavioral sciences to the challenges facing the leaders of today and tomorrow.*

## The Psychological Corporation

*Measures of Leadership* is an outgrowth of a conference held in San Antonio designed to examine whether we can identify and measure the traits and behaviors that make leaders effective. The consensus of the research and data in the 29 different investigations presented at the conference, and included in this volume, is that we can indeed identify and measure the traits and behaviors of effective leaders.

With that as a first step, we now need to investigate how we can teach those traits and behaviors and thereby increase the pool of qualified candidates for leadership roles. How we go about increasing the number of candidates for leadership roles is a central issue for education in the United States today. How we solve this pressing issue may ultimately determine whether the United States maintains its leadership role in the international community.

Effective leaders manifest traits and behaviors that are universally respected. We recognize that exemplary leaders are trustworthy and dynamic. They have the capacity not only to take the long view but also to inspire others to share their vision. By modeling the way with courage, ambition, and confidence, they help followers and subordinates to implement that vision. They encourage others to accept responsibility and persuade them to grapple with challenges.

How can these traits and behaviors best be taught? Perhaps this key question is the proper topic for the next conference and the next volume in this series on leadership.

Kenneth and Miriam Clark did a superb job of organizing the San Antonio conference and editing this volume. With vision, insight, wisdom, and patience, buttressed by a lifetime of firsthand experience in the field of leadership, they have provided an excellent synthesis of what we know today about measuring leadership traits and behaviors. Let us hope the Clarks will be our mentors and guides as we next explore how leadership can best be taught.

**Thomas A. Williamson**
President, The Psychological Corporation (1982—1988)
September 1989

*The Psychological Corporation, the nation's oldest and largest commercial test publisher, publishes tests for education, psychological assessment, admissions and credentialing, and business, industry, and government. The Psychological Corporation is a subsidiary of Harcourt Brace Jovanovich, Inc.*

*The Psychological Corporation: (1) provides the nation's schools with testing programs designed to give teachers, administrators, and parents information about student achievement and instructional needs; (2) sets the standard for psychological assessment instruments; (3) provides tests for use in business, industry, and government; and (4) offers specialized tests designed to qualify candidates for professional and technical school admissions and scholarships.*

*Committed to innovation and excellence, the Psychological Corporation is dedicated to expanding the horizons of the testing industry.*

# Preface

How do leaders help organizations accomplish more, help members work together, and somehow inspire everyone to achieve? The answer to any organizational problem is to find better leaders: leaders who inspire, leaders who motivate followers, leaders who challenge them to join in a common mission. The frequently voiced lament is, "What we need are better leaders!"

The past 20 years have seen a surge of interest and activity directed toward improving the quality of management and leadership. In America and abroad, large investments have been made in education and training, in methods of selection, and in analysis of organizational systems and processes. Great faith is placed in these efforts. They are supposed to make a difference. Do they?

A growing number of investigators have been collecting data on the effects of such efforts. This volume reports their findings. Studies are of managers and leaders. The word *leadership* is used in the title of this book because we direct attention to ways in which subordinates, members, or citizens begin to behave as followers committed to the cause when bosses, officers, or elected officials perform more like leaders. Only when people are persuaded do they show a willingness to be led and to give more of themselves. The lack of persuasive leaders diminishes a community or a society.

This book is not full of anecdotes. It is full of stories—too many to tell. Most of them are implicit: for example, what happened when 79 managers experienced training in leadership; what were the effects on profits the next year? What about the report that the young Navy officers who won competitions in the fleet could have been picked out as Academy cadets? How about the dismaying information that three out of four successful managers could not adapt enough to help their organization through a major takeover effort, or a major divestiture of part of the organization?

This book is laden with information about the final effects of good choices, good training programs, and good and poor decisions about people. It also describes in detail the procedures that were followed to find better leaders and to obtain desired results. This is new information; much of what is reported has not been generally available. Particularly, it has not been available to organizations too small or too young or too specialized to have been able to conduct massive studies on their own. To all of the entrepreneurs in the world, this book will be revealing.

Twenty-nine authors or teams of authors and two editors have written this book. The editors wrote the first nine chapters. All of the reports in Part II are the products of the authors. The book is based on a Conference on Psychological Measures and Leadership at which the research reports were discussed. The report of conference proceedings in Part III was written by Miriam B. Clark. Eighty-four persons attended the conference. All of them aided in one way or another in the completion of this book. Their names are listed in Part III.

A number of persons gave critical reading to the manuscript during its preparation. We owe a debt to John S. Bowen, Marvin D. Dunnette, John Forsyth, Robert Kaplan, Harold Kent, Morgan McCall, and Forrest L. Vance. However, the responsibility for the first nine chapters, as finally published, lies with the editors.

A project of this sort is ultimately a team effort. We are grateful to Martha Hughes, Ellen Van Velsor, and Eileene Homan for their management of the conference and their efforts to assure a good record of it; to Elizabeth Cunningham for her indexing skills; to Lynn M. Bemer for her proofreading ability; and to Judy Rock Allen and Ellen Hamman a special thanks for their invaluable aid in putting words to paper and assuring ultimate accuracy. We owe a debt to the Center for Creative Leadership and the Psychological Corporation for making the conference possible by their sponsorship, and to the nine corporations who helped share the costs of the conference. Most of all, we owe a great debt to those who attended the conference and illuminated issues so well, and to the authors of the 29 studies who have written the truly important parts of this book.

**K.E.C.** and **M.B.C.**

# Contents

**Foreword**                                    **vii**
Walter F. Ulmer, Jr., and Thomas A. Williamson

**Preface**                                      **xi**
Kenneth E. Clark and Miriam B. Clark

## Part I

**Chapter One**                                 **3**
Introduction

**Chapter Two**                               **11**
Preparing for Leadership: Yesterday and Today

**Chapter Three**                             **17**
Psychology and the Study of Leadership

**Chapter Four**                              **23**
Using Measurement to Become Objective

**Chapter Five**                               **35**
The Many Ways to Study Leadership

**Chapter Six**                               **43**
Developing Measures to Describe Leadership and
   to Select Leaders

**Chapter Seven**                            **49**
Personality Measures and Leadership

**Chapter Eight**                            **57**
Validation—The Ultimate Test

**Chapter Nine**                             **69**
Translating Knowledge Into Action

# Part II

*Section A*

## A REVIEW OF PRIOR SCHOLARLY RESEARCH IN LEADERSHIP      79

**Relational Features of Organizational Leadership and Followership**      83
Edwin P. Hollander and Lynn R. Offermann

*Section B*

## PSYCHOLOGICAL MEASUREMENTS IN LONG-TERM PREDICTION AND ASSESSMENT STUDIES      99

**Testing for Management Potential**      103
C. Paul Sparks

**Predictions of Managerial Success Over Long Periods of Time: Lessons From the Management Progress Study**      113
Ann Howard and Douglas W. Bray

**Contextual Issues in Predicting High-Level Leadership Performance: Contextual Richness as a Criterion Consideration in Personality Research with Executives**      131
V. Jon Bentz

*Section C*

## MEASURES OF LEADERSHIP AS INSPIRATION AND INFLUENCE      145

**Long-Term Forecasting of Transformational Leadership and Its Effects Among Naval Officers: Some Preliminary Findings**      151
Francis J. Yammarino and Bernard M. Bass

**Transformational Leaders: Team Performance, Leadership Ratings, and Firsthand Impressions**      171
William H. Clover

**Task Cycle Theory: The Processes of Influence**      185
Clark L. Wilson, Donal O'Hare, and Frank Shipper

Leadership Practices:  An Alternative to the    **205**
Psychological Perspective
Barry Z. Posner and James M. Kouzes

*Section D*
## MEASURES OF LEADER AND MANAGER BEHAVIOR   **217**

Preliminary Report on Validation of The Managerial    **223**
Practices Survey
Gary Yukl, Steve Wall, and Richard Lepsinger

Psychological Orientations and Leadership:    **239**
Thinking Styles That Differentiate Between
Effective and Ineffective Managers
Peter D. Gratzinger, Ronald A. Warren, and Robert A. Cooke

The Campbell Work Orientations Surveys:    **249**
Their Use to Capture the Characteristics of Leaders
David P. Campbell

*Section E*
## LEADERSHIP AT THE TOP OF AN ORGANIZATION   **275**

Military Executive Leadership    **281**
T. Owen Jacobs and Elliott Jaques

Understanding and Assessing Organizational    **297**
Leadership
Marshall Sashkin and W. Warner Burke

Leadership Behavior in Ambiguous Environments    **327**
Joseph L. Moses and Karen S. Lyness

*Section F*
## PERSONALITY AND LEADERSHIP   **337**

The Dark Side of Charisma    **343**
Robert Hogan, Robert Raskin, and Dan Fazzini

Testing for Leadership with the California    **355**
Psychological Inventory
Harrison G. Gough

The Myers-Briggs Type Indicator and Leadership    **381**
Mary H. McCaulley

Stars, Adversaries, Producers, and Phantoms at Work:            419
   A New Leadership Typology
   Ira J. Morrow and Mel Stern

Some Personality Characteristics of Senior Military           441
   Officers
   Herbert F. Barber

Leadership in Latin American Organizations:                   449
   A Glimpse of Styles Through Personality Measures
   T. Noel Osborn and Diana B. Osborn

## Section G
# INTELLECTUAL QUALITIES OF LEADERS     455

Hypotheses About the Relationship Between                     459
   Leadership and Intelligence
   Robert Most

Predicting Performance During the Apprenticeship              465
   Earl H. Potter III and Robert R. Albright II

Intellectual Styles                                          481
   Robert J. Sternberg

Street Smarts                                               493
   Richard K. Wagner and Robert J. Sternberg

## Section H
# DEVELOPMENT OF LEADERSHIP     505

Perceptual Accuracy of Self and Others and                    511
   Leadership Status As Functions of Cognitive
   Complexity
   Hal W. Hendrick

A Study of the Developmental Experiences of                   521
   Managers
   Anna Marie Valerio

BENCHMARKS: An Instrument for Diagnosing                      535
   Managerial Strengths and Weaknesses
   Cynthia D. McCauley and Michael M. Lombardo

**Assessing Opportunities for Leadership Development**   547
Marian N. Ruderman, Patricia J. Ohlott, and
Cynthia D. McCauley

**Leadership and Youth: A Commitment**   563
Frances A. Karnes

# Part III

**Proceedings of the San Antonio Conference**   569
**on Psychological Measures and Leadership**


**List of Participants**   607
**Subject Index**   617
**Index of Measures and Scales**   629

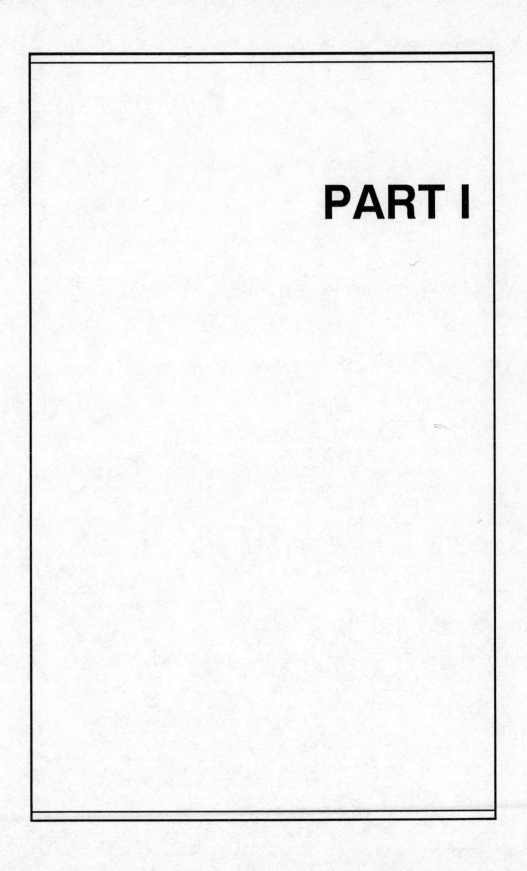

# PART I

# CHAPTER ONE

# Introduction

Whether we want to become leaders ourselves or want to set the right leaders in place, most of us spend a large part of our lives thinking about leadership and worrying about how to get better leaders. When we were children our parents exhorted us to work hard so that we might become leaders. On the school playground we hoped the other kids would point at us and yell, "Captain," or we would try to be selected by the captain we most admired. As adults we wonder whether we will get that prized promotion and become the boss, or we puzzle over which boss we would rather work for—or which candidate to vote for—or which leader would be most likely to grab hold and do what needs to be done.

In schools every day, teachers work to develop the potential of students, hoping some of them will someday lead. Business executives search for those employees who have the talent to climb the corporate ladder successfully. Civic-minded persons spend hours deciding how to choose the appropriate people to provide continuity and growth to worthwhile endeavors. Political parties debate endlessly about whether they have substantial and saleable candidates. Countries worry about their leaders' ability to maintain peace and insure prosperity and about their generals' ability to defend effectively. Villages, towns, and cities worry about how to select representatives who will be able to act for the group and cope with their problems.

Thousands of search committees are being formed every week to seek the best, the most visionary, the most endurable, the "right one" for a group or organization that needs a head. Personnel organizations flourish, and "head-hunting" firms have become almost as great a necessity as paramedics. When problems multiply, interest in leadership swells. As differences within a group spread and become irreconcilable or as problems with external forces become unmanageable, the role of the leader becomes critical and choice of the wrong leader can be disastrous. Even today the words *Il Duce* and *Der Fuhrer* continue to arouse universal revulsion. Many an organization has made errors less egregious for which they have paid dearly.

The past forty years have seen an outpouring of creative writing and analysis about leadership and management. Many excellent books have captured public attention as American executives and managers have faced the necessity of changing their ways to respond to international competition and to changing conditions in this country. There has been no lack of advice, no shortage of analyses of where past leadership erred. With each new wave of publications a new set of prescriptions is provided.

## How Does This Book Differ?

The enormous literature on leadership and management has produced fascinating insights into the effects of leadership acts of different sorts. The wise actions taken by many prominent persons have been well documented. Sets of principles have been developed and put into shorthand so that the busy manager can remember them. The topic does not lack for creative and original ideas.

Everyone who has contributed to this book owes an enormous debt to those who have studied leadership and leaders and organizations in the past. This book rests on prior work as much as it does on the work described in it. The important earlier contributions of R. M. Stogdill, H. Mintzberg, C. L. Shartle, J. K. Hemphill, E. A. Fleishman, J. P. Guilford, E. E. Ghiselli, H. A. Simon, J. M. Burns, J. Kotter, F. Herzberg, H. Levinson, F. E. Fiedler, J. Gardner, A. Zaleznik, D. Katz and J. P. Campbell, M. D. Dunnette, E. E. Lawler, and K. E. Weick are not as well known as they should be. It seems teams are better publicized: Hersey and Blanchard, Bennis and Nanus, Peters and Waterman, Peters and Austin, Blake and Mouton, and Vroom and Yetton. These lists only sample a very large group; there is in addition the list of investigators who wrote parts of this book, many of whom have already made important contributions.

For the most part, this book does not attempt to repeat or to clarify these prior contributions. Rather, it reports what happens when an organization adopts a principle or a set of ideas and puts them into practice. The idea is tested, its value determined, and the limits of its usefulness defined. The intent is to put into the hands of leaders and managers a set of procedures that will enhance their efforts to identify and develop even better leaders and managers. Those organizations that adopt tested practices will gain an advantage over those which do not. Their workers will be more productive and more satisfied in their work, and their followers will be more committed to the purposes of the organization.

The work reviewed in this book uses methods of psychological measurement to identify and to understand the nature of leadership talent and leadership behavior. As Edward Lee Thorndike put it, "Whatever exists, exists in some amount. To measure it is simply to know its varying amounts." Psychologists with an interest in measurement start with the assumption that all human characteristics can be measured and that behavior can be understood better if measures are developed. Many of them have accepted the challenge to address issues of leadership.

Psychological measurement involves the use of tests, inventories, questionnaires, and rating methods to collect and analyze data on individuals or groups of individuals.

The advantage of using such measures lies in the ability to collect data on large numbers of persons and to have data on record for each person that can be compared with other data. Compiling the data by organizations aids in the analysis. Differences in background can be assessed, as can many other influences. The heart of the matter lies in asking the right questions and measuring the right variables.

The use of psychological measures is not the only emphasis in this book. Developing measures also requires clear thinking about concepts of leadership and a great deal of basic knowledge about how humans develop and how they behave in different circumstances. A good theory, in other words, is essential. Also essential is the collection of data from a large enough group to test the generality of any theory or method. In this book, every concept and every measure that is presented has been put to some type of test.

This book deals with some of the following problems. How can we increase the number of well-prepared candidates for leadership roles? How can we describe and measure the behaviors that make leaders effective? Can we develop better concepts pertaining to leadership, so that we may understand the phenomenon better? How can we find those leaders who truly make a difference in effectiveness, or in productivity, or in profitability, or in improving the climate of an organization? Can we teach others to be equally effective? How? Can we discern the changing demands on leaders at different levels, so that we may select and develop them more effectively?

Many people helped write this book. In these first chapters we will name many of them and cite their work and report their ideas. Many of those cited have written full reports of their studies that are included in Part II. They and other investigators have important things to say and answers to many pertinent questions; for example:

**Can leadership be learned; can it be taught?** "Yes," say Clark Wilson, Donal O'Hare, and Frank Shipper, "if what you mean by leadership is the ability to make a group more effective, more productive, and, if in business, more profitable."

"Yes," say Michael Lombardo and Cynthia McCauley, "if one looks at the way experience teaches. Persons in managerial positions change as a result of their assignments, their disasters, and their successes."

"Yes," says Barry Posner. "And like any other skill it is normally distributed in the population. Some have more or less at birth, but all can increase their ability to lead."

William Rosenbach states that the more important part of the question is, Can leadership be learned? "It is an important distinction because it has implications for the many people who sincerely are attempting to learn, from youth to senior executives."

**Do special leadership qualities make a difference in work performance of persons in managerial positions?** "Yes," say Francis Yammarino and Bernard Bass. They compared later performance of U.S. Navy Officers in the fleet with their leadership qualities that had been assessed five years earlier at the Naval Academy.

"Yes," says Clark Wilson. He reports better outcomes from teams with better-trained leaders in a bank, in a health care organization, in a nuclear power plant, and in a Veterans Administration (VA) installation.

**Do "transformational" leaders really exist, and do they make a difference?** "Yes, they exist, and yes, they make a difference on the job," say Francis Yammarino and Bernard Bass. Naval Academy graduates rated high on "transformational qualities," including charisma and being inspirational, had subordinates who expressed higher satisfaction with their work in the unit, and expended more energy on the job.

"Yes," say Marshall Sashkin and Warner Burke, who have differentiated transactional and transformational leaders, found differences in performance, and studied the needs for different types of leaders at different levels of organizations.

"Transformational leaders exist and they make a difference," reports William Rosenbach. "My study of 476 business executives, fire service executives, and church leaders [presented at the XXIV International Congress of Psychology, Sydney, Australia, 1988] shows that leaders in all these groups who were rated as strong transformational leaders by their subordinates were also effective transactional leaders."

**Are mental abilities critical in jobs at the top levels?** "Yes," say Owen Jacobs and Elliott Jaques. The cognitive requirements are much greater than we often assume. Conceptual issues cover wider domains, there is more extraorganizational involvement, and the time span of planning expands. Problem-solving abilities of the highest order are required.

**Should we continue to give tests to managers on a regular basis?** "No, we don't need to, if our only emphasis is prediction," says Paul Sparks. He found that tests administered early in the career still would sort out those who would be promoted to the highest levels from those who would not quite make it.

"Yes, if we want to see how much they have changed and developed," say Ann Howard and Douglas Bray. They found that managers' abilities and motivations change somewhat with experience. A key variable that affected career progress was associated with success: the more successful ones become more caught up in their work; the less successful begin to detach.

**Isn't "Dominance" still considered the best way to describe the leader? A leader, after all, must be a "take-charge" person.** "Yes and no," says Harrison Gough. "High scores on the Dominance scale of my California Psychological Inventory [CPI] differentiate high-rated leaders from other persons better than any single scale. But leaders must operate in the context of their organizations, and must behave differently in terms of circumstances. Case studies have also revealed instances of too much dominance, where the other essential qualities are subordinated to or are overshadowed by an all-pervasive desire to control. Thus, even for the CPI Dominance scale, exceptionally high scores may be as indicative of negative as of positive potentiality for leadership."

"The question is too simple," says Mary McCaulley. "Our Myers-Briggs Type Indicator data show that extraverts are more likely to be seen as dominant, but that introverts are frequently found in leadership positions. Our data also show that management and leadership groups have a TJ bias toward people who prefer rapid, analytical decisions."

**Do these studies support the trend toward participative management?** There is little evidence either way. One point of great interest is that several studies find that subordinates are better judges of the "transformational" qualities of their immediate bosses than were those to whom the bosses reported. See the reports in Part II by Yammarino and Bass, and by Wilson, O'Hare, and Shipper.

**Do your methods allow you to show whether any practices make much difference in things that count, like earnings or performance of a unit?** "Yes," say Wilson, O'Hare, and Shipper. "Read our study!"

"Yes," say Yammarino and Bass. "Read our study!"

"Yes," reports Rosenbach. "Whether they are business executives, university administrators, fire or police chiefs, or church pastors, we found that 'better' practices led to better results, as measured against what their organizations considered important in terms of performance."

These questions and answers provide only a glimpse of a complicated picture of leadership. They are included at this point to assure you that this is not a technical report dealing in obscure language with inconsequential issues. Hundreds of organizations have participated in studies of the sort we report, and they use the results to improve their productivity.

## Authors of the Research Papers

The authors of the studies herein reported are mainly psychologists, especially psychologists interested in the use of methods of measurement for studying people and their organizations. In this book we restrict ourselves mostly to sources based on the work of these authors and to their studies that involve directly or indirectly some form of psychological measurement.

The persons who conducted the studies are well-trained behavioral scientists. Their papers were read and discussed by their colleagues at an invitational conference held in San Antonio, Texas, in October 1988. Many of the papers were revised on the basis of that discussion. The conference was sponsored by the Center for Creative Leadership and The Psychological Corporation. A number of corporations assisted in the enterprise financially and sent senior officers to the conference to participate. A list of participants and of cooperating corporations is appended to Part III, The Conference Proceedings.

This book contains reports, each of which started with a question, a concept, or a hypothesis; developed a way to address the issue; and then collected and analyzed data to provide answers or, at least, illumination. Sometimes a study involved a small number of persons in one or two organizations, sometimes a study involved a large number of organizations, and once in a while data were collected on thousands of persons in many organizations. The research reports are worth careful study. The principles developed from these studies will be taught for years to come.

The authors of these research studies include some who occupy leading roles in the field as well as a number who, with this volume, join their ranks. These authors were not invited to submit papers to the conference merely because they wrote well about leadership, although most of them do. Rather, it is the research they have completed, the data they have collected on numbers of people, their curiosity about the subject, and their consequent productivity concerning it that distinguishes them as outstanding.

Their written studies in this book stand by themselves as support for the ideas they endorse. If people study the results and are stimulated to change their practices for better ones, the authors will feel fulfilled. If the accomplishments of organizations increase and leadership improves as a result, their hopes will be fulfilled.

Many of the investigators reporting in this book are active participants in private sector organizations; they have seen some organizations work well, and they have seen some deteriorate and require attention. They have observed outstanding leaders and, on occasion, some terrible ones. These authors are not all ivory-tower scholars; they have worked as employees, consultants, volunteers, and sometimes as leaders of the organizations they have sought to improve. They become impatient at generalizations based on one case and begin to trust their own findings only when they are based on sufficient numbers of observations.

Names of some persons or organizations may be familiar: Jon Bentz of Sears, Paul Sparks of Exxon, Douglas Bray and Ann Howard of AT&T. Some test instruments may be more familiar than the names of the persons responsible for them: Harrison Gough of the California Psychological Inventory (CPI), Mary McCaulley of the Myers-Briggs Type Indicator (MBTI), David Campbell of the Strong-Campbell Interest Inventory (SCII) and also of the new Campbell Work Orientations Surveys (CWO). Some institutions are well known: the U.S. Army, the Air Force Academy, the Coast Guard, the Center for Creative Leadership. You may find, however, that the study you find most creative, stimulating, and helpful to you may have been done by none of these persons and involve none of these organizations. Good ideas and new discoveries may come from any source.

## How This Book Is Organized

Part I of this volume was written by the two editors after the San Antonio Conference concluded. Its purpose is to provide an introduction to the subject, to summarize certain topics, to present general conclusions, and to provide a basis for reading the reports in Part II. First, the whole area of leadership identification and development is put into the perspective of a free and open society (Chapter Two). A description of the growth of psychological research activities in applied settings comprises Chapter Three. Some of the issues surrounding definitions of leadership are introduced. Chapter Four describes how measurement psychologists develop measures, collect and analyze data, and come to conclusions. Chapters Five through Nine deal with the issues raised by the participants in the San Antonio Conference. The names that will appear in the review of topics will be for the most part those of the authors of the research papers prepared for the conference, whose efforts and whose insights make this volume useful. These reports appear in Part II.

In Section A of Part II, Edwin Hollander and Lynn Offermann summarize the broader field of research in leadership and followership and provide a background for the studies reported in Part II. This paper reviews the published literature in the behavioral sciences that deals with leadership and followership, covering both academic and applied psychology.

Every effort has been made to make the content of these chapters true reflections of the best judgments of the conferees about the state of the art in leadership studies. A draft of each chapter was sent to each participant for suggestions; whenever appropriate, the actual words of participants and their comments are included. This is especially true in Part III of the book.

Part II presents the papers that provided the basis for discussion at the conference. These papers were written before the conference, distributed to conferees three weeks in advance, and then revised and/or edited after the conference. The way in which results from each study help form a base for understanding leadership and what it means is left to each author to elaborate. Papers are presented in sections with a brief introduction for each section to aid in understanding their interrelationships.

The Conference Proceedings in Part III provide a running account of the conference as it proceeded—not so much as a way of reviewing the status of knowledge about leadership as to help students in the field understand the level of concerns of leading investigators about domains to be studied and areas that need to be addressed. Part III concludes with the list of participants in the conference.

This book is addressed to that large number of persons concerned about finding and supporting excellent leaders, whose responsibilities and obligations require them to play some role in this process. We hope that readers of this book will find guidance in this book that will aid their efforts. We expect that this volume will prove useful to specialists in the field of leadership research and to their students, for it assembles a diverse set of studies and data that include some sources hitherto unavailable and some studies that have just been completed or are still under way. It is also our hope that a report of the current findings will stimulate efforts to augment what is now known. We especially hope that persons in the behavioral sciences who have not heretofore considered their work relevant to a better understanding of the nature of leadership in our society will read these reports and discover they do indeed have important, relevant contributions to make.

We encourage you to read and study each of the research reports included. Each tells its own story. Each is interesting in its own right. The reports are written in the style used with scientific colleagues and may be less dramatic as a consequence, but the findings as a result have no less potential for general use. The ability to use an important finding requires being well informed about the methods that were used, how well they worked, the populations on which they were tested, and the conditions that applied. These reports incorporate all of these essential requirements. The findings still have their limits; observing them and acknowledging them is critical if practice is to improve.

# CHAPTER TWO

# Preparing for Leadership: Yesterday and Today

Issues about leaders and leadership rise periodically in societies; they seem today to be particularly salient. We may err by taking too short-range a view of the kind of leaders we need. Societies that provide for elections, that do not require a given heritage for leadership, and that encourage each person to pursue that farthest star may differ in their needs and requirements for leaders. Only one element appears to remain common across the ages: those we choose as leaders or those foisted upon us rarely seem at the time to be the ones we needed or the ones we wanted.

Leaders emerge in every society as people join together for their common good. The quality of their leadership—whether by the strong and powerful, or by the wise, or by those born to the purple, or by those elected or chosen—has been as critical to their progress toward the better life as has been the growing ability to understand the world in which we live. We may feel confident as well that the teachings of the elders of the earliest tribes also included indoctrination in modes of conduct and in respect for the leader. Leaders have been developed successfully in all societies largely through learning to be good followers. Today, one cannot study or understand the processes of leadership in its many variations without examining the relationships leaders have with followers.

As civilization progressed, the young were taught the skills and crafts of the parents. For those youngsters born of a leader or into royalty, training for leadership began almost at birth. Tutors of the best quality were found. No effort was spared. The preparation for later accession to the crown was often broad and arduous. The problems inherent in preparing the talented prince and the not-so-talented prince for the demanding roles ahead are carefully portrayed in Machiavelli's *The Prince*. That volume was a useful guide to leadership and education for its time and still has relevance for the modern era.

For centuries the highest levels of instruction were reserved for the privileged elite, with greatest attention given to those persons of high social and economic status who were expected to lead lives of professional service and leadership. It was from this elite that leaders would come. It was expected that this class would produce more than enough persons with the attributes needed to exercise power and authority and to lead.

Increasing democratization of societies and the fall of monarchies gave greater influence to less privileged segments of society and changed the processes for accession to power. The American republic, for example, was founded on a new set of principles—principles of freedom and equality that gave high priority to opportunity and to the idea of an open society—a society in which any person would be free to seek any goal, with no preferment to any. These were stated as ideals; history has demonstrated that attaining such goals takes a long time.

In the United States, the writers of the American Constitution had known and feared the oppression of tyrants and had seen the excesses that holding unlimited power allows. With a great show of creativity and wisdom, they put together a form of government that would rest on the consent of the governed and, by dividing responsibility for action, would include checks on the power of the federal government. A government was conceived that was under the control of the people, one in which the public would be sufficiently educated to know and to care about public issues, public policies, and decisions made presumably on their behalf. An informed populace was seen as essential. Without informed consent, the republic would become a democracy in name only and might soon become as tyrannical as the regimes whose excesses had caused so many people to take flight. Even such safeguards gave little support to the aspirations of women and minorities, who remain today greatly underrepresented in positions of power and influence.

The challenges that must be accepted by those who lead in open societies are enormous. The widespread mistrust of power, often expressed paradoxically in violent behavior, the abhorrence of special privilege, and the beliefs in the rights of individuals and special groups create an environment in which decision making and the exercise of authority by a leader are incalculably difficult.

Imagine the anguish of a leader who is faced day after day with incredible dilemmas, who is committed to impatient followers imbued with the ideals of democratic processes and dedicated to the equal status of all. If a decision must be made that will displease some, authoritative action may be required. Power must be exerted. The long-range goals of the cause must be served. Think of the qualities required! Gaining acceptance of decisions—not just enforcing them—requires that leaders demonstrate leadership; that is, they must not only be highly intelligent and be able to make wise decisions, but also must be deeply committed to the cause, inspirational, worthy of trust, and in turn respectful and supportive of followers.

How does one educate to assure the necessary wisdom and courage in leaders and understanding and acceptance among followers? Clearly, widespread public schooling to assure literacy and to lay a basis for an informed citizenry is only the beginning of the process of education required in such a society. The task is more formidable when, among those being educated, one cannot distinguish those who need to develop the skills of a leader from those who need to understand the role of loyal followers.

An ideal democracy declares an open competition for all positions. Only duly elected or formally appointed incumbents are authorized to enact laws and govern in the name of the people. The freedom not to follow in one's father's footsteps—critical to establishing an open society—also results in the loss of rights of the eldest son to inherit the father's position of power and authority. So we lose traditional pathways and natural successions. Thus, with the burden for developing leaders resting on all of society, not just on an elite group, major problems develop in devising appropriate educational programs.

Small wonder that education for both leaders and followers has been such a concern in open societies like America. Regardless of the purpose of the group, large or small, public or private, local or national, each needs its own system to identify, select, and develop its leaders.

Democratic societies are still struggling to find an adequate replacement for the royal system of preparing leaders. True, the old system did not prove itself a particularly beneficial way to develop competent leaders, so the loss is slight. Today, college experience is usually viewed as the first introduction to the exercise of leadership— though many who exercise leadership have skipped the process.

More serious is that too few young persons aspire to leadership, or set as a goal becoming a leader or working to develop leadership skills, or acquiring the knowledge, attitudes, and beliefs essential for leadership. College is not viewed by college students as the entry to lives of leadership and service, but rather as a time to become independent of parents and to decide on an occupation to pursue.

Not many American youth go to college today to become leaders. Only in the military academies is the attainment of leadership positions a stated goal. Most of the college population exploit the opportunity to prepare for their lives of work; they want to be engineers, businesspeople, physicians, physicists, TV stars, journalists, teachers or professors, social workers, geologists, actors, chemists, psychologists, economists, historians, or poets. In American colleges, well over half of them will change their minds about their career goals at least once. And sometimes they worry about it to the point of relinquishing their opportunities to learn and know about the world they live in and to digest what teachers and professors offer them. They spend less time than they should chewing on the tough problems that must be solved by concerned citizens if the freedoms they enjoy are to be guaranteed. It is a rare one who consistently or at any given time aspires to take on the responsibilities of a leader.

This is not to claim that going to college to prepare for a life of work is not a noble objective. Vocational education at every level is worthy, and it is the best sort of insurance for future contentment. But too high a proportion of our students (and too many parents) appear to be entirely absorbed in preparing for a career, for the first job, for "making it." Frequently, students are exclusively concerned about finding out who they are, what they can do well, what the best-paying jobs are, what they want to be, how good they will be at it, and whether anyone of the opposite sex sees merit in them (though not necessarily in that order). Many voices of experience say that the college education should prepare the student for promotion, not for the first job. Few young people listen to that word of advice.

Of course, what is missing from this scenario is any sense of obligation on the part of our citizens not only to become competent in the special field of work which they have entered or for which they are preparing, but also to commit themselves to become participants in the many areas that benefit society. For this openness of access to membership and leadership in a democracy engenders another phenomenon, the growth of an extensive structure of independent, freestanding organizations aimed at "doing something" for the local or regional community, or nationally or internationally. These organizations abound especially in America and range from garden clubs to environmental groups, sports and hobby groups, community service clubs, political support groups, religious societies, foreign affairs groups, and thousands upon thousands of others.

The growth of pluralism, ethnicity, and cultural pride is extraordinary and healthy, but it also requires responsible behavior and some training; it calls out for leadership—for literally millions of leaders. One has only to note differences among cultures and countries in the processes of getting support for a new and necessary social advance to realize how quickly one can take for granted many "helping groups" as they arise and how strange a concept it continues to be for many countries. It would be a disaster to overlook the importance of developing leaders with admirable qualities who can be counted on as community and group leaders to serve in many areas essential to a free society.

As we have tried to make clear, if students do not prepare for positions of leadership, a society will suffer. If the schools and colleges do not address the issue, other institutions move in. Past inattention to preparation for leadership is being addressed currently in a variety of ways all over the world. Business, industry, government, community organizations, and foundations, in addition to some selected schools and colleges, are generating programs and courses in leadership and leadership development.

For example, American business is reported to be spending more than $20 billion a year on training. Part of this, to be sure, is to make up for deficiencies in prior schooling, but the main portion goes to prepare employees for more responsible positions. There is growing attention to providing the experiences and the special training that will supply the effective leaders who can stimulate and accommodate to change, a major theme in business and industry today.

Recent observations in America illustrate that some public school systems have begun to incorporate leadership development training and leadership experiences at the precollege level. But these are few, and many are feeble. Most of these activities are built into extracurricular programs; only a few programs are incorporated into the curriculum. Frequently, however, the excuse given for not doing so is that there are too few hours in the day to insert something new or marginal. The question is whether the need for leadership is new; certainly it is not marginal.

In the United States, many state governors have sponsored leadership camps and leadership fellowship programs; many city officials are setting up seminars and discussion groups in an effort to achieve community goals by improving both the quality of governance and the quality of the informed consent of the governed. Surely, all this activity expresses a need. Writers and publishers have been busy as evidenced by titles about leadership and management on the best seller lists. On the nonfiction lists, heroes often are business leaders. The hot sellers of yesterday have yielded to a new set of highly touted methods, exalted personalities, and new formulations for the next round. If the publishers and media are responding to an interest, they must be receiving loud and clear messages.

The call for better leaders and for more effective leadership is also a call for the type of leadership consistent with the values that are dominant today in world societies. The domineering and autocratic leader is no longer tolerated by most followers, who want their needs and interests considered and who wish to be accorded respect for the role they play as followers. Dissatisfied followers are finding more and more ways to express their displeasure. Leaders who do not warrant trust and who are not accorded respect by their followers, and leaders who do not communicate goals and inspire followers to achieve them, are not properly called leaders.

The spirit of individual rights that has characterized the changes in governmental structure in the upheaval of societies in the past 50 years has spread widely throughout the world. The demands placed upon leaders as a result are much greater; old styles of giving orders and watching the troops fall in line no longer work. Leaders who can truly lead become harder to find and to develop. Maybe being a leader is not great fun, but the opportunities for contribution are enormous.

# Psychology and the Study of Leadership

Psychology as an independent field of study is only a bit over 100 years old. Practice of the kind of applied psychology described in this book, aiming to improve performance in the world of affairs, dates from the time of World War I. That was when psychologists in many specializations joined in an effort to mobilize and train a large army, using newly developed tests of intelligence. During the period from World War I to World War II, all sorts of psychological tests were developed.

Some of psychology's best-known students of personality helped develop the assessment programs of the Office of Strategic Services (OSS) in World War II. The Personnel Research Section of the Adjutant General's Office, U.S. Army, attracted large numbers of psychologists who worked on test development and test validation. Their work on criterion development, on scaling methods, and on biodata was pioneering. These psychologists supplied the models that led many of their colleagues to think the field had some very powerful tools to offer.

During this period prior to the end of World War II capabilities in psychometrics grew. The usefulness of assessment procedures became obvious. Behavior control and measurement techniques were being devised in laboratory studies of behavior. Assurances increased that psychologists and their fellow behavioral scientists knew a lot about learning, about personality differences, and about producing changes in behavior through clinical practice. All of this encouraged some practitioners in psychology to believe that the behavioral sciences were ready to tackle new fields and that one of them should be leadership. When the Office of Naval Research promised grant support to aid in the effort, they were ready to accept the challenge.

During that time and since, more and more psychologists have turned to areas of application. Some have engaged in applied research supported by the federal government, by business and industry, by foundations, and by private philanthropists.  Some have turned to the private practice of clinical psychology.  Some have become employees of or consultants to business, military, and governmental organizations.  Among this last group have been growing numbers of psychologists and other behavioral scientists who have studied how organizations work effectively, how managers can improve their performance, how employees can become more committed to their work and hence more productive, and how leaders can make a difference when conditions are right.

Most of the work of applied psychologists in the early years was oriented toward selection of new employees and their supervision.  Soon training of new employees came under study.  The value of psychological study throughout many parts of an organization came to be better recognized, and studies multiplied.  Today there is an enormous body of data about employees, managers, and leaders; about qualities that relate to effectiveness; and about training methods that work.  This body of information is not well disseminated, even among well-informed professionals, for the practice of encouraging publication of findings in books and journals that characterizes the academic world does not have a counterpart in the private sector.  As a result, too few know about the useful work that has been completed or is currently in progress.

Some research in leadership reminds us of the old joke about the drunk hunting for dropped car keys—who looked where there was light, because it was too dark to see in the area where they were most likely to be.  Psychologists have not studied large numbers of such obvious leaders as presidents, governors, or populist leaders.  This group is generally too preoccupied while in office or is totally unwilling to submit to psychological tests or exercises.  The large numbers of persons who have been studied fall into the not-yet-arrived group who may some day be recognized as leaders.  This tactic is not merely a fall-back position.  It is a calculated gamble.  The assumption is that those currently acting as leaders are unlikely to have unique qualities that can be examined only by studying them; instead, among the characteristics of possible contenders for high positions are to be found all of the qualities ascribed to great leaders.  Industrial organizations have supported such work because they are constantly engaged in a winnowing process with their managers, and they need to know how to pick out and develop the next generation of leaders.

Edwin Hollander of the City University of New York Graduate Center and Lynn Offermann of George Washington University provide in Part II an excellent summary of psychological and sociological research findings pertaining to leadership.  The work they summarize illustrates another assumption that characterizes much of the academic work in leadership.  That is, the study of leadership among small groups, or in situations where the stakes are not too high, or where leadership talents are in the formative stage, can yield noteworthy information about the nature of leadership that will generate principles applicable at all levels of leadership.

Hollander and Offermann call attention to the relationships between leaders and followers, especially to issues of power and authority.  Preparing such a scholarly review requires a survey of technical journals, acquaintance with research methods, knowledge of the prevailing theories and their advocates, the time and willingness to hunt for the articles of greatest relevance, and the good judgment to select those studies that are of highest quality.  Such a review, however, is limited to those articles that have been published in places normally accessible to the scholarly community. Many reports of applied efforts, especially in the military and the corporate worlds, do not appear in such journals and often are not distributed outside the organization in which they were developed.

In the beginning, the study of leadership by psychologists with a bent toward using good measures was more a study of leadership traits than of leaders. Common was the practice for specialists in the field to develop long lists of the qualities demanded of leaders. As lists grew longer, a reaction set in, and persons tried to develop short lists. The well-known study of leadership at Ohio State University ended up with a very long questionnaire that was reduced to two variables essential for leaders: structure and consideration. These terms have been translated by some into Task-Orientation and People-Orientation.

As academic psychologists broadened the scope of their inquiry, relations with followers received more attention. As their findings began to have relevance for those obligated to recruit and promote employees, psychologists were employed in increasing numbers to develop and verify new methods and to apply findings. At first the emphasis was on predicting success and on evaluating performance; these applied psychologists and other behavioral scientists are now involved in most aspects of organizational activities.

In academic social psychology, leadership is a central concept used in studies of group dynamics, with the selection of leaders within a group being part of the method, as well as part of the outcome, of the research. This left to others the issues of leader selection and the development of leadership qualities. It is this difference in the direction of research that provides the inconsistencies between results of small-group experiments and results using data collected on corporate, military, and governmental managers, executives, and other persons in positions where leadership acts might occur.

The context in which leadership may be exercised will always pose a problem in the pursuit of the secrets of leadership. Much more progress has been made in defining and measuring individual traits than in defining environmental contexts. Several of the studies in Part II (Sparks, especially) show that a combination of desired traits does indicate potential for promotion in industry. Yet only a few of the group with such good combinations of traits emerge as outstanding leaders. We must learn more about the experiences, the contexts, and the circumstances within which such persons emerge and perform with productive effect. That clever and creative person who develops an appropriate model for data collection describing how this process operates will make an enormous contribution.

## How Is Leadership Defined?

Many persons find it essential to distinguish between managers and leaders. Training programs for new managers, they argue, ought to differ in content from the set of experiences one would want to provide for developing a U.S. president or the general of an army. Such a distinction assumes, however, that leadership occurs at higher levels and is not needed at lower levels. This is contrary to the evidence. People act at low levels as managers while others act as leaders; people act at high levels as leaders while others act as managers. And sometimes the same people act in different ways. So how do we tell when leadership is being exhibited? You cannot talk about leaders with anyone until you agree on what you are talking about. That requires a definition of leadership and a criterion for leadership acts that can be agreed upon. Only then can appropriate data be collected on persons who meet that criterion, or who have exhibited qualities of leadership.

Since the words *leader* and *leadership* continue to denote different things to each of us, and since the words *manager* and *supervisor* further complicate discussions in this area, some ground rules were established before the San Antonio Conference to guide participants in discussion. It was also hoped that the papers written for the conference would follow the same guidelines. Genuine effort was expended by all participants to adhere to these rules. The following statement was sent to participants.

*The words* leader *and* leadership *will be used only as generic terms pertaining to generalities. Whenever data or research results are discussed, the method by which leadership qualities are measured will be specified, or the way in which subjects called leaders were selected will be described; some specific word shall be used instead of leader or leadership (e.g., promotability, top executives, elected officers in student government, etc.).*

*Leaders deserve to be so called only when they have been the key players in acts of leadership. Leaders are like heroes and creative persons—we only know who they are after the act of leadership, of heroism, or of creativity. Many a president, lots of CEOs, mayors and governors, chiefs, kings, generals, and premiers have been anointed, appointed, or elected who ended up with power, authority, and position, but who exhibit few instances of those behaviors we commonly associate with the word* leadership. *Many a study of "leadership" was a study of promotability, or of management committee opinion, rather than leadership. We may find that substituting the specific descriptor ("voted leader of a five-person group that had met for the first time 30 minutes earlier") instead of saying "leader" will help us sort the trivial from the profound, and thereby focus our attention appropriately.*

Having agreed to this rule of conduct, we lessen the occasions in this book when people are referred to specifically as leaders. Instead, they will be described in terms of the category to which they belong, for example, presidents, naval officers, and so forth. However, the intent all along is to discover general truths about leaders. In each study the reader shall be the judge of its relevance to leadership.

It is not our intent to avoid the provision of an adequate definition of leadership. An inductive approach might suffice, such as allowing each reader to note how each study developed a criterion or an understanding of what leadership is. Such an approach would lead the reader to view leadership as distinctly different from management, involving different relationships with followers than managers have with subordinates, and involving more of the followers' commitment and collaboration. The "transformational" leaders mentioned in chapter 1 increased the energy in the system that was available to achieve agreed-upon goals, and did so without coercion. Few definitions capture it all. Each investigator modifies the definition a little to place his or her own work in proper perspective—that is, closer to the center of the field. In an effort to enhance understanding rather than bypass the issue, a variety of approaches to definition are presented in the next two chapters.

Most studies of managers and leaders have been conducted in business and industry, in military organizations, and in governmental organizations and agencies. The vast majority of industrial and organizational psychologists working outside of colleges and universities are employed in this part of the economy. Only a small fraction of these persons' time is devoted explicitly to the problems of leadership in an organization. Yet many of their topics of study are affected by the quality of leadership. Worker motivation, accident rates, absenteeism, productivity, performance appraisal systems, turnover, quality of the work force, factors influencing advancement, quality of supervision and management, and respect for and trust in top management are regular topics for study.

Data have been accumulated that shed light on interrelations of various aspects of work life. The data also illuminate the effects of management policies, the effects of significant acts of leadership, and the effects of distrust and lack of respect for management. Most of the studies involve persons called managers. Some of the results are described as findings about leadership. That makes sense only if some managers sometimes act as leaders; it seems reasonable to assume that some managers are also leaders.

These settings where studies have been done include few community organizations, few volunteer groups, and few indigenous leaders. Such studies do exist, but they are rare. Our knowledge about all forms of leadership would be enhanced if there were more studies in the independent sector.

## The Research Studies in Part II

Most investigators have a broad analytical model (or theory) in mind while collecting data viewed as relevant to leadership. In the studies in Part II, many models are presented in detail. To skip these papers because they appear too technical is to miss some of the most important contributions of the conference and of this book. The introductory chapters (chapters 1 through 9) provide no summary or reconciliation of the various theories of leadership but instead direct attention to the measures used, the criteria established for their validation, and the ways in which the findings complement each other.

The research studies cite evidence on the effects of applications, describing measures used and how well they worked. This group of studies is not intended as a comprehensive review of all that is known about leadership. Its scope is defined by the contributors and the methods they have used. The studies are intended to be highly practical and to be of greatest use to those who are responsible or will be responsible for the leadership of any group or organization.

Methods that rely on quantitative measures set certain limits on the domains of leadership that can be studied. But in those limitations resides the strength of the assertions. As each concept is developed into a program of action, a trial procedure with appropriate measuring devices is developed, and an evaluation of the effects on work output, profits, worker satisfaction, or some other outcome is completed. How each approach or new method worked is reported in terms of real-world criteria.

# CHAPTER FOUR

# Using Measurement to Become Objective

Using solid evidence to make decisions is often more difficult than following custom or tradition. When the pressure is on and no one knows enough, superstition flourishes. We need only watch pitchers and batters in a baseball game, especially in a World Series, to see superstitious behavior exhibiting itself over and over. Tugs at the ear, touching the cap, odd body movements, or grimaces make no sense except that we guess that at some time or times before they were followed by unexpected and great success.

Plenty of superstition is evident in all that we say and do about leaders and leadership. The leaders selected by our society are taller and stronger than the average, even though today neither height nor size nor physical strength gives an advantage in doing the job. Coats of mail, shields, and swords are relegated to museums, and those who used them are long gone, but we retain the image of the warrior hero as one who wore them. We give preference for employment to those who speak well, who dress with style, whose hair length is fashionable, and who appear to be well civilized, even though we may have little evidence that these qualities are required for many jobs. When the stakes are high and no one is sure how to select the best among candidates, we rely on those variables that worked in the past. No one wants to break new ground and be wrong, or to overlook an option that might work. It is easy to say "no harm is done"; yet every senseless practice reduces the opportunities for better practice. The problem is to know for sure what is better practice. This is an important reason to study leaders, to produce solid evidence about leadership, and to disseminate the knowledge we acquire.

We have said that psychologists and other behavioral scientists have been studying and writing about leaders for years. Why, then, isn't the public better informed? Why have our practices in identifying and developing leadership talent not incorporated new methods and new procedures based on a good research base? The general public has learned a lot about introverts and extroverts, about paranoia and depression, and about which students, clerical workers, or engineers will do well. Leadership is much more important. Is there really so much to disagree about? Are there some professional secrets? Are secrets being used by insiders to make money as consultants and kept hidden so others cannot find out about them?

Those are significant questions, and their answers explain a lot about leadership and about the slow progress made in understanding the phenomenon. The answers require an examination of the ways used to discover new principles of behavior; they require an understanding and an acceptance of the methods used by psychologists and other behavioral scientists. These methods are not well known. Findings from well-done and from shoddily done studies are reported regularly in the media, without distinguishing between them. Their contradictions and their apparent superficiality turn off many thoughtful persons who deserve better.

The studies in Part II are important to the understanding of these methods. They not only review earlier work, but they also state general principles or concepts and then describe how the data were collected so as to confirm or disconfirm the original idea. We must recognize that only rarely will such studies provide an earth-shattering insight never before experienced. Human nature does not hold such secrets. We know many things about how people behave from the tales of our parents and grandparents, who in turn learned them from their ancestors. The trouble is that much of what we have learned is not quite right, or is true only in special circumstances.

Literally hundreds of concepts, ideas, theories, principles, and conjectures about leadership have been promulgated in books, essays, articles, speeches, and seminars. Many have been incorporated into training programs. Enough research data are usually collected on each idea or theory to show that it is plausible. Rare and noteworthy are the occasions when one of this host of statements is proved wrong; usually they are stated so as to be untestable. Only when our research methods are applied in a way to make it easy to disprove, rather than easy to support, will the field progress, as it must. Maybe we should offer prizes to those who show that any of our ideas are wrong.

## Problems in the Design of Leadership Studies

The task faced by a conscientious psychological scientist is to test these generally accepted items of folklore or of common practice to discover under what conditions each applies. If what such a person does is to be considered science, then whatever conclusion is drawn from such studies must be repeatable. That is, the study must be well enough described so that another person can repeat it and test anew whether the announced conclusion holds.

Merely doing the study is not enough; the research person with a new finding must publish or otherwise disseminate the result so that others may repeat it and learn from what was found. If others repeat the study and find that the reported results do not emerge, the study is discredited. A great deal of research in the social sciences has produced negative responses among readers and colleagues and ends up not influencing the course of events. If results are confirmed, other studies are done to set the limits of applicability of the findings.

Opinions drawn from years of experience are not asked to meet these standards. No matter how cogent the arguments, such evidence is not part of the body of science. It is "only" opinion. Of course, such opinions might be very valuable to an organization needing to take some action. And it may carry weight because the opinion is held by a powerful person. But the general principle does not become a part of the scholarly base of scientific psychology unless it has been tested in such a way as to be proven replicable and useful.

There are more requirements than this for knowledge to be worth reporting in standard texts and becoming "archival." The subjects must have been drawn so as to elicit confidence that the behavior being studied is characteristic of members of a defined group. Samples of executives, managers, and leaders are necessarily modest in size and frequently fortuitous. Since the classic standard of random selection will rarely be possible, other standards need to be explored and developed. More progress is likely to be made by looking for replications and for similarity of findings across various groups, and by using combinations of methods. Enough sampling of people and behavior must occur so that the investigator may say with confidence that he/she has observed something that can be generalized—that it is not merely an anecdote or a case study, or a single event in history.

## An Example: The Study of Executive Learning

We will exemplify this process of research by outlining the steps in a study of fast-track managers in major corporations and how they learned from their experiences over the years. This study started as a cooperative research project involving a number of major international corporations. Initially aimed at monitoring the progress of the most talented managers, the method used for study was in-depth interviews with the players themselves, and interviews with their associates, more senior managers, and "savvy insiders" in the corporation. These interviews were analyzed to discover themes, topics, common threads, and especially significant events that were associated with learning something important. Results of that study are now available in the book, *The Lessons of Experience*, by Morgan McCall, Michael Lombardo, and Ann Morrison.

No special measuring devices were used in that study. However, in Part II of this book, McCauley and Lombardo report on BENCHMARKS, a questionnaire that any manager can complete. This questionnaire has scoring methods that will permit any manager to compare his or her development with that of a standard group. Any corporation that uses BENCHMARKS can compare its success in providing good learning experiences for its best people with the success of other organizations.

BENCHMARKS is a long list of items to which a manager is asked to respond. The completed inventory provides the same sort of results that the research team studying executive learning obtained by four-hour intensive interviews. The items in that questionnaire came from the records of the prior study and so built upon the base of knowledge obtained at much greater expense. The scoring scheme also follows the analytical model developed in the process of the content analysis of the interview records.

Ruderman, Ohlott, and McCauley have developed another measure that aims to identify potential sources of management or leadership development by examining managerial and executive jobs in depth. Growth and development are most likely to occur when the person-job match is less than perfect. Self-ratings about experiences that helped them grow thus become useful in classifying jobs that are challenging and have growth potential. The Job Challenge Profile (JCP) was developed for this purpose.

Items for the JCP were also drawn from the study of executive learning. These items were grouped to measure 12 dimensions. One, for example, deals with revitalizing a unit in trouble, and includes items like the following:

- You manage a business or major product line that is losing money or otherwise is in serious trouble.

- Your business or unit has a long history of poor performance.

- You need to restore the credibility of your unit with the rest of the company.

Continuing research with BENCHMARKS indicates that this scale is related to reports of specific lessons learned in managerial settings. Lessons most frequently cited are:

- That most important management situations are characterized by ambiguity, uncertainty, and stress; the manager must learn to be comfortable with it and to act in spite of it.

- That decisions must be made for the sake of the business, even if they involve human cost and hurt you personally. You have to grit your teeth and do what must be done.

Although research is still preliminary, the JCP shows promise as a means of identifying sources of development which could lead to more strategic uses of the developmental aspects of managerial jobs.

These measuring devices permit more direct planning of developmental opportunities for persons with good leadership prospects. They will also permit auditing the system to assure that persons of potential from all sources have been given adequate opportunities for growth.

## Steps in Developing a Psychological Scale

As noted, most studies of leadership that use psychological measurement try to move beyond opinions to more objective factors by developing measures of the behaviors, or criteria for effectiveness in leadership, or some other way of counting or measuring. In most of the studies reported in this volume, a great deal of effort went into the development of measures of behaviors, involving the writing of many items, the grouping of items into scales, and then a factor analysis.

Each study, in other words, begins with someone's idea—a theory, a hypothesis, or a conjecture. This may have formed as the author read the published literature on leadership; or as a result of experience, successful and unsuccessful, in selecting candidates for leadership positions; or from listening to the many voices that proclaim week after week the new discoveries about leaders. The study is intended to give these conjectures credibility among an invisible college of one's colleagues, engaged in the same work, who are highly skeptical of the work of anyone else. But the study also serves another purpose. As objective evidence accumulates, these data give all workers in the field new ideas about the domain; thus, later studies become more sophisticated by getting a little bit closer to the "truth."

Measurement psychologists have learned how to devise tests and inventories so that the names given to measures will not be misleading, so that the measures will be accurate when obtained at different times or under different conditions, and so that the scores will be fair. The relations can be computed between the measures thus developed and measures of later performance that we want to predict, and other factors that may influence that performance can be discovered. When a fancy new device is only an old and familiar measure under a different name, that fact will be discovered promptly.

Psychologists have also learned how to collect measures from groups of persons under conditions that enable them to generalize about results that can be applied widely to related populations of persons. These methods (of validity generalization, for example) have been challenged in the courts and have gained judicial approval as well as professional acceptance. The use of larger samples has transformed the psychological study of leadership from a literary study of competing anecdotes to a hypothesis-testing arena in which good ideas may be shot down when wrong, even though the story is well told.

A portion of one study in this volume (both quoted and described) will be used as an example of the detailed procedures followed once a given domain of interest is identified. The editors have selected the study reported by Gary Yukl of the State University of New York at Albany and his associates, Steve Wall and Richard Lepsinger. Their study in Part II of this volume describes the development of a Managerial Practices Survey.

Yukl, Wall, and Lepsinger argue that research and theory on managerial effectiveness are highly dependent upon the concepts used to describe managerial behavior and the methods used to measure this behavior. A program of research was initiated to identify and measure categories of managerial behavior important for managerial effectiveness. This research program used a variety of research methods, including diaries, critical incidents, interviews, and questionnaires. On the conceptual side, the research led to the formulation of a taxonomy with 11 primary categories of managerial behavior. At the same time, a new questionnaire was developed to measure the managerial behaviors.

The early research of Yukl and his team relied mostly upon factor analysis of questionnaire items to identify behavior categories. Another approach was the use of judges to sort behaviors into categories on the basis of the common purpose of the behavior.

The behaviors in the new taxonomy were expected to be relevant for managerial effectiveness. One test of relevance was to ask managers to rate the importance of each defining behavior in a category. Respondents rated the importance of each behavior for doing the job of the manager being described. The questionnaire was administered to 24 managers and 130 of their subordinates. Another way of assessing relevance was to ask managers to rate the importance of a behavior category rather than to rate the importance of individual items. A sample of 119 managers from several private and public-sector organizations was given the 13 category definitions and asked to rate how important each behavior was for effective performance of their managerial job.

A good measure should have high internal consistency among the items in a scale. Internal consistency can be computed statistically and provides evidence that the scale is measuring a category of interrelated behaviors. Internal consistency was computed separately for three samples: 132 subordinates of middle managers in a large medical health insurance company, 76 subordinates of middle managers in a large chemical company, and 124 subordinates of Air Force maintenance supervisors. Additional evidence for reliability was provided by demonstrating the stability of the Managerial Practices Survey (MPS) scales: the questionnaire was administered to the same sample of subordinates on two different occasions and each scale score on the first administration was correlated with the corresponding scale on the second administration.

Measurement accuracy was tested by searching for significant differences in behavior between samples of managers expected to behave differently due to the influence of situational demands and constraints. Finding behavior differences where they have been predicted in advance provides useful evidence for the validity of the measure, as well as for the validity of the hypothesis. Several MPS scales were shown to discriminate contrasting groups.

In the final analysis, the most important indicator of utility is the capacity of a measure to predict and explain managerial effectiveness. Twenty-six beauty salon managers were described by 151 subordinates who filled out the questionnaire in the salons. Average monthly profit margin during the year following the administration of the questionnaire was found to correlate highly with scale scores computed at the group level.

The report by Yukl and his colleagues continues and describes further efforts to check on the predictive value of his measure. We will take note of his findings and their value in chapter 8.

If the reader has been slowed by reading the previous discussion of the paper done by Yukl, the intent should be obvious. Time itself is the most perfect depiction of time. Just prior to the quotation, we said that precision and large sampling and utmost care in collecting data epitomize the work of these investigators. Such work requires years of commitment and effort, and generalities drawn from it are slow in coming. Having noted the care with which descriptors were checked for accuracy, adequacy, internal consistency, stability, and inter-rater agreement, we should be cautious in suggesting radical changes to make the list of measures meet our own personal prior expectations.

We have provided this detailed description of the work of Yukl and his team to illustrate the measurement psychologist's procedures to assure that research studies are conducted objectively. The procedures involve large numbers. All data are collected in writing, and preserved. No personal judgments tilt the results in any way to satisfy the experimenter's hopes for a given result.

Many of these efforts to develop measures and adequate descriptions are not labeled studies of leadership. Often the purpose of a study is to improve organizational effectiveness or to reduce the number of fatal flaws in persons selected for major positions, or to find ways to make managers more amenable to changes in the system. We must also recognize that the psychological study of leadership is the name given to a wide variety of research designs and data collection plans that do not always involve leaders as the term is usually defined. Political scientists engage in leadership studies, too, some of them studying presidential leadership. Their criterion for a leader is easy: winning a presidential or gubernatorial election. When our definition of leadership includes middle managers, they wonder about our choice of subjects.

Yukl calls his device the Managerial Practices Survey. The correlations of scales on this survey were higher than is typical for behavior description questionnaires when used with a criterion of leader effectiveness. Although the scales for Supporting and for Conflict Management & Team Building were not correlated significantly with indicators of group performance, these behaviors were correlated with measures of subordinate satisfaction in studies that include supplementary "soft" criteria of leader effectiveness.

The scales of Yukl's Managerial Practices Survey are:

| | |
|---|---|
| Informing | Recognizing & Rewarding |
| Consulting & Delegating | Supporting |
| Planning & Organizing | Developing |
| Problem Solving | Conflict Management & Team Building |
| Clarifying | Representing |
| Monitoring | Networking/Interfacing |
| Motivating | |

This review of one research project does not provide sufficient evidence of the rich variety of information obtainable by the methods described. Even the full reading of all reports will not do that, for our selection of studies is only a beginning. The detailed description of Yukl's procedures does provide some insights into the depth of the methods and suggest some of their limitations. It should be clear that while psychologists using measurement approaches might direct attention to U.S. presidents on occasion, they could not develop a new scale using a sample of U.S. presidents; the population is too small, and the people being studied are not serving as leaders simultaneously or under similar conditions. Such small samples do not exploit the full value of the approach. With common measures, we obtain clues for early identification of leadership potential, for understanding the effects of early experiences and schooling, and for gaining a life-span perspective on the development of the various attributes considered crucial for leadership. So our methods drive us to find larger and more diverse samples, to guess about the precursors to leadership, and to capture samples of persons in the source groups from which leaders might be expected to emerge. We then can apply such measures to small samples or to special people.

Yukl made many checks to assure that his categories were properly named and that they covered the domain adequately and had desirable psychometric characteristics. Therefore, we should not take his outcome dimensions lightly; they were not obtained easily and there is a sound reason for each one. The dimensions reported by others need to be taken equally seriously. When we find different investigators reporting quite-different dimensions, we should search for the reasons and for the factors that produce such differences. Deciding which set to use will be tough. We need to ask the investigators to help us out by continuing their work in collaboration so that better interrelationships can be found.

## What Is a Leader? What Is Leadership?

Studying leadership is further complicated by the difficulty of determining who is a leader and when a leadership act has occurred. To study what makes a good engineer is much easier, for we all generally agree about who is and who is not an engineer, and we know the difference between a bridge that stands for decades and one that goes down in a gale. If one wanted to assemble a sample of American engineers, it is possible to find a list of almost all of them in the country and draw a sizable sample that would represent the total.

Identifying a group of persons as leaders is not easy. Even finding one that most persons agree would qualify is hard. It is much harder than defining a hero. You could ask, "What do you have to do to be called a hero?" (And after having arrived at an acceptable description, you might be told that a study of Congressional Medal of Honor awardees indicated that most showed great bravery and ingenuity in getting themselves out of a perilous situation that could have been avoided by prudent behavior.) However, in every case, an act of heroism is obvious and is known immediately—if observed by someone who calls attention to the act. An act of leadership is not always so easy to recognize and often is not appreciated by someone affected by it, especially when it involves the judgment of Solomon and the observer's "baby" is at stake.

Attending to excellence in criteria may be the most important step in improving the understanding of leadership. The criteria may still involve subjective judgments, but at least they will be judgments by persons who are not strongly invested in a given theory of leadership. Generalizations drawn from such studies can be tested by repeating the study with enormous skepticism about the first set of results. If a hostile critic repeats your study and finds the same results, you, as a passionate believer in your theory, have a right to feel gratified and vindicated.

Developing a "test" cannot avoid the questions about definition. The measuring device will serve a purpose only if it is developed using observations or samples of behavior, or responses characteristic of those who are, or who have prospects of becoming, a leader or who have been involved in leadership activities. It is best if those who have performed effectively are identified, for the test data will not have been worth collecting unless they prove to relate to well-defined criteria of performance in those activities the test is supposed to predict.

But how is a research psychologist to identify effective leaders when even the most prestigious organizations do it so poorly? Can the judgment of management committees be trusted, when they pick the next chief executive officer, that they have also identified a leader? Since rate of promotion and pay level are the culmination of a long process of development, observation, and screening, can we accept these indices as a proxy for leadership? Does that satisfy you? If you are satisfied, you will find several studies reported herein that are right on target for you, for they provide an understanding of what one must do to get promoted, what changes in behavior are required, and what new capabilities must be developed to handle each job of increasing scope and responsibility. Are these the primary components of leadership?

The psychologist's research function must include influencing the nature of the administrative process (if possible) and refining what that process has wrought, in order to make appropriate distinctions between and among candidates brought forth as potential leaders. Good research on leadership cannot assume that the administrative process has worked efficiently and has identified leaders. Use of more diverse sources of information, such as rating forms that collect data from supervisors, co-workers and subordinates; search for and review of records of acts of leadership; and comparisons of profiles of performance data are not new practices, but they are coming into wider use.

As psychologists develop better measures of leadership performance and better measures that predict who will do well, they also refine their own techniques for purifying their scales and supporting the evaluation procedures of their own organizations. When discrepant cases occur—that is, when the psychologist's test does not match the administrative judgment, both sides take another look. As a result, sometimes tests are changed, sometimes decisions are changed, and, then, sometimes the individual case just mystifies everyone. The process is an interesting form of the well-known practice of "bootstrapping."

The studies in this book were not intended to be limited to studies conducted within major corporations or to military organizations, but these are the organizations that have gained prominence by studying their own promotion processes and are farthest ahead in beginning to understand their merits and limitations. Leadership must emerge in many kinds of organizations, and definitions and studies in the next round must explicate how the process works in more than one special segment of the society. For now, copying the practices of those who have done studies is the best way to go.

As a general statement on leaders, and for its historical value, the following quotation from the second inaugural address of the first president of the United States is of consequence.

*One of the difficulties in bringing about change in an organization is that you must do so through the persons who have been most successful in that organization, no matter how faulty the system or organization is. To such persons, you see, it is the best of all possible organizations, because look who was selected by it and look who succeeded most within it. Yet these are the very people through whom we must bring about improvements.*

—George Washington

Leaders must become the chief critics of their own organization and the chief architects of needed change. Misplaced loyalty to the prior modes of action does not serve the organization well and does not enable the leader to serve the followers faithfully and well. Washington's point is most cogent. Every leader of an organization has the responsibility for moving that organization ahead a notch. That involves change: change that accommodates to differing conditions.

Another point hinted at in Washington's remarks was that promotion should be treated as less certain an indicator of leadership potential than it is. Especially early in a career, promotions may be based on behaviors that are important for the short term, but irrelevant or wrong for the long term—or, at least, based on different qualities than are prized later in a career. But more importantly, promotions are made by superiors and are based on past performance when what is critical in these decisions may require a vision of future behaviors often impossible for superiors to predict. Curiously, subordinates have proved to be better evaluators of potential performance than have superiors.

The work of Yammarino and Bass shows clearly that the leadership qualities of junior Navy officers, three or four years out in the fleet, are much more clearly identified by their subordinates than by their superiors. The subordinates had a better view of the level of performance of their unit than the superiors, and reported their own satisfaction with their shipboard activities when their immediate superior operated as a "transformational leader."

Conjectures about the nature of effective leadership can only be tested adequately if it is possible to establish a set of procedures to put a "handle" on the leadership variable. Before any measure of leaders can be put to the test, a cohort of proven leaders must be assembled, or some grades of leaders or leadership acts must be established. Such questions as the following must be addressed: What is adequate proof that anyone is a leader or that one person is more of a leader than another? Whose judgment is to be trusted? What behaviors can be taken as convincing evidence of leadership? Very little reflection is required to see that people asked to make such judgments might find trouble agreeing on how to grade the leaders or the leadership acts.

Small wonder that there are not a large number of comprehensive, rigorous studies of leadership! It is a tough challenge. The authors who wrote the papers in this volume came up with a variety of ingenious ways to address the issue of the criterion for leadership. After all, knowing more about the indicators of potential for effective leadership would be very useful in a society that needs effective leaders and needs them in enormous numbers.

The search for predictors of leadership assumes that we know what we want in ultimate performance, and that we know when we get it. If we are confused, or if we as a society disagree on the criteria—the nature of the person selected and the nature of the actions desired—we place a limit on the validity of our selection procedures.

Illustrations of "the criterion problem" are always inherent in political elections. Would anyone assume that the election of one candidate over another is also an endorsement of the qualities that he or she brings to the office? Does the winner have greater leadership attributes than the also-ran? Can we find more leadership qualities by studying current and past heads of state than by studying the candidates they defeated?

Are the chief executive officers of the top 100 corporations in America a good criterion group for studying leadership? Before you say yes, remember that most of these were picked by committee, that oftentimes circumstances having nothing to do with candidate qualifications led to one person being chosen rather than another, and that each person doing the selection was not a disinterested judge looking only at leadership qualities.

Would rate of promotion in a major corporation be considered a good measure of leadership potential? Take note that these promotion decisions are made by small groups of decision makers, generally on the basis of evidence of performance in a limited arena of effort and from a more limited perspective of capabilities.

If we cannot specify rather precisely the persons who deserve classification as leaders, then we cannot specify very well the life experiences that prepare one for leadership, nor the test scores that will predict, nor the character and personality that leadership requires. What the field needs is a predictable criterion that is also acceptable to most critical observers.

It is not only research on leadership that is hampered by this criterion problem. Also impaired is every decision about promotion, about selecting the next leader or the next leadership team, and about generating a fresh wave of able, vigorous, and courageous young stars who can be developed for later succession.

The authors of the studies in this book found that routinely collected performance appraisal records did not provide good criteria: they included too much error variance, or noise, produced by all the various purposes that such routine procedures were asked to serve. The best criteria that they developed involved procedures which combine information about nature of assignments, pay, promotion rate, and ratings collected for their own purposes. Some found that the very best information about leadership qualities came from ratings by subordinates.

Organizations that have developed their own assessment procedures for talented young managers gain a dividend, for participation requires supervisors to identify their most promising persons to nominate for assignment to such programs. Organizations without assessment programs can gain that advantage just as easily by mounting such identification programs for other purposes. The Eastman Kodak Company, for example, in the early eighties began a program for identifying their best young talent and finding challenging jobs that would test and develop their capabilities. Their selection procedure was outside the usual performance appraisal system: they sought nominations, kept records of unusual events, and interviewed informed observers.

To persist with the issue of the criterion for identifying leadership: just how might a good criterion for leadership be developed? Careful study of how each investigator has handled the prediction problem is quite illuminating. Each team suggests ways in which management may improve their promotion and training practices and ways in which ambitious young stars can enhance their own careers. The prediction studies reported will lead to wariness about accepting generalizations. Knowledge of the studies in Part II will help the reader develop a taste for work of quality and an aversion to the overgeneralizations that flood the literature about leadership and management. By setting one's own standard for good work, a sorting out of what works from the hopes, dreams, and horror stories can begin.

We have emphasized the importance of identifying leadership acts and trying to understand why they were or were not effective. As we look at the many studies that emphasize measurement we will find none that studies Gandhi, or Winston Churchill, or Lincoln, or any other great historic figure. Some studies in this book try to understand particular behaviors that were or were not effective. Some set as their goal the identification of those who motivate their teams to greater performance. Some study profitability of businesses, or effectiveness of work units within an organization, or the satisfaction of workers with their bosses, and develop measures that will predict such performance. Some use as the criterion success in the organization, as evidenced by pay, promotion, or increased responsibility. Some of these studies may seem to you to miss the mark. We hope that is not so. But we must heed the words of an astute observer of the scene when he says:

*All over this country, in corporations and government agencies, there are millions of executives who imagine that their place on the organization chart has given them a body of followers. And of course it hasn't. It has given them subordinates. Whether the subordinates become followers depends on whether the executives act like leaders.*

—John Gardner

# CHAPTER FIVE

# The Many Ways
# to Study Leadership

All of the insights into the nature of leaders and leadership provide precious little help to a selection committee when it is time to choose the next president of a community organization, to appoint a new college president or a new minister, or to name a next CEO of a corporation—or, for that matter, to the voting public when the time comes to elect a president of the United States. How can research studies of any sort help one to be sure that any candidate has the necessary qualities, holds to the values we cherish, and isn't just trying to give a favorable impression, isn't just providing the answers we want, isn't just "playing the role of leader" rather than revealing the true self?

How can any method improve the ability to select the best person for a leadership role when that role has dimensions none of us understands or can predict? To illustrate: our nation is today changing rapidly in its demographics, in its trade relations with the rest of the world, and in many of its stated values. The leadership in our major governmental agencies and in our multinational corporations must attend to our changing culture and the changing international scene, in addition to the usual issues of production, marketing, services to clients and customers, and preservation of the environment. If no candidate for high office has had the opportunity to deal with such issues, how shall we know who will do best?

Such questions are indeed complex and seem unanswerable. Yet it is possible to make choices among candidates in terms of their demonstrated ability to handle complex issues, their degree of flexibility in addressing problems, and their overall analytical abilities. Picking a winner may be nearly impossible, but it is easier to eliminate those who would certainly fail. It is not necessary for an investigator to have data covering every situation if there are enough studies of sufficient diversity to establish general principles.

Recent studies by Jaques, Jacobs, Stamp, Bass, Sashkin, Posner, and others, much of them reported in the studies in

Part II, have opened up new methods for studying leaders and leadership. The building of lists of desired qualities of leaders (the "trait" approach to leadership) has given way to an approach that deals with leadership events and behaviors and attempts to understand the roles of various participants in such events.

For example, Jacobs and Jaques propose in their study in Part II of this book that leadership must be viewed as a process which occurs only in situations in which there is decision discretion. To the extent discretion exists, there is an opportunity for leadership to be exercised. If there is no discretion, there is no such opportunity. They also state that leadership is not a "thing," that it probably is not useful to talk of "leaders" as either persons (in contrast to persons who are not "leaders") or as role incumbents. Leadership as defined here is an influence process which is a type of role behavior. This role behavior can be displayed by any member of a formal or informal organization. Stereotypically, it is most often directed downward. However, it may also be directed laterally (and then can be a crucially important role requirement) or upward. When directed laterally, for example, it is more likely to be given another name, such as consensus building, but nonetheless has the required properties described above and thus should be recognized for what it is.

The role behavior that is cited above is integral to most definitions of leadership. Compare it with the definition suggested by John Gardner in his forthcoming book on leadership: "Leadership is the process of persuasion or example by which an individual [or leadership team] induces a group to pursue objectives held by the leader or shared by the leader and his or her followers."

Readers should not assume that such a definition automatically leads to more concentration of efforts in the direct study of such role behaviors. General agreement on this definition is associated with an enormous range in choice of subjects for study and ways of identifying leaders and leadership events. The following sketches highlight the differences in approach.

## Other Approaches

Gough has studied husbands and wives who rated each other on leadership, adults taking part in Leaderless Group Discussions and rated on leadership by observers, high school students nominated as outstanding leaders by principals, and college students rated by peers as having leaderlike qualities. McCauley and Lombardo studied the differences in the skills and perspectives of successful managers in two types of business corporations. Wilson, O'Hare, and Shipper studied the effects of training on executives in relation to the profitability of their organizations. Hendrick compared students of different personalities to study one's sensitivity to the behaviors of others.

McCall, Lombardo, and Morrison in their book, *The Lessons of Experience*, studied the self-reported effects on learning of various experiences as recalled by managers on the fast track in a number of corporations. Howard and Bray assessed young managers early in their careers and predicted their performance using rates of promotion as a proxy for direct observation of such role behavior. Bentz and Sparks each developed a criterion to reflect the values assigned by top management to the work of individual managers and executives. Bentz noted the need to attend to quite-complex behaviors and to develop a criterion that would incorporate more than pay level and promotion rate.

All such studies were done for a mix of purposes—many at the behest of management—and all have merit for their own purposes. Which approach helps us understand best the nature of leadership? While differences in taste may commend one study over another, each study in this volume is included because it teaches something. Citing a few findings of individual studies will illustrate this point:

1. The Bentz study. There is great value in a corporation investing in a program to identify high-level managerial and leadership talent, beginning the collection of measures early. The use of predictor measures makes it possible to monitor quality and to assess various developmental programs; it is equally important to reflect appropriately the levels of complex problem-solving ability required of the most senior executives.

2. The Sparks study. Enough is known about the qualities required for growth on the job and ultimate attainment of high levels of responsibility to argue strongly for selecting young managers of high quality. Predictions of later success can still be made by test data collected as much as 25 years earlier.

3. The Howard and Bray study. Leadership abilities can be identified in individuals early in their work careers. With longer tenure in management positions, potential leaders emerge more obviously in part as they learn, in part as their motivational levels and job involvement are sustained, and in part as capabilities emerge at higher levels that were not needed and often not observed at lower levels.

4. The Gough studies. Leaders tend to be drawn from subsets in any population that differ from the rest more in personality than in cognitive attributes. These personological/motivational factors increase the willingness of the designated individuals to serve as leaders, and also enhance the probability of good performance as a leader.

5. The McCaulley summary of data collected on the Myers-Briggs Type Indicator. Various personality types behave in different manners that affect their interactions with others and their ways of interpreting the behaviors of others. Some types therefore are more likely to accept leadership roles, and to perform well in them, while others are less likely to be candidates, are less likely to accept such responsibilities, and are required to make more adaptations in their behaviors in order to perform well.

6. The McCall, Lombardo, and Morrison study on how executives learn. Longitudinal studies of managerial success give the impression that excellent choices of persons who will move high in an organization can be made at the entry level. While there may be more truth in this statement than most people accept, the predictions are not sufficiently precise to eliminate the possibility that some persons learn more from experience, change their behaviors more, and improve their position in the race to the top. In fact, opportunities to learn and change are provided for most fast-track managers; some learn a lot and change, while some learn little, do not change, and move out of the fast track. This study illuminates the varieties of learning experiences and what managers believe they teach. Wise leadership of an organization will insure the provision of such challenges to the best of candidates for top positions.

7. The work of Bass and his associates in demonstrating that transformational leadership can be measured and can be taught. James MacGregor Burns in 1978 suggested the notion of the transformational leader as one whose leadership so inspires followers that all work toward common goals with more effort and dedication than is attained merely by salary, by incentive, or by other forms of transactional leadership. A series of studies by Wilson, O'Hare, and Shipper has shown without doubt that instruction can affect style of leadership. Yammarino and Bass have shown that team performance is enhanced with such leaders in place. Rosenbach reports that use of these principles has been very effective in leadership development programs and seminars with executives, particularly with fire chiefs in the United States and Australia.

8. Sashkin and Burke, Posner and Kouzes, and Wilson, O'Hare, and Shipper have developed training and assessment methods associated with newly developed measures with novel dimensions. Their work, taken in concert, represents a considerable advance in knowledge of the behaviors associated with leadership and with achieving organizational goals. These studies relate leadership role behaviors to group outcomes, rather than merely stating them as ideals.

9. Jacobs and Jaques have ventured into the highest levels of a bureaucratic organization and have identified the components of leadership behavior evoked in the top positions in contrast to those evoked in the positions immediately below. That they find any differences is surprising. A set of studies by G. Stamp is reported that shows that essential capabilities required by very top leaders include high levels of cognitive complexity that can be measured very precisely. The Stamp measures identify almost perfectly those who are rated as most effective in top positions. The validity coefficients are at the maximum possible level when one considers the reliabilities of the test and of the criterion. This study needs to be repeated in a variety of other settings.

Most of us consider that predictions of good performance of rank-and-file workers can be made fairly well. There are good arguments for the position that prediction of performance of managers and leaders, especially at higher levels, should be easier. Consider the following points:

1. Whether a person will work hard is one of the most difficult things to predict. Dedication, continued loyalty, and enthusiasm about the work involved are all factors that affect productivity among the rank and file. Variations in motivation among workers have the effect of reducing correlations between measures of capability and measures of performance. Candidates for top positions usually have roughly equal amounts of dedication, ambition, and, as their careers progress, loyalty to the organization, so that these variables do not reduce the relation between predictors and performance.

2. Predictor devices normally assess the highest level of competence that the individual is likely to attain. Knowing a person's "ceiling" is usually not critical for predicting whether or not a factory worker, a plumber, or a stenographer will perform in a fully satisfactory way. People in such positions are only infrequently called upon to perform at their very highest level of capability. Leaders show their mettle in periods of crisis. Knowing the limits of a top manager or of a critical leader is essential to knowing how that person will perform in the most demanding tasks.

3. The behaviors that are seen as critical begin to change and become more complex at higher levels of an organization. As cognitive capabilities set limits on performance, that performance becomes more easily predicted by tests measuring high-level mental abilities. The long-term follow-up work at AT&T provided evidence that managers change in some regards: Howard and Bray report that managers' abilities, motivations, and personality characteristics do change somewhat with maturity and experience. In some cases such changes personify the typical manager, and in other cases changes can be traced to particular types of experiences, such as movement into more challenging jobs. There is still, however, a stable core of personality and ability, or predictions over long periods would not be possible. However, there is age- and experience-related variability around that core that must be attended to for an informed interpretation of psychological measures.

A study by Valerio asked explicitly about managers' self-perceptions of their own changes. Half (51%) of all responses noted that the managers experienced an increased sense of confidence over the course of their careers. Almost half (49%) stated that their orientation toward people had also increased. In particular, they noted that they were more "outgoing," "tolerant," and "considerate of others" as well as "more politically aware." A few noted that their management style tended to be more participative. Almost half also noted an improvement in their problem-solving skills (better planning, decision making, organizing) and that they were delegating more and/or delegating better.

Two research teams provide examples of alternate ways of addressing this issue. Wilson, O'Hare, and Shipper build a conceptual framework for this domain on the basic principles of learning. It is their view that leadership is best seen as one of several organizational roles that depends on skills of influencing others. They see organizational behavior as made up of a series of tasks; each task is fully equivalent to a learning trial. Their task cycle theory relates to learning theory in the context of the sequential chaining of behaviors. The notion of chaining plays an important role not only in research strategies but also in coaching and training for change. Gratzinger, Warren, and Cooke stress the development of qualities that will produce better performance. They contend that the concepts isolated in their study can serve as a basis for the development of assessment and training programs with a major focus on the reinforcement and development of these qualities in managers and other professionals who aspire to leadership excellence. To do that, they aim to show that managers who have these positive features are indeed better performers and leaders than those who do not.

## Are There Ways to Use These Findings?

The typical corporate manager who hears of this work may be intrigued by the descriptions but a bit skeptical about how practices are to improve. It is reasonable to ask, what next?, as one such conferee did: Alan Colquitt, a conference participant, noted that we have done many managerial job analyses in the name of research. We need to get beyond that and say, so what? Here are dimensions, or characteristics, of effective leader/managers...what now? What do we do with this information? He commented, "Posner is taking positive steps in the context of training; Bill Clover is using this for development purposes; what are others doing with this information? This is what we need more of."

The studies included in this volume teach lessons to all of us about leadership. We should already have learned something about the complexity of the tasks faced and about the importance of cognitive abilities for our top leaders; we have at least been told that those abilities can be assessed in tests, exercises, and interview settings prior to a person's appointment.

However, most such findings seem quite obvious to the reader and thus stimulate no changes in belief or practices. Since we ask you to examine the evidence and question every finding reported in this volume, we shall test you on what you now think about some generalizations often made about leadership. Let us review a few commonly accepted truths and see what we each believe.

### A Short Test on Leaders and Leadership

True    False    Leadership is a single personality trait, and, like other traits, can be measured.

True    False    Leaders should be smart, but not too smart.

True    False    Leaders are leaders, and are mostly alike.

True    False    Once a leader, always a leader.

True    False    A good leader brings to the task all that is required to perform effectively.

Surely you were clever enough to notice that each of these items should have been answered false. Yet note how often we all say things like this, but in different form:

"You could tell at a glance that he was a leader. He is a winner."

"He's really an intellectual. People wouldn't understand him. He's too smart to be trusted."

"He must have leadership ability. He's been elected to many community positions. People like him."

"He did a good job running that plant. He would do a good job running the company."

"We need a real leader to bail us out of this mess."

A more detailed comment on each item:

**Common Belief Number 1.** Leadership is a single personality trait and, like other traits, can be measured. Psychologists have developed measures for intelligence and for clerical, mechanical, and spatial abilities. They should be able to develop a test for leadership. This trait, if it is like intelligence or height, should be found to be relatively immodifiable, and measurements of leadership will predict later performance in jobs that require its presence in some amount for good performance.

*False.* Leadership was for a long time thought of as such a trait. Attempts to develop measures held back understanding of the nature of leadership for years.

**Common Belief Number 2.** Leaders should be smart, but not too smart.

*False.*  A summary of the studies that argued the "true" response to this question is presented in the paper by Most.  Any reader would be convinced by the evidence Most presents, especially if there were already an acceptance of the next principle.  The problem is in the definition of the leader and the context in which leadership is exercised. Some leaders are very smart and yet need even greater mental abilities to deal with the enormous complexities they face.

**Common Belief Number 3.**  Leaders are leaders.  The same demands are placed on all leaders; all leaders have the same power; all leaders have equally devoted followers; all leaders' acts are of the same consequence to their followers.

*False, if stated so baldly.*  A large part of the talk and writing about leaders and leadership mixes up what we find in studies that involve youth-group leaders, leaders of student groups in high schools and colleges, leaders of community organizations, leaders of large and influential political groups, and even persons just "elected" to be a leader in a small-group experiment.

**Common Belief Number 4.**  Once a leader, always a leader.  One who is elected, appointed, or self-anointed to a position of leadership is a leader.

*False.*  Leadership is often an event in the life of a person who in other contexts and at other times does and should yield leadership responsibilities to others.  More and more we see the need to study leadership as an experience and to consider the context in which a person leads as critical to defining the qualities needed.

**Common Belief Number 5.**  A good leader will bring to the position of leadership all that is required to perform effectively.

*False.*  Studies completed recently by McCall, Lombardo, and Morrison have taught us that those aspiring to executive positions have a lot to learn before they arrive at such positions.  Potential leaders need to have experienced the sharply increased demands after a promotion, to have been forced to handle a new type of challenge, to accept responsibility without adequate support, and to have experienced hardship, trauma, and failure.  Persons accepting the very highest offices still have things to learn; they must on occasion change their behaviors and their attitudes and beliefs, and they must open channels to learn how their actions are received by constituencies and others.

This chapter has provided an introduction to the studies of leadership which are examined in more detail in the succeeding chapters.  By now the reader must realize that the nature of leadership and the behaviors of leaders are not easily described, nor readily categorized.  One thing should be clear: there is no one type of leader, born to the role, and ready to assume the mantle.  Nor is there only one type of leadership role. Every leader still has much to learn, and every leadership act has within it some shortcomings.  Studying leadership is like viewing a great work of art: there is still much to see after the first glance.

Chapter 6 begins our examination of the dimensions of leadership presented in the 29 studies in Part II.

# Developing Measures to Describe Leadership and to Select Leaders

We asserted earlier that great benefits can accrue by developing ways to measure in individuals those qualities or behaviors that lead to more effective performance. We had not warned that such scale development produces for each study a somewhat-different set of descriptors. Each set presents a view of the manager, the leader, or the leadership event from a restricted view; only by looking at it from every angle can the full image of the phenomenon emerge.

In this chapter we will compare the different measures that have been developed, to find their common elements, if we can, and to discover the uniqueness, if any, in each. There is something to be learned by this exercise, but only by the reader who can tolerate a bit of ambiguity and who has enough patience to go back to sources (the studies in Part II of this volume) for further details. An advantage in writing this chapter was that each of the authors of the measures had the chance to add his or her comments to the synthesis being made; we thus bettered the chance of avoiding misinterpretation or overstatement.

Just how great are the differences? It is worth looking closely and making some comparisons. We then can ask questions more intelligently. First we will repeat the list of scales that resulted from the work of Yukl, Wall, and Lepsinger reported in chapter 4:

Informing
Consulting & Delegating
Planning & Organizing
Problem Solving
Clarifying
Monitoring
Motivating
Recognizing & Rewarding
Supporting
Developing

Conflict Management & Team Building
Representing
Networking/Interfacing

A much-shorter list of components is proposed by Posner and Kouzes. They conducted intensive interviews with managers who were asked to describe a "personal best as a leader"—an experience in which managers accomplished something extraordinary in an organization. The descriptors of leadership behavior that emerged were grouped in five categories:

Challenging the Process
Inspiring a Shared Vision
Enabling Others to Act
Modeling the Way
Encouraging the Heart

This list was used as the frame for their Leadership Practices Survey, comprised of 30 items, six for each dimension. A sample item for Challenging the Process is: "I seek out challenging opportunities which test my skills and abilities."

We can compare this scale to the short form of a scale developed by Bass to identify transformational leaders. Presented below are the dimensions for a version of his scale used by Clover at the Air Force Academy. "AOC" refers to Air Officer Commanding and is the immediately superior active-duty officer being rated by cadets:

Charisma (Sample item: "I am ready to trust my AOC to overcome
   any obstacle.")
Individualized Consideration (Sample item: "My AOC finds out what
   I value and helps me achieve it.")
Intellectual Stimulation (Sample item: "My AOC makes sure we think
   through what is involved before taking actions.")

Clearly, comparing the three lists does not help much. Even though one form is set for subordinates rating superiors and the others for self-rating, there is not much overlap in the content. These are more than different ways to cut a pie; they are different pies. Does it help to look at all of the Bass measures, as reported by Yammarino and Bass?

Yammarino and Bass not only identify transformational leaders as practicing the three previous activities; they also developed nine leadership scales:

Four transformational:              Four transactional:
   charisma                            contingent promises
   individualized consideration       contingent rewards
   intellectual stimulation           active management-by-exception
   inspirational leadership           passive management-by-exception
                                    One laissez-faire

One try at matching two lists is suggested by Yammarino (without total enthusiasm, however).

| The Kouzes-Posner List | The Yammarino-Bass List |
| --- | --- |
| Challenging the Process | Intellectual Stimulation |
| Inspiring a Shared Vision | Inspirational Leadership and Charisma |
| Enabling Others to Act | Intellectual Stimulation and Charisma |

Modeling the Way                        Charisma and Inspirational Leadership
Encouraging the Heart                   Individualized Consideration

It may not be profitable to try to reconcile differences between lists. The dimensions, after all, are determined in large part by the item content that entered the analysis, and that content was determined by the original conceptual framework of the study. They should be different. There is merit, however, in continuing to examine the dimensions that different teams have developed.

Sashkin and Burke began with a focus on top-level executive leadership, as opposed to mid- and lower-level management, as an organizational phenomenon. They describe how transformational and transactional leaders differ and how individuals in one or the other category can be measurably distinguished, in light of their own organizational leadership theory.

Burke's Leadership Report is based on the notion that the way power is used to empower followers is the key factor that distinguishes transformational from transactional leaders. Dimensions scored are:

Creating versus Conserving
Arousing versus Clarifying
Active versus Reactive

Each contrasting pair is characteristic of transformational leaders. Executives had significantly higher transformational scores as compared with managers.

Sashkin and Burke identify three specific personal characteristics that differentiate effective organizational leaders: such leaders (1) believe they can have an impact on the "bottom line," (2) use power to empower others, who then use power and influence to enact the leader's vision of the organization, and (3) have a cognitive time span that enables them to think and function over periods of at least a decade.

They also describe leaders as defining a common "philosophy" that they put to work by: providing a focus, communicating, engendering trust, expressing respect, and creating and taking risks. The four organizational functions described in earlier work by Talcott Parsons—adapting, achieving goals, coordinating activities, and maintaining the culture—are seen as characterizing individual work needs as well. These dimensions underlie Burke's Leader Behavior Questionnaire that has been used with 20,000 North American managers. Now revised, the LBQ has 50 items, with five items forming each of ten scales. Sashkin and Burke describe their approach as theory-based, integrating a diverse set of research work on or related to organizational leadership, and as empirically research guided.

David Campbell developed a Skills Survey Leadership Scale for a new Campbell Work Orientations (CWO). Items in his scale are:

Acquiring the necessary resources to carry out your plans
Coaching a highly skilled performance group
Cultivating leadership talents in other people
Delegating authority to others
Developing a long-range, visionary plan for your organization
Leading other people, making important things happen
Serving as an officer in a national volunteer organization

Campbell's Leadership Potential Index includes the following dimensions, illuminated by typical adjectives:

Dynamic (enthusiastic, inspiring)
Farsighted (forward-looking)
Experienced (savvy, well-connected)
Trustworthy (candid, ethical)
Confident (optimistic, well-adjusted)
Ambitious (competitive, hard-driving)
Passive (—) (fearful, meek)
Sheltered (—) (naive)

Wilson, O'Hare, and Shipper developed a survey explicitly aimed at differentiating levels of effective leadership in top-level positions. In their work, leadership is viewed as one of several organizational roles that depends upon skills of influencing others. Involved are three fundamental processes by which (1) individuals exert influence, (2) others learn to accept a person's influence, and (3) change in organizational performance is produced.

Organization behavior is made up of a series of tasks and task cycles that are repeated performances. Each task starts with (1) a purpose, (2) a plan to achieve it, (3) the provision of necessary resources, (4) tracking of progress by obtaining feedback, (5) making of adjustments, and (6) giving of or gaining reinforcement upon completion. Repetitions of these cycles round out the personality of the performer; each task is fully equivalent to a learning trial.

The six phases of the Managerial Task Cycle are operationalized into a Survey of Management Practices (SMP). This questionnaire is completed by managers, their supervisors, and their subordinates. Variables measured are:

| | |
|---|---|
| Clarifying Goals | Goal Pressure |
| Upward Communications, Participation | Delegation |
| Orderly Planning | Recognition |
| Expertise | Approachability |
| Facilitation | Team Building |
| Feedback | Interest in Subordinate Growth |
| Time Emphasis | Building Trust |
| Control of Details | |

A preliminary validation of the method with persons in leadership roles has led to the development of a Survey of Leadership Practices. It has a different set of categories, as follows:

| | |
|---|---|
| Vision | Expectations |
| Risk Taking | Excellence |
| Self-Confidence | Persuasion |
| Creativity | Push/Pressure |
| Resourcefulness | Recognition |
| Competence | Integrity |
| Modeling | Charisma |
| Mentoring | Leadership Potential |
| Caring | |

# Which Set Is Best?

Which set of variables do you prefer? What seems most appropriate? How can each be evaluated? Let us try some options.

**Option 1.** The reader might look through the lists and choose one set. That set might have variables that had been part of an organizational practice with which one has some familiarity. A brave (foolhardy?) individual might pick variables from different lists, to devise a custom-made package for his organization to try out.

That would be a pretty poor way to go.

**Option 2.** The reader might read ahead to the chapter on validation, look for the highest validity coefficients, and pick that list.

That would be better—but it might not be the best way to go.

**Option 3.** A reader might look at the institutional origins of the research workers and select the list developed by the person or persons from the best schools.

That would be worse than the first choice.

**Option 4.** A reader might read all of the reports carefully, looking for the person who had purposes in mind that matched the purposes of the organization where the work would be applied.

That would be a pretty good way to go. Many times the method used, or the interest of the investigator, will show in the results obtained; sometimes we call that "bias." Sometimes it is a reflection of the purpose of the study that is often reflected in the items written and in the measures that are developed.

**Option 5.** A reader might look for similarity in organizational settings and choose a list developed on that basis.

Not bad—the reader is beginning to see that the theoretical bent of the investigator, the preference for psychometric procedures, the nature of the groups available for making trial runs, the interests of the sponsoring organizations, and the climates of the organizations in which data are collected have effects on what eventuates as a definitive outline of behaviors or practices.

**Option 6.** A reader might examine the local setting to see what key issues face the organization and pick a method that seems to match.

Again, not bad. Obviously, different studies addressed different issues.

**Option 7.** The reader might complain that the choice should be made by the professionals, and that it is unfair to offer so many options. Why not wait until the field knows what it is doing and lets everyone know what is best?

Actually, the worst choice of all. If all of our authors spent three years together doing just this, we would end up with little more knowledge than we have now. The reader is lucky in a way. These are new findings, new insights, new measures. What will happen during the next several years is that the best of these will get better, and the least useful will disappear. And the competition will get keener as more measures are developed and tried by a large number of persons not represented in this volume. The answer for the future may even lie in a different direction.

Readers who are involved in the real world and have discovered the necessity of action will recognize that waiting is the worst of alternatives. What we will review in later pages is how well some of these measures can help decision makers in the real world select the most attractive successors, prepare them for dealing with issues even more troublesome than those of the moment, and ensure that a stream of even better successors is in the works.

What we can predict with confidence is that these investigators, having found great value in their original formulations, will see merit in looking for ways to improve their efforts. Only after someone has compared approaches and sets of dimensions in the same settings will we see any good way to choose among them. Such work may be done by a new investigator, as often happens when a promising new line of discovery attracts attention.

# CHAPTER SEVEN

# Personality Measures and Leadership

An act of great leadership leaves the observers in awe and wonderment. How could Churchill have marshalled a badly frightened nation into developing such courageous resistance? We all wish we knew in what ways such persons differ from the rest of us, and we all wonder how we would have performed under the same circumstances. Great acts of folly arouse our interest as well. We ask, "What would a person have to be like in order to behave in such a way?" Throughout history these questions must have been asked many times, and in many ways.

The approach taken in the preceding chapter did not address this aspect of leadership. Fixating on the desired behaviors of persons who have taken charge of something is not exactly the same as studying leaders and their nature. True, the approach yields insights into dimensions to which we had not given adequate attention. But we hardly wrote a word about what the managers and leaders are like. It was mostly about what they must do to succeed, how to differentiate among them, and how to measure those dimensions that make a difference.

Psychologists have been interested in differences in personality for years. Long before Freud, differences in mood and temperament had been noted, and various theories were espoused about why some people behaved in unpredictable ways. The use of written questionnaires to identify various features of the personality began about the same time as tests of intelligence became popular immediately after World War I.

The measurement of personality variables has matured substantially since those early beginnings. Psychiatric diagnosis is aided by many inventories. Differences in styles of operating (alone or with others), ways of thinking (about tasks or people), preferences for life-styles, primary values (wealth, intellectual activities, opportunities to do good), concern for others, interest in group activities, need for power, need for recognition, and need for privacy are not only personality characteristics of consequence; they are also critical differences among persons that will hinder some and help others perform effectively when leadership is needed.

Scoring schemes for most current personality inventories are developed empirically. A new dimension of personality is developed by scoring those items answered differently by groups known to be different in a specific way. Often no prior judgment is made about what items should be used in a given scale, even though a great deal of judgment may have been exercised in making up the item content of the inventory. The best known of all such inventories is the Minnesota Multiphasic Personality Inventory (MMPI). It was constructed so as to identify various groups of patients who had differing psychiatric diagnoses; the paranoia scale contains items that such patients mark in their own way; scales identify such other groups as schizoids, manics, depressed, psychopathic deviates, or psychasthenics.

Empirically developed personality measures associated with leadership have been slower in appearing on the scene for use. Finding good samples of persons who most people would agree belong in the leadership group is harder than finding clearly paranoid patients. Most personality studies of leadership groups have been made, therefore, using inventories devised for some other purpose.

The absence of measures of "leadership personality" has not deterred the widespread use of personality measures with leaders and managers. After all, the questions asked in the first paragraph of this chapter still beg for an answer, and before a new person is offered an important position, most of those involved want to know what sort of person the candidate *really* is. If there is no obvious test, all sorts of substitutes will be tried. In industry the pervasive methods are use of references and the in-depth interview, augmented often by using the advice of psychological consultants and of "headhunters."

Several of the papers prepared for the San Antonio Conference deal with personality issues. Some will satisfy your curiosity about certain groups: what senior military officers are like (Barber), differences in modes of behavior of U.S. managers and managers from Latin cultures (Osborn and Osborn), and ways in which equally intelligent persons can differ in their intellectual styles so as to behave quite differently (Sternberg).

A set of papers discusses observations obtained under quite-different circumstances, but leading to the same observation: that flaws in personality (character?) may be hidden from view until times are critical, emerging then to cause great harm and distress within the organization. These studies rely mainly on observation and may seem, on the face, to be only weakly supported. Yet the descriptions of inappropriate behavior fit closely to behaviors commonly observed and always puzzling.

Hogan describes the dark side of charisma. The attractiveness of the charismatic leader makes it easy to overlook critical weaknesses. The costs of elevating such persons are often great. Hogan reminds us of Hertzberg's finding that between 60 and 75% of American workers report that the worst or most stressful part of their jobs is their immediate supervisor. He cites three types of flawed managers: the High Likability Floater, Hommes de Ressentiment, and Narcissists.

Hogan, using his "Big 5" personality dimension, has found effective leaders to have the following profiles:

1. Intellectance—high
2. Adjustment—high
3. Prudence—high
4A. Ambition—high
4B. Sociability—variable
5. Likability—very high

Hogan's approach to linking personality dimensions and effective leadership seems to have at least two aspects that differ from the other "personality" participants at the conference:

1. He is interested in personality from the perspective of the observer, rather than an individual's self-rating.

2. He distinguishes between individuals who are able to gain high status and those whose performance is outstanding.

This second distinction Hogan sees as critical: he points out three types of people, as previously noted, who can successfully gain status but are not good leaders.

Moses studied ambiguity and its effects on managerial behavior over a five-year period prior to and during AT&T's divestiture proceedings. Two hundred fifty-eight high-potential managers participated in AT&T's Advanced Management Potential Assessment Center. Four coping styles were identified under conditions of ambiguity: Adaptive, Stylized, Unconcerned, and Overwhelmed. Only the Adaptive response was effective in ambiguous environments; most managers used one or more of the other three styles and were relatively ineffective. His study has implications for practice and for further research.

Morrow and Stern report factors that distinguish individuals who perform at superior, average, and poor levels in a management assessment program (MAP) at IBM. Superior performers scored higher on the Gordon Personal Profile/Inventory on Ascendancy, Sociability, Vigor, and Original Thinking. Poor performers scored higher on Cautiousness, were generally poor performers on tasks, were nonparticipative and passive, and had little impact on group performance. Considering all groups, four types were proposed:
The Star (Superior)—Smart, Sensitive, Social
The Adversary (Average)—Able, Analytical, Abrasive
The Producer (Poor)—Perform, Persevere, Painstaking
The Phantom (Poor)—Polite, Passive, Perturbed

Gough, the author of The California Psychological Inventory (CPI) reports that for years the Dominance scale had the highest relationship to leadership of any scale on the CPI. The Dominance scale, however, was not developed specifically for identifying leaders, but rather to characterize a set of persons of prosocial ascendancy dispositions found in persons describable as "dominant." Persons in positions of authority and decision making do tend to score higher on this scale than do other people, but this fact does not warrant the conclusion that dominance is the only, or even the primary, quality for leaders.

Gough's study in this volume summarizes a series of research projects aimed at clarifying the use of the CPI in the identification of leaders and the prediction of leadership behavior. The scales of the CPI, including Dominance, were developed by finding responses to *items* that would characterize known or specially nominated groups. The responses of any new person taking the test could then be matched against these aggregates to see how closely they agreed. A similar procedure can be used to define patterns or clusters of *scales* diagnostic of leadership. Gough's findings for these patterns should be interpreted against the methods used to define or classify leaders. For instance, in one evaluation husbands and wives rated each other on a one-sentence formulation of leadership. In another, high school principals nominated 179 students as "outstanding leaders" from a total student body of 4,073. In a third, cadets at West Point were rated by their classmates during four years of college on the concept of leadership-in-action. Altogether, six separate samples were studied, including 7,421 individuals. In all samples, the criterion was differentiated in regard to higher versus lower ratings of leadership.

The leadership criteria were strongly correlated with standard CPI scales, particularly Dominance, Capacity for Status, Sociability, Social Presence, Self-Acceptance, Independence, and Empathy. These scales are all from the "interpersonal" zone of the CPI profile and collectively point toward the initiating, enterprising, and decision-making proclivities of the leader. The CPI also has a subset of scales on its profile pertaining to the internalization and acceptance of social norms. These scales are less robustly associated with the leadership criteria. A third section contains three scales for achievement motivation and intellective functioning. In regression combinations, these three scales were often included as predictors, along with the measures of social poise and self-assurance.

At a higher level of abstraction, the CPI may be conceptualized in a theoretical model in which the two basic vectors for interpersonal orientation and normative preferences interact to form four life-styles or ways of living. For each life-style, the degree to which its potentialities are maximized and its problems minimized is indexed by a third vector scale for self-realization. Leaders in all settings tend to come from the theoretical quadrant defined by *interpersonal involvement* and *pronormative beliefs*. However, at high levels of self-realization, as assessed by the third vector scale, individuals can and do receive high ratings on leadership. For example, in situations where change and innovation are needed, persons from the theoretical quadrant defined by *interpersonal involvement* and *normative skepticism* will often assume leadership roles, with the proviso that they must also rank high on the vector for ego integration.

Mary McCaulley reports that the data bank for the Myers-Briggs Type Indicator (MBTI) contains over 500,000 records. This number substantially understates the number of American adults who have discovered their type, whether ESTP, INFJ, etc. Occupational group normative tables reveal that there are more "Feeling" types among teachers, educational administrators, and educational consultants than among the business groups. Persons in higher levels of management are more likely to reach closure (J) than to miss nothing (P); more likely to prefer impersonal, logical decision making (T) than a rational ordering of values with concern over human priorities (F); tend to be practical types (S). Types likely to be concerned with enhancing human performance (NF) are underrepresented among such leadership groups.

*(Note to reader: if these letters are unknown to you, please refer to the McCaulley study in Part II.)*

Myers-Briggs "type" distributions for the population as a whole suggest a bias toward extraversion and sensing; the majority of persons in the general population want quick, active, simple solutions. Managers show a TJ bias that predisposes toward rapid, analytical decisions.

Osborn and Osborn present data collected in a leadership development program in Mexico City, offered in Spanish, and using a translation of the MBTI. More Latin American managers are typed as Extraverted, Sensing, Feeling, and Judging than their United States counterparts. In general, these Latin managers seem to invest more energy in their expressed relationship behavior. United States executives dealing with Latin managers might expect more of a show of hospitality, more friendship activities offered and expected in business dealings, more time invested in the people than in the specific business at hand. Latin managers want more to be in the driver's seat and prefer less that others tell them what to do.

Howard and Bray call attention to differences in personalities of those who progressed rapidly in AT&T in contrast to those who did not. They note that being too much of a homebody is a negative, but acquisitiveness, desire for self-improvement, and interest in community affairs were positives. Ambition, and being strongly oriented to job and career, were positive. Successful groups looked for jobs that would depend upon their own decisions and avoided jobs that were routine or had little social contact.

The collection of data on one measure, Occupational Life Theme, over the 20 years showed that the more successful seem to be caught up more and more in their work, while the least successful begin to detach. Tolerance of Uncertainty shows the same relationship to success, perhaps because high-level jobs involve more ambiguity.

McCauley and Lombardo found that successful managers in market-driven organizations are more decisive and more adept at hiring talented staff, but that they have more difficulty making strategic transitions. Successful managers in "clannish organizations" showed more straightforwardness and composure, and were better in building and mending relationships and in team orientation. This study provides a lead to a possible fresh approach to studying corporate climate.

A large portion of those individuals likely to become the key leaders of the next generation have by this time taken one or more of the many personality measures available. Their scores are recorded in archives available for retrieval as each progresses along a career line and emerges as an important person, or falls off the fast track in the corporate progression. Some of the most interesting parts of longitudinal studies of managerial success have been the observation of flaws in personality and character that prevent individuals from using great talent in leadership positions.

## Thinking Styles

Sternberg has identified intellectual styles not as levels of intelligence but as ways of using it—a propensity. Three different styles are illustrated with case studies as he develops a model of intelligence style in terms of mental self-government. The three arms of government, executive, legislative, and judicial, form an analogy for the style preferences he postulates.

Measuring intelligence entails assessing how much of each ability the individual has; the styles model leads to assessment of how that intelligence is directed or exploited. Variables likely to affect the development of intellectual styles include (1) culture, (2) gender, (3) age ("We sometimes say that children lose their creativity in school. What they may really lose is the intellectual style that generates creative performance."), (4) parenting style, (5) schooling, and (6) occupation. Styles interact with abilities in complex ways; interactions are more synchronous in well-adjusted people. Contextually intelligent people are the ones who capitalize on their strengths and who either remediate or compensate for their weaknesses.

Can styles be measured? A validation study of an inventory aiming to do so is under way. That is a first step toward understanding people's preferences for ways of using their intelligence and teaching them how to use various styles flexibly.

Gratzinger, Warren, and Cooke identified three personal orientations of life-style by factor analysis of the Life Styles Inventory as:
  People/Security Orientation
  Satisfaction Orientation
  Task/Security Orientation

Five hundred fifty-six managers in management development programs were used to identify a top and bottom 10% on managerial effectiveness ratings by peers, subordinates, and superiors. The top group showed a predominance of styles in the Satisfaction domain; the lowest group had their lowest scores in the Satisfaction sector.

## Personality Development and Leadership

Some of the most interesting parts of longitudinal studies of managerial success have been the observation of flaws in personality and character that prevent individuals from using great talent in leadership positions, or that have blocked their consideration for positions of leadership in which they would have excelled. We also see that some who are selected have had an inadequate examination and have flaws that only emerge when the aura of a high position surrounds them.

These studies of the relevance of personality in leadership, management, and executive roles have only touched a small part of the field of personality study. The development of ambition as a result of family influence is a critical domain in which psychological studies exist in some number; there is little of this literature being used to guide public policy or business practice. This issue may become even more critical in the future if the trend persists that has been reported by Howard and Bray—that today's managers have less interest in advancing to top positions than did their predecessors.

A serious omission in our review is attention to values. The Allport-Vernon-Lindzey Scale of Values was once administered widely. There is today no commonly used measure that would aid in sorting persons into those most interested in (1) helping others or society, (2) making money, (3) advancing to positions of power and authority, (4) becoming an expert in something, (5) teaching others, (6) making things happen, (7) having a happy family life, or (8) being a person of importance in the community. There are isolated studies showing that these preferences have an impact on leadership potential and the way in which such potential should be expressed. We need additional attention here.

Personality variables are inextricably intertwined with cultural values and traditions. Our studies only tap the surface of an area of study that must expand rapidly as U.S. interests and activities become increasingly international and cross-cultural. A priority for a next conference on Psychological Measurement and Leadership is to increase the representation of persons who have studied leadership and management across national and cultural boundaries.

Neglected in our discussions, but not necessarily in some of the studies we present, is a fully adequate discussion of the role of leader as the agent of change. Our leadership definitions, as spelled out in individual studies, emphasized decision making, the need for a long time span in planning, the importance of motivating and inspiring followers, and the offering of recognition to subordinates associated with the development of their respect. The key role of the leader in repositioning an organization of the future, in identifying and developing a continuity of leadership, and in assuring the renewal of the organization may well require elements of personality that we have not yet identified.

# CHAPTER EIGHT

# Validation–
# The Ultimate Test

Some leaders perform very well and vindicate their selection. Others do less well, leading those who had been involved in the election, appointment, or advancement of the individual to wonder why obvious flaws were overlooked. As differences in performance lead to observation of weaknesses and strengths, we ask, "How can such qualities be measured in advance?" and "How can we reduce errors in choice?"

When leaders are very successful, we all ask where more of such persons can be found. From these musings have come major efforts to identify the qualities of effective or successful leaders, to develop measures for the early identification of these qualities, and to process large numbers of candidates for high positions using these measures.

## The Development of a Valid Selection Process

The advantages of psychological measures become apparent as we start asking how to pick the winners. We no longer focus on what successful leaders are like; we ask whether knowing what they are like helps us to predict subsequent good performance. We ask how much it would help us and how many persons look like winners on each measure we use. We can also ask questions about fairness: Are measures biased? Do we tend to select those who have had the advantages of birth, gender, education, family, or resources, passing over those whose native talents, when developed, might be superior? Is the measure contaminated in any way, so that preference is given to likable persons rather than winners?

Questions of the sort just sampled arise whenever psychological measures are developed for application to such important processes as selection for schooling, for employment, or for advancement. In prior chapters you have read about some of the technical processes used by measurement psychologists. Here we will introduce you to more. The introduction will be sketchy at best, and will do little more than remind some readers of what they may already have learned. Those who want to study the technical aspects of validation methods may refer to the short list of references at the end of this chapter.

Knowing there will be a lot of **variability**[*] among candidates' performance (the **criterion**), and observing a lot of variability in predictors that have proven relationships with these criteria, we use the relationship to improve our chances in making the next decision. The measures described in earlier chapters, with all their different scales, represent samples of predictors. The predictor is used to reduce the variability on the criterion and to increase the average score on the criterion. Thus we select persons who will perform better and among whom there will be fewer "mistakes."

If the test scores correlate well with the criterion, that is, with measures of later performance, we will increase the proportion of selected persons who are successful leaders or managers by taking those with the highest test scores. Discovering which test scores correlate well with leader performance is not a simple task, for it requires measuring how well leaders perform; each investigator must decide on an appropriate index of leadership success and a method of acquiring it. Often that is the most complicated task of all, which is why we hear often about "the criterion problem."

We are only able to use our predictor with confidence when we have tested a large number of applicants, followed them through a reasonable time on the job so that we can establish a criterion measure, and computed the relationship between the predictor and the criterion. This relationship is expressed in the **correlation coefficient**, which is computed whenever we have a predictor and criterion paired for a group of persons. The symbol used for the correlation coefficient is **r**.

The correlation coefficient when used in this way is an index of **validity**. The validity of a measure refers to the degree to which the measure predicts what it is supposed to predict. A test that works well is said to have high validity. As you can see, the level of validity is not a matter of judgment; it is computed. It relieves the observer of the necessity to make a judgment about whether the relationship is high or low.

A short introduction (or, for some, a reminder) to the concept of correlation may be in order. As an example: evaluating the worth of the well-known SAT as a predictor of college grades requires giving the SAT to a group of persons who then go to college and earn a grade point average (GPA) in a series of college courses. For each student we have a pair of scores: an SAT score and a GPA. Now we can compute a correlation coefficient; it will be a measure of validity of the SAT. Using the formula for the Pearson product-moment correlation coefficient, we would compute the coefficient on a set of pairs of scores: an SAT and a GPA for each student in a group. The resulting value would be +1.0, a perfect positive correlation, if every student's GPA could be predicted perfectly knowing the SAT score. That would be most unusual. Most studies that correlate SAT scores and college grades report correlations from +.30 to +.60; correlations are higher in nonselective colleges and lower in highly selective colleges. (This is not because grades are harder to predict in some colleges, but because

---

[*] *Words presented in boldface in this chapter have technical meanings. A glossary of such terms is appended to this chapter.*

coefficients are affected by the diversity within samples. As variability reduces, so do the correlations.)

Correlation coefficients range from +1.0 to -1.0. Only experience with correlations obtained under various conditions enables one to interpret their levels adequately. Three of the mathematical properties of the index are useful to keep in mind:

1. The value of the correlation coefficient provides a direct measure of predictive efficiency. To illustrate what is meant by this concept, suppose an employer needs 20 new workers. The direct way to find 20 who would be fully satisfactory would be to hire a much-larger number and try them out for six months or a year, and then retain only the 20 who had performed best. Using a test to select workers will only approximate this outcome. The correlation coefficients between a predictor test and the criterion will indicate directly the proportion of the standard criterion score of a group selected by means of the predictor to that which would be obtained by means of the criterion itself.

2. The square of the correlation coefficient tells you how much of the variance in the criterion has been explained by the predictor variable. Thus, in our example above, a correlation of +.50 between SAT and GPA would tell you that the SAT accounted for 25% of the **variance** in grade point averages. (You now face the problem of what *that* means!)

3. The **regression equation** gives a way of computing what level of criterion score can be expected for a person with a given predictor score. Thus, in our example above, we could compute that a person with an SAT score one **standard deviation** above the **mean** would be expected to earn a grade point average 0.5 standard deviations above the mean. Not knowing a person's SAT, the best prediction one can make is the mean GPA.

We will review and comment on results of validation studies that are reported in more complete detail in Part II of this volume. When validities are reported at values around +.50, you should think "25% of the variance in the criterion has been accounted for." Or: "The regression equation will help quite a bit in improving selection." When values rise to +.60 or +.70, research people get excited.

A validity coefficient usually underestimates the worth of a predictor. Why? Because there is always error in the criterion measure, either from unreliability, or from biases, or from irrelevant variability. (A student with an SAT of 600 whose GPA was 2.05 after the first semester at college may have fallen in love or joined the basketball team, and might be expected to perform better at a later time.) Predictor measures also have error in them, but until the test is improved results will not get better. Later, after the test is improved, higher validity coefficients should appear.

Validity coefficients that start out high may also diminish. As an organization changes, prediction measures that had worked well often fail to demonstrate their value. A professional in the business of making predictions needs to check regularly on the degree to which predictors are working. If the professional's work is totally accepted by the organization, and only persons who get high scores on predictors are accepted, the predictor measure will ultimately correlate zero with the criterion. All will be well, for the predictor is performing a useful function still. However, if the company decides they do not need to use the measure anymore, bad things will happen.

The business of making decisions about appointments and promotions on the basis of multiple sources of information and measures has many more intricacies than the preceding discussion might suggest. Following the logic of the analysis is easier when a specific study is described. Presented next are comments based upon studies that follow a design that involves selecting measuring devices, administering them early, then appraising later performance and developing selection strategies.

Jon Bentz introduces the report of his many years of work at Sears with the following statement: "During my tenure at Sears, my colleagues and I worked unrelentingly on the criterion problem—spending much effort on criterion development and the attendant problems of data collection." Was it worth it? Note his results: a multiple **R** of .61 between his predictor battery and the leadership component of his criterion dimensions.

Paul Sparks, in writing about his work over 25 years at Standard Oil of New Jersey, Humble Oil, and Exxon, reports: "Many man-hours were spent in developing basic criterion information. An often-overlooked consideration was given great attention. The final criterion had to make sense to top management. Significant correlations against an index that seriously violated the opinions of top management would be of no value in gaining acceptance of any tools and techniques developed by the project." Sparks used a combination of three criterion variables: position level attained, managerial effectiveness, and salary. This "success index" was adjusted to remove the effects of age and length of service. A multiple **R** of .70 was obtained between the battery of

## TABLE 1
## Predictor Scores vs. Success Index

| Rank on Test | Position on Success Index | | |
|---|---|---|---|
| | Low 1/3 | Mid 1/3 | Top 1/3 |
| 1 – 44 | 0% | 5% | 95% |
| 45 – 88 | 2 | 23 | 75 |
| 89 – 132 | 5 | 38 | 57 |
| 133 – 176 | 10 | 45 | 45 |
| 177 – 220 | 25 | 55 | 20 |
| 221 – 265 | 40 | 47 | 13 |
| 266 – 310 | 53 | 38 | 9 |
| 311 – 355 | 56 | 33 | 11 |
| 356 – 399 | 64 | 29 | 7 |
| 400 – 443 | 79 | 21 | 0 |

## TABLE 2

| Promotion Prediction | College Sample % promoted to 4th level or higher | Noncollege Sample % promoted to 3rd level or higher |
|---|---|---|
| Yes | 42% | 57% |
| No or ? | 21 | 22 |

predictor measures and this criterion. The results were presented to management in the form of a contingency table, Table 1.

It should be clear from this table that there is a substantial difference between the likelihood of success of the top tenth against the bottom tenth. The battery has high validity.

Howard and Bray chose level of promotion in the management hierarchy as their major criterion for managerial success. The major predictor was a summary judgment based upon all of the data collected in their assessment program. This judgment was expressed as answers to the question: will this person be promoted, yes or no? Their predictions are compared with standings 20 years later for their samples of college and noncollege managers (Table 2).

The assessment procedure obviously improves the predictive ability considerably.

Jacobs and Jaques report the work that Stamp began in the midseventies to develop a means of measuring "discretion in action," using an individual assessment interview, the CPA, including (1) a concept formation task, (2) a comprehensive work history, and (3) a set of phrase cards. A follow-up from 1984 to 1988 in four different companies found that the CPA as originally scored predicted the actual level occupied by the individual years later with an r of .79 for the total group, and r's of .70, .89, and .92 for three subsamples. The CPA was designed on the basis of a theoretical position that focused on cognitive capacity.

In 1985, a research program in the Army was begun to explore requirements at the senior level and devise ways to improve performance at that level. Seventy tape-recorded interviews of Army general officers of three- and four-star grade and members of the Senior Executive Service were completed, and the content was analyzed. The theory led to the expectation that executives would have far broader perspectives (frames of reference, cognitive maps) than incumbents at lower levels.

Content analysis yielded frequency counts of mentions of a type of content. Four-star generals were compared to three-stars. The former were found to have a greater multinational concern, a greater concern with Joint/Unified Relationships, and more

Envisioning/Anticipating, all as predicted by theory. Time span of work is a key tenet. Executives add the greatest value to the organization through their resource allocation decisions. Sixty-two and a half percent of three-stars, and 75% of four-stars, had time spans of ten years or longer.

The report of Jacob and Jaques was received with great interest by the psychologists at the San Antonio Conference. Those who worked in industry did not believe that such a high correlation could be obtained even with an excellent criterion and a broad range of talent. The measurement specialists asked whether there was possibility of contamination of the two measures: Could the "best" generals get ratings from their judges that were based on the same sources of evidence as those tapped in the test interviews? Are persons at this level as different from each other as the data suggest?

One person in an excellent position to comment was asked to do so. He is a former chief of staff of the Army who had supported the studies and is still associated with studies of leadership. He reacts as follows:

*I am not at all surprised at these findings. I will leave to the technical experts the examination of the very high correlations obtained. I can report that even among three-star and four-star generals there are enormous differences—more than most people would expect. Their talents run in different directions; only a few are capable of dealing with the enormously complex decisions involved in negotiating with allies, in planning for response to contingencies in the future only vaguely sensed at the moment, and in thinking broadly about issues that must be examined from all perspectives.*

*The ability to think beyond one's own time period and beyond the limits of one's own organization and culture, and to assess effects in terms of the major dimensions of a society is rare indeed. Those who possess such capability stand out sharply even in a group of persons who have gone through many selection steps and have joined the top command of the Army. I am gratified to see that the research staff involved discovered these differences.*

—General Edward C. Meyer,
USA (ret)

Posner and Kouzes established a criterion based on a questionnaire. They asked subordinates about the extent to which the manager meets job-related needs of subordinates, has built a committed work group, and has influence with upper management. Their predictor device, the Leadership Practices Inventory (LPI), explained nearly 55% of the variance around subordinates' assessments of their leaders' effectiveness ($R = .756$). A discriminant analysis to separate top-third from bottom-third managers on the criterion, using LPI, correctly classified 93% of the sample used in the analysis and 78% of an independent sample.

Yukl, Wall, and Lepsinger were able to use a variety of real-life criteria in reporting on a series of studies testing the value of Yukl's Managerial Practices Survey. Their results:

- One hundred fifty-one employees in 26 beauty salons completed the questionnaire on their managers. The variables Clarifying and Motivating correlated .47 and .49

with average monthly profit margin during the year following administration of the questionnaire.

- Three hundred ninety-three military cadets described their 42 first sergeants. Clarifying, Motivating, and Representing correlated .26, .30, and .33 with ratings of unit performance in marching competition.

- Two hundred twenty-three insurance salespersons in retail department stores described their 26 managers. Problem Solving, Clarifying, Monitoring, Motivating, and Networking/Interfacing correlated .37, .40, .49, .36, and .47 with a performance measure of managers based on sales and profits.

- Two hundred sixty-two elementary schoolteachers described their 24 principals by using the questionnaire. Problem Solving, Clarifying, Monitoring, Motivating, and Networking/Interfacing correlated .37, .40, .49, .36, and .47 with the principal's performance based mainly on student achievement and school reputation.

- Sixty-four subordinates completed questionnaires on home economics program leaders. Informing, Consulting and Delegating, Planning and Organizing, Problem Solving, Clarifying, Motivating, Recognizing and Rewarding, Supporting, Developing, Conflict Management and Team Building, and Representing correlated significantly, at .23 to .42, with a composite ranking of the county's programs in terms of quality.

- Ninety-nine teachers used the survey to describe their 42 department heads in high school. Informing, Consulting and Delegating, Planning and Organizing, Clarifying, Motivating, Supporting, Developing, and Representing correlated .23, .28, .30, .25, .23, .27, .37, and .25 with a criterion of effectiveness as a department head.

Yammarino and Bass used performance appraisals of Navy officers as the primary criterion, and their subordinates' ratings as a secondary criterion, to validate a Multifactor Officer Questionnaire designed to identify transformational leadership. Significant correlations ranged from .21 to .38 with their transformational scores for the primary criterion, and from .17 to .89 for the secondary criterion.

Wilson, O'Hare, and Shipper report three studies of change: (1) Bank. Twenty-nine managers at Director level received two weeks of training separated by six months. (2) Health Care Organization. Forty-one managers took eight half-day training sessions over a two-month period. (3) A Nuclear Power Plant. Seventy-one managers were rated by 255 subordinates in one study, and 58 managers by 327 subordinates in the second. Training sessions were conducted during the first half-year. Results in all three studies make it clear that changes can be effected in managerial practices, and that they endure over a period as long as one year. Their VA study continues; an increase of 8% in productivity of the trained group after one year compares to an increase of near zero in the untrained group, a difference significant at the .02 level.

Results of this sort compare very favorably with results obtained when psychological measures are used to identify more mundane human characteristics. These results are promising enough to warrant supporting a large number of investigators to engage in strenuous efforts to refine measures, identify the context in which performance is best, and uncover the prior learning and experiences that enhance the emergence of these desirable human qualities.

These studies have another significance that we must not overlook. The advent of measurement makes possible a more objective review of our systems to recruit and train specialists of all sorts. It should be equally useful for developing and discovering leaders. When the systems for selection and promotion are confined only to oral interviews and to unrecorded personal judgments about potential and performance, the searches for useful relationships and predictors that work, and undesired effects of flamboyant personalities, bias and error often end at the closed door behind which decisions about selection and promotion are made. When the judgments are based on a written record of careful measurement, an evaluation and postaudit is possible. Even when there is no intent to be unfair, objective analysis is more likely to suggest better ways to proceed.

In these studies, the merit of whatever selection measures were used was assessed against an agreed-upon criterion. The same assessment is just as essential when other methods of estimating capabilities are used: for example, personal observation, interview, or recommendations. While the American system can produce persons with an enormous variety of capabilities, it is not producing an adequate number of persons who can become effective leaders. It is also not drawing sufficient leadership talent from all of the likely subpopulations in the society. The system can be made fairer and more efficient by making it more objective.

To make the system work better, the entire society must provide evidence that leadership is admired, desired, respected, and rewarded. In a free and open society, young persons make independent decisions about their lives. They decide individually about which talents they will develop and the life-styles they will elect. Studies of occupational choice show that young persons also gain considerable knowledge about the world of work and select their occupations knowing pretty well the future consequences concerning lifetime earnings, possibilities for advancement, and the amount of autonomy they will have in any given pursuit. The most influential factors in their decisions are self-estimates of their capabilities and their estimate of the job potential in their field of choice.

The first major projects that studied the identification and development of managerial and leadership talent followed models developed to predict school success, occupational choice, and success in the workplace. Using the best judgment available, predictor devices were chosen from among those available (a few were devised on the spot), taking into account whatever analyses of career paths were available.

Several classic prediction studies have been cited in this volume. They involved the dedicated efforts of talented persons who committed years to the effort. They also involved enormous commitment of resources by the sponsoring organizations, a commitment that needed renewal regularly as the studies progressed. The findings of these studies warrant special study and attention, for they provide many insights into the ways in which valuable talent is identified, developed, and used. Each of the studies briefly reviewed above presents at least one major lesson that we must learn. These lessons will enable us to move forward to other important studies and build on this foundation of good work.

Yet, as we review the important findings from these major efforts, we realize that almost all of the samples studied are drawn from the United States and that most of the data were collected in the late 20th century. Some findings will surely transcend the specifics of the organizations that produced them—but which ones?

Central to these prediction studies were the decisions about the criterion. If our intent is to find how we can identify the successful leaders early, we must recognize a successful leader when we see one and know the differences in degrees of success among groups of persons we have anointed as leaders. In these decisions we observe again the necessity to attend to the context in which leadership is exercised. Is leadership of every American corporation the same? Does effective leadership of a battalion of American soldiers require the same capabilities as effective leadership of a large bakery? or of Bell Laboratories? or of the University of Chicago? Is successful leadership in America definable in the same terms as successful leadership in Russia? in Cuba? in Peru? in China? in Great Britain? Is successful leadership today definable in the same terms as successful leadership in the 19th century? in colonial times? in the times of early England? in Greek and Roman times?

We must assume that humans today and in earlier times and in different cultures and societies have similar needs and appetites, the same varieties of pathology, and similar inherent cognitive capabilities. But to what extent do different socialization processes lead to the moderating of individual selfishness in order to promote group goals? Are some societies and organizations more competitive, and some more cooperative? Is aggressive behavior prized more in some cultures and in some times, and expression of the social graces more highly prized in other settings? You will find yourself asking questions of this sort as you read the following sections, and as you read the full studies in more detail. The questions one asks about the generalizability of the findings are as critical as the knowledge one gains about what worked and what did not work in the setting specified.

Thus even the simplest prediction study makes assumptions about the nature of human beings, about the nature of leadership, and about the ways in which organizations and the society at large operate. Every step in a prediction study affects the degree of generalization that can be given to findings. The study must be interpreted in terms of the organizational context in which it was done and in terms of the implicit or explicit values associated with various activities. We must understand the criterion problem and must know for each study the way in which the criterion is defined and measured before we conclude that the findings are relevant in another setting.

This chapter provides an introduction to the reading of the individual studies in Part II. They may be read in any order. Each study is written for professional colleagues rather than for the general public but is easily readable by anyone who has proceeded thus far. We encourage you to move to the most interesting part of this volume as soon as you have read chapter 9.

Chapter 9 makes a few cognitive leaps as an aid to the reader in seeing some of the implications of the findings reviewed in these introductory chapters. There are comments about ways in which research in this field should progress as a larger number of investigators turn their attention to the better understanding of the nature of leadership and its measurement and its prediction.

# A GLOSSARY OF MEASUREMENT TERMS

These terms were used in their technical sense in this chapter. These definitions are to serve as an aid to reading the chapters and the later studies.

**analysis of variance.** Statistical procedure that divides the variance in a given variable into a variety of sources, using an F-value to indicate the probability that this source contributed to the variance at more than a chance level (indicated by a **p**-value).

**chi-squared.** Statistical test used with data sets assigned to categories. Indicates whether the classification could have resulted from chance (by testing a hypothesis that is the "chance" hypothesis).

**correlation coefficient.** A measure of the degree of relationship between any two paired measures. Varies from -1.0 to +1.0. Symbol is **r**. For no relationship, r = 0.0. **r-squared** yields an estimate of the amount of variance accounted for.

**criterion.** A measure that is accepted as being an accurate reflection of any performance, quality, or category that is to be estimated using a psychological measure. Usual use: "The criterion we were trying to predict was...." Plural is **criteria**.

**discriminant function.** Statistical procedure for using multiple measures to assign persons to categories, developing a formula for classification, and estimating within and among group variances.

**F-test.** See analysis of variance.

**mean.** The average of an array of scores. Computed by adding all scores and dividing by the number of scores.

**multiple regression equation.** Statistical procedure for using a combination of measures to predict a criterion score, and to estimate the amount of variance accounted for by the predictors. Symbol is **R**. **R squared** yields an estimate of the amount of variance accounted for.

**p.** Symbol for reporting the level of significance at which a given statistical hypothesis may be rejected. Usually seen as **p<.01** or **p<.05**.

**r.** Symbol for the correlation coefficient.

**R.** Symbol for the multiple regression coefficient.

**regression equation.** An algebraic formula for the best-fitting straight line that expresses the relationship between one variable and another. In this volume, usually a relationship between a predictor and a criterion.

**reliability.** A measure of the degree to which a measure "holds still," or has stability. Often estimated by administering the measure twice to the same persons. Coefficient is expressed as a correlation coefficient (**r**). Less-than-perfect reliability reduces the correlation of that measure with any other measure.

**restriction of range.** Refers to the common absence in a given sample of a full representation of the total population. Restriction in range gives underestimates of correlations of that variable with others.

**significant.** Refers to the probability of only chance effects producing observed effects. See probability.

**standard deviation.** A measure of the variability in an array of scores. Computed as the square root of the average sum of squares of scores around the mean. (The formula is easier than this description makes it appear.)

**t-test**. A test of the likelihood that a difference of the size observed between means of two groups sampled could have occurred if both groups were drawn randomly from the same population. A t-test is evaluated by the **p**-value associated with it.

**validity**. The degree to which a test measures what it purports to measure. Usually expressed as a **correlation coefficient**.

**variability**. The amount of dispersion in an array of scores. Measured by the **standard deviation**; often crudely estimated by noting the difference between highest and lowest scores.

**variance**. Technically, the square of the **standard deviation**.

## Suggested Readings

Anastasi, A. (1988). *Psychological testing*. New York: MacMillan.

Cronbach, L. J. (1984). *Essentials of psychological testing* (4th ed.). New York: Harper & Row.

Edwards, A. L. (1984). *Linear regression and correlation introduction* (2nd ed.). New York: W. H. Freeman.

Ghiselli, E. E., Campbell, J. P., & Zedeck, S. (1981). *Measurement theory for the behavioral sciences.* San Francisco: W. H. Freeman.

# Translating Knowledge
# Into Action

This book is directed primarily toward those persons who must make decisions about recruiting, developing, and utilizing leadership talent. The studies included provide insight into the nature of leadership and of the behaviors that make a difference in the performance of a group or an organization. The reader must plan the course of action for his or her own organization in order to gain benefits from this knowledge.

We highlight the important findings that call for action and suggest some ways to begin. The research studies themselves also provide suggested forms for action. Many of them have not only developed good measures for use, but have tested them in a meaningful way. Any organization that wants to profit from this work would do well to plan similar tests. This is prudent not merely because it provides a way of evaluating the merits of something new, but also because there are always skeptics. Without evidence a good program may be jettisoned later, and the advantages it provides for the organization may be lost.

## What We Are Learning About Leadership

1. The quality of leadership makes a difference. Productivity, quality of work, and satisfaction of members, followers, or workers increase, and the willingness to exert effort and expend energy rises when those in charge behave like leaders.

2. Many of the specific behaviors that characterize leadership have been identified and incorporated into psychological measures. These behaviors are not so exotic and difficult to perform that they must be practiced from birth. Many of them have been written about widely and recommended as good practice.

3. Individuals differ widely in their ability to behave like a leader. They also differ widely in their knowledge about which behaviors work best and in their willingness to learn better behaviors and forego behaviors that are counterproductive.

Experience is one of the teachers, but some persons do not learn from experience.

4. Training programs can affect the behaviors of persons holding positions of responsibility and will change the behaviors of many persons so that they become more like leaders.

5. Organizations can obtain fairly easily, and by methods already in use, estimates of the leadership qualities of candidates under consideration for leadership roles. Paper-and-pencil measures have been developed and are available. Procedures for collecting data from the candidate (self-ratings) are useful, but not nearly as useful as reports from superiors. These, in turn, are not nearly as useful as reports from peers and subordinates.

6. The preceding principles are sufficiently important for the way an organization functions to warrant immediate implementation. There is ample evidence that selecting and training persons who will perform more in a leadership mode than in a managerial mode will make a significant difference in attaining organizational goals. The procedures have been tested and follow-up studies have confirmed the benefits.

7. Our studies have found no single comprehensive list of leadership qualities. Every investigator who studies dimensions of leader and manager behavior comes up with a slightly different, or substantially different, list.

8. Our studies have found no best measure to differentiate leaders from managers or leaders from followers, or to identify those who someday will be leaders. There is no best battery of tests or assessment procedures either. Such measures that are useful increase the likelihood that selected persons will engage in leadership acts of consequence. The increase is enough to make investing in the selection process worthwhile.

9. Our studies have found no single path to leadership. No given training program can assure success for a person as a leader. There are training programs that have demonstrated their worth in increasing instances of effective behavior, enough of an increase to be worth investing in the program.

10. Leaders generally cannot be clearly distinguished from nonleaders. Most persons have exercised leadership in some way or other, maybe well, maybe poorly. Individuals differ in their willingness to be leaders, in their capabilities for exercising leadership, and in their feelings of responsibility for the groups that might benefit from their involvement. Increasing the number of effective leadership acts in an organization will surely have a payoff; hunting for *the* leader may not.

11. Indicators of leadership talent and predisposition can be obtained through psychological measures. These indicators identify persons who will perform better in situations calling for leadership.

12. Indicators of leadership ability are subtle and often misread. The take-charge person, the inspirational speaker, the pleasing and affable individual, or the person willing to take on every assignment may lack some of the essential qualities for effective leadership. Those who must make choices need to be wary.

13. Winning the top position does not make a person a leader. Often selection is made without adequate knowledge of the job requirements and without in-depth knowledge of how the new incumbent will perform.

14. Persons at the top of an organization have obligations far beyond those of carrying the title, presiding, and pleasing their followers. If the organization is to achieve its goals, all who support the organization must know those goals and be committed to them. If the organization is to survive, the leader must help the organization change as conditions change. If resources are to be used well, the leader must make critical decisions and take into consideration all variables that affect that decision. The leader must be able to marshal and analyze relevant information and deal with issues of enormous complexity. If the organization is to maintain its strength, the leader must develop a strong set of leaders and potential leaders; out of that set must come the leaders of tomorrow.

15. Leaders must emerge and play a role at every level of an organization if that organization is to use the full energy of all followers in achieving its objectives. Such leaders can inspire subordinates and make them followers. The team will accomplish more, and members will find greater satisfaction in their work. Managers can become leaders rather than bosses; when they do, workers are happier and more productive.

16. Some managers naturally tend to behave in ways that help them produce the effects expected of leaders. Hunting for such persons to take managerial positions can be very fruitful.

17. Leaders are more "made" than "born." Commitment to others is learned early and is an essential ingredient. The development of a sensitivity to the views of others, to the effects of context, to the high level of complexity in most issues, especially those involving conflict, is critical to good functioning as a leader.

18. Many candidates for leadership positions drop out of the competition either because of discouragement or frustration because they do not feel they are succeeding, or because they can see themselves happier doing something else. This high loss rate requires a larger pool of candidates than is usually foreseen. Often when a choice is to be made, there is too little talent available rather than too much.

19. The younger generation of persons entering managerial and leadership roles shows considerably less interest in positions of leadership and responsibility than characterizes their predecessors. This trend, if it continues, has serious consequences for society.

20. The number of instances of failed leadership is far too high. Every failure is costly both for the incumbent and for the organization. The number of egregious errors in choice is astonishingly large, considering the effort put into searches.

21. There is great value in recruiting persons of high talent into an organization and providing the experiences that will develop their leadership talents. Leaders at all levels of an organization are needed in order to multiply the influence of top leaders.

## Sample Action Plans

The preceding list of principles or generalizations is only a beginning. As you read the research studies in Part II, you will be able to add to this list. You also will begin to think about how to translate some of the ideas tested in research studies into action that will benefit your own situation.

Consider first your organization's greatest needs. Which studies are most relevant? Which address problems you are already experiencing? To help you, this chapter illustrates ways in which several different programs of action might be devised. They mimic some of the studies reported and the likely outcomes from such studies.

Suppose the organization is one that needs a bit of revitalization. Too few candidates for promotion seem good enough. Many managers seem below standard. Some of the best young managers are looking for opportunities elsewhere. What can be done? Provided are sample options; they are in no particular order.

**Option 1.** Study the Sparks, Bentz, and Howard and Bray models, and imitate them.

**Major principle involved:** An organization benefits by any program that increases the quality of members of the group.

The studies of Sparks and Bentz show that initial screening of employees, particularly managers, on a test battery that includes measures of mental abilities, personality characteristics, and measures of motivation and values can have long-term beneficial effects for the organization. Specifically, there will be a larger number of attractive candidates available for promotion to higher positions who can be developed within the organization.

### Steps to follow:

With professional help, adopt a test battery for selecting from among candidates for managerial positions. Plan a long-term validation.

Develop a program for reviewing periodically the quality of performance of all managers. Use a variety of methods of those described in a number of the studies (watch for studies that fit).

Use your test battery, retaining all past selection methods. In addition, require that no one be employed as a manager who does not score in the top 40% of applicants on that test battery. (This level is arbitrary but affects the outcome measures which follow. The level is reasonable.)

### What outcomes can you expect?

Let us assume that your organization's screening battery works exactly as well as that developed at Exxon and described by Sparks. You should find that 68% of the new managers will match the performance of the top third of managers hired without using the screening tests.

If your current top third of managers are the ones you prize and you wish the rest were like them, you now have a straightforward way to double their number. How much is that worth to your company? Or, for that matter, to any organization?

The 68% came from the table provided by Sparks in his research study; that outcome has already been noted in chapter 8. The figures in that table show the power of a predictor battery that has a validity coefficient of +.70. They also show that investing in recruiting, so that one need not choose everyone but can be selective, has a high payoff. These numbers also show why businesses like to have a good reputation as an employer—they can risk terminating marginal employees in order to replace them with better ones.

The work of Bentz at Sears or the work of Howard and Bray at AT&T could have been used as models in the same way. Their methods and objectives differ somewhat, and so the objective might have been stated differently. However, the outcomes would have been equally dramatic.

**Option 2.** Increase the proportion of managers who behave like transformational leaders.

**Major principle involved:** Transformational leaders increase commitment to group goals, increase the work output of units, and have followers who find more satisfaction in their work.

The work of Yammarino and Bass; of Clover; of Wilson, O'Hare, and Shipper; and of Posner and Kouzes points to the importance of inspirational leadership, of intellectual involvement of followers or subordinates in the work of the organization, and of attention to the individual needs of group members. Measures are illustrated that identify those candidates who will be very effective. The Wilson team has developed a training program that accomplishes similar objectives. Reported outcomes are impressive and include increased profitability of units, greater success in competition with other units, and higher ratings for the leaders both by superiors and subordinates. Interestingly, the best way to identify such leaders or managers is to inquire of subordinates, who perceive these qualities more clearly than do superiors.

**Steps to follow:**

Adopt or develop a questionnaire to administer to all managers that includes items like those in the study that appeals to you most. Scores will relate to the desirable outcomes previously outlined. Make assignments accordingly.

Verify the measures obtained from self-descriptions with data collected from superiors, peers, and especially subordinates. These ratings will correlate much more with later success than will the self-ratings provided by the managers themselves.

Supplement these ways of capitalizing on existing talent with training programs that will increase the talent in your management team. Wilson, O'Hare, and Shipper have outlined such a training program and have reported upon its success. Its scope goes well beyond accentuating the transformational aspect of leadership.

Improve your system for determining the effectiveness of each manager and increasing their motivation to succeed. That makes you a transformational leader, too. Note the methods used by Kouzes and Posner, for they represent an interesting and nonthreatening way to collect data on managers.

### What outcomes can you expect?

The studies by Yammarino and Bass; Wilson, O'Hare, and Shipper; Posner and Kouzes; and Yukl, Wall, and Lepsinger cite such levels of correlation as: .47, .49, .26, .30, .33, .37, .40, .49, .36, .47, .40, .49, .36, and .47. There are some multiple correlations that are higher and some single coefficients that are lower.

We provided an illustration of the effect of a correlation of .70 on the quality of persons selected if certain conditions prevailed. We will use this same model with correlations of the predictor at levels of .30, .40, and .50. We must first agree on some assumptions:

- You consider half of your managers satisfactory and wish all others were like the top half.

- You are willing to hire only four out of every ten applicants (or promote from within only four out of ten otherwise-acceptable candidates) who, after meeting all your other requirements, also score in the top 40% of applicants on the predictor device you have chosen.

The outcome: Of the new ones you hire or promote who meet these criteria,
    62% will be satisfactory when $r = .30$
    66% will be satisfactory when $r = .40$
    70% will be satisfactory when $r = .50$

If you are willing or able to hire or promote only one in ten of all those you consider satisfactory except for the test, then you will get the following results:
    71% will be satisfactory when $r = .30$
    78% will be satisfactory when $r = .40$
    84% will be satisfactory when $r = .50$

Note that the predictor device you will probably find most useful will involve collecting ratings of managers and candidates from their subordinates and peers. You will need to involve the manager's superiors in this decision to avoid later problems.

**Option 3.** Emphasize the growth and development of the managers in whom a great deal has already been invested. Maybe we can make them leaders.

**Major principle involved:** Some people grow on the job; some do not.

The wise organization will provide opportunities for growth, will monitor that growth, and will provide further opportunities for those who do learn and develop. The work of Howard and Bray, McCauley and Lombardo, and Ruderman, Ohlott, and McCaulley is relevant. Other work in the field, especially by McCall, Lombardo, and Morrison, highlights instances in which experience does not teach, and learning and changes of behavior are notably absent. Most such persons "derail," but some stay on, usually to the organization's disadvantage.

**Steps to follow:**

Identify those managers with the greatest promise for advancement.

Identify those jobs that offer the greatest opportunities for the development of important qualities desired in the senior leadership of the organization.

Assign the most promising managers to the positions that support development.

Monitor the process using the work of McCauley and Lombardo and the work of Ruderman, Ohlott, and McCaulley as guides. BENCHMARKS and the Job Challenge Profile can be used to support such a program.

### What outcomes can you expect?

Data do not warrant specifying these outcomes. True, the evidence of effects seems real, and results of such a program are promising. But in the absence of measures that have been applied, criteria that have been assessed, and relationships that have been tested and quantified, we can make no estimates of outcomes. With the development of BENCHMARKS and the Job Challenge Profile we can expect such basic data eventually.

There is, of course, an additional option. You may make your own choice of the most relevant studies, write out the principles that appeal to you and that meet your needs, and plan your own steps for action. A plan developed on the basis of analysis of the specific needs of an organization may appeal more to an organization than one pulled off the shelf.

Leaders of organizations report that resistance to changes in an organization is very great. Change threatens status, increases ambiguity, and thus causes anxiety and stress. Justification to make any change needs a convincing case for a crisis or near-crisis. Many leaders report that they felt it necessary to overstate their own estimates of needs for change in order to get things rolling. Thus, a homebuilt campaign can tie in with whatever dark clouds appear on the horizon, as an aid to undercutting resistance to any change.

Be certain, as part of any planned program, to include fair estimates of the beneficial outcomes to be expected and ways of measuring those outcomes.

## The Need for Much More Research

Good science leads as often to new directions for research as to knowledge that is conclusive. Even though the findings of the studies reported in this book are exciting and useful, they will have the most influence because of the new directions they suggest. Although the investigators have been creative and visionary, they recognize the limitations of the work done so far and the challenges they face.

Progress in understanding leaders and leadership has come about because persons with influence, authority, and reputation have insisted on knowing more about the phenomenon. Corporations, the military, governmental units, and even schools, small businesses, and community organizations continue to invest heavily in training programs and to support research to learn more. These organizations are also composed of the persons who need to be studied. Close collaboration between those who do research and those who will put the findings to use is essential. Most of the studies in this book are fine examples of such cooperative efforts. More must be done.

Professionals in applied areas are responding to the surge of interest in management and leadership; their numbers have increased as support has increased. The level of activity reflected in these studies is a result. The increased relevance of such studies is the direct result of close cooperation between those interested in research and those in positions of authority who have encouraged use of the organizational mechanisms to collect essential data.

Investigations of leadership phenomena by professionals in academic settings have also increased in number and in relevance. Academic studies can supply an important supportive structure required in this area of application. For example, they can provide better understanding of how individuals develop high aspirations and a commitment to build a better community, a better organization, or a better world. They can help in defining the experiences that moderate self-interest and chauvinism and produce instead a constructive and optimistic dedication to human welfare.

Today many scientists interested in behavior are examining the domain of human development from a life-span perspective. Much has been studied about the principles of learning, especially learning among successful, mature adults. In future studies of leadership, an interdisciplinary orientation is necessary to integrate the search and the knowledge obtained across age groups, class boundaries, and cultures. Only by doing so will we be able to understand more about the differences in behaviors, interrelationships, and perceptions that have surfaced so far in studies of leadership and management. Leadership is an exciting domain of research; it calls out for more and more cooperative interest and attention in the future.

This is more than just a challenge to engage more scholars in a discipline or a field of study. It is an invitation to join in making the world better. How enormously satisfying it would be to provide an emphatic yes to Richard Campbell when he asks, as he did at the conference, "Can you really develop people?" and then go on to recite confidently in detail how to do so. As it is, we have a fine start in the work reported in Part II.

Section A of Part II is written by Edwin P. Hollander and Lynn R. Offermann. It provides a background of overall principles and findings in a wide variety of studies that relate to leadership and followership, with attention to the particular issues of power and authority. Section A, with its extensive scholarly bibliography, introduces the research papers that comprise Part II. The 28 research reports that follow in succeeding sections of Part II are introduced briefly, as are the members of the research teams who produced them.

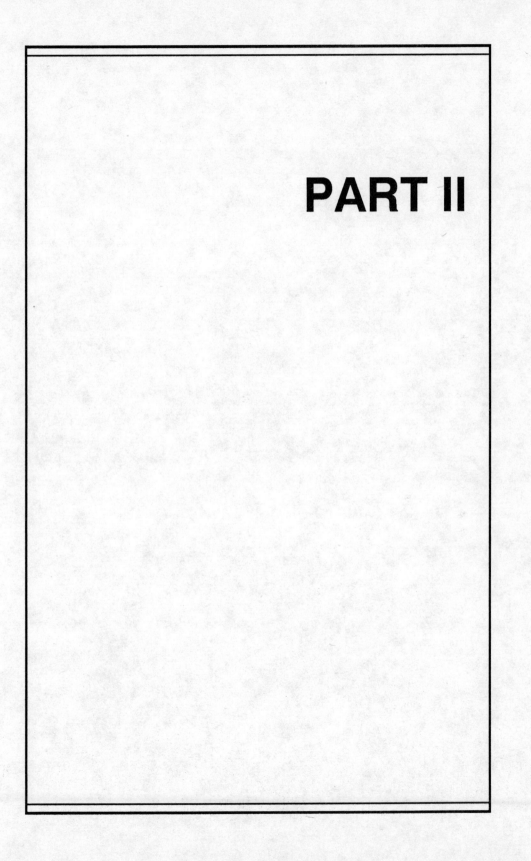

# PART II

# SECTION A

A Review of Prior
Scholarly Research
in Leadership

# A Review of Prior Scholarly Research in Leadership

The use of measurement techniques to gain a better understanding of leadership represents only one facet of a much-larger perspective on the topic. Leadership has been a subject for study in many disciplines. A perspective on this broader literature gives added meaning to the studies that are reported in the later sections. Although the methods employed and the subjects involved do not always lead directly to applications in organizations, the theories and concepts developed provide a meaningful framework for interpretation of findings in all settings.

## Relational Features of Organizational Leadership and Followership

Edwin P. Hollander and Lynn R. Offermann

This paper is a review of the development of concepts and theories of leadership up to the present time. Leadership is examined from the standpoint of leaders and their relations to followers. Various theories and approaches are described, and the development of more effective ways of thinking is traced through the post–World War II period. Origins of many of the ideas developed in the research papers in later sections can be noted in earlier work.

Edwin P. Hollander, University Distinguished Professor of Psychology, The City University of New York, I/O Psychology Doctoral Program, Baruch College & University Graduate Center, Box 512, 17 Lexington Avenue, New York, New York 10010. (212-725-3201). PhD, Columbia University. Author of various works, including *Leaders, Groups, and Influence; Leadership Dynamics*; and the "Leadership and Power" chapter in *The Handbook of Social Psychology*, third edition.

Lynn R. Offermann, Associate Professor of Psychology, The George Washington University, Washington, DC 20006. (202-676-6000). PhD, Syracuse University. Co-editor of special issue of *American Psychologist*, in press.

# Relational Features of Organizational Leadership and Followership

*Edwin P.
Hollander* *
*and*
*Lynn R.
Offermann*

In this article we intend to review some of the major findings and trends in studying leadership and followership in organizations. Our approach sees leadership as a process involving a collaboration between a leader and responsive followers. This relational view of the leadership process breaks with a tradition of seeing leadership as something possessed by a leader alone, with followers too often left out of the discussion.

The many functions performed by leadership include not only the obvious one of directing activity but also decision making, goal setting, communicating, adjudicating conflict, and otherwise maintaining the enterprise, among others. These are dispersed functions which often involve some delegation to followership. Leadership and followership therefore consist of an interlocking system of relationships.

Indeed, leadership operates within constraints as well as opportunities that are presented by external forces including followers, as Stewart (1982) has noted. The constraints include the expectations and perceptions of followers which can influence leaders (Hollander, 1985, 1986; Lord & Maher, 1989). An early exponent of this general view was Sanford (1950) who asserted that followers are crucial to any leadership event and deserve greater attention.

Leadership and followership can both be active roles, given the reality that hierarchical organizations require both functions at every level. The usual expectation of the follower role as essentially passive is misleading when considering followership as an accompaniment to leadership. Leaders do command greater attention and influence, but there now is an

---

*The authors consider their contributions to be equal, though they are listed in alphabetical order.*

increasing realization that followers affect leaders, too, and in more than trivial ways.

## Historical Background

A primary focus on leaders was evident early in the study of leadership. At its center was the emphasis on leader qualities, the so-called trait approach. It emphasized personal qualities of those occupying leader roles. Stogdill (1948) and Mann (1959) reported literature reviews which found that intelligence tended to be slightly higher for leaders, with the latter also reporting positive relationships for general adjustment, extroversion, and dominance. These reviews were part of a context for a reorientation in the 1950s called the situational approach. Its key point was that situations varied in their demands on leaders, so that traits were only appropriate as they fit a particular task and interpersonal context. This shift from the traditional trait view opened the way for a variety of approaches to the leader-follower relationship.

**From Traits to Attributions** The original trait conception of leadership was founded on the major assumption that leaders possessed universal characteristics which *made* them leaders. These characteristics were seen to be fixed, largely inborn, and applicable across situations. Broadly speaking, this was the essence of the "Great Man Theory" promulgated by Galton (1869) and his disciples. This approach began the countless attempts to discover and measure traits which distinguished leaders from followers. Among the failings of trait theory was an absence of consideration of the situation faced by the leader, including the followers to be led, and any concern with the quality of the leader's *performance*. On the latter point, interest developed in what Fiedler (1961) has called "leadership effectiveness traits," emphasizing the qualities needed to perform well as a leader, rather than those needed to become one. An example of one such quality recently investigated by Fiedler and Garcia (1987) is "cognitive resources," essentially intelligence, whose applicability Fiedler and Leister (1977) earlier found was limited by what a leader's superior would allow (see also Hendrick, 1990).

Many situational elements are now recognized as affecting the process of leadership, in addition to the characteristics of the leader and followers. Among them are the nature of the task or activity, its history and actors, the availability of human and material resources, and the quality of leader-follower relations. These relations are of course affected by the leader's attributes, including his or her perceived competence, motivation, and personality characteristics, as these relate to followers. All of these can play a part in shaping followers' perceptions and responses to the leader. Indeed, this link between perceptions and behavior is the essence of the interest now in leader attributes perceived by followers, and the followers' implicit leadership theories (ILTs) (e.g., Calder, 1977; Lord et al., 1986; Rush et al., 1977).

Today, the emphasis has shifted from traits to follower attributions of leaders that make followers respond affirmatively or otherwise to their leader. These perceptions are checked against prototypes held by followers of leader attributes and how leaders should perform (see Lord & Maher, 1989). This line of work is part of the greater attention currently being given to cognitive elements in leader-follower relations, represented by follower ILTs among other concepts. This integration of cognition and leadership is but one example of how the increasing prominence of cognitive approaches in psychology in general can be seen in organizational research (e.g., Gioia & Sims, 1986).

A related approach to leader cognition considers it to be based on relatively stable cognitive qualities, a style. This is illustrated by the work of Sternberg (1990) on "intellectual styles," reflecting individual preferences for ways of using one's intelligence. Wagner and Sternberg (1990) maintain that interest in intellectual characteristics of leaders must include assessment of "street smarts," also referred to as practical intelligence or tacit knowledge. Measurement of a leader's tacit knowledge through their new scale is situation-specific, rather than traitlike, involving a manager's judgment of specific work situations and potential responses to them.

**Leader and Follower Roles** Even with the situational and attributional approaches, ideas about leadership embodied a view of the leader and followers in sharply different roles. Yet being a follower can be an active role that holds within it the potential of leadership, and behaviors seen to represent effective leadership include attributes of good followership (see Hollander & Webb, 1955; Kouzes & Posner, 1987). Granting an imbalance of power, influence can be exerted in both roles, as part of a social exchange (Homans, 1961). Effective leadership is achieved after all by a process in which there is reciprocity and the potential for two-way influence and power sharing.

Indeed, directing followers only through the power of authority was compared unfavorably to leadership by Freud (1921), who considered it dominance. Cowley (1928) called it "headship" rather than leadership. When such assertions of power prevail, the goals of authentic leadership are undermined. This is so despite the extremes of shrinking from power and seeing its use as necessarily bad, or alternatively desiring power and abusing others in the process. The latter is seen for instance in Kipnis' (1976) work on the "metamorphoses of power." It deals with the changes that may be brought about in the "powerholder" by having high power over others, including exalted self-worth and isolation from and devaluation of less powerful others.

Leadership relies on mutual responsiveness and dependency, since the qualities needed to be a leader do not inhere in that person alone. As noted here at the outset, in any group or organization a complex of leadership functions needs to be fulfilled. No doubt the most significant early work on leadership functions was the research done by Shartle and his colleagues at Ohio State University on dimensions of leader behavior among naval officers (e.g., Shartle & Stogdill, 1953; Fleishman, 1973). One product of this research was the Leader Behavior Description Questionnaire (LBDQ), an instrument still widely used to measure the main factors of leader consideration and initiating structure.

**Contingency Models** Two other outgrowths of the situational approach occurred about 25 years ago: contingency and transactional models. They departed from the traditional dichotomy of traits or situations in determining who becomes a leader and who performs well in the role. Both developments have added conceptually and empirically to an understanding of the complexities of leadership.

The first major contingency model was Fiedler's (1964, 1967) Least Preferred Coworker (LPC) Model, followed by the Evans (1970, 1974) and House (1971) Path-Goal Model, and the Vroom and Yetton (1973) Leadership and Decision-making

Model. These and other contingency models considered leadership effectiveness to be a joint function of leader qualities and situational demands as contingencies which interact to make leader qualities variously appropriate to the task at hand.

Fiedler's LPC model distinguishes between two leader styles, task-oriented (Low LPC) and relationship-oriented (High LPC), using the LPC measure obtained by asking respondents to make ratings of the person with whom they were least able to work well. Fiedler and his colleagues find that these leader orientations can produce greater or lesser effectiveness depending upon three situational contingencies: leader-member relations, task structure, and leader position power. Where these factors are either all favorable or unfavorable, Low LPC leaders should perform best, and where mixed or intermediate, High LPC leaders should perform best, according to Fiedler (see Rice & Kastenbaum, 1983, for a literature review).

The two other contingency models noted above deal with different contingencies that affect leader-follower relations. Path-goal theory (House, 1971; House & Mitchell, 1974) is a contingency model based on the leader's effectiveness in increasing followers' motivation along a path leading to a goal. The three contingencies posited as facing the leader are the task, characteristics of the followers, and the nature of the followers' group. Central to the theory is the leader's behavior as a source of satisfaction to followers, for example, leader consideration will be more effective in situations with low role ambiguity for followers, and initiating structure with high role ambiguity and high job complexity for them; followers will respond better to the leader's direction when the task is unstructured, and less when structured (see House & Dessler, 1974).

Vroom and Yetton's (1973) normative model of decision making is concerned with increasing follower involvement, ranging from a leader's autocratic, consultative, to group decision styles, depending upon various situational factors. Choice of style is based upon such situational factors as time available, importance of decision quality, information followers have, clarity of the problem, and how much follower acceptance is necessary to implementing the decision. A useful feature of studying this model is to provide leaders with an awareness of how they make decisions, what goes into them, and how this process can be improved (Baker, 1980).

**Transactional Models** Process-oriented "transactional" models of leadership developed initially out of a social exchange perspective, emphasizing the implicit social exchange or transaction that exists between leader and followers as a feature of effectiveness (see Hollander, 1964, 1978; Hollander & Julian, 1969; Homans, 1961). The leader gives benefits to followers, such as a definition of the situation and direction, which is reciprocated by followers in heightened esteem for and responsiveness to the leader. This transactional approach fits the current social science emphasis on persuasive influence rather than coerced compliance. Indeed, Katz and Kahn (1978) define leadership in organizations as an increment of influence above compliance.

Furthermore, a transactional approach gives special emphasis to the significance of followers' perceptions of the leader. Relatedly, Graen (1975) developed a social exchange model of leader-follower relations emphasizing role making between a leader and particular followers. This Leader Member Exchange Model (LMX) has gained currency as another approach within social exchange/transactional developments (see Dienesch & Liden, 1986; Graen & Scandura, 1987). In brief, the LMX model distinguishes between the relationships a leader has with followers who are close to the leader and those who are more distant. The first have a better-quality relationship with the leader, but also have higher expectations for their loyalty and performance; the others receive fewer personal demands from the leader, but also fewer rewards. Liden and Graen (1980), for instance, found that subordinates reporting a high-quality relationship with their supervisors assumed more job responsibility, contributed more, and were rated as higher performers than those with low-quality relationships.

Generally speaking, transactional models center on the followers' perceptions of and expectations about the leader's actions and motives, in accordance with attributional analysis. Heider's (1958) earlier work on the attribution of intentions through interpersonal perception is exemplified in the distinction between "can" and "will." If a leader is perceived to be *able* to achieve a favorable outcome, but doesn't because of an apparent *failure of will*, this causes a greater loss of following than the reverse, that is, an inability to achieve something desirable but with an evident try, nonetheless. This is also related to the "idiosyncrasy credit" model of innovative leadership (Hollander, 1958), which deals with the latitude a leader has to bring about change as a function of followers' perceptions of that leader's competence and signs of loyalty that engender trust.

The main focus of the idiosyncrasy credit model is on leadership as a dynamic process of interpersonal evaluation which earns credits in the eyes of followers. These credits provide latitude for deviations that would be unacceptable for those without such credits. Credits come from perceived competence and conformity to group norms, as a sign of loyalty, and then can be used to take innovative actions expected as part of the leader's role. Unused credits can be lost by failing to fulfill follower expectations for that role, including inaction in the face of need. Also, the leader's self-serving and other negatively viewed behaviors can drain credits, as well as perceptions of weak motivation, incompetence, and the responsibility for failure (cf. Alvarez, 1968).

A closely associated question concerns how followers perceive the leader's source of authority, or "legitimacy," in responding to that leader. The evidence indicates that a leader's legitimacy has a considerable effect in shaping followers' perceptions (e.g., Ben-Yoav, Hollander, & Carnevale, 1983), and on group performance and the leader's perception of followers (cf. Green & Mitchell, 1979).

In general, election creates a heightened psychological identification between followers and the leader, insofar as followers have a greater sense of responsibility for and investment in the leader. They also have been found to have higher expectations about the leader. Elected leaders who fail to perform well are more vulnerable to criticism than appointed leaders, particularly if they are seen to be competent in the first place (Hollander & Julian, 1970, 1978). While election and appointment can be said to create different psychological climates between leaders and followers, this does not deny the very real possibility for organizational leaders to attain a "following" by doing more than exercising authority, as Katz and Kahn (1978) have observed.

One effect of the current attributional view is to make even more explicit the significance of followers' and others' perceptions of the leader as a constraint or check on leader behavior. There also are the related expectations about such leader characteristics as the necessary level of competence and motivation. But the reverse perspective of the leader's perception of followers also is significant (see Elgie, Hollander, & Rice, 1988; Mitchell, Green, & Wood, 1981). Another feature of the leader's self-presentation is how followers perceive determinants of the leader's behavior, especially in dealing with others, including followers, peers, superiors, and adversaries.

**From Charismatic to Transformational Leadership** The past decade or more has seen a revitalization of interest in the older concept of the "charismatic leader." Max Weber (1921), the eminent sociologist of bureaucracy, coined it from the Greek word "charisma" for divine gift. Such a leader has considerable emotional appeal to followers and great power over them, especially in a time of crisis when there are strong needs for direction. In an update by House (1977) in line with his path-goal theory, the leader-follower bond is seen to be based less on an emotional appeal than on the leader's program of action which grips followers, that is, a goal and the path to achieve it. From his political science perspective, Burns (1978) developed a related concept of the "transformational leader" as one who changes the outlook and behavior of followers.

Burns' idea of the leader as a transforming agent has been applied to organizational leadership by Bass (1985) and Bennis and Nanus (1985), especially regarding how exceptional performance occurs. The essential point is that the leader strives to go beyond the bounds of the usual to bring about a change in follower thinking that will redirect follower action (see Fiedler & House, 1988). Ideas of excellence, exemplified in the popular book by Peters and Waterman (1983), are another example of this thrust, as is Vaill's (1982) work on "High Performing Systems."

Transformational leadership can be seen as an extension of transactional leadership, but with greater leader intensity and follower arousal. Indeed, the Bass (1985) and Yammarino and Bass (1990) research on transformational leadership involves a measure with two transactional factors in addition to charisma—intellectual stimulation and individual attention to followers. However, it also is important to recognize that charisma may be primarily directed to the leader's self-serving ends or to those of the larger entity, which is a distinction made by Burns (1978) that may be difficult to draw at times.

The potential for damage from a leader with charismatic appeal is evident. Post (1986) observes that such a leader has narcissistic needs for continual approval from others. Coupled with personalized power needs, the outcome of a charismatic appeal can be destructive, as Hogan, Raskin, and Fazzini (1990) have observed in their paper on "the dark side of charisma" (1990). In addition to narcissists, they identify two other flawed leader types, that is, the "high likability floater" and the "homme de ressentiment," all of whom appear to have good social skills, rise readily in organizations, and take a financial and human toll in reduced productivity, poor morale, and excessive turnover. Although not all charismatic leaders provide trouble in these ways, their potential for affecting many others adversely requires attention, if only to rectify the balance of views.

**Organizational Culture and Leader Style** Also significant today is the attention being given to "organizational culture," as seen in the recent works of Deal and Kennedy (1982), Schein (1985, 1990), and Kilmann and others (1985). This emphasis extends the situational approach in keeping with an earlier interest in organizational climate, exemplified by Likert's (1961) observation that the top leader sets a climate or tone in an organization that permeates the leadership style there. In short, an autocratic leader in a high place will generate autocracy rather than participative leadership among the subordinates who are themselves leaders.

While leader style in general can be overdrawn, individual differences among leaders are perceived as real and do play a role in follower satisfaction and performance outcomes. Leader style now is understood to be more complex than just being typical behavior, as was thought earlier. Obviously, it is affected by such situational constraints as role demands, which are related to the leader's level in the organization (see Boyatzis, 1982), and the expectations of followers. Style also is a function of the particular followers with whom the leader interacts, as Graen (1975) and Dienesch and Liden (1986) point out in the leader-member exchange (LMX) model, already noted.

## Newer Developments and Future Directions

The conceptual and research developments just described show a heightened focus on the role of the follower in the leadership process. Although the study of leadership has always presumed the existence of followers, their role was viewed as essentially passive. Recent models and applications have increasingly sought to integrate followers more fully into an understanding of leadership, building on the foundation provided by contingency and transactional models (see Hollander & Offermann, 1990).

Underlying the concern for developing the role of followers in the leadership process is the inescapable factor of power. Power plays a major part in organizational life, one that cannot be ignored if we hope to understand and improve the functioning of organizations from within (Kanter, 1981; Mintzberg, 1983; Zaleznik, 1977; Zaleznik & Kets de Vries, 1975). Power is also clearly intertwined with an understanding of leadership processes, with regard both to its appropriateness and limitations (Hollander, 1985; McClelland, 1975).

Despite the relevance of power to organizations in general, and to an understanding of leadership in particular, the study of power and leadership has yet to be well integrated. Assumptions about power often remain unstated and untested. Like love, its importance and existence are acknowledged, but its study is often resisted. And those with the most power, and the most influence in organizations, have typically been most able to shield themselves from study (Kipnis, 1976).

Although there has been steady activity in leadership research over the years, further work is needed to examine and understand the leader-follower relationship. Research also should be directed toward a better understanding of the dynamics of formal and informal influence as they affect subordinates, leaders, and organizations. In this regard, the renewed interest in charismatic and transformational leadership demonstrated by the work of Yammarino and Bass (1990) ought to be viewed with appropriate caution. As discussed earlier, charismatic appeals based on emotional arousal provide ample opportunities for abuse. A major question needing consideration is how such "leader-centric" approaches mesh with the growing trend toward follower empowerment and subordinate influence.

One critical limitation of most leadership models is the failure to consider levels of leadership. Many models use the term *leader* to designate individuals occupying a wide range of supervisory positions, from first-line supervisors to executives. Until recently, most leaders studied were at the lowest levels of organizations (cf. Boyatzis, 1982). Recently, more attention has been given to more senior-level leaders and executives (e.g., Kotter, 1982; Levinson & Rosenthal, 1984). Unfortunately, it is often difficult to make comparisons across studies in regard to "supervisors," "leaders," and "executives." Not atypically, the term *executive* is operationalized as anyone to whom the firms responding attach the term, despite an awareness that the individuals so designated encompass many levels, and that *executive* is variably applied in different organizations.

Jacobs and Jaques (1987) have developed a model expressly to consider the level of leadership within an organization to understand the requisite skills needed for success at a given level. Looking at leadership as "value added" to the resources of the system at any level, what leaders must do to add value to an organizational system will differ depending on their organizational level. Tasks, goals, and time frames will differ considerably by level, with higher-level leadership requiring greater conceptual effort in dealing with uncertainty, abstraction, and longer time frames. Recent work by Jacobs and Jaques (1990) with top military leaders indicates that 63.6% of three-star and 75% of four-star generals were operating with time frames of ten years or longer.

The concept of leadership as "value-added," or incremental to basic management components, might help the leadership field address the issue of whether managers and leaders are different (see Zaleznik, 1977). Rather than being concerned about artificial distinctions between leaders and managers, leadership researchers need to consider seriously whether the "leaders" we are studying are perceived to be such. Much research on leadership is still conducted with students or supervisors without regard to their evaluations by peers or subordinates.

Attribution approaches provide a rich perspective on the leader-follower dynamic, focusing both on follower behavior as the stimulus for leader behavior and the obverse, thus expanding leadership as a process worthy of study as either a dependent or an independent variable. As noted earlier, ILTs help to understand the way in which follower perceptions and expectations about leaders may structure the leader-follower relationship and how they may adversely affect the validity of subordinate evaluations of leader behavior. Dynamic leader-member exchange relationships are key features in models noted earlier by Hollander (1958, 1978) and Graen (1975; Graen & Scandura, 1987), with an increasing interest in follower influence and follower perception of leaders. Furthermore, charismatic leaders, and therefore the charismatic component of transformational leaders, are defined by the effects they have on their followers.

Focusing on follower perceptions indicates in general that supervisors and leaders may be perceived differently. Recent work on ILTs suggests that while people use the same dimensions to describe supervisors and leaders, ratings in response to the cue *supervisor* are significantly less favorable than those given in response to the cue of *leader* (Offermann & Kennedy, 1987). This points to the need for leadership researchers to study those individuals identified as leaders by subordinates, perhaps comparing them not only with followers, but also with persons of comparable organizational authority and position who are not so identified. By implication, these "leaders" may or may not be managers. But they should be those at any level who are perceived as leaders, and whose actions move their organizations toward achieving important goals.

The dynamic features of leadership over time also need to be examined. Time frames considered could range from an episode to an entire career. Recent examples of work with a greater span of time include: the development of an episodic model of power (Cobb, 1984); looking at supervisory control as a chain or sequence of events (Green, Fairhurst, & Snavely, 1986); work on managerial careers (e.g., Howard & Bray, 1988); and leadership succession (Gordon & Rosen, 1981).

Future research must also address the values issue of *leadership toward what ends* (Hollander, 1985). Leadership processes cannot escape questions about ultimate goals and outcomes. Power, while necessary for organizational and leader effectiveness, always carries with it the specter of abuse. In the wake of scandals about insider trading and corporate violations, courses in business ethics are on the rise. The role of leaders as transmitters and upholders of organizational values is increasingly being stressed (e.g., Kouzes & Posner, 1987). Whether all this activity results in more ethical, responsive, and humane leadership remains to be seen.

In reviewing the considerable activity that has gone on in leadership research in recent years, there is good reason for optimism. As noted in Part II of this volume, continued efforts are under way to study leadership with a variety of instruments and approaches. Although many of these take a more traditional approach by measuring leader characteristics and abilities, others are taking a more developmental focus, such as encouraging leadership skills in youth (Karnes, 1990), and examining the potential of particular managerial jobs for developing leadership in the incumbent (Ruderman, Ohlott, & McCauley, 1990). Focusing on how jobs affect leadership development may be the beginning of the integration of leader and organizational context needed for successful organizational applications. While we suggest elsewhere that progress has been made toward applying what we know about leadership processes to ongoing organizational problems, significant questions remain (see Hollander and Offermann, 1990).

Substantial gains have been made in our understanding of leaders and their followers, as seen in Fiedler and House's (1988) review of gains. Granting a bias toward believing in leadership as a causal force in organizational performance, even where cause is indeterminant (Meindl, Ehrlich, & Dukerich, 1985), effective leadership *can* make a difference in important organizational outcomes (e.g., Smith, Carson, & Alexander, 1984). Our ready willingness to attribute outcomes to leadership merely underscores the importance of the concept both to individuals and to their organizations. While there is much yet to be done, understanding the processes of leadership and followership presents an exciting challenge.

# References

Alvarez, R. (1968). Informal reactions to deviance in simulated work organizations: A laboratory experiment. *American Sociological Review, 33,* 895–912.

Baker, C. (1980). The Vroom-Yetton model of leadership — model, theory or technique. *Omega, 8,* 9–10.

Bass, B. M. (1985). *Leadership and performance beyond expectations.* New York: Free Press.

Bennis, W. G., & Nanus, B. (1985). *Leaders: The strategies for taking charge*. New York: Harper & Row.

Ben-Yoav, O., Hollander, E. P., & Carnevale, P. J. D. (1983). Leader legitimacy, leader-follower interaction, and followers' ratings of the leader. *Journal of Social Psychology, 121,* 111–115.

Boyatzis, R. E. (1982). *The competent manager*. New York: Wiley-Interscience.

Burns, J. M. (1978). *Leadership*. New York: Harper & Row.

Calder, B. J. (1977). An attribution theory of leadership. In B. M. Staw and G. R. Salancik (Eds.), *New directions in organizational behavior*. Chicago: St. Clair Press.

Cobb, A. T. (1984). An episodic model of power: Toward an integration of theory and research. *Academy of Management Review, 1,* 482–493.

Cowley, W. H. (1928). Three distinctions in the study of leaders. *Journal of Abnormal and Social Psychology, 23,* 144–157.

Deal, T. E., & Kennedy, A. A. (1982). *Corporate cultures: The rites and rituals of corporate life*. Reading, MA: Addison-Wesley.

Dienesch, R. M., & Liden, R. C. (1986). Leader-member exchange model of leadership: A critique and further development. *Academy of Management Review, 11,* 618–634.

Elgie, D. M., Hollander, E. P., & Rice, R. W. (1988). Appointed and elected leader responses to favorableness of feedback and level of task activity from followers. *Journal of Applied Social Psychology, 18,* 1361–1370.

Evans, M. G. (1970). The effects of supervisory behavior on the path-goal relationship. *Organizational Behavior and Human Performance, 5,* 277–298.

Evans, M. G. (1974). Extensions of a path-goal theory of motivation. *Journal of Applied Psychology, 59,* 172–178.

Fiedler, F. E. (1961). Leadership and leadership effectiveness traits. In L. Petrullo, and B. M. Bass (Eds.), *Leadership and interpersonal behavior* (pp. 179–186). New York: Holt.

Fiedler, F. E. (1964). A contingency model of leadership effectiveness. In L. Berkowitz (Ed.), *Advances in experimental social psychology* (Vol. 1, pp. 149–190). New York: Academic Press.

Fiedler, F. E. (1967). *A theory of leadership effectiveness*. New York: McGraw-Hill.

Fiedler, F. E., & Garcia, J. E. (1987). *New approaches to effective leadership*. New York: Wiley.

Fiedler, F. E., & House, R. J. (1988). Leadership theory and research: A report of progress. In C. L. Cooper & I. Robertson (Eds.), *International review of industrial and organizational psychology* (pp. 73–92). London: Wiley.

Fiedler, F. E., & Leister, A. F. (1977). Leader intelligence and task performance: A test of a multiple screen model. *Organizational Behavior and Human Performance, 20,* 1–14.

Fleishman, E. A. (1973). Twenty years of consideration and structure. In E. A. Fleishman & J. G. Hunt (Eds.), *Current developments in the study of leadership* (pp. 1–37). Carbondale: Southern Illinois University Press.

Freud, S. (1960). *Group psychology and the analysis of the ego.* New York: Bantam. (Originally published in German in 1921.)

Galton, F. (1869). *Hereditary genius: An inquiry into its laws and consequences.* London: Macmillan. (Paperback edition by Meridian Books, New York, 1962.)

Gioia, D., & Sims, H. P. (1986). *The thinking organization.* San Francisco: Jossey-Bass.

Gordon, G. E., & Rosen, N. (1981). Critical factors in leadership succession. *Organizational Behavior and Human Performance, 27,* 227–254.

Graen, G. (1976). Role-making processes within complex organizations. In M. D. Dunnette (Ed.), *Handbook of industrial and organizational psychology* (pp. 1201–1245). Chicago: Rand McNally.

Graen, G. B., & Scandura, T. A. (1987). Toward a psychology of dyadic organizing. In B. Staw & L. L. Cummings (Eds.), *Research in organizational behavior* (Vol. 9, pp. 175–208). Greenwich, CT: JAI Press.

Green, S. G., & Mitchell, T. R. (1979). Attributional processes of leaders in leader-member interactions. *Organizational Behavior and Human Performance, 23,* 429–458.

Green, S. G., Fairhurst, G. T., & Snavely, B. K. (1986). Chains of poor performance and supervisory control. *Organizational Behavior and Human Decision Processes, 38,* 7–27.

Heider, F. (1958). *The psychology of interpersonal relations.* New York: Wiley.

Hendrick, H. R. (1990). Perceptual accuracy of self and others and leadership status as functions of cognitive complexity. In K. E. Clark & M. B. Clark (Eds.), *Measures of leadership* (pp. 511–519). West Orange, NJ: Leadership Library of America.

Hogan, R., Raskin, R., & Fazzini, D. (1990). The dark side of charisma. In K. E. Clark & M. B. Clark (Eds.), *Measures of leadership* (pp. 343–354). West Orange, NJ: Leadership Library of America.

Hollander, E. P. (1958). Conformity, status, and idiosyncrasy credit. *Psychological Review, 65,* 117–127.

Hollander, E. P. (1964). *Leaders, groups, and influence.* New York: Oxford University Press.

Hollander, E. P. (1978). *Leadership dynamics: A practical guide to effective relationships.* New York: Free Press/Macmillan.

Hollander, E. P. (1985). Leadership and power. In G. Lindzey & E. Aronson (Eds.), *The handbook of social psychology* (3rd ed.) (pp. 485–537). New York: Random House.

Hollander, E. P. (1986). On the central role of leadership processes. *International Review of Applied Psychology, 35,* 39–52.

Hollander, E. P., & Julian, J. W. (1969). Contemporary trends in the analysis of leadership processes. *Psychological Bulletin, 71,* 387–397.

Hollander, E. P., & Julian, J. W. (1970). Studies in leader legitimacy, influence, and innovation. In L. L. Berkowitz (Ed.), *Advances in experimental social psychology* (Vol. 5, pp. 33–69). New York: Academic Press.

Hollander, E. P., & Julian, J. W. (1978). A further look at leader legitimacy, influence, and innovation. In L. Berkowitz (Ed.), *Group processes* (pp. 153–165). New York: Academic Press.

Hollander, E. P., & Offermann, L. (1990). Power and leadership in organizations: Relationships in transition. *American Psychologist.* In press.

Hollander, E. P., & Webb, W. B. (1955). Leadership, followership, and friendship: An analysis of peer nominations. *Journal of Abnormal and Social Psychology, 50,* 163–167.

Homans, G. C. (1961). *Social behavior: Its elementary forms.* New York: Harcourt, Brace and World.

House, R. J. (1971). A path-goal theory of leader effectiveness. *Administrative Science Quarterly, 16,* 321–338.

House, R. J. (1977). A 1976 theory of charismatic leadership. In J. G. Hunt & L. L. Larson (Eds.), *Leadership: The cutting edge* (pp. 189–207). Carbondale, IL: Southern Illinois University Press.

House, R. J., & Dessler, G. (1974). The path-goal theory of leadership: Some post hoc and a priori tests. In J. G. Hunt & L. L. Larson (Eds.), *Contingency approaches to leadership.* Carbondale: Southern Illinois University Press.

House, R. J., & Mitchell, T. R. (1974). Path-goal theory of leadership. *Journal of Contemporary Business, 3*(4), 81–97.

Howard, A., & Bray, D. W. (1988). *Managerial lives in transition: Advancing age and changing times.* New York: Guilford Press.

Jacobs, T. O., & Jaques, E. (1987). Leadership in complex systems. In J. Zeidner (Ed.), *Human productivity enhancement* (pp. 7–65). New York: Praeger.

Jacobs, T. O., & Jaques, E. (1990). Military executive leadership. In K. E. Clark & M. B. Clark (Eds.), *Measures of leadership* (pp. 281–295). West Orange, NJ: Leadership Library of America.

Kanter, R. M. (1981). Power, leadership, and participatory management. *Theory Into Practice, 20,* 219–224.

Karnes, Frances A. (1990). Leadership and youth: A commitment. In K. E. Clark & M. B. Clark (Eds.), *Measures of leadership* (pp. 563–566). West Orange, NJ: Leadership Library of America.

Katz, D., & Kahn, R. L. (1978). *The social psychology of organizations* (2nd ed.). New York: Wiley.

Kilmann, R. H., Saxton, M. J., Serpa, R., & Associates. (1985). *Gaining control of the corporate culture*. San Francisco: Jossey-Bass.

Kipnis, D. (1976). *The powerholders*. Chicago: University of Chicago Press.

Kotter, J. P. (1982). *The general managers*. New York: Free Press.

Kouzes, J. M., & Posner, B. Z. (1987). *The leadership challenge: How to get extraordinary things done in organizations*. San Francisco: Jossey-Bass.

Levinson, H., & Rosenthal, S. (1984). *CEO: Corporate leadership in action*. New York: Basic Books.

Liden, R. C., & Graen, G. (1980). Generalizability of the vertical dyad linkage model of leadership. *Academy of Management Journal, 23,* 451–465.

Likert, R. (1961). *New patterns of management*. New York: McGraw-Hill.

Lord, R. G., & Maher, K. J. (1989). Leadership perceptions and leadership performance: Two distinct but interdependent processes. In J. Carroll (Ed.), *Advances in applied social psychology: Business settings* (Vol. 4). Hillsdale, NJ: Erlbaum.

Lord, R. G., De Vader, C. L., & Alliger, G. M. (1986). A meta-analysis of the relation between personality traits and leadership perceptions: An application of validity generalization procedures. *Journal of Applied Psychology, 71,* 402–409.

McClelland, D. (1975). *Power: The inner experience*. New York: Irvington.

Mann, R. D. (1959). A review of the relationships between personality and performance in small groups. *Psychological Bulletin, 56,* 241–270.

Meindl, J. R., Ehrlich, S. B., & Dukerich, J. M. (1985). The romance of leadership. *Administrative Science Quarterly, 30,* 78–102.

Mintzberg, H. (1983). *Power in and around organizations*. Englewood Cliffs, NJ: Prentice-Hall.

Mitchell, T. R., Green, S. G., & Wood, R. E. (1981). An attributional model of leadership and the poor-performing subordinate: Development and validation. In B. Shaw & L. Cummings (Eds.), *Research in organizational behavior* (Vol. 3, pp. 197–234). Greenwich, CT: JAI Press.

Offermann, L. R., & Kennedy, J. R., Jr. (1987, April). *Implicit theories of leadership: A look inside*. Paper presented at the meeting of the Society for Industrial and Organizational Psychology, Atlanta.

Peters, T. J., & Waterman, R. H. Jr. (1982). *In search of excellence: lessons from America's best-run companies*. New York: Harper & Row.

Post, J. M. (1986). Narcissism and the charismatic leader-follower relationship. *Political Psychology, 7,* 675–688.

Rice, R. W., & Kastenbaum, D. R. (1983). The contingency model of leadership: Some current issues. *Basic and Applied Social Psychology, 4,* 373–392.

Ruderman, M. N., Ohlott, P. J., & McCauley, C. D. (1990). Assessing opportunities for leadership development. In K. E. Clark & M. B. Clark (Eds.), *Measures of leadership* (pp. 547–562). West Orange, NJ: Leadership Library of America.

Rush, M. C., Thomas, J. C., & Lord, R. G. (1977). Implicit leadership theory: A potential threat to the internal validity of leader behavior questionnaires. *Organizational Behavior and Human Performance, 20,* 93–110.

Sanford, F. (1950). *Authoritarianism and leadership.* Philadelphia: Institute for Research in Human Relations.

Schein, E. (1985). *Organizational culture and leadership: A dynamic view.* San Francisco: Jossey-Bass.

Schein, E. (1990). Organizational culture. *American Psychologist.* In press.

Shartle, C. L., & Stogdill, R. M. (1953). *Studies in naval leadership: Methods, results, and applications* (Tech. Rep.). Columbus: Ohio State University, Personnel Research Board.

Smith, J. E., Carson, K. P., & Alexander, R. A. (1984). Leadership: It can make a difference. *Academy of Management Journal, 27,* 765–776.

Sternberg, R. J. (1990). Intellectual styles. In K. E. Clark & M. B. Clark (Eds.), *Measures of leadership* (pp. 481–492). West Orange, NJ: Leadership Library of America.

Stewart, R. (1982). *Choices for the manager.* Englewood Cliffs, NJ: Prentice-Hall.

Stogdill, R. M. (1948). Personal factors associated with leadership. *Journal of Psychology, 25,* 35–71.

Vaill, P. B. (1982). The purposing of high-performing systems. *Organizational Dynamics, 11*(2), 23–39.

Vroom, V. H., & Yetton, P. W. (1973). *Leadership and decision-making.* Pittsburgh: University of Pittsburgh Press.

Wagner, R. K., & Sternberg, R. J. (1990). Street smarts. In K. E. Clark & M. B. Clark (Eds.), *Measures of leadership* (pp. 493–504). West Orange, NJ: Leadership Library of America.

Weber, M. (1946). The sociology of charismatic authority. In H. H. Gerth & C. W. Mills (Eds. and Trans.), *From Max Weber: Essays in sociology* (pp. 245–252). New York: Oxford University Press. (Original work published 1921.)

Yammarino, F. J., & Bass, B. M. (1990). Long-term forecasting of transformational leadership and its effect among naval officers: Some preliminary findings. In K. E. Clark & M. B. Clark (Eds.), *Measures of leadership* (pp. 151–169). West Orange, NJ: Leadership Library of America.

Zaleznik, A. (1977). Managers and leaders: Are they different? *Harvard Business Review, 55,* May–June, 67–78.

Zaleznik, A., & Kets de Vries, M. F. R. (1975). *Power and the corporate mind.* Boston: Houghton Mifflin.

# SECTION B

**Psychological Measurements
in Long-Term Prediction
and Assessment Studies**

# Psychological Measurements in Long-Term Prediction and Assessment Studies

The three reports in this section are classics. Conducted over a long span of time, they used excellent methods and obtained unusual support from management. They show what can be done in early talent identification and ways to develop leadership and management capability within the organization. These studies can provide guidance to organizations that recruit and develop talent at various levels of management. The durability of the findings is worth noting. The predictive power of the measures is well known in the field of psychology, but the details of the evidence are often forgotten.

## Testing for Management Potential
C. Paul Sparks

Summarizes a 30-year research project (Early Identification of Management Potential—EIMP) in Exxon Company and its components. Measures were exclusively pencil-and-paper tests, questionnaires, and inventories, some commercially available, others specially constructed; some cognitive, some noncognitive. Much attention was given to developing meaningful criteria. The criterion variable used incorporated: (1) position level attained, (2) managerial effectiveness, and (3) salary. A "Success Index" was developed as a weighted composite of the three components.

C. Paul Sparks, Proprietor, Serendipity Unlimited, Post Office Box 810024, Houston, Texas 77281. (713-774-1668). MA, Ohio State University. Past President, Division of Industrial and Organizational Psychology of the American Psychological Association. Personnel Research Coordinator, Exxon Company. United States Army (retired). Adjunct Professor (Psychology), University of Houston.

## Predictions of Managerial Success Over Long Periods of Time: Lessons From the Management Progress Study
Ann Howard and Douglas W. Bray

A review of major findings of the Management Progress Study (MPS), a comprehensive study within AT&T of careers of managers who began work in six telephone companies in the mid- to late-1950s. Assessment factors involved both motivation and ability, such as advancement motivation, work involvement, administrative skills, interpersonal skills, intellectual ability, oral communication skills, need for advancement, inner work standards, and energy. Factors from simulations and paper-and-pencil tests were cognitive ability, administrative ability, and interpersonal ability.

Douglas W. Bray, Chairman of the Board, Development Dimensions International, 21 Knoll Road, Tenafly, New Jersey 07670. (201-894-5289). PhD, Yale University. Recipient of Professional Practice Award, American Psychological Association Division of Industrial and Organizational Psychology, and of American Psychological Association Distinguished Contributions to Applied Psychology Award. Author of "The Assessment Center and the Study of Lives" in *American Psychologist*.

Ann Howard, President, Leadership Research Institute, 21 Knoll Road, Tenafly, New Jersey 07670. (201-894-5289). PhD, University of Maryland. President, Society for Industrial and Organizational Psychology. Honorary Doctor of Science Degree, Goucher College. Author of "Measuring Management Abilities and Motivation" in *Measurement, Technology and Individuality in Education*.

## Contextual Issues in Predicting High-Level Leadership Performance: Contextual Richness as a Criterion Consideration in Personality Research with Executives
V. Jon Bentz

A report from experience with a long-term study of management succession in Sears. Among criterion variables used was an overall general effectiveness of promotion potential, with which excellent validities were associated. Predicting long-term effectiveness of management trainees required adopting more complex evaluative processes for criteria. The article documents how the contextual richness of the executive decision process forced greater complexity on the rating concepts.

V. Jon Bentz, 201 Willow Road, Elmhurst, Illinois 60126. (312-833-7149). PhD, Ohio State University. Past Director of Psychological Research and Services of the National Personnel Department of Sears, Roebuck and Company. Past member of the Board of the National Assessment of Educational Progress and of the Research Evaluation Committee of the National Manpower Commission. Member of the Committee on Military Performance for the National Council of the National Academy of Science. Author of *A View of the Top* (in press).

# Testing for Management Potential

C. Paul Sparks

The theme of this conference is research and application of psychological measures to leadership. My contribution will focus on some 30 years of research on the early identification of management potential in Exxon Company and its various affiliates and subsidiaries. While an overarching philosophy of management undoubtedly pervades the parent company and its satellites, there are adaptations to local needs and customs which keep the company from being a monolithic organization. The research has included both domestic and foreign organizations.

The psychological measures studied were exclusively paper-and-pencil tests, questionnaires, and inventories. Some were commercially available; others were constructed specifically for the initial research project. Some were cognitive; others were noncognitive. Valid prediction was the goal, not descriptive profiles full of psychological meaning but devoid of criterion relationships. To that end, much attention was given to the development of meaningful criteria.

Note that I said early identification of "management potential," not "leadership potential." Hersey and Blanchard (1982, p. 4) wrote, "It is obvious after a review of the literature that there are almost as many definitions of management as there are writers in the field....We shall define management as *working with and through individuals and groups to accomplish organizational goals*....The achievement of organizational objectives through leadership is management....In essence, leadership is a broader concept than management. Management is thought of as a special kind of leadership in which the achievement of organizational goals is paramount."

To me, leadership is Farragut saying, "Damn the torpedoes; full speed ahead." Management is never so dramatic. It is Marshall laying out a plan for renewing a war-torn world.

In the early 1950s the senior management of Exxon (then Standard Oil Company, New Jersey) became concerned that existing succession-planning programs would not be able to accomplish their purpose. The birth dearth of the thirties, decimations of World War II, and disruptions caused by reorganizations had led to a depletion of young managerial talent. Further, historical practice had been to assign men to responsible positions, evaluate performance, reassign, and evaluate over a period of several years, gradually winnowing the wheat from the chaff. Force-feeding to accelerate this process was considered to be a viable option but one that was necessarily limited as to the number of participants. A method for defining and expanding this pool was the goal of the research program embarked upon, not the identification of a small number of "crown princes."

The company had a successful postwar history of empirical research aimed at selection of first-line supervisors, petroleum products salesmen, plant operators and mechanical personnel, service station dealers, and other specialties. It seemed only natural to apply the same techniques to the identification of talent for management.

The research, entitled "Early Identification of Management Potential" (EIMP), was originally conceived as a multicompany study to be coordinated by the consulting firm of Richardson, Bellows, Henry, & Company (RBH). In fact, all of the experimental predictors were chosen or constructed by the psychologists of RBH. However, only Jersey Standard completed the collection of the necessary data and the project was moved in-house quite early. Some years later Campbell, Dunnette, Lawler, and Weick (1970) wrote, "This is a prime example of a long-term staff study, and many people contributed to it, including C. P. Sparks, A. M. Munger, Carl H. Rush, Paul F. Ross, Douglas Fryer, McE. Trawick, Paul C. Baker, Treadway Parker, Harry Laurent, and E. R. Henry" (p. 165).

The choice of predictors was intended to include one or more examples of measures that had shown validity in the limited research literature or had been hypothesized as important to management success. They are listed here, and described briefly, to show the breadth of the project:

- *Miller Analogies Test*, a standardized measure of verbal reasoning.
- *RBH Non-Verbal Reasoning Test*, a standardized measure of abstract reasoning.
- *Guilford-Zimmerman Temperament Survey*, a standardized measure of ten personality or temperament dimensions according to its authors. The 300 items were also to be considered "experimental" for item-analysis purposes.
- *Individual Background Survey*, a multiple-choice inventory of life experiences constructed specifically for the project.
- *Management Judgment Test*, verbally described situations that called for a choice of action or a decision from among several alternatives.
- *Self-Performance Report*, a forced-choice-type rating form to be completed by the job incumbent.
- *Survey of Management Attitudes*, questions of a variety of occupational, social, and educational items developed specifically for the project.
- *Picture Technique*, a set of eight TAT-type pictures flashed on a screen for ten seconds and then removed. Examinee then wrote a brief narrative describing what was going on in each picture.
- *Personal History Record*, a cumulative record of numbers and kinds of

assignments throughout his career. The record was reviewed with the incumbent and each was classified as line/staff, overseas/domestic, functional/general, etc.

—*Interview*, one-on-one interview between incumbent and researcher centering on career planning before entering the company, critical period for advancement, most important achievement, and person who contributed most to his advancement. Interview data were recorded on two checklists.

The complete file on each individual contained more than 1,000 experimental items with about 5,400 alternative responses possible.

The research was conceived as a concurrent validity study to be performed in the company headquarters and in five affiliated companies located in the greater New York City area. Possible experimental subjects were middle- to top-level managers plus specialists working at or near comparable job levels. The subjects were to include "most successful" and "less successful" individuals, and obvious failures or near failures would not be included.

Many man-hours were spent in developing basic criterion information. An often-overlooked consideration was given great attention. *The final criterion had to make sense to top management.* Significant correlations against an index that seriously violated the opinions of top management would be of no value in gaining acceptance of any tools and techniques developed by the project.

Criterion variables finally used in the study were three: *position level attained, managerial effectiveness,* and *salary.* These are simple to state and comprehend but it took four years to develop them for the 600 managers who began the study. Several pieces of information were brought to bear on each of the three before reconciliations could be achieved. The effects of age and tenure were very troublesome. Predictor scores were correlated with numerous criterion variables but the most pertinent to the researchers was a "Success Index," a weighted composite of the three majors with the effects of age and service statistically removed.

The original sample of 600 shrank to 443 because of serious gaps in either the predictor or criterion information. Individuals transferred out of the area, skipped certain testing or interview sessions, lacked rating or ranking data, or, in a few instances, declined to participate in any way.

The examinees with complete data were divided into two subsamples (A & B) of 222 and 221 for a double cross-validation of both the items and the scoring systems. Selected validity coefficients are presented above for both samples.

Using a multiple correlation approach, the selected variables were tested against different subgroups, for example, each of the six participating companies, the various function or specialty groups, persons whose careers had been general management versus professional specialization, and so forth. The researchers were looking for deviant results, information that would indicate a problem. They found none of any significance.

## Original EIMP Validities

| | Sample A | Sample B |
|---|---|---|
| #Verbal reasoning—Miller Analogies | .18** | .17* |
| #Nonverbal reasoning | .20** | .19** |
| #Guilford-Zimmerman—Empirical key | .27** | .31** |
| Self-performance Report—Forced-choice theory | .21** | .09 |
| #Self-performance Report—Empirical key | .24** | .23** |
| Interview Checklist | .21** | .19** |
| #Background—Entire form | .63** | .50** |
| Background—College items only | .32** | .24** |
| Management attitudes | .25** | .14* |
| #Management Judgment Test, 1st Choice | .32** | .31** |
| Picture Technique—*a priori* scale A | .03 | .09 |

*p<.05; ** p<.01*
*# Included in final battery*

Few managers readily translate correlation coefficients into probabilities. The researchers resorted to expectancy tables. EIMP battery scores were placed in rank order from 1–443. The Success Index criterion scores were divided into an upper third, a middle third, and a lower third. The multiple correlation of .70 was reported as a technical aside. What management saw is shown numerically in the following table.

## EIMP Battery Scores vs. Success Index

| Rank on Test | Low 1/3 | Mid 1/3 | Hi 1/3 |
|---|---|---|---|
| 1 – 44 | 0% | 5% | 95% |
| 45 – 88 | 2% | 23% | 75% |
| 89 – 132 | 5% | 38% | 57% |
| 133 – 176 | 10% | 45% | 45% |
| 177 – 220 | 25% | 55% | 20% |
| 221 – 265 | 40% | 47% | 13% |
| 266 – 310 | 53% | 38% | 9% |
| 311 – 355 | 56% | 33% | 11% |
| 356 – 399 | 64% | 29% | 7% |
| 400 – 443 | 79% | 21% | 0% |

Top management accepted the report and said, in effect, "Now go and sell it to the operating companies." Humble Oil & Refining Company in Houston was the first approached and, after several presentations, one regional vice president agreed to a tryout. He invited 21 of his managers to take the Personnel Development Series (PDS) as it had been renamed and 19 accepted. The forms were scored by RBH and reported to Jersey Standard with normative scores tentatively based on the research sample. All 19 scored above average and several were in the top decile. When informed of this the vice president smiled wryly and said that he would hope so since all of them were on his high-potential list. He then asked that PDS be given to all professional/technical employees in units under his supervision.

During this period I moved from RBH to Humble and actually spent the first few months of my new assignment giving PDS in units all across the country. The unit managers varied widely in their nomination of examinees, serendipitously creating many different research opportunities. I developed a relationship with the Psychology Department of the University of Houston and so had graduate students available to perform many of these studies.

The PDS was initially divided for operational purposes into a Series I and a Series II. Series I contained material that could be responded to by a recent college graduate while Series II required the examinee to have had work experience and adult responsibilities.

The Jersey Standard "Success Index" had been laboriously constructed with different pieces of information across six companies. Humble Oil had a coherent, well-established evaluation system administered with considerable fidelity across all the units of the company. Humble's "Success Index" combined job level attained, job performance as measured by a uniform appraisal form, and salary, with the effects of age and service partialed out. In addition, management's recorded estimate of potential job level attainment was uniformly recorded and used as a criterion for certain research studies.

Despite the preponderance of the evidence, individual managers continued to question whether the overall statistics were relevant for their particular employees. Fortunately, by that time a sufficient N was available for testing the validity for almost any subgroup. The most-often-voiced complaint involved the possibility that the specific demands of a given occupational specialty would render the PDS invalid, that technical/professional knowledge was more likely to be associated with success.

The master file was divided according to functional assignment and field of specialization. PDS scores were correlated with the Success Index computed at the time of test administration.

Shown below are the results for Series I only and for Series I & II combined. Some functions, for example, law and medicine, had insufficient numbers for meaningful data to emerge.

Your attention is invited to the particularly low SDs for the criterion for the Exploration function and for geologists wherever they might be. This was a function of supply and demand. The oversupply was so great that numerous geologists went into other operations because of the lack of promotional opportunities. One of the advantages of in-house research is that anomalies can be investigated more easily.

## Series I Only

| Function/specialization | N | PREDICTOR | | CRITERION | | |
| --- | --- | --- | --- | --- | --- | --- |
| | | M | SD | M | SD | r |
| Marketing — retail | 603 | 20.3 | 3.4 | 41.0 | 3.1 | .52** |
| Marketing — industrial | 106 | 20.8 | 3.2 | 41.8 | 2.8 | .47** |
| Marketing — operations | 73 | 17.6 | 3.8 | 37.8 | 4.2 | .52** |
| Production — engineers | 179 | 21.5 | 3.1 | 42.8 | 3.4 | .49** |
| Production — geologists | 90 | 20.9 | 3.1 | 41.9 | 1.8 | .28** |
| Exploration — geologists | 107 | 21.5 | 3.3 | 42.6 | 2.1 | .21* |
| Exploration — geophysicists | 49 | 20.3 | 2.9 | 42.5 | 1.5 | .22 |
| Exploration — landmen | 58 | 21.5 | 3.2 | 40.9 | 2.0 | .31* |
| Refining — engineers | 185 | 22.3 | 3.1 | 45.2 | 2.9 | .40** |
| Controllers — accounting | 141 | 19.5 | 3.1 | 38.8 | 3.8 | .45** |
| Employee relations | 32 | 23.2 | 3.0 | 42.4 | 2.8 | .35* |
| Planning — engineers | 38 | 21.2 | 3.2 | 41.7 | 3.3 | .45** |

$* p < .05;$  $** p < .01$

## Series I & II Combined

| Function/specialization | N | PREDICTOR | | CRITERION | | |
| --- | --- | --- | --- | --- | --- | --- |
| | | M | SD | M | SD | r |
| Marketing — retail | 145 | 21.1 | 3.4 | 41.4 | 3.3 | .56** |
| Refining — engineers | 51 | 22.5 | 3.7 | 45.9 | 4.2 | .55** |
| Production — engineers | 106 | 21.4 | 3.0 | 43.2 | 4.1 | .64** |
| Production — geologists | 51 | 19.7 | 3.0 | 42.3 | 2.5 | .30* |
| Exploration — geologists | 65 | 21.4 | 2.9 | 32.6 | 2.2 | .41** |
| Controllers — accounting | 67 | 19.5 | 3.0 | 38.9 | 3.9 | .57** |

$* p < .05;$  $** p < .01$

Employees move in and out of the parent company and among the affiliates. Fortunately, employees who moved out of Humble/Exxon USA could still be tracked, at least for "job grade attained," since the entire corporation had adopted the same job classification system. A major study involved a follow-up of persons who had completed Series I during their first two years of service and who were somewhere in the corporation ten years later. A condensed table showing the findings on 330 such individuals is shown below. The correlation for the full table was .47, both statistically and practically significant. It is a far cry from the .70 reported in the original EIMP study but it is based on only one of the major elements of that criterion.

## Predictive Validity of PDS Series I, Job Grade Ten Years after Testing

### PDS SCALE SCORE

| Job Grade | <13 | 13–15 | 16–18 | 19–21 | 22–24 | 25–27 | >27 | N |
|-----------|-----|-------|-------|-------|-------|-------|-----|-----|
| 33–34     | —   | —     | —     | —     | 2     | 2     | 1   | 5   |
| 31–32     | —   | 1     | —     | 1     | 4     | 5     | 1   | 12  |
| 29–30     | —   | 2     | 5     | 8     | 8     | 6     | 4   | 33  |
| 27–28     | 2   | 5     | 11    | 21    | 15    | 12    | 8   | 74  |
| 25–26     | 7   | 21    | 35    | 26    | 36    | 5     | —   | 130 |
| 23–24     | 11  | 15    | 17    | 17    | 7     | 2     | —   | 69  |
| 21–22     | 5   | 4     | 3     | 3     | 1     | —     | —   | 16  |
| N         | 25  | 48    | 71    | 76    | 73    | 32    | 14  | 339 |

It is conventional wisdom that validities deteriorate with the passage of time. The Exxon researchers found 304 individuals for whom job grades attained were available from their 3rd year of service through their 12th year. The validity against job grade attained was computed for Series I for each year, for the total score, and for each of the four major subscores. The results indicated an almost monotonic increase in validity. The researchers working with the data suggested that the increase was probably due to an improvement in the reliability and stability of the criterion. Certainly, there is no indication of a deteriorating validity in either the total or the subscores.

Beginning in 1965 Equal Employment Opportunity (EEO) requirements meant recruiting of minority persons and women for professional/technical jobs and attention to their advancement into higher-level positions. In 1970 EEO guidelines on use of tests mandated separate studies by sex and racial/ethnic group, if feasible. The master file was searched and sufficient representation was found to study some subgroups.

## Follow-up of PDS Series I vs. Job Grade Attained

| Years of Service | Reasoning | Background | Judgment | Temperament | Total |
|---|---|---|---|---|---|
| 3 | .29** | .27** | .22** | .16** | .31** |
| 4 | .30** | .21** | .24** | .21** | .34** |
| 5 | .30** | .28** | .22** | .20** | .35** |
| 6 | .29** | .30** | .27** | .18** | .38** |
| 7 | .28** | .30** | .30** | .14* | .40** |
| 8 | .27** | .34** | .29** | .20** | .41** |
| 9 | .28** | .34** | .32** | .20** | .44** |
| 10 | .30** | .35** | .35** | .24** | .47** |
| 11 | .30** | .35** | .32** | .24** | .45** |
| 12 | .32** | .34** | .35** | .24** | .46** |

$* p < .05; ** p < .01$

Sufficient Series I results were available to study black males, SSA males, white females, and white males. Validities against the Success Index criterion were:

.38** for 67 black males
.52** for 49 SSA males
.31** for 80 white females
.53** for 685 white males

All validities were significant at the .01 or better level.

The white females had the lowest validity. There were historical practices that could have accounted for at least some of this disparity. However, the content and wording of the biodata form and the management judgment test were obviously masculine and this was corrected.

Additional research was continued for some time but interest in the entire project began to wane about 1980. As of today no new employees are being tested according to my successor and the entire data bank has been destroyed. Why did this happen in view of the vast amount of successful demonstrations of validity? I can only conjecture that we never learned how to integrate PDS into the system. We purposefully made PDS impotent to prevent its controlling assignment and promotion. It was interesting but was never internalized into the day-to-day thinking of management.

One must also remember that Jersey Standard/Exxon had elaborate succession systems dating back to 1953. It was inability to use these systems in the early 1950s that stimulated the original EIMP research. These systems are back in place today and operating well in the opinion of top management.

# References

Campbell, J. P., Dunnette, M. D., Lawler, E. E. III, & Weick, K. E., Jr.  (1970). *Managerial behavior, performance, and effectiveness.* New York: McGraw-Hill.

Hersey, P., & Blanchard, K. H.  (1982).  *Management of organizational behavior: Utilizing human resources* (4th ed.).  Englewood Cliffs, NJ: Prentice-Hall.

# Predictions of Managerial Success Over Long Periods of Time: Lessons From the Management Progress Study

*Ann Howard
and
Douglas W.
Bray*

The Management Progress Study, a longitudinal study of Bell System managers extending over more than 30 years, provides important lessons with respect to predicting success in management and leadership roles. First, by administering psychological measures to young managers just beginning their careers, it is possible to predict eventual levels of advancement in an organization with better-than-chance accuracy. Correlations between measures and advancement after 20 or 25 years may not be strong, but many are statistically reliable and have significant utility.

Second, managers' abilities, motivations, and personality characteristics do change somewhat with maturity and experience. In some cases such changes personify the typical manager, and in other cases changes can be traced to particular types of experiences, such as movement into more challenging jobs. There is still, however, a stable core of personality and ability, or predictions over long periods would not be possible. However, there is age- and experience-related variability around that core that must be attended to for an informed interpretation of psychological measures.

The fact that people change over time leads to another important lesson about prediction: the utility of psychological measures for predicting managerial success changes over time. Some measures have more relevance early rather than later in the career. In other cases, individual differences do not emerge until managers have a certain amount of experience behind them. Finally, because promotions are related to certain types of changes in managers, greater heterogeneity among the original group results. This means that for many measures, assessments later in the career are apt to show more predictive power than those administered earlier.

Each of these points will be given greater consideration and specific illustrations in the sections that follow. More detailed information can be found in Howard and Bray (1988).

## Management Progress Study

The Management Progress Study (MPS) is a comprehensive, longitudinal study of the lives and careers of managers who began work in six telephone companies in the mid- to late-1950s. The study has remained a basic research project in which individual results have been kept confidential from the organization. The 422 participants who joined the study were all white males considered to be in the running for middle-management positions or higher.

The design of the study for its first 20 years is shown in Table 1. Participants in MPS are of two types. There were 274 new college graduates hired into the first level of management at an average age of 24. An additional 148 persons, not college graduates upon hire, had begun their careers in the nonmanagement ranks in such positions as telephone installers. All of the noncollege men had been promoted into management by the time they were 32 years of age; their average age was 30.

### TABLE 1
### Management Progress Study Design and Sample

| Year | | SAMPLE SIZE | | |
| --- | --- | --- | --- | --- |
| | | College | Noncollege | Total |
| 0 | Assessment | 274 | 148 | 422 |
| 1–7 | Annual interviews with participants, company; attitude questionnaires | | | |
| 8 | Assessment | 167 | 142 | 309 |
| 10–19 | Triannual interviews with participants, bosses, terminators; biographical questionnaires | | | |
| 20 | Assessment | 137 | 129 | 266 |

The first year, called Year 0 in Table 1, covered a span of five calendar years from 1956 to 1960. Data were collected within a three-day assessment center in which a variety of exercises were administered and evaluated by a team of assessors. The assessment process was repeated at year 8 (1964–1968) and again at year 20 (1976–1980). Interviews with participants and their bosses or other company representatives were conducted in the intervening years between the three assessment centers.

The original assessment center exercises included several simulations (in-basket exercise, competitive group discussion, and business game), an in-depth personal interview, a personal history questionnaire, several paper-and-pencil tests of abilities (School and College Ability Test or SCAT, Critical Thinking in Social Science Test, and Contemporary Affairs test of general knowledge), and work expectations and preferences questionnaires (Expectations Inventory and Work Conditions Survey). Personality and motivation were measured by several projective tests (six cards from the Thematic Apperception Test or TAT, the Rotter Incomplete Sentences Test, and the Management Incomplete Sentences Test), the results of which were summarized in a protocol and later coded into nine categories. Paper-and-pencil measures of personality were also used (Edwards Personal Preference Schedule, Guilford-Martin Inventory or GAMIN, Sarnoff Survey of Attitudes Toward Life, and the Bass version of the California F Scale) as well as a Q-sort consisting of 70 statements.

Following completion of the exercises by the assessees, the assessors wrote reports of the exercises they had observed. All reports and exercise scores were read at an integration session where the assessors rated 26 dimensions about each assessee and made predictions about his future.

The simulations and interview were subjected to additional post-hoc coding. Because of the quantity of measures used, scores and ratings were subjected to factor analysis procedures to reduce dimensionality. Three separate analyses were conducted for the dimension ratings, key ability test and exercise scores, and personality scores and ratings. A full description of the MPS assessment center as well as the components of each factor score can be found in the appendix of Howard and Bray (1988)

## Predictions of Managerial Success

The major criterion for managerial success was promotion into higher levels of management. At the time of the 20th-year assessment (dubbed MPS:20), the 266 participants still employed in the Bell System and actively involved in the study were distributed across the seven levels of telephone company management as shown in Table 2. Among the college graduates, the modal or typical management level was the third, or the entry to middle management. Among the noncollege men the typical level was second.

At the assessment center, following the achievement of consensus on the dimension ratings, the critical prediction question was "Will this man make the third level of management within ten years?" The selection of ten years was thought to represent a reasonable amount of time for a high-potential manager to be moved from the first to the third level, but the staff was really rating potential for higher-management jobs.

Comparisons of the men's actual progress after 20 years is shown in Figure 1. Advancement is indicated by the attainment of more than the modal level for each educational subgroup after 20 years. For the college men this meant reaching the fourth level and above, whereas it was the third level and above for the noncollege men.

## TABLE 2
### Management Levels at MPS:20

| Level | COLLEGE | | NONCOLLEGE | |
|---|---|---|---|---|
| | n | % | n | % |
| 6 | 3 | 2% | 0 | 0% |
| 5 | 12 | 9% | 0 | 0% |
| 4 | 27 | 20% | 4 | 3% |
| 3 | 64 | 46% | 37 | 29% |
| 2 | 27 | 20% | 61 | 47% |
| 1 | 4 | 3% | 27 | 21% |
| Total | 137 | 100% | 129 | 100% |

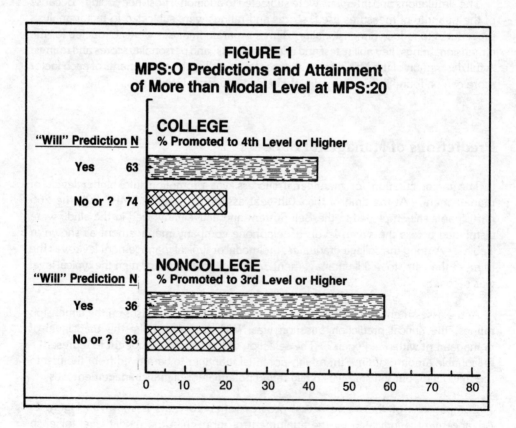

## FIGURE 1
### MPS:O Predictions and Attainment of More than Modal Level at MPS:20

**COLLEGE**
% Promoted to 4th Level or Higher

| "Will" Prediction | N |
|---|---|
| Yes | 63 |
| No or ? | 74 |

**NONCOLLEGE**
% Promoted to 3rd Level or Higher

| "Will" Prediction | N |
|---|---|
| Yes | 36 |
| No or ? | 93 |

In terms of reaching their criterion of success, the college men thought by their assessors to be good bets for promotions outnumbered those not so predicted by a ratio of more than 2:1. Among the noncollege men, the ratio was nearly 3:1 for reaching their criterion of third level. These results illustrate the power of the overall assessment center procedure for predicting success in management, even for such a distant time as 20 years hence.

The various ratings and exercises scores which comprised the assessment center process influenced the predictions illustrated above. The predictive power of each of these scores, used both alone and in combination with like scores, will be considered in turn.

**Assessment Dimensions** As mentioned previously, the 26 dimensions rated by the assessors were factor analyzed into seven primary factors as well as an overall general effectiveness factor. Factor scores were computed by averaging ratings on the dimensions that loaded significantly into each factor (unweighted by factor loadings). The relationship of the dimension factors to MPS:20 level is shown in Table 3.

### TABLE 3
### Correlations of Dimension Factors at MPS:0 with Level at MPS:20

| Dimension Factor | COLLEGE (n=137) | NONCOLLEGE (n=129) | TOTAL (n=266) |
|---|---|---|---|
| Administrative Skills | .15 | .39** | .19** |
| Interpersonal Skills | .13 | .33** | .22** |
| Intellectual Ability | .14 | .22** | .25** |
| Advancement Motivation | .22** | .30** | .28** |
| Work Involvement | .19* | .21* | .15* |
| Stability of Performance | .13 | .13 | .12 |
| Independence | .18* | .05 | .00 |

*p < .05.   **p < .005.

The factors showing significant relationships with later promotions within each educational group as well as within the total group were both motivational, with Advancement Motivation carrying more weight than Work Involvement. All three ability factors were important for the combined group and for the noncollege men.

Individual dimensions making up these factors are shown in the Appendix to this paper. Nearly all of the ability and motivation dimensions were related to later success for the noncollege and combined groups, if not the college group. Key variables related to success for both subgroups were Oral Communication Skills, Need for Advancement, Inner Work Standards, and Energy.

The last two factors in Table 3 are personality factors, and these had very little relationship to advancement 20 years later. Within the Stability of Performance factor, Resistance to Stress was unrelated to advancement in either subgroup or the total. Tolerance of Uncertainty had a low but significant correlation with MPS:20 for the combined group only. The Independence factor showed a significant correlation with MPS:20 level only for the college group, derived from dimension ratings of Need for Superior Approval and Goal Flexibility.

According to the dimensions, then, advancement was mostly related to early signs of the three basic types of ability (Administrative, Interpersonal, and Intellectual) and to motivation, especially the drive to succeed. Other variations in personality and attitudes, including love of the company, were mostly irrelevant.

**Abilities** Key scores from the simulations and paper-and-pencil ability tests produced three primary abilities factors parallel to those found in the factor analysis of the dimensions. Correlations of these three factor scores, representing Administrative, Interpersonal, and Cognitive Ability, with level at MPS:20, are shown in Table 4.

### TABLE 4
### Correlations of Ability Factors at MPS:0
### with Level at MPS:20

| Factor | COLLEGE | | NONCOLLEGE | | TOTAL | |
|---|---|---|---|---|---|---|
| | n | r | n | r | n | r |
| Administrative Ability | 135 | .05 | 126 | .36** | 261 | .16* |
| Interpersonal Ability | 103 | .21* | 128 | .36** | 231 | .20** |
| Cognitive Ability | 106 | .20* | 128 | .28** | 234 | .38** |

*p<.05. **p<.005.

Most important for the combined group was the Cognitive Ability factor. The college men scored significantly higher on this factor and they also advanced further, which boosted the correlation for the combined group. As shown in the Appendix, the SCAT and the Critical Thinking Test were both strongly related to advancement after 20 years, although the Contemporary Affairs Test was less so.

The Administrative Ability factor was a powerful predictor of success for the noncollege group but failed to demonstrate a relationship with advancement for the college group. The college group performed no better on the In-basket than had the noncollege group at the original assessment, perhaps due to their lack of business experience; the noncollege group had been with the telephone company an average of more than nine years before the original assessment, including two years in management, compared to an average tenure of only four months for the college men.

Interpersonal Ability was related to later success for both educational subgroups. The interview was a particularly good measure of Oral Communication Skills (see Appendix), which related to success within both subgroups and the combined group.

**Personality and Motivation** Several personality and motivation factors were significantly related to success 20 years later, as shown in Table 5. The Ambition factor was most closely related to career advancement for the total group, with significant relationships in each of the educational subgroups as well. For the noncollege group, this desire to rise in the organizational hierarchy among those to be most successful was also reflected in the Leadership Motivation factor (derived from the projective exercises), where they rejected a subordinate role.

## TABLE 5
## Correlations of Personality and Motivation Factors at MPS:0 with Level at MPS:20

| Factor | COLLEGE (n=137) | NONCOLLEGE (n=129) | TOTAL (n=266) |
|---|---|---|---|
| Self-Esteem | .20* | .09 | .12* |
| Leadership Motivation | .05 | .18* | .10 |
| Positiveness | .16 | .20* | .15* |
| Impulsivity | .06 | .16 | .25** |
| Affability | -.20 | -.09 | .00 |
| Ambition | .18* | .41** | .37** |

*p < .05.  **p < .005.

Within the Ambition factor, all the exercise scores except the Sarnoff scale of Forward Striving were significantly related to later advancement in the noncollege and combined groups. This meant that those rising highest in the organization scored higher than the others at the original assessment on the Edwards Dominance scale, measuring desire to lead and influence others; on the Sarnoff Motivation for Advancement scale; and on the interview ratings of Primacy of Work, Inner Work Standards, and Need for Advancement. For the college group, however, only the interview rating of Need for Advancement was significantly related to later advancement. Actually, the Need for Advancement rating from the interview showed the strongest relationship with later promotions for both groups and proved to be one of the most potent predictors of later success in the entire assessment center.

There are also indications from Table 5 that positive mental health was related to career advancement. The most successful college men and the combined group had higher scores on the Self-Esteem factor. This result derived from the GAMIN scale of Ascendance in social situations (significant for both groups and the total group) and from the GAMIN scale showing self-confidence or Lack of Inferiority Feelings (significant for the college and combined groups). General Adjustment ratings (from the projectives) on the Positiveness factor were related to career progress in both educational subgroups and the combined group.

**Life Themes** Retrospective, current, and projected involvement in nine areas or themes of life as well as current satisfaction with those areas were rated from interview protocols by a clinical psychologist. Future planned involvements in certain areas of life were frequently more indicative of future advancement than involvements at the time of the original assessment. Correlations of these projected developments with management level at MPS:20 are shown in Table 6.

## TABLE 6
## Correlations of Projected Developments in Life Themes at MPS:0 with Level at MPS:20

| Life theme | COLLEGE (n=137) | NONCOLLEGE (n=129) | TOTAL (n=266) |
|---|---|---|---|
| Marital-Familial | .03 | −.16* | −.11* |
| Parental-Familial | −.09 | −.12 | −.11* |
| Locale-Residential | −.20* | −.09* | −.06 |
| Financial-Acquisitive | .15* | .08 | .16** |
| Ego-Functional | .32** | .16* | .26* |
| Recreational-Social | .08 | .00 | .06 |
| Religious-Humanism | −.12 | −.06 | −.06 |
| Service | .03 | .23* | .26** |
| Occupational | .26** | .38** | .21** |

*p<.05.  **p<.005.

One of the implications from the life themes correlations is that being too much of a homebody was related to less advancement in the company. For the noncollege men, projections of Marital-Familial involvement related negatively to later success, while among the college men projected Locale-Residential concerns were a negative indicator. Perhaps the men who were most oriented to home and family were unwilling to make the sacrifices of time and relocation that a successful career was likely to involve. Nevertheless, the relationship of the Financial-Acquisitive life theme to success for the college and combined groups suggests that acquiring such possessions as houses and cars was important to those who would later advance in the company and may have been a reflection of their ambition.

For both educational groups, projected Ego-Functional (self-development) life-theme developments constituted a strong indicator of later success. Those destined for later advancement were clearly concerned about developing and improving themselves, both mentally and physically. Biographical data showed that those destined for greater advancement rated their health better at the original assessment. More frequent opportunities for public speaking at the time of assessment and self-reports of effectiveness as a speaker were also significantly correlated with promotions. The Service life theme, pointing to interest in community and public affairs, related to later advancement for the noncollege and combined groups.

A final life theme that differentiated the men in terms of their later advancements was projected Occupational involvement. Being oriented to job and career at a young age was clearly a strong sign that one's career would be successful. As shown in Table 6, the relationship was stronger within each educational subgroup than for the combined group. This was because the more experienced noncollege men were more involved in work at the time of assessment but would attain fewer promotions later on.

**Work Interests** In addition to the Occupational life theme, some paper-and-pencil inventories showed the relationship of early work interests to later advancement. On the Expectations Inventory, a questionnaire containing 56 statements describing various aspects of life as a manager both on and off the job, participants were asked to look ahead five years and to mark each item in terms of how likely it was to turn out to be true. Favorable attitudes toward one's anticipated experiences as a Bell System manager were a positive indicator of later success for the noncollege ($r = .24$) and combined ($r = .18$) groups but not for the college group ($r = .08$). Within both educational groups, though, having high expectations about salaries related to later management success.

On the Work Conditions Survey, participants were asked to rate the relative desirability or undesirability of 30 job characteristics, such as "irregular hours." Within both subgroups and for the total group, those who were to become more successful had stronger preferences at MPS:0 for jobs that had a lot of responsibility and that required initiative. The most successful college men wanted a job that would depend on their own decisions, while the most successful noncollege men preferred work that would require practical intelligence. In addition, the most successful from the noncollege and the combined groups showed greater antagonism toward routine work.

The most successful noncollege men had some additional work preferences that were also indicative of success when the two subgroups were combined. Those promoted most often by MPS:20 were more antagonistic toward well-defined jobs and toward jobs with little social contact. In line with this rejection of social isolation on their part was a more positive attitude toward work in personnel selection.

The overall impression from the Work Conditions results is that those who were to advance furthest had early yearnings for work conditions that higher-level jobs would provide— responsibility and opportunities to use one's initiative and intellect. They were rejecting jobs that were too routine or structured or that resulted in social isolation.

## Utility of Measures Over Time

One factor influencing the utility of psychological measures over time is that people do, in fact, change somewhat with age and experience. The MPS managers showed some changes that were relatively independent of promotions and seemed to be related primarily to aging. For example, on the Edwards they increased on the scales of Autonomy and Aggression and decreased on such people-oriented scales as Affiliation and Intraception. One implication of such changes is that normative data on psychological measures must take account of the age of respondents.

**Early- and Late-Emerging Characteristics** Repeated administrations of tests and exercises in the three assessment centers attended by the MPS men showed that measures of some of their qualities were potent predictors of advancement at the beginning of their careers but lost their impact later on. Illustrating this are indicators of advancement motivation from the Sarnoff, interview ratings, and assessment dimension ratings. Table 7 shows the correlations with level at MPS:20 of several measures of ambition taken at years 0, 8, and 20 of the study. The MPS:20 sample of 266 was used for each computation. The highest correlation in each row is underlined.

---

### TABLE 7
### Correlations of Measures of Advancement
### Motivation Over Time with MPS:20 Level

| | | YEAR MEASURED | | |
|---|---|---|---|---|
| Variable | Source | 0 | 8 | 20 |
| Need Advancement | Dimension | .35 | <u>.47</u> | .27 |
| Advancement Motivation | Sarnoff | .19 | <u>.25</u> | .15 |
| Need Advancement | Interview | <u>.46</u> | <u>.48</u> | .40 |

---

It is clear from Table 7 that measurements of advancement motivation taken concurrently with level at the 20th year do not discriminate the more successful executives as well as do measures taken earlier in the career. For the Sarnoff, year 8 looks like the most promising year to measure ambition, while the interview rating indicates that predictions could have been made equally well at year 0 or year 8.

An explanation of this phenomenon is illustrated in Figure 2, which shows mean scores on the Sarnoff Advancement Motivation scale over time. The general trend is for the participants to be high on advancement motivation early in their careers but to decline in scores later. By MPS:20 their scores had dropped so much that the average man was only at the seventh or eighth percentile of the original MPS norms. Such a decline in motivation was often due to the men achieving their promotional goals with time, realistically confronting a rapidly narrowing pyramid, or recognizing and accepting signals that they were no longer in the running for higher positions.

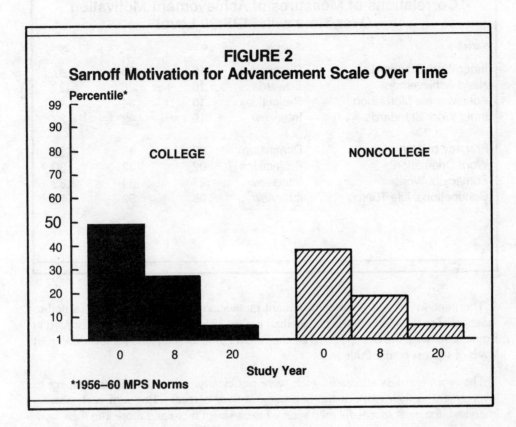

FIGURE 2
Sarnoff Motivation for Advancement Scale Over Time

The more successful men did not lose their motivation to as great an extent as the less successful men, so there was still some relationship between advancement motivation and success in the 20th year. But the overall effect of the general decline in advancement motivation is a restriction of range that lessens the impact of this personality characteristic in descriptions of the successful executive in middle age. Hence, to use ambition as a characteristic to predict executive success, it is best to measure it early in the career when youthful drive still runs strong and before achieved promotions and/or the onset of reality subdue upward striving.

The story is somewhat different for the motivation for achievement, as shown in Table 8. There are two aspects of achievement motivation, both of which fall within the Work Involvement dimension factor. Inner Work Standards reflect putting forth one's own high standards of excellence; related to this dimension are the Achievement scale of the Edwards, Achievement Motivation scored post hoc from the projectives protocols, and Inner Work Standards rated from the interview. Primacy of Work reflects the extent to which work is one of the most important aspects of one's life, providing a direction for one's efforts. Related to this dimension were ratings by the same name from the interview, the Occupational life theme, and Work Orientation rated from the projectives.

## TABLE 8
## Correlations of Measures of Achievement Motivation
## Over Time with MPS:20 Level

| Variable | Source | 0 | 8 | 20 |
|---|---|---|---|---|
| Inner Work Standards | Dimension | .16 | .35 | .47 |
| Need Achievement | Edwards | .10 | .28 | .27 |
| Achievement Motivation | Projectives | .15 | .34 | .40 |
| Inner Work Standards | Interview | .16 | .42 | .22 |
| | | | | |
| Primacy of Work | Dimension | .09 | .46 | .55 |
| Work Orientation | Projectives | .02 | .32 | .39 |
| Primacy of Work | Interview | .27 | .34 | .35 |
| Occupational Life Theme | Interview | .06 | .52 | .72 |

The trend in Table 8 is for achievement motivation to be more strongly related to managerial success later in the career than earlier. The reason for this is illustrated in Figure 3, showing the Occupational life theme over time for men who achieved different levels of success by the 20th year.

The more and less successful men were not clearly differentiated with respect to involvement in their work at the beginning of their careers. But with each passing interview, the most successful men seemed to be swept more and more into their work while the least successful began to become detached. The net result is that the later in the career one took a measure of work involvement, the more highly correlated it would be with management success, at least into the midcareer stage.

There are other examples that could be cited of late-appearing characteristics. Tolerance of Uncertainty, for instance, was more highly related to success when measured at the 20-year point than earlier, perhaps because ambiguity is more characteristic of higher-level jobs that the men had not reached earlier in their careers. Also seemingly related to higher-level jobs was the tendency for executives to become "cool at the top," declining on nurturance but remaining objective at the same time the lower-level men increased in authoritarianism.

Such late-emerging characteristics, as well as those that are more important earlier, point to the need to consider developmental changes and time of prediction when psychological measures are related to managerial success. The correlations of various MPS measures taken at two points of time (year 0 and year 8) with later advancement measured at two points in time (year 8 and year 20) are given in the Appendix.

**Increasing Heterogeneity** For both the college and noncollege groups, original predictions of advancement were most accurate only a few years (4–8) after the

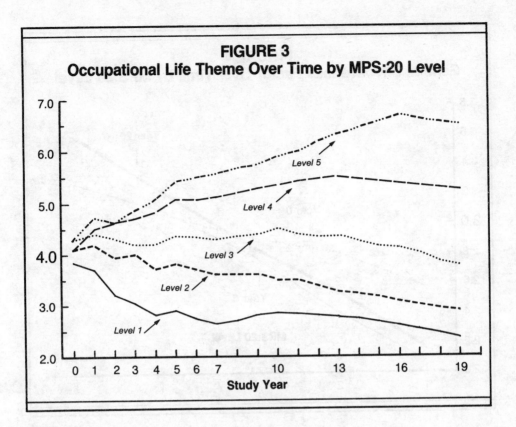

**FIGURE 3**
**Occupational Life Theme Over Time by MPS:20 Level**

Level 5

Level 4

Level 3

Level 2

Level 1

Study Year

assessment. Correlations of the overall assessment rating and level each year then began to fall, especially for the college group. The noncollege group was more stable than the college, being more mature at the time of the assessment and undergoing fewer changes in work experiences over time, especially given their lesser rates of promotion. As a result, by the time of the reassessment at year 8, predictions about the future of the college men were more likely to have changed. For both educational groups, predictions of advancement by MPS:20 were considerably more accurate from the MPS:8 assessment than from the original assessment.

One explanation for the enhanced predictive accuracy is that the men became more heterogeneous and dissimilar with time. In many cases, the differences that evolved were related to whether or not the man had been relatively successful or unsuccessful in terms of gaining promotions. A number of psychological characteristics, for example, showed the pattern of the Occupational life theme in Figure 3, where the higher-level men changed in one direction (in that case toward more work involvement) while the lower-level men changed in the opposite direction. Most of these major changes took place between the assessments at years 0 and 8.

The overall impact of these changes is reflected in the General Effectiveness factor, which may be thought of as an average across the meaningful assessment dimensions. Average scores on this factor by MPS:20 level are shown in Figure 4. The scores are shown for the 266 men who completed all three assessments.

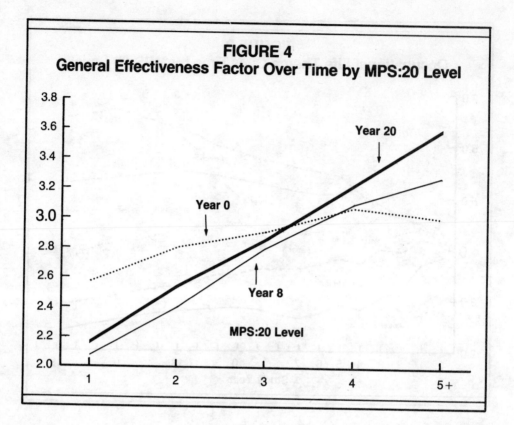

**FIGURE 4**
**General Effectiveness Factor Over Time by MPS:20 Level**

The pattern of results shown by this factor illustrates the cliché, "The rich get richer, and the poor get poorer." The fifth- and sixth-level men gained significantly in managerial effectiveness between MPS:0 and MPS:8, and again between MPS:8 and MPS:20. The fourth-level men showed little change, but each succeeding level of men below that showed greater and greater declines. The MPS:20 assessment dimension ratings were somewhat more favorable to the men in general than the MPS:8 ratings had been, but when either later period is compared to the MPS:0 results, the same pattern is evident.

All the dimension factors relating to abilities (Administrative Skills, Interpersonal Skills, and Intellectual Ability), as well as Work Involvement and Stability of Performance showed the "rich get richer, poor get poorer" phenomenon. It is very likely that motivational factors can explain much of this pattern, as the lower-level men withdrew from work involvement and the higher-level men continued to be rewarded for theirs. Where the "rich get richer, poor get poorer" phenomenon applies, psychological measures taken after a few years on the job will show more individual differences and hence be more predictive of later advancements.

# Reference

Howard, A., & Bray, D. W. (1988). *Managerial lives in transition: Advancing age and changing times*. New York: Guilford Press.

# APPENDIX
## Correlations of Techniques Used in the Management Progress Study Assessment Centers (Years 0 and 8) with Management Level Attained (Years 8 and 20): MPS:20 Sample

| | Yrs. 0–20 | | | Yrs. 0–8 | Yrs. 8–20 |
| | College | Noncollege | Total | Total | Total |
| N | 137 | 129 | 266 | 264 | 263 |
|---|---|---|---|---|---|
| **DIMENSIONS** | | | | | |
| Organizing & Planning | .14 | .36** | .20** | .27** | .47** |
| Decision Making | .14 | .38** | .16* | .27** | .46** |
| Creativity | .15 | .34** | .22** | .32** | .44** |
| Leadership Skills | .09 | .36** | .18** | .28** | .48** |
| Oral Communication Skills | .22* | .33** | .23** | .36** | .39** |
| Behavior Flexibility | .09 | .31** | .22** | .28** | .32** |
| Personal Impact | .14 | .22* | .17** | .17** | .36** |
| Social Objectivity | .02 | .08 | .05 | .02 | .24** |
| Perception of Social Cues | .06 | .24* | .16* | .24** | .34** |
| Range of Interests | .13 | .08 | .12* | .15* | .27** |
| General Mental Ability | .11 | .27** | .30** | .31** | .39** |
| Written Communication Skills | .25 | .06 | .23* | .08 | .34** |
| Tolerance of Uncertainty | .15 | .14 | .15* | .24** | .24** |
| Resistance to Stress | .08 | .12 | .08 | .20** | .27** |
| Primacy of Work | .04 | .15 | .09 | .14* | .46** |
| Inner Work Standards | .25** | .23* | .16** | .14* | .35** |
| Energy | .17* | .26** | .15* | .21** | .42** |
| Self-Objectivity | −.07 | .24* | .08 | .12 | .23** |
| Need for Advancement | .28** | .32** | .34** | .37** | .47** |
| Need for Security | −.14 | −.18* | −.13* | −.26** | −.50** |
| Ability to Delay Gratification | −.13 | −.24* | −.19* | −.25** | −.41** |
| Realism of Expectations | .04 | −.04 | −.06 | -.10 | −.15* |
| Bell System Value Orientation | −.08 | .01 | .03 | -.02 | .19* |
| Need for Superior Approval | −.18* | -.07 | −.09 | −.16* | −.21** |
| Need for Peer Approval | −.03 | -.07 | .07 | −.14* | −.11 |
| Goal Flexibility | −.17* | .04 | .03 | −.04 | .20** |
| | | | | | |
| **ABILITIES** | | | | | |
| In-Basket Overall | .05 | .31** | .11 | .14* | .27** |
| In-Basket Organ. & Planning | .04 | .30** | .18** | .23** | .33** |
| In-Basket Decision Making | .08 | .40** | .17* | .18* | .36** |
| Competitive Group Overall | .19* | .20* | .10 | .19* | .45** |
| Competitive Group Oral | .11 | .21* | .13* | .21* | .41** |
| Competitive Group Oral Comm. | .19 | .24* | .16* | .24** | .30** |
| Competitive Group Leadership | .31** | .15 | .18* | .25** | .38** |
| Business Game Overall | .00 | .34** | .00 | .18* | .38** |
| Business Game Forcefulness | −.01 | .29** | .10 | .17* | .24** |
| Interview Oral Commun. | .29** | .39** | .33** | .33** | .45** |
| SCAT Verbal | .12 | .20* | .31** | .34** | .37** |

|  | | Yrs. 0–20 | | | Yrs. 0–8 | Yrs. 8–20 |
|  | College | Noncollege | Total | | Total | Total |
| N | 137 | 129 | 266 | | 264 | 263 |
|---|---|---|---|---|---|---|

**ABILITIES (cont.)**

| | | | | | | |
|---|---|---|---|---|---|---|
| SCAT Quantitative | .18 | .31** | .39** | | .33** | .37** |
| SCAT Total | .19* | .29** | .40** | | .39** | .41** |
| Critical Thinking | .15 | .31** | .33** | | .34** | .41** |

## PERSONALITY & MOTIVATION

**EDWARDS:**

| | | | | | | |
|---|---|---|---|---|---|---|
| Achievement | .03 | .06 | .09 | | .14* | .28** |
| Deference | −.13 | .00 | −.11 | | −.01 | −.18** |
| Order | −.14 | .00 | −.17** | | −.12* | −.16* |
| Exhibition | −.10 | .00 | .09 | | .03 | .03 |
| Autonomy | .05 | −.09 | −.05 | | .02 | −.05 |
| Affiliation | .02 | −.02 | .13* | | .02 | −.04 |
| Intraception | .09 | .12 | .01 | | .08 | .04 |
| Succorance | −.09 | −.06 | .00 | | −.09 | −.06 |
| Dominance | .05 | .27** | .18** | | .23** | .28** |
| Abasement | −.10 | −.19* | −.22** | | −.22** | −.09 |
| Nurturance | .05 | −.18* | −.07 | | −.15* | −.13* |
| Change | .02 | .04 | .00 | | .07 | .02 |
| Endurance | .20* | −.08 | −.02 | | −.12 | −.02 |
| Heterosexuality | −.02 | .03 | .06 | | .01 | −.02 |
| Aggression | .09 | .11 | .10 | | .17** | .09 |

**GAMIN:**

| | | | | | | |
|---|---|---|---|---|---|---|
| General Activity | .10 | .09 | .13* | | .15* | .17** |
| Ascendance | .21* | .22* | .24* | | .21** | .21** |
| Masculinity | .09 | −.04 | .02 | | −.02 | .01 |
| Self-Confidence | .21* | .02 | .13* | | .12 | .09 |
| Emotional Stability | .10 | .00 | .01 | | −.01 | −.05 |

**SARNOFF:**

| | | | | | | |
|---|---|---|---|---|---|---|
| Advancement | .06 | .19* | .19** | | .21** | .25** |
| Money | −.08 | −.01 | −.14* | | −.02 | −.05 |
| Forward Striving | .01 | .01 | .08 | | .09 | .17** |
| **Total** | **.00** | **.05** | **.06** | | **.13*** | **.18*** |

**CALIFORNIA F**

| | | | | | | |
|---|---|---|---|---|---|---|
| | .06 | −.11 | −.05 | | −.01 | −.20** |

**PROJECTIVES:**

| | | | | | | |
|---|---|---|---|---|---|---|
| Achievement/Advancement | .04 | .14 | .15* | | .18** | .34** |
| Self-Confidence | .05 | .17 | .07 | | .13* | .38** |
| Work Orientation | .03 | .11 | .02 | | .10 | .32** |
| Dependency | −.11 | −.16 | −.14* | | −.20** | −.17** |
| Affiliation | .11 | −.05 | .09 | | .00 | −.06 |
| Optimism | .14 | .17 | .14* | | .16* | .28** |
| Leadership Role | .12 | .16 | .09 | | .16* | .25** |

| N | College 137 | Yrs. 0–20 Noncollege 129 | Total 266 | Yrs. 0–8 Total 264 | Yrs. 8–20 Total 263 |
|---|---|---|---|---|---|
| **PROJECTIVES (cont.):** | | | | | |
| Subordinate Role | −.05 | −.18* | −.11 | −.13* | −.26** |
| General Adjustment | .22* | .20* | .19** | .20** | .22** |
| **INTERVIEW RATINGS:** | | | | | |
| Primacy of Work | .08 | .29** | .27** | .35** | .34** |
| Inner Work Standards | .14 | .23* | .16* | .12 | .42** |
| Need for Advancement | .29** | .43** | .46** | .50** | .48** |
| Need for Security | −.29** | −.22* | −.36** | .33** | −.33** |

*p < .05.   **p < .005.

# Contextual Issues in Predicting High-Level Leadership Performance: Contextual Richness as a Criterion Consideration in Personality Research with Executives

V. Jon Bentz

As an explanation for nonvalidity research findings, one hears "my predictors were excellent but there seemed to be deficiencies in the criterion." My concern is with issues embedded in that statement.

During my tenure at Sears, my colleagues and I worked unrelentingly on the criterion problem, spending much effort on criterion development and the attendant problems of data generation. We were compulsive followers of prescribed psychometric procedures, making certain that precise wordings were placed within tidy undimensional items. In addition to such straightforward criterion variables, we always included an overall general effectiveness or promotion-potential criterion. Excellent validities were almost always associated with such criteria. The usual explanation for such findings is that they mirror one kind of rater bias. While this may be so, an alternative view is that the cognitive maps of experienced raters can entertain and balance several concepts simultaneously, thus producing criterion ratings which reflect the in-depth richness of their knowledge about employee performance. This notion led us to question the wisdom of an unrelenting pursuit of psychometric purity in criterion design. Nowhere did this idea seem more relevant than when we began intensive work with predicting long-term effectiveness of management trainees. The idea became a conviction during our early efforts with assessment center technology. In both instances we found it necessary to move toward more complex evaluative processes. While some of these efforts have been detailed elsewhere, let me provide examples from our earlier work.

## Long-Term Prediction of Managerial Trainee Job Performance

Immediately after selection, groups of management trainees were placed in training stores. There they received intensive developmental experiences under the constant guidance of specially selected training coordinators. The coordinators had been brought into a central location for intensive orientation in evaluation techniques. Later, when periodic ratings were to be done, either I or one of my professional colleagues and I traveled to the training stores to assist in data gathering. One such session always took place toward the end of the training cycle. The criteria used in that evaluation derived from a model reflecting behaviors related to long-term career effectiveness. Rating content consisted of comprehensive statements detailing areas of executive behavior. Ratings were made along a nine-point scale representing the normal curve of distribution. One such variable was:

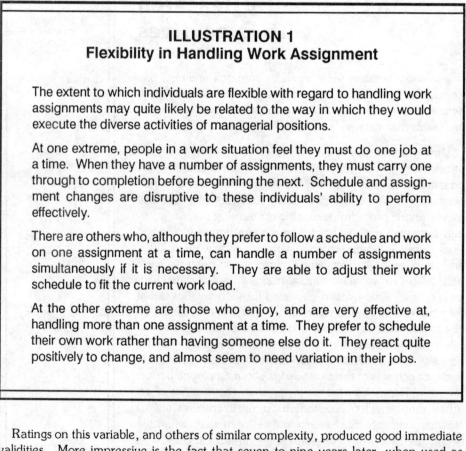

**ILLUSTRATION 1**
**Flexibility in Handling Work Assignment**

The extent to which individuals are flexible with regard to handling work assignments may quite likely be related to the way in which they would execute the diverse activities of managerial positions.

At one extreme, people in a work situation feel they must do one job at a time. When they have a number of assignments, they must carry one through to completion before beginning the next. Schedule and assignment changes are disruptive to these individuals' ability to perform effectively.

There are others who, although they prefer to follow a schedule and work on one assignment at a time, can handle a number of assignments simultaneously if it is necessary. They are able to adjust their work schedule to fit the current work load.

At the other extreme are those who enjoy, and are very effective at, handling more than one assignment at a time. They prefer to schedule their own work rather than having someone else do it. They react quite positively to change, and almost seem to need variation in their jobs.

Ratings on this variable, and others of similar complexity, produced good immediate validities. More impressive is the fact that seven to nine years later, when used as predictors in a longitudinal study, they predicted both current job performance and a series of objective criteria. The data are in Table 1. Note: the Overall Effectiveness criterion had excellent long-term predictive ability.

# TABLE 1

## Seven-to-Nine-Year Prediction of Career Progress by Earlier Performance Ratings

| LONG-RANGE CAREER PROGRAM | No. Job Evaluation | Midpoint Compensation | Compensation | 1977 Perf.Eval. Technical Knowledge | Knowledge Application | Administrative Effectiveness | Work-Related | Response to Superiors | Directive Subordinates |
|---|---|---|---|---|---|---|---|---|---|
| **EARLY EVALUATION** | | | | | | | | | |
| Original and creative production of ideas | 302** | 299** | 293** | | | | | | 261* |
| Active problem solving | 292** | 290** | 325** | | | 206* | | 205* | 304** |
| Independence in problem resolution | 211 | 197* | 200* | | | | | | 236* |
| Overall effectiveness ranking | 381** | 390** | 399** | | | | | | 282* |
| **STORE RATINGS** | | | | | | | | | |
| Flexibility | | 207* | | | | | | | 216* |
| Technical details | 259** | 251* | | | | | | | |
| Oral communications | 200* | 207* | 234** | | | | | | 275* |
| Emotional involvement | | | 243** | | | | | | |
| Aggressiveness | | | 186* | | | | | | |
| Attitude | 193* | 193* | 178* | | | | 222* | 222* | 220* |
| N = | 123 | 123 | 124 | 100 | 100 | 100 | 100 | 100 | 86 |

*p < .05.  **p < .01.
Source: Prepared by author

## Influence of Assessment Center Technology on Criterion Development

In addition to experiences of the sort just described, work with assessment center technology simultaneously developed simulations, evaluator assessments, and follow-up validity criteria. Among things developed were complex simulations involving executive decision making. We ran into problems when we began developing assessments that would capture decision-making behaviors. To begin with, we reverted to type and created nice, pure, straightforward ratings of decision making. What we produced would have been appropriate for a rudimentary decision process, but we completely failed to capture the contextual richness of the executive decision process. Our efforts to be psychometrically pure had systematically robbed the phenomenon of its meaning. When we went back to the drawing board our assessment concepts became more complex.

## A Transition to Developing More Complex Criteria

Experiences like these gradually led us away from a preoccupation with straightforward criterion development. We began to devise structurally complex items. These were frequently followed by elaborating descriptions. Examples are:

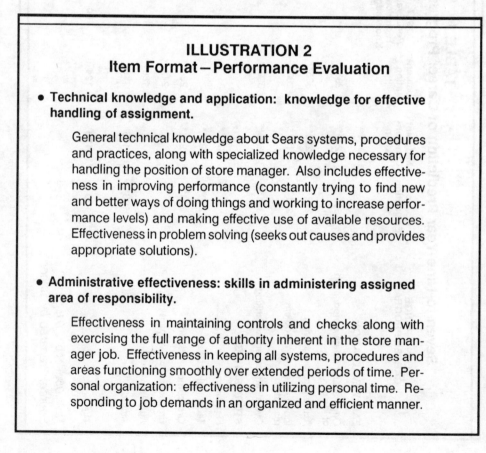

---

### ILLUSTRATION 2
### Item Format — Performance Evaluation

- **Technical knowledge and application: knowledge for effective handling of assignment.**

    General technical knowledge about Sears systems, procedures and practices, along with specialized knowledge necessary for handling the position of store manager. Also includes effectiveness in improving performance (constantly trying to find new and better ways of doing things and working to increase performance levels) and making effective use of available resources. Effectiveness in problem solving (seeks out causes and provides appropriate solutions).

- **Administrative effectiveness: skills in administering assigned area of responsibility.**

    Effectiveness in maintaining controls and checks along with exercising the full range of authority inherent in the store manager job. Effectiveness in keeping all systems, procedures and areas functioning smoothly over extended periods of time. Personal organization: effectiveness in utilizing personal time. Responding to job demands in an organized and efficient manner.

---

- **Personal organization: effectiveness in utilizing personal time.**

  Responding to job demands in an organized and efficient manner. Keeps track of the many things that must be done within a given time period. Acts according to priorities. Gets things done on time with an economy of effort. Stays organized under pressure of interruption.

The need for contextual richness in criteria became more evident when we engaged in research involving the discovery, description, and prediction of executive behavior—particularly upper-level executive behavior.

I would like to turn to such an investigation—a validity study relating an Executive Battery of Psychological Tests (the variables are listed in Table 2) to criteria reflecting high-level executive performance. I shall begin by talking about the development of a criterion called The Qualifications Questionnaire.

## TABLE 2
## Variables Contained in the
## Sears Executive Battery of Psychological Tests

**American Council on Education Psychological Test**

L—Comprehension of words, language, and verbal ideas: verbal reasoning
Q—Quantitative, numerical problem solving; logical reasoning
T—Quickness of learning

**Guilford-Martin Personality Inventories**

S—Outgoing friendliness; social ease
T—Reflective awareness of what's happening to self and surrounding
D—Freedom from depression; optimism, cheerful outlook
C—Emotional control, predictability of temperament
R—Spontaneity, flexibility, impulsiveness

G—Energy; general activity, quickness of movements

A—Social ascendancy; assume leading role when part of a group

M—Masculinity (not used in interpretation), nonsqueamishness

*Continued on next page*

**TABLE 2**—*Continued*

I — Self-confidence, assurance to act without need for support

N — Lack of nervous anxiety; composure under pressure

O — Objectivity in judging, without emotional involvement

Ag — Agreeableness, avoidance of conflict

Co — Cooperative tolerance, fair-mindedness, noncritical

## Allport-Vernon Scale of Values

| | |
|---|---|
| Theoretical | Concern for why things are as they are |
| Economic | Concern for money, profit, and general values of marketplace |
| Aesthetic | Concern for the interrelated harmony of form, line, color, and structure |
| Social | Concern for general social welfare |
| Political | Concern for personal status and prestige |
| Religion | Concern for orthodox religious values (variable not used in interpretation) |

## Kuder Preference Inventory—
## Preference for activities and tasks related to:

| | |
|---|---|
| Mechanical | Involvement with mechanical ideas, things, and principles |
| Scientific | Involvement with physical sciences |
| Computational | Involvement with numerical and computational tasks |
| Persuasive | Involvement with selling, promoting, and persuading |
| Artistic | Involvement with art and artistic production |
| Literary | Involvement with literary expression, writing, and authorship |
| Music | Involvement with music and musical production |
| Social Service | Involvement with serving, helping, and assisting others |
| Clerical | Involvement with routine, repetitive, detailed clerical tasks |

*Source: Prepared by author.*

# The Prediction of High-Level Executive Effectiveness

**Interviews Provide Content For Item Development**  Preliminary to developing the questionnaire, a series of in-depth, semistructured interviews were conducted with top-level administrators.  These interviews provided descriptions of the characteristics, skills, and abilities necessary for high-level performance.  Content analysis of interview data revealed material for developing an assessment instrument.  Again we struggled converting descriptive information into evaluation items.  We began (as we almost always did) by trying to place one specific behavioral element within each item.  As we proceeded toward descriptive specificity we distorted the phenomena.  As behaviors were removed from their contextual settings, content became trivialized.  To regain meaning it was necessary to replace behaviors within their contextual setting.  Items then combined substantive content and contextual information.  In this way we came close to recapturing content richness as it had emerged from the earlier interviews.  In the final instrument, items became definitions which frequently contained more than one idea.  Each item reflected a concept or area of executive functioning.  Nearly all represented complex skills, abilities, characteristics, or functions.  After pretesting the questionnaire and eliciting user reactions, some items were combined, thus increasing their internal complexity.

The Qualifications Questionnaire is made up of 51 items.  Content is measured on a one to four intensity scale.  Content was grouped into five *a priori* categories and appeared under the following labels:
> The Uses of Mental Ability
> Personal Characteristics
> Administrative Skills
> Relations Outside the Company
> Putting It All Together

Typical items and the measurement scale are presented in Illustration 3.

**General Background: Data Gathering**  Senior executives used the Qualifications Questionnaire to evaluate 136 people.  For inclusion in the sample, candidates had to have demonstrated accomplishment in a relatively high-level assignment.  The rating process was part of a program to select candidates for a top-level executive-continuity program.  Those surviving the selection process became members of the program and candidates for placement in top-level positions.  Because of the difficulty and sensitivity of the assessment process a slide film was developed and shown to all evaluators.  The film related rating content to higher-level executive performance.  To further support the evaluation process a booklet called "Characteristics of Higher-Level Executives" was prepared and given to evaluators as an adjunct to the rating process.

**Factor Analysis of the Qualifications Questionnaire**  Since each item represented a concept or area of executive performance, it was logical to relate each to the predictor variables.  We planned to do this.  However, since so many relationships (1,530 r's) present a number of cumbersome problems, we sought to reduce the criterion data into more compact measures through factor analysis.  We anticipated problems.  First, 136 cases represent fewer cases than ideal for factor analysis.  However, large numbers of high-level management cases are rarely available, so we decided to proceed.  Another thing we anticipated was the garbage-in/garbage-out quandary sometimes

# ILLUSTRATION 3
## Qualifications Questionnaire

**Evaluation Scale**

| Sample Item Format | Not observable<br>Not observable or developed | Observable<br>Less than the statement implies | Observable<br>As good as the statement implies | Observable<br>Better than the statement implies | Observable<br>Much better, is a model for others |
|---|---|---|---|---|---|
| *Problem Awareness*<br>Sees problems, challenges, and possibilities for change and improvement where others don't: aware of what is incomplete, inadequate, and in need of modification. Spots emerging problems. | | | | | |
| *Ability to Delegate*<br>Delegates proper responsibility to subordinates. Knows when and how much to delegate. Allows subordinates freedom to act and develop their potential, but follows up and monitors results. | | | | | |
| *Personal Courage*<br>Willingness to commit oneself in uncertain situations, ability to take risks without undue fear: absence of tendency to sidestep troublesome situations or to make concessions to avoid conflict. Can buck the tide when convinced of positions. Doesn't avoid making the unpopular decisions because of what others might think. | | | | | |
| *Ability to Set and Communicate Performance Standards*<br>Has demonstrated the ability to set specific standards or principles of performance, and communicate them in clear understandable terms: includes the ability to adapt standards to varying business conditions. | | | | | |

associated with factor analysis. Because of the complex, even eccentric, nature of item construction we anticipated only one big general factor. If this didn't happen we expected the items to separate into two factors—one dealing with personal abilities and characteristics, the other with administrative behaviors. When we performed a principal component factor analysis with varimax rotation, we found the 51 items distributed across nine factors. The titles appear in Table 3. Each factor makes good sense. Internal structure is so compelling that a full narrative description of each factor is possible simply by stringing together item word content. Such a description for one factor appears in Illustration 4.

While time does not permit lengthy discussion, I'd like to comment on the overall nature of the factor structure.

**Overview of Qualification Questionnaire Factor Structure**  The first two factors combine administrative processes with intellectual functioning. Factors I and II contain elements of personal power, strong goal orientation, decisiveness, and assurance. Both contain an integration of mental and physical health with powerful administrative and intellectual functions. These factors may tell us that upper-level administrative effectiveness is possible only when supported by flexible physical and intellectual stamina. The quality of foresight in Factor IX fits well with those qualities measured by Factors I and II.

Factors III and VII both involve leadership. Factor III deals with leadership of an interpersonal nature; VII involves concern for the welfare and development of the organization. The two factors measure people and organizational leadership respectively. Factors IV, VI, and VIII form a meaningful constellation. Factor VIII measures organization and planning activities; IV defines qualities of decisive confidence, personal courage, and the kind of fair-minded independence that supports standard setting and performance evaluation. Factor VI integrates abilities associated with the scope and scale of the extended organization and moving it forward in an orderly manner. These three factors (IV, VI, VIII, having to do with planning, setting standards, appraising performance, and effecting orderly organizational momentum) are central to effective upper-level executive functioning.

Factor V measures those abilities (communication skills, proclivity toward abstraction) and personal characteristics (social skill, knowledge of the outside world, and business perspective) that facilitate functioning as a public representative of the company.

The nine factors provide insight into the dimensionality of executive performance. Taken as a whole, they make both psychological and organizational sense: they also present a compelling portrait of top-level executive skills and characteristics. By studying the integration of personal and administrative behaviors within factors, we see that it is impossible to separate what a person *does* from what a person *is*. These findings make a contribution to our understanding of high-level executive job performance. Their richness, when used as criteria for linkage to test scores, makes the interpretative potential of validity finding equally rich. Let me turn to the results of such a linkage.

**Results–Test Scores Related to Criteria of High-Level Job Performance**
Correlations were computed between predictor variables and each of the 51 criterion items. Correlations were also done between the predictors and each of the factorial

# ILLUSTRATION 4
## Items Loading on Factor VI

**Integration of Complex and Diverse Functions to Move the Organization Forward**

| ITEM # | CONTENT | LOADING |
|---|---|---|
| 49 | Ability to coordinate diverse functions and move the organization forward in an orderly manner. | .605 |
| 48 | Ability to handle complex situations (in which there are many diverse elements, some of which may be in conflict) and co-ordinate them into single overall framework. | .575 |
| 50 | Ability to develop a strategy of administration so as to shape events (through coordinating such things as standard setting, planning, developing specific sets of priorities, and organizing). | .562 |
| 33 | Has ability to cope with new systems (such as electronic mechanization systems) and integrate them into ongoing system of administration. | .475 |
| 35 | Ability to delegate. Delegates proper responsibility to subor-dinates. Knows when and how much to delegate. Allows subordinates freedom to act and develop their potential, but follows up and monitors results. | .483 |
| 28 | Airs disagreements in the service of the business. Makes dis-agreements with superiors known primarily before decisions are made. Once decisions are made takes a proprietary inter-est in them and supports them as though they were one's own. | .474 |

# Factor VI

### INTEGRATION OF COMPLEX AND DIVERSE FUNCTIONS TO MOVE THE ORGANIZATION FORWARD

Factor VI is composed of the six items shown above. With an emphasis upon the ability to handle complex situations, Factor VI evaluates the means through which organizational momentum is achieved. There is the ability to cope with what's new and integrate it into ongoing systems of administration. If there are disagreements, differences are aired in private, before decisions are made. Once decisions are made, however, they are supported (as if they are one's own). There is also skill and follow-up on results. Such administrative actions coordinate diverse and complex functions (some of which may be in conflict) into an overall conceptual framework. A stream of interrelated activities (standard setting, planning, organizing, and developing specific sets of priorities) are coordinated so that events are shaped into a well-developed strategy of administration. Thus, orderly, forward organizational movement occurs. Since Factor VI pulls together a wide variety of personal and orga-nizational forces, it is called Integration of Complex and Diverse Functions to Move the Organization Forward.

dimension scores. Because the findings are voluminous, I will summarize some of them for you.

*Patterning of Validity Data—the 51 Criterion Items—*In commenting on the pattern of correlation between the predictors and the 51 items, let me put them within a historical perspective.

In 1951, when I did my first study with the Sears Executive Battery, a series of scores differentiated between a group of executives who had failed and a group which had made unusual job progress. The differentiating scores were Mental Ability, Sociability, Social Ascendancy, General Activity, Self-Confidence, Serious versus Carefree, Persuasive Interests, Political and Economic Values. Since that first research effort, this pattern has reappeared in study after study. So consistent has it been that we saw the pattern as a syndrome central to executive effectiveness. Now, nearly 35 years after its first appearance, the syndrome reasserts itself in the findings of this group of high-level executives.

A description of the syndrome, which we call *Competitive Leadership,* and the variables associated with it follows:

*Persuasive and socially assured, the person moves aggressively into a central role whenever part of a social or business group (Sociability, Social Ascendancy, Persuasive Interests). Confident to initiate and act without external support (Self-Confidence), the individual catches on rapidly (Mental Ability) and moves into action with energy and flexibility (General Activity, Serious versus Carefree). With heightened personal concern for status, power, and money (Political and Economic Values), the person will work hard to achieve positions which yield such rewards.*

This scoring pattern has been predictive in studies throughout the hierarchy of executive positions. I see it, therefore, as an enabling syndrome, prerequisite to executive functioning at all levels. It may well have been this combination of supportive characteristics that enabled this group of executives to ascend to top-level positions.

*Results—Multiple Correlations Between Predictors and Factorial Dimensions—*Let us turn to the multiple correlations between Executive Battery variables and the factorially defined criteria. The multiples (in Table 3), all unshrunken, range from .375 to .608. The composition and meaning of each multiple are interesting. Let me mention just a few intriguing things.
- —For all but one criterion, the first variable to enter the multiple is Social Ascendancy. This variable contributes heavily to every multiple correlation.
- —The Quantitative Mental Ability score appears in six of the nine multiples.
- —Emotional strength variables (Composure, Optimism, Stability, and Objectivity) make substantial contributions to the findings.

While there are other interesting contributions to performance prediction, let it be noted that a wide range of psychological variables predict these complex performance criteria.

It is also of practical importance that tests predict such complex performance criteria as the:

—informed competitive drive to improve and develop the business and the
—integration of complex and diverse functions to move the organization forward.

*Long-Term Prediction of Performance*—You should know that the data on the predictor side of the equation is old. The average age of test data is 21 years. These results represent long-term prediction of executive effectiveness. That psychological tests taken over 20 years ago predict current performance of high-level executives is a fact of real import.

## TABLE 3
### Multiple Correlations Between Sears Executive Battery of Psychological Tests and Factorially Defined Criteria Dimensions

| FACTOR | TITLE | MULTIPLE R |
|--------|-------|------------|
| I | Flexible physical, emotional, and intellectual strength that supports and translates into administrative action | .449** |
| II | Assured independence and ingenuity of intellectual and administrative functioning | .564** |
| III | Effective (people) leadership | .608** |
| IV | Administrative sensitivity and strength in setting standards and appraising performance | .496** |
| V | Effectiveness as a public representative of the company | .536** |
| VI | Integration of complex and diverse functions to move the organization forward | .375** |
| VII | Informed, competitive drive to improve and develop business | .535** |
| VIII | Organizing and planning activities | .482** |
| | **All items together—total score** | **.539**** |
| IX | Foresight (multiple—not computed) | |

## Conclusions

1. Psychological test variables do predict complex indices of high-level executive performance and do so over an extended time period. The predictor instruments used in this research can be labeled both as old and old-fashioned; the criteria represent an initial developmental effort. With refinements in instrumentation on both sides of the predictive equation, we should expect more important results.

2. When doing research with high-level executive behavior the criteria will nearly always be subjective ratings. We must bring all our most creative skills to both instrument development and data gathering. The challenge of the latter is equal to the former. The payoff potential can be substantial.

3. Extensive efforts were employed to develop a performance criterion that captured substantive content within its contextual setting. It is well to emphasize: context *is* meaning. As criteria are imbued with contextual richness the potential for interpretation of validity findings is extended.

4. A note about the stability of the factorial dimensions. Data from an independent executive sample (N = 340 and the organization setting was totally different from Sears) yielded a factor structure very similar to the one reported in this paper. A good case can be made that the dimensions reported are generic, not organizationally specific.

5. The job performance instrument was composed of complex items. These combined with others of equal complexity. The factorial dimensions made good psychological and organizational sense. Their internal richness provides new insight into the dynamics of high-level job performance. While it might be stretching a point, the complex mixture of elements within factorial dimensions might just possibly be giving us a beginner's portrait of the cognitive map executives use to chart their way through the complex, diverse, and ambiguous job demands that characterize the scope and scale of the extended organization. If the present research allows us an initial portrait as seen through a glass darkly, future research will allow us to see it in full.

# SECTION C

**Measures of Leadership as Inspiration and Influence**

# Measures of Leadership as Inspiration and Influence

The following three reports accent the importance of emotional components of leadership and of those behaviors that move from a transactional view of leadership to relations of influence and motivation. They illustrate ways in which organizations can benefit from these concepts and provide measuring instruments that can be adapted easily by those who want to repeat their successes.

## Long-Term Forecasting of Transformational Leadership and Its Effects Among Naval Officers: Some Preliminary Findings

Francis J. Yammarino and Bernard M. Bass

Midshipmen at the Naval Academy were identified as having varying levels of charismatic and inspirational leadership characteristics. These subjects were followed after assignment to duty in the fleet; measures of their performance, collected after five years, include ratings by superiors and their subordinates' satisfaction with work. A measure of "transformational" quality was developed.

Francis J. Yammarino, Assistant Professor of Management and Fellow, Center for Leadership Studies, Center for Leadership Studies and School of Management, State University of New York at Binghamton, Binghamton, New York 13901. (607-777-3007). PhD, State University of New York at Buffalo. Consultant to organizations including Fortune 500 companies. Author of various articles in management and social science journals. Coauthor of *Theory Testing in Organizational Behavior: The Varient Approach.*

Bernard M. Bass, Distinguished Professor of Management and Director, Center for Leadership Studies, Center for Leadership Studies and School of Management, State University of New York at Binghamton, Binghamton, New York 13901.

(607-777-4028). PhD, Ohio State University. Coauthor of Bass & Stogdill *Handbook of Leadership*, third edition. Author of *Leadership and Performance Beyond Expectations*.

## Transformational Leaders: Team Performance, Leadership Ratings, and Firsthand Impressions
William H. Clover

The nation's major military academies consider themselves leadership laboratories with the goal of developing motivated and dedicated career officers. The data collected show the impact on team performance and on subordinates' attitudes of leaders viewed by subordinates as more transformational.

William H. Clover, Director of Executive Education and Leadership Development, TRW, Inc., Cleveland, Ohio 44124. (216-291-7000). PhD, Bowling Green State University, Bowling Green, OH. Former tenured professor and director, Counseling and Leadership Center, Department of Behavioral Sciences and Leadership, U.S. Air Force Academy, Colorado Springs, Colorado.

## Task Cycle Theory: The Processes of Influence
Clark L. Wilson, Donal O'Hare, and Frank Shipper

Leadership is viewed as one of several organizational roles that depends upon skills at influencing others. Organization behavior is made up of a series of tasks and task cycles that are repeated performances. Each task is viewed as equivalent to a learning trial, with opportunities for reliable observations readily present. The six phases of the Managerial Task Cycle were operationalized into a Survey of Management Practices (SMP) and a training program developed to improve performance. Effects were tested in a Veterans Administration installation, a bank, a health care organization, and a nuclear power plant; results of each study are presented.

Clark L. Wilson, President, Clark Wilson Publishing Company, Box 471-129 Woodridge Drive, New Canaan, Connecticut 06840-0471. (800-537-7249). PhD, University of Southern California. Author of various articles on assessment of managerial, leadership, and organization skills.

Donal O'Hare, Executive Vice President, Clark Wilson Publishing Company, Box 471-129 Woodridge Drive, New Canaan, Connecticut 06840-0471. (800-537-7249). President, O'Hare Associates, 1911 North Ft. Myer Drive, Suite 1110, Arlington, Virginia 22209. (703-522-0887). MA, George Washington University. Developed Human Resource and Organization Development Client Services, Price-Waterhouse, in Europe. Past manager of the World Bank Management Development Program.

Frank Shipper, Associate Professor of Management, College of Business, Arizona State University, Tempe, Arizona 85287. (602-965-9011). PhD, University of Utah. Author of various articles on human resource management and coauthor of two books on strategic planning.

# Leadership Practices: An Alternative to the Psychological Perspective

Barry Z. Posner and James M. Kouzes

Case studies of managers' descriptions of their personal best experiences as a leader were used to develop a behavioral framework for understanding what people do when they are leading others. This qualitative data produced five key leadership practices, which were then translated into an empirical instrument (Leadership Practices Inventory). The LPI, completed by both managers and their subordinates, assesses the frequency of various leadership behaviors and strategies. Subordinate assessments are used to explain variance in their manager's (leader's) effectiveness.

Barry Z. Posner, Director, Graduate Education, Leavey School of Business and Administration, Santa Clara University, Santa Clara, California 95053. (408-554-4500). PhD, University of Massachusetts, Amherst. Coauthor of *The Leadership Challenge: How To Get Extraordinary Things Done in Organizations* and *Effective Project Planning and Management*. Author of various scholarly and practitioner-oriented articles.

James M. Kouzes, President, TPG/Learning Systems, 555 Hamilton Avenue, Suite 20, Palo Alto, California 94301. (415-326-5774). BA, Michigan State University. Member of Certified Consultants International. Past member of the American Management Association's Human Resource Council and Board of the Organizational Development Network. Past director of the Executive Development Center, the Leavey School of Business and Administration, Santa Clara University. Coauthor of *The Leadership Challenge: How to Get Extraordinary Things Done in Organizations* and The Leadership Practices Inventory. Author of various articles and chapters on management education, leadership, and organizational development.

# Long-Term Forecasting of Transformational Leadership and Its Effects Among Naval Officers: Some Preliminary Findings*

*Francis J. Yammarino and Bernard M. Bass*

The model of leadership that is limited to a transactional exchange of rewards with subordinates for the services they render also limits how much effort will be forthcoming from the subordinates, how satisfied the subordinates will be with the arrangements, and how effectively they will contribute to reaching the organization's goals. To proceed beyond such limits in subordinates' effort, satisfaction, and effectiveness calls for a new model of leadership—transformational leadership (Bass, 1985). The transformational leader articulates a realistic vision of the future that can be shared, stimulates subordinates intellectually, and pays attention to the differences among the subordinates (Bass, 1985, chapter 2).

Such transformational leadership does not need to be left to the accident of the right personality happening to show up at the right time. Transformational leadership can be increased through training and the design of role relationships. It can be fostered by the appropriate recruitment, selection, and promotion of those with potential to be transformational.

The purpose of this study was to measure and assess transformational leadership and its association with several precursors and consequences in a sample of United States Navy (USN) officers. The 186 officers were graduates of the

* This manuscript was prepared under the Navy Manpower, Personnel, and Training R&D Program of the Office of the Chief of Naval Research under Contract N0001487K0434 to B. M. Bass and F. J. Yammarino, Co-Principal Investigators. The views expressed are those of the authors. We thank David Atwater, Jose Florendo, Sheeler Kowalewski, Scott Myers, Idell Neumann, and Anne Wahrenbrock for their assistance on this project.

United States Naval Academy (USNA) and currently on active duty in the fleet. The study involved collecting and analyzing data from the officers themselves, 793 immediate subordinates of the officers, and records from the Naval Academy and the Navy.

## Background and Conceptualization

**Transactional Leadership** Current measurement of leader behavior and leadership potential is dominated by behavioral theory that suggests leaders must engage in a transaction with their subordinates—an exchange based on initiating and clarifying what is required of their subordinates and the consideration the subordinates will receive if they fulfill the requirements (e.g., Deets & Morano, 1986). These behaviors deal primarily with the two factors of initiating structure and consideration generally emphasized nowadays to be of consequence to leadership (Bass, 1981, chapter 21). This leadership consists of accomplishing well the tasks at hand while satisfying the self-interests of those working with the leader to do so. The leader sees to it that promises of reward are fulfilled for those followers who carry out successfully what is required of them.

By clarifying what is required of the subordinate, transactional leaders are able to build confidence in subordinates to exert the necessary effort to achieve expected levels of performance. Complementing this approach, transactional leaders also recognize what subordinates need and want, clarifying for them how those needs will be satisfied when necessary effort is expended to accomplish the objective. Such effort to perform or motivation to work provides a sense of direction and, to a degree, energizes subordinates to reach agreed-upon objectives.

In its active form, transactional leadership can be characterized as *contingent reinforcement*—rewards (or avoidance of penalties) contingent upon effort expended and performance level achieved. The less active form of transactional leadership is *management-by-exception* or contingent negative reinforcement; and the extreme end of inactivity is well known as *laissez-faire leadership*. In studies of 198 senior Army officers and over 800 industrial leaders who were described by their subordinates and colleagues, the correlations among such contingent rewarding by superiors and effectiveness and satisfaction ranged from .4 to .5; however, the relationships among transformational leadership by the superiors and effectiveness and satisfaction ranged from .6 to .7 (Bass, 1985; Waldman & Bass, 1986; Waldman, Bass, & Einstein, 1987).

In many instances, such transactional leadership is a prescription for mediocrity or worse: the leader relies heavily on management-by-exception, intervening with his or her group only when procedures and standards for task accomplishment are not being met. Such a manager espouses the popular adage, "If it ain't broke, don't fix it." According to subordinates, correlations of management-by-exception with effectiveness and satisfaction are about .2 for military leaders and -.1 to -.2 for industrial leaders (Bass, 1985). Using disciplinary threats to bring a group up to standards is even less efficacious and is likely to be counterproductive in the long run (Yukl, 1981).

Moreover, whether promise of rewards or avoidance of penalties is effective depends on whether the leader has control of the rewards or penalties and whether the rewards are valued or the penalties not disdained by the subordinates. Pay increases and promotions often depend on qualifications and policies about which the leader has little to say. Regulations may be the main source of penalties.

Thus, transactional leadership is good as far as it goes. However, it may fail for a variety of reasons. The transactional leader may be unable to provide rewards commensurate with subordinates' expectations due to limitations of organizational resources, ineffective appraisal systems, time pressures, and a lack of skill on the leader's part to effectively utilize positive reinforcement. Therefore something beyond transactional leadership is needed—transformational leadership.

**Transformational Leadership** Superior leadership performance—transformational leadership—is seen when leaders broaden and elevate the interests of their subordinates, when they generate awareness and acceptance among the subordinates of the purposes and mission of the group, and when they move their subordinates to go beyond their own self-interests for the good of the group (Burns, 1978). Such transformational leaders motivate subordinates to do more than originally expected. They raise the consciousness of subordinates about the importance and value of designated outcomes and ways of reaching them and, in turn, get subordinates to transcend their own immediate self-interests for the sake of the mission and vision of the organization. Subordinates' confidence levels are raised and their needs are expanded. The heightened level of motivation is linked to three empirically derived factors of transformational leadership (Bass, 1985; Avolio & Bass, 1988; Bass & Avolio, in press).

First, transformational leaders are more *charismatic and inspiring* in the eyes of their subordinates. Charismatic leaders have great referent power and influence. Charismatic leaders inspire loyalty to the organization, command respect, have an ability to see what is important (vision) which typically translates into a mission and energized response by subordinates. Subordinates want to identify with these leaders and develop intense feelings about them (Zaleznick, 1983). Subordinates have a high degree of trust and confidence in them. Charismatic leaders excite, arouse, and inspire their subordinates (House, 1977). Charismatic qualities have been observed at all levels of organizations (Bass, 1985).

A second necessary component for transformational leadership is *individualized consideration*. Although a leader's charisma may attract subordinates to the mission or vision, the leader's use of individualized consideration also significantly contributes to a subordinate achieving his/her fullest potential. The leader is attentive to individual differences in subordinates' needs for growth and development. The leader sets examples and assigns tasks on an individual basis not only to satisfy the immediate needs of subordinates, but also to elevate a subordinate's needs and abilities to higher levels. Individualized consideration is, in part, coaching and mentoring. It is a method of communicating timely information to subordinates. It provides for continuous follow-up and feedback, and, perhaps more importantly, links an individual's current needs to the organization's mission and elevates those needs when it is appropriate to do so (Bass, 1985, chapter 5).

The third component of transformational leadership is *intellectual stimulation*. An intellectually stimulating leader arouses subordinates to an awareness of problems, to their own thoughts and imagination, and to recognition of their beliefs and values.

Intellectual stimulation is evidenced by subordinates' conceptualization, comprehension, and analysis of problems they face and solutions they generate.

Leaders can fulfill the role of a transforming/intellectual leader to the extent they can discern, comprehend, conceptualize, and articulate to their subordinates opportunities and threats facing their organization, as well as the organization's strengths, weaknesses, and comparative advantages. It is through intellectual stimulation of subordinates that new methods of accomplishing the organization's mission are explored. The leaders are willing and able to show subordinates new ways of looking at old methods (Bass, 1985, chapter 6).

Overall, transformational leaders are more likely to be proactive than reactive in their thinking, to be more creative and innovative in ideas, and to be less inhibited in their ideational search for solutions. Rather than being inhibited by organizational constraints, transformational leaders see how those constraints can be turned into opportunities. In sum, transformational leaders may attain charisma in the eyes of their subordinates; transformational leaders may deal individually to meet the needs of each of their subordinates; and transformational leaders may intellectually stimulate their subordinates.

**The Greater Payoff from Transformational Leadership** Extensive survey studies of managers and technical team leaders have been completed in firms such as General Electric, IBM, Digital Equipment, Minneapolis Honeywell, Federal Express, Agway, Exxon, and Larsen & Toubro, as well as in various governmental and military organizations. Subordinates and colleagues of leaders have rated them on the extent to which they are transformational (charismatic/inspirational, individually considerate, and intellectually stimulating), transactional (contingent rewarding, managing-by-exception), and avoiding leadership (being laissez-faire). Transformational leaders contribute to their organization's effectiveness. Subordinates say they exert extra effort for such transformational leaders (see Avolio & Bass, 1988; Bass, 1985). U.S. Army combat officers were seen to be more charismatic than combat support officers (Waldman & Bass, 1986).

In contrast, if leaders are only transactional, the organizations are seen as less effective, particularly if much of the leadership practiced is management-by-exception (intervening only when standards are not being met). Subordinates say they exert much less effort for such leaders. To be effective, contingent reward by leaders requires that leaders control the rewards for compliance and the rewards have to be valued by the subordinates (Bass, 1985).

These findings, however, are based mainly on subordinates' judgments. In a recent study (Hater & Bass, 1988), leaders were evaluated by their subordinates and their superiors. Those managers described as transformational rather than transactional by their subordinates were judged much more highly in leadership potential by the managers' superiors. The transformational leaders also received higher performance ratings from their superiors (Hater & Bass, 1988).

Clearly there is a greater payoff for the organization from transformational leaders who can articulate a realistic, shared vision of the future; arouse confidence, commitment, and the desire of employees to self-actualize in alignment with organizational opportunities; as well as counter threats of mutual concern. Burns (1978) conceived transactional and transformational leadership to be bipolarities at two ends of the same continuum. However, Bass (1985) argued and demonstrated (Waldman & Bass, 1986) that transformational leadership builds on transactional, but not vice versa. Thus, in an overall way and in an additive sense, transformational leadership has a greater impact on outcomes that count.

**Perspectives on Leadership** Most previous leadership research, including that on transformational leadership, has assumed that the appropriate dynamic of consequence lies between the leader and his or her group as revealed by the average member of the group. A powerful explanatory alternative has been offered which suggests that leader-subordinate dynamics are much more complex and "individualistic," often differing in the "quality of the relationship" from one leader-subordinate dyad to another. Thus, each subordinate may view a leader differently, or a leader may interact differently with each subordinate rather than uniformly toward a group of subordinates (Graen, 1976).

The approach developed by Dansereau, Alutto, and Yammarino (1984) provides a conceptual and statistical way of looking at leadership behavior from a leader-subordinate dyadic (one-to-one) perspective, as well as in terms of a group level of analysis. It is possible then to examine those leadership behaviors that have individual and differential impact on subordinates and those which have a groupwide impact, thus refining our understanding of the transformational leadership process. To accomplish this (in addition to employing a variety of traditional statistical techniques), *Within and Between Analysis* (Dansereau, Alutto, & Yammarino, 1984) was used to compare dyadic (one-to-one) and group-based transformational leadership behaviors.

**General Model** The general model which formed the basis for this research is summarized in Figure 1. Essentially, USNA selection devices (pre-academy information) and success measures (information obtained while at the academy) were hypothesized to better predict transformational leadership (charisma, individualized consideration, intellectual stimulation, inspirational leadership) than contingent promises and rewards (transactional leadership). More specifically, based on the work of Bass (1985), it was hypothesized that verbal aptitude, high school class rank, recommendations, extracurricular activities, and humanities and social science majors (rather than engineering and science majors) would better predict transformational than transactional leadership. These precursors of leadership identified in Figure 1 (USNA selection devices and success measures) were not expected to be related to active or passive management-by-exception (transactional leadership) and to be negatively associated with laissez-faire leadership. In turn, the transformational and transactional leadership variables identified in Figure 1 were hypothesized to differentially predict the consequences; that is, USN performance as rated by supervisors of the focal leaders and outcomes as rated by subordinates of the focal leaders were expected to be more highly related to transformational than transactional leadership. In particular, transformational leadership was posited to better predict the consequences of leadership than transactional leadership, and laissez-faire leadership was hypothesized to be negatively related to the consequences identified in Figure 1. Moreover, various individual officer differences (age, rank, assignment) and ship characteristics (size, combat type) identified in Figure 1 were expected to moderate these associations.

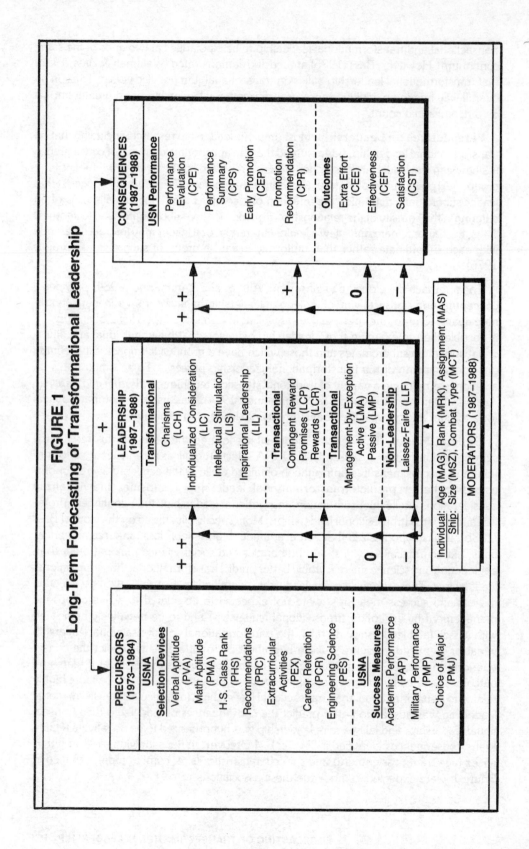

**FIGURE 1**
**Long-Term Forecasting of Transformational Leadership**

# Method

**Sample** The focal leaders for this study were all USN officers who were USNA graduates on active duty assigned to the surface warfare fleet. Originally, 330 officers were randomly selected by members of the USNA and Navy Personnel Research and Development Center (NPRDC) staffs to participate in the study. Of these, 54 officers were not reachable due to transferred assignments. From the effective sample of 276 officers, 186 participated, yielding a response rate of about 67%. In addition to gathering information from these officers and from the USNA and NPRDC records about these officers, six senior subordinates of each officer were randomly selected and asked to provide information anonymously about the officers. For officers who had less than six subordinates, all their senior subordinates were asked to provide information. In all, 793 subordinates of the focal officers participated, yielding an average of 4.26 subordinates per officer. Returns were as follows: 98 officers (53%) were described by five or six subordinates; 58 officers (31%), by three or four subordinates; and 30 officers (16%), by one or two subordinates.

The focal officers were commissioned in 1978 (n = 36), 1979 (n = 31), 1983 (n = 51), and 1984 (n = 68), and held the ranks of 0-2 or Lieutenants Junior Grade (n = 71) and 0-3 or Lieutenants (n = 114). There was one Lieutenant Commander (rank 0-4) in the sample. All but one of the officers were males and the officers were primarily 25–30 years (n = 120) and 31–35 years (n = 45) in age. They were assigned to a variety of types and sizes of ships.

All subordinate survey materials were sent to the commanding officer (CO) of the ship on which the focal officers were serving. The CO was asked to relay the materials to the appropriate senior subordinates of the focal officers. All returns were collected in sealed envelopes. The subordinates who provided information about the officers were approximately 93% males. Most were 21–25 years (n = 213), 26–30 years (n = 220), or 31–39 years (n = 275) in age. Most of the subordinates held the ranks of E-4 to E-6 (n = 171), E-7 to E-9 (n = 191), or 0-1 to 0-2 (n = 362), and generally had worked with the focal officers for three to six months (n = 184), seven months to one year (n = 243), or one to two years (n = 255). Although details about the superiors who evaluated the performance of the focal officers were not available, it is known that 5.84 reports on average about the officers were provided which constituted information from a number of superiors over several years in a variety of assignments.

**Measures** Information was obtained from multiple sources. First, precursor information was acquired from files about the officers' pre-academy and academy success scores. Second, performance information about the officers while on active duty as rated by superiors was obtained from their files. Third, from the senior subordinates, leadership and outcome measures were secured from mail surveys. Fourth, self-descriptions about leadership and outcomes were collected by mail surveys from the focal officers themselves. Although this self-report information was not used in the present analysis, it provided the focal officers with knowledge about what was being asked of their subordinates.

*Precursors: Selection Devices.* In terms of precursors (see Figure 1), data for the selection devices (e.g., aptitude, personality, interest, and biodata measures) were collected prior to admission to the USNA in 1973–1974 and 1978–1979. *Verbal and math aptitude* were measured using the Scholastic Aptitude Test (SAT). In general, a minimum score of 520 and 600 for verbal and math, respectively, is required for USNA qualification. *High school class rank* is a standardized score (M = 500, SD = 100) ranging from 200 to 800 that is based on an individual's high school rank. *Recommendations* is a score based on school officials' estimates of the individual's potential for success as a naval officer. It is an objective score ranging from 0 to 1,000 derived from evaluations of the candidate on physical abilities, academic potential, interpersonal relations, personal conduct, and participation in extracurricular activities. *Extracurricular activities* is based on an objective scoring system that ranges from 300 to 800 about a candidate's participation in both athletic and nonathletic high school activities as reported by the individual. *Career retention* (also called career interest) and *engineering-science* scales are two measures derived from the Strong-Campbell Interest Inventory (SCII) by the staff at NPRDC. Career retention is comprised of SCII items keyed to differentiate between high- and low-tenure midshipmen and officers based on motivational and academic components. Engineering-science is comprised of SCII items keyed to identify candidates with engineering and science as compared to humanities and social science interests who would be more likely to choose these majors at the USNA.

*Precursors: Success Measures.* The success measures data were collected while candidates were attending the USNA in 1974–1979 and 1979–1984. *Academic performance* is analogous to a cumulative quality or grade point average based on grades obtained and quality points for those grades. It includes all courses completed during four years at the academy. *Military performance* is analogous to a cumulative quality point score based on performance in professional, military, and physical education courses completed during four years at the USNA as well as the Second Class Summer evaluation, annual Professional Competency Review, and the semester-by-semester conduct scores. The exact formulation of these scores is a weighted combination of grades, quality points, and coefficients (values) of the components. Military performance grades are the most heavily weighted in this index. The candidates' *choice of major* is viewed at the USNA as more in line with the requirements of the Navy if it is engineering or science rather than humanities or social science. In addition, within engineering and science, the majors of "general engineering" and "physical science," respectively, are viewed as less valuable. In this study, there were 40 (22%) engineering, 67 (36%) science, 41 (22%) humanities and social science, 38 (20%) general engineering and physical science majors.

*Leadership Measures.* The leadership data (see Figure 1) were collected in 1987–1988 from the officers (not reported here) and their senior subordinates using the Multifactor Officer Questionnaire (MLQ-Forms 11R and 11S) (Bass & Yammarino, 1987). This survey is a modified version of the Multifactor Leadership Questionnaire that has been described in detail elsewhere (Avolio & Bass, 1988; Bass, 1985; Bass & Avolio, in press). In Form 11, the number of scales was increased with a consequent reduction in number of items per scale. Secondly, the content was changed wherever necessary to better suit the military setting. Respondents completing the surveys indicated how frequently they observed behaviors or reacted to the focal officers on a five-point format ranging from "not at all" (0) to "frequently, if not always" (4). These anchors have a magnitude estimation-based ratio to each other of 4:3:2:1:0 (Bass,

Cascio, & O'Connor, 1974). For each scale, items were summed and divided by the appropriate number of items, yielding a scale score that ranged from zero to four.

Nine leadership scales were created for use in the current study. The four transformational leadership scales, the number of items in each, and examples of the items were:
1. *Charisma* (6 items)—"I am ready to trust him/her to overcome any obstacle."
2. *Individualized Consideration* (6 items)—"Gives personal attention to me when necessary."
3. *Intellectual Stimulation* (6 items)—"Shows me how to think about problems in new ways."
4. *Inspirational Leadership* (6 items)—"Provides vision of what lies ahead."

The four transactional leadership scales, the number of items in each, and examples of the items were:
5. *Contingent Promises* (3 items)—"Talks about special commendations and promotions for good work."
6. *Contingent Rewards* (3 items)—"Personally pays me a compliment when I do good work."
7. *Active Management-by-Exception* (4 items)—"Would reprimand me if my work were below standard."
8. *Passive Management-by-Exception* (4 items)—"Shows he/she is a firm believer in 'if it ain't broke, don't fix it'."

The nonleadership scale was:
9. *Laissez-Faire* (6 items)—"However I do my job is OK with him/her."

*Consequences: Outcomes.* In terms of consequences (see Figure 1), the outcome data, a part of the MLQ, were collected in 1987–1988. Several items were used to measure three outcome variables. Items were summed and divided by the appropriate number of items to form scale scores that ranged from zero to four. These included:
1. *Extra Effort*—Four items were used to measure how much extra effort subordinates were willing to put forth in their jobs. For example, "I do more than I am expected to do in my work." Items from this scale used the same response format as the leadership items.
2. *Satisfaction*—Two items were used to measure subordinates' satisfaction with their leader. For example, "In all, how satisfied were you that the methods of leadership used by this officer were the right ones for getting your unit's job done?" Response alternatives were on a five-point format ranging from "very dissatisfied" (0) to "very satisfied" (4).
3. *Effectiveness*—Four items were used to measure the effectiveness of the focal officer. For example, "How effective is this officer in meeting the job-related needs of his/her subordinates?" Response alternatives were on a five-point format ranging from "not effective" (0) to "extremely effective" (4).

*Consequences: Performance.* The job performance data were collected from the year of commission (1978, 1979, 1983, or 1984) to 1987 by the USN while the officers were on active duty with the fleet. This information was provided by several different superiors of each focal officer and reflected performance over a number of years in a variety of job assignments. As shown in Figure 1, one of the measures, *performance summary*, was simply the number of performance or "fitness" reports available about a focal officer. This number was used in the calculation of two key performance measures developed by the staff at NPRDC. First, the *recommendation for early promotion* (CEP) was the officers' cumulative recommendation scores divided by the number of fitness reports. Each recommendation is on a two-point format (recommended or not recommended) that is "a consequence of the officer's exhibited performance and potential during the evaluation period." The number of times an officer was recommended was divided by the number of fitness reports. This score ranged from .00 to 1.00 with 1.00 being the highest possible score. Second, *performance evaluation* (CPE) was the officers' cumulative evaluation scores divided by the number of fitness reports. Each evaluation is on a nine-point format that assesses "the officer's performance with regard to contributions to the unit's mission, including effective integration of personnel and the mission and completion of assigned tasks." The number of times an officer was given the highest rating on this scale was divided by the number of fitness reports. This score ranged from .00 to 1.00 with 1.00 being the highest possible score. A third performance measure, *promotion recommendation* (CPR), was the officers' most recent recommendation for early promotion. Again, this recommendation was on a two-point format.

**Scale Development and Evaluation** To evaluate the modifications and new scales, internal consistency analyses of the MLQ Form 11 were conducted on a separate sample of naval officers who were attending the Naval War College in 1987–1988. The data were gathered from 318 senior officers describing their most recent immediate superiors. As shown in Table 1, the proposed scales, in general, displayed adequate reliabilities. Furthermore, the means, standard deviations, and intercorrelations among the scales follow the same pattern as in a variety of other industrial and military studies (e.g., Bass 1985; Avolio & Bass, 1988; Bass & Avolio, in press). As such, this version of the scales was used in the present study to assess connections with precursors and consequences of leadership via correlational analyses. Traditional analysis of variance procedures was also used to gain further understanding about the variables.

# Results

The findings for this study are summarized in Tables 2 to 4. Descriptive statistics and correlations among the MLQ leadership and outcome measures based on subordinates' ratings are presented in Table 2. Descriptive statistics and correlations among the USNA selection and success measures and the USN performance measures based on superiors' ratings are presented in Table 3. The interrelationships among the precursors (USNA selection and success), leadership, and consequences (USN performance and MLQ outcomes) are presented in Table 4.

**MLQ Leadership and Outcomes** Initially, the relationships among the MLQ Form 11 leadership and outcome measures were investigated based on 793 subordinates' reports about the 186 focal officers. These results displayed the same pattern as those in Table 1 and in a variety of other studies. They are not presented here because of space considerations and for the following reason: Because the relationships among these measures and the precursors and consequences also were of interest, it was necessary to aggregate the subordinates' reports about each focal leader. In this way, averaged subordinate responses for each focal officer about leadership and outcomes could be aligned with the other information about the focal officers. As a test of whether

# TABLE 1
## Descriptive Statistics and Intercorrelations Among MLQ Leadership and Outcome Measures: Naval War College

| Measure | α | M | SD | (LCH) | (LIC) | (LIS) | (LIL) | (LCP) | (LCR) | (LMA) | (LMP) | (LLF) | (CEE) | (CEF) |
|---|---|---|---|---|---|---|---|---|---|---|---|---|---|---|
| **TRANSFORMATIONAL** | | | | | | | | | | | | | | |
| Charisma (LCH) | .96 | 2.09 | 1.26 | x | | | | | | | | | | |
| Individualized Consideration (LIC) | .86 | 2.27 | .90 | .81 | x | | | | | | | | | |
| Intellectual Stimulation (LIS) | .88 | 2.33 | .88 | .80 | .74 | x | | | | | | | | |
| Inspirational Leadership (LIL) | .85 | 2.09 | .84 | .83 | .82 | .81 | x | | | | | | | |
| **TRANSACTIONAL** | | | | | | | | | | | | | | |
| Contingent Rewards (Promises) (LCP) | .67 | 1.38 | .89 | .52 | .57 | .52 | .59 | x | | | | | | |
| Contingent Rewards (Rewards) (LCR) | .92 | 2.13 | 1.14 | .68 | .80 | .64 | .73 | .68 | x | | | | | |
| Mgt-by-Exception (Active) (LMA) | .72 | 2.48 | .86 | .19 | .11 | .33 | .23 | .17 | .15 | x | | | | |
| Mgt-by-Exception (Passive) (LMP) | .61 | 2.41 | .80 | .16 | .22 | .07 | .16 | .17 | .15 | -.10 | x | | | |
| **NONLEADERSHIP** | | | | | | | | | | | | | | |
| Laissez-Faire (LLF) | .61 | 1.39 | .67 | -.55 | -.48 | -.59 | -.51 | -.21 | -.39 | -.41 | .23 | x | | |
| **OUTCOMES** | | | | | | | | | | | | | | |
| Extra Effort (CEE) | .73 | 3.36 | .57 | .12 | .11 | .11 | .10 | .02 | .03 | .15 | .08 | -.09 | x | |
| Effectiveness (CEF) | .89 | 2.68 | .95 | .83 | .73 | .73 | .73 | .48 | .62 | .20 | .10 | -.56 | .13 | x |
| Satisfaction (CST) | .93 | 2.39 | 1.36 | .90 | .80 | .74 | .77 | .51 | .67 | .12 | .18 | -.51 | .04 | .83 |

Note: $N = 318$; $r > .11$, $p < .05$; $r > .15$, $p < .01$.

this aggregation of scores was appropriate, a traditional multivariate and univariate analysis of variance was performed in which the dependent variables were the leadership and outcome measures and the independent variable was the focal leader. That is, each focal officer was a "cell" for the analysis to determine whether subordinates' ratings varied more between than within leaders. Despite numerous limitations with this traditional approach (see Dansereau, Alutto, & Yammarino, 1984), results of the MANOVA (leadership: Mult $F = 1.56$, $p < .001$, Mult $\eta^2 = .97$; outcomes: Mult $F = 1.85$, $p < .001$, Mult $\eta^2 = .73$) and all univariate ANOVA's indicated that aggregation was permissible.

As such, the intercorrelation among the MLQ leadership and outcomes measures based on 793 subordinates' averaged responses about the 186 focal officers are shown in Table 2. Compatible with prior research, the transformational leadership measures were highly correlated and had the highest associations of the leadership measures with perceived subordinate effectiveness and satisfaction. Again, consistent with previous research, charisma displayed the strongest relationships with the outcome variables, followed in magnitude by inspirational leadership, individualized consideration, and intellectual stimulation. Contingent rewards and promises and active management-by-exception (transactional leadership) were significantly related to effectiveness and satisfaction, but the magnitudes of these associations were less than those involving transformational leadership. Passive management-by-exception was not significantly related to the outcomes, and laissez-faire (nonleadership) was significantly, negatively associated with effectiveness and satisfaction. The relationship between perceived subordinate extra effort and the leadership measures followed the same pattern, but the magnitudes of the associations were much less.

**USNA and USN Measures** The intercorrelations among the USNA selection and success measures (precursors) and USN performance (consequences) as reported by the focal leaders' superiors are shown in Table 3. Consistent with forecasting success in college from preadmissions assessments, and then forecasting subsequent on-the-job performance, high school class rank and tested verbal and math aptitudes predicted academic and military success at the USNA but did not correlate with USN performance following graduation. Preadmissions recommendations displayed a modest association with military success at the USNA but neither with academic success nor subsequent performance in the fleet.

In addition, based on ANOVA results (3 and 173 degrees of freedom), verbal aptitude ($F = 4.62$, $p < .01$, $\eta^2 = .07$), math aptitude ($F = 6.44$, $p < .001$, $\eta^2 = .10$), engineering-science scores ($F = 8.83$, $p < .001$, $\eta^2 = .13$), academic success ($F = 6.24$, $p < .001$, $\eta^2 = .10$), and military success ($F = 8.20$, $p < .001$, $\eta^2 = .13$), differed by the officers' choices of major. As might be expected, humanities and social science majors had the highest verbal scores, the lowest math scores, and the lowest engineering-science scores. Engineering majors had the highest math scores and the greatest academic and military success scores. General engineering and physical science majors, despite the highest engineering-science scores, had the lowest verbal scores and the least academic and military success. Choice of major, however, was not a significant predictor of subsequent on-the-job performance.

## TABLE 2
### Intercorrelations Among MLQ Leadership and Outcome Measures Based on 793 Subordinates' Averaged Responses: Navy Fleet

| Measure | α | M | SD | (LCH) | (LIC) | (LIS) | (LIL) | (LCP) | (LCR) | (LMA) | (LMP) | (LLF) | (CEE) | (CEF) |
|---|---|---|---|---|---|---|---|---|---|---|---|---|---|---|
| **TRANSFORMATIONAL** | | | | | | | | | | | | | | |
| Charisma (LCH) | .94 | 2.40 | 1.16 | x | | | | | | | | | | |
| Individualized Consideration (LIC) | .86 | 2.50 | .91 | .80 | x | | | | | | | | | |
| Intellectual Stimulation (LIS) | .88 | 2.47 | .88 | .78 | .71 | x | | | | | | | | |
| Inspirational Leadership (LIL) | .82 | 2.26 | .83 | .84 | .83 | .83 | x | | | | | | | |
| **TRANSACTIONAL** | | | | | | | | | | | | | | |
| Contingent Rewards (Promises) (LCP) | .67 | 1.61 | .92 | .61 | .62 | .60 | .67 | x | | | | | | |
| Contingent Rewards (LCR) | .91 | 2.38 | 1.10 | .72 | .80 | .65 | .78 | .61 | x | | | | | |
| Mgt-by-Exception (Active) (LMA) | .71 | 2.65 | .85 | .46 | .41 | .62 | .52 | .39 | .42 | x | | | | |
| Mgt-by-Exception (Passive) (LMP) | .59 | 2.26 | .82 | .14 | .18 | .10 | .17 | .16 | .16 | -.04 | x | | | |
| **NONLEADERSHIP** | | | | | | | | | | | | | | |
| Laissez-Faire (LLF) | .63 | 1.31 | .67 | -.57 | -.54 | -.67 | -.56 | -.33 | -.45 | -.57 | .15 | x | | |
| **OUTCOMES** | | | | | | | | | | | | | | |
| Extra Effort (CEE) | .81 | 3.24 | .69 | .17 | .27 | .24 | .22 | .04 | .22 | .25 | .03 | -.35 | x | |
| Effectiveness (CEF) | .89 | 2.75 | .94 | .87 | .73 | .74 | .79 | .48 | .66 | .50 | .11 | -.60 | .27 | x |
| Satisfaction (CST) | .92 | 2.82 | 1.22 | .89 | .81 | .73 | .82 | .53 | .72 | .44 | .19 | -.55 | .22 | .86 |

Note: $N = 186$; $r > .14$, $p < .05$; $r > .19$, $p < .01$.

None of the other precursors displayed significant relationships with the USNA success measures or subsequent USN performance. However, assessed military performance at the USNA correlated .23 with superiors' performance appraisals (CPE) and .25 with early promotion evaluations (CEP) many years later, but not with recommendations for promotion (CPR). Evidently a single, two-point item (CPR) obtained just once lacks much reliability and remains unpredictable. However, when it is accumulated over a number of time periods (CEP), it becomes more predictable as shown in the next section.

**Precursors, Leadership, and Consequences** The intercorrelations among the precursors (USNA selection and success), leadership (MLQ), and consequences (USN performance and MLQ outcomes) measures are shown in Table 4. First, with one exception, none of the USNA selection devices (preadmissions assessments) correlated significantly with the MLQ leadership measures. The exception was that the preadmissions extracurricular activities score was correlated .15 with active management-by-exception. Second, with two exceptions, the USNA success measures, including choice of major (as based on ANOVA results), were not associated with the MLQ leadership measures. The first exception was that the military performance grade at the USNA correlated with being seen as a charismatic (.18) and inspirational (.14) officer in the fleet. The military performance score did not correlate with being viewed as a transactional leader. The second exception was that the academic performance grade at the USNA correlated with being seen as an active management-by-exception (.14) officer in the fleet. The academic performance score did not correlate with being viewed as a transformational leader. In addition, although the results lacked statistical significance, humanities and social science majors were rated as being the most transformational (charismatic, individually considerate, intellectually stimulating, inspirational), most transactional (contingent rewards and promises, active management-by-exception), and least laissez-faire as compared to officers who had chosen other majors.

Third, as in industrial studies (e.g., Hater & Bass, 1988), a similar pattern of correlations emerged for the naval fleet officers between subordinates' descriptions of their leaders' transformational and transactional behavior and outcomes (MLQ) and the performance appraisals (USN) of those leaders by their superiors. As shown in Table 4, significant correlations ranged from .21 to .38 for the performance appraisals (CPE) with the officers' transformational scores, -.05 to .22 for the performance appraisals with their transactional scores, and -.31 for the performance appraisals with laissez-faire leadership. As in industry, early promotability correlated in a similar fashion with subordinates' descriptions. Transformational leadership of the officers correlated significantly .24 to .37 with an average of recommendations by the superiors for early promotion (CEP). Transactional leadership correlated -.04 to .28, and laissez-faire leadership correlated -.31, with early promotability. Promotion recommendation (CPR) yielded the same pattern of results with somewhat less magnitude for the correlations.

Note that these findings parallel those for the relationship between the MLQ leadership and outcome measures as described above (Table 2) and reproduced in the lower portion of Table 4. This is not surprising given that subordinates' ratings of the focal officers' effectiveness (MLQ) significantly correlated .38, .37, and .25 with superiors' ratings (USN) of early promotion, performance evaluation, and promotion recommendations, respectively. Moreover, subordinates' perceived satisfaction (MLQ) with the

## TABLE 3

## Descriptive Statistics and Intercorrelations Among Precursors and Consequences: Navy Fleet

| Measure | M | SD | Pre-Academy (Selection) | | | | | | | Success at the Academy | | USN Performance in the Fleet | |
|---|---|---|---|---|---|---|---|---|---|---|---|---|---|
| | | | (PVA) | (PMA) | (PHS) | (PRC) | (PEX) | (PCR) | (PES) | (PAP) | (PMP) | (CEP) | (CPE) |
| **USNA Selection** | | | | | | | | | | | | | |
| Verbal Aptitude (PVA) | 578.15 | 80.49 | x | | | | | | | | | | |
| Math Aptitude (PMA) | 650.16 | 68.32 | .45 | x | | | | | | | | | |
| H.S. Class Rank (PHS) | 570.46 | 111.31 | .07 | .19 | x | | | | | | | | |
| Recommendations (PRC) | 851.60 | 108.54 | -.16 | -.19 | .06 | x | | | | | | | |
| Extracurricular Activities (PEX) | 519.21 | 68.20 | -.29 | -.19 | -.07 | .21 | x | | | | | | |
| Career Retention (PCR) | 517.17 | 89.68 | -.09 | .08 | .09 | -.08 | -.06 | x | | | | | |
| Engineering Science (PES) | 493.20 | 90.24 | -.11 | .17 | .11 | .04 | -.19 | .22 | x | | | | |
| **USNA Success** | | | | | | | | | | | | | |
| Academic Performance (PAP) | 261.57 | 40.82 | .33 | .31 | .42 | .10 | -.12 | .01 | -.02 | x | | | |
| Military Performance (PMP) | 292.39 | 35.96 | .18 | .24 | .35 | .17 | .00 | -.04 | .05 | .70 | x | | |
| **USN Performance** | | | | | | | | | | | | | |
| Early Promotion (CEP) | .46 | .35 | -.01 | .04 | -.02 | -.02 | .12 | -.02 | -.04 | .12 | .25 | x | |
| Performance Evaluation (CPE) | .32 | .34 | -.08 | .02 | .02 | .07 | .04 | .00 | .07 | .08 | .23 | .65 | x |
| Promotion Recommendation (CPR) | 1.39 | .49 | -.13 | .00 | -.05 | -.12 | .07 | .03 | -.02 | -.02 | .06 | .71 | .44 |

Note: $N = 186$; $r > .14$, $p < .05$; $r .19$, $p < .01$.

focal officers significantly correlated .25 and .29 with superiors' assessments (USN) of early promotion and performance evaluation, respectively.


## Discussion

The purpose of this study was to propose and assess the association between transformational leadership and various precursors and consequences in a sample of naval fleet officers. Data were gathered from a variety of sources (USNA records, officers' senior subordinates via the MLQ, officers' superiors via USN records) to empirically assess a general model summarized in Figure 1. Although preliminary, the findings of this study lead to several conclusions and suggest directions for future research.

**Key Findings** First, in terms of precursors, it appears that the USNA selection paradigm works reasonably well. High school class rank and verbal and math aptitude test scores from preadmissions assessments predict academic and military performance at the USNA as well as the identification of choice of majors. Although extracurricular activities and academic performance were predictors of active management-by-exception, of all the precursors, only military performance at the USNA was a significant predictor of transformational leadership and consequences as rated by subordinates or superiors of the focal officers.

Second, the relationships among the leadership measures, and between the leadership and outcome measures (consequences rated by subordinates), were consistent with prior research (Avolio & Bass, 1988; Bass, 1985; Bass & Avolio, in press). Transformational leadership and the outcomes were highly, positively related; transactional leadership and the outcomes less so; and laissez-faire and the outcomes were negatively associated.

Third, the relationships between the leadership measures (as rated by subordinates) and performance measures (consequences rated by superiors) also were consistent with previous research (Hater & Bass, 1988). Transformational leadership had the highest positive associations with the performance appraisals, followed by transactional leadership, and laissez-faire was negatively related to these evaluations.

Fourth, the different types of consequences were generally related to one another. That is, using different rating forms (MLQ versus USN), different types of raters (subordinates versus superiors of focal officers) agreed in their evaluations of focal officers and those evaluations were more highly related to transformational than transactional leadership.

Fifth, military performance at the USNA was a predictor of charismatic and inspirational leadership of the focal officers rated by their subordinates as well as early promotion and performance evaluation rated by their superiors. As such, this USNA success measure seems to be a key for understanding the long-term forecasting of transformational leadership and its consequences. However, subordinate and peer ratings of leadership performance at the academy might be more likely to predict the future MLQ measures and superiors' fitness reports for the focal officers.

## TABLE 4
## Intercorrelations Among Leadership, Precursors, and Consequences: Navy Fleet

| Measure | TRANSFORMATIONAL | | | | TRANSACTIONAL | | | | NONLEADER |
| --- | --- | --- | --- | --- | --- | --- | --- | --- | --- |
| | LCH | LIC | LIS | LIL | LCP | LCR | LMA | LMP | LLF |
| **USNA Selection** | | | | | | | | | |
| Verbal Aptitude (PVA) | -.08 | -.07 | -.13 | -.10 | -.06 | -.04 | -.05 | -.02 | .01 |
| Math Aptitude (PMA) | -.08 | -.04 | -.09 | -.08 | -.12 | .01 | -.10 | .03 | .07 |
| H.S. Class Rank (PHS) | .10 | .06 | .03 | .08 | .06 | .09 | .05 | -.03 | .01 |
| Recommendations (PRC) | .12 | .06 | .04 | .11 | .07 | .06 | .11 | -.02 | -.06 |
| Extracurricular Activities (PEX) | .06 | .10 | .07 | .06 | .07 | .11 | .15 | .09 | -.05 |
| Career Retention (PCR) | -.02 | -.01 | .00 | -.03 | -.06 | -.07 | -.04 | -.10 | -.13 |
| Engineering Science (PES) | .00 | -.06 | -.06 | -.11 | -.12 | -.06 | -.08 | -.03 | .08 |
| **USNA Success** | | | | | | | | | |
| Academic Performance (PAP) | .07 | .02 | .05 | .09 | .05 | .11 | .14 | -.11 | -.06 |
| Military Performance (PMP) | .18 | .06 | .10 | .14 | .03 | .12 | .13 | -.10 | -.06 |
| **USN Performance** | | | | | | | | | |
| Early Promotion (CEP) | .37 | .24 | .34 | .28 | .17 | .24 | .28 | -.04 | -.31 |
| Performance Evaluation (CPE) | .38 | .21 | .31 | .25 | .17 | .20 | .22 | -.05 | -.31 |
| Promotion Recommendation (CPR) | .26 | .16 | .27 | .22 | .16 | .18 | .24 | -.01 | -.25 |
| **Outcomes** | | | | | | | | | |
| Extra Effort (CEE) | .17 | .27 | .24 | .22 | .04 | .22 | .25 | .03 | -.35 |
| Effectiveness (CEF) | .87 | .73 | .74 | .79 | .48 | .66 | .50 | .11 | -.60 |
| Satisfaction (CST) | .89 | .81 | .73 | .82 | .53 | .72 | .44 | .19 | -.55 |

*Note: N = 186; r > .14, p < .05; r > .19, p < .01.*

**Future Research** Clearly, the importance of military performance in the network of variables assessed in this study should be the subject for additional future research. Given the results of this study, several other directions for future work also are warranted.

First, potential moderators of the relationships proposed in Figure 1 can be investigated. The lack of some relationships and the nature of other associations can be clarified by examining the role of individual moderators such as the age, rank, and assignment of the officers, and of ship moderators such as size and combat type. Second, the relationship between subordinates' ratings of the officers and the officers' self-ratings can also be investigated. This work can provide some insight into the issue of congruence between self- and other ratings of leadership and outcomes. Third, an evaluation of nonresponse bias can be made. Of the 330 officers who were originally selected, 144 did not participate in the study because of either transferred assignments ($n = 54$) or nonresponse ($n = 90$). Precursors (USNA selection and success measures) and consequences (USN performance) data are available, however, for these 144 officers. As such, a comparison on these measures can be made between the 186 participating and 144 nonparticipating officers to assess potential differences.

Fourth, because a new version of the MLQ was used in this study, additional scale refinement seems necessary in future work. Using the Naval War College sample (Table 1), a new sample of midshipmen at the USNA, and the present sample of officers (Table 2), factor analyses, creation of new scales, and cross-validation of these can be conducted to enhance the measurement of transformational leadership. Fifth, Within and Between Analysis (Dansereau, Alutto, & Yammarino, 1984) can be employed in future research to address levels-of-analysis issues in this study. These procedures permit a more rigorous test of whether aggregation of the subordinates' reports is appropriate. Moreover, they provide an assessment of variation and covariation in the leadership and outcome measures within and between the focal officers and the groups of subordinates that they lead. In addition, the use of within and between analysis provides tests of the magnitudes of the obtained effects independent of, yet compatible with, tests of statistical significance.

In conclusion, this study has obtained new, valid, and reliable measures of transformational leadership and has shown the forecasting potential of the USNA military grade for predicting subsequent transformational leadership and appraised performance. However, early forecasting of prospective leaders suggests that more attention needs to be paid to various biodata in addition to differential aptitudes of this highly preselected group admitted to the academy, and rated military performance in addition to academic performance at the USNA. These preliminary findings are likely to have further implications for identifying, selecting, training, and developing transformational leaders in a variety of settings.

## References

Avolio, B. J., & Bass, B. M. (1988). Transformational leadership, charisma and beyond. In J. G. Hunt, B. R. Baliga, H. P. Dachler, & C. A. Schriesheim (Eds.), *Emerging leadership vistas* (pp. 29–50). Lexington, MA: Lexington Books.

Bass, B. M. (1981). *Stogdill's handbook of leadership* (2nd ed.). New York: Free Press.

Bass, B. M. (1985). *Leadership and performance beyond expectations*. New York: Free Press.

Bass, B. M., & Avolio, B. J. (in press). *The multifactor leadership questionnaire (MLQ)*. Palo Alto, CA: Consulting Psychologists Press.

Bass, B. M., Cascio, W. F., & O'Connor, E. (1974). Magnitude estimates of frequency and amount. *Journal of Applied Psychology, 59*, 313–320.

Bass, B. M., & Yammarino, F. J. (1987). *Multifactor officer questionnaire: MLQ forms 11r and 11s*. Binghamton, NY: Center for Leadership Studies, State University of New York at Binghamton.

Burns, J. M. (1978). *Leadership*. New York: Harper & Row.

Dansereau, F., Alutto, J. A., & Yammarino, F. J. (1984). *Theory testing in organizational behavior: The varient approach*. Englewood Cliffs, NJ: Prentice-Hall.

Deets, N., & Morano, R. (1986). Xerox's strategy for changing management styles. *Management Review*, March, 31–35.

Graen, G. (1976). Role-making processes within complex organizations. In M. D. Dunnette (Ed.), *Handbook of industrial and organizational psychology* (pp. 1201–1245). Chicago: Rand McNally.

Hater, J., & Bass, B. M. (1988). Superiors' evaluations and subordinates' perceptions of transformational and transactional leadership. *Journal of Applied Psychology, 73*, 695–702.

House, R. J. (1977). A 1976 theory of charismatic leadership. In J. G. Hunt & L. L. Larson (Eds.), *Leadership: The cutting edge* (pp. 189–207). Carbondale, IL: Southern Illinois University Press.

Waldman, D. A., & Bass, B. M. (1986). Adding to leader and follower transactions: The augmenting effect of transformational leadership. *Working Paper* (No. 86–108). Binghamton, NY: State University of New York at Binghamton.

Waldman, D. A., Bass, B. M., & Einstein, W. O. (1987). Leadership and outcomes of performance appraisal processes. *Journal of Occupational Psychology, 60*, 177–186.

Yukl, G. A., (1981). *Leadership in organizations*. Englewood Cliffs, NJ: Prentice-Hall.

Zaleznick, A. (1983). The leadership gap. *Washington Quarterly, 6* (1), 32–39.

# Transformational Leaders: Team Performance, Leadership Ratings, and Firsthand Impressions*

*William H. Clover*

The nation's major military academies consider themselves leadership laboratories. This is no accident. Their mission is not simply to provide an undergraduate education but to produce motivated and dedicated second lieutenants who will serve their country in numerous capacities for the duration of a lifetime career.

This goal of developing motivated and dedicated career officers requires a multifaceted approach which involves both the development of basic supervisory skills and the inculcation and clarification of values central to the organization. One goal over the past several years has been to develop a systematic and integrated leadership and organizational assessment process to track the relation of various climate and leadership variables to various outcome indices. Some of those outcome indices were standard attitude measures. Others were the subjective and qualitative comments of cadet subordinates regarding key officer superiors. Finally, rated team performance was tracked.

*The Organization.* The Air Force Academy is composed of 4,400 cadet undergraduate students who complete their academic program while being assigned to one of 40 different organizational units called squadrons. Each squadron consists of approximately 110–115 male and female cadets. Females make up approximately 12%–15% of each class at any given time. The 40 squadrons are organized into four groups of ten squadrons each. Squadrons are rated regularly on several dimensions within three major areas of performance: military, athletic, and academic. Each of the 40 squadrons is organized along the lines of a traditional active duty military

---

* *The opinions in this paper represent solely those of the author and do not reflect any opinions of the United States Air Force Academy or the United States Air Force.*

squadron so cadets may learn academy organization and important aspects of Air Force organization before they graduate.

Each cadet squadron is supervised by an active duty officer who is called the Air Officer Commanding (AOC). This officer plays multiple roles such as counselor, mentor, disciplinarian, supervisor, parent, role model, and teacher. AOCs are charged with overseeing the activities of the cadets (freshmen through seniors) in their squadrons. Cadets within a squadron move through a series of developmental roles intended to increase their understanding of the Air Force and to enhance their own leadership development. Freshman cadets spend the year as followers; sophomore through senior cadets systematically take on progressively greater leadership roles. Senior cadets literally run their own cadet squadrons under the tutelage of their AOCs.

## Why Transformational Leadership?

Transformational leadership represents a significant qualitative step beyond previous leadership models. The leadership setting for both cadets and officers as just described makes this concept particularly relevant to achieving academy goals as highlighted by the following paragraphs.

**Rational versus Emotional Leadership** Richard Nixon has said that "people are persuaded by reason, but moved by emotion; [the leader] must both persuade them and move them" (1982, p. 4). It is this author's belief, shared by many, that transformational leadership is changing the focus of leadership research in two ways. First, we are moving away from the issue of solely rational models of supervisory behavior. Such models as the Hersey and Blanchard model, Fiedler's contingency theory, House's path-goal theory, the Vroom and Yetton model (see Hellriegel et al., 1986), and Hollander's (1978) social exchange model were generally rational approaches and prescriptions as to how a supervisor should deal with a subordinate. Transformational models, starting with the work of Burns (1978), House (1977), Zaleznik (1977), and Bass (1985) are pursuing the issue of using and dealing with emotion in the leadership process. For many the issue is equated to the distinction between leadership and management.

**Value Formation and Clarification** Schein (1980, pp. 107–110) uses Etzioni's concepts to discuss the different types of leaders needed in different cultural contexts. He differentiates three types of organizations—coercive, utilitarian, and normative— which require distinct types of leadership. A value-laden organization, such as a military academy, would be considered a normative organization. In normative organizations the basic form of involvement is moral and the basis for authority is charismatic or rational authority based on experience. McCloy and Clover (1988) have argued that a military academy is clearly a place where values regarding duty, honor, country, and service before self are either inculcated or clarified. Dealing with values is a primary purpose of a military academy. It must be recognized that values have a large emotional component since they are "explicit or implicit conceptions of the desirable held by an individual or a group" (Miner, 1988, p. 240). Given this emotional side of a military academy, transformational leadership should have a bearing on motivation and performance.

**A Time of Change** Authors such as Tichy and Devanna (1986) have postulated that transformational leadership is needed most at times of change. While this can be said of all college students, most are unlikely to find as much change demanded of their personal value system. While their work deals with organizational change, it seems relevant that personal change in a group setting is also a relevant locus for leadership that helps young people understand the change around them. A military academy represents a significant time of change for individual cadets.

**Scrutinizing Role Models** Bass's original research (1985) indicated that modeling and charisma were related. Kouzes and Posner (1987) note that role modeling and emotional leadership played a key role in the behavior of effective leaders. In a November 1985 unpublished survey of the cadet wing at the Air Force Academy, cadets were asked to choose from a list of nine different possible roles what they believed was the primary role of the AOC. Nearly 55% of the cadets chose the role of "officer model" defined as a "person who exemplifies what you want to be, acts the way you would like to act, and balances a task and people orientation." This particular role and definition was chosen five times as often as the next-highest choice. These data indicate that being perceived as a role model is very important to the successful fulfillment of the job of an AOC. If being a role model is important to the subordinate, then transformational leadership seems to be a relevant type of leadership for concern at a military academy.

The purpose of this paper is to show the impact of transformational leaders on their subordinates and their organization using several measures.

## Method

Toward the end of each semester, cadet squadrons complete an organizational climate survey which assesses various attributes of their squadron (cohesiveness, training standards, cadet leadership, rewards, trust, goals, etc.). Additionally, cadet subordinates rate their AOC on a series of leadership dimensions including abbreviated versions of Bass's (1985) transformational leadership scales. These scales cover charisma, inspiration, intellectual stimulation, and individualized consideration. One of Bass's transactional leadership scales labeled contingent reward is also used. Finally, all cadets are generally requested to respond to two open-ended questions dealing with the best and worst aspects of their AOC's leadership style.

The data are analyzed and written comments are typed. Data are then given to each AOC in what has been termed a "benign feedback" system. That is, each AOC is provided information about the climate in their respective squadron and comparison data for the overall Cadet Wing of all 40 cadet squadrons. However, no one other than the AOC sees the data on his/her own particular squadron. There are two parts to the feedback data provided to the AOC. Part 1 deals with overall squadron climate data on several measures. These data the AOC is encouraged to share with his or her squadron. Part 2 of the feedback deals with the actual leadership ratings of the AOC, provided by the subordinates, on the Bass scales and other leadership measures. The AOC is advised to discuss aspects of these data with the subordinates who rated him/her. The AOC is also encouraged to see a member of the research team to go over these data in more detail if the scores are low. Few of the AOCs who obviously need the feedback take advantage of this offer.

# FIGURE 1

## Charisma

"My AOC makes me proud to be associated with him/her."

"I have complete faith in my AOC."

"In my mind, my AOC is a symbol of success and accomplishment."

"I am ready to trust my AOC to overcome any obstacle."

## Individualized Consideration

"My AOC gives personal attention to cadets who seem neglected."

"My AOC finds out what I value and helps me achieve it."

"We can count on my AOC to express his/her appreciation when we do a good job."

"My AOC gives us a lot of help."

## Intellectual Stimulation

"My AOC provides me with reason to change the way I think about problems."

"My AOC places heavy emphasis on careful problem solving before taking action."

"My AOC makes sure we think through what is involved before taking actions."

"My AOC gets us to use reasoning and evidence rather than unsupported opinion."

## Inspiration

"My AOC arouses in me the effort to work harder and better."

"My AOC enables me to get a lot more done than I thought I could have if he/she weren't around."

"We work faster, higher, and/or farther in reaching objectives because of my AOC."

"My AOC stimulates our efforts to excel."

*Figure 1 items used in abbreviated Bass Transformational Leadership Scales.*

**Measures** Figure 1 shows the questions used in the abbreviated Bass transformational leadership scales. These questions are answered on Bass's five-point scale. Questions within a factor are combined to create a scale score.

**Performance Rankings** Each squadron is rated on several measures. The objective measures include a wide range of individual and group measures. One individual measure is a key exam called the Professional Competency Exam (PCE). This exam measures each cadet's knowledge of information they should know as cadets and professional officers. Another area of individual effort, which is combined for the entire squadron, is the overall academic performance of members of the squadron. An area of team performance that is measured includes cadet ratings in athletic events in their intramural competition. Additionally, once per semester each cadet squadron must undergo a "standardized evaluation" test in which the squadron is evaluated in all areas of performance.

Each cadet squadron is continually evaluated on such measures as daily marching, periodic marching in parades, disciplinary actions occurring in the squadron, daily and weekly squadron room inspections, and evaluation of how each squadron is conducting a primary task of indoctrinating and training freshmen into the ways of the Air Force Academy and the Air Force. At first blush, these may seem trivial criteria; we would argue just the opposite. Admittedly, they may appear too simple to be taken seriously; and yet, that is their strength. In general, these are behaviors that anyone can perform. They are not dependent on unique skills or exceptionally long training. Rather, they are behaviors that are a function of pure motivation and attitude. Anyone can do well on these tasks with sufficient motivation. Therefore, they give a good indication of when motivational leadership may be present. *

The Group AOC (a supervisor of ten squadron AOCs) combines all objective and subjective measures at the end of each month and provides a cumulative ranking at the end of each semester. These cumulative rankings serve as the performance criteria used to differentiate upper- and lower-performing squadrons in this research. These criteria are not perfect; in fact, they are filled with bias of one form or another. Yet, they are one relevant measure by which squadrons are judged. Therefore, these measures have been used as realistic standards by which to judge the relevance of transformational leadership. Most criteria in the real world are sloppy or "contaminated" in some fashion (Cascio, 1978, pp. 51–53). However, it is these criteria that organizations and bosses use. Therefore, we have chosen deliberately to stay with this real, but messy, criterion as a test of the validity of transformational leadership concepts.

**Naturally Occurring Results** In general, all the data in this research represent naturally occurring results. That is, no systematic intervention occurred to try to change specifically the behavior of those officers who were either identified by their ratings as transformational or nontransformational. During the past four-year period, we have tried to incorporate two broad interventions into the entire system. The first is a systematic feedback system on climate and leadership variables. The second is a series of overall team-building workshops in which the results of much of this work have been presented. In reality, while some might see these workshops as an intervention, the

---

* *I am grateful to Richard Hughes for this insight concerning the relevance of these tasks as measures of motivation.*

author has painfully come to the conclusion that even in organizations "love is more than just a little speech, it's got to find a common ground" (song titled "I've Been To Town," sung by Glen Yarborough). Unless a leader not only intellectually but emotionally understands and embraces these concepts, I see very little chance of significant change.

In sum, data are collected at the end of each semester. Approximately one to two months after data are collected, criterion data are accumulated from the various groups of ten squadrons each. Data presented here come from the academic year 1987–1988 and are the basis for the results that follow.

## Results and Discussion

The data will be viewed in three different ways. First, we will look at the actual performance rankings achieved by squadrons in relation to the transformational leadership ratings received by the officers in charge of those squadrons. Second, we will look at the differences in the ratings of the officers in charge of upper- versus lower-performing squadrons on such transformational leadership variables as charisma, intellectual stimulation, inspiration, and so forth. Third, we will look at the qualitative reactions of subordinates to transformational and nontransformational leaders.

Tables 1 and 2 show the transformational leadership ratings (a combination of charisma, intellectual stimulation, inspiration, and individualized consideration) and the overall performance rankings (an overall subjective and objective summary of each squadron's performance that semester) of each of the squadrons. Performance rankings can range from 1–10. Table 1 shows the transformational leadership ratings of officers in charge of these cadet squadrons during the fall semester, 1987. The overall transformational leadership rating is 3.24 with a standard deviation of 1.10 ($N = 1966$). The range is from a low of 2.10 to a high of 4.63 on a five-point scale. Individual officer ratings are based on an average sample size of 49 and a standard deviation of 10. In general, approximately 3,500 cadets responded to the November 1987 survey, or approximately 88 cadets per squadron. The reduction in sample size for the overall transformational leadership rating is due to the fact that a significant proportion of respondents chose the response "can't answer/doesn't apply" to individual items within the different transformational leadership scales. In April 1988 (see Table 2), the overall transformational leadership rating is 3.03 with a standard deviation of 1.11 ($N = 1913$). The range is from a low of 1.85 to a high of 4.22 during this semester. Approximately 3,000 cadets responded to the April 1988 survey. The average N per squadron on which the transformational leadership ratings are based is 48 with a standard deviation of 12.

**Performance and Transformational Leadership** A most important question is whether performance is higher in the groups led by perceived transformational leaders. Calculating the average rank of each transformational leadership quartile in Table 1 shows that the average performance ranking in Quartiles 1 through 4 is 4.9, 4.8, 5.5, and 6.1. Calculating the average rank of each transformational leadership quartile in Table 2 shows that the average performance ranking in Quartiles 1 through 4 is 4.2, 5.3, 6.5 and 6.0. A comparison of the upper two quartiles versus the lower two quartiles in Table 1 indicates an average performance rank of 4.89 versus 5.8. Likewise, a

# TABLE 1
## Transformational Leadership Ratings, Nov '87, and Overall Performance Rankings by Squadron, Dec '87

| LINE | Coded Squadron | Transform Nov '87[1] | Rank Dec '87[2] | Nov '87 Quartile[3] |
|------|------|------|------|------|
| 1 | 1322 | 4.63 | 4 | 1 |
| 2 | 117 | 4.18 | 5 | 1 |
| 3 | 1914 | 4.06 | 7 | 1 |
| 4 | 1526 | 4.05 | 6 | 1 |
| 5 | 1523 | 4.03 | 1 | 1 |
| 6 | 808 | 3.98 | 7 | 1 |
| 7 | 1225 | 3.89 | 5 | 1 |
| 8 | 614 | 3.89 | 3 | 1 |
| 9 | 120 | 3.87 | 2 | 1 |
| 10 | 1304 | 3.87 | 9 | 1 |
| 11 | 618 | 3.79 | 1 | 2 |
| 12 | 1218 | 3.74 | 9 | 2 |
| 13 | 1104 | 3.68 | 10 | 2 |
| 14 | 1714 | 3.62 | 4 | 2 |
| 15 | 119 | 3.61 | 5 | 2 |
| 16 | 915 | 3.59 | 7 | 2 |
| 17 | 1426 | 3.55 | 5 | 2 |
| 18 | 1616 | 3.53 | 2 | 2 |
| 19 | 1919 | 3.45 | 4 | 2 |
| 20 | 418 | 3.43 | 1 | 2 |
| 21 | 307 | 3.37 | 10 | 3 |
| 22 | 502 | 3.35 | 2 | 3 |
| 23 | 1904 | 3.21 | 3 | 3 |
| 24 | 116 | 3.18 | 7 | 3 |
| 25 | 1609 | 3.08 | 8 | 3 |
| 26 | 320 | 3.02 | 4 | 3 |
| 27 | 603 | 3.01 | 10 | 3 |
| 28 | 1603 | 2.95 | 3 | 3 |
| 29 | 1308 | 2.81 | 1 | 3 |
| 30 | 416 | 2.74 | 6 | 3 |
| 31 | 207 | 2.71 | 9 | 4 |
| 32 | 1710 | 2.65 | 8 | 4 |
| 33 | 1719 | 2.63 | 10 | 4 |
| 34 | 203 | 2.62 | 8 | 4 |
| 35 | 1822 | 2.58 | 9 | 4 |
| 36 | 304 | 2.55 | 2 | 4 |
| 37 | 906 | 2.46 | 3 | 4 |
| 38 | 726 | 2.11 | 6 | 4 |
| 39 | 1019 | 2.11 | 6 | 4 |
| 40 | 1814 | 2.10 | 8 | 4 |

[1] Overall subordinate ratings of AOC's on abbreviated Bass Scales measuring charisma, intellectual stimulation, inspiration, and individualized consideration.
[2] Overall squadron rankings within each group of ten squadrons at the end of the Fall Semester, 1987. A ranking of 1 is best and a ranking of 10 is worst.
[3] Quartile classification is based on overall transformational leadership score.

# TABLE 2
## Transformational Leadership Ratings, APR '88, and Overall Performance Rankings by Squadron, MAY '88

| LINE | Coded Squadron | Transform Apr '88[1] | Rank May '88[2] | Apr '88 Quartile[3] |
|------|------|------|------|------|
| 1 | 1322 | 4.22 | 1 | 1 |
| 2 | 1304 | 4.17 | 3 | 1 |
| 3 | 1019 | 3.98 | 9 | 1 |
| 4 | 1523 | 3.90 | 4 | 1 |
| 5 | 117 | 3.87 | 7 | 1 |
| 6 | 618 | 3.86 | 2 | 1 |
| 7 | 1914 | 3.81 | 6 | 1 |
| 8 | 116 | 3.80 | 3 | 1 |
| 9 | 1225 | 3.77 | 3 | 1 |
| 10 | 915 | 3.61 | 4 | 1 |
| 11 | 1104 | 3.55 | 7 | 2 |
| 12 | 1526 | 3.54 | 5 | 2 |
| 13 | 808 | 3.52 | 10 | 2 |
| 14 | 1919 | 3.44 | 1 | 2 |
| 15 | 119 | 3.41 | 5 | 2 |
| 16 | 614 | 3.37 | 5 | 2 |
| 17 | 120 | 3.33 | 1 | 2 |
| 18 | 1822 | 3.22 | 10 | 2 |
| 19 | 1904 | 3.08 | 3 | 2 |
| 20 | 1426 | 3.07 | 6 | 2 |
| 21 | 502 | 3.05 | 1 | 3 |
| 22 | 203 | 2.87 | 8 | 3 |
| 23 | 1616 | 2.86 | 10 | 3 |
| 24 | 418 | 2.76 | 2 | 3 |
| 25 | 1609 | 2.68 | 8 | 3 |
| 26 | 1714 | 2.66 | 4 | 3 |
| 27 | 320 | 2.64 | 6 | 3 |
| 28 | 1218 | 2.62 | 9 | 3 |
| 29 | 1710 | 2.60 | 8 | 3 |
| 30 | 1719 | 2.57 | 9 | 3 |
| 31 | 304 | 2.51 | 7 | 4 |
| 32 | 726 | 2.47 | 6 | 4 |
| 33 | 1603 | 2.45 | 2 | 4 |
| 34 | 1308 | 2.42 | 7 | 4 |
| 35 | 307 | 2.37 | 8 | 4 |
| 36 | 603 | 2.25 | 4 | 4 |
| 37 | 416 | 2.20 | 5 | 4 |
| 38 | 207 | 2.11 | 9 | 4 |
| 39 | 906 | 1.91 | 2 | 4 |
| 40 | 1814 | 1.85 | 10 | 4 |

[1] Overall subordinate ratings of AOC's on abbreviated Bass Scales measuring charisma, intellectual stimulation, inspiration, and individualized consideration.
[2] Overall squadron rankings within each group of ten squadrons at the end of the Spring Semester, 1988. A ranking of 1 is best and a ranking of 10 is worst.
[3] Quartile classification is based on overall transformational leadership score.

comparison of the upper two quartiles versus the lower two quartiles in Table 2 indicates an average performance rank of 4.75 versus 6.25. Clearly, we find some performance differences in the direction we would expect on this murky, but real, criterion measure. That is, in general transformational leaders have higher-performing squadrons. Conducting a Mann-Whitney U Test (Hinkle et al., 1979, pp. 354–357) indicates that the performance differences between the ranks in Table 1 are marginally significant, at the .10 level (U = 148, Critical Value = 152 at $p < .10$). A Mann-Whitney U Test on the performance ranks in Table 2 again indicates a significance $< .10$ (U = 139, Critical Value = 152 at .10). Some would say these results are "close, but no cigar." Yet we are encouraged. As John Gardner (1988, p. 214) notes:

*Leaders act in the stream of history. As they labor to bring about a result, multiple forces beyond their control, even beyond their knowledge, are moving to hasten or hinder the result. So there is rarely a demonstrable causal link between a leader's specific decisions and consequent events. Consequences are not a reliable measure of leadership.*

We think that Gardner's comments are relevant to leaders at all levels. Some may see this as a mere excuse. Perhaps the triangulation of the rest of the data will provide more support.

**Perceived Transformational Leadership in the Eyes of Subordinates** Another way to view the data is to separate the upper- and lower-performing squadrons and compare how subordinates rate their officer leaders on transformational and selected transactional scales. In this analysis, we have grouped all of the upper-performing squadrons—those with a rank of 1–5 and compared them against all the lower-performing squadrons—those with a rank of 6–10. Tables 3 and 4 show these differences for the transformational variables.

There are clear differences in the way that subordinates see their officer leaders in upper- versus lower-performing squadrons. As shown in Tables 3 and 4, the overall transformational leadership ratings of officers in the upper-performing squadrons were 3.46 and 3.23 in November 1987 and April 1988, respectively. The overall transformational leadership ratings of officer leaders in the lower-performing squadrons were 3.03 and 2.84, respectively, for the Fall and Spring semesters. Additionally, every component variable that made up the transformational leadership score was also significantly different between the upper- and lower-performing groups. The largest differences in terms of effect can be seen in the ratings on the charisma and inspiration variables. Clearly, these two represent the emotional reaction to a group leader.

Finally, one other pair of differences shown in Table 4 should be noted: between ratings of officers in upper- versus lower-performing groups on the perception of them as "role models." Perception as a role model was assessed with the following two questions: "My AOC is a good model of the way I would like to be as an officer," and "My AOC provides a good model of a professional military officer." Bass's original work shows that the issue of modeling loads on the charisma factor. We have separated it from that factor and assessed it separately since being perceived as a role model is a critical element of officer behavior at a military academy. The concept of role modeling has also been placed recently as a focal leadership behavior in the ideas presented by

# TABLE 3
## Comparison of Transformational Leadership Ratings Given by Subordinates to Officers in Charge of Upper- Versus Lower-Performing Squadrons, November 1987

| Variable | | Upper Squadrons[1] | Lower Squadrons[2] | F[3] | Sig |
|---|---|---|---|---|---|
| Individualized | X | 3.34 | 3.06 | 45.44 | <.001 |
| Consideration | SD | 1.02 | 1.08 | | |
| | N | 1230 | 1298 | | |
| Charisma[4] | X | 3.75 | 3.31 | 100.16 | <.001 |
| | SD | 1.18 | 1.32 | | |
| | N | 1623 | 1628 | | |
| Intellectual | X | 3.56 | 3.24 | 56.56 | <.001 |
| Stimulation | SD | .98 | 1.10 | | |
| | N | 1221 | 1291 | | |
| Inspiration | X | 3.30 | 2.85 | 105.97 | <.001 |
| | SD | 1.14 | 1.20 | | |
| | N | 1396 | 1459 | | |
| Overall – | X | 3.46 | 3.03 | 78.14 | <.001 |
| Transformational | SD | 1.02 | 1.13 | | |
| Leadership | N | 945 | 1021 | | |
| Perception | X | 4.35 | 3.84 | 111.28 | <.001 |
| of AOC as a | SD | 1.31 | 1.53 | | |
| Role Model[5] | N | 1765 | 1754 | | |

[1] Upper-Performing Squadrons are those ranked 1 through 5 in their respective groups.
[2] Lower-Performing Squadrons are those ranked 6 through 10 in their respective groups.
[3] One way ANOVA was conducted using SPSSx (Statistical Programs for the Social Sciences, 1986) computer programs.
[4] All transformational leadership variables are measured on a five-point scale found in Bass, 1985.
[5] Role model ratings were obtained using a six-point Likert scale ranging from "strongly disagree" to "strongly agree."

## TABLE 4
## Comparison of Transformational Leadership Ratings, Given by Subordinates, to Officers in Charge of Upper- Versus Lower-Performing Squadrons, April 1988

| Variable | | Upper Squadrons | Lower Squadrons | F | Sig |
|---|---|---|---|---|---|
| Individualized | X | 3.19 | 2.87 | 53.07 | < .001 |
| Consideration | SD | 1.10 | 1.05 | | |
| | N | 1140 | 1260 | | |
| Charisma | X | 3.48 | 2.99 | 102.17 | < .001 |
| | SD | 1.27 | 1.26 | | |
| | N | 1306 | 1421 | | |
| Intellectual | X | 3.38 | 3.04 | 60.36 | < .001 |
| Stimulation | SD | 1.07 | 1.08 | | |
| | N | 1143 | 1235 | | |
| Inspiration | X | 3.05 | 2.61 | 82.33 | < .001 |
| | SD | 1.23 | 1.15 | | |
| | N | 1167 | 1252 | | |
| Overall — | X | 3.23 | 2.84 | 59.35 | < .001 |
| Transformational | SD | 1.12 | 1.06 | | |
| Leadership | N | 916 | 994 | | |
| Perception of | X | 4.01 | 3.48 | 95.34 | < .001 |
| AOC as a | SD | 1.46 | 1.46 | | |
| Role Model | N | 1392 | 1525 | | |

Kouzes and Posner (1987, pp. 187–239). The differences in ratings between upper- and lower-performing groups are dramatic.

**Qualitative Differences Between Transformational and Nontransformational Leaders** It is one thing to interpret numbers and quite another to calculate their emotional impact. The following comments about officers perceived as transformational give a flavor for the meaning of charisma, individualized consideration, inspiration, being a role model, and so forth, as seen through the eyes and feelings of subordinates.

*Our AOC is great! Good job in picking her. I've had five AOCs–she's by far the best. She helps us out instead of trying to hurt us. She isn't insecure and power hungry like the other four AOCs I've had. She's concerned about teaching us to be capable officers instead of about teaching us to be capable cadet regulation followers.*

*You know what? We follow the regs more now than we did when we were forced to be cadet reg followers. INCREDIBLE!! Did someone catch a clue? (Senior, Sq 1019)*

*My AOC is always around to "just talk." And, when you "just talk" you work out your gripe with the system and he helps you look at all sides–maybe you still disagree with the system but you feel better just by looking at all issues. (Senior, Sq 1322)*

*She gives cadets enough rope to hang themselves with and yet never relinquishes her command or responsibility of the squadron. Oftentimes she's taken a lot of heat for one or more squadron members from her superiors and yet she doesn't change her style–I like that. (Senior, Sq 1225)*

*Lets us run things. Trusts and treats us responsibly. Doesn't act like we are a threat to his career. Acts as if his experience with us will enhance his career...is very reasonable and accepts and considers suggestions. I believe he cares about us. Is approachable. (Senior, Sq 1304)*

*He is very approachable and is around often enough that when you need him, he's there. But, in my opinion, his greatest strength is that he allows us to run our own squadron–he trusts us enough to do it. In essence, he treats us like junior officers... (Senior, Sq 1523)*

*He lets the cadets run things and supports them all the way. He is secure enough with his role that he doesn't have to force his rule on us in an effort to get things done. He will listen to all opinions and isn't afraid of changing his mind or being wrong. He gets our respect for treating us as people and adults. (Junior, Sq 117)*

*His emphasizing those parts of our development that will be relevant after graduation. (Junior, Sq 1914)*

*He's always around when you need him and he's intelligent and intellectual enough to talk to when there is a problem. He's very experienced in the Air Force and relates a lot of what is going on in our squadron to "real-life" areas. (Junior, Sq 614)*

The picture and feelings are quite different, literally opposite, when dealing with comments about perceived nontransformational leaders. Comments about these officers deal with such things as experienced frustration, decreased morale, perceived lack of integrity, self-serving behavior, lack of trust, inequity, poor interpersonal skills, lack of insight into others, and harsh arbitrary judgments.

Needless to say, none of the above comments are rational reactions to leadership. Rather, they represent emotional reactions to role models. In the emotionality, however, we see a definite impact on the motivation of cadets who are exposed to different kinds of leadership. As I read these statements, I cannot help but be struck by how much they represent two different types of leaders described in recent literature. AOCs who are seen as positive role models and transformational leaders represent the characteristics that Kouzes and Posner (1987) describe in their sample of leaders. Nontransformational AOCs seem to possess many of the characteristics that McCall and Lombardo (1983) describe in their "derailed" executives. That is, many of the nontransformational AOCs seem arrogant or aloof, or at the least, lack interpersonal skills.

Experience with supervisors and leaders of this kind can have an impact. McCall et al. (1988, pp. 67–85) argue that bosses teach four lessons which deal with management values, human values, what executives are like, and politics. They recognize that most subordinates will take away the message of what not to be like. However, as social learning theory would predict, some significant proportion will absorb the lessons of these leaders as the correct ones and propagate such behavior in much the same way that abused children learn to become abusing adults. Hopefully, over time, our feedback systems and emphasis on transformational leadership will cause changes in officer leaders who are perceived as nontransformational and also help to mitigate their negative impact on subordinates.

## Summary

The data presented here represent data collected during academic year 1987–1988. However, they are similar to data collected at the Air Force Academy over the past four to five years. Our conclusion is that transformational leadership, as perceived in the eyes of subordinates, has an impact on team performance, member attitudes, and strong emotional reactions. To be sure, we are not convinced that transformational leadership rules out the need for good transactional leadership. In fact, we are convinced of just the opposite: good transformational leadership is balanced and aided by good transactional leadership. We believe that transformational leadership is an important component in an organization where a central part of its mission is the transmission of pivotal values such as "duty, honor, country," and service before self to a group of young people, many of whom are in Erikson's identity and intimacy stages of life (DiCaprio, 1983, pp. 188–195).

## References

Bass, B. M. (1985). *Leadership and performance beyond expectations*. New York: Free Press.

Burns, J. M. (1978). *Leadership*. New York: Harper & Row.

Cascio, W. F. (1978). *Applied psychology in personnel management*. Reston, VA: Reston.

DiCaprio, N. S. (1983). *Personality theories: A guide to human nature* (2nd ed.). New York: Rinehart & Winston.

Gardner, J. W. (1988). The nature of leadership. In J. L. Gibson, J. M. Ivancevich, & J. H. Donnelly, Jr. (Eds.), *Organizations close-up* (6th ed.), (pp. 210–218). Plano, TX: Business Publications.

Hellriegel, D., Slocum, J. W., & Woodman, R. W. (1986). *Organizational behavior* (4th ed.). St. Paul, MN: West.

Hinkle, D., Wiersma, W., & Jurs, S. J. (1979). *Applied statistics for the behavioral sciences*. Boston: Houghton-Mifflin.

Hollander, E. P. (1978). *Leadership dynamics: A practical guide to effective relationships*. New York: Free Press/Macmillan.

House, R. J. (1977). A 1976 theory of charismatic leadership. In J. G. Hunt & L. L. Larson (Eds.), *Leadership: The cutting edge* (pp. 189–207). Carbondale, IL: Southern Illinois University Press.

Kouzes, J. M., & Posner, B. Z. (1987). *The leadership challenge: How to get extraordinary things done in organizations.* San Francisco: Jossey-Bass.

McCall, M. W., Jr., & Lombardo, M. M. (1983). *Off the track: Why and how successful executives get derailed.* (Tech. Rep. No. 21). Greensboro, NC: Center for Creative Leadership.

McCall, M. W., Jr., Lombardo, M.M., & Morrison, A. (1988). *The lessons of experience.* Lexington, MA: Lexington Books.

McCloy, T. M., & Clover, W. H. (1988). Value formation at the Air Force Academy. In C. C. Moskos & F. R. Wood (Eds.), *The military: More than just a job?* (pp. 129–149). Washington, DC: Pergamom-Brassey's International Defense.

Miner, J. (1988). *Organizational behavior: Performance and productivity.* New York: Random House.

Nixon, R. (1982). *Leaders.* New York: Warner Books.

Schein, E. H. (1980). *Organizational psychology* (3rd ed.). Englewood Cliffs, NJ: Prentice-Hall.

*SPSS-X: User's guide* (2nd ed.) (1986). Chicago: SPSS Inc.

Tichy, N., & Devanna, M. A. (1986). *The transformational leader.* New York: John Wiley & Sons.

Zaleznik, A. (1977). Managers and leaders: Are they different? *Harvard Business Review, 55* (3), 59–70.

# Task Cycle Theory: The Processes of Influence

Clark L.
Wilson
Donal O'Hare
and
Frank Shipper

It is our view that leadership is best seen as one of several organizational roles that depend on skills at influencing others. Executives, managers, supervisors, technical and professional peers, and outside sales representatives all depend heavily on influence skills to perform their roles. Therefore, to make research on leadership fully meaningful, one must differentiate these various roles for greater clarity.

This has led us to think in terms of the processes in the most elementary meaning of the term. By so doing, we feel we can better identify the similarities and differences between the roles under study. We suggest that there are three fundamental processes involved, the dictionary listing of a process being a systematic series of actions directed to some end.

First is the process by which individuals exert influence; second, the process by which others learn to accept a person's influence; and third, the process by which we as investigators show that we have identified the factors, skills, and attributes that influence change in individual and organization performance.

For purposes of explication, we dwell on the roles of managing and leading.

## Task Cycle Theory: The Process of Exerting Influence

Organization behavior is made up of a series of tasks. Tasks are iterated and the sum of those iterations totals up to the work of the unit or individual. While tasks of different groups and individuals differ from one to the other, the fundamental nature of a task does not change. This perspective of task iteration led to the notion of the task cycle, in that repeated performance of a task involves repeating a process—a systematic series of actions directed to some end.

Table 1 lays out a sequence of behaviors involved in executing a generic task. Then it translates the phases of task activity into other organization roles for illustration. Note that all of these are roles in which one person or group of people aims to influence one or more others.

## TABLE 1
## The Task Cycle Model

| A GENERIC TASK | EXECUTIVES | LEADERS | MANAGERS | PEERS | SELLERS |
|---|---|---|---|---|---|
| **I. THE GOAL** | | | | | |
| What do I do? | Clarify and direct mission achievement | Envision and initiate change for future | Clarify and communicate today's goals | Give service, keep own goals clearly in mind | Meet client needs, earn revenues |
| **II. THE PLAN** | | | | | |
| How do I do it? | Develop and communicate strategies | Solve novel problems resourcefully | Plan and solve problems encountered | Solve client problems as advisor | Give service, be professional, analyze needs |
| **III. RESOURCES** | | | | | |
| How do I carry out the plan? | Develop supportive culture | Modeling, mentoring, and challenging | Facilitate by coaching, training | Professional/ technical skills | Product knowledge, empathy, probing skills |
| **IV. FEEDBACK** | | | | | |
| How do I know I am performing? | Track and share information | Develop awareness of impact | Obtain and give feedback on performance | Inquire, follow up for impact | Ask; identify questions, resistances |
| **V. ADJUSTMENT** | | | | | |
| How do I fix my mistakes? | Direct/oversee other managers | Use persuasion to gain/ maintain commitment | Correct time and details to meet goals | Self-control to meet service commitments | Answer objections, ask for order |
| **VI. REINFORCEMENT** | | | | | |
| Satisfaction from achievement of the task | Share rewards for organization success | Share rewards for supporting change | Recognize/ reinforce performance | Recognize/ reinforce cooperation | Express appreciation to clients |
| **RESULT** | | | | | |
| Task achievement | Mission accomplishment | Change for the better | Goals achieved | Service rendered | A sale |

For illustration purposes, we examine the Managerial Task Cycle more closely: Every task starts with a purpose, a goal of some sort (Phase I). Once you have a goal, you must develop a plan to achieve it (Phase II). Then, to carry out your plan, you provide or acquire the necessary resources such as time, training, coaching, materials, and so forth (Phase III). As you proceed, you keep track of your progress by obtaining feedback (Phase IV). If your feedback indicates you are off track or behind time, you make adjustments (Phase V). And, finally as you reach your goal, you give and gain reinforcement in whatever form is appropriate (Phase VI). Ultimately, the repeated implementation of this behavioral cycle produces an outcome and leaves a residual profile of attributes which round out the personality of the task performer or manager.

We make no brief for there being precisely six phases in these task cycles. The relevant point is that they are processes, sequences of chained activities by which influence is exerted by managers and leaders. These processes are spelled out in sufficient detail to serve as a source of hypotheses for the creation of scales with which to operationalize the behaviors involved in the model.

Note that the behavior phases in the task cycle are sufficiently generic to be applicable to the wide range of tasks. At the top of the organization, a goal may be a mission; a plan, a strategy. At the first line level, we think more in terms of an immediate work goal and an operating procedure. But generally, the behaviors of all phases of the cycle can be seen in the work of executives, leaders, managers, and supervisors at any level, or independent contributors and organization representatives who contact internal and external clients and prospects.

**Task Cycle Theory in the Context of Leadership Literature** We see a major problem with the literature on leadership in that it is narrowly focused and fails to distinguish organizational roles clearly. Instead, considerable effort is expended to identify and validate the characteristics of leaders, however loosely defined. There is an abundance of anecdotal reporting but that contributes only at the level of hypothesis, not systematic investigation.

Because of this narrowed focus, relatively little attention has been paid to other key organization roles such as managers, independent contributing professionals or technicians, and outside representatives. As indicated, we consider all of these roles to have certain common characteristics, the main one being that effective performance is based on one's ability to influence others. This restricted focus of the literature has also led writers to speak of a whole array of kinds of leadership such as transactional leadership, transformational leadership, and even communications leadership, trust leadership, bottom-line leadership (Sashkin & Burke, 1990), and so forth.

So, let us put our views in context with some of the other contributors to this volume who focus on the measurement and validation of leadership characteristics. Then we can expand on our thinking, once we have things in perspective.

Harrison Gough (1987), with the California Personality Inventory (CPI) has shown that Dominance, Independence, Empathy, and other traits relate to leadership in a variety of situations. He goes further to categorize people into four quadrants by dichotomizing Extraversive–Introversive and Norm-Accepting–Norm-Questioning continua: Alpha, the Leader; Beta, the Saint; Delta, the Artist; and Gamma, the Innovator.

Alpha and Gamma respondents, both on the Extraversive side, are more frequently rated high on leadership. It should be noted that Gough's Dominance measure is oriented toward positive aims and objectives, not raw power.

Similarly, substantial experience with the Myers-Briggs Type Indicator (MBTI) reported by Mary McCaulley (1990) places leaders in the four categories of ISTJ, INTJ, ENTJ, and ESTJ.

In a different vein, Bernard Bass (in press), with a long history of leadership research, treats it at a more behavioral level, speaking of Charisma, Intellectual Leadership, Individual Consideration, and Inspirational Leadership as the prime behaviors of transformational leaders; the basic thrust being that they strive to change or transform organizations and operations for the better. Posner and Kouzes (1987) relate transformational leadership to such behaviors as Challenging the Process, Inspiring a Shared Vision, Encouraging the Heart, and so forth.

Bass further categorizes transactional leaders as those who rely largely on Contingent promises and rewards. He also notes a reliance on both Active and Passive Management-by-Exception. We feel, however, that the notion of transactional leadership is not operationally meaningful in that it encompasses only a small number of the characteristics or skills of leadership or management. To confine managerial scope to reinforcement and control activities is to overlook the familiar skills of goal clarification, coaching, and other support functions. As we see it, transactional leadership essentially serves as a foil or stalking horse to set the notion of transformational leadership apart. We see transactional leaders as outliers or extremes of a continuum. In our terms the shortfalls, noted by Bass and others, are not due to types of leadership but failure to balance relevant skills. With us, they are unbalanced on the hard or soft side.

However, all of these perspectives give insights into the underlying variables of leadership and the measures used by these writers to meet adequate psychometric standards.

We, however, have a mission that goes beyond investigation of the personalities or broad behavior patterns of leaders: It is to develop assessments which can be more readily used to train individuals in the skills and attributes that constitute leaderlike and other important influencing role behaviors. To accomplish this end, we have oriented our assessments at a more operational level. Our measures are stated in terms of operational skills and attributes as distinct from personality traits (Gough and McCaulley), or broad behavior patterns (Bass, Posner and Kouzes).

We believe that all of us are observing the same activities or operations but describing them in different ways and levels; we overlap each other to a greater extent than might be apparent at first glance. For our part, we consider that our Survey of Leadership Practices reflects the skills and attributes as well as the spirit of transformational leadership but at a more operational level than the others. We have captured the vision, venturesomeness, and charisma of the concept along with an array of over 20 amplifying skills and attributes to try to make the concept more trainable. Yet, it is also plain to see from the operational profiles our methods produce that personality patterns emerge quite clearly. One can also, with data from our Survey of Management Practices, view patterns generally associated with Bass's view of transactional leadership and personality patterns which portray Dominance, Empathy, and so forth. Further, in the Survey of Peer Relations for independent contributing specialists and Survey of Sales Relations for relations between sales personnel and customers, the same wide range of patterns emerges.

So, we relate to contemporary literature but we differ in our level of observations, preferring to assess the specifics of what participants actually do and to speak in their terminologies. Our orientation is that, in order to train people to influence others, it is necessary to utilize models and speak in terms to which operating personnel can more readily relate.

## The Process of Learning to Be Influenced

Every manager—or leader—potentially goes though the relevant phases of the cycle with every task he or she supervises. This means that, with successive tasks and with multiple people, a manager iterates task cycle behaviors many times over. This puts forward two important and basic implications:

1. Each task is fully equivalent to a learning trial. Managers learn about the individuals they supervise. But, equally important, if not more so, the relevant others learn a lot about the manager or leader. Especially, they learn what behaviors to expect on the next task so they can adapt to those expectations. This means very clearly that we can lean on the learning literature to get a better understanding of the dynamics of adaptation and change in organizations.

It is important, therefore, to see how this model ties into the cognitive learning paradigm of E. C. Tolman (1932). Two more recent sources amplified the original insights that underpin this research program: Bolles's (1972) updating of Tolman's cognitive theory contributed greatly to the original formulation of the task cycle model. Then, Hilgard's elaborations (1956; Hilgard & Bower, 1966) helped materially in putting task cycle theory into the Tolman perspective.

Hilgard observed that stimulus-response theories—those of Hull, Skinner, and others—"...imply that an individual is goaded along a path by internal and external stimuli, learning the correct movement sequences so that they are released under appropriate circumstances of drive and environmental stimulation" (Hilgard, 1956, p. 191; Hilgard & Bower, 1966, p. 196).

By contrast, he referred to Tolman's theory as sign learning in that "...the learner is following signs to a goal, is learning his way about, is following sort of a map...learning not movements but meanings." The individual learns "sign-significate relations; ...a behavior route, not a movement pattern." Further: Tolman's theory included the concept of expectancy: that with repeated experiences, an individual learns to discriminate a probability that a given behavior will lead to the expected end result. Hilgard added that these expectancies are confirmed or modified by reinforcement of the level of success in repeated trials.

Task cycle theory relates readily to Tolman's formulations. In the terminology of the managerial task cycle, the early phases of the cycle—goal clarification, planning, facilitation, and feedback—are conceived as equivalent to Tolman's signs. These up-front phases of the cycle signal direction and support to co-workers in the task execution process. The level of these behaviors and their interaction with control behaviors, are instrumental in generating levels of expectancy of success. Similarly, the final phase of the task cycle (VI—Reinforcement) is instrumental in generating expectancies of reward.

To view this point clearly, see the role of the manager in the Tolman context: it is to raise the expectation of successfully reaching a work goal that satisfies a need of the worker and the organization.

How are these expectancies generated? By providing the meaning and the signs— clear goals, effective planning, good coaching, continuous feedback, supportive control, and positive reinforcement—so that co-workers have higher levels of expectation of reaching worthwhile goals. If we don't pay attention to the early signs in the sequence, and the skills of sign givers—managers and leaders—we have, in effect, a leaderless leadership literature. We are not attending to how expectancies, valences, and probabilities of success are developed in the first place (c.f., Vroom, 1964; Vroom & Yetton, 1973).

So, in the Tolman context, the aim of task cycle theory is to provide a practical and meaningful conceptual framework to study the sequence of skills—the process—by which managers and leaders influence others by communicating appropriate behavioral signs to their co-workers; and co-workers learn to be influenced by their expectations of these signs being repeated.

Task cycle theory also relates to learning theory in the context of the sequential chaining of behaviors (Skinner, 1938; Gagne, 1985). The notion of chaining plays an important role, not only in research strategies but also in coaching and training for change. Presenting desirable role behaviors as sequentially chained models gives participants a more complete integrated picture of the process one is trying to impart. It thus provides a conceptual strategy or what Gagne and others would call a "learning strategy."

2. The second inference to be drawn from the repeated cycling through task behaviors is that, with iteration and the consequent opportunity to repeat observations, reliability is generated in assessments. The proof of this will be in the data, of course. And that is where we go next.


## The Process of Verification

This is the most fundamental process of all in many respects. We cannot rest with developing models and instruments. Up to that point all is hypothesis. The verification process tests whether or not hypotheses are of operational value. We see four steps after hypotheses have been posited:

    A. Translating the hypothesized model into measurable variables.
    B. Testing the utility of the variables by showing a correlation with performance; testing for validity.
    C. Evaluating the ability to change valid measured behaviors by training.

D. Demonstrating that changes in the measured behaviors are accompanied by concomitant changes in desired individual and organization performance; validating the model as a whole.

An overview of this process and our progress to date is shown in Table 2. The following section refers to this process.

We have conducted studies to bring us up through cell C in both the Manager and Leader rows. A study to explore changing managerial on-the-job performance (Manager cell D) is currently under way with results reported on later pages.

## TABLE 2
## The Verification Process

| Role | Model | A Measure | B Validity | C Behavior Change | D Performance Change |
|------|-------|-----------|------------|-------------------|----------------------|
| Leader | Leader Task Cycle (Change) | Survey Of Leadership Practices | External/ Internal Ratings | In Process | How? |
| Manager | Manager Task Cycle (Goals) | Survey Of Management Practices | Objective Output And Ratings | Five Studies With Positive Results | VA Medical Center, Phoenix |

All studies fitting in cell D are difficult to accomplish in the field, but especially for leadership. How do we validate change in performance for leaders? The dilemma arises from one's distinction between management and leadership: We define management as the responsibility for achieving operating goals, whether implicit or explicit; plus, of course, the skills to build quality into working life. Leadership involves both goal achievement and the skills to bring about positive changes.

If one accepts that distinction, as we do, then observing leaders making positive changes becomes a largely clinical exercise and not readily subject to systematic observation, but only by anecdote. Anecdotal observations are not substitutes for organized testing of hypotheses.

The way around this problem has often been to accept promotions to top positions as tantamount to the manifestation of leadership. But there lies the dilemma. One has to believe that in many organizations, accession to high positions is more survivorship which means adaptation, conforming to the local culture. The skills of adaptation are the logical antithesis of the skills for bringing about positive change. Adaptation implies following rather than leading.

Our answer to this problem has been to take management as a starting point, measuring and validating our model with the Survey of Management Practices. Then, given these steps, we have hypothesized an operational model of leadership skills and attributes different from those of managers. We have operationalized these in the Survey of Leadership Practices. These scales have been shown to be reliable and valid for ratings of leadership. The overlap with the management scales has been minimal with about five percent of intercorrelations being significant at the .05 level. We are now in the process of testing our ability to change leadership skills and attributes as we have done with managers.

What follows is our progress to date by way of verification:

A. *Translating the Model into Measurable Variables: The Survey of Management Practices*

The six phases of the Managerial Task Cycle were operationalized into the Survey of Management Practices (SMP) which assesses 11 operational dimensions representing the six phases of the Task Cycle and four relating to Interpersonal Relations (Wilson, 1975, 1978; Morrison, McCall & DeVries, 1978). The variables are presented in Table 3 in the following section.

B. *Testing and Retesting for Validity: Hospital Weighted Equivalent Work Units (WEWU's)*

The first requirement of any proposed model—and scaling instrument derived from it—is to demonstrate that it makes a difference; that one can make valid operational inferences from the data produced.

Over the past 15 years, more than 20 such studies have been conducted. The most recent, which produced results similar to the rest, is currently being conducted by Frank Shipper with the cooperation of the Director and Staff of the Veterans Administration (VA) Medical Center in Phoenix. Your interest will be heightened by the WEWU criterion and the results shown in Table 3, following.

The VA evaluates productivity by a measure of Weighted Equivalent Work Units or WEWU's, an approach adapted from industrial engineering. The basic quantity is an estimate of the standard number of personnel hours it should take to perform each task or work unit. Various laboratory tests carry various WEWU's or earned hours; operations on patients carry a WEWU value depending on complexity, and so forth. Administrative departments also earn WEWU's. With repeated measures over successive periods, standards or norms are established to evaluate performance in later periods.

In practice, the sum of WEWU's at the end of a period is divided by the number of staff hours charged to the department. The resulting ratio of earned WEWU's divided by actual hours charged, is a direct engineering-type measure of productivity on which an operating unit can be evaluated.

In Shipper's study, SMP was administered for 64 managers for whom he was able to calculate WEWU ratios over a period of five quarters to use as criteria in a concurrent validity study. The results are reported as an analysis of variance of direct reports' ratings in Table 3. The subordinate ratings on SMP discriminated much more significantly than either supervisors' or self-ratings. In fact, no F-values were meaningfully significant for either of the latter two groups. Those that approached or reached statistical significance reflected curvilinear relationships with the Middle group usually lower than the other two and thus providing the discriminating variance.

As in many such field studies, certain anomalies arose in the data-gathering process: Because several managers from a single department participated, it was not possible to sort out direct WEWU values for each one separately. Therefore, all managers within these departments were credited with the same number of WEWUs though it was apparent that their SMP scores varied from one to the other.

Further, and of special significance in this study, the distribution of WEWU's was highly leptokurtic ($g_2 = 14.2$ when 0 fits the normal curve; SMP scales typically were between plus or minus 1.0). In fact, WEWU scores ranged from .845 to 2.23, but 22 of the 64 were squeezed between 1.040 and 1.125, bunched about the median of the distribution. This may not be too surprising because the VA has evolved WEWU standards over time and the departments have become adjusted to working to meet those levels.

This study was repeated a year later after all survey participants had been given feedback on their results and a number of volunteers had participated in a training program based on Managerial Task Cycle skills. In that program, special emphasis was placed on Upward Communications and Participation, Delegation, Reinforcement, and so forth, to attend to those scales whose validity in the pretest was lower than some of the others.

In reviewing the results of this pre-post study it is important to keep the sample sizes clearly in mind. Like many field studies, attrition was a fact of life.

Seventy-two (72) managers participated in the administration of the Survey of Management Practices at the start of the study. Some of these had no subordinates.

Sixty-four (64) out of the 72 had WEWU data available both at the beginning and end of the study.

Twenty-eight (28) of the original 72 participated in the Survey of Management Practices at both the beginning and end.

Thirty-five (35) participated in the training program.

The test-retest reliability of the WEWU criterion was .48 based on the data of the 64.

The multiple correlation (R) between the SMP variables and the WEWU measures for the year prior to administration was .42 which becomes .60 when corrected for attenuation in the criterion (N = 64). On the post-test after one year it was .57 which corrects to .80 (N = 28).

The pattern of significant scales in the first administration is of interest: Clarification of Goals, Orderly Work Planning, Expertise, Work Facilitation, Feedback, Time Emphasis, Control of Details, and Building Trust (1, 3, 4, 5, 6, 7, 8, and 15 in Table 3). If we consider that a one-tailed test is appropriate, then Recognition, Teambuilding, and Interest in Subordinate Growth (11, 13, and 14) join the significant group.

# TABLE 3
## Differences in Subordinate Ratings
## of High, Middle, and Low WEWU Unit Managers

| Dimension | High[1] Mean | SD | Middle[1] Mean | SD | Low[1] Mean | SD | High-Low Diff[2] | F | p-value |
|---|---|---|---|---|---|---|---|---|---|
| **TASK CYCLE PHASE I: MAKING GOALS CLEAR AND IMPORTANT** | | | | | | | | | |
| 1. Clarification of Goals | 63[3] | 16 | 53[3] | 18 | 49[3] | 16 | +14 | 4.00 | .023* |
| **TASK CYCLE PHASE II: PLANNING AND PROBLEM SOLVING** | | | | | | | | | |
| 2. Upward Communications | 64 | 17 | 57 | 18 | 56 | 18 | + 8 | 1.23 | .300 |
| 3. Orderly Planning | 65 | 16 | 55 | 21 | 50 | 18 | +15 | 3.75 | .029* |
| 4. Expertise | 73 | 14 | 63 | 17 | 57 | 14 | +16 | 5.74 | .005* |
| **TASK CYCLE PHASE III: FACILITATING THE WORK OF OTHERS** | | | | | | | | | |
| 5. Work Facilitation | 66 | 16 | 57 | 19 | 51 | 18 | +15 | 3.78 | .028* |
| **TASK CYCLE PHASE IV: OBTAINING AND PROVIDING FEEDBACK** | | | | | | | | | |
| 6. Feedback | 64 | 16 | 53 | 18 | 52 | 15 | +12 | 3.86 | .026* |
| **TASK CYCLE V: MAKING CONTROL ADJUSTMENTS** | | | | | | | | | |
| 7. Time Emphasis | 71 | 12 | 62 | 16 | 57 | 12 | +14 | 6.19 | .004* |
| 8. Control of Details | 52 | 13 | 45 | 14 | 40 | 9 | +12 | 4.93 | .010* |
| 9. Goal Pressure | 39 | 14 | 38 | 11 | 36 | 16 | + 3 | 0.30 | .743 |
| 10. Delegation (Permissiveness) | 65 | 13 | 59 | 13 | 61 | 13 | + 4 | 1.29 | .284 |
| **TASK CYCLE VI: REINFORCING PERFORMANCE** | | | | | | | | | |
| 11. Recognition | 66 | 17 | 57 | 18 | 54 | 21 | +12 | 2.38 | .102 |
| **INTERPERSONAL RELATIONS** | | | | | | | | | |
| 12. Approachability | 69 | 17 | 61 | 19 | 62 | 18 | + 7 | 1.12 | .334 |
| 13. Teambuilding | 65 | 16 | 58 | 19 | 52 | 20 | +13 | 2.87 | .064 |
| 14. Interest in Subs | 63 | 18 | 55 | 19 | 52 | 19 | +11 | 2.37 | .102 |
| 15. Building Trust | 72 | 17 | 62 | 20 | 58 | 18 | +14 | 3.22 | .047* |

[1]N=20 High, 21 Middle, 23 Low.
[2]Diff + = High is above Low; − = vice versa; degrees of freedom: 2,61.
[3]All scores are percent of maximum possible.

*p=.05 or less, two-tailed test.

And the omissions are especially interesting. The four dimensions usually associated with the tone of personal relations—good or bad—are all nonsignificant: Encouraging Upward Communications and Participation, Goal Pressure, Delegation (Permissiveness) and Approachability (2, 9, 10, and 12).

In short, in the pre-feedback/training period, the significant dimensions pertain to structuring the work in a positive supportive way. While they do not imply strong positive tone, neither do they lend a negative note. For example Work Facilitation, Feedback, Expertise, and Building Trust are all very favorable supportive scales in their primary thrust.

In the posttest, the multiple R of .57 included Clarification of Goals and Objectives again but also included Approachability and Teambuilding as the other primary independent variables to this raised multiple. So Shipper's emphasis on what we refer to as the tone of a profile bore results. More on the change in survey scores appears in the following section in Table 4.

*C. Changing Measured Behaviors*

Having demonstrated that the instruments could differentiate skills from which to draw inferences of validity, the next question was that in cell C of Table 2: "Can training change those skills and attributes?"

We have conducted five change studies, four of which are reported here. The fifth was a five-week assessment of the effect of feedback alone in an aerospace company. It resulted in significant positive changes in the experimental group and none in the controls. However, the effect dissipated in about six months in the absence of follow-up training.

The results of the four studies are in Table 4, with the Shipper VA study last in order.

*Study 1. A Multinational Bank (BANK)* Twenty-nine managers at the Director level participated in the Survey of Management Practices (SMP) prior to the first and second weeks of a three-week residential training program, the sessions being six months apart. This presented the opportunity to assess change from feedback and training over a six-month period.

The first week's training consisted of feedback from SMP along with a discussion of the Managerial Task Cycle. Other instruments, such as the Myers-Briggs Type Indicator, were also administered and the results discussed along with their respective rationales. Actual training included instruction on listening and feedback communications, exerting influence, videotaping of interactive sessions in which participants applied feedback and listening principles, and so forth.

*Study 2. A Health-Care Organization (CARE)* This organization manages intermediate term health-care facilities, home health-care services, and so forth, in a midwestern city. An outside consultant, Gene Morton, administered SMP at the beginning of the program and a year later.

Feedback from SMP was given to each of 41 participants, followed by a series of eight half-day training sessions over a two-month period. The training modules, based on the shortfalls identified in the SMP preadministration, covered goal setting, planning and problem solving, coaching, giving feedback, time management, and related topics; all designed to implement Task Cycle concepts. The surveys were readministered the following year.

*Study 3. A nuclear power plant (NUKE)* In this study, understandably, some of the specifics of the data are confidential. The user has made available through the consultant, Daniel Booth, the aggregated composites of SMP administrations one year apart. There were 71 managers rated by 255 subordinates in the first administration and 58 managers rated by 327 subordinates in the second. The training program, in general terms, consisted of modules available in the firm, with emphasis on goal setting, planning, and interpersonal relations. The training sessions were conducted during the first six months of the study period.

*Study 4. The VA Medical Center Study (VAMC)* Because of the shifting numbers of participants in this yearlong study it was not possible to match pre- and post-wave participants to utilize an analysis of variance. Aggregated results from 413 subordinates of the 64 managers from the first administration were compared with 238 ratings of 28 managers in the second.

From these studies it is clear that changes can be effected in managerial practices and that they can endure over a period as long as one year. It is also apparent that there are differences in effect, partly as a consequence of the content and manner of the training.

In CARE, significant changes—some with very substantial F-values—were observed in 14 of the 15 measured dimensions: in VAMC, 13 out of 15; in BANK and NUKE, 9 each. The sole exception in CARE was in Goal Pressure, which was reduced but not as significantly as in BANK, NUKE, and VAMC. However, it is argued in Task Cycle theory that one can exert pressure when necessary as long as the up-front scores are strong. Under those conditions, Interpersonal Relations will not suffer. It is apparent here that the Interpersonal Relations in CARE did not suffer but, instead, were significantly enhanced in training.

The CARE and VAMC studies differed from the others in two important ways: (1) The training was spaced in half-day or full day increments. BANK's was massed in one week. (2) CARE and VAMC training was focused on the Managerial Task Cycle, which underlies the Survey of Management Practices. This could be a case of teaching to the test which may or may not be all bad. So long as the changes from training reflect differences in skills and attributes identified in validity studies, then those changes are on target.

## D. Changes in Productivity

The final evaluation of the effect of the feedback/training program in the VAMC study was made by multiple regression. The independent variables were three:

> *Size of work group.* It was logical to Shipper that the effect of any change in managerial behavior would be more apparent in small groups than in larger ones. And work units varied considerably in size.

> *Prior performance.* These were the pretest WEWU values for control.

# TABLE 4
## Changes in Management Practices Following Training

| Dimension | | PRE[#] Mean | SD | POST[#] Mean | SD | PRE-POST Diff[#]— | F/t-val | p |
|---|---|---|---|---|---|---|---|---|
| **TASK CYCLE PHASE I** | | | | | | | | |
| 1. Clarifying Goals | BANK | 59.7 | 13 | 63.2 | 11 | + 3.5 | F 2.86 | .102 |
| | CARE | 57.4 | 12 | 68.1 | 14 | +10.7 | F 20.05 | .000* |
| | NUKE | 49 | 19 | 54 | 19 | + 5 | t 2.7 | .01* |
| | VAMC | 54 | 24 | 58 | 22 | + 4 | t 2.27 | .05* |
| **TASK CYCLE PHASE II** | | | | | | | | |
| 2. Upward Communications, Participation | BANK | 64.7 | 14 | 70.3 | 11 | + 5.6 | F 6.25 | .019* |
| | CARE | 59.7 | 14 | 70.1 | 15 | +10.4 | F 28.03 | .000* |
| | NUKE | 55 | 20 | 61 | 19 | + 6 | t 3.95 | .001* |
| | VAMC | 57 | 26 | 63 | 23 | + 6 | t 3.20 | .01* |
| 3. Orderly Planning | BANK | 59.9 | 15 | 62.1 | 13 | + 2.2 | F 0.88 | .357 |
| | CARE | 61.8 | 14 | 69.5 | 14 | + 7.7 | F 8.73 | .005* |
| | NUKE | 48 | 19 | 49 | 20 | + 1 | t 0.66 | ns |
| | VAMC | 55 | 25 | 60 | 23 | + 5 | t 2.71 | .01* |
| 4. Expertise | BANK | 61.6 | 12 | 65.6 | 10 | + 4.0 | F 4.32 | .047* |
| | CARE | 66.4 | 13 | 74.8 | 14 | + 8.4 | F 11.97 | .001* |
| | NUKE | 59 | 19 | 61 | 18 | + 2 | t 1.35 | ns |
| | VAMC | 62 | 24 | 67 | 21 | + 5 | t 2.91 | .01* |
| **TASK CYCLE PHASE III** | | | | | | | | |
| 5. Work Facilitation | BANK | 57.5 | 13 | 60.9 | 10 | + 3.4 | F 2.96 | .096 |
| | CARE | 59.9 | 12 | 69.1 | 14 | + 9.2 | F 13.56 | .001* |
| | NUKE | 51 | 19 | 52 | 20 | + 1 | t 0.66 | ns |
| | VAMC | 56 | 25 | 60 | 23 | + 4 | t 2.17 | .05* |
| **TASK CYCLE PHASE IV** | | | | | | | | |
| 6. Feedback | BANK | 58.5 | 13 | 63.7 | 11 | + 5.2 | F 6.67 | .015* |
| | CARE | 59.4 | 12 | 68.4 | 13 | + 9.0 | F 15.41 | .000* |
| | NUKE | 50 | 18 | 53 | 19 | + 3 | t 2.03 | .050* |
| | VAMC | 55 | 25 | 60 | 23 | + 5 | t 2.71 | .01* |
| **TASK CYCLE PHASE V** | | | | | | | | |
| 7. Time Emphasis | BANK | 66.8 | 13 | 64.4 | 13 | − 2.4 | F 1.46 | .237 |
| | CARE | 67.4 | 13 | 72.3 | 11 | + 4.9 | F 4.12 | .049* |
| | NUKE | 62 | 16 | 63 | 16 | + 1 | t 0.73 | ns |
| | VAMC | 64 | 21 | 66 | 19 | + 2 | t 1.30 | ns |
| 8. Control of Details | BANK | 50.7 | 12 | 51.6 | 10 | + 0.9 | F 0.28 | .602 |
| | CARE | 51.9 | 12 | 56.5 | 14 | + 4.6 | F 5.09 | .030* |
| | NUKE | 42 | 16 | 41 | 17 | − 1 | t 0.72 | ns |
| | VAMC | 46 | 21 | 48 | 19 | + 2 | t 1.30 | ns |
| 9. Goal Pressure | BANK | 36.4 | 13 | 31.2 | 14 | − 5.2 | F 10.37 | .003* |
| | CARE | 40.5 | 18 | 37.4 | 16 | − 3.1 | F 1.80 | .187 |
| | NUKE | 40 | 19 | 35 | 19 | − 5 | t 3.36 | .001* |
| | VAMC | 38 | 22 | 33 | 19 | − 5 | t 3.18 | .01* |

*Continued on next page*

**TABLE 4**—*Continued*

| Dimension | | PRE[#] Mean | SD | POST[#] Mean | SD | PRE-POST Diff[#]— | F/t-val | p |
|---|---|---|---|---|---|---|---|---|
| 10. Delegation | BANK | 58.7 | 11 | 61.9 | 9 | + 3.2 | F 3.59 | .069 |
| (Permission) | CARE | 58.6 | 12 | 65.4 | 14 | + 6.8 | F 17.98 | .000* |
| | NUKE | 58 | 17 | 62 | 16 | + 4 | t 3.36 | .001* |
| | VAMC | 59 | 21 | 63 | 18 | + 4 | t 2.68 | .01* |

**TASK CYCLE PHASE VI**

| Dimension | | PRE Mean | SD | POST Mean | SD | Diff | F/t-val | p |
|---|---|---|---|---|---|---|---|---|
| 11. Recognition | BANK | 64.7 | 14 | 70.1 | 12 | + 5.4 | F 7.13 | .013* |
| | CARE | 61.0 | 16 | 70.7 | 16 | + 9.7 | F 13.92 | .001* |
| | NUKE | 55 | 22 | 60 | 22 | + 5 | t 3.10 | .02* |
| | VAMC | 57 | 28 | 64 | 25 | + 7 | t 3.56 | .001* |

**INTERPERSONAL RELATIONS**

| Dimension | | PRE Mean | SD | POST Mean | SD | Diff | F/t-val | p |
|---|---|---|---|---|---|---|---|---|
| 12. Approachability | BANK | 68.2 | 16 | 74.3 | 16 | + 6.1 | F 6.36 | .018* |
| | CARE | 65.3 | 17 | 72.7 | 17 | + 7.4 | F 10.36 | .003* |
| | NUKE | 61 | 24 | 67 | 23 | + 6 | t 3.61 | .001* |
| | VAMC | 62 | 28 | 68 | 25 | + 6 | t 3.05 | .01* |
| 13. Teambuilding | BANK | 60.8 | 13 | 65.8 | 11 | + 5.0 | F 6.08 | .020* |
| | CARE | 63.1 | 13 | 71.6 | 14 | + 8.5 | F 13.88 | .001* |
| | NUKE | 53 | 18 | 57 | 19 | + 4 | t 2.7 | .01* |
| | VAMC | 56 | 25 | 63 | 22 | + 7 | t 3.90 | .001* |
| 14. Interest in | BANK | 59.4 | 13 | 66.7 | 11 | + 7.3 | F 10.52 | .003* |
| Subordinate | CARE | 57.5 | 13 | 68.0 | 15 | +10.5 | F 20.37 | .000* |
| Growth | NUKE | 50 | 19 | 54 | 21 | + 4 | t 2.6 | .01* |
| | VAMC | 54 | 28 | 60 | 24 | + 6 | t 3.02 | .01* |
| 15. Building Trust | BANK | 66.2 | 13 | 70.7 | 12 | + 4.5 | F 4.79 | .037* |
| | CARE | 68.2 | 13 | 75.4 | 13 | + 7.2 | F 9.62 | .004* |
| | NUKE | 60 | 21 | 62 | 20 | + 2 | t 1.28 | ns |
| | VAMC | 61 | 26 | 66 | 23 | + 5 | t 2.67 | .01* |

\# = Scores are percent of maximum possible.
\* = *Significance approaching or bettering .05. Degrees of freedom: BANK=2, 28; CARE=2, 40. In BANK and CARE it was possible to match participants pre and post by averaging scores for individual managers. N=BANK, 29; CARE, 41. In NUKE, pre-post scores are composites of 71 managers rated by 255 subordinates in the first administration and 58 managers rated by 327 subordinates in the second. In VAMC pre-post scores are composites of 64 managers rated by 413 subordinates and 28 rated by 238.*

*Training/No Training.* A dummy variable with the 35 managers who participated in the training versus those who did not.

The total N was 64. The results are shown in Table 4A.

From this we see indications that the training actually produced an increase in productivity. The positive sign on the B-weight for Training indicates that productivity increased more among those who attended the training course after feedback than among those who did not.  The negative signs in the B-weights show that, as unit size increased and as pretest WEWU scores increased, there was less average improvement.

The summary statement is that the correlation between the three variables and productivity as measured by WEWU's was very significant.

---

### TABLE 4A
### Effects of Training on Productivity

| Variable | B | T | P |
|---|---|---|---|
| # of Subordinates | − .00065 | − 3.092 | .0029 |
| Prior Performance | − .38547 | − 5.875 | .0000 |
| Training | + .07891 | + 2.681 | .0092 |

**OVERALL** $\quad$ **n = 64**

| R | $R^2$ | F | P |
|---|---|---|---|
| .67 | .45 | 18.541 | .0000 |

---

It is appropriate to consider the B-weights as multipliers to assess how much difference this increase in productivity could make in terms of savings.  While this exercise is relatively theoretical, it is, at least, a step in the direction our research will go from here on.

Consider that the + .07891 is rounded to .08 and that it represents the amount of savings to be gained from this training.  Considering that there are an estimated 829 affected employees, the net reduction in costs to do the same work if such an increase could be realized would be the equivalent of 66 people (.08 X 829).  At an estimated $35,000 per year for salaries and fringe benefits, a reduction of 66 employees would mean avoiding a cost in excess of $2,300,000 per annum (66 X $35,000).

## The Leadership Replication

Having demonstrated that we could differentiate between levels of managers' performance and change their practices over time, the next step was to try to do the same for leadership.  The instrument is the Survey of Leadership Practices which in its current form (SLP-G) encompasses 24 dimensions. But we start by reporting our first field trial using an earlier form D which assessed 16 dimensions as shown in Table 5.

**A Preliminary Validation of the Survey of Leadership**  This was a pilot study of bank managers in a chain of medium- to small-sized banks.  The chief executive officer (CEO) and President selected 17 managers all of whom they considered to be good managers, but they rated 10 as good leaders and the other 7 with lesser leadership characteristics. The Survey of Leadership Practices (Form D) was answered by the 17 participants about themselves and, in turn, each was rated by the CEO and President and by five to eight subordinates. The data in Table 5 come from the subordinate ratings, but the criterion separation into high and low groups was made jointly by the CEO and President.

From Table 5, it is clear that the CEO and President made their criterion evaluations on the basis of the managers' ability to get things done—a reflection and expansion of Ohio State's Initiating Structure. The subordinates' ratings bear this out in that the most significant differences are on such dimensions as Self-confidence, Modeling, Expectations of Excellence, and Push/Pressure (3, 7, 10, and 12). Risk Taking (2) almost came through but the scales on Vision, Creativity, Resourcefulness, Competence, Mentoring, Caring, Recognition, and Integrity (1, 4, 5, 6, 8, 9, 13, and 14), all with an interpersonal orientation, missed significance, in some cases by a substantial margin. Some of these shortfalls may be ascribed to the state of development of the instrument; others to the environment.

**A Replication of the Survey of Leadership Practices** In this study, Dr. Dennis Cohen of Strategic Management Group (SMG) in Philadelphia, administered Form G in a program for executives in a high-tech company. Each participant was rated by his or her boss, three peers, and three direct reports. The boss's ratings were used to separate them into high and low criterion groups. Table 6 shows the comparison of the peers' ratings of those levels.

In this case, Peers evaluate Leadership in the same general manner as their Superiors: They perceive the highly rated leaders to be higher in Vision/Imagination, Risk Taking/Venturesomeness, Persuasiveness, and Persistence (1, 3, 4, and 9) on the structural side; balanced with good Teaming, Mentoring, Personal Awareness, and Recognition/Reinforcement (6, 8, 10, and 11) on the interpersonal side. The net is high scores on Effectiveness/Outcomes (12) and especially on Integrity and Charisma (15 and 16). And note that they put significantly less reliance on Position or Job Title (19) as a source of influence (French and Raven, 1968), but greater reliance on Technical Competence and Teaming with Other Executives (21 and 23).

All in all, the results are as hypothesized: this instrument is beginning to show the same results as we have experienced with the Survey of Management Practices.

**Operationalizing Leadership** The last entry in Tables 5 and 6 is a Leadership scale embedded in the instrument (alpha reliability .83). It is a capstone scale that serves both internal and external validation purposes, it being extremely difficult to obtain sound performance-based criteria for leadership if we define it as bringing about change for the better. So, we use this dimension as an internal criterion to correlate with other scales to identify which of the measured attributes are most closely related to perceived leadership. Whenever possible, we also correlate it with an external criterion—as we have here with superiors' ratings—to see if that assessment does, indeed, measure something other survey respondents might agree is leadership.

In summary, we are aiming at validating surveys of management and leadership to the fullest extent possible. We have shown that we can identify valid differences

## TABLE 5
## The Leadership Practices of
## High- and Low-Rated Bank Managers

| Dimension | High-[1]<br>Rated<br>Mean | SD | Low-[1]<br>Rated<br>Mean | SD | Diff | Hi-Lo<br>t-val | p-val[2] |
|---|---|---|---|---|---|---|---|
| **PHASE I INITIATIVE** | | | | | | | |
| 1. Vision | 73.5[3] | 14 | 70.5[3] | 15 | + 3.0[4] | 1.02 | .309 |
| 2. Risk Taking | 75.0 | 13 | 79.7 | 14 | + 5.3 | 1.88 | .062 |
| 3. Self-confidence | 84.5 | 12 | 77.6 | 15 | + 6.9 | 2.52 | .013* |
| **PHASE II RESOURCEFULNESS** | | | | | | | |
| 4. Creativity | 65.0 | 15 | 67.8 | 15 | − 2.8 | 0.88 | .383 |
| 5. Resourcefulness | 68.1 | 15 | 67.0 | 15 | + 1.1 | 0.35 | .730 |
| 6. Competence | 75.8 | 15 | 75.0 | 17 | + 0.8 | 0.23 | .819 |
| **PHASE III EXEMPLARY BEHAVIOR** | | | | | | | |
| 7. Modeling | 67.3 | 14 | 57.2 | 11 | + 10.1 | 3.62 | .000* |
| 8. Mentoring | 64.3 | 16 | 60.7 | 19 | + 3.6 | 1.00 | .318 |
| 9. Caring | 61.4 | 22 | 59.3 | 22 | + 2.2 | 0.93 | .353 |
| **PHASE IV MONITORING** | | | | | | | |
| 10. Expectations of Excellence | 79.4 | 12 | 70.4 | 16 | + 9.0 | 3.18 | .002* |
| **PHASE V FOLLOW-THROUGH** | | | | | | | |
| 11. Persuasion | 64.5 | 15 | 60.2 | 15 | + 4.3 | 1.38 | .172 |
| 12. Push/Pressure | 54.9 | 19 | 45.4 | 17 | + 9.5 | 2.50 | .014* |
| **PHASE VI RECOGNITION/REINFORCEMENT** | | | | | | | |
| 13. Recognition | 61.8 | 21 | 59.3 | 22 | + 2.5 | 0.55 | .584 |
| **RESIDUAL IMPACT** | | | | | | | |
| 14. Integrity | 74.5 | 18 | 75.8 | 16 | − 1.3 | 0.35 | .728 |
| 15. Charisma | 68.0 | 17 | 63.5 | 18 | + 4.5 | 1.23 | .220 |
| **LEADERSHIP** | | | | | | | |
| 16. Leadership | 73.9 | 18 | 65.0 | 22 | + 8.9 | 2.12 | .031* |

1=76 ratings of 10 highly regarded Leaders; 33 raters of Lower 7.  2=p-values for a two-tailed test; *p = .05 or better.  3=Scores are in percent of maximum possible. 4=Differences are + if high-rated managers received higher scores on a dimension and vice versa.

# TABLE 6
## Comparison of Peer Ratings of Executives Rated Above or Below Norms on Leadership by Their Bosses

| Phase/Scale | Highs[#] Mean | SD | Lows[#] Mean | SD | Diff | Hi-Lo t-val | p-val |
|---|---|---|---|---|---|---|---|
| **I VISION** | | | | | | | |
| 1. Vision/Imagination | 72 | 15 | 64 | 17 | + 8 | 2.88 | .01 |
| **II INITIATION** | | | | | | | |
| 2. Organizational Sensitivity | 71 | 13 | 70 | 13 | + 1 | ns | |
| 3. Risk Taking/Venturesomeness | 74 | 14 | 66 | 17 | + 8 | 2.96 | .01 |
| **III GAINING COMMITMENT** | | | | | | | |
| 4. Persuasiveness | 70 | 13 | 63 | 15 | + 7 | 2.88 | .01 |
| 5. Expectation of Excellence | 72 | 15 | 68 | 13 | + 4 | 1.65 | ns |
| **IV IMPLEMENTATION** | | | | | | | |
| 6. Teaming | 67 | 15 | 60 | 16 | + 7 | 2.61 | .01 |
| 7. Modeling by Example | 64 | 15 | 61 | 14 | + 3 | 1.20 | ns |
| 8. Mentoring | 69 | 15 | 62 | 15 | + 7 | 2.70 | .01 |
| 9. Persistence | 72 | 12 | 67 | 14 | + 5 | 2.21 | .05 |
| **V FEEDBACK** | | | | | | | |
| 10. Personal Awareness | 68 | 13 | 63 | 14 | + 5 | 2.14 | .05 |
| **VI REINFORCEMENT** | | | | | | | |
| 11. Recognition/Reinforcement | 71 | 17 | 64 | 17 | + 7 | 2.38 | .05 |
| **OUTCOMES** | | | | | | | |
| 12. Effectiveness/Outcomes | 74 | 16 | 66 | 15 | + 8 | 2.99 | .01 |
| **RESIDUAL IMPACT** | | | | | | | |
| 13. Stress Management | 69 | 14 | 69 | 15 | 0 | ns | |
| 14. Push/Pressure | 56 | 18 | 55 | 16 | + 1 | ns | |
| 15. Integrity | 80 | 16 | 72 | 18 | + 8 | 3.28 | .001 |
| 16. Charisma | 71 | 18 | 55 | 18 | + 16 | 6.08 | .001 |
| **SOURCES OF INFLUENCE** | | | | | | | |
| 17. Control of Incentives/Pay | 43 | 22 | 44 | 22 | − 1 | ns | |
| 18. Connections with Influential People | 53 | 25 | 50 | 25 | + 3 | ns | |
| 19. Job Title/Position | 56 | 20 | 64 | 13 | − 8 | 2.76 | .01 |
| 20. Pressure on Subordinates | 45 | 24 | 48 | 19 | − 3 | ns | |
| 21. Technical Competence | 75 | 21 | 67 | 23 | + 8 | 2.10 | .05 |
| 22. Managerial Competence | 68 | 19 | 62 | 21 | + 6 | 1.73 | ns |
| 23. Teaming with Other Executives | 70 | 18 | 60 | 21 | + 10 | 2.95 | .01 |
| 24. Values Compatible with Mine | 71 | 21 | 64 | 23 | + 7 | 1.84 | ns |
| **LEADERSHIP** | | | | | | | |
| 25. Leadership Rating | 70 | 19 | 59 | 17 | + 11 | 3.54 | .001 |

#=Rated above/below norm on Leadership (Variable 25) by superiors;
N=HIGHS=ratings of 30 executives by 69 peers; LOWS=28 by 65 peers.
Scores are percent of maximum possible.

between managerial levels of performance and independent ratings of leadership skills and attributes. We have shown that we can facilitate measurable changes in managerial practices in four studies. Further, we have shown in one study that these changes are accompanied by improvements in productivity. We are pursuing our research plan in the direction of replicating the managerial results with leadership.

# References

Bass, B. M., & Avolio, B. J. (in press). *Manual for the multifactor leadership questionnaire MLQ*. Palo Alto, CA: Consulting Psychologists Press.

Bolles, R. C. (1972). Reinforcement, expectancy, and learning. *Psychological Review, 79,* 394–409.

French, J. R. P., & Raven, B. (1968). The bases for social power. In D. Cartwright & A. Zander (Eds.), *Group dynamics*. New York: Harper & Row.

Gagne, R. M. (1985). *Conditions of learning* (4th ed.). New York: Holt, Rinehart, & Winston.

Gough, H. G. (1987). *Administrator's guide for the California Psychological Inventory*. California: Consulting Psychologists Press.

Hilgard, E. R. (1956). *Theories of learning* (2nd ed.). New York: Appleton Century.

Hilgard, E. R., & Bower, G. H. (1966). *Theories of learning* (3rd ed.). New York: Appleton Century.

McCaulley, M. H. (1990). The Myers-Briggs type indicator. In K. E. Clark & M. B. Clark (Eds.), *Measures of leadership* (pp. 381–418). West Orange, NJ: Leadership Library of America.

Morrison, A. M., McCall, M. W., Jr., & DeVries, D.L. (1978). *Feedback to managers: A comprehensive review of twenty-four instruments*. Greensboro, NC: Center for Creative Leadership.

Posner, B. Z., & Kouzes J. M. (1987). *The leadership challenge: How to get extraordinary things done in organizations*. San Francisco: Jossey-Bass.

Sashkin, M., & Burke, W. W. (1990). Understanding and assessing organizational leadership. In K. E. Clark & M. B. Clark (Eds.), *Measures of leadership* (pp. 297–325). West Orange, NJ: Leadership Library of America.

Skinner, B. F. (1938). *The behavior of organisms: An experimental approach*. Englewood Cliffs, NJ: Prentice-Hall.

Tolman, E. C. (1932). *Purposive behavior in animals and men*. New York: Appleton Century Crofts.

Vroom, V. (1964). *Work and motivation*. New York: Wiley.

Vroom, V. H., & Yetton, P. W. (1973). *Leadership and decision-making*. Pennsylvania: University of Pittsburgh Press.

Wilson, C. L. (1975). Multi-level management surveys: feasibility studies and initial applications. *JSAS: Catalog of selected documents in psychology*, 5, (Ms. No. 1137). Washington, DC: American Psychological Association.

Wilson, C. L. (1978). The Wilson multi-level management surveys: Refinement and replication of the scales. *JSAS: Catalog of selected documents in psychology*, 8, (Ms. No. 1707). Washington, DC: American Psychological Association.

# Leadership Practices: An Alternative to the Psychological Perspective

*Barry Z.
Posner
and
James M.
Kouzes*

A timeworn debate over whether leaders are made or born lies at the heart of a search for the mystical psychological characteristics which separate leaders from the rest of the population. If leaders are born and not made, then the answer to the question "Can leadership be taught?" is moot. Our glib response to this question is that all leaders are definitely born. We have little if any concrete evidence to the contrary. But the only honest answer to this question of whether leaders are made or born must be "no one knows for sure."

We strongly believe, however, that leadership is a skill and like any other talent is distributed normally in the population. Clearly, some individuals have a higher probability of succeeding at leadership than others. But even in the most comprehensive and conscientious longitudinal studies of executive progress (e.g., Bray & Howard, 1983), often more than one-third of those *not* predicted to be were in fact successful as leaders. An alternative perspective on leadership shifts the focus away from the psychological characteristics of leaders themselves to what it is that people (managers, leaders, administrators, salespeople, politicians, homemakers, military officers, priests, scientists, teachers, carpenters, and so on) *do when they are leading.*

A plethora of research studies on leadership has been conducted over the past three decades (see, for example, Bass, 1981). A host of recent books focus on leadership and leaders (e.g., Bass, 1985; Bennis & Nanus, 1985; Bradford & Cohen, 1984; Kotter, 1987; Leavitt, 1986; Levinson & Rosenthal, 1984; Peters & Austin, 1985; Tichy & Devanna, 1986). Currently, the leadership research field is in transition about the essential behaviors of leaders, moving from earlier versions of initiating consideration and structure (Fleishman,

1953) and transactional leaders to what Burns (1978) has referred to as transformational leadership. Still, the field lacks consensus around such issues as what leadership is, how it differs from management, and whether it can be measured or taught.

Leaving aside these important arguments for the moment, there is ample evidence of a viable construct called leadership and attempts to understand and measure this phenomenon are worthwhile. In this paper we present first a brief review of our qualitative efforts to develop a conceptual framework for understanding leadership. Described in more detail are the empirical efforts utilized in developing a reliable and valid instrument to measure this leadership model. *

## Stage One: Qualitative Perspective on What Leaders Do

We asked managers attending a variety of public and contract management development seminars to describe a "personal best as a leader"—an experience in which they got something extraordinary accomplished in an organization. This was their personal best experience as a *leader*. This was an experience in which they felt they had led, not managed, their project to plateaus beyond traditional expectations. These were experiences in which "everything came together."

The personal best survey is 12 pages long and consists of 37 open-ended questions. Several sample questions include: Who initiated the project? What made you believe you could accomplish the results you sought? What special, if any, techniques or strategies did you use to get other people involved in the project? Did you do anything to mark the completion of the project, at the end or along the way? What did you learn most from the experience? What key lessons would you share with another person about leadership from this experience? Completing the personal best survey generally requires about one to two hours of reflection and expression. More than 850 of these surveys have been collected. A short form (one to two pages) of the survey was also developed and has been completed by an additional 450 managers.

In addition to these case studies we conducted 38 in-depth interviews primarily with managers in middle- to senior-level organizational positions in a wide variety of public and private sector companies. These interviews have generally taken 45–60 minutes, but in some cases have lasted four or five hours. The various case studies (from surveys and interview notes) were content analyzed first by the authors and then validated by two separate outside raters. While the category labels have gone through several iterations, the fundamental pattern of leadership behavior which emerges when people are accomplishing extraordinary things in organizations is best described by the following five practices, each of which consists of two basic strategies:

---

* A more complete explanation of the methodology and conceptual framework is available in our book The Leadership Challenge: How to Get Extraordinary Things Done in Organizations (San Francisco, CA: Jossey-Bass, 1987). Similarly, a more extensive psychometric report can be found in "Development and Validation of the Leadership Practices Inventory," Educational and Psychological Measurement (1988), Vol 48: 483–496.

*1) Challenging the Process*
   a. Search for opportunities
   b. Experiment and take risks

*2) Inspiring a Shared Vision*
   a. Envision the future
   b. Enlist the support of others

*3) Enabling Others to Act*
   a. Foster collaboration
   b. Strengthen others

*4) Modeling the Way*
   a. Set the example
   b. Plan small wins

*5) Encouraging the Heart*
   a. Recognize contributions
   b. Celebrate accomplishments

More than 80 percent of the behavior and strategies described in respondents' personal best case studies and interviews can be accounted for by these factors. While there may appear to be a somewhat linear or sequential flow to these practices the actual dynamics are more complex. In the course of personal best experiences individuals are likely to describe an iterative, or developmental, flow to the leadership process. Their cases provided illustrative examples of the dynamic interconnectedness among the various behaviors and strategies.

## Stage Two: Measuring What Leaders Do

The Leadership Practices Inventory (LPI) was designed on the basis of lengthy and repeated feedback from respondents, and factor analyses of various sets of behaviorally based statements. Each statement was cast on a five-point Likert scale. A higher value represented greater use of a leadership behavior: (1) Rarely or never do what is described in the statement, (2) Once in a while do what is described, (3) Sometimes do what is described, (4) Fairly often do what is described, and (5) Very frequently, if not always, do what is described in the statement. Sample statements include: "I seek out challenging opportunities which test my skills and abilities." "I let others know my beliefs on how to best run the organization I manage." "I treat others with dignity and respect."

The LPI was originally completed by 120 MBA students. These students were employed full-time and attending school on a part-time basis at a small private West Coast university. Their average age was 29 years, nearly 60 percent were males, and almost half had supervisory experience. An item-by-item discussion was conducted after the subjects completed the instrument. Difficult, ambiguous, or inconsistent items were either replaced or revised. Feedback discussions with nine professionals in psychology, organizational behavior, and human resource management—familiar with psychometric issues, the conceptual framework, and management development—further refined the inventory.

Successive administrations of the instrument in the early stages of development involved more than 2,100 managers and their subordinates. Analysis of data from these respondents included tests of internal reliability and construct validation through evaluating the underlying factor structure (Kerlinger, 1973). Statements which loaded poorly or on an uninterpretable factor were either discarded or rewritten. Additional discussions with respondents resulted in further modification of the instrument.

The outcome of the above procedures is the current form of the instrument, which contains 30 statements—six statements measuring each of the five leadership practices. There are two forms of the Leadership Practices Inventory—Self and Other—which differ only in whether the behavior described is that of the respondent's (Self) or is the respondent's behavior being described by a third party (Other).

## Sample

The sample for the current version of the Leadership Practices Inventory consists of 2,876 managers and executives involved in several public and in-company management development seminars and their subordinates. For the LPI-Self there are 708 respondents whose backgrounds represent a full array of functional fields from both public and private sector organizations. Twenty-two percent are female. There are approximately three subordinate respondents (LPI-Other) for each managerial subject ($N = 2,168$). A separate sample of foreign managers was also collected, including managers from Australia, England, Germany, and Holland. While no attempts have been made to generate "representative" sample populations of managers, the relatively large total sample size involved increases the potential generalizability of these findings. The .01 level was adopted throughout the analyses as the appropriate level of statistical significance.

Procedurally, individuals completing the LPI-Self also request four to five other people familiar with their behavior to complete the LPI-Other (although in some workshop settings only the LPI-Self is completed). The LPI-Other is voluntary and confidential. The form is returned directly to the researchers (or seminar facilitators). The LPI-Self can be self-scored, but is typically returned directly to the researchers for scoring and feedback purposes.

## Results

**Means, Standard Deviations, and Reliability** Means and standard deviations for each scale of the Leadership Practices Inventory are represented in Table 1, as well as the scores on various reliability measures. Enabling Others to Act was the leadership practice most frequently being used. This was followed by Challenging the Process, Encouraging the Heart, and Modeling the Way. Inspiring a Shared Vision was the leadership practice perceived as least frequently engaged in by managers, although there was the greatest amount of variance associated with this practice.

---

* The Leadership Practices Inventory is available from University Associates (8517 Production Avenue, San Diego, CA 92121). Scholars interested in utilizing the LPI in their research, rather than executive development programs, should contact the authors directly.

# TABLE 1
## Standard Deviations and Reliability Indices
## for the Leadership Practices Inventory

| | Mean | Standard Deviation | INTERNAL RELIABILITY | | | Test-Retest Reliability (N = 57) | Social Desirability (N = 30) |
|---|---|---|---|---|---|---|---|
| | | | LPI (N = 2,876) | LPI-Self (N = 708) | LPI-Other (N = 2,168) | | |
| Challenging the Process | 22.53 | 3.95 | .77 | .73 | .79 | .93 | .13 |
| Inspiring a Shared Vision | 20.01 | 5.04 | .88 | .83 | .89 | .94 | .04 |
| Enabling Others to Act | 23.68 | 4.23 | .84 | .70 | .86 | .94 | .24 |
| Modeling the Way | 22.30 | 4.10 | .80 | .72 | .81 | .95 | .29 |
| Encouraging the Heart | 22.31 | 4.92 | .90 | .84 | .91 | .93 | .27 |

Internal reliabilities on the Leadership Practices Inventory ranged from .77 to .90, with reliabilities ranging from .70 to .84 on the LPI-Self to .81 to .91 on the LPI-Other. Test-retest reliability from a convenience sample of 57 MBA students averaged nearly .94. These students were employed full-time and attending graduate school on a part-time basis. More than 50 percent had supervisory responsibility. Forty percent were women.

Tests for social desirability response bias using the Marlowe-Crowne Personal Reaction Inventory (Crowne & Marlowe, 1960) were also conducted. This scale consists of 33 items representing behaviors that are culturally sanctioned and approved but are improbable of occurrence. The sample involved 30 middle-level managers and none of the correlations were statistically significant.

## Comparisons Between the LPI-Self and LPI-Other

Table 2 presents means and standard deviations for the five leadership practices on the LPI-Self compared with those on the LPI-Other. Frequency scores on the LPI-Self were generally higher ($p < .001$) than those on the LPI-Other for all five practices. The relative rank ordering of the leadership practices on the LPI-Self was identical with the rank ordering on the LPI-Other, and in agreement with the pattern observed in Table 1. The variances for each of the leadership practices were notably greater on the LPI-Other than the LPI-Self. On the LPI-Other there was considerable variance about the Inspiring a Shared Vision practice, closely followed by Encouraging the Heart. This same configuration was found on the LPI-Self. Enabling Others to Act was reported by managers (LPI-Self) to be the practice they engaged in most frequently and there tended to be considerable agreement (low variance) among them. Others, responding about these managers, also reported this practice as most frequently engaged in but there was considerably more disagreement among them. Inspiring a Shared Vision was the

## TABLE 2
## T-Tests of Differences Between Scores
## on the LPI-Self and LPI-Other*

| | LPI-SELF | | LPI-OTHER | |
|---|---|---|---|---|
| | Mean | Standard Deviation | Mean | Standard Deviation |
| Challenging the Process | 23.44 | 3.11 | 22.23 | 4.14 |
| Inspiring a Shared Vision | 21.02 | 4.17 | 19.69 | 5.25 |
| Enabling Others to Act | 25.09 | 2.63 | 23.22 | 4.54 |
| Modeling the Way | 23.04 | 3.16 | 22.05 | 4.34 |
| Encouraging the Heart | 23.30 | 3.87 | 21.99 | 5.18 |

* All two-tailed t-tests were statistically significant (p <.001).

practice both managers and their subordinates felt was least frequently engaged in, although this practice showed the greatest variance on both the LPI-Self and LPI-Other.

**Factor Structure of the LPI** The factor structure of the Leadership Practices Inventory is presented in Table 3. Responses to the 30 leadership behavior items were factor analyzed, using principal factoring with iteration and varimax rotation. The analysis extracted five factors with eigenvalues greater than or equal to 1.0 and accounted for 59.9 percent of the variance. These factors were quite consistent with a priori expectations. The individual item factor loadings were also generally as expected. The stability of the five factors was tested by factor analyzing the data from different subsamples. In each case the factor structure was similar to the one shown in Table 3 which involves the entire sample (N = 2,876).

**Managerial Effectiveness and the Leadership Practices Inventory** In addition to the creation of the Leadership Practices Inventory, a leadership effectiveness scale was developed and included in the investigation with several samples. This measure also went through several iterations in its development. It contained six Likert-type items on five-point scales. The questions asked about the extent to which this manager (the person who requested they complete the LPI) meets the job-related needs of his/her subordinates, has built a committed work group, and has influence with upper management. Additional items gauge the extent to which the respondents are satisfied with the leadership provided by the manager, believe that the manager's leadership practices are appropriate, and feel empowered by the manager. Coefficient alpha for the leadership effectiveness scale was .98. The test-retest reliability over ten days for a sample of 57 MBA students was better than .96. The leader effectiveness scale was found, in a sample involving 30 middle-level managers, not to be significantly correlated with the Marlowe-Crowne social desirability measure.

Utilizing only the responses from the LPI-Other (N = 514), the relationship between a leader's effectiveness and their behavior as measured on the Leadership Practices

## TABLE 3
### Factor Structure (Factor Loadings)
### for the Leadership Practices Inventory
### (N = 2,876)

| Item Number | FACTOR 1 Enabling Others to Act | FACTOR 2 Encouraging the Heart | FACTOR 3 Inspiring a Shared Vision | FACTOR 4 Challenging the Process | FACTOR 5 Modeling the Way |
|---|---|---|---|---|---|
| 8 | .719 | .173 | .096 | .008 | .098 |
| 18 | .694 | .200 | .176 | .088 | .214 |
| 23 | .680 | .198 | .189 | .231 | .273 |
| 13 | .526 | .169 | .092 | .085 | .006 |
| 28 | .509 | .280 | .206 | .195 | .290 |
| 3 | .459 | .208 | .235 | .069 | .256 |
| 5 | .111 | .731 | .220 | .099 | .109 |
| 25 | .152 | .725 | .255 | .143 | .128 |
| 15 | .402 | .689 | .102 | .129 | .113 |
| 20 | .451 | .673 | .163 | .148 | .172 |
| 10 | .400 | .635 | .079 | .154 | .189 |
| 30 | .224 | .532 | .194 | .250 | .240 |
| 7 | .185 | .215 | .709 | .251 | .119 |
| 2 | .156 | .165 | .657 | .276 | .136 |
| 27 | .223 | .255 | .623 | .384 | .239 |
| 17 | .173 | .225 | .615 | .270 | .240 |
| 22 | .223 | .151 | .506 | .362 | .136 |
| 12 | .166 | .114 | .481 | .345 | .107 |
| 16 | .180 | .169 | .266 | .641 | .233 |
| 26 | .164 | .185 | .241 | .637 | .057 |
| 11 | .043 | .082 | .184 | .622 | .145 |
| 1 | .182 | .128 | .219 | .548 | .153 |
| 21 | .354 | .194 | .178 | .473 | .145 |
| 6 | .170 | .049 | .138 | .392 | .173 |
| 29 | .218 | .185 | .144 | .192 | .609 |
| 9 | .343 | .158 | .031 | .107 | .512 |
| 14 | .164 | .164 | .239 | .228 | .509 |
| 4 | .232 | .142 | .353 | .238 | .411 |
| 19 | .109 | .156 | .334 | .315 | .409 |
| 24 | .319 | .120 | .115 | .227 | .372 |

Inventory, was examined. Including only the responses from "other people" about the manager provided relatively independent assessments, thereby minimizing any potential self-report bias. Using stepwise regression analysis the five leadership factors/practices were entered as the independent variables and leader effectiveness as the dependent variable. The results (not shown) revealed a highly significant regression equation ($F = 318.9$, $p < .0001$). The leadership practices model explained nearly 55 percent (adjusted R = .756) of the variance around subordinates' assessments of their leaders' effectiveness.

Another method for examining the validity of the Leadership Practices Inventory is to determine how well LPI scores can differentiate between high- and low-performing managers. This issue was investigated using discriminant analysis as a classification technique. This assessment of predictive validity examined how well the Leadership Practices Inventory could group managers into various performance-based categories.

The lowest third and highest third of the managers on the LPI-Other leader effectiveness scale formed the low- and high-performance categories. Approximately 85 percent of the sample of LPI-Other respondents (N = 325) were used to create the canonical discriminant function with the remaining respondents (N = 54) used to create a holdout sample for classification purposes. One discriminant function was derived. As shown in Table 4, the discriminant function correctly classified 92.62 percent of the known cases. In the holdout sample 77.78 percent of the cases were correctly classified. Both of these results are statistically significant ($p < .001$).

## TABLE 4
## Classification Results from Discriminant Analysis on Effectiveness by Leadership Practices Inventory for Two- and Three-Group Cases

| TWO-GROUP CASE | LOW | HIGH | PERCENTAGE CORRECT |
|---|---|---|---|
| **Known Sample** | | | |
| Actual Members | 169 | 156 | |
| Predicted Members | 154 | 147 | 92.62 |
| **Holdout Sample** | | | |
| Actual Members | 23 | 31 | |
| Predicted Members | 16 | 26 | 77.78 |

| THREE-GROUP CASE | LOW | MODERATE | HIGH | PERCENTAGE CORRECT |
|---|---|---|---|---|
| **Known Sample** | | | | |
| Actual Members | 169 | 108 | 156 | |
| Predicted Members | 123 | 64 | 121 | 71.13 |
| **Holdout Sample** | | | | |
| Actual Members | 23 | 27 | 31 | |
| Predicted Members | 16 | 16 | 23 | 67.90 |

When the middle third of the sample (that is, managers with moderate effectiveness scores) was included, the discriminant functions derived were able to correctly classify 71.13 percent of the cases in the known sample and 67.90 percent in the holdout sample (see Table 4). Both of these percentages are significantly beyond probabilities due to chance ($p < .001$). That scores on the Leadership Practices Inventory are related to managerial (leader) effectiveness is reinforced by the classification results from the discriminant analyses.

## Conclusions

The Leadership Practices Inventory was developed to measure empirically the conceptual framework developed in the case studies of managers' personal best experiences as leaders—times when they had accomplished something extraordinary in an organization. Various analyses suggest that the LPI has sound psychometric properties.

The factor structure of the Leadership Practices Inventory is quite consistent with the a priori conceptual model. The internal reliabilities of the LPI (both Self and Other forms) are substantial. The reliability of the LPI over time seems very good. Finally, the LPI does not seem to be significantly affected by possible social desirability response biases.

There are differences between respondents' self scores and scores provided by others about the respondent (LPI-Self versus LPI-Other). In itself this is not a remarkable finding because this same phenomenon is characteristic of many psychological inventories. Caution, however, should be exercised when interpreting the LPI-Self scores independent of LPI-Other feedback.

For both feedback (self-development) and research purposes the LPI-Other appears to provide relatively reliable and valid assessments of respondent behavior. More than one-half of subordinates' evaluations of their managers' effectiveness can be explained by their perceptions of the managers' behavior along the conceptual framework of the Leadership Practices Inventory. Moreover, significantly better-than-chance predictions about subordinates' assessments of their managers' effectiveness can be made based upon information provided by the LPI. Research is currently under way to investigate how the Leadership Practices Inventory is related to other independent measures of managerial effectiveness.

Returning to the initial question of whether or not leadership can be taught, it is interesting to note that people seldom ask: "Can management be taught?" "Are managers born or made?" These questions are central to debates about leadership, yet are never raised about management. Why should management be viewed as a set of skills and abilities but leadership be seen as a set of innate personality characteristics? It has simply been assumed that management can be taught and on the basis of that assumption hundreds of business schools and thousands of management courses have been established. Certainly some of these managers are better than others. However, on average, the caliber of managerial performance is undoubtedly better today than years ago because of the assumption that people can learn the attitudes, skills, and knowledge associated with good management practice. Why should leadership education and development require a loftier or more genetically based set of assumptions?

Preliminary research utilizing a pre- and posttest administration of the LPI suggests that leadership skills can be taught and/or enhanced. Participants in a week-long leadership development program (conducted by AT&T) showed an average 15 percent increase in leadership behaviors (as measured on the LPI-Other) ten months following the program. Qualitative analyses revealed even more dramatic changes in leadership practices as reported to company officials by both participants and their subordinates. The search continues for specific psychological traits which predict leaders. We suggest, however, that a more fruitful approach is to examine and identify key behaviors of leaders, how these behaviors manifest themselves, and how these practices can be nurtured and developed in people.

## References

Bass, B. M. (1981). *Stogdill's handbook of leadership: A survey of theory and research*. New York: Free Press.

Bass, B. M. (1985). *Leadership and performance beyond expectations*. New York: Free Press.

Bennis, W., & Nanus, B. (1985). *Leaders: The strategies for taking charge*. New York: Harper & Row.

Bradford, D. L., & Cohen, A. R. (1984). *Managing for excellence*. New York: Wiley.

Bray, D. W., & Howard, A. (1983). The AT&T longitudinal studies of managers. In K. W. Schaiel (Ed.), *Longitudinal studies of adult psychological development*. New York: Guilford Press.

Burns, J. M. (1978). *Leadership*. New York: Harper & Row.

Crowne, D. P., & Marlowe, D. (1960). A new scale of social desirability independent of psychopathology. *Journal of Consulting Psychology, 14,* 349–354.

Fleishman, E. A. (1953). The description of supervisory behavior. *Journal of Applied Psychology, 37,* 1–6.

Kerlinger, F. N. (1973). *Foundations of behavioral research* (2nd ed.). New York: Holt, Rinehart, & Winston.

Kotter, J. (1987). *The leadership factor*. New York: Free Press.

Kouzes, J. M., & Posner, B. Z. (1987). *The leadership challenge: How to get extraordinary things done in organizations*. San Francisco, CA: Jossey-Bass.

Leavitt, H. J. (1986). *Corporate pathfinders*. Homewood, IL: Dow Jones–Irwin.

Levinson, H., & Rosenthal, S. (1984). *CEO: Corporate leadership in action*. New York: Basic Books.

Peters, T. J., & Austin, N. (1985). *A passion for excellence*. New York: Random House.

Tichy, N. M., & Devanna, M. A. (1986). *The transformational leader*. New York: Wiley.

# SECTION D

## Measures of Leader and Manager Behavior

# Measures of Leader and Manager Behavior

By developing psychological measures of behavior, a score can be provided for each person which reflects differences that can be studied. Important characteristics of organizational behavior or performance can then be related to these scores. Several such measures are described in this section. The rationale behind their development and the relationship of the scores to effectiveness in leading or managing are also reported.

## Preliminary Report on Validation of The Managerial Practices Survey

Gary Yukl, Steve Wall, and Richard Lepsinger

The Managerial Practices Survey (MPS) measures categories of managerial behavior that are relevant to managerial effectiveness and are applicable to all types of managers. Developed over a period of 12 years from research involving over 2,000 managers, it has been tested with employees in a variety of managerial positions and organizations. Information on reliability and validity of the MPS scales is presented. Criterion-related validity is presented for managers of beauty salons, military cadets, insurance sales managers, elementary school principals, home economics program leaders, and department heads in high schools.

Gary Yukl, Professor of Management, Management Department, School of Business, State University of New York at Albany, 1400 Washington Avenue, Albany, New York 12222. (518-442-4932). PhD, University of California, Berkeley. Member of Editorial Board of *Journal of Applied Psychology*. Fellow of American Psychological Association Division 14. Consulting Editor for *Academy of Management Review*. Author of *Leadership in Organizations* and *Skills for Managers and Leaders* (in press).

Steve Wall, President, Manus Associates, 175 Fifth Avenue, Suite 712, New York, New York 10010. (212-475-0404). MS, New York University. Author of various articles in *The International Strategy Yearbook, Issues and Observa-*

*tions,* and *Society of Trainers and Educators Journal,* and a chapter in *The Practice of Management Development.*

Richard Lepsinger, Vice President, Manus Associates, 175 Fifth Avenue, Suite 712, New York, New York 10010. (212-475-0404). MS, University of Southern California; MA, State University of New York at New Paltz. Coauthor of article in *Society of Insurance Trainers and Educators Journal* and chapters in *The Practice of Management Development* and *Applying Psychology in Business.*

## Psychological Orientations and Leadership: Thinking Styles That Differentiate Between Effective and Ineffective Managers
Peter D. Gratzinger, Ronald A. Warren, and Robert A. Cooke

Management style descriptors obtained from managers' self-ratings are used to predict actual effectiveness of managers as perceived by their co-workers. Three major orientations of life-style are identified by factor analysis: (1) a people/security orientation, (2) a satisfaction orientation, and (3) a task/security orientation. Effectiveness ratings by peers, subordinates, and superiors are compared with scores obtained on the Life Styles Inventory.

Peter Gratzinger, Research Psychologist, Human Factors Advanced Technology Group, 4340 Redwood Highway, Suite 26, San Rafael, California 94903. (415-492-9190). PhD, Charles University, Prague, Czechoslovakia. Coauthor of ACUMEN products. Engaged in research on personality and cognitive training at Stanford University.

Ronald A. Warren, Director of Research and Development, Human Factors Advanced Technology Group, 4340 Redwood Highway, Suite 26, San Rafael, California 94903. (415-492-9190). PhD, University of Chicago. Principal author of ACUMEN products. Engaged in research on high-performance practices and team communication.

Robert A. Cooke, Assistant Professor of Management, Department of Management, College of Business Administration, University of Illinois at Chicago, Chicago, Illinois 60680. (312-996-3000). PhD, Northwestern University. Author of various published works and several instruments. Consultant with corporations and government agencies.

## The Campbell Work Orientations Surveys: Their Use to Capture the Characteristics of Leaders
David Campbell

The Campbell Work Orientations Survey includes four psychological assessment inventories designed to reflect an individual's orientation toward work, with particular emphasis on leadership and creativity. The four sections cover interests, skills, leadership potential (self versus observer), and an organization survey. The steps in the development and perfection of each section, and of obtaining adequate interpretative material, are described, with illustrations of uses to date.

David Campbell, Smith Richardson Senior Fellow, Center for Creative Leadership, Post Office Box 1559, Colorado Springs, Colorado 80901. (719-633-3891). PhD, University of Minnesota. Past Distinguished Visiting Professor, U.S. Air Force Academy, Colorado Springs, Colorado. Recipient of E. K. Strong, Jr. Gold Medal for excellence in psychological testing research. Author of the Campbell Work Orientations. Coauthor of the Strong-Campbell Interest Inventory. Author of various works, including *If You Don't Know Where You're Going, You'll Probably End Up Somewhere Else*; *Take the Road to Creativity and Get Off Your Dead End*; and *If I'm in Charge Here, Why Is Everybody Laughing?*

# Preliminary Report on Validation of The Managerial Practices Survey

*Gary Yukl*
*Steve Wall*
*and*
*Richard*
*Lepsinger*

Research and theory on managerial effectiveness are highly dependent upon the concepts used to describe managerial behavior and the methods used to measure this behavior. Progress in learning about effective manager behavior has been slowed by a proliferation of behavior concepts and a lack of accurate measures of these concepts. In most cases, the behavior concepts have been measured by a questionnaire constructed hastily without the slow and tedious research needed to properly validate this type of measuring device.

In 1975, a program of research was initiated to identify and measure categories of managerial behavior important for managerial effectiveness. This research program used a variety of research methods, including diaries, critical incidents, interviews, and questionnaires. On the conceptual side, the research led to the formulation of a taxonomy with 11 primary categories of managerial behavior (Yukl, 1987). At the same time, a new questionnaire was developed to measure the managerial behaviors. Initially called the Managerial Behavior Survey, the most recent versions of this questionnaire are called the Managerial Practices Survey (MPS). The purpose of this paper is to describe how the behavior categories were formulated and to present results of research conducted to validate the questionnaire.

**Early Developmental Research** The early research relied mostly upon factor analysis of questionnaire items to identify behavior categories. In a preliminary report of the factor analysis research, Yukl and Nemeroff (1979) found support for 14 categories of managerial behavior. As the research progressed, scales were refined and items measuring other aspects of managerial behavior were added. The number of behavior categories continued to increase and, by 1981, there were 22 behaviors with corresponding orthogonal factors in two or more studies. However, several of the factors accounted for only a small amount of common factor variance, and overlap in content was evident for some factors, despite the use of orthogonal rotation. Additional factor analyses, including higher-order analyses of scale scores and hierarchical analyses of item scores, failed to provide a stable solution across samples for a more parsimonious taxonomy. It became obvious that development of a meaningful and parsimonious taxonomy would require a variety of approaches in addition to factor analysis.

**Identification of Behavior Categories** Since 1981, other approaches have been used to supplement factor analysis in identifying behavior categories and selecting questionnaire scales. One approach was the use of judges to sort behaviors into categories on the basis of common purpose of the behavior. This approach allows some aspects of behavior to appear in the same category, even though they are not necessarily intercorrelated highly with respect to frequency of use. Another approach involved testing categories by using them to code behavior descriptions from diaries and critical incidents (e.g., Yukl & Clemence, 1984; Yukl & Van Fleet, 1982). This approach considered the extent of overlap between pairs of categories, the extent of interjudge agreement in coding incidents into each category, and the extent to which a behavior category had observable examples of the behavior. If there was substantial overlap with another category in coding incidents, if there was low agreement between judges in coding incidents into a category, or if a category lacked observable examples, then the category was eliminated or redefined.

Another consideration was continuity with behavior categories found in three decades of literature on leadership and managerial effectiveness. Prior research and theory provide clues about potentially important aspects of managerial behavior that should be included in a comprehensive taxonomy. The comparison with earlier research provided a good basis for resolving some inconsistencies stemming from the other forms of analysis. A major objective was to develop a behavior taxonomy that would integrate the major earlier ones, including taxonomies describing managerial behavior (e.g., Morse & Wagner, 1978), taxonomies describing leader behavior (e.g., Stogdill, 1963), taxonomies describing observed managerial activities (e.g., Mintzberg, 1973; Luthans & Lockwood, 1984), and taxonomies describing behavioral position responsibilities (e.g., Page, 1985; Tornow & Pinto, 1976).

The determination of category width and number of categories in a behavior taxonomy is highly arbitrary; different theorists have different perspectives about the "correct" categories, even when empirical methods such as factor analysis and multidimensional scaling are used. Two criteria used for the current taxonomy were parsimony and a middle level of generality. We tried to keep the taxonomy as parsimonious as possible, which is the reason for collapsing some narrow categories into more general ones. We also tried to have categories that are general enough to be applicable to most leaders but specific enough to be relevant for assessing how well a leader copes with situational role requirements. Finally, as noted later, generalizability to external as well as internal contexts was desired for the behavior categories. That is, we sought to identify categories of behavior that are important for interactions with peers, superiors, and outsiders in addition to subordinates. However, we did not expect all of the elements of a category to be relevant to all contexts. In the questionnaire, some subcategories are dealt with separately because they have a special importance for interactions with subordinates but little relevance for interactions with peers and superiors.

## Description of the Questionnaire

The 1982 version of the MBS had 115 items grouped into 23 scales. The 1986 version of the MPS had 110 items grouped into 13 scales. In addition to collapsing some scales into broader ones, the wording of items was changed from group-oriented wording ("praises subordinates for...") to dyadic wording (e.g., "praise me for...") in order to reduce ambiguity and to make the questionnaire more suitable for research on dyadic relationships. The 1988 version of the MPS has 110 items grouped into 11 major scales plus 3 supplementary scales. A major change between the 1986 and 1988 versions was to modify the wording of items to make them suitable for use by peers as well as subordinates. Moreover, the wording of some items that were focused on supervisors was changed to make them suitable for describing the behavior of managers at all levels, including executives. The supplementary scales (Delegating, Rewarding, Mentoring) are used for two reasons. First, factor analyses on the MPS, including the latest factor analysis of 1,049 subordinates who used the 1986 version to describe their managers, find a separate orthogonal factor corresponding to each of the 14 scales in the current version of the questionnaire. Second, the supplementary scales involve managerial behavior that applies mostly to subordinates rather than peers. In order to make the questionnaire suitable for use with peers as well as subordinates, aspects of managerial behavior that apply mostly to subordinates were put into supplementary scales that are used only by subordinates. However, conceptually, each of the narrowly defined supplementary scales is considered to be an element of a broader category in Yukl's (1989) taxonomy of midrange managerial behaviors. The behavior categories are labeled and defined in Table 1. Note that rewarding is a part of a more general category of positive reinforcement (Recognizing and Rewarding), delegating is part of a more general category of participative leadership (Consulting and Delegating), and mentoring is part of a broader category of supportive-considerate leadership (Supporting and Mentoring).

---

**TABLE 1**
**Definitions of the Eleven Managerial Practices**

- **INFORMING:** disseminating relevant information about decisions, plans, activities to people that need it to do their work; answering requests for technical information; and telling people about the organizational unit to promote its reputation.

- **CONSULTING AND DELEGATING:** checking with people before making changes that affect them, encouraging suggestions for improvement, inviting participation in decision making, incorporating the ideas and suggestions of others in decisions, and allowing others to have substantial responsibility and discretion in carrying out work activities and making decisions.

- **PLANNING AND ORGANIZING:** determining long-term objectives and strategies for adapting to environmental change, determining how to use personnel and allocate resources to accomplish objectives, determining how to improve the efficiency

---

of operations, and determining how to achieve coordination with other parts of the organization.

- **PROBLEM SOLVING:** identifying work-related problems, analyzing problems in a timely but systematic manner to identify causes and find solutions, and acting decisively to implement solutions and resolve important problems or crises.

- **CLARIFYING ROLES AND OBJECTIVES:** assigning tasks, providing direction in how to do the work, and communicating a clear understanding of job responsibilities, task objectives, deadlines, and performance expectations.

- **MONITORING OPERATIONS AND ENVIRONMENT:** gathering information about work activities, checking on the progress and quality of the work, evaluating the performance of individuals and the organizational unit, and scanning the environment to detect threats and opportunities.

- **MOTIVATING:** using influence techniques that appeal to emotion, values, or logic to generate enthusiasm for the work; commitment to task objectives; and compliance with requests for cooperation, assistance, support, or resources; also setting an example of proper behavior.

- **RECOGNIZING AND REWARDING:** providing praise, recognition, and rewards for effective performance, significant achievements, and special contributions.

- **SUPPORTING AND MENTORING:** acting friendly and considerate, being patient and helpful, showing sympathy and support, and doing things to facilitate someone's skill development and career advancement.

- **MANAGING CONFLICT AND TEAM BUILDING:** encouraging and facilitating the constructive resolution of conflict, and encouraging cooperation, teamwork, and identification with the organizational unit.

- **NETWORKING:** socializing informally; developing contacts with people who are a source of information and support; maintaining contacts through periodic interaction, including visits, telephone calls, correspondence, and attendance at meetings and social events.

---

Each item in the 1986 and 1988 versions of the MPS has the following six response choices:

|     |                               |
| --- | ----------------------------- |
| 1   | Never, Not at All             |
| 2   | Seldom, To a Limited Extent   |
| 3   | Sometimes, To a Moderate Extent |
| 4   | Usually, To a Great Extent    |
| NA  | Not Applicable                |
| ?   | Don't Know                    |

---

Various alternative response formats were tested during the 12 years of research on the questionnaire, including formats with three, four, five, and six graduated choices, and variations of the extra choices such as "Don't Know" and "Not Applicable." Supplemental research on response accuracy for different formats indicated that discrimination was poor for formats with as few as three choices. On the other hand, feedback was confusing for formats with many choices. We compromised on the current format, which appeared to offer a good balance on these trade-offs. When scale scores are computed, the Not Applicable and Don't Know responses are recorded as a "1" response, because these responses indicate absence of the behavior. However, for item feedback, the frequency of use for each response is shown, including respondent use of the extra choices.

# Results

The remainder of this paper describes the principal studies conducted during the past few years to assess the meaningfulness, validity, and reliability of the behavior scales.

**Content Validity** One test of the content validity of the scales in the MPS is the extent to which items are seen as defining examples of the behaviors. This test was carried out several times, and most of the data were collected by Tom Taber and Cecilia Falbe.

The first study was conducted in 1984. A panel of 32 MBA students served as judges. They were given all of the items on separate slips of paper, then asked to classify each item into the appropriate behavior category based on the definitions of the categories which were also provided. The results are shown in Table 2. The numbers represent the mean coding accuracy across the seven to nine items defining a scale. As shown in the table, coding accuracy was relatively high for all of the scales, indicating that the defining items were viewed as representative examples of the appropriate behavior categories by the judges.

## TABLE 2
## Mean Correct Classification of Defining Examples

| Managerial Behavior | 1984 Study | 1985 Study | 1986 Study | 1988 Study |
|---|---|---|---|---|
| Informing | 96% | 86% | 92% | 84% |
| Consulting & Delegating | 88% | 91% | 91% | 82% |
| Planning & Organizing | 87% | 91% | 91% | 82% |
| Problem Solving | 91% | 90% | 91% | 85% |
| Clarifying | 85% | 79% | 86% | 87% |
| Monitoring | 96% | 94% | 92% | 89% |
| Motivating | 81% | 82% | 81% | 72% |
| Recognizing & Rewarding | 86% | 95% | 94% | 95% |
| Supporting | 85% | 91% | 85% | 89% |
| Mentoring/Developing | 89% | 91% | 88% | NI |
| Conflict Mgt. & Team Bldg. | 91% | 89% | 86% | 73% |
| Representing | 94% | 86% | 84% | NI |
| Networking/Interfacing | NI | 87% | 86% | 87% |
| **Number of Judges** | **32** | **24** | **36** | **41** |

*Note: NI indicates the scale was not included in a study.*

A second study was conducted in 1985 using a variation of the initial approach. Instead of having defining items on separate slips of paper, the items were put in random order and judges were asked to indicate for each item the behavior category it best represented. There were eight to nine items for each scale. The sample of judges consisted of 24 MBA students. Coding accuracy was measured in terms of percentage of judges who accurately coded the item, averaged across the items in a scale. As before, the accuracy index was quite good for all of the behavior scales, as well as for most of the individual items within scales.

In 1986, a third study was conducted with 36 MBA students and undergraduates serving as judges. The method was similar to the one used in the second study. The purpose of the replication was to check on the effects of making minor changes in item wording and category definitions. The definitions were shortened and less information was provided about the category content. Coding accuracy was measured as before. Once again, the behavior examples were correctly assigned to their respective behavior categories by most of the judges.

In 1988, another study was conducted to assess coding accuracy for the new and revised items and the newly defined categories in the 11-category taxonomy. The judges were 41 undergraduates in a course in organizational behavior. The method was the same as in the third study. The results show that accuracy of classification was a little lower for most scales, although still good for untrained judges. The change in results may be due to use of broader categories with a wider range of examples, or perhaps it was due to the use of undergraduates without work experience instead of MBA students.

**Relevance** The behaviors in the new taxonomy are assumed to be relevant for managerial effectiveness. One test of relevance is to ask managers to rate the importance of each defining behavior in a category. Three studies of importance were conducted, and most of the data were collected by Steve Wall and Rick Lepsinger.

In a study conducted in 1984, respondents rated the importance of each behavior for doing the job of the manager being described. The questionnaire was administered to 24 managers and 130 of their subordinates. Half of the respondents were employed in a large multinational chemicals company and half were employed in a health-care insurance company. Respondents were asked to rate importance on a four-point scale with the following four choices: 1 = Not Relevant, 2 = Slightly Important, 3 = Moderately Important, 4 = Very Important. The ratings for an item were averaged within the manager sample; then the item means were averaged across the items in a scale to obtain a mean rating of item importance for each scale. This procedure was repeated for the sample of subordinates. The results are shown in Table 3, and it is evident that the defining examples of the behaviors were perceived to be quite relevant for the manager's job, especially by the managers themselves.

Another way of assessing relevance is to ask managers to rate the importance of a behavior category rather than to rate the importance of individual items. In 1985, a sample of 119 managers from several private- and public-sector organizations was given the 13 category definitions and asked to rate how important each behavior was for effective performance of their managerial job. Ratings were made on a five-point scale, with the following rating choices: 1 = Not Relevant, 2 = Slightly Important, 3 = Moderately Important, 4 = Very Important, 5 = Absolutely Essential. The frequency of 4 and 5 ratings for a behavior category was compared to the frequency of 1 or 2 ratings for the same category. The results are shown in Table 3. Each of the 13 behaviors was viewed by a large percentage of the managers as very important or essential for effective performance of their managerial jobs.

## TABLE 3
## Perceived Importance of Managerial Behaviors

| Behavior | 1984 STUDY Mean Item Rating By: | | 1985 STUDY | | 1987 STUDY Mean Scale Rating By: | |
|---|---|---|---|---|---|---|
| | Mgr. | Subord. | % Mgrs. Rating 4 or 5 | % Mgrs. Rating 1 or 2 | Mgr. | Boss |
| Informing | 3.3 | 3.2 | 96% | 2% | 4.6 | 4.4 |
| Consulting & Delegating | 3.4 | 3.2 | 87% | 2% | 4.0 | 3.9 |
| Planning & Organizing | 3.3 | 3.2 | 82% | 2% | 4.1 | 4.0 |
| Problem Solving | 3.6 | 3.4 | 87% | 2% | 4.2 | 4.2 |
| Clarifying | 3.4 | 3.2 | 82% | 2% | 4.1 | 4.2 |
| Monitoring | 3.3 | 3.0 | 77% | 3% | 3.8 | 3.8 |
| Motivating | 3.2 | 2.9 | 73% | 4% | 4.1 | 4.3 |
| Recognizing & Rewarding | 3.3 | 3.0 | 84% | 2% | 3.9 | 3.7 |
| Supporting | 3.5 | 3.2 | 78% | 2% | 3.9 | 3.6 |
| Developing/Mentoring | 3.2 | 3.0 | 79% | 6% | 3.9 | 3.9 |
| Conflict Mgt. & Team Bldg | 3.2 | 2.9 | 84% | 1% | 3.9 | 4.2 |
| Representing | 3.3 | 3.3 | 80% | 2% | 4.0 | 3.8 |
| Networking/Interfacing | 3.0 | 2.9 | 78% | 7% | 4.0 | 4.0 |
| **Sample Size** | **24** | **130** | **119** | | **135** | **126** |

*Note: Rating choices in 1984 Study ranged from 1 ("not relevant") to 4 ("very important"). Rating choices in l985 and l987 studies ranged from 1 ("not relevant") to 5 ("absolutely essential").*

The 1986 version of the MPS has a separate questionnaire for rating the importance of the 13 behaviors included in this version. The questionnaire is administered to managers themselves and to each manager's boss. Both respondents rate the importance of each behavior category (based on the category definitions) for effective performance of the manager's job. Ratings are made on a five-point scale with the same response choices described for the preceding study. Mean importance ratings are shown in Table 3 for managers in a variety of business organizations participating in feedback workshops conducted by Manus Associates. Each behavior category was rated at least moderately important, and most were rated very important.

**Internal Consistency** Internal consistency is the degree of intercorrelation among the items in a scale. A high value means that managers tend to use the behaviors defining a scale to the same extent. High internal consistency is evidence that the scale is measuring a category of interrelated behaviors. Although it is not necessary for all of the defining examples within a behavior category to be highly intercorrelated, it is reasonable to expect that an item will correlate more with the items in its own category than with items in other categories. This condition is unlikely to occur unless the items in a scale have at least moderate internal consistency.

Internal consistency was computed separately for managerial behavior descriptions from three samples of subordinates. Most of the data were collected by Steve Wall and

## TABLE 4
## Internal Consistency for MPS Scales

| Managerial Behavior | Sample 1 | Sample 2 | Sample 3 | Sample 4 |
|---|---|---|---|---|
| Informing | .84 | .80 | .83 | .84 |
| Consulting & Delegating | .86 | .86 | .87 | .88 |
| Planning & Organizing | .90 | .86 | .88 | .85 |
| Problem Solving | .93 | .84 | .88 | .86 |
| Clarifying | .88 | .81 | .86 | .86 |
| Monitoring | .88 | .80 | .83 | .87 |
| Motivating | .90 | .87 | .90 | .90 |
| Recognizing & Rewarding | .92 | .86 | .90 | .84 |
| Supporting | .90 | .89 | .89 | .90 |
| Developing/Mentoring | .93 | .87 | .90 | .91 |
| Conflict Mgt. & Team Bldg. | .91 | .85 | .90 | .90 |
| Representing | .90 | .87 | .89 | .88 |
| Networking/Interfacing | .87 | .84 | .87 | .84 |
| **Sample Size** | **132** | **76** | **124** | **1,173** |

*Note: The index for internal consistency was Cronbach's alpha.*
*Sample 4 includes samples 1 and 2.*

Rick Lepsinger. The first sample consisted of 132 subordinates of middle managers in a large medical health insurance company, the second sample consisted of 76 subordinates of middle managers in a large chemical company, and the third sample consisted of 124 subordinates of Air Force maintenance supervisors at several bases around the United States. The results are shown in Table 4, and it is evident that internal consistency was very high for all of the scales. Also shown in Table 4 is the internal consistency computed for a composite sample of the 1,173 managers in several organizations who used the 1986 version of the MPS. This sample includes managers in samples 1 and 2. Again, internal consistency was quite high.

**Stability** Additional evidence for construct validity is provided by demonstrating stable measurement of a behavior over a time interval in which the behavior is expected to be the same. The stability of the MPS scales was tested by administering the questionnaire to the same sample of subordinates on two different occasions and correlating each scale score on the first administration with the corresponding scale score on the second administration. Three studies of this type were conducted using different time intervals. In each study, the subordinates were night MBA students with regular jobs during the day. The time interval between administrations was three weeks in the first study, six weeks in the second study, and four weeks in the third study. In the first study, the questionnaire had a four-choice response format. In the other two studies, the questionnaire had the current six-choice format. The results are shown in Table 5. Stability was satisfactory for all of the scales, although not as high as desired for a few scales. This test is currently being repeated for the 1988 version.

# TABLE 5
## Retest Stability for MPS Scales

| Managerial Behavior | 1984 Study | 1985 Study | 1986 Study |
|---|---|---|---|
| Informing | .67 | .84 | .76 |
| Consulting & Delegating | .81 | .63 | .66 |
| Planning & Organizing | .61 | .67 | .78 |
| Problem Solving | .79 | .58 | .79 |
| Clarifying | .80 | .79 | .75 |
| Monitoring | .71 | .81 | .61 |
| Motivating | .78 | .75 | .86 |
| Recognizing & Rewarding | .82 | .74 | .80 |
| Supporting | .94 | .91 | .75 |
| Developing/Mentoring | .75 | .70 | .64 |
| Conflict Mgt. & Team Bldg. | .78 | .86 | .86 |
| Representing | .81 | .73 | .65 |
| Networking/Interfacing | .67 | .65 | .48 |
| | | | |
| **Sample Size** | **36** | **24** | **42** |

*Note: The index for stability was Pearson r, with measurement repeated over a time interval of three weeks in the 1984 study, six weeks in the 1985 study, four weeks in the 1986 study.*

**Interrater Reliability** It is reasonable to assume that descriptions of a manager's behavior provided by different subordinates should be similar if a manager treats each subordinate the same way in dyadic interactions, and if each subordinate has an adequate opportunity to observe nondyadic behavior (e.g., planning). For behaviors defined at a middle level of abstraction there should be a moderate level of agreement among subordinates. However, perfect agreement is not expected, since there is likely to be some differential treatment of subordinates by a manager, and subordinates are likely to differ somewhat in their opportunity to observe a manager doing nondyadic behaviors.

Two alternative indices of interrater agreement were computed for 50 groups of subordinates having at least four subordinates describing the same manager. The leaders described by the subordinates included 22 middle managers in a large medical insurance company, 16 middle managers in a large chemical company, 7 middle-level administrators in a municipal housing authority, and 5 managers of real estate offices. Data were collected on the first three samples by Rick Lepsinger and Steve Wall, and data on the fourth sample were provided by David Van Fleet. A one-way analysis of variance was computed on each scale score for the 50 groups. The F-tests were significant at the .01 level for each of the 13 scales. These results indicate that the within-group variance in ratings of a behavior was smaller than the between-group variance. In other words, the managers differed in their behavior, and there was enough agreement among subordinates to detect this difference. The proportion of variance in

# TABLE 6
## Agreement Among Subordinates
## Describing the Same Manager

| Managerial Behavior | Eta | Intraclass Correlation |
|---|---|---|
| Informing | .49 | .63 |
| Consulting & Delegating | .48 | .61 |
| Planning & Organizing | .48 | .62 |
| Problem Solving | .43 | .55 |
| Clarifying | .56 | .71 |
| Monitoring | .52 | .67 |
| Motivating | .65 | .72 |
| Recognizing & Rewarding | .52 | .66 |
| Supporting | .56 | .71 |
| Developing/Mentoring | .57 | .72 |
| Conflict Mgt. & Team Bldg. | .43 | .55 |
| Representing | .50 | .64 |
| Networking/Interfacing | .70 | .56 |

**Sample Size**          **50 groups/261 subordinates**

*Note: All F values for the one-way ANOVA were significant at .01 level. The index of interrate reliability is the intraclass correlation coefficient (ICC) for group means.*

behavior descriptions (scale means) accounted for by managers was determined by computing eta squared for each F-test, and the eta squared values were converted to eta values (shown in Table 6).

An alternate index for interrater agreement is the intraclass correlation coefficient. Based on the article by Shrout and Fleiss (1979), the ICC coefficient selected was the one for group means showing the extent to which the mean rating by one group of raters is similar to the mean rating made by another group of raters of the same size. Results for this ICC coefficient are also shown in Table 6. In general, the results for both omega and ICC indicated moderate levels of interrater agreement for all of the behaviors. The amount of agreement is at least as high as that found in earlier research on retrospective behavior descriptions obtained from subordinates or peers.

The 1988 version will permit an analysis of interrater agreement between subordinates and peers. Research is under way to examine this question and to assess the agreement between subordinate descriptions and leader self-reported behavior.

**Discrimination of Contrasted Groups** Measurement accuracy is indicated by significant differences in behavior between samples of managers expected to behave differently due to the influence of situational demands and constraints. Except where differences in behavior across situations have been established previously with another type of behavior measure, this test is only as good as the assumption that the situation will affect manager behavior in the manner predicted. Absence of a significant difference may be due to an incorrect hypothesis rather than to lack of accurate measurement. Nevertheless, finding behavior differences where they have been predicted in advance is considered useful evidence for the validity of the measure, as well as for the validity of the hypothesis. Preliminary supporting evidence on the capacity of several MBS scales to discriminate contrasting groups was presented in a paper by Yukl and Carrier (1986). A more comprehensive study of this type is now in progress.

**Criterion-related Validity** In the final analysis, the most important indicator of utility is the capacity of a measure to predict and explain managerial effectiveness. This type of study is one of the most difficult to conduct due to the problems in finding a set of similar leaders with a comparable and dependable criterion of unit effectiveness. Several studies have been conducted on the criterion-related validity of the MPS and earlier MBS with a variety of different criteria of leader effectiveness. We will report only the results for research with an independent criterion of leader effectiveness. Results for studies with subjective same-source criteria (e.g., subordinate satisfaction and role clarity, subordinate ratings of leader effectiveness) will not be reported because the correlations are inflated by a variety of artifacts and are not very dependable.

The first analysis of criterion-related validity was a study conducted by Yukl and Kanuk (1979) on 26 beauty salon managers, using a very early version of the questionnaire that did not include some of the current scales. The study is reported here because the questionnaire still includes many items similar to the ones used in that version, and because the study had an objective criterion of managerial effectiveness. Subordinates who filled out the questionnaire were 151 employees in the salons. There were multiple performance criteria, but results are only reported here for one of the objective criteria, namely average monthly profit margin during the year following the administration of the questionnaire. Correlations between scale scores computed at the group level (i.e., averaging across a leader's multiple subordinates) and profit margin for the salon are shown in Table 7. In spite of the weaker power for such a small sample, results were quite good.

The second study was conducted with military cadets at Texas A & M University by Yukl and Van Fleet (1982). The leaders were 42 first sergeants. The questionnaire was filled out by subordinates who were cadets of lower rank in each sergeant's unit. A total of 393 usable questionnaires were returned. The criterion was a composite rating by observers of unit performance in marching competition. As in the first study, this early version of the questionnaire did not include all of the current scales. Correlations between group level scale scores and unit performance ratings are shown in Table 7. The correlations were generally lower, but considering how weak the criterion was and the part-time nature of the leadership position, the results were encouraging.

The third study was conducted by Gary Yukl and Maurice Cayer on 26 managers of insurance salespersons who work in retail department stores in one of the largest department store chains in the United States. Having insurance sales centers in the stores was a new development for this chain and most of the centers had been in existence less than two years. This study used the 1982 version of the questionnaire, which had 23 scales, but results were recomputed for 13 scales corresponding to those in the 1986 version. Questionnaires describing the manager's behavior over the prior

## TABLE 7
## Criterion-related Validity for MPS Scales

| Behavior Study: | 1 | 2 | 3 | 4 | 5 | 6 |
|---|---|---|---|---|---|---|
| Informing | NI | .07 | .21 | .06 | .23 | .40* |
| Consulting & Delegating | .10 | −.10 | .12 | .03 | .30* | .38 |
| Planning & Organizing | .28 | −.02 | .08 | .33 | .37** | .44* |
| Problem Solving | NI | NI | .39* | .37 | .41** | .26 |
| Clarifying | .47** | .26* | .27 | .40* | .24 | .43* |
| Monitoring | NI | NI | .14 | .49** | .21 | .27 |
| Motivating | .49** | .30* | .13 | .36 | .35* | .30 |
| Recognizing & Rewarding | .13 | .00 | .42* | .07 | .23 | .28 |
| Supporting | .01 | −.21 | −.04 | .09 | .24 | .37 |
| Developing | NI | .24 | .11 | .25 | .37** | .58** |
| Conflict Mgt. & Team Bldg. | .22 | .05 | .26 | .09 | .34* | .13 |
| Representing | NI | .33* | .05 | .25 | .42** | .34 |
| Networking/Interfacing | NI | NI | .22 | .47** | NI | .18 |
| **Sample Size:** | | | | | | |
| Leaders | 26 | 42 | 26 | 24 | 48 | 24 |
| Subordinates | 151 | 393 | 223 | 262 | 64 | 90 |

Note: NI means scale not included in this version of the questionnaire.
Results for Study 5 are at individual level of analysis.

*p <.05.   **p <.01.

six months were filled out anonymously by several of the manager's subordinates (i.e., the sales representatives). Responses for each group of subordinates were averaged by scale and correlated with the criterion of managerial effectiveness. The criterion was a three-level classification (high, medium, low effectiveness) based on the ratings made by four persons in the company who were familiar with most or all of the managers in the sample. Their judgments were based in turn on information about the objective performance (i.e., sales, profits) of each center. The results are shown in Table 7. Two aspects of manager behavior (Problem Solving and Recognizing & Rewarding) were correlated significantly with the criterion of managerial effectiveness. Some individual items in the Clarifying scale also had highly significant correlations with the criterion, even though the correlation for the scale mean was only marginally significant by a conservative two-tailed test.

The fourth study also used the 1982 version of the questionnaire. The sample in this study consisted of 24 elementary school principals who participated in a larger research project carried out by Martinko and Gardner (1984). The elementary schools were all in the same state, and information about school performance (e.g., school reputation, test scores of students on standardized tests) was used by a panel of judges as the basis for identifying outstanding principals. The sample consisted of roughly equal numbers of outstanding and mediocre principals. Several teachers in each school filled out the questionnaire describing the managerial behavior of their principal. Responses were averaged by scale across respondents in the same school and correlated with the performance criterion. As before, scale scores were defined in terms of the 13 behaviors in the 1986 version of the MPS. The results are shown in Table 7. Three behaviors (Clarifying, Monitoring, Networking/Interfacing) were correlated significantly with the criterion of managerial effectiveness. Some individual items in the Problem Solving and Motivating scales were highly significant, even though the correlation for the overall scales was only marginally significant with a conservative two-tailed test.

The fifth study was a dissertation conducted by Sue Miles (1985) on 48 home economics program leaders employed by the Cornell County Cooperative Extension Associations in New York State. Program leaders are responsible for the management of educational and research programs conducted by the associations; they have a variety of administrative managerial responsibilities, including some important external functions with clients and county officials. The study used an intermediate version of the questionnaire that had a three-choice item format. The questionnaire was mailed to one or two of the program leader's subordinates, such as staff associates and volunteer leaders. Respondents included 64 subordinates. The criterion of leader effectiveness was a composite ranking of county programs by the Associate Director for home economics programs, based in turn on separate rankings by eight members of the Director's staff. Correlations between scale scores and the criterion were conducted at the individual level of analysis, because in many cases there was only one subordinate respondent per leader. Despite the lower discrimination afforded by the three-choice format, the correlations between leader behavior scales and the independent criterion were quite good. At the most conservative .01 level of significance for a two-tailed test, four of the scales correlated significantly with the managerial effectiveness, including Planning/Organizing, Problem Solving, Developing, and Representing. Next-highest correlations were for Motivating and Conflict Management/Team Building, both significant at the .05 level for a two-tailed test.

The sixth study is a dissertation conducted by Don Hindman on department heads in high schools. Effective and less effective department heads in six high schools were identified by principals, superintendents, and staff personnel. The department heads selected for the study were ones for which high agreement occurred among judges on rankings of effectiveness. Teachers who were subordinates of the leaders filled out the 1986 version of the MPS. Although the major analysis was in terms of t-tests, in order to be consistent with the other results in Table 7 correlations were computed at the group level between scale scores and the dichotomous criterion. Again, several scales correlated significantly with managerial effectiveness, including Informing, Planning/Organizing, Clarifying, and Developing.

Across the six studies there was evidence for the relevance of most scales in at least one study. The correlations were higher than is typical for behavior description questionnaires when used with a criterion of leader effectiveness that is independent of the behavior descriptions and is reasonably accurate. The different pattern of correlations across studies is to be expected for situations as diverse as those in the six studies. Although Supporting and Consulting/Delegating seldom correlated significantly with indicators of group performance, these behaviors were correlated with measures of subordinate satisfaction in studies that included supplementary "soft" criteria of leader effectiveness. Additional research is now in progress to assess the criterion-related validity of the scales in the 1988 version of the MPS.

## Summary

Construct validation of behavior categories is a slow process taking many years. It is a "bootstrap operation" in which behavior categories and measures are simultaneously assessed. The present validation program has been more intensive and comprehensive than the validation research done on any previous leader behavior questionnaire. To date, the results are very promising. Nevertheless, the validation program continues, and it includes plans for some other types of studies, such as the simultaneous use of different measurement methods, and the experimental manipulation of managerial behavior.

Much of the data used in the development and validation research for the MPS comes from ongoing applications of the questionnaire, which provide further evidence for its practical utility. Manus Associates is currently using the MPS for a variety of different types of interventions, including individual training needs analysis, development of leadership skills, and team building (Yukl & Lepsinger, in press). The feedback workshop developed for the MPS has been administered to middle-level managers and executives in several major corporations, managers in a public-sector organization, and military officers in the United States Army Reserve. Responses by in-house trainers and by managers participating as trainees have been a major source of ideas for the improvement of both the questionnaire and the feedback workshop. Reaction to the MPS by managers has been overwhelmingly favorable. They report that the categories and items are meaningful and relevant, and that the feedback is informative and useful. The favorable reception by managers, combined with the favorable validation results, is very encouraging and helps to justify the immense investment of time and money to develop the questionnaire and related workshops by a large contingent of researchers and practitioners over a period of 12 years.

## References

Luthans, F., & Lockwood, D. L. (1984). Toward an observation system for measuring leader behavior in natural settings. In J. G. Hunt, D. Hosking, C. A. Schriesheim, & R. Stewart (Eds.), *Leaders and managers: International perspectives on managerial behavior and leadership* (pp. 117–141). New York: Pergamon Press.

Martinko, M. J., & Gardner, W. L. (1984). *The behavior of high-performing educational managers: An observation study.* Tallahassee, FL: Florida State University.

Miles, C. S. (1985). *Leadership effectiveness of professional home economists in Cornell Cooperative Extension.* Unpublished dissertation, Cornell University, New York.

Mintzberg, H. (1973). *The nature of managerial work.* New York: Harper & Row.

Morse, J. J., & Wagner, F. R. (1978). Measuring the process of managerial effectiveness. *Academy of Management Journal, 21,* 23–35.

Page, R. (1985). *The position description questionnaire.* Unpublished manuscript, Minneapolis, MN: Control Data Business Advisors.

Shrout, P. E., & Fleiss, J. L. (1979). Intraclass correlations: Uses in assessing rater reliability. *Psychological Bulletin, 86,* 420–428.

Stogdill, R. M. (1963). *Manual for the leader behavior description questionnaire–Form XII.* Columbus: Ohio State University.

Tornow, W. W., & Pinto, P. R. (1976). The development of a managerial job taxonomy: A system of describing, classifying, and evaluating executive positions. *Journal of Applied Psychology, 61,* 410–418.

Yukl, G. A. (1987). *A new taxonomy for integrating diverse perspectives on managerial behavior.* Paper presented at the American Psychological Association Meetings, New York.

Yukl, G. A. (1989). *Leadership in organizations* (2nd ed.). Englewood Cliffs, NJ: Prentice-Hall.

Yukl, G. A., & Carrier, H. (1986). An exploratory study on situational determinants of managerial behavior. *Proceedings of the 22nd Annual Meeting of the Eastern Academy of Management,* 40–43.

Yukl, G. A., & Clemence, J. (1984). A test of path-goal theory of leadership using questionnaire and diary measures of behavior. *Proceedings of the 21st Annual Meeting of the Eastern Academy of Management,* 174–177.

Yukl, G. A., & Kanuk, L. (1979). Leadership behavior and the effectiveness of beauty salon managers. *Personal Psychology, 32,* 663–675.

Yukl, G., & Lepsinger, R. (in press). An integrating taxonomy of managerial behavior: Implications for improving managerial effectiveness. In J. W. Jones, B. D. Steffy, & D. W. Bray (Eds.), *Applying psychology in business: The manager's handbook.* Lexington, MA: Lexington Press.

Yukl, G. A., & Nemeroff, W. (1979). Identification and measurement of specific categories of leadership behavior: A progress report. In J. G. Hunt & L. L. Larson (Eds.), *Crosscurrents in leadership.* Carbondale: Southern Illinois University Press.

Yukl, G. A., & Van Fleet, D. (1982). Cross-situational, multi-method research on military leader effectiveness. *Organizational behavior and human performance, 30,* 87–108.

# Psychological Orientations and Leadership: Thinking Styles That Differentiate Between Effective and Ineffective Managers

*Peter D.
Gratzinger
Ronald A.
Warren
and
Robert A.
Cooke*

Is there a leadership style that differentiates effective managers from ineffective managers? It is not difficult to reach consensus on certain shared traits, values, and behaviors—such as confidence, emphasis on results and personal vitality, the ability to listen to and motivate others—that set effective leaders apart from ineffective ones. In this study we demonstrate how a set of management style descriptors obtained from managers' self-ratings relates to the actual effectiveness of managers as perceived by their co-workers.

Much of leadership research is based on the descriptions of leaders' behaviors, interpersonal styles, and effectiveness (Kotter, 1988; Bennis & Nanus, 1985; Hollander, 1978; Stogdill, 1974; Fiedler, 1967). These assessments are obtained either from the managers themselves or from their superiors, peers, or subordinates. The primary concepts, orientation towards tasks and orientation towards people, have served both as personality dimensions (Fiedler, 1967) and behavioral styles (Evans, 1970; House, 1971; Schriesheim & Van Glinow, 1977) in leadership research. At the same time they provide major focus in many leadership assessment and training programs (Hersey & Blanchard, 1982; Mitchell, 1979).

Leaders with a focus on people are usually described as supportive and interested in others. They enjoy working with others, have a positive view of contributions made by others, and want to be perceived positively by others. Task-oriented leaders are usually portrayed as results- and goal-oriented and apt at commanding resources to facilitate performance.

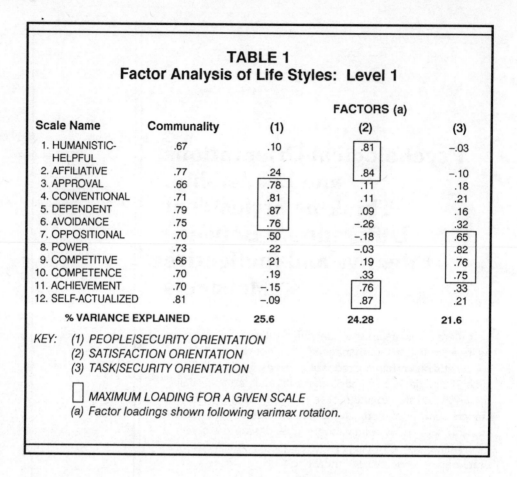

**TABLE 1**
**Factor Analysis of Life Styles: Level 1**

| Scale Name | Communality | FACTORS (a) (1) | (2) | (3) |
|---|---|---|---|---|
| 1. HUMANISTIC-HELPFUL | .67 | .10 | .81 | −.03 |
| 2. AFFILIATIVE | .77 | .24 | .84 | −.10 |
| 3. APPROVAL | .66 | .78 | .11 | .18 |
| 4. CONVENTIONAL | .71 | .81 | .11 | .21 |
| 5. DEPENDENT | .79 | .87 | .09 | .16 |
| 6. AVOIDANCE | .75 | .76 | −.26 | .32 |
| 7. OPPOSITIONAL | .70 | .50 | −.18 | .65 |
| 8. POWER | .73 | .22 | −.03 | .82 |
| 9. COMPETITIVE | .66 | .21 | .19 | .76 |
| 10. COMPETENCE | .70 | .19 | .33 | .75 |
| 11. ACHIEVEMENT | .70 | −.15 | .76 | .33 |
| 12. SELF-ACTUALIZED | .81 | −.09 | .87 | .21 |
| **% VARIANCE EXPLAINED** | | 25.6 | 24.28 | 21.6 |

KEY:  (1) PEOPLE/SECURITY ORIENTATION
(2) SATISFACTION ORIENTATION
(3) TASK/SECURITY ORIENTATION

☐ MAXIMUM LOADING FOR A GIVEN SCALE
(a) Factor loadings shown following varimax rotation.

These two basic styles have been found to be relatively stable and independent of each other (Blake & Mouton, 1964). It is important to note that several leading researchers have proposed—and to a certain extent demonstrated experimentally—that the most effective leadership style should be a blend of the two styles; however, they were not able to operationalize and measure this combining of effective leadership styles directly. *

While other researchers have built on two major constructs—task- and people-orientation—the Level I: Life Styles Inventory as well as ACUMEN scales measure 12 thinking styles in three, instead of two, separate domains (Cooke & Rousseau, 1983; Ware, Leak, & Perry, 1985; Gratzinger & Cooke, 1985). These three domains correspond to three factors obtained using an orthogonal factor analysis on the results of self-assessments of 1,000 managers. This analysis was performed on both the

---

* The operationalization and direct measurement of critical aspects of leadership style using self-description was undertaken using the Human Synergistics Level I: Life Styles Inventory, Self Description (1973, 1976, 1981, 1982 by Human Synergistics, Plymouth, Michigan). A revised and upgraded version of this instrument has been used by Acumen International as a basis for ACUMEN: INSIGHT FOR MANAGERS (1985 by Acumen International, San Rafael, CA) and subsequent programs in the ACUMEN family of products.

original and revised instruments and yielded similar loadings on all three factors (Tables 1 and 2), confirming a robust underlying factorial structure. The three factors together explain 69.5 and 72.3% of the variance respectively. These factors indicate the presence of the following personal orientations:

*People/Security Orientation* encompassing the scales measuring Approval, Conventional, Dependence, Apprehension (Avoidance in Life Styles: Level 1).

*Satisfaction Orientation* encompassing the scales measuring Achievement, Self Actualization, Humanistic-Helpful, and Affiliation.

*Task/Security Orientation* encompassing the scales measuring Power, Competition, Perfectionism (Competence in Life Styles: Level 1), and Oppositional.

By looking at the content areas of the three domains isolated in Life Styles and ACUMEN, one can draw preliminary conclusions about the relationship of the two-factor models consisting in people and task orientations to our three-factor solution:

*The People/Security Orientation is related to the people orientation and the Task/Security Orientation is related to the task orientation found by other theorists. Both Security Orientations, however, sample heavily ineffective and counterproductive attitudes and behaviors. The Satisfaction Orientation, on the other hand,*

## TABLE 2
### Factor Analysis of Acumen Self-Assessment Scales

| Scale Name | Communality | FACTORS (a) (1) | (2) | (3) |
|---|---|---|---|---|
| 1. HUMANISTIC-HELPFUL | .57 | −.01 | .83 | .05 |
| 2. AFFILIATION | .67 | −.18 | .81 | .27 |
| 3. APPROVAL | .62 | .33 | −.00 | .76 |
| 4. CONVENTIONAL | .54 | .03 | .13 | .83 |
| 5. DEPENDENCE | .72 | .13 | .05 | .88 |
| 6. APPREHENSION | .63 | .43 | −.32 | .67 |
| 7. OPPOSITIONAL | .56 | .73 | −.17 | .30 |
| 8. POWER | .66 | .87 | −.03 | .07 |
| 9. COMPETITION | .63 | .78 | .22 | .21 |
| 10. PERFECTIONISM | .59 | .72 | .38 | .14 |
| 11. ACHIEVEMENT | .65 | .25 | .80 | −.16 |
| 12. SELF-ACTUALIZATION | .70 | .17 | .85 | −.09 |
| % VARIANCE EXPLAINED | | 23.8 | 25.5 | 23.0 |

KEY:  (1) *TASK/SECURITY ORIENTATION*
      (2) *SATISFACTION ORIENTATION*
      (3) *PEOPLE/SECURITY ORIENTATION*

☐ *MAXIMUM LOADING FOR A GIVEN SCALE*
(a) *Factor loadings shown following varimax rotation.*

*touches on both the people and task areas, but it focuses on productive action and positive values, beliefs, and attitudes. Thus, the Satisfaction Orientation provides direct operationalization and measure of the "blend" of effective people- and task-related values, attitudes, and behaviors predicted by other theorists.*

It is our contention that the concept isolated in this study can serve as a basis for the development of assessment and training programs with a major focus on the reinforcement and development of these qualities in managers and other professionals who aspire to leadership excellence. To do that, we need to show that managers who have these positive features are indeed better performers and leaders than those who do not.

## Hypothesis

Ratings of behavioral outcomes of focal managers—such as effectiveness and relationships with others—by their peers, superiors, and subordinates will discriminate between those self-perceptions falling into the Security domains and those falling into the Satisfaction Orientation.

This will show that managers who perceive in themselves qualities related, for instance, to the Task Security Orientation (e.g., Power) will be rated as less effective than those who have task-related qualities representative of the Satisfaction Orientation (e.g., Achievement). Similar results are hypothesized for the People/Security and people-oriented aspects of the Satisfaction Orientation. Moreover, the most effective managers will possess a blend of positive aspects of people- and task-oriented management styles measured directly by the scales comprising the Satisfaction Orientation domain.

To appreciate this contribution to the theory of effective leadership, it is important to note that none of these results could be predicted or measured using other approaches subscribing to the two-factor solution of people and task orientations.

## Method

**Subjects** The sample in this study consisted of 556 managers who were involved in management development programs. Also obtained were behavioral outcome ratings ("summary perceptions") from 2,923 others, of which 1,177 were peers, 788 subordinates, and 518 superiors. On average there were 4.7 observers per manager. The participants came from different sectors (manufacturing, public utilities, government, public accounting) and geographical areas (Great Lakes, Middle Atlantic, and southern areas of the United States). Their organizational positions varied from foremen through all management levels to key executives; they were predominantly white (96%), male (94%), between 30 and 49 years old (60%), and college educated (75%).

**Data** The self-report data used in this study were gathered using the ACUMEN revision of the Life Styles: Level 1 instrument. This revised instrument, used for self-assessment in the ACUMEN family of products, consists of 120 items measuring the 12 management styles that are described by our three-factor model, namely the People/Security, Task/Security, and Satisfaction Orientations.

The behavioral outcomes rated by co-workers encompassed four key areas of management—on-the-job effectiveness, interest in self-improvement, handling negative feedback, and social relationships. These ratings by others were used to estimate managerial effectiveness of the focal managers who were administered the self-reports.

## Results

Behavioral ratings usually obtain predictable but weak correlations with self-report data. This is due to situational factors and response sets such as a "leniency factor" which narrows the range of the responses used. To minimize this confounding, we factor analyzed the ratings and obtained a single weighted factor score for each individual (Table 3). Each focal manager was given a rank based on the weighted ratings score. We then created two subsamples out of the top and bottom 10% of the sample. The top 10% with highest weighted effectiveness ratings were called the "Effective Manager" group and the bottom 10% with lowest ratings formed the "Ineffective Manager" group. We then averaged the self-assessment scale scores for each group and thus obtained the Effective Manager and the Ineffective Manager Profiles.

Our objective was to demonstrate that behavioral ratings clearly differentiate between managers who are effective or ineffective in terms of styles. A comparison of the scale scores between the two groups shows the direction of the differences between the scale scores in the predicted direction: The Effective Profile (top 10%) shows a predominance of styles in the Satisfaction domain—comprised of the Achievement, Self-Actualization,

---

### TABLE 3
### Analysis of the Behavioral Outcome
### Ratings by Co-Workers

| Item Description | Communality | Factor (a) |
|---|---|---|
| A. How do you see this person's level of effectiveness in his/her job? | .44 | .67 |
| B. How interested does this person appear to be in improving him/herself? | .47 | .68 |
| C. How do you think this person will handle any negative feedback received from this program? | .63 | .79 |
| D. How would you describe the quality of this person's relationship with others? | .49 | .70 |
| **% VARIANCE EXPLAINED** | **50.8** | |

(a) Factor loadings shown are scaled loadings.

# TABLE 4A
## Best Managers (Top 10%) Vs.
## Worst Managers (Bottom 10%)
## on Acumen Scales (a)

| Scale Name | | Top 10% (a) | Bottom 10% | T-Test (b) | Direction of Difference Between Means |
|---|---|---|---|---|---|
| HUMANISTIC-HELPFUL | MEAN | 1.49 | 1.31 | t = 2.77** | TOP > BOTTOM |
| | SD | .14 | .13 | | |
| AFFILIATION | MEAN | 1.51 | 1.40 | t = 1.53(*) | TOP > BOTTOM |
| | SD | .15 | .13 | | |
| APPROVAL | MEAN | .55 | .60 | t = -.61 | BOTTOM > TOP |
| | SD | .13 | .16 | | |
| CONVENTIONAL | MEAN | .82 | .88 | t = -.85 | BOTTOM > TOP |
| | SD | .15 | .15 | | |
| DEPENDENCE | MEAN | .74 | .84 | t = -1.70* | BOTTOM > TOP |
| | SD | .08 | .11 | | |
| APPREHENSION | MEAN | .23 | .36 | t = -2.03* | BOTTOM > TOP |
| | SD | .10 | .13 | | |
| OPPOSITIONAL | MEAN | .32 | .49 | t = -2.78** | BOTTOM > TOP |
| | SD | .09 | .12 | | |
| POWER | MEAN | .29 | .43 | t = -2.01* | BOTTOM > TOP |
| | SD | .14 | .16 | | |
| COMPETITION | MEAN | .55 | .74 | t = -2.41* | BOTTOM > TOP |
| | SD | .19 | .16 | | |
| PERFECTIONISM | MEAN | 1.08 | 1.14 | t = -.84 | BOTTOM > TOP |
| | SD | .17 | .15 | | |
| ACHIEVEMENT | MEAN | 1.59 | 1.47 | t = 1.80* | TOP > BOTTOM |
| | SD | .10 | .13 | | |
| SELF-ACTUALIZATION | MEAN | 1.37 | 1.29 | t = 1.14 | TOP > BOTTOM |
| | SD | .15 | .10 | | |

$**p < .01$; $*p < .05$; $(*)p < .075$

(a) The TOP 10% (N=55) and BOTTOM 10% (N=54) have been selected from a sample of 556 managers based on high and low effectiveness ratings by their co-workers. The table shows mean raw scores/number of items (10) and standard deviations.

(b) The test used is t-test for two independent samples; the levels of significance are reported for a one-tailed test in the indicated direction.

Humanistic-Helpful, and Affiliation Scales. The Ineffective Profile (bottom 10%) shows the opposite—with the highest scores on the Dependence, Apprehension, Oppositional, Power, and Competition Scales, and the lowest scores in the Satisfaction sector. The t-test values indicate that on eight out of the 12 scales the differences are such that each scale alone would reliably differentiate between the groups of effective and ineffective managers (Table 4A).

Taken together, the 12 scales differentiate between the two groups with a very high degree of significance ($F = 64.80$; df 25,83; $p < .001$) (Table 4B).

## TABLE 4B
## Analysis of Variance Comparing the Groups
## of Best (Top 10%) and Worst (Bottom 10%)
## Managers on the Acumen Scales (a)

| Source | Sum-of-Squares | DF | Mean-Square | F-Ratio | P |
|--------|----------------|-----|-------------|---------|-------|
| REGRESSION | 274.01 | 25 | 10.96 | 64.80 | 0.001 |
| RESIDUAL | 14.04 | 83 | 0.17 | | |

(a) Managers were divided into these groups on an aggregated overall effectiveness measure obtained from co-workers and applied to Self-Assessment of the individual managers.

The results thus show that managerial effectiveness ratings by co-workers differentiate between self-described People/ and Task/Security-oriented versus Satisfaction-ori-
ented behaviors and thinking styles of the target managers. This makes Satisfaction
Orientation traits, which subsume general leadership constructs like an achievement
orientation, self-respect, high energy, willingness to help others, and affiliation, important predictors of leader effectiveness.

## Discussion

The managers who describe themselves as having the traits, values, and attitudes
measured by the ACUMEN scales in the Satisfaction domain are, at the same time,
perceived by others as overall more effective. At the opposite end of the spectrum
within our managerial sample, those managers who describe themselves as low on these
scales could be identified by pooling profiles from managers seen as least effective by
others. The findings for the remaining domains, People/Security and Task/Security,
which embody the less effective aspects of people and task orientations, also point in
the corresponding, predictable directions. This finding has important implications for
the use of self-descriptions to study leadership in general, and the usefulness of the
ACUMEN three-domain model in particular.

In the first place, these findings strengthen the position that personal orientations play
an important role in interactions with others and in molding others' perceptions of one's
effective or ineffective behaviors and attitudes (Cooke, Rousseau, & Lafferty, 1987).
This aspect should not be underestimated when compared to the role played by
situational factors (Mitchell, 1979). The consistency of the results could not be possible
if there were not a consistency in the underlying perceptual data—demonstrating that
self-perceptions reflect relatively accurately the management style of the self-rating
person as judged in turn by others by its behavioral outcome.

The findings also argue strongly for the usefulness of using the ACUMEN three-factor-based domains for such assessments. Of special interest to anyone practically involved with increasing people's effectiveness and leadership abilities, the Satisfaction/Security distinction is an extremely valuable indicator of the potential behavior outcomes for a leader or a manager. To strengthen this contention, we carried out additional analyses of the demographic data for the Effective Manager subsample to show the association between the characteristics that typify the Effective Profile and successful management functioning. We will address here salary and organizational rank. The top 10% of the sample (again, selected by co-worker ratings on the four effectiveness criteria) have significantly higher salaries (chi-square $= 14.78$, df $= 6$, $p < .05$) and higher organizational rank (chi-square $= 16.75$, df $= 4$, $p < .01$) than the other 90% in the study. Thus, these identified top 10% have a track record of success perceived by their co-workers and recognized by their organizations in the form of promotions and remuneration.

While the finding that the top 10% have achieved higher organizational ranks supports the notion that high scores in the Satisfaction domain are related to effective outcomes, an important question remains: Is the Effective Manager Profile only a function of the position of an individual in the company; that is, do individuals in higher ranks have healthier profiles? The answer is no. This answer is based on a series of analyses of the self-profiles of the 1,000 managers in the normative sample, regardless of any ratings by co-workers (Cooke & Rousseau, 1983). In this sample, organizational rank differences are not significantly related to a scale configuration (F $= 1.25$, df $= 5$, 911; $p = .28$). However, salary differences, possibly a more sensitive indicator of actual performance, did show a weak association to having a certain profile (F $= 2.20$; df $= 4$, 994; $p = .06$).

The finding that there is no statistically significant relationship between organizational rank and the self-profiles in the normative sample indicates that there is no general trend for certain types of profiles to be found at certain levels in the organization. By the same token, managers who happen to have profiles similar to the Effective Manager Profile can, in all probability, be found at different levels in the organization and are thus not restricted to the top ranks in the organization. High scores in the Satisfaction sector of the scales, or the Effective Manager type of profile, are not just a function of high organizational rank. We can then assume that there are always managers who possess an Effective Manager Profile and who, given the visibility of key positions, would stand out in the eyes of their co-workers and superiors as excellent managers.

The findings in the study as well as these additional analyses strongly support the notion that the ACUMEN assessment tool measures relatively well-defined aspects of attitudes and thinking styles demonstrably relevant to effective leadership behavior as perceived by others and by the organization. In the domains it measures—the Task/ and People/Security and the Satisfaction Orientations—it also provides a valuable predictor of management effectiveness and leadership abilities observed by others.

## Acknowledgements

Level 1: Life Styles Inventory, Self-Description. Copyright 1973, 1976, 1981, 1982, by Human Synergistics, Plymouth, MI.

# References

Bennis, W. G., & Nanus, B. I. (1985). *Leaders: The strategies for taking charge*. New York: Harper & Row.

Blake, R. R., & Mouton, J. C. (1964). *The managerial grid*. Houston, TX: Gulf Publishing.

Cooke, R. A., & Rousseau, D. M. (1983). The factor structure of level 1: Life styles inventory. *Educational and Psychological Measurement*, *43*, 449–457.

Cooke, R. A., Rousseau, D. M., & Lafferty, J. C. (1987). Thinking and behavioral styles: Consistency between self-descriptions and descriptions by others. *Educational and Psychological Measurement*, *47*, 815–823.

Evans, M.G. (1970). The effects of supervisory behavior on the path-goal relationship. *Organizational Behavior and Human Performance*, *5*, 277–298.

Fiedler, F. (1967). *A theory of leadership effectiveness*. New York: McGraw-Hill.

Gratzinger, P. D., & Cooke, R. A. (1985). Moving from traditional self-assessment inventories to computerized self-development programs. *ACUMEN: Insight for managers program manual*. San Rafael, CA: Acumen International.

Hersey, P., & Blanchard, K. H. (1982). *Management of organizational behavior: Utilization of human resources*. Englewood Cliffs, NJ: Prentice-Hall.

Hollander, E. P. (1978). *Leadership dynamics: A practical guide to effective relationships*. New York: Free Press.

House, R. J. (1971). A path-goal theory of leadership effectiveness. *Administrative Science Quarterly*, *16*, 321–328.

Kotter, J. P. (1988). *The leadership factor*. New York: Free Press.

Lafferty, J. C. (1973). *Level 1: Life styles inventory, self-description*. Plymouth, MI: Human Synergistics.

Mitchell, T. R. (1979). Organizational behavior. *Annual Review of Psychology*, *30*, 243–281.

Schriesheim, C., & Van Glinow, M. A. (1977). The path-goal theory of leadership: A theoretical and empirical analysis. *Academy of Management Journal*, *20*, 398–405.

Stogdill, R. M. (1974). *The handbook of leadership: A survey of theory and research*. New York: Free Press.

Ware, M. E., Leak, G. K., & Perry, N. W. (1985). Life styles inventory: Evidence for its factorial validity. *Psychological Reports*, *56*, 963–968.

# The Campbell Work Orientations Surveys: Their Use to Capture the Characteristics of Leaders

*David P. Campbell*

This is a report of the development of a new battery of psychological assessment inventories designed to reflect the individual's orientation toward work, with particular emphasis on the factors of leadership and creativity; collectively, the battery is entitled "Campbell Work Orientations [CWO™]." Currently, there are four surveys in the battery:

1. Campbell Interest Survey (CIS). A 200-item questionnaire asking about the individual's preferences or aversions for a wide range of occupational activities, some of which are associated with leadership and creativity. Each respondent is provided with a profile containing standard scores for 29 scoring scales. Two of the scales specifically cover "Leadership" and "Management" interests.

2. Campbell Skills Survey (CSS). A 120-item questionnaire asking respondents to evaluate their skills in the same occupational activities as those covered by the Interest Survey. Each respondent is given a profile showing standard scores for self-reported skills on the same 29 scales as provided on the Interest Profile. Again, two of the scales specifically cover "Leadership" and "Management" skills.

3. Campbell Leadership Potential Index Self vs. Observers (CLPI). A 160-adjective checklist, designed to be filled in both by the individual and by a set of three through five observers, describing the individual on 33 scales, grouped into six Orientations, each of which has a fairly direct relationship to leadership and creativity. Each respondent is given a profile comparing self-reported scores on the 33 scales and six Orientations with average scores on the same scales based on observers' responses.

4. Campbell Organizational Survey (COS). A 44-item questionnaire focused on the individual's working satisfactions and frustrations, including reactions to the quality of organizational leadership and degree of freedom to innovate. The scores provide a means of checking on the perceived quality of leadership in an organization, as well as providing specific data to each respondent on individual personal perceptions.

Although each survey can stand alone as an individual assessment instrument, several steps have been taken to convert them into an integrated battery; these steps include:

1. Use of a *uniform typography, form layout, and logo* for all surveys.

2. Use of the *same (six-point) response style format* throughout all of the surveys.

3. Use of the *same raw-score-to-standard-score conversion* method for each form.

4. Use of a *similarly designed profile report* form for all surveys.

5. Inclusion of *scales relative to leadership and creativity on all surveys*, where possible.

6. A concerted *effort to present the respondent's scores in a straightforward, easy-to-understand way*, with an absence of arcane jargon or mysterious analytic schemes. The major emphasis is on face valid scores, with obvious content validity.

## Samples Tested to Date

Table 1 lists the samples tested on the various surveys thus far. Obviously, from the motley nature of the list, many of these were samples of opportunity. When developing a new test, one is faced with the dilemma that you cannot test people effectively until you have some norms, and you cannot get norms without testing some people. We now have enough people for most of the surveys to offer tentative norms, but as more appropriate samples are gathered, the norms may change.

Following is a review of where we are currently on each of the surveys.

**Campbell Interest Survey (CIS)** The Campbell Interest Survey is a "typical" vocational interest survey, following in the tradition of other inventories such as the Kuder Preference Record, the Career Assessment Inventory, and the Strong Interest Inventory. It differs from the last in being shorter (200 vs. 325 items), more comprehensive in coverage (29 vs. 23 Basic Scales), plus being more "modern" in coverage, including occupational areas such as Animal Care, Fashion, Financial Services, International Activities, Leadership, and Plants and Gardens. The CIS also has a more flexible response format (a six-point scale ranging from "Strongly Like" to "Strongly Dislike" vs. a three-point "Like-Indifferent-Dislike" scale), and more comprehensive procedural checks to make certain that the individual has filled in the inventory properly.

*Reliability of the CIS.* The reliability of the CIS scoring scales has been studied in two ways: first, by calculating Cronbach's Alpha coefficient—the median scale value was .87, with a range of .78 to .94, using a sample of 821 people, and second, by using a three-week test-retest sample of 87 college fraternity leaders—the median test-retest correlation was .88, with a range of .75 to .93. Both of these techniques indicate a

# TABLE 1
## Samples Tested To Date [a][b]

- **Roughly 1,000 people in "General Reference Sample"**
  Basically, Campbell's 1,000 closest friends
- **College Fraternity Leaders (N = 87)**
  Tested twice over 3-wk. period to calculate test-retest reliability
- **University Students**
  One group in student leadership positions (N = 50)
  One group in student organizations (N = 50)
  One group "just students" (N = 50)
- **Community College Students (N = 140)**
  Students in a leadership-oriented educational program
- **Military Academy Cadets (N = 90)**
  Seniors in psychology courses
- **Military Academy Psychology Faculty (N = 33)**
  All military officers, and all psychologists
- **Women's Networking Group (N = 20)**
- **Corporate Managers (Fortune 500 Co.) (N = 47)**
- **Senior Executives attending business school management program Spring 1988 (N = 163) and Fall 1988 (N = 162)**
- **Hospital Chaplains (N = 30)**
- **Life Insurance Sales (N = 18)**
- **I/O Psychologists (Div. 14) (N = 43)**
- **State Leaders (N = 33)**
- **Municipal Fire Chiefs (N = 250)**
  Attendees at National Leadership Course for Fire Chiefs
- **Large Manufacturing Corporation HR Staff (N = 14)**
- **Clinical Psychologists (N = 14)**
- **College Student Leaders (N = 92)**
  College students participating in a summer leadership development program
- **Leadership Seminar Participants — 1987 (N = 24) and 1988 (N = 13)**
- **Leadership Seminar Trainers (N = 27)**
- **Leadership Seminar Participants (N = 17)**
- **Sales and Training Executives (N = 92)**
- **Computer Co. Sales Staff (N = 21)**
- **Food Company Marketing Division (N = 25)**
- **Nonprofit R & D Organization (N = 128)**
- **Chemical Co. R & D Managers (N = 48)**
- **Manufacturing Conglomerate Middle Managers (N = 107)**

[a] *Not all samples completed all surveys.*
[b] *Sample sizes listed in Table 1 do not always equal sample sizes listed on other tables because some participants from each group did not complete some tests.*

## TABLE 2
## Item Intercorrelations for the CIS Leadership Scale Items

|  | St.Gov. | TopExec. | U.Pres. | StudyLdr. | Dev.Ldr. | Persuade |
|---|---|---|---|---|---|---|
| State Gov. |  | .60 | .66 | .40 | .41 | .40 |
| Top Exec. |  |  | .59 | .43 | .38 | .32 |
| Univ. Pres. |  |  |  | .42 | .44 | .40 |
| Study Ldrshp. |  |  |  |  | .65 | .44 |
| Dev. Ldrshp. Talent |  |  |  |  |  | .50 |
| Persuade others |  |  |  |  |  |  |

respectable degree of reliability. Reliability statistics for the scoring scales of the other surveys fell in the same general range.

*Scale Development for the CIS*. The scoring scales for the CIS were developed by clustering together similar items, using a combination of statistical cohesion; that is, the items on any given scale show a high level of intercorrelation, and common sense; that is, the items on each scale intuitively seem to be drawn from the same cluster of interests. For example, the LEADERSHIP scale includes the items listed in Table 2, where their item intercorrelations are reported.

Obviously, the items have a strong flavor of leadership running through them, which is reflected in their high intercorrelations. (For those who have never worked with correlations at the item level, an item intercorrelation of .30 is usually considered "high.")

The scoring scales for the CIS are listed in Table 3, along with some representative activities covered in each scale, and with examples of occupations that would presumably score high on each scale.

*Norming the CIS*. Interest inventories are usually normed in one of two ways, or both. The first method is to use a representative sample of the working population; test them with a collection of homogeneous scales, which are scales covering only one interest area such as Mechanical Activities; and then calculate the scores of this representative sample, using some familiar standard scoring system, such as T-Scores (with a mean of 50, standard deviation of 10, the system used here), stanines, or percentiles. Once the system has been selected, future respondents can be scored on this standardized system, which permits a quick comparison between their scores and those of the general working population on the various homogeneous scales. This approach allows interpretive statements such as, "You have reported strong mechanical interests and an aversion for artistic activities," where the implication is "compared to most people." These homogeneous scales are easy to interpret because their content is obvious and straightforward, but the implications for the respondent are not so obvious. For example, what occupations are good candidates for an individual who has high scores on Mechanical interests and low scores on Artistic interests?

## TABLE 3
## CWO™ Campbell Interest Survey—
## Explanatory Notes

| Scale | Activities Covered | Preferred Occupations |
|---|---|---|
| Farming/Forestry<br>Plants/Gardens<br>Animal Care | Raising crops, managing timber, caring for livestock.<br>Planting gardens, working with flowers, landscaping.<br>Caring for pets, raising and training animals. | Farmer, Forester, Rancher<br>Florist, Gardener, Landscaper<br>Animal Trainer, Pet Shop Owner |
| Woodworking<br>Mechanical/Crafts | Carpentry, building furniture and decks.<br>Working with cars, machines, and electrical systems. | Cabinetmaker, Carpenter<br>Electrician, Inventor, Mechanic |
| Military/Law<br>Enforcemt.<br>Risk Taking<br>Athletics/Phys. Fitness | Military strategies, commanding troops, solving crimes.<br>Dangerous, exciting, physically strenuous activities.<br>Exercising, coaching, competing, staying fit. | Military Officer, Police Captain<br>Auto Racer, Bush Pilot, Explorer<br>Athletic Coach, Professional Athlete |
| Mathematics<br>Physical Science | Computers, studying and teaching mathematics.<br>Lab research, chemistry, physics, scientific concepts. | Computer Programmer, Math Teacher<br>Chemist, Med. Researcher, Physicist |
| Writing<br>Music/Dramatics<br>Internat'l. Activities<br>Art/Design | Literature; writing stories, novels, newspaper articles.<br>Music, acting, singing, dancing, directing plays.<br>Traveling, working overseas, foreign languages.<br>Architecture, creating artworks, designing room layouts. | Author, Poet, Reporter, Writer<br>Actor, Dancer, Entertainer, Musician<br>Foreign Serv., Tour Guide, Translator<br>Architect, Artist, Interior Designer |
| Food Service<br>Child Development<br>Adult Development<br>Social Service<br>Medical Practice<br>Religious Activities | Cooking, serving food, managing food services.<br>Teaching, playing with children, telling stories.<br>Teaching, doing psychological research, working with students.<br>Counseling, helping, advising people who are in trouble.<br>Healing, caring for patients with physical problems, first aid.<br>Conducting religious programs and services, preaching. | Baker, Chef, Restaurant Manager<br>Day-Care Worker, Schoolteacher<br>Principal, Psychologist, Teacher<br>Career Counselor, Social Worker<br>Dentist, Doctor, Nurse, Paramedic<br>Minister, Priest, Rabbi |
| Public Speaking<br>Law/Politics<br>Leadership<br>Management<br>Office Practices<br>Financial Services | Speaking, debating, telling jokes to audiences.<br>Politics, diplomacy, legal activities, negotiating.<br>Directing corporations, universities, state governments.<br>Managing factories, offices, hotels, retail stores.<br>Typing, maintaining files, secretarial work.<br>Economics, investments, financial planning. | Media Announcer, Public Official<br>Diplomat, Judge, Lawyer, Legislator<br>Corporate CEO, Governor, President<br>Manager, Supervisor<br>Office Worker, Receptionist<br>Banker, Finan. V.P., Stockbroker |
| Advertising/Marketing<br>Sales<br>Fashion | Advertising, marketing, and developing new products.<br>Making sales calls; selling merchandise, homes, services.<br>Creating fashion, buying and selling clothes, jewelry. | Advertiser, Marketing Director<br>Realtor, Salesperson<br>Designer, Fashion Buyer, Jeweler |

9/88

The second scoring method is the so-called "empirical" method, whereby an occupational sample of some kind is identified, say military officers or elementary schoolteachers, and their responses are used to develop a scoring scale which can then be used to score future respondents. These scores are usually interpreted by saying, "You have interests similar to military officers or elementary schoolteachers." Because empirical scales are normally longer and statistically developed against some outside criterion (occupational membership), they are usually more reliable and more predictive of future behavior. Their disadvantage is that the content of any given scale is seldom intuitively obvious, and counselors and other users are left to grapple with what exactly it means "to have the interests of military officers."

A combination of the two scoring systems has many advantages; the homogeneous scales are easy to interpret, and the empirical scales provide a statistical tie-in to the occupational world.

At the moment, the CIS has only the homogeneous scales; development of the occupational scales has yet to be accomplished. The homogeneous scales have been normed by using an amalgamation of all of the samples tested thus far, each approximately equally weighted.

*Preliminary Results for the CIS.* Roughly 2,000 people have filled in the Campbell Interest Survey thus far; mean profiles for several samples are shown in Tables 4 through 9. Because the norms are still preliminary, the absolute level of the scale scores should be considered tentative, but the relative values are illustrative of the separation between groups that the CIS provides.

The samples include a senior executive sample attending an advanced management program at one of the leading business schools (Table 4); a sample of state community leaders (Table 5); a sample of military cadets, all seniors and mostly psychology majors (Table 6); a sample of municipal fire chiefs (Table 7); a sample of community college students (Table 8); and a sample of professional women in a variety of different occupations (Table 9).

Scanning these tables is reassuring; even with these preliminary norms, the patterns of scores look quite reasonable; occupational samples are scoring high on the appropriate scales, and their low scores are also about as expected. The more general groups, such as the community college students and the women's network sample, show lower peaks indicating more variability in these samples, but again they score high on scales that make intuitive sense.

**Campbell Skills Survey (CSS)** The Skills Survey is not as well-developed as the Interest Survey because of two unfortunate decisions early in its development. First, a five-point response scale was used instead of a six-point scale. At the time, we were still experimenting with various approaches and the benefits of using a common response format across all surveys had not yet become apparent. Second, and more deleterious, we did not attempt to force congruence between the Interests and Skills profiles; we simply developed two item pools, one containing interest-type items, the other containing skill-type items, and then let the scales fall out as they may, using the statistical-intuitive scale construction process. It was not until the first crude profiles were

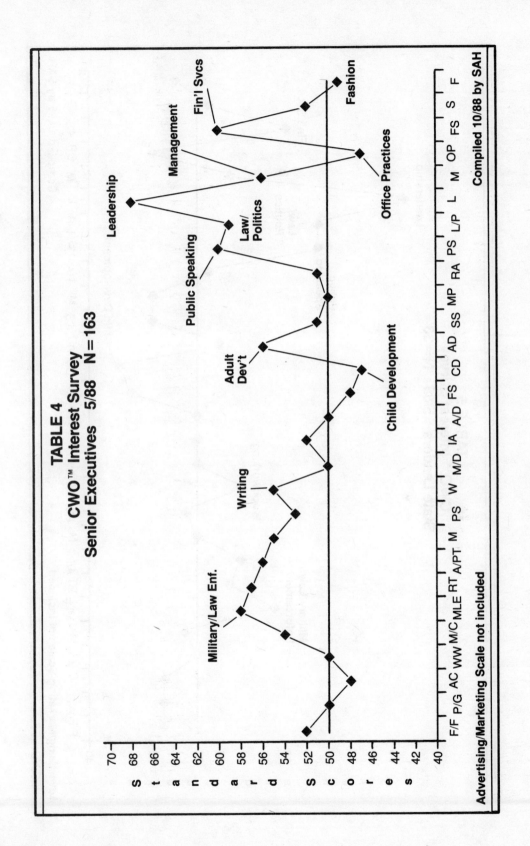

TABLE 4
CWO™ Interest Survey
Senior Executives 5/88 N = 163

Compiled 10/88 by SAH

Advertising/Marketing Scale not included

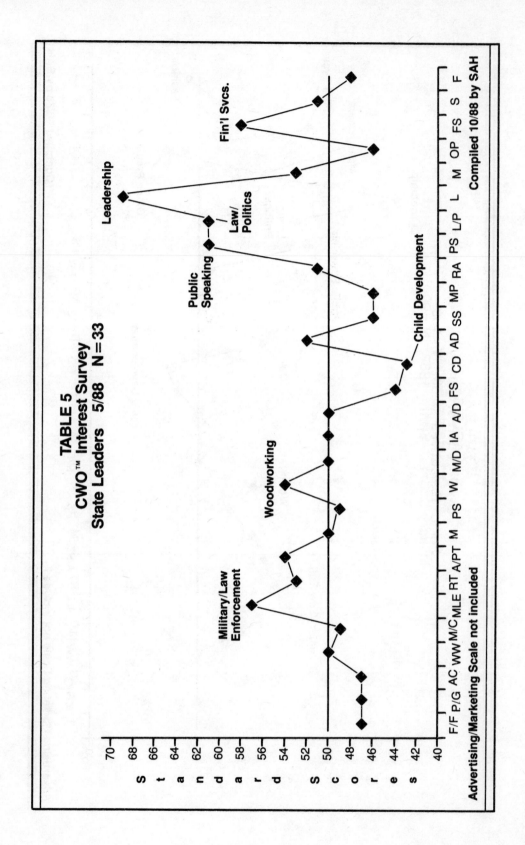

TABLE 5
CWO™ Interest Survey
State Leaders 5/88 N=33

Leadership

Public Speaking

Law/Politics

Fin'l Svcs.

Military/Law Enforcement

Woodworking

Child Development

F/F P/G AC WW M/C MLE RT A/PT M PS W M/D IA A/D FS CD AD SS MP RA PS L/P L M OP FS S F

Advertising/Marketing Scale not included          Compiled 10/88 by SAH

70 68 66 64 62 60 58 56 54 52 50 48 46 44 42 40

S t a n d a r d   S c o r e s

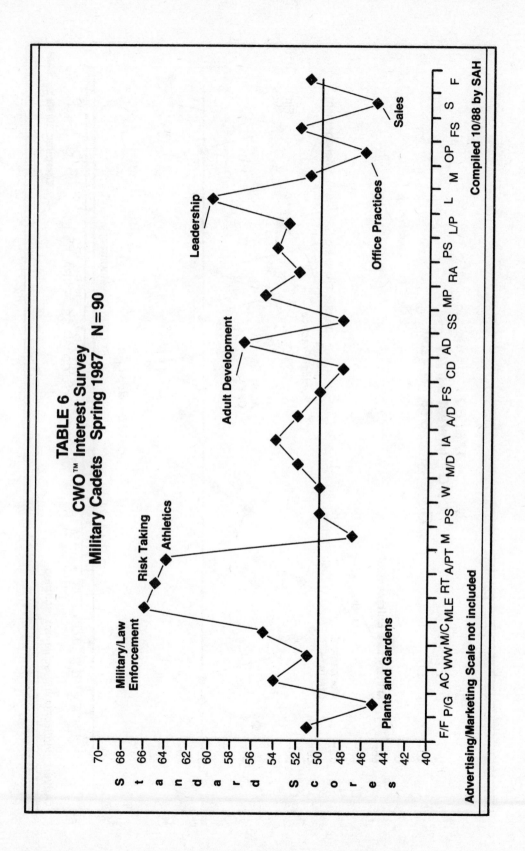

## TABLE 6
## CWO™ Interest Survey
## Military Cadets   Spring 1987   N = 90

Military/Law Enforcement

Risk Taking

Athletics

Leadership

Adult Development

Office Practices

Sales

Plants and Gardens

|  |  |
|---|---|
| 70 | S |
| 68 | t |
| 66 | a |
| 64 | n |
| 62 | d |
| 60 | a |
| 58 | r |
| 56 | d |
| 54 |  |
| 52 | S |
| 50 | c |
| 48 | o |
| 46 | r |
| 44 | e |
| 42 | s |
| 40 |  |

F/F   P/G   AC   WW   M/C   MLE   RT   A/PT   M   PS   W   M/D   IA   A/D   FS   CD   AD   SS   MP   RA   PS   L/P   L   M   OP   FS   S   F

Advertising/Marketing Scale not included

Compiled 10/88 by SAH

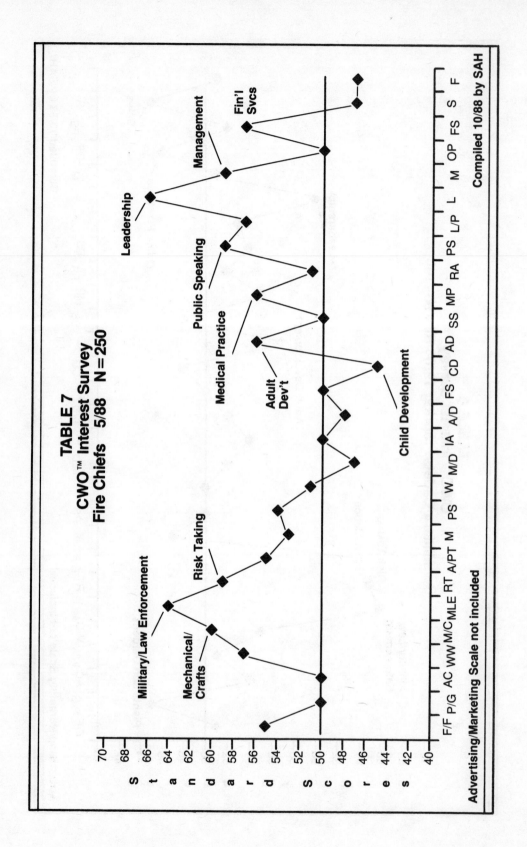

TABLE 7
CWO™ Interest Survey
Fire Chiefs  5/88   N = 250

Compiled 10/88 by SAH

Advertisting/Marketing Scale not included

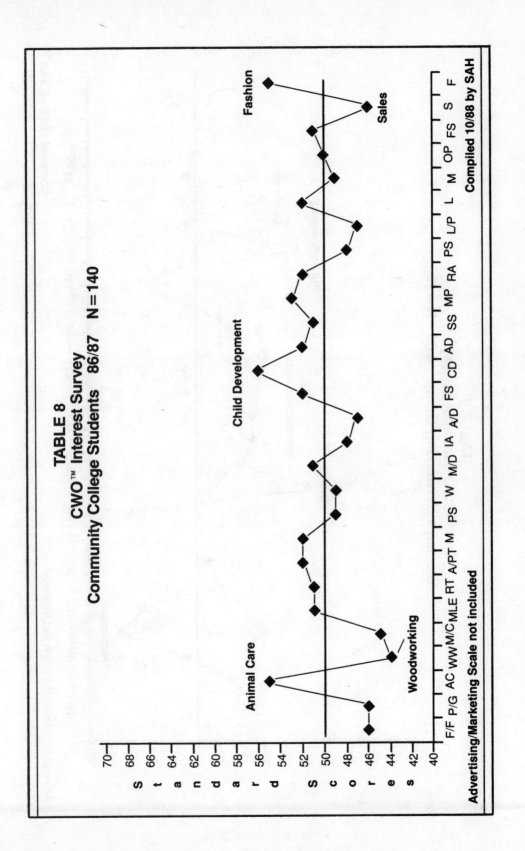

**TABLE 8**

CWO™ Interest Survey
Community College Students  86/87   N=140

Compiled 10/88 by SAH

Advertising/Marketing Scale not included

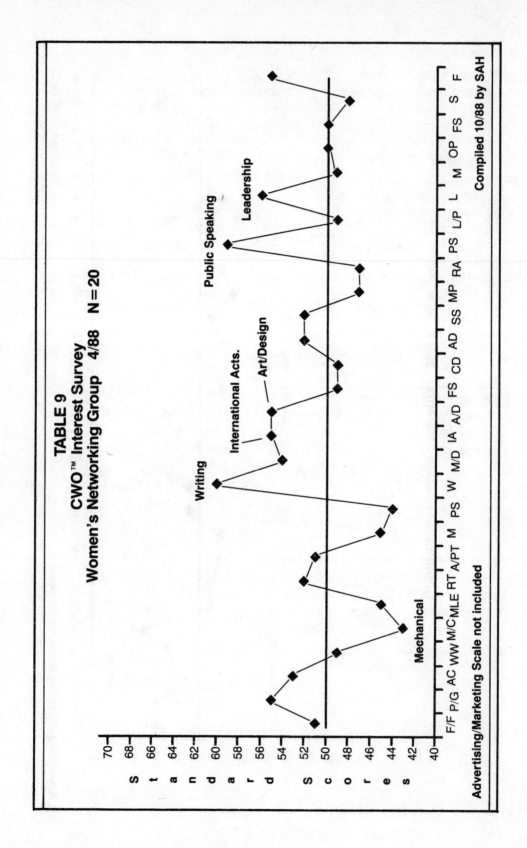

TABLE 9
CWO™ Interest Survey
Women's Networking Group   4/88    N = 20

Compiled 10/88 by SAH

prepared and returned to respondents that we realized it was confusing to be given scores for one set of interests and a different set of skills.

Consequently, at that point, the Skills Survey was redone, changing it to a six-point response format, and arbitrarily making certain that the Skills profile exactly mirrored the Interest profile. To do this required adding some new skill items to the survey and eliminating some other items that were no longer necessary. Because of this late start, we do not yet have any normative data for the Skills Survey.

We have collected enough data with the earlier version, and analyzed it at the item level, to suggest that asking people to report their self-evaluated skills is a viable approach. Tables 10 and 11, for example, show the ten most and ten least frequently reported skills among the senior executive sample, and these data make intuitive sense. Table 12 has the response frequencies for some other interesting skills from the same sample; note that 60 percent of them see themselves as either "good" or "expert" in charming members of the opposite sex, and 49 percent see themselves as either "good" or "expert" at predicting future economic trends.

For comparison with the item content of the Interest Survey Leadership Scale, the items on the Skills Survey Leadership Scale are listed in Table 13. As yet, no intercorrelation data are available.

**TABLE 10**
**CWO™ Skills Survey**
**Senior Executives   10/88   N = 154**

**Ten Most Frequently Reported Skills**
**(Percent Responding "Expert" or "Good")**

| | |
|---|---|
| Leading other people, making things happen | 91% |
| Distinguishing right from wrong | 90 |
| Acquiring the necessary resources for your plans | 90 |
| Inspiring teammates to superior performance | 88 |
| Competing against others in challenging situations | 88 |
| Following a plan of action, seeing projects through... | 86 |
| Delegating authority to others | 85 |
| Negotiating compromises between conflicting parties | 83 |
| Staying calm in crisis situations | 83 |
| Supervising the work of others | 83 |

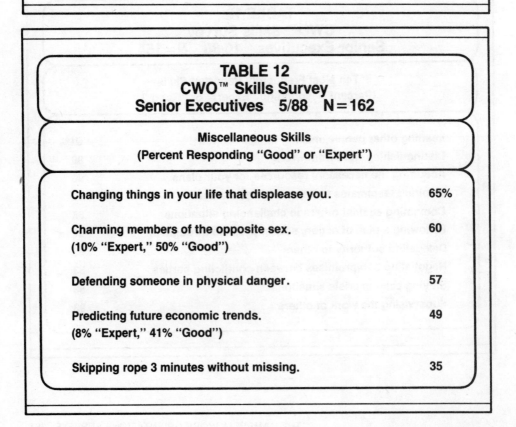

## TABLE 11
### CWO™ Skills Survey
### Senior Executives   10/88   N=154

**Ten Least Frequently Reported Skills**
**(Percent Responding "Poor" or "None")**

| | |
|---|---|
| Tailoring new shirts. . . | 89% |
| Raising exotic plants. . . | 78 |
| Performing in public on a musical instrument . . . | 76 |
| Doing major auto repairs. . . | 75 |
| Dancing in a professional style. . . | 72 |
| Sketching drawings of people or objects. . . | 72 |
| Caring for a wild bird sanctuary. . . | 70 |
| Maintaining a herd of livestock. . . | 68 |
| Operating scientific instruments. . . | 67 |
| Diagnosing physical health. . . | 65 |

## TABLE 12
### CWO™ Skills Survey
### Senior Executives   5/88   N=162

**Miscellaneous Skills**
**(Percent Responding "Good" or "Expert")**

| | |
|---|---|
| Changing things in your life that displease you. | 65% |
| Charming members of the opposite sex. (10% "Expert," 50% "Good") | 60 |
| Defending someone in physical danger. | 57 |
| Predicting future economic trends. (8% "Expert," 41% "Good") | 49 |
| Skipping rope 3 minutes without missing. | 35 |

## TABLE 13
## Items on the Skills Survey Leadership Scale

- Acquiring the necessary resources to carry out your plans.
- Coaching a highly skilled performance group.
- Cultivating leadership talents in other people.
- Delegating authority to others.
- Developing a long-range, visionary plan for your organization.
- Leading other people, making important things happen.
- Serving as an officer in a national volunteer organization.

We have been able to plot the senior executives' Skills and Interests, and those data are graphed in Table 14. The two curves are gratifyingly close to each other, but it should be recognized that these are raw scores, so all this really means is that the average item popularity within the Skills clusters is roughly the same as in the Interests clusters. Until we have both surveys standardized, we won't know how to interpret score discrepancies between Skills and Interests.

Of course, the other interesting analysis will be to do intracorrelations with each person to study the relationship between interests and self-reported skills.

Collection of skills data from other samples is also proceeding.

**Campbell Leadership Potential Index Self Versus Observers (CLPI)** The Leadership Potential Index is a list of 160 adjectives which the individual uses for self-description. Each adjective, such as "Active," "Brooding," or "Creative," is to be answered on a six-point scale from "Always" to "Never" according to how descriptive respondents think that adjective is for them. Similarly, three through five observers who know the person's working style are also asked to use the same list of 160 adjectives to describe the person.

*Scale Development for the CLPI.* The scales for the CLPI were developed in the same statistical/intuitive manner as the Interest Survey, with the additional consideration of trying to develop a list of scoring scales that was particularly related to the factors underlying successful leadership. This latter consideration guided the selection of adjectives to be included in the Index, the construction of the scoring scales, and the grouping of the scales on the profile. At each step, statistical data were used when available to guide the decisions, but it was also necessary to use a fair amount of reasoned judgment, what in the past has been called "armchair psychology," to decide just what factors should be included on the profile, and how they should be grouped. Future research will eventually determine whether these judgments were made correctly.

The six major Orientations, the components included in each, examples of adjectives in each of the components, and a brief psychological description of each component are listed in Table 15.

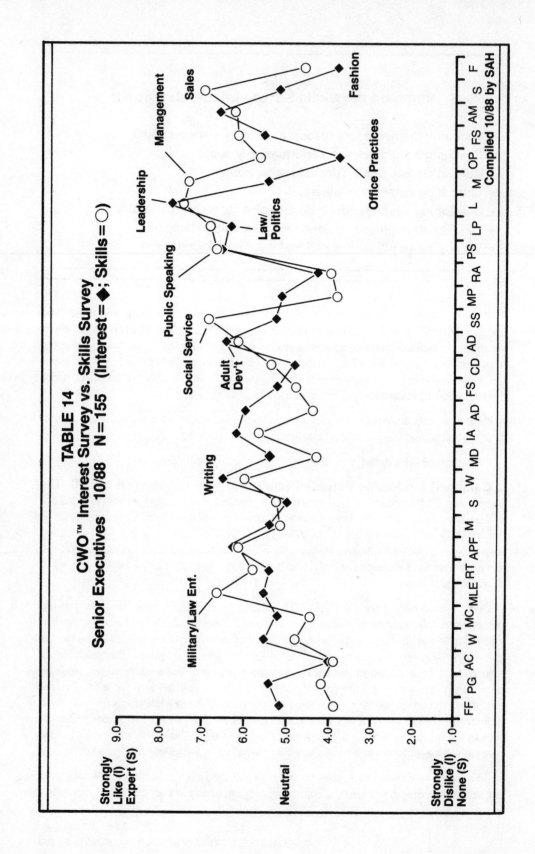

**TABLE 14**
**CWO™ Interest Survey vs. Skills Survey**
**Senior Executives  10/88  N = 155   (Interest = ◆; Skills = ○)**

# TABLE 15
## CWO™ Campbell Leadership Potential Index
## (Self Versus Observers)

| Orientations | Components | Typical Adjectives | Psychological Interpretation |
|---|---|---|---|
| **LEADERSHIP** | | | |
| | + Dynamic | Enthusiastic, inspiring | Takes charge, inspires others, seen as a leader. |
| | + Farsighted | Farsighted, forward-looking | Looks ahead, planful, a visionary. |
| | + Experienced | Savvy, well-connected | Has a good background, has been around. |
| | + Trustworthy | Candid, ethical | Demonstrates a sense of integrity and candor. |
| | + Confident | Optimistic, well-adjusted | Self-confident, has a comfortable feeling of self. |
| | + Ambitious | Competitive, hard-driving | Determined to make progress, drives others. |
| | − Passive | Fearful, meek | Often fearful, timid, cannot move forward. |
| | − Sheltered | Naive, sheltered | Inexperienced, perhaps young, or at least new. |
| **CREATIVITY** | | | |
| | + Enterprising | Resourceful, insightful | Works well with the complexities of change. |
| | + Original | Imaginative, inventive | Sees the world differently, has many new ideas. |
| | + Daring | Bold, impulsive | Willing to try new experiences, risk-oriented. |
| | + Colorful | Dramatic, flamboyant | Likes to stand out from the crowd, a character. |
| | − Conforming | Cautious, obedient | Does what is told, tries nothing risky. |
| | − Conventional | Conservative, traditional | Prefers the world as it has always been. |
| **PHYSICAL ENERGY** | | | |
| | + Active | Athletic, rugged | Has lots of energy, good physical endurance. |
| | − Sedentary | Inactive, sedentary | Lives an inactive life with no exercise. |
| **PRODUCTIVITY** | | | |
| | + Effective | Persistent, productive | Gets things done, stays on target. |
| | + Dependable | Orderly, reliable | Can be depended on, especially for routine matters. |
| | + Thrifty | Frugal, prudent | Uses and manages money wisely. |
| | − Careless | Irresponsible, wasteful | Neglects obligations and daily details. |
| | − Procrast'ng. | Distractible, fickle | Cannot get things done on time. |
| **LIKEABILITY** | | | |
| | + Friendly | Cheerful, likeable | Pleasant to be around, makes others feel good. |
| | + Affectionate | Emotional, loving | Acts close, warm, and nurturing. |
| | + Helpful | Considerate, generous | Shows a strong, unselfish concern for others. |
| | + Entertaining | Outgoing, witty | Has the power to please and delight others. |
| | − Solitary | Aloof, autonomous | Self-sufficient, often prefers to be alone. |
| | − Quiet | Private, serious | Says little, difficult to get to know. |
| | − Self-centered | Egotistical, sarcastic | Thinks continually of self, disregards others. |
| **PSYCHOLOGICAL COMFORT** | | | |
| | + Confident | Optimistic, well-adjusted | Self-confident, has a comfortable feeling of self. |
| | + Calm | Calm, peaceful | Has an unhurried, unruffled manner. |
| | − Temperam'tl. | Irritable, stubborn | Firmly fixed in own ways, can be petty and fiery. |
| | − Suspicious | Cynical, resentful | Often complains, does not trust others. |
| | − Brooding | Depressed, pessimistic | Continually worries, feels gloomy and discouraged. |

9/88

## TABLE 16
## Item Intercorrelations for the Dynamic Component

|  | Charismatic | Dynamic | Enthusiastic | Inspiring | A Leader |
|---|---|---|---|---|---|
| Charismatic |  | .65 | .44 | .44 | .57 |
| Dynamic |  |  | .58 | .47 | .59 |
| Enthusiastic |  |  |  | .33 | .39 |
| Inspiring |  |  |  |  | .47 |
| A Leader |  |  |  |  |  |

*Scale Development for the CLPI.* As with the other surveys, the scoring scales (also termed components) were developed with a combination of statistical data, that is, item intercorrelations and intuition. As an example, the adjectives comprising the Dynamic component, and their intercorrelations, are listed in Table 16.

Once again, it is worth pointing out that item intercorrelations above .30 are usually considered high, so the items in the Dynamic Component are indeed highly inter-correlated. Obviously, these five adjectives form a tightly knit measuring scale.

The other scoring components were developed in a similar manner, with similar intercorrelations.

*Naming the CLPI Scoring Components.* Naming the components was an important step because the choice of a name dictates the overt psychological meaning of the scale; as such, the name should convey the sense of the cluster of items as accurately as possible.

Three general guidelines were followed in selecting the name for each component: first, the names were restricted to the adjectives actually included in the component; second, in general, the adjective with the highest average intercorrelation with the remaining adjectives was usually chosen as the component name; third, some arbitrary judgment was used when the decision was close, with the intent of choosing a component name that would be acceptable to the respondent. For example, one component was named "Temperamental" even though another adjective in that component, "Hotheaded," actually had slightly higher item intercorrelations (average of .45 vs. .43). "Temperamental" seems more appropriate for a component name because it is more professional sounding than "Hotheaded," which sounds a bit slangy.

Another component that has been troublesome to name has been the "Brooding" component. In some of the preliminary tryouts, this cluster was named "Depressed," which is the adjective in that component with the highest average intercorrelation (average = .50). That name "Depressed" created some concern, especially among some of the psychologists who were being used as sounding boards during the develop-ment phase. They were afraid that respondents would be upset when told that the test indicated that they were "Depressed"—the name seemed too potent. Consequently, the name was changed to "Anxious" for several more tryout samples. That didn't feel quite right; "Anxious" implies a more temporary emotion than this component probably taps, so the name was changed once again to "Brooding," which is what we are now experimenting with.

There may be no good solution because of the nature of the measure itself. Those who describe themselves as some combination of Anxious, Brooding, and Depressed, all adjectives within that component, need to be dealt with in a professionally sound, emotionally sensitive manner. By definition, these people are already somewhat down, and the test results should not contribute more to that depression. In the several dozen cases that I have reviewed in the developmental stage of this inventory, my impression is that none of the high scorers, that is, the depressed people, have been surprised by the outcome. They feel down, and they know it. For at least some of them, the statistical manifestation of their emotional state seemed to be useful, for it vividly highlighted their situation. People dealt with the high scores in various ways, but at least some said, "I'm not surprised, but it has caught my attention and suggests that I had better do something about it."

*Preliminary Results for the CLPI.* Table 17 shows the results from preliminary scoring for the senior executives sample, including both Self and Observer profiles. The highest and lowest components are labelled, and the data look quite reasonable; this sample scored highest on the Leadership, Ambition, and Productivity components, lowest on Passivity, Affection, and Helpfulness.

It must again be emphasized that the scoring norms used here are tentative, and they may need to be modified somewhat as more data are collected. The true test will come when we have better outside criteria on which to compare groups.

Still, at this time, these observer ratings are at least as good as most criteria used in a typical leadership study. For each person, we have ratings from at least three observers on an extensive checklist of adjectives. In a sense, concurrent validity is built right into the scoring system.

**Campbell Organizational Survey (COS)** The Organizational Survey was developed for different reasons from the other surveys. The Interest, Skills, and Leadership Potential Surveys were developed for use as individual assessment tools, while the Organizational Survey came into existence in order to assess the characteristics of work groups. The initial thinking behind the development of the Organizational Survey was concerned with developing a criterion measure which could be used to evaluate some of the other survey instruments. People who are good leaders should score high on the appropriate scales of the individual surveys; their subordinates should score high on appropriate measures of job and organizational satisfaction. In working with some of the initial tryout samples, this issue of trying to evaluate the quality of leadership within an organization kept coming up, so the Organizational Survey was developed to study this point.

The Organizational Survey went through several experimental iterations, and finally emerged as a short questionnaire (44 items) with 13 scoring scales. The same six-point response format was used, and the same statistical/intuitive scale construction techniques were followed.

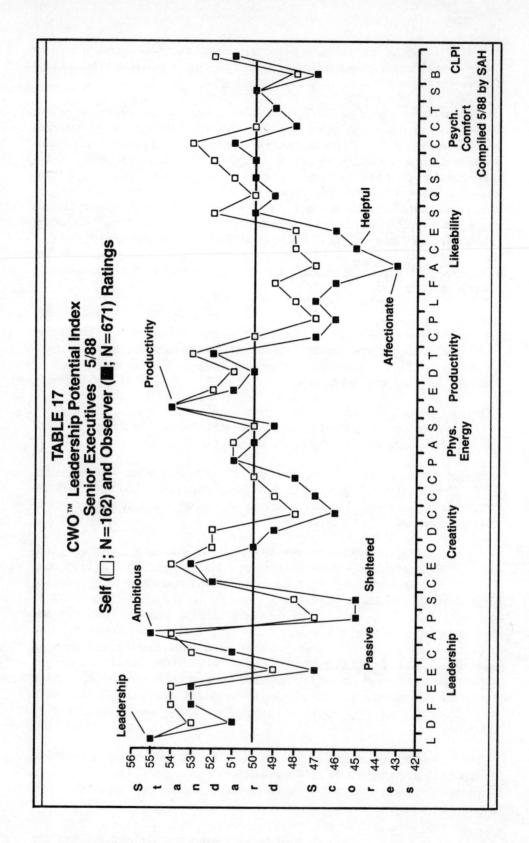

**TABLE 17**
**CWO™ Leadership Potential Index**
**Senior Executives   5/88**
**Self (□; N=162) and Observer (■; N=671) Ratings**

Compiled 5/88 by SAH

Table 18 lists the current scoring scales for the Organizational Survey, along with sample items from each scale, and a brief statement about the meaning of high scores.

Table 19 has some preliminary results, in raw score form (scores from 1 through 9), for three samples who filled in an earlier version of the COS: 162 senior executives; 128 employees of a nonprofit R & D Organization, including a wide range of professional, clerical, janitorial, and other support staff; and a sample of 11 members of a CCL Leadership Development Class. The last sample, quite small, contains a diverse collection of people from the corporate world, the military, and nonprofit settings. Clearly, senior executives in this sample, which includes mostly successful corporate executives on their way up, are quite satisfied with their working situation.

Table 20 has other data which demonstrate another application of the COS; it shows individual scores for two people: one the highest scoring and thus most satisfied R & D employee; the other, the lowest scoring and thus the least satisfied R & D employee, along with the mean of all R & D employees who filled in the questionnaire. An obvious conclusion is that the nature of the leadership or supervision required for the most satisfied employee is likely to be much different from that required for the least satisfied employee. For the most satisfied employee, the major leadership task is probably to stay out of the way. In contrast, regarding the least satisfied employee, one cannot help wondering why such employees stay around. They appear not to like anything about their job: not their work, not their co-workers, certainly neither their supervisor nor top leadership, not their pay—nothing seems to satisfy them.

As a result of looking at data like this, another scale was added to the COS, that of Job Security, under the rationale that this must be a missing component. Some people may stay in miserable jobs just because the jobs are secure. At the same time, the Working Conditions scale was split into two scales, one concerned with physical comfort (Working Conditions), the other concerned with psychological conditions (Freedom From Stress).

Some data using the expanded, and final, version are reported in Table 21. Another sample of senior executives from the same business school has filled in this version, along with several other samples. One sample, N = 107, contains midlevel managers from a large Fortune 100 conglomerate that has recently been involved in much merger, acquisition, and divestiture activity, which shows up in the low Job Security score; another sample (N = 48) contains the R & D directors of a large chemical/drug firm. Most of these were MDs or PhDs and their skepticism about organization constraints shows up in their low regard for supervision and leadership.

A fourth sample (N = 29) includes only the top executives—Vice-Presidents, Presidents of Foreign Subsidiaries, and so forth—of an international publishing company. From their data, this appears to be a highly satisfied, highly motivated sample.

A fifth sample (N = 57; Federal Government Managers—New) reports the data for a less satisfied sample, that of newly promoted managers in the federal government. They are substantially less happy with most aspects of their working environment, compared to the other samples.

The Organizational Survey seems to be working well, producing information that is related to the perceived quality of many aspects of the working environment. The

# TABLE 18
## CWO™ Campbell Organizational Survey— Explanatory Notes

| COMPONENTS | SAMPLE ITEMS<br>([+] indicates item is weighted positively,<br>[−] negatively) | PSYCHOLOGICAL INTERPRETATION OF<br>HIGH SCORES<br>(Low scores indicate the reverse) |
|---|---|---|
| **The Work Itself** | + On my job, I use a wide range of skills.<br>− My job is dull and boring. | People like their work, feel stretched by their job, and believe that what they do is important. |
| **Working Conditions** | + I work in a pleasing, attractive setting.<br>− I work under unpleasant conditions, such as crowding. . . . | Indicates satisfaction with the physical environment—space, equipment, lighting, etc. |
| **Freedom From Job Stress** | + When I am under stress, I have someone at work to talk to.<br>− Because the pace is so demanding here, mistakes often happen. | Level of job stress is comfortable, i.e., not too high. |
| **Co-workers** | + People help each other out when the work load is heavy.<br>− Around here, people take advantage of others to get ahead. | Reflects a sense of camaraderie and teamwork among colleagues. |
| **Supervision** | + My supervisor is skilled and experienced.<br>− My supervisor is difficult to work for. | Indicates respect, trust, and appreciation for the immediate supervisor; a feeling of being listened to, and of being valued as a contributor. |
| **Top Leadership** | + The people in charge have a clear vision of where we are going.<br>− The people at the top are conservative and slow to take advantage of new opportunities. | Shows faith in and admiration for the people at the top, a sense of being well-led. |
| **Pay** | + I am satisfied with my pay.<br>− We are not paid as well as people in other organizations. . . . | People feel well-rewarded and equitably treated in an economic sense. |
| **Fringe Benefits** | + Our fringe benefits—such as holidays, insurance, vacations, and retirement plans—are good. | Basic benefits are seen as adequate. |
| **Job Security** | + I know that as long as I do good work, my job here is secure.<br>− I am afraid that some unexpected change might eliminate my job. | Job security is certain, based on good performance by the individual and the company. |
| **Promotions/ Opportunities** | + This job is a good stepping-stone for the future.<br>− Promotions depend more on having the right connections than on performance. | Opportunities for advancement are perceived as good, and fairly administered. |
| **Feedback/ Communications** | + Feedback on performance for people at my level is timely, accurate, and constructive.<br>− Our organization does a poor job of keeping us informed. . . . | People feel well-informed and accurately evaluated. |
| **Organizational Planning** | + New projects are usually well-planned.<br>− There is very little planning here; we just go from crisis to crisis. | Planning is taken seriously, and change is managed well. |
| **Freedom to Innovate** | + New ideas are welcomed and nurtured here.<br>− Change comes slowly; people would rather do things the old way. | People believe they have the necessary resources and freedom to try new ideas, and feel appreciated for being innovative. |
| **Overall Index** | Includes all items, weighted either positively or negatively as appropriate. | An overall high score reflects satisfaction with all, or mostly all, of the individual's working life. |

9/88

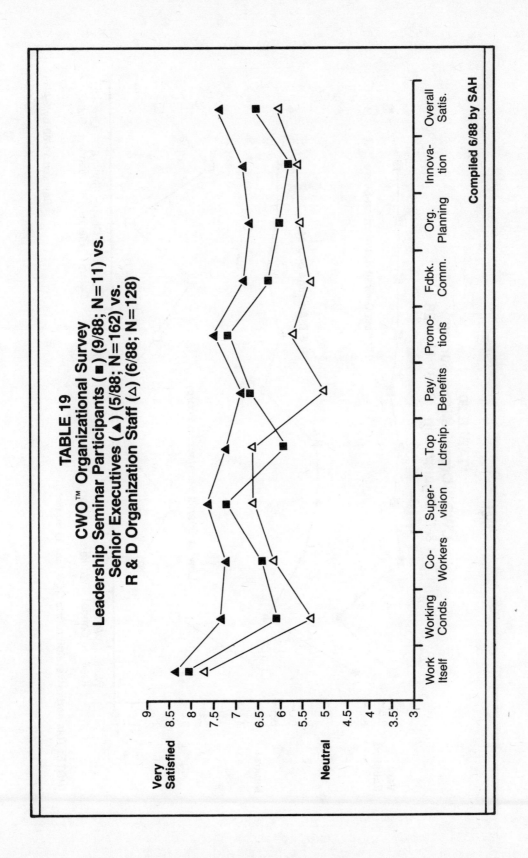

**TABLE 19**
**CWO™ Organizational Survey**
**Leadership Seminar Participants (■) (9/88; N=11) vs.**
**Senior Executives (▲) (5/88; N=162) vs.**
**R & D Organization Staff (△) (6/88; N=128)**

Compiled 6/88 by SAH

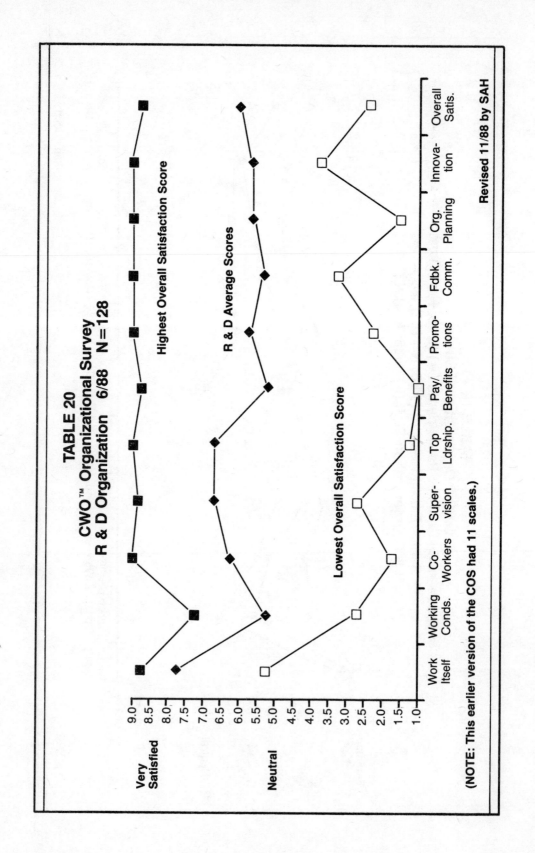

**TABLE 20**
CWO™ Organizational Survey
R & D Organization   6/88   N = 128

Highest Overall Satisfaction Score

R & D Average Scores

Lowest Overall Satisfaction Score

Very Satisfied

Neutral

9.0
8.5
8.0
7.5
7.0
6.5
6.0
5.5
5.0
4.5
4.0
3.5
3.0
2.5
2.0
1.5
1.0

Work Itself   Working Conds.   Co-Workers   Supervision   Top Ldrship.   Pay/Benefits   Promotions   Fdbk. Comm.   Org. Planning   Innovation   Overall Satis.

Revised 11/88 by SAH

(NOTE: This earlier version of the COS had 11 scales.)

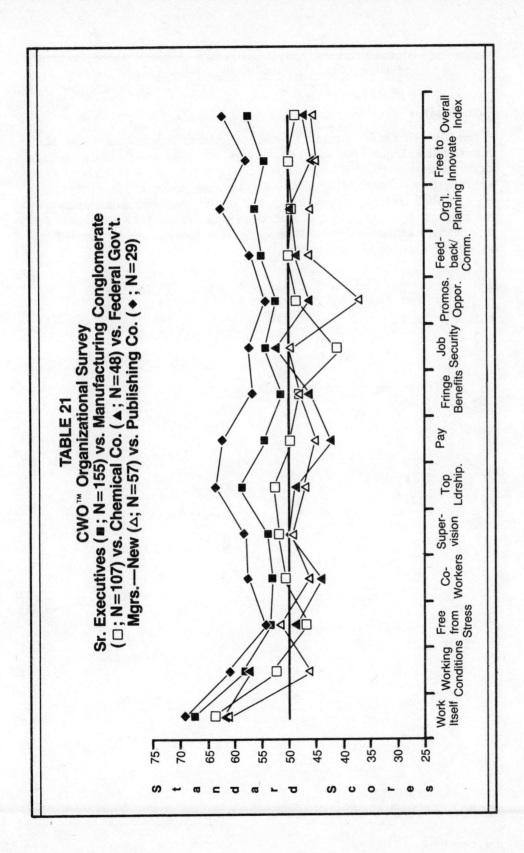

**TABLE 21**
**CWO™ Organizational Survey**
**Sr. Executives (■; N=155) vs. Manufacturing Conglomerate**
**(□; N=107) vs. Chemical Co. (▲; N=48) vs. Federal Gov't.**
**Mgrs.—New (△; N=57) vs. Publishing Co. (♦; N=29)**

challenge now is to see if these measures correlate with the individual leadership qualities measured by the Interest, Skills, and Leadership Potential surveys.

## Conclusion

This has been a brief overview of a new battery of surveys designed to tap many factors in the individual's orientation toward work, with special attention paid to those factors particularly related to leadership and creativity. The goal is to be able to study a wide range of personal characteristics within the individual, spread over the areas of interests, skills, leadership characteristics, and working satisfactions and frustrations. Much more work has to be done to develop interpretative aids to help individuals and organizations use these surveys, but the research to this point suggests that their technical underpinnings are sound.

# SECTION E

**Leadership at the Top
of an Organization**

# Leadership at the Top of an Organization

Most studies of leadership that involve collecting psychological measures have been conducted in laboratories with college students as subjects or have used samples of lower- and middle-level managers. However, leadership theorizing has developed, with particular heed paid to leadership at the top. Consequently, data and theories often do not relate well to each other. The articles in this section represent new ventures in the study of top organizational leadership and provide new insights into its nature. For example, one set of measures is collected on lieutenant generals and generals in the United States Army. Sets of behaviors and capabilities emerge that relate to both good and poor performance.

## Military Executive Leadership
T. Owen Jacobs and Elliott Jaques

This paper outlines an organizational theory and presents results of research efforts based on it. Leadership is viewed as a process which occurs only in situations where there is decision discretion. Leadership is more important at higher organizational levels because of the greater uncertainty, ambiguity, and complexity at these levels. A means of measuring "discretion in action," the CPA, was designed to focus on cognitive capacity; it has been tested in various settings as a measure of high-level cognitive functioning. Four-star generals are compared to three-stars in terms of multinational concern, a concern with joint/unified relationships, and envisioning/anticipating with time span of work as a key component.

T. Owen Jacobs, Chief, Executive Development Research Group, U.S. Army Research Institute for the Behavioral and Social Sciences, 5001 Eisenhower Avenue, Alexandria, Virginia 22333-5600. (202-274-9045). PhD, University of Pittsburgh. Author of *Leadership and Exchange in Formal Organizations*.

Elliott Jaques, 902 1101 South Arlington Ridge Road, Arlington, Virginia 22202. (703-521-3873). MD, Johns Hopkins University; PhD, Harvard University. Author of various articles and publications.

## Understanding and Assessing Organizational Leadership
Marshall Sashkin and W. Warner Burke

Only recently have psychologists engaged in the study of top-level executive leadership—as opposed to mid- and lower-level management—as an organizational phenomenon. This paper describes and discusses how transformational and transactional leaders differ and how individuals in one or the other category can be measurably distinguished. The way power is used to empower followers is posited as a key factor that distinguishes transformational from transactional leaders. Described is a questionnaire, developed to assess three aspects of transformational leadership: interpersonal behavior, personal characteristics, and organizational culture-building actions. Research is described which suggests or demonstrates that organizations with leaders who score high on this Leader Behavior Questionnaire are more effective, as compared with organizations with low-scoring leaders.

Marshall Sashkin, OERI Senior Associate, Educational Networks Division, Programs for the Improvement of Practice, Office of Educational Research and Improvement, United States Department of Education, Washington, DC 20208-5644. (202-357-6120). PhD, The University of Michigan. Past Chair of the Organization Development Division of the Academy of Management. Past Editor of *Group and Organization Studies*. Editorial Board member of *Academy of Management Executive*, the *Human Resource Development Quarterly*, and the *Journal of Executive Development*. Author or coauthor of various publications on leadership, group dynamics, and organizational change.

W. Warner Burke, Professor of Psychology and Education and Coordinator for the Graduate Program in Organizational Psychology, Teachers College, Columbia University, 525 West 121st Street, New York, New York 10027 (212-678-3249). PhD, The University of Texas. Editor of *Academy of Management Executive*. Member of Board of Governors of the American Society for Training and Development. Diplomate in Industrial/Organizational Psychology, American Board of Professional Psychology. Author, coauthor, or editor of various publications on organization development, training, and social and organizational psychology.

## Leadership Behavior in Ambiguous Environments
Joseph L. Moses and Karen S. Lyness

A study of ambiguity and its effects on high-level managerial behavior conducted over a five-year period (prior to and during AT&T's divestiture). Only about one in four high-potential managers was found to be effective in ambiguous environments. Adaptive styles, ability, and comfort levels were critical in affecting performance effectiveness.

Joseph L. Moses, Corporate Psychologist, AT&T and Applied Research Group, 550 Madison Avenue, Room 3225, New York, New York 10022. (212-605-7624). PhD, Baylor University. Fellow, Division 14 American Psychological Association. Diplomate, American Board of Professional Psychology. Coauthor of *Ambiguity, Uncertainty and Change: Assessing Behavior and Improving Coping Styles* (in press).

Karen S. Lyness, Vice President, Corporate Human Resources, Citicorp, 399 Park Avenue, 26th Floor, Zone 3, New York, New York 10043. (212-559-0488). PhD, Ohio State University. Member, SIOP and Academy of Management. Director of Professional Development for the Metropolitan New York Association for Applied Psychology. Coauthor of *Ambiguity, Uncertainty and Change: Assessing Behavior and Improving Coping Styles* (in press) and "Stimulating High-Potential Career Development Through an Assessment Center Process" in *Career Growth and Human Resource Strategies: The Role of the HR Professional in Employee Growth.*

# Military Executive Leadership

*T. Owen
Jacobs
and
Elliott
Jaques*

In 1978, Elliott Jaques completed his *General Theory of Bureaucracy*. In this book, he integrated observational experience over a period in excess of 35 years to produce a set of descriptions of requisitely structured organizations and of the work required at each organizational level. This general theory has quite significant implications concerning the nature of leadership within the total organization, and for the development of capacity to exercise leadership at the various levels of such an organization.

This paper will briefly outline the theory and its implications. It will then present the results of two research efforts which seem to provide substantial support for the theory itself.

## Theoretical Structure

**Leadership Definition** It seems useful first to define leadership. The following is proposed:

*Leadership is a process of giving purpose [meaningful direction] to collective effort, and causing willing effort to be expended to achieve purpose.*

This definition at first glance appears to be a content-free generality with little utility. It is quite esoteric when compared with the many definitions Yukl (1989) cites. However, this kind of abstractness may be necessary if one construct is to encompass all the levels of the organization as Jaques describes it. The definition sets two criteria for determining that leadership has occurred. One is that member(s) of a collectivity are left with a perception of a goal and that what they are doing is focused on goal attainment. The second is that they are internally committed to expend effort toward goal attainment.

To be consonant with the theory to be described below, leadership must be viewed as a process which occurs only in situations in which there is decision discretion. To the extent discretion exists, there is an opportunity for leadership to be exercised. If there is no discretion, there is no such opportunity. This follows the logic of Hunt, Osborn, and Martin (1981).

One final assertion is that leadership is not a "thing" and that it probably is not useful to talk of "leaders" as either persons (in contrast to persons who are not "leaders") or as role incumbents. Leadership as defined here is an influence process which is a type of role behavior. This role behavior can be displayed by any member of a formal or informal organization. Stereotypically, it is most often directed downward. However, it may also be directed laterally (and then can be a crucially important role requirement) or upward. When directed laterally, for example, it is more likely to be given another name, for example, consensus building, but it nonetheless has the required properties described above and thus should be recognized for what it is. It is, in fact, so recognized by Osborn, Hunt, and Jauch (1980).

As thus defined, leadership is a systems requirement which is fundamentally related to the process of organizing and gaining collective unity of movement. It can be exercised by anyone in the collectivity, though it is the superordinate who most often does. At its most fundamental level, it is an exchange of information about what ought to be done (or how it ought to be done, or some other discretionary issue) that, if successful, impacts on the belief systems which support action. (This ignores the special case of charismatic "leadership" in crisis situations: there, the compulsion to action by the "follower" may cause emulation of any "leader" action, whether it is correct and proper or not. It may or may not be useful to include this as a "type" of leadership.)

Leadership as so defined probably is more important at higher organizational echelons because of the greater uncertainty, ambiguity, and complexity at these levels. This is because an essential precursor to the exercise of the leadership process is a resolution of situational uncertainty, ambiguity, and complexity to a sufficient extent that clarity is achieved about what directions *should* be taken. Such resolution may require information exchange processes, much like those already described (Jacobs, 1972), as essential in the leadership process at lower levels. In large-scale formal organizations, this degree of uncertainty and complexity almost never will be found at lower levels. It almost never is *not* found at the higher levels.

**Organizational Structure** In earlier work (Jacobs & Jaques, 1987), a theoretical model relating leadership, complexity, and organizational level was presented, based on the earlier theory developed by Jaques (1978). Jacobs and Jaques suggest that well-configured large-scale organizations will have approximately seven distinguishable levels which are divided into three broad bands. Simon (1977) describes three organizational "layers" much like these three bands; he spoke of them as "layers of a cake." Each band, or layer, is conceptually more complex than the one below it and thus poses unique new conceptual requirements for decision makers and leaders. These new requirements do not replace those of earlier levels, but rather are superimposed on them. The capacity to deal with these requirements is based on development of a causal map (frame of reference) which is capable of "patterning" the encountered complexity. A substantial part of "learning the new job" is completing the causal map needed for that job to a sufficient extent that it permits adequately reliable and effective decisions to be made.

The theory also suggests that the decisions, and therefore the required thinking skills, may also be qualitatively different in nature at successively higher echelons. Here, the theory parallels and draws on observations made by Katz and Kahn (1966) concerning shifts in broad skill categories required at different organizational levels. The lowest "layer" of an organization generally focuses on the accomplishment of concrete tasks, and thus demands a focus on technical and interpersonal skills. Superordinates *generally* have, or can have, direct face-to-face contact with subordinates involved in task accomplishment, and thus can achieve results through direct assignment of tasks and direct motivation of effort toward task accomplishment. Leadership in this lowest "layer" thus is "direct." While conceptual skills may be of some importance, they are *less* important than technical and interpersonal skills.

Superordinates in the middle "layer" do not generally have direct access to the direct production level. They are generally well removed from those involved in direct task accomplishment, and, in addition, are concerned with critical tasks that do not involve the direct supervision of those doing the task work. Their responsibilities are more in the area of finding indirect means for facilitating task accomplishment at the direct level. The work strongly focuses on the management of interdependencies among subordinate elements and their differential resourcing in relation to requirements, as well as coordination of effort over time. Because "indirect" means are not "concrete" and "direct," there is a greater requirement for conceptual skills and for the capacity for abstract thought. For these reasons, the theory postulates that abstract analytic thinking skills are substantially more important in the middle "layer" than at lower levels. By contrast, technical skills may be less important.

Superordinates in the top, or executive, "layer" are confronted with even more complex requirements. Executives "add value" to their organizations in at least two critical areas: providing a sense of understanding and purpose to the general activities of the organization, and tapping sources of resources not available to others. They do the first (either single-handedly or in collaboration with others) by "patterning" the ambiguity, uncertainty, and complexity of the organization's environment through use of an appropriately complex causal map. By uncertainty reduction, they enable unity of organization effort to emerge. They do the second by building consensus about proposed courses of action among those who hold needed resources, generally outside the organization.

These two broad functions by no means exhaust the role requirements at the executive level, as Mintzberg (1973) pointed out nearly a generation ago. However, they *are* critical functions, and they draw attention to the conceptual skills required at this level. For example, executive time horizons must be quite long, uniformly in excess of ten years, according to Jaques. Causal maps are essentially patterns of cause-and-effect relationships. The executive must in theory be able to build into his frame of reference enough cause-and-effect "chains" to enable inference to the overarching rules and principles that pertain to the system at his level. His capacity to perceive effects over time therefore must be at least as great as the cause-and-effect time intervals in the real system. And his capacity to infer rules and principles is crucial for generalization from one application of the map to another. This suggests that abstract integrative thinking skills are essential at the executive level.

**Summary of Theoretical Structure** The theoretical position outlined above is a synthesis of a number of relatively diverse elements, among them Jaques' general theory, exchange theory, and representation theory as it is developing in the cognitive sciences. Many of its predictions are untested, and a substantial amount of data gathering will be needed to answer questions it raises. Among those critical questions are the following:

a. Theory suggests that there is a progression of thinking skill requirements from concrete to abstract analytic to abstract integrative. Is there really such a progression? If so, is individual development progressive, or were executives always capable of abstract integration?

b. Is development maturational (Fischer, 1980) or is it dependent on experience and/or proclivity? If a mixture, what proportion of total variance is contributed by each of the contributors, and how can nonmaturational development be impacted to enhance conceptual skill growth?

c. What is proclivity, and, in general, how can the factors suggested above be operationally defined?

The remainder of this paper reports data from two separate efforts which support the theory at least in part, and which may provide insight concerning further directions that should be taken. The first is a longitudinal study of methods for assessing managerial potential conducted at the Brunel Institute of Social Studies by Stamp (1988). The second is a study of military executives conducted at the Army Research Institute by the Executive Development Research Group (Jaques, Clement, Rigby, & Jacobs, 1985; Harris, Rigby, & Jacobs, in preparation).

## Assessment of Managerial Potential

In the mid-1970s, Stamp undertook to develop a means of measuring "discretion in action," a construct central to the work Jaques was then doing as he was developing his general theory. The outcome was an individual assessment interview, called the CPA, which is built around three components and which lasts two hours or more. The first component was a concept formation task which uses the same card-sorting task Bruner (1966) used. The second was a comprehensive work history. The third was a set of phrase cards, that is, cards with short phrases which are sorted as to preference (a "comfort" criterion) and then discussed by assessees.

The procedure for conducting an assessment is to administer the CPA according to a rigid protocol which involves not only the individual's performance, for example, on the card-sort task, but also the manner in which the various tasks are pursued. The administrator must be trained in the use of the procedure, and must in addition be rather substantially knowledgeable of Jaques' general theory. For reasons that will become apparent later, precise understanding of his classification of levels of work, that is, the *nature* of work by level, is crucial. The CPA is essentially a tool for locating an individual's current position in this schema with coordinates representing current age and current level. The outcome of the assessment is then evaluated against a standard set of "growth" curves derived by Jaques from extensive study of managerial progression in formal organizations to obtain a prediction of probable future organizational level at any given future age.

Over a period of 14 years, Stamp and her associates have done many assessments with this procedure. For a subset of those, it was possible in the time period from 1984 to 1988 to conduct a follow-up of the individuals initially assessed in four different companies. They were a multinational oil company (N=84), a multinational engineering company (N=35), a fertilizer company (N=38), and a mine in a developing country (N=25). In the follow-up, the predictor variable was the CPA outcome as described above. The criterion was the actual level occupied by the individual at the time of follow-up. In essence, the CPA provided a prediction of what that level would be. The correlations reported in the study are between those two variables.

Because the assessment procedure developed over time, only 76 assessees received the most current version of the CPA. Nonetheless, the predictive validities were impressive. Stamp broke out several different subsamples:

a. Total Sample (N=182). Individual follow-ups occurred over periods from four to thirteen years. As suggested by the description of organizational settings in which assessment occurred, assessees were diverse. Stamp notes educational level ranged from school dropout at age 11 to PhD. The sample included both men and women, of different cultural backgrounds. A correlation of .79 was obtained between predicted and actual organizational level at follow-up.

b. Multinational Oil Company (N=84). Individual follow-up occurred after a period of nine years. The original data collection occurred in 1974, with follow-up initiated in 1984. The initial sample contained 100 assessees, with 84 remaining within the company at the time of follow-up. The form of CPA used was the first form, which contained the card-sort task and a brief work history. The correlation between predicted and actual organizational level was .70. This may be an underestimate of the actual correlation if attrition from the original sample occurred from one extreme end of the distribution on the criterion measure.

c. Mixed sample (N=76). This sample consisted of assessees who received the current form of the CPA. Individual follow-up period ranged from four to eight years. The correlation between predicted and actual organizational level was .89. Stamp comments that the increase in predicted variance in this sample (79.6%) over that obtained in the multinational oil company (49.9%) resulted from the refinement of the CPA, a reasonable assertion.

d. Subsample (N=59). This is a subsample of the mixed sample, above, who were employed by a single organization and who remained in the organization over the period of time during which the follow-up occurred. The correlation between predicted and actual organizational level for this subsample was .92.

**Summary and Discussion** In her report, Stamp also cites findings from other assessment methodologies, relying on five earlier reviews. It goes without saying that the findings from follow-up of CPA assessments revealed considerably higher predictive validities than were found in these reviews. Most assessment centers elicit assessee data on a wide variety of dimensions. The time requirements for this are in many cases formidable. That a highly transportable assessment procedure examining performance on a single cluster of conceptual skills (construct validity has not yet been fully explored) should so outperform them constitutes a strong mandate to undertake confirmatory work using this technology.

However, two further points are cogent here. The first is that required assessor skill is not trivial. The second is that the CPA findings, in addition to suggesting its potential as a tool for early identification of executive potential, give powerful support to Jaques' general theory, on the basis of which the CPA was designed.

In regard to the first, Stamp is convinced, as is the present writer, that the pool of trainable assessors is small. In essence, the assessor must be at Jaques' current level IV or higher in order to administer the CPA well. The reason is simple. Satisfactory administration requires the ability to perceive and correctly note the significance of assessee behaviors from which the inference of conceptual skill level can be made. In Jaques' schema, this requires at least level IV capability.

Given this caution, the importance of the second point above can hardly be over-emphasized. The CPA was designed on the basis of a theoretical position which focused on cognitive capacity. Predictions of future organizational level rely on "growth" curves which are an integral part of the theory. It would appear that Stamp's findings strongly confirm key elements of the general theory. In particular, the importance of cognitive capability for upward movement seemingly has been confirmed. In addition, these findings confirm the existence of a "growth" process which is reliably predicted by Jaques' growth curves and which is anchored by initially assessed capability and age.

The question remains why IQ is not nearly as good an assessment tool as the CPA. This will be addressed at the end of this paper.

## Interviews of Military Executives

In 1985, research was initiated by the Executive Development Research Group of the Army Research Institute to improve the Army's leadership development process. The objective was to explore requirements at the senior level and devise ways to improve performance at that level. A number of logical options were evident at the outset, but all depended on understanding of executive-level performance requirements. To develop that understanding, an effort was launched which resulted in 70 tape-recorded interviews of Army general officers of three- and four-star grades and members of the Senior Executive Service. These interviews were transcribed and the content analyzed. The findings reported below are from this content analysis (Harris, Rigby, & Jacobs, in preparation).

The theoretical base for this research was Jaques' general theory. As described earlier, the schema envisions three broad domains within a large-scale organization: direct, organizational, and systems. The organizational domain is thought to top out at the level of a strategic business unit (SBU). The corresponding Army element is a division. The executive domain is thought to extend above these organizational domain elements. There consequently is thought to be a qualitative difference between successfully performing executives and strategic business unit heads. The latter operate from *within* the context of their organizations, operating them to achieve a positive balance of resources relative to costs in competition with other similar entities. The organization typically satisfies the definitional requirements of a system. By contrast, the executive operates above the context of a single system. A corporation headquarters typically will control a number of systems. While the head of a SBU seeks to bring to life new products and diversifies through product lines, the corporate CEO will bring to life new organizations and will diversify through lines of product lines. Vertical integration is, for example, most properly conceived to be in the domain of executive action.

The theory thus led to the expectation that executives would have far broader perspectives (frames of reference, cognitive maps) than incumbents at the organizational level. Because SBU establishment involves consideration of broad issues of resourcing and of political climate, concern for political issues, long-term resourcing issues, and proper strategic role were expected to surface. Large-scale industrial resourcing and marketing are now multinational. Industrial executives now of necessity have multinational world views. We expected our Army executives to have multinational world views from a military perspective but, in addition, to understand international political dynamics from more than a purely force projection perspective. Finally, we expected our military executives to have wide-ranging personal networks that extended beyond purely military counterparts. We expected these to be used both for information gathering to resolve uncertainty and complexity, and for consensus building among contemporaries as to broad directions that should be pursued, that is, to impact on external opinion leaders to create an external environment more favorable to the total system for which the executive is responsible.

**Research Findings** This section summarizes findings from Harris, Rigby, and Jacobs (in preparation). In essence, the findings were obtained from content analysis of the transcribed tape-recorded interviews; the analysis itself yields a frequency count of mentions of a type of content. A summary of the areas mentioned is shown in Table 1, in response to general questions to describe knowledges and skills required to do the work at the level. The sample consisted of eight of the then-current thirteen four-star generals, and 33 of the then-current 47 three-star generals.

Though eight of the available thirteen four-star general officers permitted an interview, the N is too small to permit rigorous statistical analysis. However, at the risk of error, some observations will be made concerning the percentages in Table 1.

First, the expected multinational concern was found, and it appears to be more strongly emphasized by the more senior generals, again as expected. Two examples of coded comments in this area are:

*We must develop an understanding of our own foreign policy and the policies of other countries in the minds of our officers. This development should begin at least by the one-star level, and no later than two-star.*

*A division commander is running inside the umbrella of a corps, but a corps commander's domain intersects with almost the whole world. He had better know what's out there.*

Comments on Joint/Unified Relationships also support theoretical expectations. The issue here is "outside the company." That is, in a Joint command, all elements of the armed forces may be represented. While there is a chain of command, it is lacking

## TABLE 1
### Content Areas by Rank of Respondent

| CONTENT AREAS | RESPONDENT | |
| --- | --- | --- |
| | Three-Star | Four-Star |
| 1. Multinational Knowledge | 60.6% | 87.5% |
| 2. Joint/Unified Relationships | 54.5% | 75.0% |
| 3. Understanding of Total Army System | 42.4% | 37.5% |
| 4. Consensus Building/Networking | 87.9% | 87.5% |
| 5. Envisioning/Anticipating | 63.6% | 87.5% |

in the "enforcement" options available to a division commander, for example. Instead of a unified company (e.g., strategic business unit), it is more like a coalition (e.g., corporate headquarters in which different major players each have come from different operating companies). While there is unified direction, members come from separate services which have different languages, concepts, and procedures. If mutual understanding is absent, effective operations may be quite difficult. Examples of comments recognizing the need for this understanding are:

*In this position, we are focusing on the Joint interface; we're working the seams. . . .*

*Everything we do should stem from national strategy, and that strategy is Joint. . . .*

By contrast, there were fewer comments on need for knowledge or skill on organization and requirements of the total Army. This outcome may reflect either the interviewee's perception that his/her skills in that area were adequate or a perception that the worldview had to extend beyond the Army. Significantly, the comments that did occur reflect a tendency toward integrated thinking. An example is:

*Whoever invented the "tooth-to-tail" analogy should be hung. That gives the impression of the combat forces dragging a big dead piece of fat and that's not so. You have to understand the systems–all of them. It does no good to know how to shoot if you don't have any bullets.*

Though the Ns were too small for rigorous analysis, it should be noted that comparison of lines two and three in Table 1 are in line with theoretical expectations. The awareness of understanding of Joint/Unified Relationships was greater at the four-star level, and emphasis on Total Army less. A growth process leading to greater "external" emphasis would produce these relationships. Such a growth process would also produce the noted lower frequency of mention of Total Army concerns at both levels.

Three comments illustrate the near-universal recognition of the importance of consensus building:

*With subordinates at the top levels, a number of things cannot get done by orders. You correct the rocket slowly, and you do so by persuasion and consensus building.*

*To be directive at this level is to be unsuccessful; you must deal collegially and through consensus.*

*At this level, one's successes can be measured by the degree to which you are able to deal with the amorphousness, the lack of definite subordination, and to exercise leadership through co-option and building support for a common mission.*

Two comments illustrate the sensitivity found in the interviews about the importance of networking and interfacing beyond merely military counterparts.

*We are implementing an expanded relations program with all the countries in the region. It is done through persuasion and negotiating with civilian and military leaders.*

*I have been accused of being a diplomat in this job. You are dealing with royalty, with a number of other countries. You have both the military and the internal hierarchy, and you have to know what the power is in the country.*

Again, the interviews confirmed the theoretical expectations that Army executives would regard consensus building and negotiating (with other-than-military counterparts) skills to be important. There is, in addition, a sense of representational (Mintzberg, 1973) responsibility, in the sense of the incumbent's feeling that he is representing not just Army interests, but rather national interests as well.

Finally, the following comments illustrate the envisioning codings:

*At this level, there is a great premium on anticipation. If I'm not drawing on my experience and intuitive understanding of the situation, I'm not functioning as a four-star. If I am anticipating right, I can shape the issues, rather than having the issues shape me.*

*You have to be able to understand what is making environmental changes before you can chart your own objectives and set your long-term goals. Everything is connected in interrelated systems.*

*All of the work at this level is in concepts and visions of what should be . . . force structure and hardware for the year 2000 and beyond are being set right now and the strategic mix must be right. The decisions that we make in the 86–89 POM will come to fruition in 2020, 35 years from now.*

Two observations are relevant here. First is the sense of time horizon, the individual's sense of outreach into the future. (Time horizons in both this sample and another will be addressed in the following section.) The second is the sense of being proactive, which was found in many of the interviews.

One other category of comment occurred frequently enough to warrant inclusion here. The theoretical expectation was that executive-level job requirements would include abstract integrative thinking skills. However, it was not necessarily expected that verbalization of awareness of the thinking skill requirement would also exist. Contrary to expectation, such comments were found in roughly one-third of the interviews. Examples are:

*The role at this level should be devoted to concepts, abstracts, visions of what we should have as a military defense structure.*

*A synthesis is required to produce doctrine, a very different set of skills than managing weapons systems or commanding troops.*

*You must be able to visualize, to deal in concepts and abstracts.*

**Time Span of Work**  One of the key tenets of the theory is that higher-level position incumbents have longer time horizons.  There are several reasons why this expectation is logical.  Perhaps the most important is that executives, in particular, add the greatest value to their organizations through their resource allocation decisions.  Resource decisions at the executive level assume mammoth proportions.  The "star-wars" Strategic Defense Initiative is an example of an executive-level resourcing decision with the following characteristics:

- It is a zero-sum decision.  That is, its choice will close other options both in the defense budget and in governmental operations at large.

- The fiscal resources to pay for it are not presently in hand.  They will need to be generated over time—a long time—because discretionary fiscal resources will flow only so fast, either in industry or government.

- The development could not be concretely programmed at present, even if fiscal resources were adequate, because the end product depends on concepts which have not yet been proven.  Concept proof is an integral element of the total developmental process and must be acknowledged in planning just as any other element in the system development must be.

- The decision to develop has profound impact on the international political balance of power, and thus must be considered from a variety of perspectives, though there is substantial uncertainty about the exact impact and about the response that will be made by other governments.  Further, it can be expected that any U.S.S.R. response will be complex, that is, aimed at multiple objectives.  The impact will extend far beyond military considerations, and the response may well be nonmilitary.  (Soviet initiatives to reduce military pressure on Eastern Europe, Soviet aims at reducing public acceptance of SDI in the United States, Soviet aims of reducing European support for maintenance of the NATO alliance, and Soviet aims at improving long-term economic capacity for renewal of international competition are all closely related.)

There are two sources of information about time span of Army executives.  One is the interview data base, and the second is data obtained in a separate effort by the Professional Development of Officers Study (PDOS).  Figures 1 and 2 show the stated time span of work for the three-star and four-star general officers in our interview sample.  Of the three-stars, 63% had time spans of ten years or longer; 75% of the four-stars did.  Though the frequencies are too small to permit generalization, it appears that the time horizon of our four-star generals was longer than that of the three-stars, again in accord with theoretical expectations.

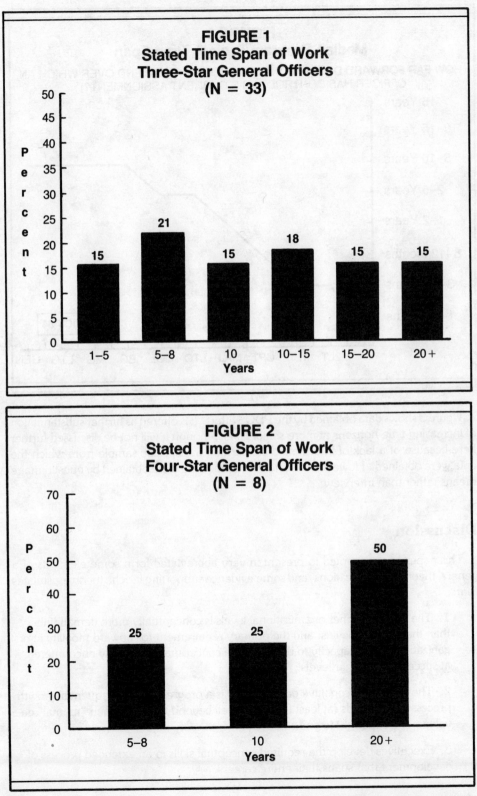

**FIGURE 1**
**Stated Time Span of Work**
**Three-Star General Officers**
**(N = 33)**

**FIGURE 2**
**Stated Time Span of Work**
**Four-Star General Officers**
**(N = 8)**

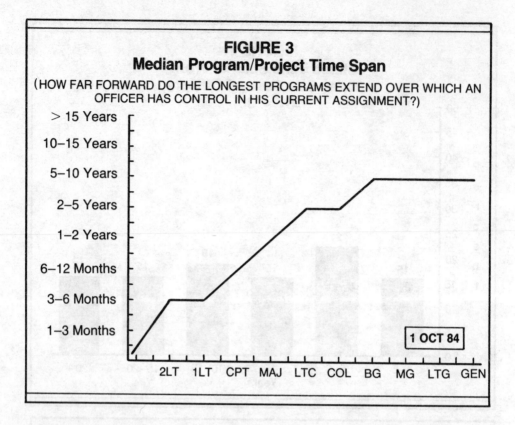

**FIGURE 3**
**Median Program/Project Time Span**
(HOW FAR FORWARD DO THE LONGEST PROGRAMS EXTEND OVER WHICH AN OFFICER HAS CONTROL IN HIS CURRENT ASSIGNMENT?)

> 15 Years
10–15 Years
5–10 Years
2–5 Years
1–2 Years
6–12 Months
3–6 Months
1–3 Months

2LT   1LT   CPT   MAJ   LTC   COL   BG   MG   LTG   GEN

1 OCT 84

Figure 3 shows data obtained by the PDOS effort. It is offered as further substantiation of increasing time horizons at more senior levels, though it will not be discussed further here because of a lack of information concerning the specific sample from which the data were obtained. However, it is known that the data were obtained by questionnaire means rather than interview.

## Discussion

This paper has attempted to present in very abbreviated form some elements of a general theory of organizations, and some evidence supporting it. The theory postulates that:

1. The work at higher organizational levels is conceptually more demanding than that at lower levels, and the primary requirement for upward mobility in organizations is the capacity to deal with the conceptual complexity encountered at successively higher levels.

2. The process of cognitive development is a progressive and sequential growth process that extends (at least for some) well beyond the time when "mental" development is thought to end.

3. Executives develop the required conceptual skills in an extended process of development that spans their entire careers.

As has been noted earlier, the theory makes a case for focusing primarily, though not exclusively, on conceptual skill development as a key dimension in executive development. It proposes that progressive conceptual development takes place gradually as the skills and capabilities that comprise any given current level are "overgrown" by the skills required at the next-higher level. The growth process probably consists of construction of a progressively more extensive and complex causal map (conceptual frame of reference) which can be used as a tool to pattern and thereby understand the progressively greater complexity encountered at successively higher organizational levels. A fascinating article by Turlington (1987) seems to use this notion as an implicit thesis in a discussion of how to develop strategic thinking skills.

The two sets of research findings reported above seem to provide very strong support for the theory. First, the central construct in the theory is the increase in complexity across organizational levels, and the corresponding requirement for growth in "conceptual grasp," as opposed to native intelligence, as managers move up. Stamp's work clearly shows that measured conceptual ability predicts an enormous proportion of the variance of upward mobility. Second, the theory provides the basis for asserting the nature of the specific critical requirements at each level, and their associated time horizons. Our content analysis of Army executive interviews revealed critical tasks of the type predicted, particularly in regard to conceptual grasp, forward outreach in time, and strategic thinking skills. As a further interesting note, the similarity between critical tasks described by members of our sample and those in other studies suggests that many of these critical high-level organizational tasks are generic.

As depicted in the theory, in the interviews, and in the general literature, the executive role is probably too complex to yield to skill enumeration (list building). Without repetition of findings previously discussed, it is enough to comment that creating organizational understanding of environmental (political, economic, sociological, technological, and informational) complexity is at the heart of the executive's job. And this process is qualitatively different from apparently similar processes at lower organizational levels.

A consistent finding in the literature is that leaders at the executive level comprehend both direct and indirect effects that combine to produce outcomes over very long time intervals. At lower levels, there is less understanding of indirect ("second-order") effects, and particularly of how to generate "direct" effects "indirectly." (An example might be organizational policies that create a context conducive for the appearance of apparently unrelated but desired behavior at a distant level.) Their approach to decision making is also different and more challenging. It appears not to be selection from among formulated alternatives, based on an advantages-disadvantages comparison, but rather the formulation of "workable" solutions to problem situations which are difficult to fathom. Jacobs and Jaques (1987) provide several examples and a discussion of the process. The executive approach thus is to develop a workable course of action and then to manage the outcome over time so that it will be successful. The "management" process may require solution of a substantial number of smaller "problems" along the way. The conceptual skills required for this process include those developed for use at lower levels, including abstract analytic skills, and, in addition, abstract synthesis skills. Where analytic skills are essential for separating out the elements of a problem or situation, skills in synthesis are essential for seeing patterns—and probably for creating patterns—within a highly complex and seemingly disordered problem situation.

One last observation is that the predictive validity of the CPA is substantially higher than the predictive validity of measures of intelligence against the criterion of upward organizational mobility. This begs for an answer. The present findings offer no solution, but speculation is still possible. It seems likely that a part of the answer is found in what an individual does with the intelligence s/he has. If we can safely conclude that the *sine qua non* is the development of mental models (cognitive maps), we may well be addressing the issue of how an individual chooses to expend energy in work. There can be little doubt that the building of mental models does require time and energy, and that this is in mutually exclusive relationship with other activities. The issue then is whether such activity is intrinsically rewarding to the individual. (The issue is posed in this manner because it is assumed that this activity is not *extrinsically* rewarded at the lower organizational levels, but yet that it must be developed at a relatively early age, certainly early in a career.)

At the present state of development of the theory, this is termed *proclivity*. It is a reflection of what Jaques calls *temperament*. Individuals who find mental model development intrinsically rewarding are likely to be the ones who do it early in life (or a career), and it probably must be started early in order that adequate metacognitive model-building skills will develop in parallel with the increase in organizational complexity that accompanies upward movement. Our early thinking on this issue is that the Myers-Briggs Type Indicator may well be measuring this proclivity. In theory, the NT (iNtuitive-Thinking) individual is a mental model builder. It clearly would be useful to determine if the proportion of NTs increases at progressively higher organizational echelons.

Research at the executive level has barely begun, in comparison with the vast literature on direct supervisory leadership. There are at least three thrusts which must be a part of any broad strategy calculated to improve leadership development in formal organizations:

- Defining the major dimensions of the executive conceptual frame of reference to confirm the "end point" for the developmental process so as to enable both better aiding of executive work, and shaping or "fine-tuning" of early development processes.

- Determining if there is a "best" developmental sequence.

- Developing performance assessment and training methodologies to mediate the developmental sequence.

## References

Bruner, J. (1966). *Toward a theory of instruction*. New York: Norton.

Fischer, K. W. (1980). A theory of cognitive development: The control and construction of hierarchies of skills. *Psychological Review, 87*, 477–531.

Harris, P., Rigby, C., & Jacobs, T. O. (in preparation). *Executive leadership: Requisite skills and developmental processes for three- and four-star assignments*. Alexandria, VA: U.S. Army Research Institute.

Hunt, J. G., Osborn, R. N., & Martin, H. J. (1981). *A multiple influence model of leadership* (Tech. Rep. No. 520). Alexandria, VA: U.S. Army Research Institute.

Jacobs, T. O. (1972). *Leadership and exchange in formal organizations*. Alexandria, VA: Human Resources Research Organization.

Jacobs, T. O., & Jaques, E. (1987). Leadership in complex systems. In J. A. Zeide (Ed.), *Human productivity enhancement. Organizations and personnel*. (Vol. II). New York: Praeger.

Jaques, E. (1978). *General theory of bureaucracy*. Exeter, NH: Heinemann Books.

Jaques, E., Clement, S., Rigby, C., & Jacobs, T. O. (1985). *Senior leadership: Performance requirements at the executive level*. Alexandria, VA: U.S. Army Research Institute.

Katz, D., & Kahn, R. L. (1966). *The social psychology of organizations*. New York: John Wiley & Sons.

Mintzberg, H. (1973). *The nature of managerial work*. New York: Harper & Row.

Osborn, R. N., Hunt, J. G., & Jauch, L. R. (1980). *Organization theory: An integrated approach*. New York: John Wiley & Sons.

Simon, H. A. (1977). *The new science of management decision* (3rd ed.). Englewood Cliffs, NJ: Prentice-Hall.

Stamp, G. (1988). *Longitudinal research into methods of assessing managerial potential*. Alexandria, VA: U.S. Army Research Institute.

Turlington, J. E. (1987). Truly learning the operational art. *Parameters, 17,* 51–64.

Yukl, G. A. (1989). *Leadership in organizations* (2nd ed.). Englewood Cliffs, NJ: Prentice-Hall.

# Understanding and Assessing Organizational Leadership

*Marshall Sashkin and W. Warner Burke*

Only in the past decade has there appeared a serious interest in *leadership*, as opposed to management. The study of leadership has, in our view, been neglected in favor of a focus on what might best be called "supervisory management," the role of individuals at middle and lower levels of the organizational hierarchy. Katz and Kahn (1978) define the central activities of persons at these levels as "interpolation" at middle levels, and "administration" at lower levels. Interpolation means adding to and interpreting structures and policies developed and defined at the top of the hierarchy, while administration is simply operating within defined structures, carrying out the policies developed at the top and modified by midlevels of managers.

With only a few exceptions, organizational psychologists and behavioral scientists have failed to pay attention to top-level executive leadership—as contrasted with mid- and lower-level management—as an organizational phenomenon. This has resulted in much significant knowledge about management at these lower levels, some of which has even been of considerable practical use, but proportionately little real knowledge about leadership, the process by which those at the top level of an organization design and direct social-organizational processes. Indeed, the study of organizational leadership has been left to individually centered psychologists such as Kets de Vries (1988), Levinson (1981), and Zaleznik (1977), whose typical approach is that of psychodynamic or Freudian psychology on the one hand, and, on the other hand, to political scientists and sociologists such as Burns (1978) and Weber (1947), whose interests lie primarily in the mass-movement or societal effects of such leadership. In this paper we offer an alternative approach to understanding organizational leadership. First, let us briefly review "where we have come from" in terms of the conceptual and empirical work on leadership over the past 50 years or so.

## The Nature of Leadership: A Historical Overview

We observed above that traditional approaches to understanding leadership have in fact dealt not with leadership but with supervision and lower-level management, activities that—while certainly of great organizational importance—are quite different from leadership. We described the work of some of those who have taken the lead in what we see as a paradigm shift in how leadership is conceptualized—Bass (1985), Bennis and Nanus (1985), and Burns (1978), for example. We noted that these and other scholars (such as House [1988]) had begun to explore some of the specific variables that identify and distinguish transformational leaders and transformational leadership.

Looking back to the history of the study of leadership, we find that the earliest coherent thrust centered on an approach now referred to as the "Great Man" or "Great Person" theory of leadership. That approach centered on identifying and measuring the specific personal characteristics of leaders, under the assumption that great leaders are born, not made. Thus, a host of research was conducted under the assumption that there are certain, specific, measurable personal traits and characteristics that clearly distinguish such leaders. In reviewing and synthesizing the results of 25 and more years of such research Stogdill (1948) came to two major conclusions. First, he pointed out that no specific traits or personal characteristics stood out as strong, certain markers of leadership. But, second, he also identified five specific sets of personal characteristics that were consistently associated with leadership across many research studies. Unfortunately, it was the first and not the second of these points that other scholars and researchers seized on, all but ignoring the second. Thus, almost all research on personal characteristics stopped for over 25 years, until House (1977) first suggested that charisma might be based on specific personal traits and characteristics that could be measured.

What followed was a focus on the behavior of leaders. If the key was not who they were, perhaps it could be found in what they did, if we looked closely enough. Two different research programs, conducted over a decade or more, one at Harvard and the other at Ohio State University, offered hope that a behavioral answer had been found. In work with college undergraduates at Harvard, Bales (1958) identified two critical types or dimensions of behavior, behavior centered on task accomplishment and behavior that was directed toward interpersonal relations, which he labelled "socio-emotional relationship" behavior. Individuals who consistently exhibited high levels of both of these types of behavior in small group discussions were typically reported as leaders by their peers. Those who only engaged in a high level of task-directed activity but less relationship-centered behavior were often designated as leaders. Those who engaged only in a high volume of socio-emotional relationship behavior were rarely designated as "the leader" by their peers, after the discussion was over. Thus, perhaps leadership consisted of high levels of behavior in both of these categories or, at least, of task-relevant behavior.

In independent studies, conducted mostly in factories, researchers at Ohio State also identified two types of behavior on the part of foremen and supervisors. Their two categories, "initiating structure"—giving task directions—and "consideration" (of employees and their feelings) boil down, in essence, to the same two dimensions identified by Bales. At that point it seemed that the puzzle might have been solved: the most effective leaders exhibit high quantities of both task- and relationship-centered behavior, while leadership itself is characterized by a high degree of task-oriented activity. Some, such as Blake and Mouton (1964), promptly developed training programs designed to help managers learn to be "high-high" (or, in their jargon, "9,9") leaders. Unfortunately, another 20 years of research consistently failed to confirm that effective leaders actually engage in such high-high behavior, leading one group of scholars to call it the "high-high leadership myth" (Larson, Hunt, & Osborn, 1976).

Of course, not all research results were negative; some work did suggest that high levels of both types of behavior can have performance relevance. One study, for example, found that high-high supervisors had lower grievance and turnover rates (Fleishman & Harris, 1962). But by the late 1960s it was clear that there was much more to leadership effectiveness than simply exhibiting a lot of task- and relationship-centered behavior.

One new path taken by some was to suggest that perhaps effectiveness depended on engaging in different combinations of task and relationship behavior in different situations (Hersey & Blanchard, 1969; House, 1971). Further research did yield support for some such formulations (e.g., see House & Baetz, 1979), but the support was not extremely strong; there was still more to the "mystery" of leadership.

A second and different path was to combine the situational hypothesis with some variations on the old personal characteristics approach and even some intimations of behavior according to the two categories. This is the approach taken by Fiedler (1965, 1967) whose personality measure, degree of liking for one's "least preferred co-worker" (LPC), supposedly indicates a deep personal motivational preference in terms of task or relationship motivation. This motivational preference is then shown to be associated with effectiveness or ineffectiveness in each of eight situational combinations of three variables: employee relations (good or poor), the degree to which the task is structured (high or low), and the amount of power the leader has (high or low).

Fiedler (1967) developed many complex explanations for why this should be so. For example, low LPC leaders do better in the best possible situation, when leader-member relations are good, the task is clearly structured, and the leader's power is high. Fiedler suggests this is so because they engage in more relationship-centered behaviors, the opposite of their LPC-based motivational pattern. That is, these low LPC leaders are concerned most with task accomplishment. The situation is, however, so positive that such task accomplishment seems assured.

Thus, the low LPC leader, unworried about getting the job done, can relax and engage in relationship-oriented activities. The high LPC leader, however, seeing that everything is fine in terms of relationships (the primary concern of this type of leader) spends his or her time on task-directed activity. That, however, is the wrong thing to do; the task is moving along fine. The leader irritates and perhaps even alienates followers, resulting in poor performance.

Similar arguments are made for each of the other eight situations, explaining why one or another type of leader does better. And, make no mistake, in at least five of the situations one or the other does, clearly, do better. Unfortunately, neither Fiedler nor anyone else has ever been able to demonstrate that leaders actually *behave* in the ways suggested. Nor has anyone ever found any motivational measure—or any other psychological measure, for that matter—that relates to the LPC score.

In sum, the situational approaches seem to work either weakly, for clear reasons, or modestly well, but for very unclear reasons. Again, there is a partial answer here that leaves much to be resolved. And keep in mind that most, if not all, of the theory and research up to the 1970s concerned supervisors and lower-level managers, not top executive leaders.

**Beginnings of the Study of Organizational Leadership** We initially criticized most of the psychological work on leadership for its overwhelming focus on supervisory leadership. We "blasted" others, including political scientists and historians, for ignoring organizations while concentrating on the leadership of large social systems—mass movements and nations. Still, it is the work of the psychologist House (1977, 1987, 1988) and of the political scientist and social historian Burns (1978) that has had the most influence on the research on organizational leadership that has developed over the past decade. House has persistently pursued the study of psychological characteristics of charismatic leaders, insisting that such factors can be identified and measured. His work has focused on the power need of effective charismatic leaders (which was defined and studied even earlier by McClelland [1975] and McClelland and Burnham [1976]). Burns' work served to reacquaint scholars with a critical distinction first raised by Weber (1924/1947): the difference between economic and noneconomic sources of authority, which served as one basis for Weber's discussion of charisma. Burns amplified and focused this important definition, using leadership illustrations (such as Gandhi and Roosevelt), that made the distinction between leaders and managers so striking that it could not be ignored.

The work of House (1977) and Burns (1978) has led to the development of several new approaches to the study of what many now refer to as "transformational" leadership. This term is used to contrast this "new leadership" with the old "transactional" leadership—or management—approach. The transactional approach is based on economic or quasi-economic transactions between a leader and followers, while the new transformational approaches all incorporate the idea that leadership involves what Weber called noneconomic sources of authority. House (1988) has, for example, in his more recent work focused on the leadership of the U.S. presidents. Bass (1985) has built on the foundation of Burns and others (e.g., Bennis & Nanus [1985], Schein [1985], Kouzes & Posner [1987]) and has incorporated key elements of the transformational construct.

The approach to be reported here shares much with these others (more with some than with others), yet it has enough unique characteristics that we must spend some time in definition, prior to reporting the results of normative and experimental research. We will first describe and discuss how transformational and transactional leaders differ and how individuals in one or the other category can be measurably distinguished (Burke, 1988). We will then briefly review our own organizational leadership theory, presenting and discussing the instrument developed for researching our approach. Finally, we will briefly review recent and ongoing research using the *Leader Behavior Questionnaire*. Appended to this report are the normative data developed using the Leadership Report (Burke, 1988) and the data tables from the technical manual supporting the *Leader Behavior Questionnaire* (Sashkin, 1988a).

## Differentiating Transformational from Transactional Leaders

House (1988) and some others (e.g., see Winter, 1987) see transformational leadership as primarily based on the extent to which a leader can effectively express his or her need for power by using imagery that presents socially desirable examples and applications. House (1977, 1988) is explicit in arguing that transformational leadership is a matter of degree rather than a simple either-or issue. Nonetheless, his research has yielded some striking results that differentiate effective from ineffective national leaders (as judged by panels of historians) on the basis of power need imagery in public speeches and writings that is characteristic of transformational rather than transactional leaders.

We agree, with House, that power need and its organizational application lie at the very heart of the issue of transformational leadership. However, we also believe that there are other significant personal factors that can contribute to the identification of transformational (or more transformational) leaders. (In fact, so does House, who has suggested several such factors in addition to power need and power need direction; see House [1977] or House & Baetz [1979].)

Bass (1985) also distinguishes transformational from transactional leaders, using a questionnaire derived through empirical factor analytic methods. Research by Bass and his associates (Bass, 1988; Avolio & Gibbons, 1988) seems supportive of Bass' Multifactor Leadership Questionnaire, in differentiating transactional from transformational leaders. Our view, however, is that the MLQ does not adequately incorporate key theoretical elements of transformational leadership, particularly that of power and its use.

**A New Questionnaire Instrument** Burke's (1988) Leadership Report is based on the notion that the way power is used to empower followers is the key factor that distinguishes transformational from transactional leaders. The report is an 18-item modified forced-choice questionnaire. Each item consists of a stem followed by two alternative choices. The respondent allocates five points between the two alternatives, in any combination he or she desires (5-0, 4-1, 3-2, 2-3, 1-4, 0-5). One choice is designed to represent how a typical transactional leader would think or act, the other being characteristic of transformational leaders. While some items are behaviorally oriented, most are intended to tap the attitudes and values characteristic of transformational and transactional leaders. For example, item six reads:

*As a leader I spend considerable energy in:*
  *(A) managing separate but related goals.*
  *(B) arousing hopes, expectations, and aspirations in my followers.*

Item 16 gets more at a basic belief, the question of effectance (belief that one can control one's environment or make a difference):

*I feel that my destiny is:*
  *(A) essentially within my control.*
  *(B) largely determined by circumstances outside my control.*

And items three and thirteen are clearly aimed at the essence of a transactional versus a transformational approach:

*I am concerned:*
  *(A) that my followers are rewarded equitably for their work.*
  *(B) about what my followers want in life.*

*Regarding my work:*
  *(A) I have a strong sense of mission.*
  *(B) It is a means to an end, a way to make a living.*

The alternative choices comprising each item are both worded positively, to minimize social desirability concerns. In addition, instructions emphasize that there are no "right" or "wrong" answers. It should be noted that this is done not merely to "soothe" transactional individuals or convince them to expose themselves by responding honestly. It is basic to our position that effective organizations call for both leadership *and* management, a point that is explicit in Katz and Kahn's (1978) early analysis (the more recent version of which we referred to above). In fact, we believe that effective transformational leaders rely on effective transactional leaders—managers.

While the Leadership Report items were developed based on the concepts of transactional and transformational leadership, even more explicit was the focus on power and how it is used. A factor analysis showed that the 18 items form three coherent groups. Each group of items centers on a particular aspect of power use/empowerment.

The first group of items (1B, 11A, 14B, 15A) center on the use of power to make creative changes and solve problems in creative ways. We have called this dimension of transformational leadership "Creating versus Conserving." This distinction between a creative approach to situations and a conservative approach may be central to the difference between how transformational and transactional leaders act and use power. Transactional leaders focus on maintaining stability in the short run, while transformational leaders empower others to make creative changes for the long run. Bass (1985) points out in the title of his book that transformational leadership often results in performance beyond expectations, but this goes both ways, as shown by item 14:

*My requests of followers are:*
  *(A) only what is required.*
  *(B) typically more than they expect.*

The second set of five items (6B, 9A, 10B, 12B, 18A) describes the difference between a person who concentrates on creating energy and arousing hopes and one who separates and clarifies assignments and derives power from established roles. We have called this dimension "Arousing versus Clarifying," but another label might be "Empowering Through Excitement." Power issues become quite explicit in item 18:

*What power I have to influence others comes primarily from my:*
  *(A) ability to get others to identify with me and my ideas.*
  *(B) status and position.*

The third and final dimension consists of just three items (2A, 5A, 7A), all of which center on the distinction between an active use of power and a more reactive or passive approach. A transformational leader sees him- or herself as a cause of events, one who actively teaches others the right way to go. This approach contrasts with a more reactive one in which the leader sees him- or herself as a facilitator, helping a follower to go in the direction that person (but perhaps not the leader) wants to go. Bennis and Nanus (1985) express well this "Active versus Reactive" distinction in the use of power through their aphorism, "Managers do things right; leaders do the right things."

Six additional items (3, 4, 8, 13, 16, 17) on the Leadership Report are not part of the three dimensions. The content of these items, however—a sense of mission, destiny, and morality—has been noted by various writers and researchers, and the items do differentiate between transactional and transformational leaders as part of the total score.

Table 1 shows the means for the total transformational leadership scores on the Leadership Report, as well as for the three dimensions just defined.

## TABLE 1
## Mean and Standard Deviation for
## Original Norms—"The Leadership Report"

|  | N | $\overline{x}$ | sd |
|---|---|---|---|
| Transformational Score (Overall) | 257 | 50.38 | 10.09 |
| **Dimensions** | | | |
| • Creating (4 items) | | 11.9 | 1.78 |
| • Arousing (5 items) | | 14.0 | 1.78 |
| • Active (3 items) | | 7.0 | 2.58 |

**Differentiating Managers from Leaders** In Table 1 we presented normative data using the Leadership Report. These data were obtained from managers at various organizational levels in a diverse set of organizations. More to the point in terms of our basic aims, one must ask whether the Leadership Report can actually differentiate leaders from managers. We have some initial and admittedly limited data that shed some light on this question.

Using some new data sets, we created two groups of respondents, "executives" and "managers." Those in the first group were all high-level executives from business and industry as well as from government. Those in the manager group were midlevel managers in two high-technology business firms. We then compared the transactional and transformational scores on the Leadership Report for the two groups. The results are shown in Table 2. The executives had significantly higher transformational scores as compared with the managers ($p < .01$), while the managers scored significantly higher on transactional leadership. (The latter result is not independent; because of the forced-choice construction of the Leadership Report, it is almost guaranteed that if the first difference were found the second would follow.)

It does, then, seem that the Leadership Report is able to differentiate top- from midlevel organizational members. Of course, some of those at midlevels may well be leaders while some of those close to the top are very likely to be managers rather than leaders. Thus, the differentiation shown here is a very conservative estimate; we have been calling some managers "leaders" and some leaders "managers," thus weakening the comparison. Were we independently to identify individuals clearly acting as leaders and another group that could quite definitively be labelled managers, it is very likely that the two groups' Leadership Report scores would differ much more than is indicated by the results reported here.

## TABLE 2
## Leadership Report Results
## Differentiating Executives From Midlevel Managers

| | | | | | | | Pooled variance estimate | | | Separate variance estimate | | |
|---|---|---|---|---|---|---|---|---|---|---|---|---|
| Variable | Number of cases | Mean | Standard Deviation | Standard Error | F Value | 2-tail Prob. | T Value | Degrees of Freedom | 2-tail Prob. | T Value | Degrees of Freedom | 2-tail Prob. |
| **TRANFORM** | | | | | | | | | | | | |
| GROUP 1 | 78 | 53.2051 | 9.190 | 1.041 | | | | | | | | |
| | | | | | 1.24 | .397 | 2.61 | 128 | .010 | 2.56 | 101.35 | 0.012 |
| GROUP 2 | 52 | 48.7115 | 10.214 | 1.416 | | | | | | | | |
| **TRANACT** | | | | | | | | | | | | |
| GROUP 1 | 78 | 37.0513 | 9.107 | 1.031 | | | | | | | | |
| | | | | | 1.26 | .353 | -2.48 | 128 | .014 | -2.43 | 100.55 | 0.017 |
| GROUP 2 | 52 | 41.3077 | 10.228 | 1.418 | | | | | | | | |

LEGEND:  Group 1: 78 executives from a large autonomous government agency and from a major manufacturer of pharmaceuticals (latter N = 18).
Group 2: 52 midlevel managers from two different high-technology firms: one a service-centered business, the other a manufacturer (Ns = 31 and 21, respectively).
Over 95% of the samples are male.

# A New Theory of Organizational Leadership

Burke has demonstrated that it is possible to assess individuals on a dimension of transactional-transformational leadership and has shown that a strong element in making such a distinction is how one uses power to empower others. A more comprehensive and clear understanding of organizational leadership, however, calls for a more structured theory, a theory that examines how organizational leaders—not supervisors and foremen—function. The approach that follows is a further extension of one presented in detail by Sashkin and Fulmer (1987) and Sashkin (1988c). Rather than provide another detailed presentation, we will sketch the outlines of this theory, adding some new details, and then go on to review in greater depth its operational implementation by means of the *Leader Behavior Questionnaire*.

A more comprehensive understanding of organizational leadership must go beyond earlier approaches in several respects. The present approach does so by incorporating three key elements: (1) the leader's personal characteristics, (2) the leader's effect on organizational functioning and culture, and (3) the leader's behavior. These are the three foundation elements of the organizational leadership theory we shall describe.

**Personal Characteristics** We believe that there are at least three specific personal characteristics that differentiate effective organizational leaders from others. This conclusion is based on work by House (1977, 1988), referred to earlier, as well as on the research of McClelland (1975) and on Jaques' (1976, 1986) theory of adult cognitive development and its relationship to organizational functioning.

*Impact Belief.* Building on House's (1977; House & Baetz, 1979) and on Stogdill's (1948) work suggesting that leaders are more assertive and self-confident, as well as on research findings regarding effectance—the belief that one can control or affect one's environment—we suggest that effective leaders start with a strong belief in themselves and their ability to affect their organizational environment. They believe they can have an impact on the "bottom line." Such a belief seems to us to be a prerequisite if the second personal characteristic is to have any organizational effect.

*Power Need.* The work of McClelland and his associates (McClelland, 1975; McClelland & Burnham, 1976; Winter, 1987) as well as more recent work by House (1988) and by Howell (1988) offers strong support for the view that effective leaders have a high need for power (*n*Pow). Moreover, their work shows that such leaders direct their need for power in socially positive ways, that is, ways that benefit others and the organization rather than merely contributing to the leader's personal status or material condition. Effective leaders want power and influence because they know that it is through power and influence that things get done in organizations. And they realize that such power and influence must be widely shared, not just exercised at top levels by a few. In effective organizations everyone has a strong sense of influence, especially over one's own job (Tannenbaum, 1968). Effective leaders use power to empower others, who then use power and influence to enact the leader's vision of the organization.

*Cognitive Time Span.* Some years ago Jaques (1979) developed and elaborated a practical theory of job analysis and evaluation, tying the worth of a job to the span of time for which the incumbent is held responsible without supervision. Jaques then argued that time span capability—the longest span of time over which an individual can function autonomously and effectively on a task—is not a continuous variable. Rather, it occurs in several stages which, in turn, are linked to the nature of work itself (in terms of complexity and difficulty). Moreover, Jaques (1976) also argued that organizations are naturally "stratified" in terms of these same six levels of complexity (and concluded that in no case should an organization have more than six levels of hierarchy). Regardless of whether one accepts Jaques' (1989) comprehensive theory, his work and that of his associates suggest strongly that effective organizational leaders, at the top levels of an organization, have—and must have—relatively long time spans of vision (this is our term; Jaques would say "higher levels of cognitive development"). Such executives must think and function over periods of at least a decade or two. Thus, our third critical personal characteristic is cognitive time span.

Shortly we shall discuss and provide examples of the questionnaire scales we have developed to measure the three personal characteristics. Of course, we do not suggest that these three are the only personal characteristics that are associated with effective organizational leadership. But we do believe that there is strong evidence that they are important parts of the set of such variables.

**Organizational Context** Parsons (1960) points out that all organizations must effectively carry out four critical functions if they are to survive over time. Parsons' argument is based on an extension of Weber's (1947) means-ends analysis, combined with an open systems approach. He identifies the four functions as *adapting*, *attaining goals*, *coordinating* or *integrating* the efforts of organizational members and groups, and *maintaining* the organization's culture, the pattern of values and beliefs that supports effective operation of the other three functions. There is evidence (Hoy & Ferguson, 1985) that organizations judged more effective in terms of these four functions are also more effective in terms of "bottom-line" performance indicators.

Schein (1985) suggests that it may be that the only really important function of organizational leaders is building or changing the organization's culture by creating and inculcating certain specific values and beliefs that support effective operation of the four functions. Of course, the specific values may differ somewhat depending on the type of organization and its goals (e.g., see Sashkin, 1987), but overall we think it is possible to assess whether a leader is, in fact, having a positive impact on the organization's functioning (in terms of the four specific functions) as well as the extent to which the leader is successful in defining and inculcating within the organization's culture the values that support these functions.

**Leadership Behavior** Finally we come to the most overt aspect of our theory of organizational leadership, the actions taken by leaders. Our reason for dealing first with personal characteristics and organizational context is our belief in Kurt Lewin's dictum, $B = f(P,S)$ or, behavior is a function of the person and the situation in interaction with one another. Thus, we see leadership behavior as purposefully conceived and directed by leaders capable (having the requisite personal characteristics) of dealing with specific organizational conditions and needs.

At the organizational level, leaders define a common "philosophy" that is the basis for shared values and beliefs. They then act to put that philosophy to work in the organization in two important ways. Again at the larger level they create or direct the development of policies and programs that serve as vehicles for the organizational philosophy. That is, such policies and programs show that the philosophical statements—and the values that underlie them—do not consist merely of words with no real effects. The leader aims to demonstrate that organizational actions are consistent with the statement of philosophy, that there is truth, consistency, and reliability here, not hypocrisy.

At the individual level of behavior and action, organizational leaders inculcate and reinforce the values contained in an organizational philosophy. They do so in interpersonal interaction, using at least five specific types of behavior, as first defined by Bennis (1984). We will briefly review each, since a major part of our assessment instrument is devoted to the measurement of the extent to which leaders behave in these ways in interaction with other organizational members.

Bennis (1984) observed that exceptional CEOs were able to focus others on key points and concepts, in interpersonal discussions. Supporting this was a generally high level of basic communication skills. That is, the CEOs exhibited the sorts of behaviors associated with effective communication—they paid attention, used active listening skills, attended to feelings that others expressed, were good at giving helpful feedback, used questions effectively, and so on. A third category of behaviors centered on actions that demonstrated that others could place trust in the leader. This was done through consistency of action, by following through on commitments, and by matching words with actions. Throughout interactions with others, Bennis observed that these effective CEOs were consistent in their frequent expressions of respect and personal concern, and that this sense of respect extended to include a base of self-respect. Finally, Bennis noted that the effective CEOs he studied created and took risks, not in the sense of "gambling" but by constructing opportunities for others to "buy in" to the leader's ideas and programs and take an active, "ownership" role in making real the leader's vision.

**Visionary Leadership Theory** Effective transformational leaders believe they can have a major impact on their organization by using power and influence to empower organization members to make real the leader's long-range organizational vision. For this reason we often refer to the present leadership approach as "visionary leadership theory." Leaders enact their visions by constructing and/or modifying organizational cultures, that is, by defining and promulgating shared values and beliefs that form the foundation supports for the organizational reality the leader envisions.

Thus, visionary leaders are, in essence, long-range culture builders, as has been suggested by Schein (1985). But not just any vision and not just any culture will do; visionary leaders create cultures that strengthen and support the critical organizational functions identified by Parsons (1960) and described above. Thus, both Schein (1985) and Sashkin (1988c) have suggested certain specific values and beliefs that lend support to one or another of the functions such as, for example, the belief that one's actions can have a significant effect on one's environment; this is one reason that this belief is such an important personal characteristic of visionary leaders.

Sashkin (1987) and Sashkin and Morris (1984) have argued that Parsons' four organizational functions—adapting, attaining goals, coordinating activities, and maintaining the culture—are paralleled at the individual level in terms of human work needs. The "pattern maintenance" function, defining the organization's culture, is, of course, paralleled at the individual level by values and beliefs. The other three functions are also intimately related to individual-level human work needs. Sashkin and Morris (1984) show this in the context of the historical development of the nature of work over the past 100 years. Marx (1844/1961) identified the need for control and autonomy over one's work activity. Durkheim (1897) pointed out the importance of meaningfulness (and the dangers of anomie) in work. Mayo (1933) described the significance of interpersonal work relationships. These themes are also clearly seen in the more recent work of McClelland and his colleagues, using a modified version of Murray's (1938) Thematic Apperception Test to assess the need for power (McClelland, 1975; McClelland & Burnham, 1976), the need for meaningful achievement (McClelland, 1961; McClelland & Winter, 1969), and the need for interpersonal contact in the context of work (McClelland, 1955, 1958). Thus, effective visionary leaders build into their visions and into organizational cultures strong support for both the critical organizational functions *and* critical human work needs.

The process by which leaders go about creating cultures is another important aspect of our approach. This concerns the way in which visionary leaders use power and influence to construct organizational cultures that embody their visions. One reason for the importance of the personal leadership characteristics we defined is that they enable leaders to use power and influence effectively, to empower followers. The use of power is directed toward the construction of an organizational culture that will support the leader's vision; such cultures are developed by defining and internalizing among followers specific values and beliefs and by designing policies and programs that permit work activities that followers can control, from which followers can derive a sense of completion and achievement, and within which individuals can work together to construct elements of the leaders' vision. Finally, visionary leaders empower followers through their, the leaders', actions, both on an organizational level (defining a philosophy and creating policies and programs) and on an individual, interpersonal level by means of the sorts of behaviors described briefly above.

We believe that our approach to organizational leadership is unique, differing from other transformational leadership theories in at least three important ways. First, we incorporate all three critical variables: personal characteristics of leaders, organizational contexts in which leaders act, and the specific actions leaders take, both organizationally and interpersonally. Second, we focus on the ways that transformational or visionary leaders empower followers, in order to construct their organizational visions. Finally, we incorporate a micro-macro integration, showing how individual-level variables mesh with social-organizational level factors.

Having outlined our organizational leadership theory, we will turn to the means we have developed for assessing visionary leadership in organizations, the *Leader Behavior Questionnaire*.

## Assessing Organizational Leadership

The *Leader Behavior Questionnaire* was first developed as a 24-item research and training instrument, based on work by Bennis (1984) on the characteristics of exceptionally effective chief executives, across a wide range of organizational settings. Initial studies to determine and improve scale coherence and reliability were conducted using managers and graduate students (most of whom were managers in part-time MBA programs; Sashkin & Fulmer, 1985b). This work led to the first widely available version of the LBQ, published in 1984. For that second edition a variety of minor changes were made in item wording, an additional item was added to each of the six original scales (to increase reliabilities), and four new scales, based on the Michigan Four-Factor Theory of Leadership (Bowers & Seashore, 1966), were added. Although some further minor wording changes were made in some items over the past few years (based on continued research studies), the present revision of the LBQ represents the first major change since its publication in 1984.

Over 20,000 managers in North America have experienced the LBQ during the past five years, and almost ten percent of those data have been used in various research activities. Since the LBQ is, then, one of the most widely used measures of organizational leadership, why was a revision undertaken?

The revision was carried out for two reasons. First, the last five scales of the LBQ were too often seen as either minimally useful or as actually distracting from the utility of the instrument. Scale Six assessed the emotional reactions of followers to the leader, a measure of the leader's "charisma." It was originally included as a research measure, to see if leaders who were reported as engaging in the five key visionary leadership behaviors were then perceived as charismatic, producing a characteristic pattern of affective responses among followers. Research showed that this was indeed the case (Sashkin & Fulmer, 1985b, 1987). But those using the LBQ for training often found Scale Six's use as a "check" on the first five scales to be confusing.

The final four scales measured traditional leadership functions, summing into the two more basic categories often referred to as "task" and "relationship" orientations or styles. But those using the LBQ were interested in new conceptions of transformational or visionary leadership, not in the old theories. Those using the LBQ for training often found the final four scales irrelevant and, sometimes, dysfunctional in that they distracted participants from the more significant points the trainer was trying to communicate.

In sum, the last five scales were sometimes acting as distractors rather than as facilitators of learning. As this was becoming clear, a second and more important reason for revising the LBQ was developing. The LBQ was, originally, an operationalization of concepts developed by Bennis in his study of characteristics of exceptional leaders cited above. But Bennis' theory, as well as the theories of several of his colleagues, continued to develop (e.g., see Bennis & Nanus, 1985), as did the theory constructed by the author of the LBQ (Sashkin, 1988b). While the leader's behavior is one critical factor in visionary leadership, there are two other equally important sets of variables which we have defined above: personal characteristics and organizational context.

Scales Six, Seven, and Eight of the newly revised LBQ assess three personal characteristics defined earlier. Scale Six measures effectance, the belief that one can make a real difference and have an impact on the organization by means of one's vision and the actions one takes to implement that vision. Scale Seven assesses the need for power, used in organizationally positive and productive ways. Scale Eight gives a measure of one's typical time span, as applied to one's managerial and leadership activities. All together, these three new scales give an overall measure of the extent to which one's personal characteristics are similar to those of effective visionary leaders. Note, however, that we take the explicit viewpoint that none of these scales tap what are fixed personality traits or characteristics. All three of these variables, while they do refer to personal characteristics of the respondent, are clearly changeable through training and/or experience, as shown by research on effectance, on training in need for achievement (McClelland & Winter, 1969), and on Jaques' (1986) theory of cognitive development.

Scales Nine and Ten provide an assessment of the leader's effectiveness at building the organization's culture. Scale Nine gets at the extent to which the leader is able to have a direct positive effect on the operation of Parsons' (1960) four critical organizational functions (adapting, attaining goals, coordinating the activities of individuals and groups, and maintaining the patterns of values and beliefs that define the organizational culture). Scale Ten asks whether the leader has developed, in the organization, the sort of values and beliefs that Schein (1985) and others (e.g., Peters & Waterman, 1982; Sashkin, 1988c) suggest are the foundation of organizational cultures that create and support excellence.

**Technical Information** While the latest edition of the LBQ is the third major revision, minor improvements in item wording have been made in successive printings since the first printing of the 1984 second edition. These changes have been made mostly on the basis of scale reliability analyses using Cronbach's alpha, a measure of the strength of the relationships among the items that make up a particular scale. A recent analysis by Stoner-Zemel (1988), using the previous edition of the LBQ, provides reliability coefficients (Cronbach alpha) for the first five scales, based on data from several hundred employees in a manufacturing plant in the Midwest. These respondents were reporting on the behavior of their managers. Stoner-Zemel obtained Cronbach alphas consistently better than those found in earlier studies (Sashkin & Fulmer, 1985b). Thus, it appears that the minor item modifications made since 1984 have in fact improved scale reliabilities. The lowest reliability score reported by Stoner-Zemel was .52 for Scale One, Focused Leadership. This is low but acceptable. Reliabilities for the remaining four scales were as follows: .74 (Scale Two, Communication Leadership); .75 (Scale Three, Trust Leadership); .71 (Scale Four, Respectful Leadership); .60 (Scale Five, Risk Leadership). Because scales six through ten of the current edition are new, we are still in the process of obtaining adequate samples for statistical analysis. The scales being used have, however, been through two or more developmental iterations, using various—and generally quite small—samples.

We have not attempted to use other reliability assessment methods, but we are about to examine interrater scale reliabilities, having obtained a moderately large sample of leaders (about 20) and raters (between five and nine raters for each leader).

Our experience has been (and examination of the norms in the appended data tables confirms) that there is generally little difference between self-ratings and ratings by others. While one might, as is often the case, expect self-reports to be more positive than the reports of others, this is not generally the case. It is more often true that self-ratings are actually a bit less positive than the ratings of others. This general convergence of self- and others' reports is important, because it alerts users to look closely at cases in which self-reports differ greatly from the reports of others. Our training experience has been that such gross discrepancies are rare but that when they occur they are a strong indicator that the individual being rated has serious problems. Normative LBQ data from a wide range of samples are shown in the tables in Appendix A.

**LBQ Scales**   The LBQ consists of 50 items, with five items forming each of ten scales. On each scale two items (40%) are negatively stated (this is not always obvious), while three (60%) are stated in positive terms, in order to help reduce social desirability bias. Items are ordered so that respondents read and make a choice about an item on each of the ten scales, repeating this four times. Positive and negative items are sequenced so as to eliminate any long chains of either. We will briefly describe each of the ten scales.

*Scale One: Focused Leadership.* Bennis found that effective visionary executives paid especially close attention to people with whom they were communicating. They "focused in" on the key issues under discussion and helped others to see these issues clearly. And they had clear ideas about the relative importance or priorities of different issues under discussion, concentrating only on the most important issues. Overall this scale comes together as the ability to manage one's attention and to direct the attention of others. Examples of items are:

*I pay attention to what others say when we are talking.*

*I have a clear set of priorities.*

*Scale Two: Communication Leadership.* This scale is composed of a set of items centering on the leader's basic skills in interpersonal communication. These skills allow the leader to get across the essential meaning of a message, even if this means devising some innovative, unusual way to ensure that the idea is understood. The skills include the basic interpersonal communication skills of attending to both ideas and feelings, rephrasing for clarification ("active listening"), giving feedback, asking questions, and summarizing. Sample items are:

*I make points in strikingly clear and even unusual ways.*

*I sometimes don't notice how others feel.*

*Scale Three: Trust Leadership.* The key issue here is the leader's perceived trustworthiness, as shown by willingness to take clear positions, to avoid "flip-flop" shifts in position, and to follow through on commitments. This scale assesses the leader's reliability, the extent to which one can trust the leader to be consistent and not act in surprising or unexpected ways. Some sample items are:

*I am extremely dependable.*

*I often find it desirable to change or alter my position.*

*Scale Four: Respectful Leadership.* This scale concerns the way the leader treats others (and him- or herself, as well) in daily interactions. Visionary leaders consistently and constantly express concern for others and their feelings. The visionary leader has a high degree of self-regard, too, as well as regard for others, since only when one has positive regard for one's self can one extend this to others. In essence, this scale measures what Carl Rogers calls "unconditional positive regard," an expressed respect for self and others that is maintained independent of whether an individual engages in "good" or "bad," in "desirable" or "undesirable" behavior. Because unconditional positive regard must apply to one's self as well as to others, we include within this scale the leader's sense of how he or she fits into the organization. Some sample items are:

*I recognize others' strengths and contributions.*

*I show that I really care about other people.*

Scale Five: *Risk Leadership.* Effective visionary leaders are deeply involved in what they do. They don't spend excessive amounts of time or energy on plans to protect themselves against possible failures; they don't worry particularly about covering their butts. These leaders are willing to take risks, not on a hit-and-miss basis but, rather, only after a careful examination of factors favoring success and failure. All the leader's energy is then invested in actions to ensure success. Thus, the "risks" the leader takes are, from the leader's own perspective, not risky in the way an outside observer might judge, because the leader is confident that he or she can do what is required to make happen what must be done. In other words, visionary leaders may take some risks in implementing their visions, but they see their actions as steps forward in creating their visions, not as "chancy" or "risky bets." Finally, visionary leaders design risks—challenges and opportunities—that others can "buy into" so that followers can participate in and "own" the vision. Some sample items are:

*I worry a lot about the possibility of failing.*

*I find ways to get everyone fully committed to new ideas and projects.*

Scale Six: *Bottom-Line Leadership.* Effective visionary leaders have a basic sense of self-assurance, an underlying belief that they can personally make a difference and have an impact on people, events, and organizational achievements. They believe, in other words, that they can have an impact or effect on final, "bottom-line" outcomes in the organization. They know that people make a difference and they believe that they, personally, can do so. This scale measures a leader's effectance, the sense that one can have an effect over one's own destiny. Sample items are:

*I can see clear effects resulting from my action.*

*I have found that no one person can make very much of a difference in how this organization operates.*

Scale Seven: *Empowered Leadership.* While the concepts of power and empowerment are central and recurring themes appearing throughout our theory of organizational leadership, this scale assesses the specific personal characteristic defined as the need-for-power motive (McClelland, 1975), in terms of both its strength and its manner of application. That is, some people desire power primarily or solely in order to obtain and enjoy the material rewards it can bring, or even to experience the "pleasure" of imposing their wills on and dominating over others. Visionary leaders have a high need for power, not for its personal rewards or to dominate others, but because they know that it is through power and influence that things get done in organizations. Power and influence are the necessary means for affecting one's world, for realizing one's vision. Visionary leaders realize that power and influence must be widely shared, not just exerted at top levels by a few key persons. In effective organizations, everyone feels he or she has a lot of influence, especially over the job for which one is personally responsible. Effective visionary leaders use power to *empower* others, who then use their power and influence to help create the leader's vision. The chief measure of the power motive has been McClelland's adaptation of Murray's Thematic Apperception

Test, a projective test used to generate written or verbal vignettes that are then scored for power-relevant imagery. While there have been efforts to develop paper-and-pencil questionnaire measures, these attempts have not been particularly successful. Thus, this LBQ scale should be treated as experimental; meaningful validation will call for correlation with TAT-based assessments. Some sample items on this LBQ scale are:

*I think that the real value of power is in being able to accomplish things that benefit both the organization and its members.*

*I believe that some of the most significant aspects of my position are the little "perks" that demonstrate my importance to the organization and its members.*

*Scale Eight: Long-Term Leadership.* Effective visionary leaders are able to think clearly over relatively long spans of time, at least several years. That is, their visions, and the more specific goals along the way, are not short-term "to do" lists but are instead conditions that these leaders are committed to creating, over the long run. They know what actions must be taken to stay on the right track, they are able to clearly explain their long-range views to others (at least in basic outline), they see how their plans can be extended to take into consideration added elements of their organizations, and they can conceive of how their visions might be expanded beyond their current views and plans. The methods developed by Jaques' associates (Stamp, 1978) for assessing the level of cognitive complexity are fairly complex and involve a long clinical interview. We are not at all certain how well this LBQ scale will do at providing a similar measure, even one that is defined in a simpler and more limited sense. Thus, this scale must be treated as experimental at this time, and it may be that it proves useful only as a training tool for use in teaching and training visionary leadership and is not an acceptable measure of time span of vision. Some sample items are:

*I focus on clear short-term goals rather than being concerned with longer-range aims.*

*I think about how the plans and programs I've developed in my own unit might be expanded to benefit the entire organization.*

*Scale Nine: Organizational Leadership.* All organizations must deal with certain basic issues. One concerns changes in their environments. A second has to do with achieving goals based on customer/client demands. A third centers on coordinating the activities of individuals and teams. A fourth and final basic issue is that of maintaining the system of shared values and beliefs that drives the organization's "culture" and determines how well the organization will deal with problems of adaptation, goal attainment, and coordination. These issues are, of course, based on the four organizational functions defined by Parsons (1960) and discussed earlier. This scale examines the degree to which the leader has a positive impact on these matters, helping the organization to adapt more effectively, to attain goals, to get people working together effectively in teams and between teams, and to maintain a strong set of shared values and beliefs. In other words, this scale assesses the degree to which the leader "connects" with the organization in terms of its four critical functions. To the extent that visionary leaders can do these things, they can both improve organizational functioning and construct elements of their organizational visions. Some sample items on this scale are:

*I have not generally been able to help the organization attain its goals.*

*I try to express and support a set of basic values about how people should work together in this organization to solve common problems and reach shared goals.*

*Scale Ten: Cultural Leadership.* An organization's culture is defined by the stable pattern of values and beliefs that is shared by most or all of the organization's members. Some values and beliefs are more likely to support effective functioning—and the leader's vision—than are other values and beliefs. This scale measures the extent to which the leader is able to develop or inculcate those values that will strengthen organizational functioning—adapting to change, attaining goals, working together, and maintaining the culture—and, at the same time, help build and support the leader's vision. Schein (1985) has suggested that constructing the organization's culture may be the only really important task of leadership. It is surely one of the most basic and difficult of the leader's tasks, being at the heart of what Bennis and Nanus (1985) define as the leader's role as a "social architect." Sample scale items are:

*I strive to take actions to reach goals rather than contributing to keeping things the way they are.*

*I help others understand that there is often little we can do to control important factors in the environment.*

**Validation Research** Most of the research on the LBQ is quite recent and much is still in process. Research has generally addressed the question of whether scores on the LBQ are related to such things as organizational performance and productivity (Major, 1988; Godwin, in process), the perceived quality of work life of organizational members (Stoner-Zemel, 1988), or the quality of the organization's culture (Ray, in process).

In the first research study, conducted by Valley (1986), the question was whether pastors of high- versus low-growth church congregations could be differentiated by the LBQ. While some differences were found, none were strikingly significant. More extended exploration suggested that the key dependent variable, congregation growth, was not seen as a strong goal by any of the pastors, although it was a major goal for those at higher levels in the church hierarchy.

Stoner-Zemel (1988) developed a questionnaire measure to assess the perceptions of organization members with respect to quality of work life on a variety of dimensions (including self-perceptions of productivity). She then obtained LBQ-other assessments from employees with regard to all of the managers in a small organization. She also obtained results using the LBA, a situational leadership questionnaire developed by Kenneth Blanchard and widely used in management training and development (but supported by no validity or psychometric research). Stoner-Zemel found that both the LBQ and the LBA were very strongly and significantly correlated with employees' quality-of-work-life perceptions. The LBQ, however, made much more of a difference in quality-of-work-life perceptions, when managers were separated into high and low LBQ groups, than did the LBA, when managers were, similarly, separated into high and low groups.

Ray (in process) obtained LBQ data from about 200 employees in each of two manufacturing plants, along with a measure of organizational excellence culture (Sashkin, 1984b; Sashkin & Fulmer, 1985a). Initial data analyses show that culture scores on the *Organizational Beliefs Questionnaire* (Sashkin, 1984b) are strongly and significantly related to LBQ scores. Moreover, one plant was significantly higher than the other with respect to OBQ scores and was similarly significantly higher with respect to the LBQ. Thus, a clear association has been demonstrated between organizational leadership and organization culture.

Finally, in the strongest demonstration yet of the LBQ's relevance to organizational performance, Major (1988) identified 30 high-performing high schools and 30 low-performing high schools in Southern California. Major used a set of quantitative criteria to assess performance, including student achievement test scores, and equated the high- and low-performance sets of schools on such factors as minority student population and socioeconomic status. Major then administered the LBQ to the principals of the 60 schools. He found a strong and highly significant difference, with principals of the high-performing schools scoring substantially higher than principals of low-performing high schools (p < .001). It is clear that leaders' LBQ scores are strongly associated with bottom-line organizational performance in the case of public high schools.

All of the studies just described used the previous edition of the LBQ and are, therefore, based only on the five behavior scales. Studies now in progress will examine the ways in which the five new scales relate to organizational performance. In one study nearing completion, Godwin (in process) obtained LBQ-self measures from 20 residence hall directors at a state university. She also obtained from five to eight LBQ-other reports for each director, from the 90 associate directors. Finally, she modified Stoner-Zemel's measure of perceived quality of work life and administered it to a sample of the student residents in each of the 20 residence hall units. These data are now being analyzed and will prove of great value both in the further psychometric development of the LBQ and as a first test of the new edition, examining the relationships of the scales to bottom-line outcome measures.

The author and publisher of the LBQ have been active in assisting those wishing to use the LBQ in organizational leadership research, providing permission to use the instrument (in exchange for copies of the data sets) and even providing copies of the instrument gratis in some cases. This policy will be continued.

## Conclusion

We believe that over the past decade a paradigm shift (Kuhn, 1970) has occurred with respect to leadership theory, a shift which is just now appearing in terms of research and application. Bass (1985), Bennis and Nanus (1985), Burke (1988), Kouzes and Posner (1987), and Sashkin (1984a) are all speaking, writing, and doing research on a similarly conceived new vision of leadership, a vision based on the transformational, culture-shaping organizational leadership role of top-level leaders. And the distinction is clearer than ever between this sort of leadership activity and the important but different role of managers, whose activities have been the prime, if not the sole, purview of so-called leadership research for over 50 years.

We believe it is time to clarify our research directions and, concurrently, to apply what we have learned and are still discovering about real leadership, in order to benefit organizations and their members. The approach presented here is theory-based, integrating a diverse set of research work on or related to organizational leadership. It is also empirically research guided. While we have only provided an outline in this report, and while there is much to be dealt with in concrete detail, we believe that we have made substantial progress toward the aim of practical, data-based theory of organizational leadership. Perhaps we will add new weight to another of Kurt Lewin's dictums: there is nothing so practical as a good theory.

## Appendix A: *Leader Behavior Questionnaire* Norms

Since the first general publication of the LBQ, norms have been collected on a wide range of managerial/professional groups. The tables that follow show the averages for each scale and, where available, for the three cluster scores (Visionary Leadership Behavior, Visionary Leadership Characteristics, and Visionary Culture Building) and the Visionary Leadership Total Score. Most of the data presented here were obtained using the earlier versions of the LBQ, so those data do not include the current scales six through ten, representing the Visionary Leadership Characteristics score and the Visionary Culture Building score. Included with all of these data are the number of individuals responding and whether the data represent self-ratings, or ratings by others, of a particular individual. Most data sets also give the standard deviation for each scale, a measure of how variable the scores are, how wide a range they cover.

---

## LBQ Scales — Key to Samples

   I: Midlevel managers in a rural electric utility

  II: "Fast track" plant managers in an international manufacturing organization (consumer and industrial products)

 III: Executive program MBA students, large urban university, southeast United States

 IV: MBA students, evening/part-time program, large metropolitan area, mid-Atlantic United States

   *: Combined data, all above samples, except "self" excludes II

  V: Senior managers, electric utility firms, diverse organizations

 VI: Senior-level U.S. government agency program managers (GS14 + )

 VII: Senior-level U.S. government agency program managers (GS13 + )

VIII: Midlevel managers and engineers, large industrial manufacturing organization in India

 IX: U.S. military officers, staff training professionals

 **: All data from samples I through IX combined, except "self" data from sample II

  X: Top executives, large multinational oil company

 XI: Mid- to lower-level managers and professionals, large multinational oil company

 XII: Cross section of all employees, consumer product manufacturing firms, southwest United States (part of national firm)

XIII: Top executives (paid and unpaid); large, decentralized, voluntary community service organization; United States (sample of approximately 20%)

XIV: Top executives (paid and unpaid), large decentralized, voluntary community service organization, United States (small sample; no overlap with XIII)

*Continued on next page*

XV: Principals of high-performing public high schools, Southern California

XVI: Principals of low-performing public high schools, Southern California

XVII: Directors of residence halls, residential university, northeast United States

XVIII: Public school principals, south central United States

XIX: Community educators, national sample

XX: Adult educators, college and community college faculty, various institutions of higher education, south central United States

***: Samples XVIII, XIX, and XX, combined data

XXI: Managers and professionals, national telecommunication services organization

## LBQ Scales

1   Focused Leadership
2   Communication Leadership
3   Trust Leadership
4   Respectful Leadership
5   Risk Leadership
6   Bottom-Line Leadership
7   Empowered Leadership
8   Long-Term Leadership
9   Organizational Leadership
10  Cultural Leadership

## Code

N = refers to the number of respondents in the sample
S = LBQ-Self data
O = LBQ-Other data
X = mean score
sd = standard deviation
VLB = Visionary Leadership Behavior Score
VLC = Visionary Leadership Characteristics Score
VCB = Visionary Culture Building Score
Ttl. = Total Visionary Leadership Score

## LBQ Scales

| Sample | | N | | 1 | 2 | 3 | 4 | 5 | VLB |
|--------|----|-----|----|------|------|------|------|------|------|
| I | (S) | 18 | X | 16.4 | 17.6 | 19.3 | 20.7 | 18.1 | 92.1 |
| | | | sd | 1.65 | 2.57 | 2.27 | 2.33 | 2.75 | 7.70 |
| | (O) | 36 | X | 18.2 | 18.5 | 18.2 | 20.3 | 15.9 | 91.1 |
| | | | sd | 1.98 | 4.00 | 3.24 | 3.21 | 2.33 | 12.89 |
| II | (S) | 21 | X | 18.3 | 18.6 | 18.9 | 21.4 | 19.2 | 96.4 |
| | | | sd | 1.83 | 2.34 | 1.91 | 1.84 | 2.31 | 6.58 |
| | (O) | 42 | X | 18.5 | 20.0 | 19.7 | 21.9 | 18.1 | 97.8 |
| | | | sd | 1.89 | 2.83 | 2.00 | 2.11 | 2.55 | 9.46 |
| III | (S) | 24 | X | 18.0 | 19.2 | 20.5 | 22.0 | 18.5 | 98.2 |
| | | | sd | 1.91 | 2.41 | 1.21 | 2.36 | 1.59 | |
| IV | (S) | 30 | X | 17.3 | 19.2 | 20.2 | 21.0 | 18.9 | 96.6 |
| | | | sd | 2.23 | 2.51 | 2.09 | 2.36 | 2.26 | |
| | (O) | 30 | X | 18.0 | 21.2 | 20.3 | 22.6 | 19.1 | 101.2 |
| | | | sd | 2.04 | 2.86 | 2.81 | 2.61 | 2.45 | |
| * | (S) | 72 | X | 17.3 | 18.8 | 20.1 | 21.2 | 18.5 | 95.9 |
| | | | sd | 2.06 | 2.55 | 1.93 | 2.38 | 2.19 | |
| | (O) | 108 | X | 18.5 | 19.8 | 19.4 | 21.6 | 17.7 | 97.0 |
| | | | sd | 2.00 | 3.43 | 2.83 | 2.81 | 2.93 | |
| V | (S) | 7 | X | 18.0 | 18.4 | 21.0 | 21.6 | 19.1 | 98.1 |
| | | | sd | 1.82 | 1.72 | 1.41 | 1.81 | 1.86 | 4.18 |
| | (O) | 16 | X | 19.1 | 19.0 | 19.0 | 21.4 | 17.3 | 95.8 |
| | | | sd | 1.53 | 1.94 | 1.93 | 1.48 | 1.42 | 5.98 |
| VI | (S) | 11 | X | 18.1 | 19.4 | 20.4 | 21.1 | 19.6 | 98.6 |
| | | | sd | 2.17 | 1.63 | 2.20 | 2.17 | 2.25 | 6.80 |
| VII | (S) | 16 | X | 18.4 | 19.2 | 20.4 | 21.1 | 19.6 | 98.6 |
| | | | sd | 1.93 | 1.91 | 1.87 | 1.71 | 1.86 | 5.74 |
| VIII | (S) | 15 | X | 18.6 | 19.8 | 18.3 | 19.2 | 19.4 | 95.3 |
| | | | sd | 1.88 | 2.46 | 2.02 | 2.46 | 2.53 | 7.84 |
| IX | (S) | 12 | X | 19.7 | 20.5 | 19.3 | 21.9 | 17.9 | 99.3 |
| | | | sd | 1.80 | 2.36 | 2.43 | 1.66 | 1.71 | 6.98 |
| ** | (S) | 121 | X | 17.7 | 19.0 | 20.0 | 21.2 | 18.9 | 96.8 |
| | | | sd | 2.0 | 2.3 | 1.9 | 2.1 | 2.1 | |
| | (O) | 136 | X | 18.7 | 19.8 | 19.3 | 21.6 | 17.7 | 97.1 |
| | | | sd | 1.9 | 3.2 | 2.7 | 2.6 | 2.6 | |
| X | (S) | 80 | X | 18.5 | 18.6 | 21.2 | 21.0 | 19.6 | 98.9 |
| | | | sd | 2.24 | 2.99 | 1.76 | 2.60 | 2.04 | |
| | (O) | 157 | X | 19.4 | 20.3 | 21.4 | 21.7 | 19.1 | 101.9 |
| | | | sd | 1.81 | 2.54 | 2.43 | 2.29 | 2.76 | |

*Continued on next page*

**LBQ Scales—***Continued*

| Sample | | N | | 1 | 2 | 3 | 4 | 5 | VLB |
|---|---|---|---|---|---|---|---|---|---|
| XI | (S) | 52 | X | 17.5 | 17.4 | 21.0 | 20.2 | 17.9 | 94.0 |
| | | | sd | 2.19 | 2.77 | 2.37 | 2.49 | 2.41 | 9.02 |
| | (O) | 203 | X | 18.6 | 19.1 | 20.7 | 20.8 | 17.9 | 97.1 |
| | | | sd | 2.30 | 2.78 | 2.34 | 2.54 | 2.82 | 9.25 |
| XII | (O) | 264 | X | 17.9 | 17.7 | 18.8 | 19.8 | 16.5 | 90.7 |
| | | | sd | 2.52 | 4.09 | 3.66 | 3.66 | 3.13 | 14.4 |
| XIII | (S) | 183 | X | 18.3 | 18.6 | 20.7 | 21.9 | 19.6 | 99.2 |
| | | | sd | 1.80 | 2.38 | 1.91 | 2.02 | 2.34 | 6.92 |
| XIV | (S) | 70 | X | 18.1 | 18.2 | 20.2 | 21.2 | 18.5 | 96.7 |
| | | | sd | 1.86 | 2.57 | 1.94 | 2.49 | 2.23 | 7.23 |
| XV | (S) | 30 | X | 19.3 | 19.7 | 20.3 | 20.8 | 18.9 | 99.3 |
| | | | sd | 1.76 | 2.00 | 2.09 | 2.27 | 1.74 | 5.36 |
| XVI | (S) | 30 | X | 17.8 | 17.0 | 18.0 | 17.7 | 16.2 | 86.8 |
| | | | sd | 2.07 | 2.61 | 2.62 | 3.09 | 3.14 | 11.03 |

| | | N | | 1 | 2 | 3 | 4 | 5 | VLB | 6 | 7 | 8 | VLC | 9 | 10 | VCB | Ttl. |
|---|---|---|---|---|---|---|---|---|---|---|---|---|---|---|---|---|---|
| XVII | (S) | 18 | X | 18.1 | 19.1 | 20.3 | 20.9 | 20.3 | 98.7 | 19.1 | 18.9 | 16.6 | 54.6 | 20.6 | 20.0 | 40.6 | |
| | | | sd | 1.92 | 2.54 | 2.91 | 1.88 | 2.49 | 8.44 | 2.59 | 2.24 | 3.58 | 6.37 | 2.26 | 1.91 | 3.26 | |
| | (O) | 93 | X | 17.9 | 18.9 | 18.7 | 21.0 | 18.7 | 95.2 | 18.6 | 18.4 | 17.7 | 54.7 | 19.6 | 19.3 | 38.9 | |
| | | | sd | 2.29 | 3.64 | 3.28 | 2.75 | 3.16 | 12.4 | 2.99 | 2.89 | 3.41 | 6.87 | 3.78 | 2.96 | 6.25 | |
| XVIII | (S) | 155 | X | 18.3 | 18.8 | 20.7 | 21.5 | 19.7 | 98.0 | 21.2 | 19.4 | 20.7 | 61.2 | 21.3 | 19.4 | 40.7 | |
| | | | sd | 1.70 | 2.40 | 2.37 | 1.99 | 2.71 | 7.87 | 2.30 | 2.50 | 2.67 | 5.81 | 2.52 | 2.59 | 4.28 | |
| XIX | (S) | 55 | X | 18.0 | 17.6 | 20.3 | 20.7 | 20.7 | 97.3 | 20.4 | 19.9 | 20.3 | 60.7 | 20.5 | 20.5 | 41.0 | |
| | | | sd | 1.83 | 2.27 | 1.90 | 2.03 | 2.09 | 6.79 | 2.82 | 2.50 | 2.03 | 5.45 | 2.26 | 2.25 | 3.82 | |
| XX | (S) | 67 | X | 17.8 | 18.7 | 19.7 | 21.2 | 18.9 | 96.4 | 19.4 | 18.2 | 19.2 | 56.7 | 19.8 | 19.1 | 39.0 | |
| | | | sd | 2.09 | 2.73 | 2.02 | 2.52 | 2.78 | 8.87 | 2.81 | 2.80 | 2.66 | 5.50 | 3.23 | 2.43 | 4.71 | |
| *** | (S) | 277 | X | 18.1 | 18.6 | 20.4 | 21.3 | 19.7 | 98.0 | 20.6 | 19.2 | 20.2 | 60.1 | 20.8 | 19.5 | 40.4 | |
| | | | sd | 1.83 | 2.50 | 2.25 | 2.16 | 2.67 | 7.98 | 2.65 | 2.63 | 2.63 | 5.98 | 2.72 | 2.54 | 4.37 | |
| XXI | (S) | 39 | X | 19.0 | 18.0 | 20.5 | 20.4 | 18.4 | 97.0 | 19.8 | 19.4 | 17.9 | 57.3 | 19.6 | 19.4 | 39.0 | 193.3 |
| | | | sd | 2.63 | 2.90 | 2.06 | 3.06 | 2.85 | 10.38 | 2.75 | 2.46 | 3.69 | 6.45 | 2.84 | 2.41 | 4.61 | 17.98 |

## Endnotes

Prepared especially for the Conference on Psychological Measures and Leadership, sponsored by the Center for Creative Leadership and the Psychological Corporation, San Antonio, Texas, October 23 through 26, 1988.

This report and all associated data tables copyright 1988, Marshall Sashkin and W. Warner Burke. May be reproduced only with the express permission of the authors.

The views expressed in this report are those of the authors and do not necessarily represent the positions or policies of the Office of Educational Research and Improvement or the United States Department of Education.

## References

Avolio, B. J., & Gibbons, T. C. (1988). Developing transformational leaders: A life span approach. In J. A. Conger & R. N. Kanungo (Eds.), *Charismatic leadership: The elusive factor in organizational effectiveness* (pp. 276–308). San Francisco: Jossey-Bass.

Bales, R. F. (1958). Task roles and social roles in problem-solving groups. In E. E. Maccoby, T. M. Newcomb, & E. L. Hartley (Eds.), *Readings in social psychology* (3rd ed.) (pp. 437–447). New York: Holt, Rinehart & Winston.

Bass, B. M. (1985). *Leadership and performance beyond expectations*. New York: Free Press.

Bass, B. M. (1988). Evolving perspectives of charismatic leadership. In J. A. Conger & R. N. Kanungo (Eds.), *Charismatic leadership: The elusive factor in organizational effectiveness* (pp. 40–77). San Francisco: Jossey-Bass.

Bennis, W. G. (1984). The four competencies of leadership. *Training and Development Journal, 38*(8), 15–18.

Bennis, W. G., & Nanus, B. (1985). *Leaders*. New York: Harper & Row.

Blake, R. R., & Mouton, J. S. (1964). *The managerial grid*. Houston: Gulf.

Bowers, D. G., & Seashore, S. E. (1966). Predicting organizational effectiveness with a four factor theory of leadership. *Administrative Science Quarterly, 11*, 238–263.

Burke, W. W. (1988). *Leadership report* (rev. ed.). Pelham, NY: W. Warner Burke and Associates.

Burns, J. M. (1978). *Leadership*. New York: Harper & Row.

Durkheim, E. (1897). *Le suicide*. Paris: F. Alcan.

Fiedler, F. E. (1965). Engineer the job to fit the manager. *Harvard Business Review, 43*(5), 115–122.

Fiedler, F. E. (1967). *A theory of leadership effectiveness*. New York: McGraw-Hill.

Fleishman, E. A., & Harris, E. F. (1962). Patterns of leadership behavior related to employee grievances and turnover. *Personnel Psychology, 15*, 43–56.

Godwin, K. (in process). *Leadership of college residence hall directors and its effects on student perceptions of residence life.* Doctoral dissertation in process, University of Maine at Orono.

Hersey, P., & Blanchard, K. H. (1969). Life-cycle theory of leadership. *Training and Development Journal, 23*(5), 26–34.

House, R. J. (1971). A path-goal theory of leader effectiveness. *Administrative Science Quarterly, 16*, 321–338.

House, R. J. (1977). A 1976 theory of charismatic leadership. In J. G. Hunt & L. L. Larson (Eds.), *Leadership: The cutting edge* (pp. 189–207). Carbondale, IL: Southern Illinois University Press.

House, R. J. (1988). Leadership research: Some forgotten, ignored, or overlooked findings. In J. G. Hunt, B. R. Baliga, H. P. Dachler, & C. A. Schriesheim (Eds.), *Emerging leadership vistas* (pp. 245–260). Lexington, MA: Lexington Books.

House, R. J., & Baetz, M. L. (1979). Leadership: Some empirical generalizations and new research directions. In B. M. Staw (Ed.), *Research in organizational behavior* (pp. 341–423). Greenwich, CT: JAI Press.

House, R. J., Woycke, J., & Folor, E. M. (1988). Charismatic and noncharismatic leaders: Differences in behavior and effectiveness. In J. A. Conger & R. N. Kanungo (Eds.), *Charismatic leadership: The elusive factor in organizational effectiveness* (pp. 98–121). San Francisco: Jossey-Bass.

Howell, J. M. (1988). Two faces of charisma. In J. A. Conger and R. N. Kanungo (Eds.), *Charismatic leadership: The elusive factor in organizational effectiveness* (pp. 213–236). San Francisco: Jossey-Bass.

Hoy, W. L., & Ferguson, J. (1985). A theoretical framework and exploration of organizational effectiveness of schools. *Educational Administration Quarterly, 21*(2), 117–134.

Jaques, E. (1976). *A general theory of bureaucracy.* London: Heinemann.

Jaques, E. (1979). Taking time seriously in evaluating jobs. *Harvard Business Review, 57*(5), 124–132.

Jaques, E. (1986). The development of intellectual capability. *Journal of Applied Behavioral Science, 22*, 361–383.

Jaques, E. (1989). *Requisite organization.* Arlington, VA: Cason Hall.

Katz, D., & Kahn, R. L. (1978). *The social psychology of organizations* (rev. ed.). New York: Wiley.

Kets de Vries, M. F. R. (1988). Origins of charisma. In J. A. Conger & R. N. Kanungo (Eds.), *Charismatic leadership: The elusive factor in organizational effectiveness* (pp. 237–252). San Francisco: Jossey-Bass.

Kouzes, J. M., & Posner, B. Z. (1987). *The leadership challenge: How to get extraordinary things done in organizations*. San Francisco: Jossey-Bass.

Kuhn, T. S. (1970). *The structure of scientific revolutions* (2nd ed.). Chicago: University of Chicago Press.

Larson, L. L., Hunt, J. G., & Osborn, R. N. (1976). The great hi-hi leader behavior myth: A lesson from Occam's Razor. *Academy of Management Journal, 19,* 628–641.

Levinson, H. (1981). *Executive*. Boston: Harvard University Press.

McClelland, D. C. (Ed.). (1955). *Studies in motivation*. New York: Appleton-Century-Crofts.

McClelland, D. C. (1958). Methods of measuring human motivation. In J. W. Atkinson (Ed.), *Motives in fantasy, action, and society* (pp. 7–45). Princeton, NJ: Van Nostrand.

McClelland, D. C. (1961). *The achieving society*. New York: Van Nostrand.

McClelland, D. C. (1975). *Power: The inner experience*. New York: Irvington.

McClelland, D. C., & Burnham, D. H. (1976). Power is the great motivator. *Harvard Business Review, 54,*(2), 100–110.

McClelland, D. C., & Winter, D. G. (1969). *Motivating economic achievement*. New York: Free Press.

Major, K. D. (1988). *Dogmatism, visionary leadership, and effectiveness of secondary schools*. Unpublished doctoral dissertation, University of La Verne, La Verne, California.

Marx, K. (1961). *Economic and philosophical manuscripts of 1844*. Moscow: Foreign Languages Publishing House. (Original work published 1844)

Mayo, E. (1933). *The human problems of an industrial civilization*. New York: Macmillan.

Murray, H. A. (1938). *Explorations in personality*. New York: Oxford University Press.

Parsons, T. (1960). *Structure and process in modern societies*. New York: Free Press.

Peters, T. J., & Waterman, R. H., Jr. (1982). *In search of excellence*. New York: Harper & Row.

Ray, B. (in process). *Leadership and organizational culture in two manufacturing plants*. Doctoral dissertation in process, East Texas State University.

Sashkin, M. (1984a). *The leader behavior questionnaire*. King of Prussia, PA: Organization Design and Development.

Sashkin, M. (1984b). *The organizational beliefs questionnaire*. King of Prussia, PA: Organization Design and Development.

Sashkin, M. (1987, April). *Explaining excellence in leadership in light of Parsonian theory*. Paper presented at the annual meeting of the American Educational Research Association, Washington, DC.

Sashkin, M. (1988a). *Trainer guide: Leader behavior questionnaire*. King of Prussia, PA: Organization Design and Development.

Sashkin, M. (1988b). The visionary leader. In J. A. Conger & R. N. Kanungo (Eds.), *Charismatic leadership: The elusive factor in organizational effectiveness* (pp. 122–160). San Francisco: Jossey-Bass.

Sashkin, M. (1988c). The visionary principal: School leadership for the next century. *Education and Urban Society, 20*, (3), 239–249.

Sashkin, M., & Fulmer, R. M. (1985a, August). *Measuring organizational culture*. Paper presented at the annual meeting of the Academy of Management, Organization Development Division, San Diego.

Sashkin, M., & Fulmer, R. M. (1985b, July). *A new framework for leadership: Vision, charisma, and culture creation*. Paper presented at the Biennial International Leadership Symposium, Texas Tech University, Lubbock, TX.

Sashkin, M., & Fulmer, R. M. (1988). Toward an organizational leadership theory. In J. G. Hunt, B. R. Baliga, H. P. Dachler, & C. A. Schriesheim (Eds.), *Emerging leadership vistas* (pp. 51–65). Lexington, MA: Lexington Books.

Sashkin, M., & Morris, W. C. (1984). *Organizational behavior: Concepts and experiences*. Englewood Cliffs, NJ: Prentice-Hall.

Schein, E. H. (1985). *Organizational culture and leadership: A dynamic view*. San Francisco: Jossey-Bass.

Stamp, G. (1978). Assessment of individual capacity. In E. Jaques, R. O. Gibson, & D. J. Isaac (Eds.), *Levels of abstraction in logic and human action*. London: Heinemann.

Stogdill, R. M. (1948). Personal factors associated with leadership: A survey of the literature. *Journal of Psychology, 25*, 35–71.

Stoner-Zemel, M. J. (1988). *Visionary leadership, management, and high performing work units*. Unpublished doctoral dissertation, University of Massachusetts, Amherst.

Tannenbaum, A. S. (Ed.). (1968). *Control in organizations*. New York: McGraw-Hill.

Valley, C. A. (1986). *The relationship between the leader behaviors of pastors and church growth*. Unpublished doctoral dissertation, Western Michigan University, Kalamazoo.

Weber, M. (1947). *The theory of social and economic organization*. (A. M. Henderson & T. Parsons, Trans.; T. Parsons, Ed.). New York: Free Press. (Original work published 1924)

Winter, D. G. (1987). Leader appeal, leader performance, and the motive profiles of leaders and followers. *Journal of Personality and Social Psychology, 52,* 196–202.

Zaleznik, A. (1977). Managers and leaders: Are they different? *Harvard Business Review, 55*(3), 67–78.

# Leadership Behavior in Ambiguous Environments

*Joseph L.*
*Moses*
*and*
*Karen S.*
*Lyness*

The best predictor of future behavior is past behavior. This statement is at the heart of many of our assumptions about leadership behavior. It drives many of our selection strategies, longitudinal research efforts, and models about effective leadership performance.

In order to predict from past events, there needs to be continuity between past and future events. What happens when the future is no longer an incremental extension of the past? What happens when the leaders of stable, predictable organizations enter a turbulent and uncertain world? What happens when the forces of change increase so fast that the rules of the game change while the game is being played?

For many leaders, the future is now. The past decade has been extremely turbulent. Mergers and acquisitions, deregulation of major sections of our economy, and unparalleled global competition have significantly changed the ways leaders operate. In addition to responding to externally induced change, many leaders face internal change as well. Corporate reorganizations, downsizing of staffs, or the redeployment of people to respond to shifting markets have impacted on millions of managers and employees. Change has a major impact on managerial lives. It introduces ambiguity, particularly if there are significant discontinuities between the past and the future.

While ambiguity has always been viewed as part of a manager's job, little is really known about ambiguity and its effects on managerial behavior. This is troublesome, because the modern manager's job is one, which for many, occurs in an increasingly more ambiguous world of divestitures, mergers and acquisitions, corporate restructuring, deregulation, and an increasing rate of change brought about by new technologies, new markets, and new competition.

What behaviors are appropriate in ambiguous situations? How do people and organizations adapt to a more ambiguous world? What behavioral styles inhibit or facilitate responses to ambiguity? These are some of the questions that we attempted to answer with our research.

The Ambiguity Research Study began as an exploratory analysis of individual behavior in ambiguous environments. At the time that we initiated our research in 1980, we had no indication that our organization, AT&T, would undergo the largest corporate reorganization on record (Tunstall, 1985). As we became both subjects and researchers as the divestiture of the Bell system unfolded, we were able to study managers as they were experiencing major ambiguity in their lives and careers.

The study continued for over five years, spanning both the pre- and post-divestiture period. We collected data on hundreds of managers both inside and outside AT&T. Our units of analysis included both the individual and the organization. Our research objectives were designed to:

1. Gain a better understanding of ambiguity and its effects on managerial behavior.

2. Study the types of ambiguous situations faced by managers inside and outside AT&T.

3. Identify ways to help individuals and organizations cope more effectively with ambiguity.

We defined ambiguity as: "A global characteristic of the situation that is determined by the summation and interaction of the specific components of the immediate work context, members of the organization, and the external environment" (Lyness, Zedeck, Jackson, & Moses, 1985).

This paper briefly summarizes some of the rich data that we have collected on individuals. A more extensive treatment of this topic can be found in our forthcoming book (Lyness & Moses, 1990).

## The Interview Study

In order to learn firsthand about managers' experiences with ambiguity, we conducted a series of in-depth interviews with individuals who had been identified as people who had experienced considerable ambiguity in their jobs (Moses & Lyness, 1983). Over 40 executives were interviewed, representing a broad spectrum of industries including computer services, international banking, retailing, investment, manufacturing, investment services, advertising, and education. The sample was a senior-level one and represented a wide assortment of staff and line responsibilities, functions, and strategic initiatives.

We asked each executive to define ambiguity and its characteristics, to provide us examples of ambiguous situations that they had faced, and to provide critical incidents of effective and ineffective behavior in ambiguous situations.

We were impressed with the level of candor and insight provided by our respondents. The ambiguous situations that they described tended to be important situations for them—ones that they had thought about a great deal.

Four major findings emerged from these interviews.

1. Ambiguity is an important and pervasive part of these managers' jobs.

2. Ambiguity is very personal and is a highly individualized perception. Situations that are very ambiguous for one manager might be much less so for another. Ambiguous situations were seen as uncertain or unpredictable, lacking clarity or definition, or often novel.

3. Ambiguity tends to be stressful. It can be viewed as a challenge or opportunity that serves to energize the manager and bring out maximal effort. Or it can be seen as a threat which inhibits effective performance. Often both feelings can be experienced.

4. Several key determinants were identified which differentiate executives who were effective in ambiguous situations from others who experienced difficulty.

This last finding became a key basis for understanding which behaviors helped determine effectiveness in ambiguous situations. The interview data clearly indicated that no single characteristic determined whether or not a manager will be effective in ambiguous settings. This was due in part to the unique nature of ambiguity for each individual. Two underlying factors, however, helped explain why managers behaved so differently in ambiguous situations. These were: the manager's level of the skills needed to effectively respond to an ambiguous situation *and* the manager's level of comfort with the ambiguity present in the situation.

Both of these factors could vary greatly. For example, the necessary skills to be effective in one ambiguous situation may not be applicable in another. In one setting, where interpersonal problems provide most of the ambiguity, individuals who are perceptive, flexible, and capable of effective interaction might be most effective. In another setting, where the ambiguity results from incomplete, inconsistent, or contradictory information, skills stressing analytical problem-solving skills would be most appropriate.

While possessing the right kinds of skills is important, the skills themselves are not sufficient to determine whether or not a manager will be effective in ambiguous situations. We also need to determine the manager's degree of comfort in ambiguous settings. Some managers are quite upset with ambiguity and work to eliminate or control it. Other managers acknowledge ambiguity as part of their role and respond to ambiguity in a more relaxed and accepting manner. Or other managers may actively seek out ambiguous situations because of their challenges and opportunities.

Figure 1 presents the four distinct coping styles that can result from high and low levels of managerial skills and comfort with ambiguity. Each cell in the model represents a distinct coping style.

*Adaptive managers* have both the requisite managerial skills and the comfort level to deal effectively with a wide range of ambiguous situations. They recognize and accept

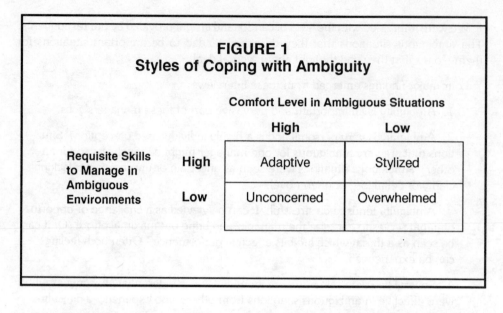

**FIGURE 1**
**Styles of Coping with Ambiguity**

|  | | Comfort Level in Ambiguous Situations | |
|---|---|---|---|
|  | | High | Low |
| **Requisite Skills to Manage in Ambiguous Environments** | **High** | Adaptive | Stylized |
|  | **Low** | Unconcerned | Overwhelmed |

ambiguity and can adapt their behavior and approach to the situation at hand. Adaptive managers maintain a broad perspective, are sensitive to feedback, and can use both intuition and logic when solving problems. In addition to responding well to ambiguous situations, Adaptive managers may actually seek out these situations because of the opportunities provided by the lack of preexisting boundaries or limitations.

*Stylized managers* have the potential to handle ambiguous situations well, but rarely do so, because they focus their energies and talents on removing the ambiguity, rather than responding to its opportunities and challenges. While they have the managerial skills needed to take appropriate actions, their lack of comfort inhibits their effectiveness. They can be so uncomfortable with the ambiguity that its removal or containment becomes their prime objective, often with disastrous results. We have called them Stylized because they tend to rely on habitual responses, particularly if these have worked well in the past. These managers also like to create or follow rules, procedures, or precedent because these provide a structure for action. When confronted with an ambiguous situation they seek structure, resulting in actions designed to minimize ambiguity rather than deal with the real issues presented.

*Unconcerned managers* are not bothered by ambiguity. They give the appearance of being unconcerned about most problems and may trivialize their importance. Although these managers are comfortable with ambiguity, they lack the skills to respond effectively in ambiguous situations. Their lack of inhibition is often compounded by an inflated self-image and insensitivity to feedback, particularly if the feedback is negative. Unconcerned managers are quick to take action in ambiguous settings, with little reality testing about the appropriateness of their actions. They may appear to be self-assured and confident when they confront ambiguous situations. Their action orientation, coupled with minimal self-insight, is often dangerous. Outwardly self-confident, they may persuade others who are less comfortable with the ambiguity to follow their early lead, frequently with disastrous results.

*Overwhelmed managers* have considerable difficulty in ambiguous situations since they lack the necessary skills and are extremely uncomfortable with ambiguity. They are often hesitant to take action in ambiguous situations and may deny or fail to understand the critical aspects of the problem or situation. Often they tend to focus on an insignificant part of the problem and "work it to death," while avoiding the more complex issues. Although these managers are overwhelmed in ambiguous situations, they often are very effective in structured, familiar environments where proven procedures or past experiences can guide their actions.

Even though the factors in our model are continuous variables, we have found that most people tend to manifest a dominant or characteristic style. We were able to reliably classify individual managers using this model. In two separate studies conducted in 1981 and 1982, there was perfect interrater agreement in 79% and 83% of the managers classified (Lyness & Moses, 1983). Thus, our model could be used as a basis for predicting performance in ambiguous settings.

## The Assessment Center Ambiguity Study

We learned a great deal about individual responses to different ambiguous situations through our assessment center research. We used our operational assessment program, Advanced Management Potential Assessment (AMPA), to conduct additional research.

AT&T's AMPA Program was designed to identify the further potential among high-potential middle-level managers. This program, designed to evaluate senior-level potential (Moses, 1985) was redesigned based on our interview study as well as other research concerning contemporary management behavior at AT&T.

As described elsewhere (Lyness & Moses, 1983) we incorporated a multimethod approach to measure managerial behavior in ambiguous situations. New measures and techniques were developed for the assessment process that reflected the various types of ambiguity that managers encounter. Our ambiguity measures included group and individual simulation exercises, clinical interviews, projective instruments, personality inventories, biographical as well as other background data, as well as modifications of contemporary pencil-and-paper tolerance-of-ambiguity instruments.

The assessment center lasted for five days. Participants were assessed during a three-and-one-half-day period by senior-level managers and an internal and external professional staff composed of clinical, counseling, and industrial-organizational psychologists. A total of 25 separate dimensions were assessed using six separate simulations, two interviews, and a battery of projective and pencil-and-paper instruments. The staff made independent predictions on each of these managerial dimensions as well as an overall assessment of senior-level potential.

The ambiguity study was embedded within the assessment center. Specially designed rating and interview forms were used to independently classify each manager. This data was not used as part of the assessment of potential; nor was it shared with the assessment team.

After the assessment procedures and evaluation sessions had been completed, two psychologists independently reviewed all of the assessment data and classified the managers according to their coping styles in ambiguous situations. These ambiguity classification judgments required the synthesis of a great deal of complex information based on each psychologist's understanding of the coping styles model. The psychologists making these judgments had worked as the directors of the assessment program and thus were quite familiar with all of the assessment procedures and resulting data. In all cases, at least one of the psychologists had not participated in the initial assessment decision. Previous analyses (Lyness & Moses, 1983) indicated that the interrater agreement among these psychologists was quite high, with perfect interrater agreement in 79% of a sample of 108 cases and 83% perfect agreement in a subsequent sample of 107 individuals. This suggested that the assessment center data provided a sufficient basis for reliable judgments about a manager's characteristic coping style in ambiguous situations.

Once an individual had been classified, comparisons could then be made between his or her coping style and performance on a wide variety of assessment instruments and ratings. A total of 258 high-potential middle-level managers were classified over a three-year period.

Figure 2 provides the overall distribution of coping styles for this sample. Since this is a high-potential group, we would expect to see similar distribution of coping styles among managers in other organizations as well. While the frequency in different cells of the model might change somewhat based on organizational history, selection, and socialization processes, we would expect to see similar patterns among high-potential managers in well-managed organizations who had not experienced any extensive ambiguity in their careers or organizational history.

The data are consistent with the impressions we obtained in our initial interview study and other reviews of management populations. We would expect about half of all existing managers to possess the requisite skills to perform effectively in ambiguous environments. Based on many discussions and examination of other managerial groups, we had estimated that less than one-third of all contemporary managers, however, were comfortable with ambiguity.

## FIGURE 2
## Distribution of Ambiguity Coping Styles
## Among High-Potential Managers

**Comfort Level in Ambiguous Situations**

| | | High | Low |
|---|---|---|---|
| **Requisite Skills to Manage in Ambiguous Environments** | **High** | Adaptive 12% | Stylized 33% |
| | **Low** | Unconcerned 8% | Overwhelmed 47% |

To some extent, we would expect the distribution of styles to vary in different organizations as a function of selection and development practices. Organizations that rely on validated selection procedures would be expected to have a high percentage of Adaptive or Stylized managers. We were not surprised, for example, with the relatively low number of Unconcerned managers in our sample. Organizations that rely on extensive independent verification of performance would tend to weed out these individuals from their ranks. On the other hand, organizations that relied on superficial selection procedures or who hired many key executives from outside the organization with minimal evaluation of real potential could be expected to have many more Unconcerned managers seeded in key positions.

In addition to the finding that differences in behavior predicted by our model for the differing coping styles were confirmed by actual observation and evaluation of behavior, a number of other key findings emerged. There was a strong relationship between the individual's coping style and further management potential. There were no sex differences noted among the different coping styles. No startling differences in paper-and-pencil personality measures were found other than for obvious comparisons—such as Stylized managers reporting a high need for cautiousness. In fact, few of the existing, traditional pencil-and-paper measures were related to coping style, a not surprising finding since the literature had only focused on tolerance of ambiguity as an assessment of one's comfort with ambiguity. In most cases, our projective and clinical ratings, made independently and not used in the assessment program, supported the actual behavioral data of these participants.

Since the Adaptive managers are the only group which displays consistently effective behavior in ambiguous settings, a number of analyses were conducted to differentiate key differences in behavior between Adaptive managers and managers exhibiting the other coping styles. An example of the type of analysis for a given coping style is shown in Table 1, which shows some key differences in behavior between Adaptive and Stylized managers. Table 1 presents four distinct managerial dimensions which differ between Adaptive and Stylized coping styles using Scheffe's Test of Differences between means. All of the ratings were based on a five-point rating scale, with five as the highest rating. Only differences at the .01 level of confidence are shown.

In many respects, the differences between these two groups are very interesting. Our model suggests that both Adaptive and Stylized managers are competent in most business situations, and from an ability level should have little difficulty in handling ambiguous problems and situations. Our assessment data supports this, as these two groups display similar management talents on most of the management dimensions associated with performance outcomes (leadership, decision making, problem solving, etc.).

On the other hand, we predicted that these two groups would differ in comfort levels associated with ambiguity. This is clearly seen in Table 1 where large differences in the ratings of tolerance of ambiguity of these groups of managers are evident. Other differences are noted as well. Adaptive managers are significantly more effective in tasks requiring considerable risk taking, creativity, and decisiveness than Stylized managers.

This latter finding is quite suggestive. It may be that one's approach to ambiguity can impact other performance variables. For example, the structuring activities that we so

**TABLE 1**
**Some Key Differences in Behavior**
**Adaptive — Stylized Managers**

| Dimension Assessed | Mean Ratings | |
| --- | --- | --- |
| | Adaptive | Stylized |
| Tolerance of Uncertainty | 4.22 | 2.89 |
| Risk Taking | 3.66 | 2.65 |
| Creativity | 4.00 | 3.02 |
| Decisiveness | 4.13 | 3.26 |

*Note: All ratings are on a 5-point scale, 5 is high;*
*all differences are significant, p<.01.*

often find among Stylized managers may affect their risk taking, creativity, and willingness to make decisions.

Similar analyses suggested that there were distinct behavioral differences among the various coping styles for all of the managers based on our prediction of their coping behaviors. Overwhelmed and Unconcerned managers differed from Adaptive managers in interesting ways. For example, we would expect Unconcerned managers to be as comfortable with ambiguity as Adaptive managers. We found no differences in the tolerance-of-ambiguity ratings for these two groups. These groups were similar in risk taking as well, as measured by their willingness to take risks. However, marked ability differences emerged. The Unconcerned managers, as a group, had significantly poorer performance outcomes on such dimensions as Problem Solving. Thus, while as willing to take risks as an Adaptive manager, the Unconcerned manager was far less likely to effectively solve problems, and consequently, the willingness to take risks could be a key liability rather than an asset for this type of manager.

A key behavioral difference between the Overwhelmed manager and the Adaptive manager, in addition to predicted differences in tolerance of ambiguity, was in behavior flexibility. Overwhelmed managers were rated as significantly less flexible than Adaptive managers, an outcome predicted by our model.

These are but a few of the many findings that emerged among the distinct groups of management coping styles. The interested reader can find additional examples in Lyness and Moses (1990) or can write to the authors.

This paper has merely scratched the surface of the rich behavioral and psychological data that was assessed. A complete analysis is reported in our forthcoming book. We can, however, summarize our findings as follows:

1. Ambiguity is a significant part of many management jobs, but in general, it is a concept which is poorly understood.

2. Most managers do not have effective coping styles to behave effectively in ambiguous environments. We estimate that less than 25% of most managerial groups are truly effective in ambiguous situations.

3. Previous approaches at assessment have focused on tolerance-of-ambiguity measures and have ignored other critical performance determinants.

4. In order to evaluate managerial performance in ambiguous environments, both ability and comfort levels need to be assessed.

5. A new model for examining behavior in ambiguous settings was developed, with particular emphasis on four distinct coping styles, only one of which represents effective performance in ambiguous environments.

6. Data collected from a high-level assessment center supports the model of four distinct coping styles.

7. The model predicts performance and can be used to classify individuals. This diagnosis can be extremely helpful in determining appropriate intervention strategies to help managers cope more effectively with ambiguity. (See, for example, Moses & Lyness, 1988.)

8. Numerous research possibilities exist for further exploration of both individual and organizational coping styles.

## References

Lyness, K. S., & Moses, J. L. (1983, August). Measurement strategies for studying ambiguity and managerial behavior. In S. Zedeck (Chair), *Ambiguity, uncertainty, and change: A theoretical view.* Symposium conducted at the meeting of the American Psychological Association, Anaheim, CA.

Lyness, K. S., & Moses, J. L. (1990). *Ambiguity, uncertainty and change in organizations: Assessing behavior and improving coping styles.* Boston: Unwin Hyman.

Lyness, K. S., Zedeck, S., Jackson, S., & Moses, J. L. (1985). *Ambiguity: A review and conceptual framework.* (AT&T Tech. Rep.). New York: Author.

Moses, J. L. (1985). Using clinical methods in a high level management assessment center. In H. J. Bernardin & D. A. Bownas (Eds.), *Personality assessment in organizations* (pp. 177–192). New York: Praeger.

Moses, J. L., & Lyness, K. S. (1983, August). A conceptual model for studying ambiguity and managerial behavior. In S. Zedeck (Chair), *Ambiguity, uncertainty, and change: A theoretical view.* Symposium conducted at the meeting of the American Psychological Association, Anaheim, CA.

Moses, J. L., & Lyness, K. S. (1988). Individual and organizational responses to ambiguity. In F. D. Schoorman & B. Schneider (Eds.), *Facilitating work effectiveness* (pp. 165–181). Lexington, MA: Lexington Books.

Tunstall, W. B. (1985). *Disconnecting parties: Managing the Bell system breakup.* New York: McGraw-Hill.

# SECTION F

## Personality and Leadership

# Personality and Leadership

The personality of leaders fascinates everyone. Did Napoléon excel because his diminutive stature drove him to winning? Was Hitler a true paranoid? Could Gandhi be characterized as a passive-aggressive type? Of such stuff are constructed wonderful cocktail conversations.

Psychological measurement of personality characteristics makes it possible to obtain insights into character and personality through evidence reported by persons about their own customary modes of thought and motivation. Even if the responses are questioned, the data often turn out to be stable and to discriminate successes and failures. They are also useful as we attend to differences among cultural and national groups. The articles in this section highlight the importance of these personal qualities for the effectiveness of leaders and provide insight into the nature of selected measures.

## The Dark Side of Charisma
Robert Hogan, Robert Raskin, and Dan Fazzini

The relationship between personality and managerial competence and incompetence and the prevalence of mistakes in elevating certain types of persons are portrayed. Cited is Hertzberg's finding that between 60% and 75% of workers report that the worst or the most stressful aspect of their jobs is the immediate boss. Included is an identification and description of flawed managers of three types, all of whose flaws are hidden behind social graces and likeability: floaters, full-of-resentment types, and narcissists, each of whom imposes high costs on the organization.

Robert Hogan, Director of Research, Tulsa Psychiatric Center, University of Tulsa, 1620 12th Street, Tulsa, Oklahoma 74120. (918-584-5992). PhD, University of California–Berkeley. McFarlin Professor and Chair, Department of Psychology, University of Tulsa. Past editor of "Personality Processes and Individual Differences" section of *Journal of Personality and Social Psychology*.

Robert Raskin, Research Scientist, Tulsa Psychiatric Center, University of Tulsa, 1620 12th Street, Tulsa, Oklahoma 74120. (918-584-5992). PhD, University of California, Berkeley. Coauthor of "The Narcissistic Regulation of Self-Esteem" (in press) in *Journal of Personality and Social Psychology*.

Dan Fazzini, Chief Executive Officer, Tulsa Psychiatric Center, University of Tulsa, 1620 12th Street, Tulsa, Oklahoma 74120. (918-584-5992). PhD, University of Wisconsin. Director, Idaho State School and Hospital.

## Testing for Leadership with the California Psychological Inventory
Harrison G. Gough

This paper describes the way in which the California Psychological Inventory (CPI) has been made especially useful in identifying leadership. Six leadership measures are developed using as criteria principals' ratings of students, data collected from spouses, ratings by observers and by peers in an assessment program, performance in Leaderless Group Discussions, and West Point ratings on Aptitude for Service. High leadership scores are associated with high scores on Dominance, Capacity for Status, Sociability, Social Presence, Self-acceptance, Independence, and Empathy, and somewhat less with scores on Responsibility through Tolerance, Achievement via Conformance, and Intellectual Efficiency. A new Type/Level Model for interpreting the CPI is reported in some detail.

Harrison G. Gough, Professor of Psychology–Emeritus, Institute of Personality Assessment and Research, University of California–Berkeley, Berkeley, California 94720. (415-642-5050). PhD, University of Minnesota. Coauthor of *The Adjective Check List* and the *Personnel Reaction Blank*. Author of the *California Psychological Inventory*.

## The Myers-Briggs Type Indicator and Leadership
Mary H. McCaulley

The theory underlying the Myers-Briggs Type Indicator (MBTI) and the significance of each of the types is described. Profiles are presented for many groups. These data suggest that leaders are more likely to reach closure (J) than to miss nothing (P); are more likely to prefer impersonal, logical decision making (T) than a rational ordering of values with concern over human priorities (F); and tend to be practical (S) types. Understanding type supports better understanding of differences and, therefore, more productive teamwork.

Mary H. McCaulley, President, Center for Applications of Psychological Type (CAPT), 2720 N.W. 6th Street, Gainesville, Florida 32609. (904-375-0160). PhD, Temple University. Psychologist formerly at University of Florida. Founder (with Isabel Briggs Myers) of Center for Applications of Psychological Type which provides publications, professional training, computer scoring, and research consultation for the Myers-Briggs Type Indicator. Author of *MBTI Manual*, second edition.

## Stars, Adversaries, Producers, and Phantoms at Work:
## A New Leadership Typology
Ira J. Morrow and Mel Stern

Measures collected during IBM's management assessment program (MAP) are analyzed to discover what factors distinguish individuals who are given overall assessment ratings at superior, average, and poor levels. Superior performers in the MAP work effectively with difficult problems and new ideas and prefer an active role in both social and business settings; they are diplomatic and sensitive leaders. Poor performers are typically nonparticipative and passive, with little impact on group performance; some seem overwhelmed by the MAP experience, while others work feverishly but do not attempt to lead, functioning instead in a support or staff role.

Ira J. Morrow, Associate Professor and Assistant Chairman, Department of Management, The Lubin Graduate School of Business, Pace University, One Pace Plaza, New York, New York 10038-1502. (212-488-1846). PhD, New York University. Past Visiting Professor, International Business Machines Corporation's International Finance, Planning, and Administration School. Consultant in public and private sector on managerial and nonmanagerial assessment and testing.

Mel Stern, Senior Communications Research Analyst, Communications Research, International Business Machines Corporation, 1133 Westchester Avenue, White Plains, New York 10605. (914-642-3324). PhD, Case Western Reserve University.

## Some Personality Characteristics of Senior Military Officers
Herbert F. Barber

Students at the U.S. Army War College, mostly lieutenant colonels and colonels, are tested with the Myers-Briggs Type Indicator, the Schutz "Element B," and the Rokeach Terminal and Instrumental Values Survey. Scores are reported and interpreted. Studied are such variables as: need to be in control during interaction with others; acceptance that someone should be in control of the situation even if the person in control is someone else; wanting openness from others; willingness to be open themselves; and the importance attached to being competent, logical, intellectual, imaginative, ambitious, courageous, forgiving, cheerful, and polite. The officers gave rankings to self-respect, a sense of service, wisdom, mature love, a world at peace, a comfortable life, happiness, and equality that are compared with rankings by a norm group.

Herbert F. Barber, Professor of Behavioral Science; Department of Command, Leadership, and Management; U.S. Army War College; Carlisle Barracks; Pennsylvania 17013. (717-245-3131). PhD, Southern Illinois University. Chairholder, Brehon Burke Somervell Chair of Management.

## Leadership in Latin American Organizations:
## A Glimpse of Styles Through Personality Measures
T. Noel Osborn and Diana B. Osborn

Presents data collected in Center for Creative Leadership leadership development programs offered in Latin America in Spanish by Tecnología Administrativa Moderna, S.C. (TEAM). Myers-Briggs and FIRO-B scores are reported and results interpreted.

U.S. and Latin managers and administrative assistants are compared on type preferences and self-reported relationship behaviors.

Diana B. Osborn, Director, Leadership Development Program, Tecnología Administrativa Moderna (TEAM), S.C., 14206 Arbor Oak, San Antonio, Texas 78249. (512-493-1452). MA, U.S. International University. Engaged in research and publication in cross-cultural management styles.

T. Noel Osborn, President, Tecnología Administrativa Moderna (TEAM), S.C., 14206 Arbor Oak, San Antonio, Texas 78249. (512-493-1452). PhD, University of Colorado–Boulder. Author of *Higher Education in Mexico*. Coeditor of *U.S.-Mexico Economic Relations* and *El Dilema de Dos Naciones*. Author of various journal articles.

# The Dark Side of Charisma

Robert Hogan
Robert Raskin
and
Dan Fazzini

This paper is intended to make three points: (1) there is a systematic relationship between personality and managerial competence, (2) there is a systematic relationship between personality and managerial incompetence, (3) certain kinds of people with identifiable personality characteristics tend to rise to the tops of organizations and these people are potentially very costly to those organizations.

The relationship between leadership or managerial effectiveness and personality is one of the more extensively studied topics in applied psychology. The authoritative reviews of this subject (e.g., Campbell, Dunnette, Lawler, & Weick, 1971; Stogdill, 1974) tend to conclude that the relationship is complex and difficult to interpret precisely. Nonetheless, there are certain consistent trends in the literature, and the following are three examples.

Ghiselli (1971) developed a pool of 64 self-descriptive adjectives matched for scaled social desirability. Ghiselli argues (p. 40) that, although conditions change, "there certainly is some communality across situations in the capacity to direct the efforts of others," and on this basis he developed a "supervisory ability scale," using his self-descriptive adjectives, to assess this capacity. He formed two groups (N = 210) "closely matched for occupation, sex, and age"; one group contained people in supervisory positions, the second group contained people not nominated by their organizations for supervisory roles. He then compared their responses on his 64 items and developed a scoring key for "supervisor ability." In four samples of managers (N = 152), Ghiselli found correlations ranging from .35 to .75 (average = .55) between scores on this scale and rated job success. There are three points to note about Ghiselli's study: (1) his index of supervisory ability is a personality measure and persons with high scores on it tend to be bright, initiating, self-assured, decisive, masculine, achievement-oriented, upwardly mobile, and unconcerned with job security (cf. Ghiselli, 1971, p. 129); (2) Ghiselli endorses the concept of a "g" factor (i.e., generalized competence) in management potential; and (3) managerial performance was defined in terms of supervisors' ratings.

In what is perhaps the best-known study of managerial performance in industry, the staff of the Standard Oil Company of New Jersey tested 443 managers with an extensive battery, including cognitive tests, a personality inventory, and a biographical inventory. A composite measure of managerial effectiveness was defined, and scoring keys were developed to predict that criterion. Sparks (1966) reports correlations above .70 between job performance and scores on the managerial key. Three findings from this research parallel those reported by Ghiselli: (1) the evidence supports the notion that people differ in terms of a construct that we may call "general potential for management" (i.e., there is a "g" factor in management); (2) this general factor is a personality syndrome, the key features of which involve being forceful, dominant, assertive, confident, and active in taking advantage of leadership opportunities (Campbell et al., 1971, p. 169); and (3) managerial performance was defined so as to take account of a person's entire career and "minimize the effects of favorable or unfavorable biases held by one or a few supervisors" (Laurent, 1966, p. 9).

One final example supports these generalizations regarding personality and managerial effectiveness. Bentz (1967) summarizes 30 years of research at Sears, Roebuck concerning the relationship between an "executive test battery" and various indices of executive effectiveness. The test battery included cognitive measures and a personality, a vocational preference, and a values inventory. Executive effectiveness was typically defined by supervisors' ratings, but sometimes it was defined in terms of employee morale. Bentz reports many correlations between test scores and criterion measures of effectiveness and the multiple Rs range between .40 and .75. We would like to highlight three findings from this impressive research effort: (1) Bentz (1967) argues that "a cluster of psychological characteristics contributes to general executive competence that transcends the boundaries of specialized or nonspecialized assignments" (once again, there is a "g" factor in management); (2) the general factor is a personality syndrome whose defining features Bentz (1967) describes as persuasiveness, social assurance, ambition for leadership, initiation, energy, mental ability, and "heightened personal concern for status, power and money"; (3) managerial performance was typically defined in terms of ratings provided by higher organizational officials.

This brief overview conveys the general flavor of the research literature regarding personality and leadership (see also Aronoff & Wilson, 1986, p. 214). On the basis of this it seems safe to conclude that there are some reliable covariations between certain aspects of normal personality and rated managerial performance. In the context of this generalization, however, there are certain systematic ambiguities that cloud its interpretation. We will mention two; these concern how managerial effectiveness and personality are defined.

Managerial effectiveness is typically defined by ratings and when defined this way, the ratings are usually provided by supervisors. Campbell et al. (1971) make two interesting points about these ratings: (1) They are confounded by halo (e.g., supervisors tend to give higher ratings to managers they like whether or not they are doing a good job), (2) Correlations between supervisors' and subordinates' ratings of managerial performance are often low to nonexistent. These two points raise serious questions about the relationship between supervisors' ratings of managerial effectiveness and the "true" effectiveness of a manager's performance. Campbell et al. (1971) suggest that the most appropriate way to evaluate a manager is to compare the performance of his or her unit/team/group with the performance of comparable units/teams/groups in terms of productivity and efficient use of resources. This is a sensible suggestion regarding how to define effectiveness, but this definition rarely appears in the research literature.

The definition of personality is also murky. Certain writers (e.g., MacKinnon, 1944; Hogan, 1982) argue that there are two conceptually distinct definitions of the term that are routinely confounded; this confounding makes it difficult to interpret the link between personality and leadership. On the one hand, personality refers to a person's reputation, to the unique impression that he or she creates among his or her colleagues, friends, and neighbors. On the other hand, personality refers to the dynamic forces, structures, and processes within a person that are somehow associated with his or her unique personality. We believe that the relationship between these two definitions of personality in any single person is, at best, obscure. Moreover, although the concept of personality as reputation can be treated in a reliable and quantitative way (i.e., there is some consensus in the research community regarding the structure of personality defined as reputation), there is no consensus regarding the structure of personality defined in terms of internal processes.

Despite the reliable correlations between scores on personality measures and rated managerial performance, there are some unexplained vagaries, some residual ambiguities in those relationships. Before proceeding with an analysis of these ambiguities, it might be useful to specify how we intend to use the word *personality* in the context of this paper. We assume that most people desire or are concerned with acquiring attention and approval from their social communities; at the same time they also desire status, power, or respect in those communities. In the course of development people choose identities for themselves, identities that they like and think they can support—that is, athlete, scholar, devout Christian, mountain man—and these identities are used to structure interactions and tell other people how the actor would like to be regarded. Sometimes these images are confidently assumed; sometimes they are used defensively to guard against the loss of status and social acceptance. Part of these identities includes life or occupational goals, for example, money, recognition, power, security, or piety. Sometimes people choose sensible identities and goals for themselves and sometimes they choose less wisely. Hogan and Jones (1983) argue, for example, that criminals (incarcerated felons) have often chosen a particular deviant identity whose components include toughness, alienation, thrill-seeking, and exhibitionism. Criminals use this identity to negotiate status and social acceptance from the groups with whom they typically interact. The more general point is that behind each person's everyday social behavior lies an identity, a preferred self-image, and a dominant goal, and the images and goals are chosen so as to enhance individual status and social approval.

People's behavior during social interaction creates a response in the other people with whom they interact. It is an evaluative response, and these responses have been the subject of considerable research attention over the past 20 years. There is a fair degree of consensus in the personality research community that observers' reactions to actors can be grouped in five broad categories; that is, each of us has a social reputation which reflects our relative degree of status and social acceptance. These reputations can be coded in terms of five broad evaluative categories. The first category concerns intellectual activity and acumen, where judgments vary along a continuum ranging from dull, literal-minded, and unimaginative to bright, conceptually oriented, and open-minded. The second category concerns self-acceptance and social self-confidence; here judgments vary along a continuum ranging from anxious, guilt-ridden, and moody to confident, self-accepting, and stable. The third category entails judgments along a continuum varying from impulsive, careless, and undependable to self-controlled, conscientious, and reliable. The fourth dimension includes judgments ranging from meek, complacent, and unassertive to outgoing, assertive, and ambitious. The final dimension involves judgments varying from blunt, outspoken, and independent to mannerly, diplomatic, and charming.

To bring this somewhat abstract discussion back to the topic at hand, leadership is normally related to the personal goals of power, recognition, and money, and to being perceived as bright, stable, dependable, assertive, and charming; people who are perceived as bright, mature, reliable, ambitious, and socially skilled and who desire power, fame, and financial rewards are overrepresented in the ranks of leadership.

## Flawed Leadership

This section of the paper concerns the notion that there are certain (identifiable) kinds of people who tend to rise to the tops of organizations but who subsequently have a negative impact on the organization. These are people with well-developed social skills and an attractive interpersonal style who, in reality, have little or no talent for management. Unfortunately, there are more of these people around than we often realize.

**The Base Rate of Flawed Leadership** Survey research on job satisfaction and on job-related stress over the past 35 years reveals a consistent and disturbing trend. Beginning with Hertzberg's (1966) research on worker motivation and hygiene factors, study after study across time, occupational group, and geographical location shows a surprising rate of dissatisfaction with supervision. Between 60% and 75% of workers surveyed report that the worst, or the most stressful, aspect of their jobs is their immediate supervisor (cf. Hertzberg, 1968). Moreover, virtually every employed adult reports that he or she had to spend considerable time during the course of his or her career working for an "intolerable" boss.

The following examples happen to be on our desks at the moment; the phenomenon is so pervasive that rigorous documentation is unnecessary. *Newsweek* of April 25, 1988, ran a feature article in the business section entitled "Stress on the Job." In a nutshell, the argument, supported by a variety of surveys and research studies, is that: (1) stress in the workplace is rampant, (2) stress in the workplace is very costly (in terms of lawsuits, worker compensation claims, and other medical costs, possibly up to $18 billion dollars per year in the near future), and (3) the most frequently cited source of this stress is a "tyrannical boss." *The New York Times*, on June 14, 1988, reported the results of a Louis Harris poll of 1,031 office workers and 150 top-level executives from around the country, a poll paid for by Steelcase (a large office furniture manufacturer). The survey concerned gaps between workers' perceptions and expectations about management, and management's perceptions of the same issues. The largest single gap concerned giving employees a "lot of freedom to decide how they do their own work"; 77% of office workers said this was very important to them, but only 37% of the executives thought this was an important issue for their employees. The most ominous gap, however, concerned the fact that 89% of the employees said it was very important that management be "honest, upright, and ethical in its dealings with employees and the community," but only 41% said this was actually true of their present employers. Finally, the May 27, 1988 edition of *Modern Healthcare* reports studies indicating that the annual turnover rate of hospital chief executive officers is about 30% nationwide. The heads of two large research firms (who profit nicely from this turnover) remark that "most of the CEOs who leave their jobs are terminated, forced to resign, or quit before they're fired." The article also notes that the 30% turnover rate may be an underestimate of the true figure.

We propose, based on our reading of these surveys over the past six years, that the base rate for flawed leadership is somewhere between 60% and 75%; rephrasing this point, we estimate that somewhere between six and seven out of every ten managers in corporate America are not very good as managers. The consequences of this in terms of lost productivity, employee alienation, and stress-related medical costs are staggering. If we assume that the same base rate applies to the military, then it follows that there are also serious consequences for military preparedness.

**Causes of Managerial Incompetence** If, as seems to be the case, the performance of many people in managerial or supervisory roles is less than adequate as judged by their subordinates (and sometimes by their supervisors), what are the reasons for this? One way of answering this question is to consult studies of managerial failure. Bentz (1967) describes his observations regarding managerial failure at Sears, Roebuck and concludes that a key factor is a lack of emotional stability and social and leadership skills—that is, insensitivity to the needs and expectations of one's subordinates and co-workers.

Lombardo, Ruderman, and McCauley (1988) extend Bentz's analysis with fascinating data of their own. They ask whether executive derailment is a function of the absence of positive qualities of leadership (as described above) or the presence of negative qualities of leadership. They studied a sample of 169 mid- to upper-level managers, 83 of whom had been involuntarily terminated. Each person in the sample was rated by his or her supervisor on 61 items related to managerial performance, and the two groups were compared on these ratings. Lombardo et al. (1988) conclude that derailment is a function of both the absence of positive characteristics and the presence of negative characteristics. Their figure 3 lists the following as characterizing the failed managers: unable to build a cohesive team; over- and undermanaging; overly ambitious; not supportive and demanding of subordinates; overly emotional; insensitive, cold, and arrogant; maintained poor relations with staff; and overriding personality defects (this last theme was present in every dimension of failure).

## Personality Disorders and Managerial Incompetence

The Lombardo et al. (1988) paper is the best study of executive failure to date and clearly highlights flawed personality as the causal agent in derailment. We believe a key to understanding their data is provided by the newly emerging research on the personality disorders (Kernberg, 1979). Specifically, Hogan and Jones (in press) argue that there are certain people who have good social skills, who rise readily in organizations, and who ultimately derail; but before they fail, they cost their organizations large sums of money by causing poor morale, excessive turnover, and reduced productivity. We postulate three ideal types, three kinds of executive failures, described below, and we provide a small amount of original data to support some of our speculations.

### Three Types of Flawed Managers

### • 1. The High Likeability Floater

We find it convenient to describe normal personality in terms of the so-called "Big Five Theory" which suggests that observers' impressions of actors can be expressed in terms of five broad dimensions of interpersonal appraisal. Much of our research is based on the *Hogan Personality Inventory* (HPI; Hogan, 1986) which is designed to assess these dimensions, all of which are related to individual differences in occupational performance. One particular pattern of scores is common in executive nonperformance, and that pattern consists of high scores for Likeability and average to low scores for Ambition in a profile that is otherwise normal.

Persons with this profile are exceedingly pleasant, congenial, charming, and attractive. They are wonderful colleagues and dinner companions; they are supportive and understanding; they facilitate meetings; and they never complain, argue, or criticize. Because they are so well-liked, they rise steadily in organizations, but they accomplish very little along the way. At the same time, they don't represent anything, they don't have a point of view, they don't have an agenda, and they rarely take a stand on issues that matter. In any case, sooner or later these people find themselves in charge of a unit of an organization and little happens under their guidance beyond the maintenance of good morale.

When the nonperformance of these people is finally perceived, their supervisors are faced with a dilemma—high likeability floaters are very difficult to fire because they have no enemies, but they have lots of friends all of whom will be angry when good old George is terminated. As a consequence, the arteries of large organizations tend to be clogged by congenial but unambitious midlevel managers.

### • 2. Hommes de Ressentiment

As a model for this second type we have in mind Kim Philby, the legendary British spymaster who was also a Russian double agent. By all accounts Philby was a handsome, devastatingly charming, bright, and highly effective man. Many who worked for him in British intelligence (e.g., Malcom Muggeridge and Graham Greene) described him as a brilliant and unusually competent administrator. Philby rose steadily through the ranks of British intelligence. At the end of his career, Philby was in charge of the Soviet desk and lived for a long time in Washington, DC, where he had access to the most sensitive and secret information that the British and American intelligence networks were able to assemble—and which he passed on to the Russians.

The key to Philby's character seems to be that, beneath the charm, composure, and social skill was a deep strain of resentment, smoldering hostility, and a desire for revenge. Although this resentment is normally attributed to Philby's dismay over the British and

American reactions to fascism, we believe it had characterological roots. Our reasoning is as follows. Jones (1988) developed a psychometrically sound inventory of personality disorders; designed to assess the standard DSM III, Axis 2 diagnostic categories, it is called the *Inventory of Personality Disorders* (IPD). Jones finds the categories to be complex, overlapping, and heterogeneous. He has developed a set of homogeneous subscales into which the DSM III categories (e.g., Histrionic, Borderline, etc.) can be decomposed. One of these subscales is called Resentment. Resentment is common to the scales for the Paranoid and Passive-Aggressive disorders, and it correlates quite substantially with self-reported episodes of interpersonal betrayal.

The Kim Philbys of the world always do well in interviews and on assessment center exercises because the ability to appear charming, bright, and leaderlike is independent of the resentful tendencies implicit in the paranoid and passive-aggressive personality disorders. In fact the interpersonal style associated with these disorders leads to watchfulness, caution, and minimal self-disclosure, and these tendencies are advantageous in interpersonal negotiations.

## ● 3. Narcissists

In the modern literature on personality disorders narcissism is defined as a constellation of attitudes that includes exhibitionism, feelings of entitlement, the expectation of special privileges and exemptions from social demands, feelings of omnipotence in controlling others, intolerance of criticism, and a tendency to focus on one's own mental products and to see others as extensions of oneself.

Clinical psychology has been interested in narcissism for some time, and several measures of the construct have been developed. The best-validated of these is the *Narcissistic Personality Inventory* (NPI; Raskin & Hall, 1979, 1981). This 54-item "self-report" measure yields alpha reliability coefficients in the .80 to .86 range and has some interesting relationships with indices of leadership. Consequently, several points from recent research with the NPI are important for this discussion. First, consider some of the NPI items: "I see myself as a good leader"; "I will be a success"; "I have a natural talent for influencing people"; "I am a born leader." Although these are among the more benign items on the inventory, they are, nonetheless, components of narcissism. Second, consider some of the correlations between the NPI and the standard scales of the California Psychological Inventory (Gough, 1988), one of the more useful predictors of leadership and managerial effectiveness: Dominance (.71), Sociability (.66), Social Presence (.62), and Capacity for Status (.37). Persons with high scores on the CPI scales for Dominance, Sociability, Social Presence, and Capacity for Status will tend to be self-confident, assertive, outgoing, and leaderlike, with a distinct overlay of narcissism. Third, consider how persons with high scores on the NPI are described by others: highly energetic, extraverted, self-confident, competitive, achievement-oriented, aggressive, exhibitionistic, egotistical, manipulative, and self-seeking. Fourth, the most pathological aspects of narcissism are exploitiveness and entitlement (Raskin & Novacek, 1989). The following items define the exploitiveness factor of the NPI: "I can read people like a book"; "I can make anybody believe anything I want them to." The following items define the entitlement factor: "I will never be satisfied until I get all that I deserve"; "I expect a great deal from other people." Fifth, Raskin and Novacek (1989) report the following correlations between the NPI and the Harris and Lingoes'

(1968) MMPI content scales (N = 173): Denial of Social Anxiety .35, Social Imperturbability .48, Ego Inflation .29, Subjective Depression -.20. Raskin and Novacek also report the following correlations between the NPI and Wiggins' (1969) MMPI content scales (N = 173): Social Maladjustment -.43, Poor Morale -.30. Finally, Raskin and Novacek (1989) report the following MMPI items have the highest correlations in the item pool with scores on the NPI: "I am entirely self-confident"; "I am an important person"; and "In a group I would not be embarrassed to be called upon to start a discussion or give an opinion about something I know well." The point of this section is that recent research on narcissism, using Raskin's NPI, shows a persistent and surprisingly large relationship between measures of narcissism and attitudes and characteristics often thought to typify aggressive managers, athletic coaches, military commanders, and political leaders, and this relationship needs to be acknowledged, interpreted, and explained.

As noted above, Jones (1988) has developed a personality inventory designed to assess the primary personality disorders. He reports (personal communication) that most of the external correlates of his Narcissism scale are positive; that is, Jones' IPD measure of narcissism is associated with a variety of indicators of positive adjustment. Table 1 contains correlations between the IPD Narcissism scale and the standard scales of the Hogan Personality Inventory (HPI) for a sample of 132 police applicants. These correlations suggest that persons with high scores on the IPD Narcissism scale are ambitious, upwardly mobile, and self-aggrandizing (Ambitious); tough and single-minded (Likeability); and privately self-doubting (Adjustment).

### TABLE 1
### Correlations Between the IPD Narcissism Scale
### and the Hogan Personality Inventory
#### (N = 132)

| HPI Scale | Narcissism | |
| --- | --- | --- |
| Intellectance | −.18 | (p < .02) |
| Adjustment | −.32 | (p < .01) |
| Prudence | −.09 | (NS) |
| Ambition | .33 | (p < .01) |
| Sociability | .10 | (NS) |
| Likeability | −.28 | (p < .01) |

Hogan and Jones (1988) have developed an Inventory of Personal Motives (IPM) that is designed to reveal the pattern of a person's motives, values, and interests. Table 2 contains correlations between the IPD Narcissism scale and the standard scales of the IPM for the same sample. These correlations suggest that persons with high scores on the IPD Narcissism scale are strongly motivated by needs for recognition and pleasure

**TABLE 2**
**Correlations Between the IPD Narcissism Scale
and the Inventory of Personal Motives**

(N = 132)

| IPM Scale | Narcissism | |
|---|---|---|
| Aesthetic Motives | .17 | (p < .03) |
| Affiliative Motives | .00 | (NS) |
| Altruistic Motives | .03 | (NS) |
| Commercial Motives | .15 | (p < .04) |
| Hedonistic Motives | .35 | (p < .01) |
| Power Motives | .20 | (p < .01) |
| Recognition Motives | .46 | (p < .01) |
| Intellectual Motives | −.04 | (NS) |
| Security Motives | .14 | (p < .05) |
| Religious Motives | −.26 | (p < .01) |

and less so by needs for achievement and success (Power); the typical motive pattern for managers is high Power and Commercial and moderate Recognition.

Recent research on attribution theory suggests some disturbing elements in the narcissist's cognitive style that have implications for his or her performance in leadership roles. Our conclusions are based on the well-documented relationships between measures of narcissism and measures of self-esteem, and we would like to highlight five implications. First, narcissists will resist accepting suggestions (Taylor & Brown, 1988). For the narcissist to accept suggestions from others may make him or her appear weak, because presenting oneself confidently is a major method of self-enhancement (Powers & Zuroff, 1988), and because narcissists are concerned with self-enhancement (recall the correlation with IPM Recognition), it will be very difficult to give them advice. In addition, narcissists tend to be so self-confident that they truly don't believe others have anything useful to tell them.

Second, narcissists are biased to take more credit for success than is legitimate (Taylor & Brown, 1988). Third, they are biased to avoid acknowledging responsibility for their failures and shortcomings for the same reasons that they claim more success than is their due. Fourth, narcissists typically make judgments with greater confidence than other people (Cutler, 1988) and, because their judgments are rendered with such conviction, other people tend to believe them and the narcissists become disproportionately more influential in group situations. Finally, because of their self-confidence and strong needs for recognition, narcissists tend to "self-nominate"; consequently, when a leadership gap appears in a group or organization, the narcissists rush to fill it.

Recent research presents a picture of the narcissist as a self-confident, assertive person who is concerned about recognition and advancement, who self-nominates, and who exploits his or her subordinates while currying favor with his or her supervisors. This is part of what we mean by the dark side of charisma.

## Final Thoughts

Consider for a moment our three types of flawed leadership—the High Likeability Floater, the Resentful Person, and the Narcissist. All three are typified by considerable talent for self-presentation and the capacity to create favorable impressions. Consider next that CEOs are chosen largely on the basis of interviews. The May 27, 1988 issue of *Modern Healthcare* reports a study of more than 1,300 governing board chairmen of not-for-profit hospitals in which they were asked what characteristics they looked for when hiring a CEO. In descending order these characteristics were (p. 122): commitment to quality care, undisputed reputation, strong leadership qualities, ability to make tough decisions, effective communication skills, persuasiveness, confidence and self-esteem, energy, and executive presence and image. Our point is that boards typically search for those qualities in potential CEOs that our three types of flawed leaders (especially the Narcissists) are best able to project.

Managerial selection procedures seem well-advised to look beyond the degree to which candidates seem committed and have executive presence and examine the dark side of charisma. In this way they may be able to improve on the base rate for flawed leadership.

## References

Aronoff, J., & Wilson, J. (1986). *Personality in the social process*. Hillsdale, NJ: Erlbaum.

Bentz, V. J. (1967). The Sears experience in the investigation, description, and prediction of executive behavior. In F. R. Wickert & D. E. McFarland (Eds.), *Measuring executive effectiveness* (pp. 147–206). New York: Appleton-Century-Crofts.

Campbell, J. P., Dunnette, M. D., Lawler, E. E. III, & Weick, K. E., Jr. (1971). *Managerial behavior, performance, and effectiveness*. New York: McGraw-Hill.

Cutler, B. (1988, March). *The confidence of self-monitors*. Paper presented at the meeting of the Eastern Psychological Association, Buffalo, NY.

Ghiselli, E. E. (1971). *Explorations in managerial talent*. Pacific Palisades, CA: Goodyear.

Gough, H. G. (1988). *Manual for the California Psychological Inventory* (3rd ed.). Palo Alto, CA: Consulting Psychologists Press.

Harris, R., & Lingoes, J. (1968). Subscales for the Minnesota Multiphasic Personality Inventory. Mimeographed materials, Langley Porter Clinic.

Hertzberg, F. (1966). *Working and the nature of man*. New York: Crowell.

Hertzberg, F. (1968). One more time: How do you motivate employees? *Harvard Business Review, 46*, 53–62.

Hogan, R. (1982). A socioanalytic theory of personality. In M. Page & R. Dienstbier (Eds.), *Nebraska symposium on motivation* (pp. 55–89). Lincoln, NE: University of Nebraska Press.

Hogan, R. (1986). *Manual for the Hogan Personality Inventory.* Minneapolis: National Computer Systems.

Hogan, R., & Jones, W. H. (1983). A role-theoretical model of criminal conduct. In W. S. Laufer & J. M. Day (Eds.), *Personality theory, moral development, and criminal behavior* (pp. 3–21). Boston: Lexington.

Hogan, R., & Jones, W. H. (1988). *Manual for the inventory of personal motives.* Tulsa, OK: University of Tulsa.

Hogan, R., & Jones, W. H. (in press). Trust and betrayal: The psychology of trust violation. In T. R. Sarbin, R. M. Carney, & C. Eoyang (Eds.), *Espionage: Studies in trust and betrayal.* New York: Pergamon.

Jones, W. H. (1988). *Manual for the inventory of personality disorders.* Tulsa, OK: University of Tulsa.

Kernberg, O. F. (1979). Regression in organizational leadership. *Psychiatry, 42,* 24–39.

Laurent, H. (1966). *EIMP applied to the International Petroleum Company.* (Tech. Rep.) New Jersey.

Lombardo, M. M., Ruderman, M. N., & McCauley, C. D. (1988). Explanations of success and derailment in upper-level management positions. *Journal of Business and Psychology, 2,* 199–216. Greensboro, NC: Center for Creative Leadership.

MacKinnon, D. W. (1944). The structure of personality. In J. McV. Hunt (Ed.), *Personality and the behavior disorders* (pp. 3–48). New York: Ronald Press.

Powers, T. A., & Zuroff, D. C. (1988). Interpersonal consequences of overt self-criticism: A comparison with neutral and self-enhancing presentations of self. *Journal of Personality and Social Psychology, 54,* 1054–1062.

Raskin, R., & Hall, C. S. (1979). A narcissistic personality inventory. *Psychological Reports, 45,* 590.

Raskin, R., & Hall, C. S. (1981). The narcissistic personality inventory: Alternate form reliability and further evidence of construct validity. *Journal of Personality Assessment, 45,* 159–162.

Raskin, R., & Novacek, J. (1989). An MMPI description of the narcissistic personality. *Journal of Personality Assessment, 53,* 66–80.

Sparks, C. P. (1966). *Personnel development series: Humble Oil & Refining Company.* Unpublished mimeographed report, Humble Company. Houston, TX.

Stogdill, R. M. (1974). *Handbook of leadership*. New York: Free Press.

Taylor, S. E., & Brown, J. D. (1988). Illusion and well-being: A social psychological perspective on mental health. *Psychological Bulletin, 103*, 193–210.

Wiggins, J. S. (1969). Content dimensions in the MMPI. In J. N. Butcher (Ed.), *MMPI: Research developments and clinical applications*. New York: McGraw-Hill.

# Testing for Leadership with the California Psychological Inventory

*Harrison G. Gough*

Although this paper will deal primarily with the relationships of personality to leadership, it should be acknowledged at the outset that an adequate conceptualization of leadership must go far beyond the personological realm. For instance, there are cognitive, experiential, familial, morphological, physiological, and situational factors related to the occurrence of leadership, and to its effectiveness. For analyses of these and other phenomena pertaining to leadership, comprehensive surveys such as those of Burns (1978) and Simonton (1987) in the political sphere and Stogdill (1974) in the managerial may be consulted.

Leadership may also be approached from the standpoint of what leaders do. Among other things, leaders may define and clarify goals, motivate and inspire followers, decide on courses of action, and direct the behavior of subordinates. Each of these functions, and others that could be listed, constitutes a useful topic for study. One hopes that studies of this kind will produce incremental accumulations of knowledge, so as to yield a broad and ecologically valid understanding of leadership in all of its facets and circumstances.

In regard to personality, one goal is to identify attributes that (a) characterize leaders in all settings; (b) cut across boundaries of age, gender, and other classifications; and (c) predict future attainment of leadership positions. A second goal is to discover ways in which these attributes may be developed and enhanced. These aims carry clear implications for strategies of research, in that samples of varied composition and background need to be observed in a variety of settings. Prospective or longitudinal designs, as well as concurrent analyses, are also mandatory, so that the predictive power of attributes discriminating between leaders and nonleaders may be appraised. In the applications of the California Psychological Inventory (CPI; Gough, 1987) to be described, careful attention has been paid to these strategic imperatives.

# The New CPI

In the new edition of the CPI there are 20 scales addressed to the assessment of folk concepts. A folk concept is a way of describing or conceptualizing personality used by ordinary people in everyday life, and therefore to be found in all societies and social groups. Examples of such concepts are "dominance," "self-control," and "flexibility." The first version of the CPI (Gough, 1957) included 18 folk measures. The two new scales are for Independence and Empathy.

Each of the 20 folk scales has two fundamental purposes: (1) to predict what people will say and do in defined situations and (2) to identify persons who will be described by others in distinctive and interpersonally consequential ways. The scales are not intended to assess or define personality "traits"; nor are any claims made that the scales are unifactorial or psychometrically homogeneous. The two instrumental goals just mentioned for the scales of the CPI should be differentiated from the possibly more common definitional goals in assessment, that is to develop scales having certain internal psychometric qualities.

The set of 20 measures is intended to be large enough to permit the prediction and conceptualization of any recurring form of social or interpersonal behavior. If behaviors are noted that the inventory cannot accommodate, new scales can be added. If the set of 20 proves not to be necessary for these purposes, scales can be dropped. That is to say, the set constitutes an "open system," subject to expansion or contraction according to demonstrable pragmatic criteria. Since the CPI was first used in its complete form in 1951, scales have been deleted and scales have been added.

Another designated requirement of the set of 20 scales is to mirror or reflect the ways in which the same notions are used by people in their everyday life. Thus, for example, if ratings or evaluations of "sociability" and "sense of well-being" correlate about .50 in large samples, then the CPI scales for these same attributes should correlate at the same level. This topographical principle should be distinguished from the common psychometric aim of merely minimizing all interscale correlations.

A fourth theoretical principle in the construction of the scales for the CPI was to achieve intensity or saturation of measurement. An analogy to the assessment of cognitive ability will make this intention clear. There are single-score ability or intelligence tests, such as the Stanford-Binet, that furnish an overall appraisal of the function. There are also multivariate tests, such as the WAIS, that provide a profile of scores on slightly different facets of the same general dimension. Many psychologists who deal with individual clients find the multiscore approach more useful than the single score. The MMPI furnishes another example. It could be asserted that the clinical scales on the MMPI represent merely minor and highly correlated aspects of the single overall notion of personal adjustment or maladjustment. Few users of the MMPI, however, would be willing to trade in the multivariate profile for a single, overall measure.

In the CPI, this principle of intensity or concentration of measurement holds within specific regions. For instance, in the realm of interpersonal behavior there are seven scales, each focused on a particular kind of interpersonal effectiveness. A respondent with very high scores on Dominance and Independence, but moderately high scores on Sociability and Empathy, will be resourceful, self-confident, and persuasive. The same will hold for the respondent very high on Sociability and Empathy, but only moderately high on Dominance and Independence. But in the style and manner in which these social qualities are manifested, the two persons will be very different from each other, and in most circumstances friends, co-workers, and so forth will want and find it useful to be aware of these differences.

The 20 profiled scales, with their folk concepts and instrumental, topographical, and incremental characteristics, are now buttressed by three vector scales to assess the basic metathemes of the inventory. The first is called v.1. It serves as a measure of interpersonal orientation, going from involvement and externality at one pole to detachment and internality at the other. The v.2 scale depicts the respondent's normative orientation, going from a norm-favoring, rule-cathecting perspective at the high end to a norm-doubting, rule-questioning viewpoint at the low.

The v.1 and v.2 scales are quasi-orthogonal, thus classifying about 25 percent of the population into each of the four quadrants defined by median splits on each scale. The quadrants themselves define four life-styles or ways of living, designated the Alpha, Beta, Gamma, and Delta. The Alpha life-style combines normative cathexes with active interpersonal engagement. The Beta life-style combines pronormative feelings with a strong sense of detachment or privacy. Gammas combine a liking for interpersonal involvement with doubts about the wisdom of most normative constraints. Deltas combine normative skepticism with an internalized, introversive orientation.

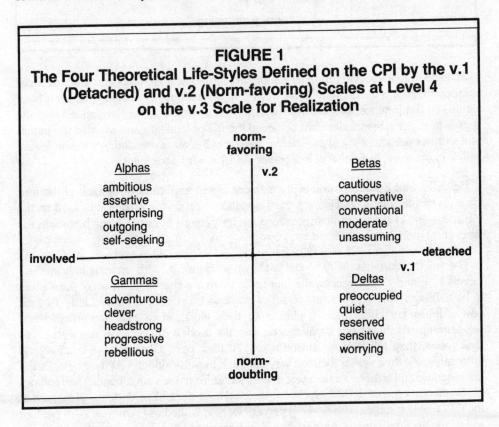

**FIGURE 1**
**The Four Theoretical Life-Styles Defined on the CPI by the v.1 (Detached) and v.2 (Norm-favoring) Scales at Level 4 on the v.3 Scale for Realization**

norm-favoring

v.2

Alphas
ambitious
assertive
enterprising
outgoing
self-seeking

Betas
cautious
conservative
conventional
moderate
unassuming

involved — detached

v.1

Gammas
adventurous
clever
headstrong
progressive
rebellious

Deltas
preoccupied
quiet
reserved
sensitive
worrying

norm-doubting

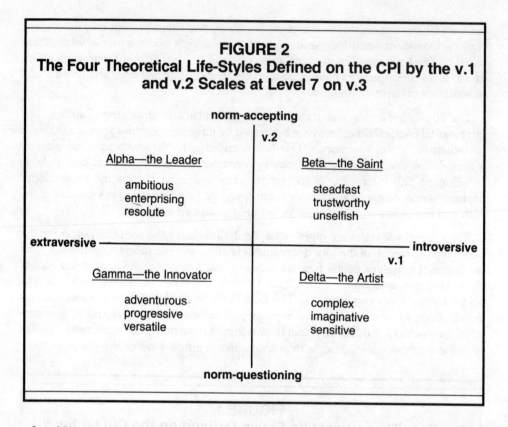

**FIGURE 2**
**The Four Theoretical Life-Styles Defined on the CPI by the v.1 and v.2 Scales at Level 7 on v.3**

norm-accepting

v.2

Alpha—the Leader

    ambitious
    enterprising
    resolute

Beta—the Saint

    steadfast
    trustworthy
    unselfish

extraversive ———————————————————— introversive

v.1

Gamma—the Innovator

    adventurous
    progressive
    versatile

Delta—the Artist

    complex
    imaginative
    sensitive

norm-questioning

In addition to these two fundamental orientations (towards others and towards social values), there is a third metatheme having to do with self-realization, as seen from within, or competence as seen from without. A v.3 scale for realization indexes the degree to which a respondent has achieved the full potentiality and avoided the pitfalls of his or her particular life-style. Scores on the v.3 scale are coded into seven levels, with 7 indicating a high level of integration and 1 a very poor level.

Figures 1 and 2 sketch some of the personological implications for each of the four life-style classifications. In Figure 1 the descriptions pertain to persons at Level 4 on the v.3 scale, and in Figure 2 the implications are for persons at Level 7, the highest in the theoretical model.

The full cuboid personality model is shown in Figure 3, with sections indicated for Levels 1, 4, and 7. For each of the four types there is a characteristic set of possibilities to be achieved, and a characteristic set of negative outcomes to be avoided. At their best, Alphas are charismatic leaders. At their worst, they are manipulative and self-serving. At their best, Betas can be saintlike models of goodness and virtue. At their worst, they are conformist and rigid. At their best, Gammas are creative and innovative. At their worst, they are wayward and impulse-ridden. At their best, Deltas are visionary and artistic. At their worst, they suffer from deep inner conflict and feelings of fragmentation. Of 1,023 psychologists for whom normative data are presented in the *CPI Guide* (Gough, 1987), 47.8 percent were classified as Gammas, 27.9 percent as Deltas, 16.8 percent as Alphas, and 7.5 percent as Betas. On the other hand, for

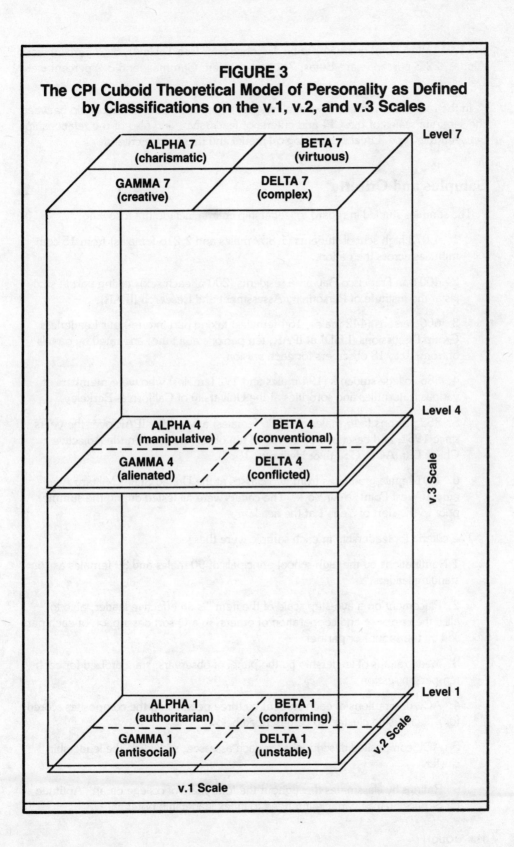

**FIGURE 3**
**The CPI Cuboid Theoretical Model of Personality as Defined by Classifications on the v.1, v.2, and v.3 Scales**

Level 7

ALPHA 7
(charismatic)

BETA 7
(virtuous)

GAMMA 7
(creative)

DELTA 7
(complex)

Level 4

ALPHA 4
(manipulative)

BETA 4
(conventional)

GAMMA 4
(alienated)

DELTA 4
(conflicted)

v.3 Scale

Level 1

ALPHA 1
(authoritarian)

BETA 1
(conforming)

GAMMA 1
(antisocial)

DELTA 1
(unstable)

v.2 Scale

v.1 Scale

the 1,014 West Point graduates to be described later (see Table 4), 67.2 percent were Alphas, 22.3 percent were Betas, 7.4 percent were Gammas, and 3.2 percent were Deltas.

In the remainder of this paper analyses will be reported of the relationship between the separate scales of the CPI and criteria of leadership, and also of the relationships between the Type/Level personological model and these same criteria.

## Samples and Criteria

The samples studied in regard to leadership criteria include the following:

1. 4,073 high school students (1,857 males and 2,216 females) from 15 communities across the nation.

2. 400 San Francisco Bay area residents (200 of each sex), taking part in studies at the Institute of Personality Assessment and Research (IPAR).

3. 606 persons (442 males, 164 females) taking part in one-hour Leaderless Group Discussions (LGD) at IPAR, ten persons at a time, and rated by panels of from 10 to 18 observers for each session.

4. 386 college students (194 males and 192 females) who were members of various fraternities and sororities at the University of California–Berkeley.

5. 852 persons (546 males and 306 females) assessed at IPAR over the years since 1951, and described by panels of ten observers each on the Adjective Check List (ACL; Gough & Heilbrun, 1983).

6. 1,014 male graduates from two classes at the United States Military Academy at West Point, New York. The cadets were all tested during the summer prior to the start of Year 1 at the academy.

The criteria for leadership in each sample were these:

1. Nominations by the high school principals of 90 males and 89 females as "outstanding leaders."

2. Placement on a five-step scale of the item "Is an effective leader; able to elicit the response and cooperation of others" in a Q-sort description of each person by the spouse or partner.

3. Mean ratings of leadership by the panel of observers, standardized for each ten-person session.

4. ACL descriptions of each student by three peers, with the composites scored for a "leadership cluster" to be described below.

5. ACL composited descriptions for each assessee, scored on the leadership cluster.

6. Ratings by classmates throughout the four years of college on an "Aptitude for Service" (AFS) variable intended to index leadership potential.

Reliabilities of the leadership nominations by principals and of the Q-sorting of the leadership item by spouses or partners are indeterminate. In the IPAR LGD sessions, no interjudge reliabilities were less than .90 and the median was .95. The median interjudge alphas for the 386 students, each described by three classmates, was .81. The median interjudge alpha for the 852 ten-judge panels at IPAR was .77. In unpublished studies at West Point, the interrater reliabilities for the AFS ratings approached 1.00.

The criteria themselves are either self-explanatory or well-known in all instances save that of the ACL leadership cluster. To select items for this cluster, two computations were carried out. In the first, all 300 items in the ACL were correlated with LGD leadership ratings for 95 college males and 98 college females. The observers in this instance rated participants on leadership and also completed ACL descriptions of each participant. The other analysis was a correlation of each of the 300 adjectives in the sample of 200 couples with the placement of the Q-sort leadership item for each person. Table 1 presents the correlations obtained, by sex, for the items retained for the cluster.

The correlations in the first two columns in Table 1 are based on the 1-0 dummy weight for each adjective (1 = checked and 0 = left blank), whereas those in the third and fourth columns are based on sums from 0 to 10 for each item, depending on how many of the ten observers for each student checked the word. This difference will account, in part, for the generally larger coefficients for the LGD relationships than for the spouses' ratings. All 300 items were reviewed to identify those with statistically significant (p < .01) values in at least two columns, and nonzero correlations in the same direction in the other two. Endorsement rates were also noted so as to screen out any items whose correlations might rest on just a few applications. An example of a selected item with a positive diagnostic value for leadership is "self-confident." For both males and females in both settings its correlations with the leadership criteria were significant at or beyond the .01 level. An example of a contraindicative item is "worrying," with coefficients of -.16 and -.15 for the spouses and -.39 and -.29 for the students observed in LGD.

Altogether, 47 items were chosen for the ACL leadership cluster, with 28 classified as indicative and 19 as contraindicative. The content of these items seems reasonable, with terms such as assertive, capable, outgoing, and strong scored as indicators, and terms such as awkward, immature, mild, and weak scored as contraindicators. The interitem reliability of the 47-item cluster was evaluated on four different samples. For the 194 male fraternity members the alpha coefficient was .77, and for the 192 female sorority members the alpha was .82. Note that these alphas were computed on the descriptions obtained from peers. For the 546 male IPAR assessees the interitem alpha, computed on the staff description, was .87, and the same coefficient was found for the 306 female assessees.

# TABLE 1
## Correlations of ACL Descriptions
## by Observers
## with Criteria of Leadership

| | Positive correlations | | | | | Negative correlations | | | |
|---|---|---|---|---|---|---|---|---|---|
| | With spouse's Q-sort rating | | With leadership rating in LGD | | | | With spouse's Q-sort rating | | With leadership rating in LGD |
| ACL items | M N=200 | F N=200 | M N=95 | F N=98 | ACL items | M N=200 | F N=200 | M N=95 | F N=98 |
| 2. active | .08 | .14 | .72 | .68 | 20. awkward | −.15 | −.14 | −.57 | −.48 |
| 3. adaptable | .09 | .12 | .32 | .35 | 37. commonplace | −.18 | −.11 | −.30 | −.39 |
| 7. aggressive | .10 | .10 | .62 | .67 | 61. dependent | −.07 | −.19 | −.41 | −.46 |
| 8. alert | .13 | .06 | .70 | .60 | 85. fearful | −.06 | −.18 | −.42 | −.46 |
| 10. ambitious | .15 | .24 | .55 | .61 | 119. immature | −.26 | −.11 | −.28 | −.26 |
| 17. assertive | .22 | .17 | .85 | .84 | 133. interests narrow | −.11 | −.14 | −.42 | −.46 |
| 26. capable | .14 | .20 | .57 | .51 | 149. meek | −.05 | −.21 | −.67 | −.62 |
| 33. clear-thinking | .10 | .16 | .38 | .43 | 151. mild | −.14 | −.16 | −.67 | −.62 |
| 34. clever | .17 | .12 | .49 | .54 | 175. pessimistic | −.13 | −.12 | −.10 | −.22 |
| 41. confident | .21 | .25 | .72 | .74 | 192. quitting | −.18 | −.12 | −.33 | −.32 |
| 50. courageous | .17 | .19 | .13 | .29 | 207. retiring | −.15 | −.25 | −.66 | −.59 |
| 63. determined | .17 | .15 | .44 | .59 | 230. shy | −.20 | −.14 | −.81 | −.65 |
| 78. energetic | .10 | .09 | .65 | .62 | 231. silent | −.14 | −.16 | −.72 | −.67 |
| 79. enterprising | .16 | .09 | .53 | .66 | 232. simple | −.11 | −.11 | −.39 | −.53 |
| 91. foresighted | .10 | .10 | .28 | .50 | 268. timid | −.08 | −.27 | −.68 | −.63 |
| 122. independent | .09 | .18 | .49 | .59 | 274. unambitious | −.15 | −.19 | −.42 | −.43 |
| 130. initiative | .16 | .08 | .65 | .75 | 293. weak | −.27 | −.17 | −.52 | −.49 |
| 167. outgoing | .14 | .21 | .65 | .59 | 297. withdrawn | −.05 | −.21 | −.63 | −.58 |
| 168. outspoken | .13 | .21 | .76 | .80 | 299. worrying | −.16 | −.15 | −.39 | −.29 |
| 180. polished | .14 | .18 | .26 | .34 | | | | | |
| 204. resourceful | .11 | .11 | .63 | .61 | | | | | |
| 213. self-confident | .15 | .20 | .71 | .73 | | | | | |
| 226. sharp-witted | .10 | .10 | .53 | .44 | | | | | |
| 239. sociable | .13 | .20 | .62 | .39 | | | | | |
| 241. sophisticated | .13 | .16 | .41 | .44 | | | | | |
| 251. strong | .10 | .22 | .52 | .69 | | | | | |
| 265. thorough | .09 | .16 | .25 | .24 | | | | | |
| 296. wise | .15 | .15 | .42 | .30 | | | | | |
| r(.05) | .14 | .14 | .20 | .20 | | | | | |
| r(.01) | .18 | .18 | .27 | .26 | | | | | |

# TABLE 2
## Correlations of CPI Scales with the Criteria of Leadership Indicated

### Criteria, Samples, and Ns

| CPI scales | Ratings by spouses | | Nominations by principals | | Rating of leadership in LGD | | AFS ratings | Staff ACL leadership cluster | | Peer ACL leadership cluster | | Median |
|---|---|---|---|---|---|---|---|---|---|---|---|---|
| | M (200) | F (200) | M (1,857) | F (2,216) | M (442) | F (164) | M (1,014) | M (546) | F (306) | M (194) | F (192) | |
| Do | .34 | .27 | .17 | .18 | .20 | .33 | .13 | .39 | .36 | .33 | .42 | .33 |
| Cs | .17 | .19 | .15 | .16 | .32 | .22 | .07 | .24 | .35 | .20 | .23 | .20 |
| Sy | .16 | .20 | .15 | .17 | .18 | .21 | .15 | .25 | .32 | .33 | .38 | .21 |
| Sp | .05 | .13 | .09 | .13 | .15 | .21 | .06 | .33 | .30 | .28 | .37 | .15 |
| Sa | .17 | .26 | .14 | .18 | .29 | .25 | .10 | .33 | .38 | .29 | .32 | .26 |
| In | .28 | .20 | .14 | .14 | .27 | .24 | .13 | .39 | .34 | .26 | .33 | .28 |
| Em | .15 | .23 | .13 | .17 | .36 | .27 | .13 | .33 | .36 | .25 | .26 | .25 |
| Re | .21 | .04 | .16 | .10 | .25 | .05 | .11 | −.01 | .12 | .10 | .19 | .11 |
| So | .15 | .00 | .14 | .06 | .01 | .02 | .12 | .01 | .03 | .17 | .08 | .06 |
| Sc | .07 | −.04 | .06 | −.02 | .00 | −.04 | .03 | −.12 | −.13 | −.05 | −.10 | −.04 |
| Gi | .13 | −.01 | .07 | .02 | .06 | .01 | .05 | −.07 | −.03 | .08 | −.05 | .02 |
| Cm | .02 | .15 | .10 | .02 | .10 | .09 | .10 | .06 | .18 | .15 | .16 | .10 |
| Wb | .17 | .07 | .12 | .05 | .23 | .04 | .09 | .08 | .13 | .16 | .16 | .12 |
| To | .16 | .02 | .13 | .11 | .23 | .07 | .06 | .05 | .12 | .03 | .14 | .11 |
| Ac | .22 | .12 | .18 | .12 | .22 | .17 | .13 | .09 | .11 | .21 | .16 | .16 |
| Ai | .15 | .06 | .11 | .09 | .32 | .17 | .04 | .18 | .26 | .15 | .16 | .15 |
| Ie | .16 | .12 | .15 | .12 | .30 | .17 | .09 | .21 | .30 | .15 | .16 | .16 |
| Py | .18 | .08 | .11 | .06 | .22 | .06 | .02 | .14 | .18 | .02 | .19 | .11 |
| Fx | .08 | −.05 | −.03 | .02 | .04 | .04 | −.08 | .13 | .15 | .02 | .09 | .04 |
| F/M | −.08 | −.08 | .00 | −.03 | −.09 | −.07 | −.06 | −.01 | −.12 | −.30 | −.07 | −.07 |
| v.1 | −.26 | −.24 | −.12 | −.17 | −.17 | −.31 | −.09 | −.42 | −.34 | −.33 | −.44 | −.26 |
| v.2 | .13 | .08 | .13 | .07 | .11 | .02 | .10 | −.06 | −.01 | .10 | .10 | .10 |
| v.3 | .22 | .11 | .13 | .10 | .26 | .14 | .06 | .12 | .15 | .13 | .12 | .13 |
| Mp | .28 | .16 | .16 | .14 | .23 | .15 | .13 | .18 | .18 | .20 | .22 | .18 |
| Wo | .16 | .12 | .10 | .05 | .18 | .03 | .13 | .00 | .04 | .16 | .14 | .12 |
| Anx | −.04 | −.10 | −.08 | −.03 | −.16 | −.11 | −.11 | −.13 | −.13 | −.16 | −.05 | −.11 |

## Findings

Table 2 presents the correlations obtained when the CPI folk, structural, and certain special purpose scales were correlated with the criteria available for each sample. In the far right column, medians based on the 11 prior correlations for each scale are listed. These medians range from a high of .33 for Dominance to a low of -.11 for the Leventhal (1966, 1968) Anxiety scale. Positive medians greater than .20 were noted for Dominance, Independence, Self-acceptance, the 38-item version of Hogan's (1969) Empathy scale now included in the CPI, and Sociability. The only negative correlation in this same range was that of -.26 for the v.1 scale for detachment or internality. All of these findings point towards the realm of interpersonal style as critical. The finding that

Dominance was the single best predictor is in agreement with the conclusion of Megargee and Carbonell (1988) that this scale is the strongest indicator of leadership potential in the inventory.

The data in Table 2 suggest the possibility of regression analyses, to see if combinations of scales might be discovered that could reliably exceed the level of prediction afforded by Do alone. Earlier (Gough, 1969), such an analysis was carried out on the sample of 4,073 high school students, using the old versions of the CPI scales. An equation based on Dominance, Self-Acceptance, Well-Being, and Achievement via Independence with positive weights, and Good Impression with negative, gave rise to a cross-validational correlation of .34 when applied to 164 college students rated as high, average, or low on leadership in a study by Carson and Parker (1966). Although encouraging, this coefficient is about the same as the median figure in Table 2 of .33 for the Dominance scale alone.

Joyce Hogan (1978) later cross-validated the equation on a sample of 50 male members of a college football squad, rated by two coaches on a seven-point scale for leadership. The interjudge reliability was .80. Scores from the equation correlated .62 with the sum of the two ratings, but the Dominance scale alone produced precisely this same coefficient. Self-Acceptance was in second place in Hogan's study, with a coefficient of .49. It is apparent that scales of the CPI do relate to leadership, but it is less apparent that the initial regression equation for leadership can improve on the predictions derivable from the Dominance scale alone.

To check on this conclusion, the 1969 leadership equation, using the old scales, was computed for several of the samples in Table 2. For the 194 males and 192 females described on the ACL by peers, the scores on the equation correlated .34 (males) and .42 (females) with the criterion. These values are almost identical to those for the Do scale alone. For the 442 males rated in LGD, scores from the equation correlated .30 with this criterion, higher than the coefficient of .20 for Do, but lower than those of .32 for Capacity for Status and .36 for Empathy. For the 164 females rated in LGD, scores from the equation correlated .33 with the criterion, precisely the same value as noted for the Do scale alone.

New regression analyses are currently being carried out on the various samples reported in Table 2, with cross-validations on the other samples, to see if a stable subset of scales can be identified that will improve on the relationships given by Do alone. It appears that modest increments may be obtainable, particularly if the Independence scale (not available in 1969) is included in the equation. An example is the equation derived from analysis of the spouses' ratings in the sample of 200 couples: Leadership = 38.47 + .82Do - .72Sp + .43In + .27Em, whose new-sample validity approximated .40. To compute scores on this equation, raw scores from each of the four CPI scales should be used. The constant of 38.47 is included so as to place the mean of an array of scores from any heterogeneous sample at approximately 50.0.

## Comparative Analyses

Table 3 presents comparative data for predicting LGD leadership ratings of 95 male and 98 female college students for the ACL (Gough & Heilbrun, 1983), the CPI, the

## TABLE 3
## Correlations of the Variables Indicated with Leadership Ratings in One-Hour Ten-Person LGD Sessions for 95 Male and 98 Female College Sophomores

| Variables | Males | Females |
|---|---|---|
| *Adjective Check List (ACL)* | | |
| Number Checked | .02 | .16 |
| Number Favorable | .07 | .06 |
| Number Unfavorable | .02 | −.04 |
| Communality | .02 | −.01 |
| Achievement | .14 | .22* |
| Dominance | .33** | .29** |
| Endurance | .02 | .01 |
| Order | −.06 | −.09 |
| Intraception | .04 | .04 |
| Nurturance | −.04 | −.04 |
| Affiliation | .03 | −.01 |
| Heterosexuality | .19 | .22* |
| Exhibition | .35** | .38** |
| Autonomy | .22* | .30** |
| Aggression | .27** | .37** |
| Change | .11 | .16 |
| Succorance | −.08 | −.11 |
| Abasement | −.25* | −.24* |
| Deference | −.21* | −.30** |
| Counseling Readiness | −.20* | −.12 |
| Self-control | −.27** | −.42** |
| Self-confidence | .27** | .27** |
| Personal Adjustment | .07 | .08 |
| Ideal Self | .09 | .12 |
| Creative Personality | .20* | .37** |
| Military Leadership | .13 | .01 |
| Masculinity | .26* | .26** |
| Femininity | −.07 | −.04 |
| Critical Parent | .16 | .28** |
| Nurturing Parent | −.03 | −.08 |
| Adult | .11 | −.05 |
| Free Child | .23* | .33** |
| Adapted Child | −.01 | −.07 |
| High Origence/Low Intellectence | .00 | −.18 |
| High Origence/High Intellectence | .00 | .24* |
| Low Origence/Low Intellectence | −.01 | −.18 |
| Low Origence/High Intellectence | .12 | .00 |
| *California Psychological Inventory (CPI)* | | |
| Dominance | .40** | .36** |
| Capacity for Status | .17 | .39** |
| Sociability | .13 | .29** |
| Social Presence | .13 | .23* |
| Self-Acceptance | .24* | .46** |

*Continued on next page*

**TABLE 3** — *Continued*

| Variables | Males | Females |
|---|---|---|
| *California Psychological Inventory (CPI) — concluded* | | |
| Independence | .27** | .41** |
| Empathy | .13 | .47** |
| Responsibility | −.03 | .22* |
| Socialization | −.02 | −.03 |
| Self-Control | −.03 | −.11 |
| Good Impression | −.04 | .01 |
| Communality | .11 | .04 |
| Well-Being | .11 | .19 |
| Tolerance | .01 | .08 |
| Achievement via Conformance | .10 | .20* |
| Achievement via Independence | .14 | .32** |
| Intellectual Efficiency | .19 | .32** |
| Psychological-Mindedness | .12 | .22* |
| Flexibility | .00 | .03 |
| Femininity/Masculinity | −.15 | −.07 |
| v.1 (detachment) | −.35** | −.33** |
| v.2 (norm-favoring) | .08 | .06 |
| v.3 (realization) | .08 | .20* |
| Managerial Potential | .20* | .17 |
| Work Orientation | .02 | .10 |
| Baucom Masculinity | .23* | .32** |
| Baucom Femininity | −.08 | −.11 |
| Levanthal Anxiety | −.18 | −.18 |
| *Minnesota Multiphasic Personality Inventory (MMPI)* | | |
| L | .00 | .01 |
| F | −.21* | −.17 |
| K | .18 | .19 |
| Hs + .5K | .08 | −.06 |
| D | −.07 | −.20* |
| Hy | .13 | .18 |
| Pd + .4K | .05 | .13 |
| Mf | .00 | .10 |
| Pa | −.04 | −.01 |
| Pt + K | −.06 | −.13 |
| Sc + K | −.17 | −.10 |
| Ma + .2K | −.02 | .13 |
| Si | −.20* | −.29** |
| Welsh A | −.17 | −.20* |
| Welsh R | −.01 | −.10 |
| Barron ES | .22* | .10 |
| Oettel LP (Leadership) | .26* | .33** |
| *Myers-Briggs Type Indicator (MBTI)* | | |
| E (Extraversion) | −.01 | .18 |
| I (Introversion) | −.01 | −.23* |
| EI (Continuous Scale) | .00 | −.21* |
| S (Sensing) | −.02 | −.17 |
| N (Intuiting) | −.04 | .13 |
| SN (Continuous Scale) | −.01 | .15 |
| T (Thinking) | .16 | .09 |
| F (Feeling) | −.25* | −.08 |
| TF (Continuous Scale) | −.13 | −.09 |

*Continued on next page*

**TABLE 3**—Continued

| Variables | Males | Females |
|---|---|---|
| *Myers-Briggs Type Indicator (MBTI)*—concluded | | |
| J (Judging) | .02 | .02 |
| P (Perceiving) | .01 | .00 |
| JP (Continuous Scale) | .00 | −.02 |
| *Other Variables* | | |
| High School Grade Point Average | .03 | .16 |
| College Grade Point Average | .22* | .22* |
| SAT—Verbal | .17 | .34** |
| SAT—Mathematical | .11 | .08 |
| Gottschaldt Figures Test | .12 | .05 |
| Drug & Alcohol Info Survey | .21* | −.12 |
| Sexual Knowledge Questionnaire | .13 | .19 |
| (external) Locus-of-Control | −.05 | −.17 |
| Barron-Welsh Art Scale | −.11 | .12 |
| Revised Art Scale | −.10 | .12 |

\* $p<.05$;  \*\* $p<.01$

MMPI, the Myers-Briggs Type Indicator (MBTI; Myers & McCaulley, 1985), high school and college academic performance, SAT Verbal and Mathematical aptitude, Crutchfield's version of the Gottschaldt Figures Test (CGFT; Crutchfield, Woodworth, & Albrecht, 1958), the Drug and Alcohol Information Survey (Gough, 1985), the Sexual Knowledge Questionnaire (SKQ; Gough, 1974), Rotter's (1966) Locus-of-Control scale, the Barron-Welsh Art Scale (Barron & Welsh, 1952), and the Revised Art Scale (Welsh, 1969, 1975). Altogether, 101 correlations with the leadership ratings are given for each sex.

In spite of some minor differences, the coefficients are quite similar for both males and females, an observation compatible with the notion of a common core of characteristics pertinent to leadership for both sexes. Another observation is that distinctly higher correlations are obtained for certain personality variables than for any of the academic performance, aptitude, and information tests. It cannot be asserted, therefore, that for these students the manifestation of leadership attributes in LGD performance is primarily a function of intellectual and cognitive qualities, and only secondarily a function of personality characteristics.

For the 95 males, the seven measures with largest correlations are the CPI scales for Dominance (r=.40), Independence (r=.27), and detachment or internality (v.1, r=−.35), and the ACL scales for Exhibition (r=.35), Dominance (r=.33), Self-Confidence (r=.27), and Self-Control (r=.27).

For the 98 females, the seven measures with largest correlations are the CPI scales for Self-Acceptance (r=.46), Empathy (r=.47), Independence (r=.41), and Capacity for Status (r=.39), and the ACL scales for Self-Control (r=−.42), Exhibition (r=.38), and Aggression (r=.37).

For all 193 students, the largest correlations (not shown in Table 3) are for CPI Dominance (r = .38), Self-Acceptance (r = .34), Independence (r = .34), and detachment (v.1, r = -.34); the ACL scales for Exhibition (r = .36), Self-Control (-.33), and Aggression (.30); and the MMPI Oettel (1953) scale for leadership (r = .30). The conclusion seems reasonable that for both males and females, the CPI folk and structural scales afford a stronger base for the prediction of leadership than either intellective/cognitive measures, or scales from other personality inventories. It should also be noted that, in agreement with the conclusions of Megargee and Carbonell (1988), the CPI Dominance scale is the strongest single indicator of leadership potential among those reviewed in Table 3.

## Type/Level Analyses

The theoretical Type/Level model has clear implications for leadership. In general, Alphas should seek and be accepted in leadership roles, particularly Alphas at higher levels. Gammas should be interested in leadership, but at lower levels should be relatively unacceptable to others in such roles; at higher levels, their acceptability should increase. Betas and Deltas will tend to avoid leadership roles, although in certain circumstances and certain individuals, Betas will be sought out and nominated by others.

There are also environmental/personological congruences inherent in the theoretical model. High school is an Alpha environment, with its emphasis on achievement via defined pathways. West Point, with its emphasis on compliance, initiative, and leadership, is or should be an Alpha environment. Other colleges, such as the University of California–Berkeley, with its tradition of protest and rule-rejection, will be more Gamma-like.

The contingency table for a CPI Type/Level analysis against leadership is shown in Table 4 for students from two classes at West Point. The cadets (all males) were tested prior to the start of Year 1, and the Aptitude for Service (AFS) leadership ratings were gathered from classmates throughout the following four years of college. The study is therefore prospective, in that the personality measures were taken four years before the AFS criterion was completed.

Because of the minimal number of cadets at Levels 1 and 2, and also the fairly small number at Level 7, grouping on Level was necessary, into categories formed by Levels 1 + 2 + 3, then Level 4, and finally Levels 5 + 6 + 7. There were 265, 361, and 388 cadets in each of these groups, respectively. In regard to CPI Types, 681 or 67.2 percent were Alphas, 226 or 22.3 percent were Betas, 75 or 7.4 percent were Gammas, and only 32 or 3.2 percent were Deltas.

The ANOVA for Type gave a significant (p = .01) F-ratio, with a ranking on AFS (standardized to a mean of 50 and a sigma of 10 by class) of Alphas (highest), Betas, Gammas, and Deltas. The differences were slight among the first three, but the 32 Deltas had a mean of only 44.75. The F-ratio for Level was not significant (p = .17), although the trend was in the expected direction with Levels 5 + 6 + 7 highest, Level 4 intermediate, and Levels 1 + 2 + 3 lowest. A contingency table like this one is hard to visualize. An easier picture of trends is provided by the graph in Figure 4, which gives the findings for the principals' nominations in the 15 high schools.

## TABLE 4
## CPI Types and Levels versus Aptitude
## for Service Ratings of West Point Cadets
## from Two Classes

| Type | | LEVELS 1+2+3 | 4 | 5+6+7 | Total |
|------|---|------|---|-------|-------|
| Alpha | N | 164 | 231 | 286 | 681 (67.2%) |
|  | M | 49.93 | 50.67 | 50.81 | 50.55 |
|  | SD | * | * | * | 10.05 |
| Beta | N | 65 | 86 | 75 | 226 (22.3%) |
|  | M | 48.23 | 49.13 | 50.67 | 49.38 |
|  | SD | * | * | * | 10.18 |
| Gamma | N | 23 | 32 | 20 | 75 (7.4%) |
|  | M | 48.61 | 49.66 | 49.30 | 49.24 |
|  | SD | * | * | * | 9.21 |
| Delta | N | 13 | 12 | 7 | 32 (3.2%) |
|  | M | 40.77 | 45.58 | 50.71 | 44.75 |
|  | SD | * | * | * | 7.36 |
| Total | N | 265 | 361 | 388 | 1,014 |
|  | M | 48.95 | 50.04 | 50.70 | 50.01 |
|  | SD | 10.36 | 9.84 | 9.85 | 10.00 |

| ANOVA for | df | F | p |
|-----------|----|---|---|
| Type | 3 | 3.64 | .01 |
| Level | 2 | 1.75 | .17 |
| T x L | 6 | 0.73 | .62 |

*SD not computed

The baseline for nominations was 4.64 percent, indicated in Figure 4 by a line at this point. The Alpha students had a higher rate of nomination for all four groupings on Level, and an upward progression from Levels 1+2 through Levels 3 and 4, up to Levels 5+6+7. Next came the Gammas, with nominations below the norm for Levels 1 through 3, but above for Levels 4 through 7. Betas started below the norm, but at Levels 5+6+7 just barely exceeded it. For none of the four groupings of Deltas did nominations ever reach the base rate. The trends for both Type and Level were significant beyond the .001 level of confidence.

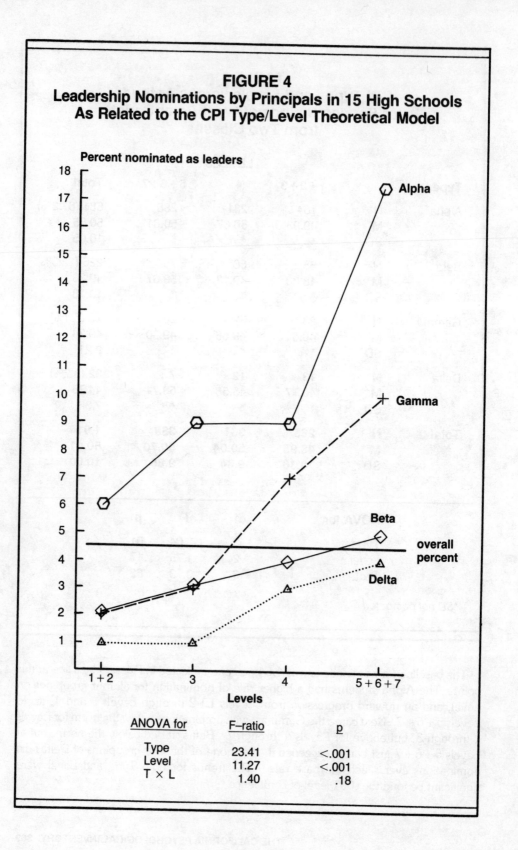

**FIGURE 4**
**Leadership Nominations by Principals in 15 High Schools As Related to the CPI Type/Level Theoretical Model**

Percent nominated as leaders

Alpha

Gamma

Beta

overall percent

Delta

Levels

| ANOVA for | F–ratio | p |
|---|---|---|
| Type | 23.41 | <.001 |
| Level | 11.27 | <.001 |
| T × L | 1.40 | .18 |

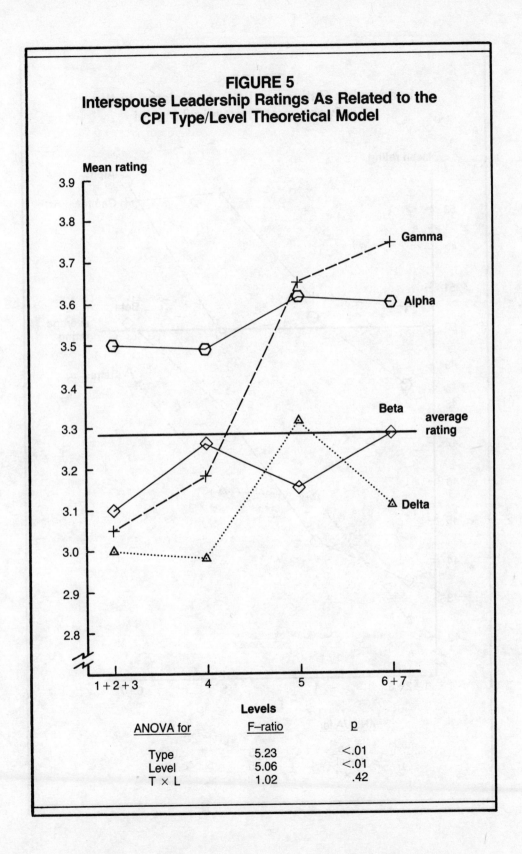

**FIGURE 5**
**Interspouse Leadership Ratings As Related to the CPI Type/Level Theoretical Model**

| ANOVA for | F-ratio | p |
|-----------|---------|------|
| Type | 5.23 | <.01 |
| Level | 5.06 | <.01 |
| T × L | 1.02 | .42 |

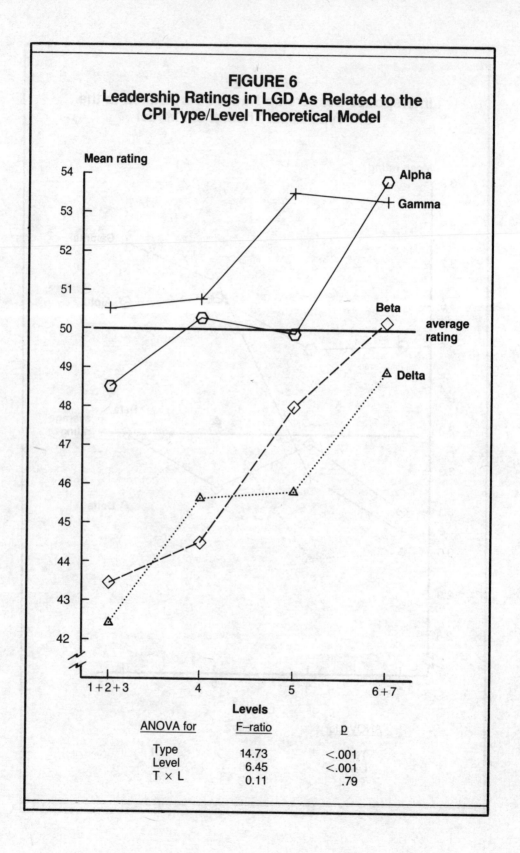

**FIGURE 6**
**Leadership Ratings in LGD As Related to the CPI Type/Level Theoretical Model**

| ANOVA for | F–ratio | p |
|-----------|---------|------|
| Type | 14.73 | <.001 |
| Level | 6.45 | <.001 |
| T × L | 0.11 | .79 |

Figure 5 displays a Type/Level analysis against leadership for the Q-sort ratings within the 200 couples. The mean placement of the leadership item on a five-step scale in the sample of 400 persons was 3.29; a line has been drawn to mark this value. The mean ratings for all four Alpha clusters are above this baseline, as are the ratings for Gammas at Levels 5 to 7. Gammas in the lower two groupings on Level are rated below the norm. Betas are either below or just at the norm for all groupings on Level, and Deltas are below except for a slight elevation at Level 5. The ANOVAs for both Type and Level were significant (p < .01), but there was no observable interaction.

Figure 6 offers the trend lines for the 442 males and 164 females rated for leadership in one-hour LGD sessions by IPAR staff observers. The mean rating for all 606 persons was 49.98, as indicated by the line at that value. Alphas at Level 1 + 2 + 3 were slightly below this norm, but at or above the average at all other Levels. Gammas were rated above this norm for all groupings on Levels. Betas were at or below the norm for each grouping, and Deltas were always below the norm. The F-ratios were significant (p < .001) for both Type and Level, but once again there was no detectable interaction. The superior leadership performance of the Gammas in this analysis sheds light on the nature of the LGD procedure, stressing as it does talk and interpersonal competition. It will be recalled from Table 3 earlier that among the strongest correlations for leadership in LGD in the sample of 193 college students were the ACL scales for Exhibition and Aggression, with equally negative coefficients for Self-Control, Abasement, and Deference. This element of self-aggrandizement in the LGD procedure will appeal to Gammas, and will tend to favor the Gamma-like forms of leadership.

The peer ACL clusters for leadership as related to the Type/Level model are given in Figure 7, for the 194 male and 192 female college students. The average ACL cluster score was approximately 450, and a line has been drawn at this point. Because of the relatively small N (386), only three groupings on Level were possible. All three of the Alpha subsamples had mean peer ratings above this baseline, as did the Gammas at Level 4 and at Levels 5 + 6 + 7. Betas and Deltas in all three groupings had ratings well below the average, and for the Betas there was an unusual downward trend from the lower to the higher Levels on the v.3 scale. The ANOVA for this sample was significant (p < .001) only for Type. Had it not been for the downward slope for the Betas, the F-ratio for Level would have had a lower probability than the observed value of .13.

The ACL descriptive cluster for leadership as applied to the 852 IPAR assessees is related to the CPI Type/Level model in Figure 8. The mean score on the staff ACL descriptions was approximately 274. All four Alpha and all four Gamma subsamples ranked above this norm, and all eight of the Beta and Delta subsamples ranked below. The F-ratio for Type was significant beyond the .001 level of probability, and that for Level had a p-value of .02. There was no observable interaction between Type and Level. The Gammas in this analysis were highest-rated at all levels. This finding should be interpreted while recognizing that the IPAR subjects were chosen primarily for their creativity and effectiveness in a variety of fields, such as architecture, mathematics, the natural sciences, and literature. Because of this screening, no "unrealized" or obviously unsuccessful Gammas would have been invited to take part. This means that the IPAR Gammas at the lower levels would be unrepresentative of the ordinary Gamma population at Levels 1, 2, and 3, and probably at 4.

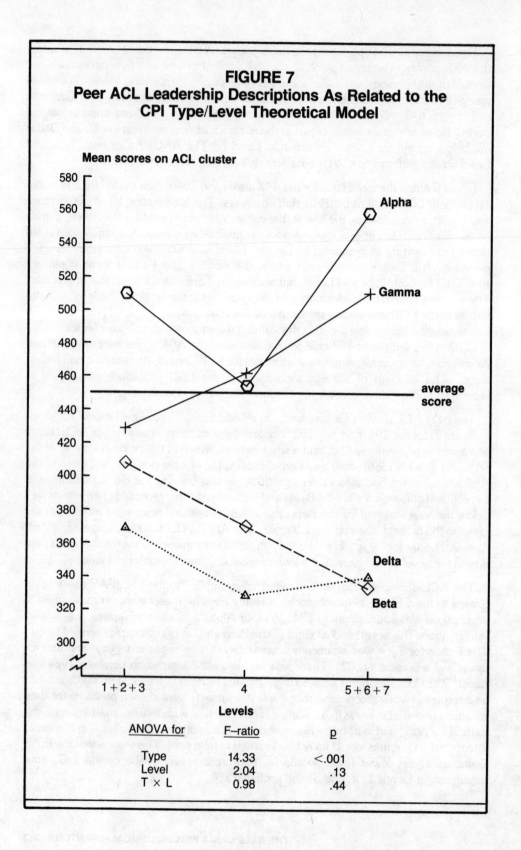

**FIGURE 7**
**Peer ACL Leadership Descriptions As Related to the CPI Type/Level Theoretical Model**

Mean scores on ACL cluster

| ANOVA for | F–ratio | p |
|-----------|---------|---|
| Type | 14.33 | <.001 |
| Level | 2.04 | .13 |
| T × L | 0.98 | .44 |

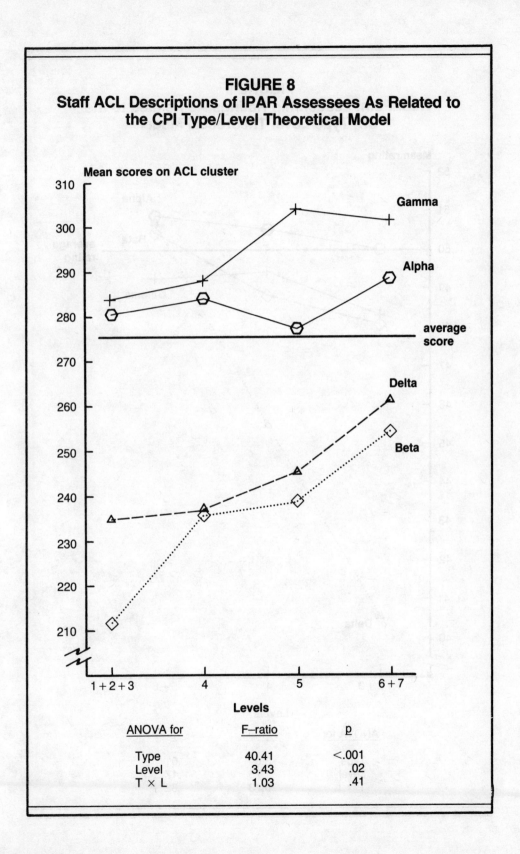

**FIGURE 8**
**Staff ACL Descriptions of IPAR Assessees As Related to the CPI Type/Level Theoretical Model**

Mean scores on ACL cluster

Gamma

Alpha

average score

Delta

Beta

Levels

| ANOVA for | F–ratio | p |
|---|---|---|
| Type | 40.41 | <.001 |
| Level | 3.43 | .02 |
| T × L | 1.03 | .41 |

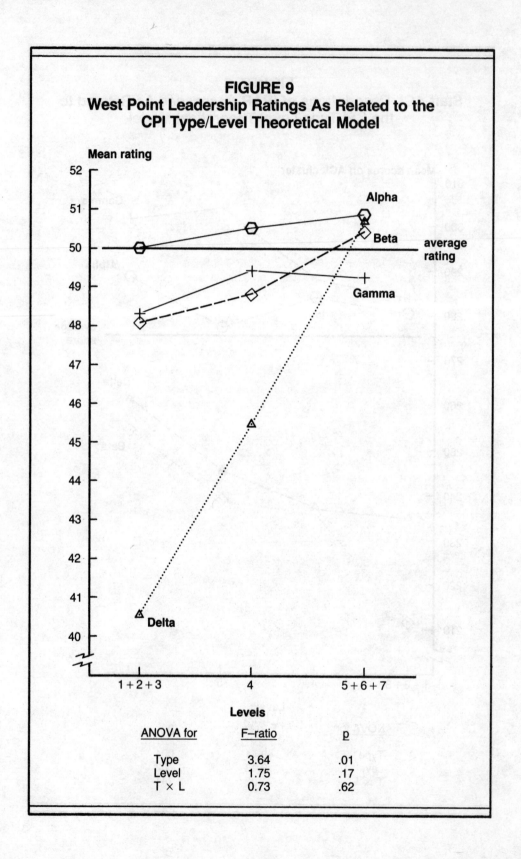

**FIGURE 9**
**West Point Leadership Ratings As Related to the CPI Type/Level Theoretical Model**

Figure 9 presents the West Point data from Table 4 in graphic form. The AFS (leadership) ratings were standardized within each class to a mean of 50 and a sigma of 10. The Alpha cadets were at or above this baseline for each grouping, and the Gammas were always below the mean of 50. The Betas in the lower two clusters on Level ranked below the average of 50, but at Levels 5 to 7 ranked slightly above. The Deltas at Levels 1, 2, and 3 had a very low AFS mean rating; then at Level 4 the Deltas moved up, and at Levels 5, 6, and 7 the Delta mean was second only to that of the Alphas. The trend for Type was significant ($p = .01$), but that for Level with a probability of .17 did not reach the customary .05 level.

## Conclusions

Two kinds of analysis have been presented in this paper. The first dealt with the CPI scales in direct correlations with the leadership criteria for both sexes in different settings. There was a strong trend for the CPI scales from the interpersonal sector (Dominance through Empathy) to be positively related to leadership in all instances. The scales in the realm of intrapersonal values (Responsibility through Tolerance) had distinctly lower correlations, although there was a trend towards positive coefficients. In the regression analyses, only minimally presented, the interpersonal scales more consistently entered into the combination of variables affording maximized prediction than did the intrapersonal measures. The three scales for intellective and achievement modes (Ac, Ai, and Ie) had positive correlations in every instance, and in the regressions usually added something to what was available in the interpersonal cluster. Psychological-Mindedness was also positive in its correlations in every sample, but Flexibility and Femininity/Masculinity were either close to zero or negative.

In the comparative analysis reported for LGD leadership ratings of 193 college students only, the relationships for the CPI appeared to be stronger than those for the other personality inventories considered, and also stronger than those for scholastic aptitude tests, observed academic achievement, range of information, and cognitive independence as assessed by a hidden figures test. Analyses of this kind are continuing and additional results will be reported in subsequent papers.

In regard to the CPI Type/Level theoretical personality model, the findings were unequivocal. In every sample and against every criterion, Alphas were rated as having good leadership potential and as exhibiting leaderlike behavior. In fact, their high ranking was contested only by Gammas at Levels 5, 6, and 7. Alphas, it will be recalled, enter happily into the interpersonal milieu and while so doing strive hard to maintain and advance consensual social values and traditions. From case analyses (not reported in the paper) it appears that their leadership style stresses open and candid communication with subordinates, and a preference for delegating both responsibilities and decision-making prerogatives. At Levels 6 and 7, Alphas can also manifest the charisma that most people associate with leaders functioning in an optimum manner.

In the LGD situation Alphas can do well, and do receive generally good marks. However, this is not the ideal Alpha setting, as in direct interpersonal give-and-take Alphas will often listen and even seem to defer in acquiescence to others. High-level Gammas, in contrast, take well to the LGD situation, and generally get the highest ratings. This may well be a defect in the LGD procedure as a method for spotting effective leaders, in that too many Gammas and too few Alphas will be identified.

From case studies in the CPI archives it appears that the problem in Gamma leadership is a certain impatience with and distrust of followers, which may result in unwillingness to delegate and in arbitrary, unshared decision making. The strong need of Gammas for change may also produce problems in those situations in which continuity and maintenance of past practices are advisable.

From the West Point and LGD Type/Level analyses it is apparent that Betas at high v.3 levels can achieve and carry out leadership roles. Case studies suggest that Betas almost never seek out such roles, but will accept them when asked to do so by followers. The logic seems to be that the sincerity and ethical integrity of high-level Betas are seen in certain settings as mandatory for a leader. Deltas also almost never seek leadership positions, and contrary to the Betas also resist strongly any entreaties from others to take on such roles. The Delta is always an outsider in one way or another, with a private, doubting view of the social enterprise. At high v.3 levels, these Delta views can be prescient, discerning of things that others cannot even imagine. Thus there is an important social function for the Delta type, but this function is seldom, if ever, that of the chosen leader.

Finally, there are some dispositional/situational interactions embodied in these findings. Certain settings, such as the military, seem to be Alpha-like in what is wanted and indeed demanded of leaders. Others, such as settings where old ways are failing and new ways are needed, are Gamma-like in what is called for. In those occasional settings where followers have become disillusioned or feel the need for some sort of incorruptible moral force in the leader, Betas at Levels 6 and 7 will respond to a draft. It is hard to visualize a Delta environment, but in all settings and in every context the disposition of the Delta to look into the future and to imagine better and more restorative social and intellectual systems is vital.

## References

Barron, F., & Welsh, G. S. (1952). Artistic perception as a factor in personality style: Its measurement by a figure-preference test. *Journal of Psychology*, *33*, 199–203.

Burns, J. M. (1978). *Leadership*. New York: Harper and Row.

Carson, G. L., & Parker, C. A. (1966). Leadership and profiles on the MMPI and CPI. *Journal of College Student Personnel*, *7*, 14–18.

Crutchfield, R. S., Woodworth, D. G., & Albrecht, R. E. (1958). *Perceptual performance and the effective person* (Tech. Note WADC-TN-58-60, ASTIA No. 151039). Lackland Air Force Base, TX: Personnel Laboratory, Wright Air Development Command.

Gough, H. G. (1957). *Manual for the California Psychological Inventory*. Palo Alto, CA: Consulting Psychologists Press.

Gough, H. G. (1969). A leadership index on the California Psychological Inventory. *Journal of Counseling Psychology*, *16*, 283–289.

Gough, H. G. (1974). A 24-item version of the Miller-Fisk Sexual Knowledge questionnaire. *Journal of Psychology, 87*, 183–192.

Gough, H. G. (1985). Development of a drug and alcohol information survey. *International Journal of the Addictions, 20*, 519–526.

Gough, H. G. (1987). *California Psychological Inventory administrator's guide.* Palo Alto, CA: Consulting Psychologists Press.

Gough, H. G., & Heilbrun, A. B., Jr. (1983). *The Adjective Check List manual*–1983 edition. Palo Alto, CA: Consulting Psychologists Press.

Hogan, J. C. (1978). Personological dynamics of leadership. *Journal of Research in Personality, 12*, 390–395.

Hogan, R. (1969). Development of an empathy scale. *Journal of Consulting and Clinical Psychology, 33*, 307–316.

Leventhal, A. M. (1966). An anxiety scale for the California Psychological Inventory. *Journal of Clinical Psychology, 22*, 459–561.

Leventhal, A. M. (1968). Additional data on the CPI anxiety scale. *Journal of Counseling Psychology, 15*, 479–480.

Megargee, E. I., & Carbonell, J. L. (1988). Evaluating leadership with the CPI. In C. D. Spielberger & J. N. Butcher (Eds.), *Advances in personality assessment* (Vol. 7, pp. 203–219). Hillsdale, NJ: Lawrence Erlbaum Associates.

Myers, I. B., & McCaulley, M. H. (1985). *Manual: A guide to the development and use of the Myers-Briggs Type Indicator.* Palo Alto, CA: Consulting Psychologists Press.

Oettel, A. (1953). *Leadership: A psychological analysis.* Unpublished doctoral dissertation, University of California, Berkeley.

Rotter, J. B. (1966). General expectancies for internal versus external control of reinforcement. *Psychological Monographs, 80* (1, Whole No. 609).

Simonton, D. K. (1987). *Why presidents succeed: A political psychology of leadership.* New Haven, CT: Yale University Press.

Stogdill, R. M. (1974). *Handbook of leadership.* New York: Free Press.

Welsh, G. S. (1969). *Gifted adolescents: A handbook of test results.* Greensboro, NC: Prediction Press.

Welsh, G. S. (1975). *Creativity and intelligence: A personality approach.* Chapel Hill, NC: University of North Carolina, Institute for Research in Social Science.

# The Myers-Briggs Type Indicator and Leadership

*Mary H.
McCaulley*

This paper is concerned with questions about individual differences in leadership. The theoretical approach is based on C. G. Jung's theory of psychological types (Jung, 1971). The instrumentation is the Myers-Briggs Type Indicator (MBTI), a questionnaire developed to make it possible to test Jung's theory and to put it to practical use. Jung's theory and the MBTI are concerned with the conscious use of four mental processes—assessment of reality, vision of the future, logical decision making, and value-oriented decision making—and the attitudes in which these are used. These processes appear in the exercise of leadership, for example, in:

accurate assessment of existing situations
vision of new possibilities
logical analysis of causes and effects, immediate and
     long-range
clarity in weighing values, immediate and long-range
alertness in perceiving changes—immediate or future
decisiveness in reaching good judgments
clarity in conceptualizing the issues
ability to build and maintain the momentum for action

Type theory suggests that individuals have different patterns of interest and effectiveness in these aspects of leadership. A person effective in one setting may be ineffective where leadership demands are different. Jung's model and the data generated about individuals and groups from the MBTI can be useful in refining our understanding of leadership styles and the match or mismatch with situations in which leadership is exercised. The paper is divided into the following sections:

A. Outline of Key Concepts in Jung's Theory of Psychological Type

B. Brief Description of the Development and Uses of the MBTI

C. Brief Description of Data Resources for the MBTI

D. Summary Types Tables of Patterns in Different Leadership Settings

E. Comments on Tables and Related Research

F. Leadership Research Issues and Psychological Type

References

Sections D, E, and F provide the substance for the paper. Section D shows that across settings where leadership can be exercised, the same types tend to be frequent, and the same types tend to be rare. Section E comments on the tables of Section D and other MBTI research related to leadership. Section F raises issues for leadership research. Not all persons in the management positions shown on the tables exercise good leadership or creative leadership; but these patterns have implications for understanding the relationship between individuals and the specific leadership qualities required in different settings.

## A. Outline of Key Concepts in Jung's Theory of Psychological Type

The basic concepts of Jung's theory of psychological types, which are also "indicated" in the Myers-Briggs Type Indicator, are:

- **Extraversion (E) or Introversion (I)**

  In the extraverted (E) attitude, persons seek engagement with the environment and give weight to events in the world around them.
  In the introverted (I) attitude, persons seek engagement with their inner world and give weight to concepts and ideas to understand events.

- **Sensing perception (S) or Intuitive perception (N)**

  When using sensing perception (S), persons are interested in what is real, immediate, practical, and observable by the senses.
  When using intuitive perception (N), persons are interested in future possibilities, implicit meanings, and symbolic or theoretical patterns.

- **Thinking (T) or Feeling (F)**

  When using thinking judgment (T), persons rationally decide through a process of logical analysis of causes and effects.
  When using feeling judgment (F), persons rationally decide by weighing the relative importance or value of competing alternatives.

- **Judgment (J) or Perception (P)**

  When the orientation toward the world uses judgment (J), persons enjoy organizing, planning, and moving quickly to a decision.
  When the orientation to the world uses perception (P), persons enjoy being curious and open to changes, preferring to keep options open in case something better turns up.

Every person uses all eight processes, E, I, S, N, T, F, J, and P, but type theory postulates that one of each pair is intrinsically preferred over the other. Interests, motivations, and skills follow from these basic preferences. Thus, a person preferring ESTJ is expected to have different interests, motivations, and skills than a person preferring INFP, and similarly with other combinations.

The theory assumes that youth is a time to specialize and develop the skills associated with the preferred processes; in later life, there is time to become a generalist, that is, to develop and appreciate the processes which were less preferred earlier. The ESTJ who has favored action (E), common sense (S), analytical logic (T), and a planned life (J) will not become an INFP in mid-life, but may find contemplation (I), imagination (N), values (F), and flexibility (P) becoming more understandable, and even appealing.

## B. Brief Description of the Development and Uses of the MBTI

The MBTI is a questionnaire which was developed by Isabel Briggs Myers and her mother Katharine Cook Briggs, with the aim of making Jung's ideas testable and usable. They had studied Jung's ideas and tested them out on acquaintances for 20 years before they began construction of the MBTI in 1941, a process continued by Isabel Briggs Myers until her death in 1980.

After a long incubation and testing period in the 1940s and 1950s, Educational Testing Service published the MBTI in 1962 as a research tool. During this period it was discovered by a Japanese psychologist and translated into Japanese. The Nippon Recruit Center in Tokyo has used the MBTI extensively for career guidance since the 1960s. In 1975 the MBTI was considered ready to move from research to applications status and Consulting Psychologists Press became its publisher. It is now one of the most widely used tests for normal people and it is being translated into languages worldwide. Users include:

Counselors who use it with individuals, couples, families, and groups for individual understanding, communications, and career guidance;

Educators at all levels who use it to understand teaching and learning styles, aptitude, achievement, and motivation;

Organizations in business, industry, government, and the military who use it to understand communications, motivation, teamwork, work styles, and leadership;

Religious groups of many denominations interested in individual differences in ministry and spirituality; and relatively recently

The public which has been introduced to type theory through an increasing number of popular books.

The MBTI questions force choices between E or I, S or N, T or F, and J or P. Scores generated from answers to the MBTI show the direction of preference by a letter, and the consistency of preference by a number (example E 29, T 15, etc.). The types are denoted by four letters reflecting the direction of preferences—ESTJ, INTP, ENFJ, and so forth. Myers wrote descriptions for each of the 16 types, using the developmental dynamics implicit in Jung's theory. Descriptions show the characteristics of a type at optimum development, and potential problems when development is incomplete. These descriptions are based on the theory, long years of observation, and empirical data.

In addition to reports for individuals, the MBTI generates descriptions of groups called "type tables," which are useful in looking at careers patterns and team interactions. Type tables are presented in Section D. The *MBTI Manual* (Myers and McCaulley, 1985) provides extensive data on reliability and validity, and applications in many areas.

## C. Brief Description of Data Resources for the MBTI

**The Center for Applications of Psychological Type (CAPT)** Sections E and F report MBTI data from resources at the Center for Applications of Psychological Type (CAPT). CAPT is a public, not-for-profit organization which grew out of a Typology Laboratory formed with Isabel Briggs Myers in 1969 at the University of Florida. At that time the MBTI was relatively unknown. The mission of CAPT is "to extend and teach the accurate understanding and ethical and practical applications of Jung's theory of psychological types." CAPT provides MBTI scoring, publications, and professional training and consultation to MBTI users and the public.

**The MBTI Data Bank** CAPT created the first computer scoring service for the MBTI and continues to provide scoring with reports for the individual, the professional MBTI user, and the researcher. As part of its mission to expand knowledge of type, CAPT codes answer sheet information for occupations and other research data. The scoring service has generated the CAPT MBTI Data Bank of nearly 500,000 records. Other MBTI users send answer sheets to archive and add to the data bank.

The MBTI Data Bank is used for normative studies, and composites from the data bank appear in tables of the *MBTI Manual* and in the *Atlas of Type Tables* (Macdaid, McCaulley, & Kainz, 1987). Data from the atlas and other sources were used to create the summaries in Section D.

Because the MBTI generates data on groups of types as well as data on individuals, CAPT has developed and makes available software for comparing type tables.

**The MBTI Library Collections** The Isabel Briggs Myers Memorial Library at CAPT is the largest collection of research and applications of the MBTI. Nearby, the Isabel Briggs Myers papers are housed in the archives of the University of Florida.

MBTI users donate to the library published and unpublished research reports, including type tables for the *MBTI Atlas*.

CAPT publishes the *MBTI Bibliography* and the *Compendium of Research Involving the Myers-Briggs Type Indicator* (Carskadon, McCarley, & McCaulley, 1987).

**Research Reports** The *Journal of Psychological Type* is a refereed journal under the editorship of Thomas Carskadon of the Psychology Department of Mississippi State University. It is distributed by the publisher and by CAPT.

CAPT distributes reports of its own and others' research from time to time.

**Other MBTI Data Sources** The Center for Creative Leadership (CCL) has important data sets of managers and others trained at Greensboro and satellite programs. These data sets are important because they include many other test data and behavioral and rating data which can be analyzed in terms of type differences. Examples of CCL data shared with CAPT appear on Tables 2, 4, and 11–15. MBTI users in organizations and consulting firms have also collected large numbers of MBTI records as part of their training and development operations. Most of these data are unavailable for research; many have been returned to participants or are filed where access is difficult.

## D. Summary Types Tables of Patterns in Different Leadership Settings

This section summarizes representative samples of persons in leadership positions. Each table gives a picture of frequent and rare types in a leadership setting. Most of the data are from the *MBTI Atlas of Type Tables* where more detail can be found. Some tables are from the CAPT MBTI Data Bank; others are from published research or data sent to CAPT to be archived. Career data in the MBTI Data Bank and atlas are based on CAPT coding of the occupations recorded on MBTI answer sheets.

Tables 1–8 show abbreviated names for tables at the left margin. Within each type appears the percentage for the type in the total sample followed by a bar graph making the percentage more visible. In the bar graphs, there are some occasions where more than 20% of a sample occur in a single type; in these cases the bar graph is followed by a + .

### Table 1. Leaders in Business and Industry in the United States

Group 1A is a composite of 7,463 persons who wrote "manager" or "administrator" on their MBTI answer sheets; these data from the MBTI Data Bank appear in the atlas.

Group 1B shows 150 chief executives of Texas small businesses that experienced comparatively limited growth. The data were reported in Hoy and Hellriegel (1982) and appear in the atlas.

Group 1C shows 316 managers in a national chain of retail scores described by Gaster (1982) and reported in the atlas.

Group 1D is a composite group of 756 financial managers and bank officers. These data from the MBTI Data Bank appear in the atlas.

Group 1E shows 101 middle and high executives of a midwestern telephone company, reported in the dissertation of Dietl (1981).

Group 1F shows 159 founders/cofounders (133 males and 26 females) from the 1987 *Inc* 500 list of fastest-growing privately held firms in the United States, reported by Ginn and Sexton (1988).

Group 1G shows 216 partners in accounting firms described in Jacoby (1981) and Otte (1984).

Groups 1H, 1I, and 1J compare three subgroups of 298 organizational decision-makers from a number of large organizations reported in Roach (1986). Group 1H are 70 line supervisors, 1I are 161 managers, and 1J are 67 executives. The executives include significantly more extraverts and intuitives than

# TABLE 1
## Myers-Briggs Type Indicator Percentages
## for Managers in Business and Industry in the United States

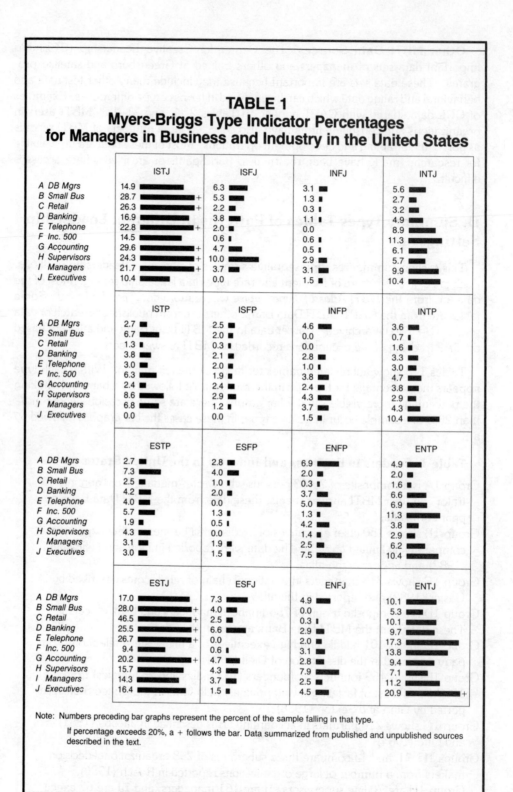

| | | ISTJ | ISFJ | INFJ | INTJ |
|---|---|---|---|---|---|
| A | DB Mgrs | 14.9 | 6.3 | 3.1 | 5.6 |
| B | Small Bus | 28.7 + | 5.3 | 1.3 | 2.7 |
| C | Retail | 26.3 + | 2.2 | 0.3 | 3.2 |
| D | Banking | 16.9 | 3.8 | 1.1 | 4.9 |
| E | Telephone | 22.8 + | 2.0 | 0.0 | 8.9 |
| F | Inc. 500 | 14.5 | 0.6 | 0.6 | 11.3 |
| G | Accounting | 29.6 + | 4.7 | 0.5 | 6.1 |
| H | Supervisors | 24.3 + | 10.0 | 2.9 | 5.7 |
| I | Managers | 21.7 + | 3.7 | 3.1 | 9.9 |
| J | Executives | 10.4 | 0.0 | 1.5 | 10.4 |

| | | ISTP | ISFP | INFP | INTP |
|---|---|---|---|---|---|
| A | DB Mgrs | 2.7 | 2.5 | 4.6 | 3.6 |
| B | Small Bus | 6.7 | 2.0 | 0.0 | 0.7 |
| C | Retail | 1.3 | 0.3 | 0.0 | 1.6 |
| D | Banking | 3.8 | 2.1 | 2.8 | 3.3 |
| E | Telephone | 3.0 | 2.0 | 1.0 | 3.0 |
| F | Inc. 500 | 6.3 | 1.9 | 3.8 | 4.7 |
| G | Accounting | 2.4 | 2.4 | 2.4 | 3.8 |
| H | Supervisors | 8.6 | 2.9 | 4.3 | 2.9 |
| I | Managers | 6.8 | 1.2 | 3.7 | 4.3 |
| J | Executives | 0.0 | 0.0 | 1.5 | 10.4 |

| | | ESTP | ESFP | ENFP | ENTP |
|---|---|---|---|---|---|
| A | DB Mgrs | 2.7 | 2.8 | 6.9 | 4.9 |
| B | Small Bus | 7.3 | 4.0 | 2.0 | 2.0 |
| C | Retail | 2.5 | 1.0 | 0.3 | 1.6 |
| D | Banking | 4.2 | 2.0 | 3.7 | 6.6 |
| E | Telephone | 4.0 | 0.0 | 5.0 | 6.9 |
| F | Inc. 500 | 5.7 | 1.3 | 1.3 | 11.3 |
| G | Accounting | 1.9 | 0.5 | 4.2 | 3.8 |
| H | Supervisors | 4.3 | 0.0 | 1.4 | 2.9 |
| I | Managers | 3.1 | 1.9 | 2.5 | 6.2 |
| J | Executives | 3.0 | 1.5 | 7.5 | 10.4 |

| | | ESTJ | ESFJ | ENFJ | ENTJ |
|---|---|---|---|---|---|
| A | DB Mgrs | 17.0 | 7.3 | 4.9 | 10.1 |
| B | Small Bus | 28.0 + | 4.0 | 0.0 | 5.3 |
| C | Retail | 46.5 + | 2.5 | 0.3 | 10.1 |
| D | Banking | 25.5 + | 6.6 | 2.9 | 9.7 |
| E | Telephone | 26.7 + | 0.0 | 2.0 | 17.3 |
| F | Inc. 500 | 9.4 | 0.6 | 3.1 | 13.8 |
| G | Accounting | 20.2 + | 4.7 | 2.8 | 9.4 |
| H | Supervisors | 15.7 | 4.3 | 7.9 | 7.1 |
| I | Managers | 14.3 | 3.7 | 2.5 | 11.2 |
| J | Executives | 16.4 | 1.5 | 4.5 | 20.9 + |

Note: Numbers preceding bar graphs represent the percent of the sample falling in that type.

If percentage exceeds 20%, a + follows the bar. Data summarized from published and unpublished sources described in the text.

# TABLE 2
## Myers-Briggs Type Indicator Percentages
## for Managers in Business and Industry
## in Japan, England, & Latin America

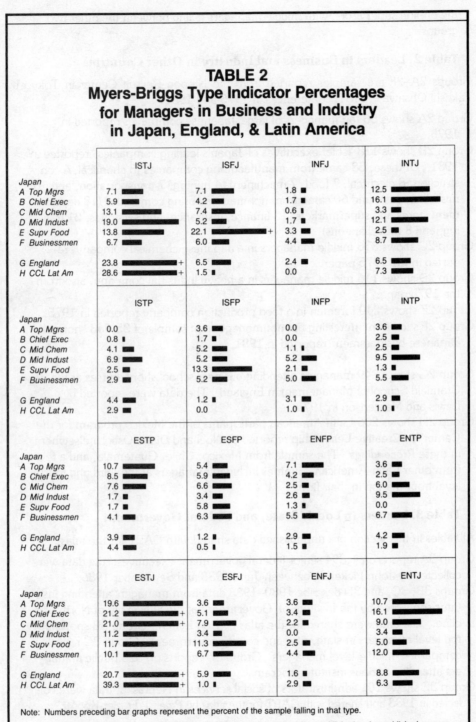

| | ISTJ | ISFJ | INFJ | INTJ |
|---|---|---|---|---|
| **Japan** | | | | |
| A Top Mgrs | 7.1 | 7.1 | 1.8 | 12.5 |
| B Chief Exec | 5.9 | 4.2 | 1.7 | 16.1 |
| C Mid Chem | 13.1 | 7.4 | 0.6 | 3.3 |
| D Mid Indust | 19.0 | 5.2 | 1.7 | 12.1 |
| E Supv Food | 13.8 | 22.1 + | 3.3 | 2.5 |
| F Businessmen | 6.7 | 6.0 | 4.4 | 8.7 |
| G England | 23.8 + | 6.5 | 2.4 | 6.5 |
| H CCL Lat Am | 28.6 + | 1.5 | 0.0 | 7.3 |

| | ISTP | ISFP | INFP | INTP |
|---|---|---|---|---|
| **Japan** | | | | |
| A Top Mgrs | 0.0 | 3.6 | 0.0 | 3.6 |
| B Chief Exec | 0.8 | 1.7 | 0.0 | 2.5 |
| C Mid Chem | 4.1 | 5.2 | 1.1 | 2.5 |
| D Mid Indust | 6.9 | 5.2 | 5.2 | 9.5 |
| E Supv Food | 2.5 | 13.3 | 2.1 | 1.3 |
| F Businessmen | 2.9 | 5.2 | 5.0 | 5.5 |
| G England | 4.4 | 1.2 | 3.1 | 2.9 |
| H CCL Lat Am | 2.9 | 0.0 | 1.0 | 1.0 |

| | ESTP | ESFP | ENFP | ENTP |
|---|---|---|---|---|
| **Japan** | | | | |
| A Top Mgrs | 10.7 | 5.4 | 7.1 | 3.6 |
| B Chief Exec | 8.5 | 5.9 | 4.2 | 2.5 |
| C Mid Chem | 7.6 | 6.6 | 2.5 | 6.0 |
| D Mid Indust | 1.7 | 3.4 | 2.6 | 9.5 |
| E Supv Food | 1.7 | 5.8 | 1.3 | 0.0 |
| F Businessmen | 4.1 | 6.3 | 5.5 | 6.7 |
| G England | 3.9 | 1.2 | 2.9 | 4.2 |
| H CCL Lat Am | 4.4 | 0.5 | 1.5 | 1.9 |

| | ESTJ | ESFJ | ENFJ | ENTJ |
|---|---|---|---|---|
| **Japan** | | | | |
| A Top Mgrs | 19.6 | 3.6 | 3.6 | 10.7 |
| B Chief Exec | 21.2 + | 5.1 | 3.4 | 16.1 |
| C Mid Chem | 21.0 + | 7.9 | 2.2 | 9.0 |
| D Mid Indust | 11.2 | 3.4 | 0.0 | 3.4 |
| E Supv Food | 11.7 | 11.3 | 2.5 | 5.0 |
| F Businessmen | 10.1 | 6.7 | 4.4 | 12.0 |
| G England | 20.7 + | 5.9 | 1.6 | 8.8 |
| H CCL Lat Am | 39.3 + | 1.0 | 2.9 | 6.3 |

Note: Numbers preceding bar graphs represent the percent of the sample falling in that type.

If percentage exceeds 20%, a + follows the bar. Data summarized from published and unpublished sources described in the text.

the on-line supervisors, with middle managers falling between the other two groups.

## Table 2. Leaders in Business and Industry in Other Countries

Groups 2A–2F are samples reported from the Nippon Recruit Center in Tokyo by Takeshi Ohsawa in MBTI conferences in 1975 and 1981.

Group 2A shows 56 top managers of large Japanese companies reported in 1975.

Group 2B shows 118 "chief executives of Japan's leading companies" reported in 1981. Of these, 58 came from manufacturing companies (5 chemical, 4 construction, 8 electrical, 7 food, 7 machinery, 4 mining, 7 transportation, and 16 miscellaneous), and 60 came from nonmanufacturing companies (18 department stores and supermarkets; 13 finance, insurance, and securities; 21 trading; and 8 miscellaneous).

Group 2C shows 336 middle managers in a Japanese chemical company, reported in the 1975 paper.

Group 2D shows 116 middle managers in a heavy industrial company, also from the 1975 paper.

Group 2E shows 240 foremen in a food production company reported in 1975.

Group 2F shows an interesting but nonmanagement sample of 35,663 "normal Japanese businessmen" reported in 1981.

Group 2G shows 849 managers attending business school short courses at the Cranfield School of Management in England. The data were reported by Lewis and Margerison in 1979.

Group 2H shows 206 Latin American participants of the Mexico program for the Center for Creative Leadership reported by Noel and Diana Osborn elsewhere in these *Proceedings*. The sample from Mexico, Chile, Guatemala, and a few from other Latin-American countries included managers at the third and fourth level from the top in their firms.

## Table 3. Leaders in Local, State, and Federal Government

All tables in this section are unpublished data shared with CAPT for the atlas.

Group 3A reports on 1,394 senior federal government executives; the data were collected by John Pickering between June 1983 and September 1986.

Groups 3B, 3C, and 3D describe 1980–1983 data from managers attending institutes sponsored by the Institute of Government at the University of North Carolina. The data were shared for the atlas by Ron Lynch. Group 3B shows 257 top level managers in state, city, and county government. Group 3C reports comparable middle-level managers. Group 3D reports on 523 public managers attending various institute programs.

Group 3E shows 101 administrators of social services in Nebraska; data were collected in 1983 and shared with CAPT for the atlas by Peter J. Frazier-Koontz.

## Table 4. Participants in Programs of the Center for Creative Leadership

Table 4 shows largely unpublished data shared with CAPT by the Center for Creative Leadership. Data describe participants in CCL leadership programs. The typical

## TABLE 3
## Myers-Briggs Type Indicator Percentages
## for Managers in Federal, State, and Local Government

| | ISTJ | ISFJ | INFJ | INTJ |
|---|---|---|---|---|
| *Federal*<br>A Senior | 26.3 + | 2.7 | 1.8 | 14.9 |
| *State—City*<br>B Top Level | 30.7 + | 6.2 | 2.0 | 7.4 |
| C Midlevel | 17.9 | 9.7 | 0.7 | 5.9 |
| D Public | 26.4 + | 5.5 | 1.5 | 5.5 |
| E Soc Serv | 16.8 | 19.8 | 1.0 | 2.0 |

| | ISTP | ISFP | INFP | INTP |
|---|---|---|---|---|
| *Federal*<br>A Senior | 5.4 | 0.4 | 2.4 | 9.1 |
| *State—City*<br>B Top Level | 4.7 | 1.6 | 1.2 | 3.9 |
| C Midlevel | 3.1 | 3.1 | 1.7 | 2.1 |
| D Public | 4.8 | 1.9 | 1.5 | 2.9 |
| E Soc Serv | 5.0 | 3.0 | 2.0 | 4.0 |

| | ESTP | ESFP | ENFP | ENTP |
|---|---|---|---|---|
| *Federal*<br>A Senior | 2.0 | 0.6 | 2.4 | 5.8 |
| *State—City*<br>B Top Level | 1.6 | 1.6 | 2.0 | 1.6 |
| C Midlevel | 5.5 | 2.1 | 2.4 | 3.8 |
| D Public | 2.7 | 1.9 | 3.4 | 2.7 |
| E Soc Serv | 3.0 | 2.0 | 1.0 | 2.0 |

| | ESTJ | ESFJ | ENFJ | ENTJ |
|---|---|---|---|---|
| *Federal*<br>A Senior | 12.3 | 1.4 | 1.9 | 10.6 |
| *State—City*<br>B Top Level | 22.2 + | 3.9 | 2.7 | 7.0 |
| C Midlevel | 24.1 + | 6.2 | 3.1 | 8.6 |
| D Public | 22.8 + | 7.1 | 2.5 | 6.9 |
| E Soc Serv | 19.8 | 10.9 | 5.0 | 3.0 |

Note: Numbers preceding bar graphs represent the percent of the sample falling in that type.

If percentage exceeds 20%, a + follows the bar. Data summarized from published and unpublished sources described in the text.

# TABLE 4
## Myers-Briggs Type Indicator Percentages for Participants in Center for Creative Leadership Programs—1979–84

| | ISTJ | ISFJ | INFJ | INTJ |
|---|---|---|---|---|
| A 74–78 | 14.0 | 2.9 | 2.8 | 10.8 |
| B 79–82 | 21.3 + | 1.9 | 1.3 | 11.3 |
| C Males | 23.7 + | 1.7 | 1.2 | 11.6 |
| D Females | 7.2 | 2.8 | 1.7 | 9.4 |
| E Top Exec | 24.3 + | 0.0 | 0.7 | 11.0 |
| F Rank High | 17.8 | 2.4 | 0.6 | 10.4 |
| G Rank Low | 31.4 + | 1.6 | 0.4 | 12.2 |
| H Lat America | 28.6 + | 1.5 | 0.0 | 7.3 |

| | ISTP | ISFP | INFP | INTP |
|---|---|---|---|---|
| A 74–78 | 1.8 | 0.7 | 3.0 | 7.1 |
| B 79–82 | 4.1 | 0.7 | 2.6 | 5.6 |
| C Males | 4.3 | 0.7 | 2.3 | 5.3 |
| D Females | 2.8 | 1.1 | 4.4 | 7.2 |
| E Top Exec | 4.4 | 0.7 | 2.2 | 2.9 |
| F Rank High | 1.8 | 0.6 | 2.4 | 7.4 |
| G Rank Low | 6.7 | 0.8 | 2.4 | 5.9 |
| H Lat America | 2.9 | 0.0 | 1.0 | 1.0 |

| | ESTP | ESFP | ENFP | ENTP |
|---|---|---|---|---|
| A 74–78 | 3.2 | 0.9 | 6.1 | 10.0 |
| B 79–82 | 3.2 | 0.8 | 5.1 | 6.9 |
| C Males | 3.0 | 1.0 | 3.1 | 6.3 |
| D Females | 3.9 | 0.0 | 16.6 | 10.5 |
| E Top Exec | 2.9 | 2.9 | 0.7 | 8.1 |
| F Rank High | 3.7 | 0.0 | 5.5 | 8.0 |
| G Rank Low | 3.9 | 1.2 | 5.1 | 2.8 |
| H Lat America | 4.4 | 0.5 | 1.5 | 1.9 |

| | ESTJ | ESFJ | ENFJ | ENTJ |
|---|---|---|---|---|
| A 74–78 | 16.1 | 2.6 | 4.5 | 13.5 |
| B 79–82 | 17.1 | 3.2 | 1.9 | 13.1 |
| C Males | 18.6 | 3.0 | 1.2 | 12.8 |
| D Females | 8.3 | 3.9 | 6.1 | 14.4 |
| E Top Exec | 19.8 | 2.2 | 0.7 | 16.2 |
| F Rank High | 15.3 | 4.3 | 3.7 | 16.0 |
| G Rank Low | 14.5 | 2.0 | 2.0 | 7.4 |
| H Lat America | 39.3 + | 1.0 | 2.9 | 6.3 |

Note: Numbers preceding bar graphs represent the percent of the sample falling in that type.

If percentage exceeds 20%, a + follows the bar. Data summarized from published and unpublished sources described in the text.

participant is a male in his forties, in upper to middle management in business and industry. Women who participate in CCL programs tend to come from middle- to lower-level management, nonmanagement, and/or the professions.

Group 4A shows the type distribution of 997 participants in CCL seven-day modular programs from 1974–1978, reported by Douglas Mills.

Group 4B shows 1,232 CCL Leadership Development Program (LDP) participants from January 1979 through December 1982 reported by Ellen Van Velsor.

Groups 4C and 4D show the subsamples of 4B for the 1,051 males and 139 females respectively.

Group 4E shows a subsample of 136 "high-level corporate executives" made up of presidents, vice-presidents, or chief executive officers in business or industrial organizations of more than ten employees.

Group 4F is the subsample of 163 executives ranked first or second by trained observers, by their peers, and by themselves, in a competitive leaderless group discussion during the behavioral assessment portion of the LDP.

Group 4G shows another subsample of 255 executives ranked fourth, fifth, or sixth (in groups of five or six) in the same LDP exercise.

Group 4H repeats the Osborn and Osborn CCL Latin American sample also shown in Table 2 as Group 2H.

### Table 5. Consultants to Organizations

This table was prepared to look at the question, "Are consultants to leaders different from those leaders, or are consultants of the types with similar strengths and blind spots?"

Group 5A shows 111 Canadian consultants who volunteered from firms in the Canadian Association of Management Consultants. Wade (1981) collected the data in 1980 and made them available for the atlas.

Group 5B shows 71 officers and principals of an international consulting firm. The unpublished data were collected by Mary McCaulley in 1984 and reported with permission in the atlas.

Group 5C shows 192 people coded "consultants" from self-descriptions on MBTI answer sheets in the CAPT MBTI Data Bank. The data appear in the atlas.

Group 5D shows 89 people coded "management analyst" in the CAPT MBTI Data Bank.

Group 5E was included to show the contrast with business consultants in a small sample of 54 consultants coded as "educational consultants" in the Data Bank. The data appear in the atlas.

Group 5F shows 108 members of the New York City Human Resources Planners Association. These unpublished data were collected in 1982 by Randall Ruppart and Nancy Hutchens, and are reported with permission in the atlas.

### Table 6. Leaders in Schools, Colleges, and Universities

This summary was designed to show that education, which has more feeling types among teachers, also has among its administrators more feeling types than are found in business, industry, and government.

Group 6A shows 1,024 elementary and secondary school administrators in the Data Bank, and reported in the atlas.

# TABLE 5
## Myers-Briggs Type Indicator Percentages
### for Consultants to Organizations

| | ISTJ | ISFJ | INFJ | INTJ |
|---|---|---|---|---|
| A Canadian | 20.7 + | 0.0 | 0.0 | 16.2 |
| B US Internat | 15.5 | 1.4 | 1.4 | 15.5 |
| C DB Consult | 9.4 | 4.2 | 5.2 | 6.2 |
| D DB Mgmt Anal | 13.5 | 4.5 | 6.7 | 7.9 |
| E DB Education | 13.0 | 3.7 | 14.8 | 7.4 |
| F NYC Hum Res | 11.1 | 0.9 | 3.7 | 14.8 |

| | ISTP | ISFP | INFP | INTP |
|---|---|---|---|---|
| A Canadian | 4.5 | 0.0 | 1.8 | 15.3 |
| B US Internat | 1.4 | 1.4 | 0.0 | 5.6 |
| C DB Consult | 1.6 | 1.6 | 6.2 | 3.6 |
| D DB Mgmt Anal | 3.4 | 2.2 | 7.9 | 2.2 |
| E DB Education | 0.0 | 3.7 | 13.0 | 0.0 |
| F NYC Hum Res | 2.8 | 0.9 | 0.9 | 4.6 |

| | ESTP | ESFP | ENFP | ENTP |
|---|---|---|---|---|
| A Canadian | 2.7 | 0.9 | 1.8 | 4.5 |
| B US Internat | 1.4 | 0.0 | 1.4 | 8.4 |
| C DB Consult | 3.6 | 1.6 | 11.5 | 8.3 |
| D DB Mgmt Anal | 0.0 | 0.0 | 12.4 | 7.9 |
| E DB Education | 0.0 | 1.8 | 14.8 | 3.7 |
| F NYC Hum Res | 1.8 | 0.0 | 12.0 | 6.5 |

| | ESTJ | ESFJ | ENFJ | ENTJ |
|---|---|---|---|---|
| A Canadian | 11.7 | 0.0 | 0.0 | 19.8 |
| B US Internat | 21.1 + | 0.0 | 2.8 | 22.5 + |
| C DB Consult | 8.3 | 4.7 | 11.5 | 12.5 |
| D DB Mgmt Anal | 11.2 | 4.5 | 6.7 | 9.0 |
| E DB Education | 1.8 | 7.4 | 1.8 | 13.0 |
| F NYC Hum Res | 4.6 | 7.4 | 7.4 | 20.4 + |

Note: Numbers preceding bar graphs represent the percent of the sample falling in that type.

If percentage exceeds 20%, a + follows the bar. Data summarized from published and unpublished sources described in the text.

# TABLE 6
## Myers-Briggs Type Indicator Percentages for Administrators in Schools, Colleges, and Universities

| | ISTJ | ISFJ | INFJ | INTJ |
|---|---|---|---|---|
| **Grades K–12** | | | | |
| A DB Elem—Sec | 12.5 | 7.4 | 3.9 | 5.3 |
| B Principals | 25.4 + | 4.7 | 2.2 | 8.7 |
| C Canada Adm | 11.3 | 9.7 | 7.3 | 8.1 |
| D Top Leaders | 9.6 | 3.6 | 4.8 | 8.4 |
| E Fut Leaders | 9.0 | 0.0 | 3.4 | 6.7 |
| **College—Univ** | | | | |
| F DB Coll—Un | 10.3 | 5.3 | 7.0 | 8.5 |
| G Stud't Pers | 11.8 | 5.9 | 3.9 | 7.8 |
| H DB Educ Adm | 13.2 | 6.5 | 4.4 | 6.9 |
| I Danforth Fac | 7.9 | 4.3 | 10.2 | 18.6 |

| | ISTP | ISFP | INFP | INTP |
|---|---|---|---|---|
| **Grades K–12** | | | | |
| A DB Elem—Sec | 1.5 | 2.6 | 5.4 | 2.5 |
| B Principals | 2.5 | 2.5 | 1.1 | 1.1 |
| C Canada Adm | 0.0 | 0.8 | 2.4 | 0.8 |
| D Top Leaders | 0.0 | 1.2 | 3.6 | 1.2 |
| E Fut Leaders | 0.0 | 0.0 | 0.0 | 3.4 |
| **College—Univ** | | | | |
| F DB Coll—Un | 1.8 | 0.6 | 6.4 | 5.3 |
| G Stud't Pers | 0.0 | 0.0 | 7.8 | 2.0 |
| H DB Educ Adm | 1.7 | 2.0 | 5.9 | 3.3 |
| I Danforth Fac | 1.3 | 1.1 | 7.1 | 6.1 |

| | ESTP | ESFP | ENFP | ENTP |
|---|---|---|---|---|
| **Grades K–12** | | | | |
| A DB Elem—Sec | 2.4 | 2.7 | 9.3 | 3.7 |
| B Principals | 2.2 | 1.8 | 2.2 | 1.4 |
| C Canada Adm | 0.8 | 2.4 | 4.8 | 1.6 |
| D Top Leaders | 1.2 | 0.0 | 8.4 | 9.6 |
| E Fut Leaders | 0.0 | 0.0 | 13.5 | 3.4 |
| **College—Univ** | | | | |
| F DB Coll—Un | 2.4 | 2.4 | 9.4 | 4.1 |
| G Stud't Pers | 0.0 | 0.0 | 15.7 | 5.9 |
| H DB Educ Adm | 2.2 | 2.6 | 8.9 | 3.8 |
| I Danforth Fac | 0.4 | 1.3 | 7.7 | 5.1 |

| | ESTJ | ESFJ | ENFJ | ENTJ |
|---|---|---|---|---|
| **Grades K–12** | | | | |
| A DB Elem—Sec | 13.2 | 10.6 | 8.4 | 8.6 |
| B Principals | 26.1 + | 5.4 | 2.5 | 10.1 |
| C Canada Adm | 21.8 + | 12.1 | 5.6 | 10.5 |
| D Top Leaders | 8.4 | 4.8 | 13.2 | 21.7 + |
| E Fut Leaders | 19.1 | 2.2 | 15.7 | 23.6 + |
| **College—Univ** | | | | |
| F DB Coll—Un | 10.0 | 5.3 | 7.0 | 14.4 |
| G Stud't Pers | 3.9 | 17.6 | 7.8 | 9.8 |
| H DB Educ Adm | 12.7 | 8.2 | 7.4 | 10.2 |
| I Danforth Fac | 4.1 | 4.0 | 7.5 | 13.3 |

Note: Numbers preceding bar graphs represent the percent of the sample falling in that type.

If percentage exceeds 20%, a + follows the bar. Data summarized from published and unpublished sources described in the text.

Group 6B shows 276 school principals who attended programs of the Institute of Government at the University of North Carolina from 1984–1986. Ron Lynch shared these otherwise-unpublished data for the atlas.

Group 6C shows 58 school principals and 66 superintendents tested in Canada by Erich von Fange in 1960 and reported in his dissertation in 1961. They appear in the atlas.

Group 6D shows 83 volunteers from a list of "100 Top Executive Educators" appearing in *The Executive Educator* (February 1984, pp. 15-17). The executive educators of the sample included 63 males and 27 females, mainly superintendents but also assistant superintendents, directors, and principals. Groups 6D and 6E were reported by Donald Lueder (1986a, 1986b).

Group 6E shows 89 "rising stars" in education from a list of "100 Executive Educators to Watch" in *The Executive Educator* (Spring of 1985). Of the 100, 39 of the 44 women and 50 of the 56 men responded to an offer to take the MBTI. Rising stars had 31% superintendents, 17% assistant or associate superintendents, 22% directors, and 30% principals.

Group 6F shows 341 administrators in technical schools, colleges, and universities from the CAPT Data Bank, and reported in the atlas.

Group 6G shows 51 student personnel administrators from 22 colleges and universities in Virginia. The unpublished data were collected in 1983 by David Robertson and appear in the atlas.

Group 6H is a composite of 1,857 educational administrators at all educational levels, from the CAPT Data Bank, and reported in the atlas.

Group 6I shows college and university faculty, *not* in administrative posts, but nominated as Danforth Associates because of excellence in scholarship and student development. They were introduced to the MBTI as a tool for student-faculty understanding at biennial regional meetings of Associates. The unpublished data are in the *MBTI Atlas*.

### Table 7. Managers in Public Safety

Group 7A are 105 persons who described themselves as police supervisors on MBTI answer sheets. Data are from the MBTI Data Bank and are reported in the atlas.

Group 7B are 92 police supervisors in a large southeastern urban community. Data were collected in the late 1970s by Wayne Hanewicz (1978). They appear in the atlas.

Group 7C are 912 police managers from the southeastern United States who attended institutes at the University of North Carolina Institute of Government. The unpublished data were reported by Ron Lynch and appear in the atlas.

Group 7D are 57 police commanders from the same programs.

Group 7E are 99 police attending senior officers' courses at the Australian Police College. Data were collected at the Australian Police College in 1978–80 by Ron Cacioppe and appear in the atlas.

Group 7F are 60 fire managers attending the University of North Carolina institutes. Data were collected by Ron Lynch from 1980 to 1986 and are included in the atlas.

# TABLE 7
## Myers-Briggs Type Indicator Percentages
## for Managers in Public Safety

| | ISTJ | ISFJ | INFJ | INTJ |
|---|---|---|---|---|
| **Police** | | | | |
| A DB Supv | 21.9 + | 10.5 | 1.9 | 2.9 |
| B Urban Supv | 14.1 | 10.9 | 0.0 | 3.3 |
| C SE Supv | 32.9 + | 4.4 | 0.7 | 4.5 |
| D SE Comm'drs | 35.1 + | 7.0 | 0.0 | 5.3 |
| E Australia | 25.2 + | 15.2 | 2.0 | 1.0 |
| **Fire** | | | | |
| F SE Mgrs | 15.0 | 10.0 | 0.0 | 1.7 |

| | ISTP | ISFP | INFP | INTP |
|---|---|---|---|---|
| **Police** | | | | |
| A DB Supv | 4.8 | 1.9 | 6.7 | 1.9 |
| B Urban Supv | 4.4 | 3.3 | 1.1 | 0.0 |
| C SE Supv | 5.4 | 1.4 | 0.6 | 2.3 |
| D SE Comm'drs | 3.5 | 1.8 | 0.0 | 1.8 |
| E Australia | 3.0 | 2.0 | 1.0 | 1.0 |
| **Fire** | | | | |
| F SE Mgrs | 5.0 | 6.7 | 0.0 | 0.0 |

| | ESTP | ESFP | ENFP | ENTP |
|---|---|---|---|---|
| **Police** | | | | |
| A DB Supv | 5.7 | 3.8 | 3.8 | 1.9 |
| B Urban Supv | 7.6 | 7.6 | 2.7 | 5.4 |
| C SE Supv | 2.4 | 1.4 | 2.2 | 2.2 |
| D SE Comm'drs | 1.8 | 0.0 | 3.5 | 3.5 |
| E Australia | 2.0 | 3.0 | 2.0 | 0.0 |
| **Fire** | | | | |
| F SE Mgrs | 6.7 | 5.0 | 3.3 | 5.0 |

| | ESTJ | ESFJ | ENFJ | ENTJ |
|---|---|---|---|---|
| **Police** | | | | |
| A DB Supv | 19.0 | 4.8 | 2.9 | 5.7 |
| B Urban Supv | 29.4 + | 1.1 | 2.2 | 6.5 |
| C SE Supv | 26.6 + | 3.7 | 1.6 | 7.1 |
| D SE Comm'drs | 24.6 + | 1.8 | 3.5 | 7.0 |
| E Australia | 25.2 + | 11.1 | 2.0 | 4.0 |
| **Fire** | | | | |
| F SE Mgrs | 36.7 + | 1.7 | 1.7 | 1.7 |

Note: Numbers preceding bar graphs represent the percent of the sample falling in that type.

If percentage exceeds 20%, a + follows the bar. Data summarized from published and unpublished sources described in the text.

# TABLE 8
## Myers-Briggs Type Indicator Percentages
## for High School and College Student Leaders

| | ISTJ | ISFJ | INFJ | INTJ |
|---|---|---|---|---|
| **High School** | | | | |
| A SE Gifted | 7.9 | 4.3 | 1.8 | 5.5 |
| B NE Red Cross | 9.8 | 4.9 | 3.3 | 4.1 |
| **Junior College** | | | | |
| C SE Stu Govt | 4.9 | 2.7 | 4.0 | 0.9 |
| **College** | | | | |
| D SE PA Ldrs | 3.6 | 0.0 | 1.8 | 5.4 |
| E NE Female | 0.0 | 6.0 | 0.0 | 0.0 |
| F NE Female | 6.0 | 8.0 | 2.0 | 4.0 |

| | ISTP | ISFP | INFP | INTP |
|---|---|---|---|---|
| **High School** | | | | |
| A SE Gifted | 2.4 | 4.3 | 6.7 | 15.2 |
| B NE Red Cross | 4.1 | 3.3 | 8.2 | 0.8 |
| **Junior College** | | | | |
| C SE Stu Govt | 3.6 | 1.3 | 3.6 | 2.7 |
| **College** | | | | |
| D SE PA Ldrs | 0.0 | 0.0 | 1.8 | 3.6 |
| E NE Female | 2.0 | 2.0 | 4.0 | 2.0 |
| F NE Female | 0.0 | 6.0 | 4.0 | 4.0 |

| | ESTP | ESFP | ENFP | ENTP |
|---|---|---|---|---|
| **High School** | | | | |
| A SE Gifted | 1.2 | 4.3 | 16.5 | 9.8 |
| B NE Red Cross | 2.5 | 5.7 | 13.1 | 7.4 |
| **Junior College** | | | | |
| C SE Stu Govt | 3.6 | 5.8 | 12.0 | 8.0 |
| **College** | | | | |
| D SE PA Ldrs | 5.4 | 0.0 | 5.4 | 7.3 |
| E NE Female | 4.0 | 4.0 | 12.0 | 6.0 |
| F NE Female | 4.0 | 8.0 | 22.0 + | 0.0 |

| | ESTJ | ESFJ | ENFJ | ENTJ |
|---|---|---|---|---|
| **High School** | | | | |
| A SE Gifted | 3.0 | 5.5 | 5.5 | 6.1 |
| B NE Red Cross | 15.6 | 4.9 | 10.7 | 1.6 |
| **Junior College** | | | | |
| C SE Stu Govt | 20.9 + | 7.1 | 3.6 | 15.6 |
| **College** | | | | |
| D SE PA Ldrs | 27.3 + | 9.1 | 10.9 | 18.2 |
| E NE Female | 14.0 | 14.0 | 18.0 | 10.0 |
| F NE Female | 10.0 | 12.0 | 6.0 | 4.0 |

Note: Numbers preceding bar graphs represent the percent of the sample falling in that type.

If percentage exceeds 20%, a + follows the bar. Data summarized from published and unpublished sources described in the text.

## Table 8. High School and College Student Leaders

These summaries are included to permit comparison of the adults now in leadership positions (Tables 1 to 7) with the next generation.

Group 8A are 164 gifted Florida high school seniors (48% male, 52% female) participating in an internship in community leadership and development. The unpublished data were collected by Carol Clark, Barbara Cloud, and Gerald Macdaid during 1981 through 1986 and appear in the atlas.

Group 8B are 122 high school student leaders (30% male, 70% female) who held leadership positions in Red Cross activities and organizations in Pennsylvania, New York, and Maryland. The unpublished data were collected in 1982 and 1983 by Charlotte Jacobsen and appear in the atlas.

Group 8C are 225 community college students (44% male, 56% female) from Florida who were active in student government. The unpublished data were collected by Alice Hadwin in 1983 and appear in the atlas.

Group 8D are 55 college students (45% male, 55% female) who held leadership positions in southeastern Pennsylvania colleges and universities. The unpublished data were collected at a student leadership conference in 1984 by Charlotte Jacobsen and appear in the atlas.

Group 8E are 50 female college students elected to positions in student government in a Pennsylvania women's college. The unpublished data were collected by Charlotte Jacobsen in 1982 and 1983, and appear in the atlas.

Group 8F are 50 elected leaders in student government, student academic groups, or social groups at a female liberal arts college in Boston. The unpublished data were collected in 1988 and 1989 by Joan Wofford and are included with permission.

## Tables 9A and 9B. Normative Samples of College Students

Two tables are presented to provide a basis for comparing the type distributions of Tables 1–8. These tables are in the standard format used in the *MBTI Atlas*.

Table 9A is a composite of 14,138 MBTI Data Bank samples of male college students. The composite is made up of 12,637 "traditional-age" college students between the ages of 18 and 25 when they answered the MBTI, and 1,501 "nontraditional" college students 25 years of age and older.

Table 9B is a composite of 18,070 MBTI Data Bank samples of female college students. The composite is made up of 14,519 "traditional-age" college students between the ages of 18 and 25 when they answered the MBTI, and 3,551 "nontraditional" college students 25 years of age and older.

## Table 10. The Pattern of Type Distribution for Educators

Table 10 summarizes data from the Data Bank for teachers at different levels of education. This table has two purposes. First, it demonstrates that there are samples with many more feeling types and different patterns from the "leadership" samples of earlier tables. It is designed to break any mental sets that the reader may have formed from the overrepresentation of TJ in Tables 1–7. Second, it lets the reader estimate the probabilities that leaders of any type had a "kindred spirit" among teachers as they progressed through school.

# TABLE 9A
## Male College Students
## N = 14,138

| | SENSING | | INTUITION | |
|---|---|---|---|---|
| | THINKING | FEELING | FEELING | THINKING |

| ISTJ | ISFJ | INFJ | INTJ |
|---|---|---|---|
| N = 1,852 | N = 757 | N = 371 | N = 809 |
| % = 13.10 | % = 5.35 | % = 2.62 | % = 5.72 |

| ISTP | ISFP | INFP | INTP |
|---|---|---|---|
| N = 960 | N = 558 | N = 746 | N = 953 |
| % = 6.79 | % = 3.95 | % = 5.28 | % = 6.74 |

| ESTP | ESFP | ENFP | ENTP |
|---|---|---|---|
| N = 892 | N = 587 | N = 854 | N = 938 |
| % = 6.31 | % = 4.15 | % = 6.04 | % = 6.63 |

| ESTJ | ESFJ | ENFJ | ENTJ |
|---|---|---|---|
| N = 1,838 | N = 770 | N = 420 | N = 833 |
| % = 13.00 | % = 5.45 | % = 2.97 | % = 5.89 |

JUDGMENT — INTROVERSION — PERCEPTION — PERCEPTION — EXTRAVERSION — JUDGMENT

| | N | % |
|---|---|---|
| E | 7,132 | 50.45 |
| I | 7,006 | 49.55 |
| S | 8,214 | 58.10 |
| N | 5,924 | 41.90 |
| T | 9,075 | 64.19 |
| F | 5,063 | 35.81 |
| J | 7,650 | 54.11 |
| P | 6,488 | 45.89 |
| I J | 3,789 | 26.80 |
| I P | 3,217 | 22.75 |
| E P | 3,271 | 23.14 |
| E J | 3,861 | 27.31 |
| S T | 5,542 | 39.20 |
| S F | 2,672 | 18.90 |
| N F | 2,391 | 16.91 |
| N T | 3,533 | 24.99 |
| S J | 5,217 | 36.90 |
| S P | 2,997 | 21.20 |
| N P | 3,491 | 24.69 |
| N J | 2,433 | 17.21 |
| T J | 5,332 | 37.71 |
| T P | 3,743 | 26.47 |
| F P | 2,745 | 19.42 |
| F J | 2,318 | 16.40 |
| I N | 2,879 | 20.36 |
| E N | 3,045 | 21.54 |
| I S | 4,127 | 29.19 |
| E S | 4,087 | 28.91 |
| E T | 4,501 | 31.84 |
| E F | 2,631 | 18.61 |
| I F | 2,432 | 17.20 |
| I T | 4,574 | 32.35 |
| S dom | 4,088 | 28.91 |
| N dom | 2,972 | 21.02 |
| T dom | 4,584 | 32.42 |
| F dom | 2,494 | 17.64 |

Note: ■ = 1% of sample

ccl

This table is one of a series of tables from the CAPT-MBTI Data Bank of MBTI records submitted to CAPT for computer scoring between 1971 and June 1984. This sample was drawn from 59,784 records with usable occupational codes from the total data bank of 232,557. This data bank has 51% Form F cases from 1971 to March 1978, 35% Form F cases from 1978 to June 1984, and 14% Form G cases from 1978 to December 1982. An analysis of Form F and G data banks showed the data banks were comprised of 56% females and 44% males; education level completed: 6% some grade school, 30% high school diploma, 25% some college, 18% bachelor degrees, 11% masters degrees, 3% doctoral or postdoctoral work, and 6% unknown. Age group percentages were: 11% under 18, 29% 18 to 20, 12% 21 to 24, 10% 25 to 29, 16% 30 to 39, 10% 40 to 49, 5% 50 to 59, 2% 60 plus, and 5% unknown.

# TABLE 9B
## Female College Students
## N = 18,070

| | SENSING | | INTUITION | | | | N | % |
|---|---|---|---|---|---|---|---|---|
| | THINKING | FEELING | FEELING | THINKING | | | | |

| ISTJ | ISFJ | INFJ | INTJ | | E | 10,459 | 57.88 |
|---|---|---|---|---|---|---|---|
| N = 1,375 | N = 2,125 | N = 723 | N = 440 | | I | 7,611 | 42.12 |
| % = 7.61 | % = 11.76 | % = 4.00 | % = 2.43 | | S | 11,094 | 61.39 |
| ▪▪▪▪▪▪▪▪ | ▪▪▪▪▪▪▪▪▪▪▪ | ▪▪▪▪ | ▪▪ | | N | 6,976 | 38.61 |
| | ▪▪ | | | | T | 6,041 | 33.43 |
| | | | | | F | 12,029 | 66.57 |
| | | | | | J | 10,626 | 58.80 |
| | | | | | P | 7,444 | 41.20 |

| | | | | | I J | 4,663 | 25.81 |
|---|---|---|---|---|---|---|---|
| ISTP | ISFP | INFP | INTP | | I P | 2,948 | 16.31 |
| N = 467 | N = 1,052 | N = 1,020 | N = 409 | | E P | 4,496 | 24.88 |
| % = 2.58 | % = 5.82 | % = 5.64 | % = 2.26 | | E J | 5,963 | 33.00 |
| ▪▪▪ | ▪▪▪▪▪▪ | ▪▪▪▪▪▪ | ▪▪ | | | | |
| | | | | | ST | 3,949 | 21.85 |
| | | | | | SF | 7,145 | 39.54 |
| | | | | | NF | 4,884 | 27.03 |
| | | | | | NT | 2,092 | 11.58 |

| | | | | | SJ | 7,719 | 42.72 |
|---|---|---|---|---|---|---|---|
| ESTP | ESFP | ENFP | ENTP | | SP | 3,375 | 18.68 |
| N = 488 | N = 1,368 | N = 2,014 | N = 626 | | NP | 4,069 | 22.52 |
| % = 2.70 | % = 7.57 | % = 11.15 | % = 3.46 | | NJ | 2,907 | 16.09 |
| ▪▪▪ | ▪▪▪▪▪▪▪▪ | ▪▪▪▪▪▪▪▪▪▪▪ | ▪▪▪ | | | | |
| | | ▪ | | | TJ | 4,051 | 22.42 |
| | | | | | TP | 1,990 | 11.01 |
| | | | | | FP | 5,454 | 30.18 |
| | | | | | FJ | 6,575 | 36.39 |

| | | | | | I N | 2,592 | 14.34 |
|---|---|---|---|---|---|---|---|
| ESTJ | ESFJ | ENFJ | ENTJ | | E N | 4,384 | 24.26 |
| N = 1,619 | N = 2,600 | N = 1,127 | N = 617 | | I S | 5,019 | 27.78 |
| % = 8.96 | % = 14.39 | % = 6.24 | % = 3.41 | | E S | 6,075 | 33.62 |
| ▪▪▪▪▪▪▪▪▪ | ▪▪▪▪▪▪▪▪▪▪▪ | ▪▪▪▪▪▪ | ▪▪▪ | | | | |
| | ▪▪▪▪ | | | | ET | 3,350 | 18.54 |
| | | | | | EF | 7,109 | 39.34 |
| | | | | | I F | 4,920 | 27.23 |
| | | | | | I T | 2,691 | 14.89 |
| | | | | | S dom | 5,356 | 29.64 |
| | | | | | N dom | 3,803 | 21.05 |
| | | | | | T dom | 3,112 | 17.22 |
| | | | | | F dom | 5,799 | 32.09 |

Note: ▪ = 1% of sample                    ccl

This table is one of a series of tables from the CAPT-MBTI Data Bank of MBTI records submitted to CAPT for computer scoring between 1971 and June 1984. This sample was drawn from 59,784 records with usable occupational codes from the total data bank of 232,557. This data bank has 51% Form F cases from 1971 to March 1978, 35% Form F cases from 1978 to June 1984, and 14% Form G cases from 1978 to December 1982. An analysis of Form F and G data banks showed the data banks were comprised of 56% females and 44% males; education level completed: 6% some grade school, 30% high school diploma, 25% some college, 18% bachelor degrees, 11% masters degrees, 3% doctoral or postdoctoral work, and 6% unknown. Age group percentages were: 11% under 18, 29% 18 to 20, 12% 21 to 24, 10% 25 to 29, 16% 30 to 39, 10% 40 to 49, 5% 50 to 59, 2% 60 plus, and 5% unknown.

# TABLE 10
## Myers-Briggs Type Indicator Data Bank: Percentages of Teachers at Different Levels of Education

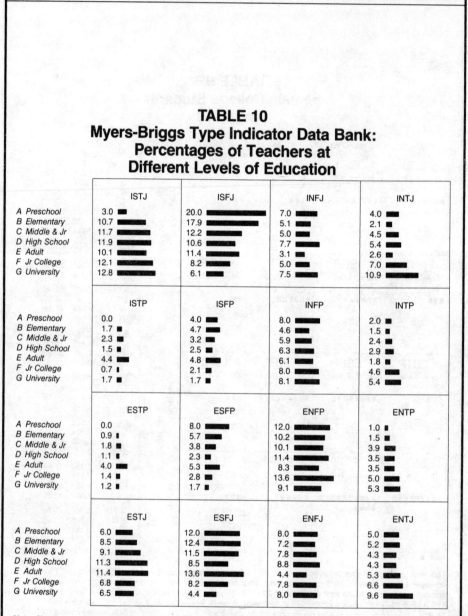

| | ISTJ | ISFJ | INFJ | INTJ |
|---|---|---|---|---|
| A Preschool | 3.0 | 20.0 | 7.0 | 4.0 |
| B Elementary | 10.7 | 17.9 | 5.1 | 2.1 |
| C Middle & Jr | 11.7 | 12.2 | 5.0 | 4.5 |
| D High School | 11.9 | 10.6 | 7.7 | 5.4 |
| E Adult | 10.1 | 11.4 | 3.1 | 2.6 |
| F Jr College | 12.1 | 8.2 | 5.0 | 7.0 |
| G University | 12.8 | 6.1 | 7.5 | 10.9 |

| | ISTP | ISFP | INFP | INTP |
|---|---|---|---|---|
| A Preschool | 0.0 | 4.0 | 8.0 | 2.0 |
| B Elementary | 1.7 | 4.7 | 4.6 | 1.5 |
| C Middle & Jr | 2.3 | 3.2 | 5.9 | 2.4 |
| D High School | 1.5 | 2.5 | 6.3 | 2.9 |
| E Adult | 4.4 | 4.8 | 6.1 | 1.8 |
| F Jr College | 0.7 | 2.1 | 8.0 | 4.6 |
| G University | 1.7 | 1.7 | 8.1 | 5.4 |

| | ESTP | ESFP | ENFP | ENTP |
|---|---|---|---|---|
| A Preschool | 0.0 | 8.0 | 12.0 | 1.0 |
| B Elementary | 0.9 | 5.7 | 10.2 | 1.5 |
| C Middle & Jr | 1.8 | 3.8 | 10.1 | 3.9 |
| D High School | 1.1 | 2.3 | 11.4 | 3.5 |
| E Adult | 4.0 | 5.3 | 8.3 | 3.5 |
| F Jr College | 1.4 | 2.8 | 13.6 | 5.0 |
| G University | 1.2 | 1.7 | 9.1 | 5.3 |

| | ESTJ | ESFJ | ENFJ | ENTJ |
|---|---|---|---|---|
| A Preschool | 6.0 | 12.0 | 8.0 | 5.0 |
| B Elementary | 8.5 | 12.4 | 7.2 | 5.2 |
| C Middle & Jr | 9.1 | 11.5 | 7.8 | 4.3 |
| D High School | 11.3 | 8.5 | 8.8 | 4.3 |
| E Adult | 11.4 | 13.6 | 4.4 | 5.3 |
| F Jr College | 6.8 | 8.2 | 7.8 | 6.6 |
| G University | 6.5 | 4.4 | 8.0 | 9.6 |

Note: Numbers preceding bar graphs represent the percent of the sample falling in that type.

If percentage exceeds 20%, a + follows the bar. Data summarized from published and unpublished sources described in the text.

## Rankings of the Samples by the Four Preferences EI, SN, TF, and JP

The following four tables bring together the samples in Tables 1–10 to allow the reader to identify easily the groups at the extremes for each of the four MBTI preferences. Each entry gives the table and group number, an abbreviated description of the sample, the source (followed by * if the table appears in the atlas), the number in the sample, and the percentage of those in the sample holding the preference in question. A break in the table at 50% shows when the favored preference changes (e.g., from a majority of extraverts, to a majority of introverts).

Table 11—Ranking of the Samples in Percentage of Extraverts
Table 12—Ranking of the Samples in Percentage of Sensing Types
Table 13—Ranking of the Samples in Percentage of Thinking Types
Table 14—Ranking of the Samples in Percentage of Judging Types

## Table 15. Example of MBTI Type Differences on Other Tests

Table 15 summarizes data shared with CAPT by Douglas Mills on 997 participants in the seven-day module programs at the Center for Creative Leadership during the years 1974–1978. The original data show the means and standard deviations for each of the MBTI types on each of the scales of the California Psychological Inventory. Table 10 names the scales with means significantly higher than the group mean (H) or means significantly lower than the group mean (L). This method of presentation lets the reader evaluate clusters of CPI characteristics for each type, to see if they are consistent with type theory. In this case, for example, extraverts tended to score higher on Self-Acceptance and Social Presence. The independent spirits, the NP types, tended to score low on Communality and high on Flexibility. The table also poses some surprises. Why did the 26 ESFJs of the CCL sample—usually the most friendly and sociable of the types—average low among Extraverts in Capacity for Status, Sociability, and Social Presence?

# TABLE 11
## Ranking of the Samples in Tables 1–10:
## Percentage of Extraverts (E)

| Sample Number and Description | Source | Number | E% |
|---|---|---|---|
| 8D. College student leaders Penna. | Jacobsen* | 55 | 83.64 |
| 8E. College student gov't. leaders—female | Jacobsen* | 50 | 82.00 |
| 6E. Educators named "rising stars" K–12 | Lueder | 89 | 77.53 |
| 8C. Community college student leaders | Hadwin* | 225 | 76.44 |
| 6D. Educators named top executives K–12 | Lueder | 83 | 67.47 |
| 2B. Japan chief exec's. large co's. 1981 | Ohsawa* | 118 | 66.95 |
| 8F. College student gov't. leaders—female | Wofford | 50 | 66.00 |
| 1J. Organiz. decision-makers—executives | Roach | 67 | 65.67 |
| 1C. Managers of national retail chain | Gaster* | 316 | 64.87 |
| 2A. Japan top managers large co's. 1975 | Ohsawa* | 56 | 64.29 |
| 4D. CCL LDP 79–82: females | Van Velsor* | 181 | 63.54 |
| 7B. Police supervisors Florida—urban | Hanewicz* | 92 | 63.04 |
| 2C. Japan mid-mgmt.—chemical company | Ohsawa* | 366 | 62.84 |
| 5C. Management consultants | MBTI Data Bank | 192 | 61.98 |
| 7F. Fire managers—southeast US | Lynch* | 60 | 61.67 |
| 8B. High school Red Cross leaders in NE | Jacobsen* | 122 | 61.48 |
| 1D. Officers of banks/financial inst. | MBTI Data Bank | 756 | 61.24 |
| 6H. College student personnel admin. | Robertson* | 51 | 60.78 |
| 5E. Human Resources Planners Assoc. NYC | Ruppart/Hutchens* | 108 | 60.19 |
| 6C. Principals–supervisors in Canada | von Fange* | 124 | 59.68 |
| 6A. Elementary & secondary school admin. | MBTI Data Bank | 1,024 | 58.89 |
| 9B. Female college students | MBTI Data Bank | 18,070 | 57.88 |
| 2H. Latin America mgrs. at CCL Mexico | Osborn et al. | 206 | 57.77 |
| 5B. Principals of internat. consult. firm | CAPT* | 71 | 57.75 |
| 4A. CCL Leadership Devel. Program 74–78 | Mills | 997 | 56.77 |
| 1A. Managers & administrators | MBTI Data Bank | 7,463 | 56.67 |
| 4F. CCL LDP 79–82: high ranked by CCL | Van Velsor | 136 | 56.44 |
| 6G. Education administrators—all levels | MBTI Data Bank | 1,857 | 56.06 |
| 3B. Senior city, county, & state execs. | Lynch* | 257 | 55.86 |
| 2F. Japan normative sample businessmen | Ohsawa | 35,663 | 55.80 |
| 6F. College/university administrators | MBTI Data Bank | 341 | 54.84 |
| 4E. CCL LDP 79–82: top corporate execs. | Van Velsor* | 136 | 53.68 |
| 1B. Managers of small Texas businesses | Hoy & Hellriegel* | 150 | 52.67 |
| 8A. Gifted high school student leaders | Clark et al.* | 164 | 51.83 |
| 6B. School principals—North Carolina | Lynch* | 276 | 51.81 |
| 5D. Management analysts | MBTI Data Bank | 89 | 51.69 |
| 4B. CCL Leadership Devel. Program 79–82 | Van Velsor | 1,232 | 51.30 |
| 9A. Male college students | MBTI Data Bank | 14,138 | 50.45 |
| | | | |
| 3D. Public managers from southeast US | Lynch* | 523 | 49.90 |
| 7E. Senior police officers—Australia | Cacioppe* | 99 | 49.49 |
| 2G. England mgrs. at small bus. courses | Lewis, Margerison | 849 | 49.35 |
| 4C. CCL LDP 79–82: males | Van Velsor* | 1,051 | 49.19 |
| 1E. Telephone company top executives | Dietl | 101 | 48.33 |
| 7C. Police managers—southeast US | Lynch* | 912 | 47.92 |
| 7A. Police supervisors | MBTI Data Bank | 105 | 47.62 |
| 1G. Partners in accounting firms | Jacoby, Otte | 213 | 47.42 |
| 1F. Founders, fast-growing *Inc* 500 firms | Ginn & Sexton | 159 | 46.54 |
| 3E. Admin. social services, Nebraska | Frazier-Koontz | 101 | 46.53 |
| 7D. Police commanders—southeast US | Lynch* | 57 | 45.61 |
| 1I. Organiz. decision-makers—managers | Roach | 161 | 45.34 |
| 5F. Educational consultants | MBTI Data Bank | 54 | 44.44 |
| 6I. College faculty Danforth Associates | CAPT* | 705 | 43.40 |
| 3C. Middle city, county, & state execs. | Lynch* | 290 | 42.41 |
| 5A. Members of Canadian Assoc. Mgmt. Cons. | Wade* | 111 | 41.44 |
| 2E. Japan foremen; food production co. | Ohsawa | 240 | 39.17 |
| 4G. CCL LDP 79–82: low ranked by CCL | Van Velsor | 255 | 38.82 |
| 1H. Organiz. decision-makers—supervisors | Roach | 70 | 38.57 |
| 3A. Senior federal executives | Pickering* | 1,394 | 37.02 |
| 2D. Japan mid mgmt.—heavy industry co. | Ohsawa* | 116 | 35.34 |

Note: * indicates the table for the sample can be found in the *MBTI Atlas*.

# TABLE 12
## Ranking of the Samples in Tables 1–10:
## Percentage of Sensing Types (S)

| Sample Number and Description | Source | Number | S% |
|---|---|---|---|
| 7E. Senior police officers—Australia | Cacioppe* | 99 | 86.87 |
| 7F. Fire managers—southeast US | Lynch* | 60 | 86.67 |
| 1B. Managers of small Texas businesses | Hoy & Hellriegel* | 150 | 86.00 |
| 1C. Managers of national retail chain | Gaster* | 316 | 82.59 |
| 2E. Japan foremen; food production co. | Ohsawa | 240 | 82.08 |
| 3E. Admin. social services, Nebraska | Frazier-Koontz* | 101 | 80.20 |
| 7C. Police managers—southeast US | Lynch* | 912 | 78.29 |
| 7B. Police supervisors Florida—urban | Hanewicz* | 92 | 78.26 |
| 2H. Latin America mgrs. at CCL Mexico | Osborn et al. | 206 | 78.16 |
| 7D. Police commanders—southeast US | Lynch* | 57 | 75.44 |
| 3D. Public managers from southeast US | Lynch* | 523 | 73.04 |
| 2C. Japan mid-mgmt.—chemical company | Ohsawa* | 366 | 72.95 |
| 7A. Police supervisors | MBTI Data Bank* | 105 | 72.38 |
| 3C. Middle city, county, & state execs. | Lynch* | 290 | 72.37 |
| 3B. Senior city, county, & state execs. | Lynch* | 257 | 71.72 |
| 6B. School principals—North Carolina | Lynch* | 276 | 70.65 |
| 1H. Organiz. decision-makers—supervisors | Roach | 70 | 70.00 |
| 2G. England mgrs. at small bus. courses | Lewis, Margerison | 849 | 67.49 |
| 1E. Telephone company top executives | Dietl | 101 | 66.67 |
| 1D. Officers of banks/financial inst. | MBTI Data Bank* | 756 | 65.08 |
| 4G. CCL LDP 79–82: low ranked by CCL | Van Velsor | 255 | 61.96 |
| 9B. Female college students | MBTI Data Bank | 18,070 | 61.39 |
| 1G. Partners in accounting firms | Jacoby, Otte | 213 | 61.20 |
| 6C. Principals–supervisors in Canada | von Fange* | 124 | 58.87 |
| 9A. Male college students | MBTI Data Bank | 14,138 | 58.10 |
| 4E. CCL LDP 79–82: top corporate execs. | Van Velsor* | 136 | 57.35 |
| 2A. Japan top managers large co's. 1975 | Ohsawa* | 56 | 57.14 |
| 1I. Organiz. decision-makers—managers | Roach | 161 | 56.52 |
| 1A. Managers & administrators | MBTI Data Bank* | 7,463 | 56.32 |
| 4C. CCL LDP 79–82: males | Van Velsor* | 1,051 | 56.04 |
| 2D. Japan mid mgmt.—heavy industry co. | Ohsawa* | 116 | 56.03 |
| 8F. College student gov't. leaders—female | Wofford | 50 | 54.00 |
| 2B. Japan chief exec's. large co's. 1981 | Ohsawa* | 118 | 53.39 |
| 6A. Elementary & secondary school admin. | MBTI Data Bank* | 1,024 | 52.93 |
| 4B. CCL Leadership Devel. Program 79–82 | Van Velsor | 1,232 | 52.19 |
| 3A. Senior federal executives | Pickering* | 1,394 | 51.08 |
| 8B. High school Red Cross leaders in NE | Jacobsen* | 122 | 50.82 |
| 8C. Community college student leaders | Hadwin* | 225 | 49.78 |
| 6G. Education administrators—all levels | MBTI Data Bank* | 1,857 | 49.17 |
| 2F. Japan normative sample businessmen | Ohsawa | 35,663 | 48.00 |
| 4F. CCL LDP 79–82: high ranked by CCL | Van Velsor | 136 | 46.01 |
| 8E. College student gov't. leaders—female | Jacobsen* | 50 | 46.00 |
| 8D. College student leaders Penna. | Jacobsen* | 55 | 45.45 |
| 5B. Principals of internat. consult. firm | CAPT* | 71 | 42.25 |
| 4A. CCL Leadership Devel. Program 74–78 | Mills | 997 | 42.23 |
| 5A. Members of Canadian Assoc. Mgmt. Cons. | Wade* | 111 | 40.54 |
| 1F. Founders, fast-growing *Inc* 500 firms | Ginn & Sexton | 159 | 40.25 |
| 5D. Management analysts | MBTI Data Bank* | 89 | 39.33 |
| 6H. College student personnel admin. | Robertson* | 51 | 39.22 |
| 6F. College/university administrators | MBTI Data Bank* | 341 | 37.83 |
| 5C. Management consultants | MBTI Data Bank* | 192 | 34.90 |
| 8A. Gifted high school student leaders | Clark et al.* | 164 | 32.93 |
| 1J. Organiz. decision-makers—executives | Roach | 67 | 32.84 |
| 5F. Educational consultants | MBTI Data Bank* | 54 | 31.48 |
| 6E. Educators named "rising stars" K–12 | Lueder | 89 | 30.34 |
| 4D. CCL LDP 79–82: females | Van Velsor* | 181 | 29.83 |
| 5E. Human Resources Planners Assoc. NYC | Ruppart/Hutchens* | 108 | 29.63 |
| 6D. Educators named top executives K–12 | Lueder | 83 | 28.92 |
| 6I. College faculty Danforth Associates | CAPT* | 705 | 24.40 |

Note: * indicates the table for the sample can be found in the *MBTI Atlas*.

# TABLE 13
## Ranking of the Samples in Tables 1–10:
## Percentage of Thinking Types (T)

| Sample Number and Description | Source | Number | T % |
|---|---|---|---|
| 5A. Members of Canadian Assoc. Mgmt. Cons. | Wade* | 111 | 95.50 |
| 1C. Managers of national retail chain | Gaster* | 316 | 93.04 |
| 2H. Latin America mgrs. at CCL Mexico | Osborn et al. | 206 | 91.75 |
| 5B. Principals of internat. consult. firm | CAPT* | 71 | 91.55 |
| 4E. CCL LDP 79–82: top corporate execs. | Van Velsor* | 136 | 89.71 |
| 1F. Founders, fast-growing Inc 500 firms | Ginn & Sexton | 159 | 86.79 |
| 3A. Senior federal executives | Pickering* | 1,394 | 86.44 |
| 4C. CCL LDP 79–82: males | Van Velsor* | 1,051 | 85.73 |
| 4G. CCL LDP 79–82: low ranked by CCL | Van Velsor | 255 | 84.71 |
| 7C. Police managers—southeast US | Lynch* | 912 | 83.44 |
| 4B. CCL Leadership Devel. Program 79–82 | Van Velsor | 1,232 | 82.47 |
| 7D. Police commanders—southeast US | Lynch* | 57 | 82.46 |
| 1J. Organiz. decision-makers—executives | Roach | 67 | 82.09 |
| 1B. Managers of small Texas businesses | Hoy & Hellriegel* | 150 | 81.33 |
| 4F. CCL LDP 79–82: high ranked by CCL | Van Velsor | 136 | 80.37 |
| 3C. Middle city, county, & state execs. | Lynch* | 290 | 78.99 |
| 1G. Partners in accounting firms | Jacoby, Otte | 213 | 77.93 |
| 1I. *Organiz. decision-makers—managers | Roach | 161 | 77.64 |
| 6B. School principals—North Carolina | Lynch* | 276 | 77.54 |
| 4A. CCL Leadership Devel. Program 74–78 | Mills | 997 | 76.53 |
| 2G. England mgrs. at small bus. courses | Lewis, Margerison | 849 | 75.27 |
| 1D. Officers of banks/financial inst. | MBTI Data Bank* | 756 | 75.00 |
| 3D. Public managers from southeast US | Lynch* | 523 | 74.57 |
| 1E. Telephone company top executives | Dietl | 101 | 74.17 |
| 2B. Japan chief exec's. large co's. 1981 | Ohsawa* | 118 | 73.73 |
| 2D. Japan mid mgmt.—heavy industry co. | Ohsawa* | 116 | 73.28 |
| 7F. Fire managers—southeast US | Lynch* | 60 | 71.67 |
| 1H. Organiz. decision-makers—supervisors | Roach | 70 | 71.43 |
| 3B. Senior city, county, & state execs. | Lynch* | 257 | 71.03 |
| 8D. College student leaders Penna. | Jacobsen* | 55 | 70.91 |
| 7B. Police supervisors Florida—urban | Hanewicz* | 92 | 70.65 |
| 2A. Japan top managers large co's. 1975 | Ohsawa* | 56 | 67.86 |
| 2C. Japan mid-mgmt.—chemical company | Ohsawa* | 366 | 66.67 |
| 5E. Human Resources Planners Assoc. NYC | Ruppart/Hutchens* | 108 | 66.67 |
| 6E. Educators named "rising stars" K–12 | Lueder | 89 | 65.17 |
| 9A. Male college students | MBTI Data Bank | 14,138 | 64.19 |
| 7A. Police supervisors | MBTI Data Bank* | 105 | 63.81 |
| 4D. CCL LDP 79–82: females | Van Velsor* | 181 | 63.54 |
| 7E. Senior police officers—Australia | Cacioppe* | 99 | 61.62 |
| 1A. Managers & administrators | MBTI Data Bank* | 7,463 | 61.56 |
| 6D. Educators named top executives K–12 | Lueder | 83 | 60.24 |
| 8C. Community college student leaders | Hadwin* | 225 | 60.00 |
| 6I. College faculty Danforth Associates | CAPT* | 705 | 56.88 |
| 2F. Japan normative sample businessmen | Ohsawa | 35,663 | 56.70 |
| 6F. College/university administrators | MBTI Data Bank* | 341 | 56.60 |
| 3E. Admin. social services, Nebraska | Frazier-Koontz* | 101 | 55.45 |
| 5D. Management analysts | MBTI Data Bank* | 89 | 55.06 |
| 6C. Principals–supervisors in Canada | von Fange* | 124 | 54.84 |
| 6G. Education administrators—all levels | MBTI Data Bank* | 1,857 | 54.01 |
| 5C. Management consultants | MBTI Data Bank* | 192 | 53.65 |
| 8A. Gifted high school student leaders | Clark et al.* | 164 | 51.22 |
| 6A. Elementary & secondary school admin. | MBTI Data Bank* | 1,024 | 49.71 |
| 8B. High school Red Cross leaders in NE | Jacobsen* | 122 | 45.90 |
| 6H. College student personnel admin. | Robertson* | 51 | 41.18 |
| 8E. College student gov't. leaders—female | Jacobsen* | 50 | 40.00 |
| 5F. Educational consultants | MBTI Data Bank* | 54 | 38.89 |
| 2E. Japan foremen; food production co. | Ohsawa | 240 | 38.33 |
| 9B. Female college students | MBTI Data Bank | 18,070 | 33.43 |
| 8F. College student gov't. leaders—female | Wofford | 50 | 32.00 |

Note: * indicates the table for the sample can be found in the MBTI Atlas.

# TABLE 14
## Ranking of the Samples in Tables 1–10:
## Percentage of Judging Types (J)

| Sample Number and Description | Source | Number | J% |
|---|---|---|---|
| 1C. Managers of national retail chain | Gaster* | 316 | 91.46 |
| 2H. Latin America mgrs. at CCL Mexico | Osborn et al. | 206 | 86.89 |
| 6C. Principals–supervisors in Canada | von Fange* | 124 | 86.29 |
| 7E. Senior police officers—Australia | Cacioppe* | 99 | 85.86 |
| 6B. School principals—North Carolina | Lynch* | 276 | 85.14 |
| 7D. Police commanders—southeast US | Lynch* | 57 | 84.21 |
| 3C. Middle city, county, & state execs. | Lynch* | 290 | 82.10 |
| 7C. Police managers—southeast US | Lynch* | 912 | 81.58 |
| 5B. Principals of internat. consult. firm | CAPT* | 71 | 80.28 |
| 6E. Educators named "rising stars" K–12 | Lueder | 89 | 79.78 |
| 3E. Admin. social services, Nebraska | Frazier-Koontz* | 101 | 78.22 |
| 3D. Public managers from southeast US | Lynch* | 523 | 78.20 |
| 1G. Partners in accounting firms | Jacoby, Otte | 213 | 77.93 |
| 8D. College student leaders Penna. | Jacobsen* | 55 | 76.36 |
| 2G. England mgrs. at small bus. courses | Lewis, Margerison | 849 | 76.21 |
| 3B. Senior city, county, & state execs. | Lynch* | 257 | 76.21 |
| 1B. Managers of small Texas businesses | Hoy & Hellriegel* | 150 | 75.33 |
| 4E. CCL LDP 79–82: top corporate execs. | Van Velsor* | 136 | 75.00 |
| 6D. Educators named top executives K–12 | Lueder | 83 | 74.70 |
| 4C. CCL LDP 79–82: males | Van Velsor* | 1,051 | 74.02 |
| 2B. Japan chief exec's large co's. 1981 | Ohsawa* | 118 | 73.73 |
| 1H. Organiz. decision-makers—supervisors | Roach | 70 | 72.86 |
| 2E. Japan foremen; food production co. | Ohsawa | 240 | 72.08 |
| 3A. Senior federal executives | Pickering* | 1,394 | 71.88 |
| 1D. Officers of banks/financial inst. | MBTI Data Bank* | 756 | 71.43 |
| 4G. CCL LDP 79–82: low ranked by CCL | Van Velsor | 255 | 71.37 |
| 4B. CCL Leadership Devel. Program 79–82 | Van Velsor | 1,232 | 71.02 |
| 4F. CCL LDP 79–82: high ranked by CCL | Van Velsor | 136 | 70.55 |
| 5E. Human Resources Planners Assoc. NYC | Ruppart/Hutchens* | 108 | 70.37 |
| 1I. Organiz. decision-makers—managers | Roach | 161 | 70.19 |
| 6I. College faculty Danforth Associates | CAPT* | 705 | 69.93 |
| 6A. Elementary & secondary school admin. | MBTI Data Bank* | 1,024 | 69.82 |
| 6G. Education administrators—all levels | MBTI Data Bank* | 1,857 | 69.57 |
| 7A. Police supervisors | MBTI Data Bank* | 105 | 69.52 |
| 1A. Managers & administrators | MBTI Data Bank* | 7,463 | 69.32 |
| 6H. College student personnel admin. | Robertson* | 51 | 68.63 |
| 5A. Members of Canadian Assoc. Mgmt. Cons. | Wade* | 111 | 68.47 |
| 7F. Fire managers—southeast US | Lynch* | 60 | 68.33 |
| 6F. College/university administrators | MBTI Data Bank* | 341 | 67.74 |
| 7B. Police supervisors Florida—urban | Hanewicz* | 92 | 67.39 |
| 4A. CCL Leadership Devel. Program 74–78 | Mills | 997 | 67.10 |
| 2A. Japan top managers large co's. 1975 | Ohsawa* | 56 | 66.07 |
| 1J. Organiz. decision-makers—executives | Roach | 67 | 65.67 |
| 2C. Japan mid-mgmt.—chemical company | Ohsawa* | 366 | 64.48 |
| 5D. Management analysts | MBTI Data Bank* | 89 | 64.04 |
| 8E. College student gov't. leaders—female | Jacobsen* | 50 | 64.00 |
| 1E. Telephone company top executives | Dietl | 101 | 63.33 |
| 5F. Educational consultants | MBTI Data Bank* | 54 | 62.96 |
| 5C. Management consultants | MBTI Data Bank* | 192 | 61.98 |
| 8C. Community college student leaders | Hadwin* | 225 | 59.56 |
| 2F. Japan normative sample businessmen | Ohsawa | 35,663 | 59.00 |
| 9B. Female college students | MBTI Data Bank | 18,070 | 58.80 |
| 2D. Japan mid mgmt.—heavy industry co. | Ohsawa* | 116 | 56.03 |
| 8B. High school Red Cross leaders in NE | Jacobsen* | 122 | 54.92 |
| 9A. Male college students | MBTI Data Bank | 14,138 | 54.11 |
| 1F. Founders, fast-growing *Inc* 500 firms | Ginn & Sexton | 159 | 54.09 |
| 4D. CCL LDP 79–82: females | Van Velsor* | 181 | 53.59 |
| 8F. College student gov't. leaders—female | Wofford | 50 | 52.00 |
| 8A. Gifted high school student leaders | Clark et al.* | 164 | 39.63 |

Note: * indicates the table for the sample can be found in the *MBTI Atlas*.

# TABLE 15
## MBTI Types Scoring Significantly High (H) or Low (L) on the California Psychological Inventory

| ISTJ | ISFJ | INFJ | INTJ |
|------|------|------|------|
| N 140    14.0% | N 29    2.9% | N 28    2.8% | N 108    10.8% |
| (H) Self control | (H) Self control<br>(H) Femininity | (H) Femininity | (H) Capacity for status<br>(H) Self control<br>(H) Achieve via independ<br>(H) Flexibility |
| (L) Dominance<br>(L) Capacity for status<br>(L) Sociability<br>(L) Social presence<br>(L) Self-acceptance<br>(L) Flexibility | (L) Dominance<br>(L) Capacity for status<br>(L) Sociability<br>(L) Social presence<br>(L) Self-acceptance<br>(L) Flexibility | (L) Dominance<br>(L) Capacity for status<br>(L) Sociability<br>(L) Social presence<br>(L) Self-acceptance<br>(L) Sense of well-being | (L) Dominance<br>(L) Sociability<br>(L) Social presence |

| ISTP | ISFP | INFP | INTP |
|------|------|------|------|
| N 18    1.8% | N 7    0.7% | N 30    3.0% | N 71    7.1% |
| (H) Flexibility | | (H) Achieve via independ<br>(H) Flexibility | (H) Achieve via independ<br>(H) Flexibility |
| (L) Dominance<br>(L) Capacity for status<br>(L) Sociability<br>(L) Social presence<br>(L) Self-acceptance | (L) Dominance<br>(L) Capacity for status<br>(L) Sociability<br>(L) Social presence<br>(L) Self-acceptance<br>(L) Sense of well-being<br>(L) Flexibility | (L) Capacity for status<br>(L) Sociability<br>(L) Social presence | (L) Dominance<br>(L) Capacity for status<br>(L) Sociability<br>(L) Social presence<br>(L) Self-acceptance<br>(L) Sense of well-being<br>(L) Communality<br>(L) Femininity |

| ESTP | ESFP | ENFP | ENTP |
|------|------|------|------|
| N 32    3.2% | N 9    0.9% | N 61    6.1% | N 100    10.0% |
| (H) Capacity for status<br>(H) Social presence<br>(H) Self-acceptance<br>(H) Flexibility | (H) Flexibility | (H) Capacity for status<br>(H) Sociability<br>(H) Social presence<br>(H) Self-acceptance<br>(H) Achieve via independ<br>(H) Flexibility<br><br>(L) Self control<br>(L) Communality | (H) Dominance<br>(H) Capacity for status<br>(H) Sociability<br>(H) Social presence<br>(H) Self-acceptance<br>(H) Flexibility<br><br>(L) Communality |

| ESTJ | ESFJ | ENFJ | ENTJ |
|------|------|------|------|
| N 160    16.1% | N 26    2.6% | N 44    4.5% | N 134    13.5% |
| (H) Dominance<br>(H) Capacity for status<br>(H) Sociability<br>(H) Social presence<br>(H) Self-acceptance<br>(H) Sense of well-being<br>(H) Self control<br>(H) Communality<br><br>(L) Flexibility | (H) Femininity<br><br><br><br><br><br>(L) Capacity for status<br>(L) Sociability<br>(L) Social presence<br>(L) Achieve via independ<br>(L) Flexibility | (H) Dominance<br>(H) Capacity for status<br>(H) Sociability<br>(H) Social presence<br>(H) Self-acceptance<br>(H) Flexibility | (H) Dominance<br>(H) Capacity for status<br>(H) Sociability<br>(H) Social presence<br>(H) Self-acceptance<br>(H) Flexibility<br><br>(L) Femininity |

Note: Data collected by Douglas Mills of the Center for Creative Leadership from 997 participants in the seven-day module programs at the Center during the years 1974–1978.
(H) indicates CPI scale means significantly (p .01) higher than sample mean, (L) indicates means significantly (p .01) lower.

# E. Comments on Tables and Related Research

This section looks at issues in leadership research from the perspective of the data in Section F, and from examples of research on type differences in constructs considered important for understanding leadership.

**1. Extraversion and Introversion** Type theory would predict that extraverts will place more emphasis on the external situation and quick rapid action in reaching decisions; introverts will place more emphasis on conceptualizing the problem clearly and thoughtful deliberation before making decisions. Extraverts are estimated at 65% to 75% of the general population of the United States. In comparable male and female samples, the proportion of extraverts is often higher for females. (For example, compare the college student Tables 9A and 9B, and the male and female CCL participants in Table 4.) Relatively more introverts seek higher education; as expected, the percentage of introverts equals or exceeds that of extraverts in samples of university faculty, scientists, and other fields requiring graduate training. In the type tables of Tables 1–10, introverts appear in the top two rows and extraverts in rows three and four. An inspection of the tables shows sizeable numbers of introverts. Only in the student samples are extraverts clearly in the majority. Table 11 shows the rankings of extraverts in the 59 samples of Tables 1–10. The samples range from 84% extraverts to 65% introverts; the median is 56% extraverts, about what would be expected from a college population.

In the CCL subset of participants rated high and low in the leaderless group discussion exercise, the highest-rated participants were 56% extraverts, not significantly different from the sample as a whole. However, the lowest-rated participants were 61% introverts, with significantly more of the thoughtful, careful, quiet, laconic IST types. The extraverted, logical, innovative ENT types were significantly underrepresented among low-rated participants in the leaderless group discussions. Many leadership measures and leadership training programs assume that extraversion is essential for leadership. Clearly, much of leadership requires sociability, communication, and action which come easier to extraverts. Leadership also requires a thoughtful consideration of issues and an understanding of the enduring principles which persist despite changing environments—these come more easily to introverts. Unless one assumes that the large numbers of introverts in the MBTI data are inadequate leaders, it is wise for leadership research to allow for successful leaders with both the extraverted and introverted orientations. Research would then examine the ways in which extraverted and introverted leaders each develop the skills of their less-preferred attitude.

**2. Sensing and Intuition** In the general population, sensing types outnumber intuitive types roughly 3:1. From type theory we predict sensing leaders to put more weight on practical experience, continuity with the past ("If it's not broken, don't fix it"), and evaluation of success in terms of tangible products. We predict that intuitive leaders will be more concerned with the "big picture," visions and projections which are not immediately objectified, and change for the sake of change ("There has to be a better way"). Table 12 shows a range in the 59 samples from 87% sensing types to 76% intuitive types, with the median sample at 56% sensing. Samples with high percentages of sensing types tend to be concerned with practical action, production of tangibles, or fields with many details to manage. Groups at the intuitive end of Table 12 are more likely to include educators, consultants, and student leaders.

Some of the most serious misunderstanding and lack of respect in organizations come from the differences between the realistic, practical, hands-on sensing types and the innovative, more theoretical intuitives. Many organizational problems have been solved when people holding these opposite preferences learn to respect and use their differences constructively.

**3. Thinking and Feeling** The expectation in the general population is that about two-thirds of males prefer thinking, and about two-thirds of females prefer feeling. However, female samples with thinking types in the majority do occur among engineering students, graduate students, and business executives. Male samples with a majority of feeling types occur in the arts and in some health professions, including counseling. Thinking types (T) are clearly in the majority in the 59 samples. The range in Table 13 is from 96% T to 68% F with a median at 71% T; 21 of the samples are above 75% T and in only eight samples are F types in the majority. Tables 1–10 picture the weight of thinking types in the two outside columns of the type tables. Only in the samples of educational leaders, student leaders, and teachers are substantial numbers found in the middle feeling columns.

The NF types in the third column, postulated to be most skilled in communications and most likely to be the inspiring leaders, are underrepresented in leader samples. Some appear among the student leaders and the human development consultants.

In a comparison of managers in health systems and in business, Hai (1983) found more feeling types among managers in health systems than in business, but thinking types were clearly in the majority at CEO levels in both settings.

**4. Judgment and Perception** The style of judging types is to collect enough data to make a decision, and then move on. The style of perceptive types is to cast a broad net, trying not to miss anything, leaving options open in case new factors turn up. In the general population we expect about 55% judging types. Table 14 provides a stark contrast to this expectation, with its range from 91% J to 52% J. Only one exception, the gifted high school leaders, preferred perception. It is not surprising to find that the J types who enjoy being decisive are found in leadership positions where decisions need to be made. The preference for judging types is also clear in Tables 1–10, where the top and bottom J rows are full and the second and third P rows are almost empty.

To summarize, it is clear from the data that MBTI types are not equally represented in samples of persons in leadership/management positions. The data suggest that the majority of leaders are of the types wanting to reach closure (J) rather than those wanting to have their antennae out to make sure they miss nothing (P). In business, government, the military, and even education, leaders are more likely to favor impersonal, logical, analytical decision making (T) than a rational ordering of values with concern over personal and human priorities (F). The "tough-minded" TJs clearly outnumber the more "gentle" FPs. One can argue that the tasks call for TJ leadership and all is well. One can also ask whether it is wise in a democratic society to have a TJ power structure so one-sided that decisions may be made too quickly (J) with insufficient consideration of important human and value concerns (F).

**5. Creativity in Leadership** Creativity is concerned with creating the new, the yet unknown. Intuition is concerned with future possibilities which have not yet occurred. Extensive research reported in the *MBTI Manual* (Myers & McCaulley, 1985) shows that creativity is associated with preferences for intuition and, to a lesser extent, introversion and perception. Type theory predicts the boldest leaps will come from the intuitives; sensing types are more likely to use their less-preferred intuition to make innovative changes in existing systems. Given the large number of sensing executives who can be expected to be more comfortable with established ways, and given our rapidly changing society in which often the old ways no longer work, the attempts of organizations such as CCL to help executives develop new ways of problem solving are well-timed.

**6. Type Differences in Orientation to Time** Leadership involves attention to the past, the present, and the future; to short-range and long-range planning. Leaders balance the need to retain past values and the need for change. Issues relating to time confront leaders daily. Predictions of type differences in orientation to time include:

Time will seem more episodic for extraverts and more continuous for introverts. Supported by Seiden (1970).

Sensing types are more oriented to the present and intuitives toward the future. Supported by Evans (1976), Evered (1973), Seiden (1970), and Yang (1981). The "future" is seen short-term by sensing types, long-term by intuitives. Supported by Harrison and Lawrence (1985) in children and by Nightingale (1973).

Thinking types are more likely to experience time as a past-present-future continuum with no special emphasis on any stage. Supported by Evans (1976) and Yang (1981).

Feeling types, rooted in values, are more oriented toward the past and retaining the values of that past. Supported by Seiden (1970) and Yang (1981).

Achieving management by objectives by target dates comes more easily to types with sensing, with thinking, and with judging preferences (Jaffe, 1980).

**7. Type Differences in Assessment of Risk** Leadership involves decisions which take into account conditions of risk. One leader's "considered action" may seem very risky to a leader of a different type. From type theory, one might expect riskier decisions to come from the impulsivity associated with extraversion, the willingness to rely on minimal cues associated with intuition, and the desire for harmony associated with feeling. Reluctance to take risks might be associated with the delay for reflection associated with introversion, the practicality of sensing, and the analysis of probable consequences associated with thinking.

Rifkind (1976) found that intuitive undergraduates in a risky-shift exercise made significantly more risky decisions than did sensing undergraduates. Blaylock (1980, 1981) developed a model for interactions of three aspects of risk—decision environment, available information, and cognitive style (indicated by the MBTI); he found significant interactions. For example, facts about people and community relationships were considered important by feeling types five times oftener than by thinking types. The possibility of environmental change was a more serious problem to feeling than thinking types. McKenney and Keen (1974) found that sensing and intuitive types differed in the kinds of problems they liked and were good at, with sensing types liking problems that could be programmed and intuitives preferring open-ended problems. They noted that sensing and intuitive types "often treat the same project as two entirely different problems." Sensing types are most likely to look for structure, reduce the unknowns, and define the constraints; intuitives are more likely to use the given model to get an overall sense of the problem, play with unknowns, use random trials, and, after an incubation period, see the necessary steps to completion. Henderson and Nutt (1980) noted that the practical, matter-of-fact ST organization decision-makers saw more risk in situations that SF types in the same group perceived as reasonably safe.

Research on the risk-taking tasks of leadership can be enriched by going beyond examination of general effects to look at differences in type-related effects.

**8. Type Differences in Stress and Burnout** Garden (1985, 1988) reports ongoing studies of type differences in burnout. As energy is depleted, sensing types report feeling bored and less grounded in reality; intuitives lose enthusiasm; feeling types find themselves more distant, less nurturing, and more hostile; and thinking types find their desire for achievement drops. Garden is developing a differentiated model for understanding and treating burnout symptoms. Her data suggest that in burnout we may move from our preferred to our less-preferred functions.

**9. Type Differences in Teamwork** Early writing on type differences and teamwork (Doering, 1972; Myers, 1974; McCaulley, 1975) described behavioral observations and posed hypotheses that diverse teams might have more difficulty achieving team goals, but that, if successful, their team products would be better than those of teams whose types were similar. Doering described a team where members chose working partners in terms of type, not academic discipline, and where a talkative extravert was frozen out by the quiet introverts.

Blaylock (1981, 1983) has created models for teams which take into account past research on teams and Jungian theory. In one study, teams with complementary types did better than teams with compatible types. Sensing types remained interested in doing the task after it became repetitive; intuitives dropped out as the task became less challenging, leading to a loss of effectiveness of the team overall.

**10. Type Differences in Changing Organizational Environments** Leaders must often create changes in organizational environments. From type theory one would predict that the vision of possibilities in intuitives would lead them to seek change more often than sensing types, that extraverts with intuition would be the most active change agents, and that feeling types would manage the human side of change with more finesse than thinking types.

Evered (1977) found that intuitives were more likely to activate change. Slocum (1978) studied "change agents" (e.g., consultants from universities or in independent practice, and members of training departments). An analysis of the factors the change agents considered important showed that the practical and matter-of-fact ST types put weight on tasks, the SF and NF feeling types put weight on people, and the logical, ingenious NT types put weight on organizational structure. Slocum also reported on differences in tactics to effect change: the STs used job enrichment and behavior modification; the SFs used job enrichment and transactional analysis; the NFs used decision centers, T-groups, and confrontation meetings; and the NTs used survey feedback.

Mitchell (1981) factor-analyzed a large number of instruments in a sample of 474 employees from all levels of a large southeastern bank. The types differed significantly on mean scores of the factors. For example, the sympathetic and friendly SF types had high scores on a factor named Harmonious Work Climate. The independent ENTP scored high on Variety and Challenge. The active, conservative ESTJ rated highest on Achievement within the System. The extraverts with feeling, ESFJ and ENFJ, were high on Outgoing Affiliation and Business Sociability. Logical, ingenious NTs were high on Financial Analysis.

Mitroff and Kilmann (1975) and Kilmann and Mitroff (1976) have described their experiences in asking clients to describe their "ideal organization." The STs—shown so often in Tables 1–10 managing operations—describe an ideal organization with clear procedures, meticulously followed. The affiliative SFs' ideal company is a friendly place where people like working together and feel included. The idealistic NFs envision a company with enough resources to serve humanitarian goals fully; and the logical and ingenious NTs envision a place where there are clear strategic plans and the organization is moving toward its long-range goals.

Leaders must direct and change organizations that are worlds within worlds. Each leader will see some of these worlds clearly and value them; each leader, with the blind spots of his or her type, will overlook, and even deplore, other worlds. Type theory highlights the complexity of leadership but also provides a model for understanding why leaders differ in those aspects of leadership that come easily, and those that cause the greatest difficulty.

**11. Who Reaches Top Management?** All 16 types may become presidents or chief executive officers, but Tables 1–10 indicate that some types are more likely to reach these heights than others.

Very early in her work, Isabel Myers, in an undated manuscript, commented that top management had more intuitive types than line management. In Table 12, management samples are heavily weighted toward sensing types. However, top management samples tend to be more evenly divided between sensing and intuitive types (executives in CCL programs, top executives in Japan, senior federal executives). Intuitives are in the majority among innovative leaders, such as the founders of *Inc.* 500 firms, top executives, and "rising stars" in education.

In summary, though any type can reach the top, executives most likely to do so are somewhat more likely to prefer extraversion and intuition, and are highly likely to prefer thinking and judgment. Leaders who inspire by communicating a vision of a better future may come from the intuitives, especially the intuitives with feeling.

**12. Leadership and Individual Type Development** Given the fact that all types become leaders, how does one predict which members of any given type are most likely to reach the top? In her early paper on leadership, Myers (undated) and a new book, *The Leadership Equation*, Barr and Barr (1989) discuss the need for leaders to develop all the processes of type—those that come naturally, and those less preferred. Myers describes the challenge of type development for leaders in this way:

*Under all the shifting problems that cross an executive's desk lie three basic necessities:*
  *1. He must decide.*

*2. He must be right.*

*3. He must convince certain key people of his rightness . . . .*

*There is, then, no perfect executive type . . . . No type is naturally endowed with everything that would be useful for the necessary decision, the necessary analysis, and the necessary communication.*

*For maximum effectiveness in this field, a man must add to his natural endowment the use of the opposites when necessary. He may accomplish this by the use of the opposites in other people. Or he may, if he can, develop controlled use of the opposites within himself.*

*This last is the top and final stage in type development. It is quite impossible before a man has achieved full scale development of his inborn type. Undeveloped types use all the opposites indiscriminately, without controlling any of them or acquiring any skill in their use. Type development demands the preferential use of the better judging function and the better perceptive function with increasing skill and increasing degree of direction and control.*

*Once a man has full control of his first and second functions, he knows not only their strengths but their deficits; not only how to use them but when not to use them because the opposite function or attitude is more appropriate. Then he can in some measure control the use of these opposites, crossing over at need from that which is natural to that which is appropriate. This is difficult, but perfectly possible to a sufficiently well-developed type, always providing that he understands why the thing which he naturally and automatically does is not appropriate at the moment.*

In her type descriptions for the 16 types, Myers described each type in its well-developed state, ending with a caution about the problems when development has not yet been achieved. Barr and Barr (1989) give many examples of executive actions which involve good or poor type development.

# F. Leadership Research Issues and Psychological Type

Type theory provides a dynamic model for understanding why individuals see the world differently and make different decisions from the same data. The MBTI provides information about individuals and about groups. From the type perspective, one would not ask the question, "What type is the best leader?" Rather, one would ask, "How does each type show leadership?"

Research on type differences among leaders is just beginning. The following questions are suggestions for research. They also demonstrate the kinds of issues raised by the Jungian type model.

**1. Understanding the Performance of Different Types of Leaders** The facts about leader types are established through many samples in this country and in some samples in Canada, Great Britain, and Japan. They provide a framework for such questions as:

*a. Leadership styles and work settings.* What are the characteristic leadership styles of each MBTI type? What is the interaction between the leadership style and the setting in which leadership is exercised?

*b. Leadership styles of the "rare" types.* In what settings are the rare types in managers/leaders successful? How were they chosen? How do they lead?

*c. Development of leadership abilities.* Which strategies are best to enhance the human performance of the *more typical* STJ or NTJ leaders? Does one work with what comes naturally—logical analysis and decision making—or with the qualities often discounted or overlooked by TJ types—listening, communication, and understanding people?

Which strategies enhance human performance of the less typical persons who have achieved leadership positions?

Teach them to become like (turn into) TJ types?
Teach them to exercise TJ skills while remaining true to their own styles?
Teach them to be excellent at the skills that come naturally to their types?
Teach them to surround themselves with types whose skills complement their own?

*d. Comparisons with other instruments.* How do the types differ in scores on other personality tests? Sometimes the comparison of patterns for each type on other personality tests can confirm, clarify, or raise questions about the MBTI types (see the CPI data in Table 10 for example). Sometimes analysis by types casts light on the meaning of the scales of other tests. For example, rankings of the MBTI types on the Omnibus Personality Inventory Altruism Scale placed the four extraverts with intuition (EN types) at the top and the quiet ISFJs, often found among priests, nuns, health care workers, and teachers, at the bottom. OPI "altruism" appears to be the kind that actively tries to change the world, not the quiet laborers in the vineyard.

**2. Enhancing Performance of Subordinates** Little is known about the motivation, skills, and strategies of different types of leaders in enhancing the performance of different types of subordinates. We would predict that the TJ leaders (especially early in their careers before experience broadens them) will see enhancement of subordinate performance in terms of tangible, analytical skills. The types to whom communications skills do not come easily may be slow in recognizing communications problems in themselves or their subordinates.

**3. Teamwork** The few research studies of teams support the general expectation that teams of similar types will show cohesion early, but may be limited in scope; teams of diverse types take longer to "become a team" but solve problems more successfully.

The MBTI is used extensively to teach teamwork. Participants and leaders report that a knowledge of type leads to better appreciation of differences and more productive teamwork. From an empirical standpoint, most current MBTI teaching for teamwork is in settings where time pressures and confidentiality issues preclude gathering careful data on the actual functioning of ongoing teams.

Research on ad hoc teams can track initial team building. The picture may be quite different in ongoing teams of people who have worked together for long periods of time. Organizational users of the MBTI have the capability to conduct studies using ongoing teams whose members know each other well. Studies of such ongoing teams could provide important information not found in short-term studies of ad hoc teams.

**4. Methodological Issues** The foundation of type theory rests on differences in taking in information and making decisions. Type differences are frequent in variables about what is interesting or dull, important or useless; in the processes of reaching conclusions and the content of decisions.

Research variables related to leadership styles, communication, information processing, decision making, risk taking, behavioral ratings by self and others, or scales of any personality test, can be analyzed to identify type differences.

One strategy is to correlate scores on other measures with MBTI continuous scores (which are a linear transformation of the preference scores). Many such correlations are presented in the validity chapter of the *MBTI Manual*. However, since each leader represents only one of the 16 types, research designs which include analyses of the 16 types (and the type groupings) will yield more valuable and practical information.

A special problem in MBTI research in leadership comes from the fact that type distributions from organizations tend to be one-sided, as shown in Section D. It is not uncommon to find a reasonable distribution of extraverts and introverts, and of sensing types and intuitive types. But often there are so few feeling types and perceptive types that research questions comparing TF and JP cannot be answered. Some studies may need larger samples, or even nonorganization samples.

Issues of type development are important in understanding leadership. Looking at within-type differences with other more clinical measures can help identify effective and ineffective members of a type.

Designs involving cluster analyses of other variables can identify subjects in each cluster; type tables of these subjects will show whether the empirically derived clusters bring together theoretically related types.

As type differences in leadership variables are identified, the next step will be to see if these type differences hold up in persons who differ in education, ethnic background, gender, or age.

Addition of the MBTI to ongoing studies adds a new level for explaining data. Partitioning the average group response by type may reveal instances where types behave in ways that have canceled each other out in the overall analysis.

**5. Type Differences in Attitudes Toward Research Itself** Research by Peters (1981) identified type differences in attitudes toward what constitutes "good research." Researchers praise highly research with the qualities valued by their types, and criticize research with qualities valued by other types. Even in research, where we strive for common high standards, we human researchers can be blindsided by our type preferences.

## Summary

In summary, there is evidence that all 16 MBTI types assume leadership positions. Some are found more frequently than others. Types differ in many aspects of leadership—the facts considered important, assessment of risk, style of decision making, orientation to time, ability to persuade, clarity of concepts, enjoyment of action, and ability to go beyond what comes naturally to use less-preferred skills.

The bias for the population as a whole is toward extraversion and sensing. This fact has implications for leaders. How does one deal with complex, long-range problems in a society where the majority want quick action and simple solutions? How does one lead toward necessary change to meet the challenges of the future, when the majority trust and want to preserve the ways of the past?

The bias toward thinking and judging TJ managers in business, government, and the military predisposes those in power in this country, and in other countries, to emphasize logical analysis and organization in accomplishing goals. Is there a danger that leaders' emphasis on objectivity and logic (T) may handicap them in dealing constructively with problems that need the input from feeling values (F), such as protection of the environment, prevention of war, safety of food and equipment, death with dignity, or respect for privacy, to name just a few?

Will the bias toward rapid decision making provided by judgment (J) lead to premature closure based on inadequate data?

Type data tell us much about individuals. They also raise questions for our society. How do we recognize the strengths of the types most drawn to leadership? How do we recognize our blind spots as a society, and the blind spots of those most likely to lead us? And, most important, how do we create a system for giving respectful consideration to viewpoints of types seldom found in positions of power?

## References

Barr, L., & Barr, N. (1989). *The leadership equation: Leadership, management and the Myers-Briggs*. Austin, TX: Eakin Press.

Blaylock, B. K. (1980). *Interactive effects of classificatory and environmental variables in decision making under conditions of risk*. Unpublished doctoral dissertation, Georgia State University.

Blaylock, B. K. (1981). Method for studying perception of risk. *Psychological Reports, 49*(3), 899–902.

Blaylock, B. K. (1983). Teamwork in a simulated production environment. *Research in Psychological Type, 6*, 58–67.

Carskadon, T. G., McCarley, N. G., & McCaulley, M. H. (1987). *Compendium of research involving the Myers-Briggs Type Indicator*. Gainesville, FL: Center for Applications of Psychological Type.

Center for Applications of Psychological Type (1988). *Bibliography: The Myers-Briggs Type Indicator*. Gainesville, FL: Center for Applications of Psychological Type. (Available as computer listing or diskette)

Dietl, J. A. (1981). *A study reflecting the dominant personality style most effective in exemplifying effective situational leadership within a corporate organization*. Unpublished doctoral dissertation, United States International University.

Doering, R. D. (1972). New dimensions for staff talents: Enlarging scientific task team creativity. *Personnel, 49*,(2), 43–52.

Evans, L. N. (1976). A psycho-temporal theory of personality: A study of the relationship between temporal orientation, affect, and personality type. *Dissertation Abstracts International, 37*, 1875B. (University Microfilms No. 76-22, 381)

Evered, R. D. (1973). Conceptualizing the future: Implications for strategic management in a turbulent environment. *Dissertation Abstracts International, 34*, 3625A–3626A. (University Microfilms No. 73-32, 663)

Evered, R. D. (1977). Organizational activism and its relation to "reality" and mental imagery. *Human Relations, 30*(4), 311–334.

Garden, A. M. (1985). Burnout: The effect of Jungian type. *Journal of Psychological Type, 10*, 3–10.

Garden, A. M. (1988). Jungian type, occupation and burnout: An elaboration of an earlier study. *Journal of Psychological Type, 14*, 2–14.

Gaster, W. D. (1982). A study of personality type as a predictor of success in retail store management (Doctoral dissertation, Louisiana Technical University, 1982). *Dissertation Abstracts International, 43*(12), 4020A.

Ginn, C. W., & Sexton, D. L. (1988). Psychological types of Inc. 500 founders and their spouses. *Journal of Psychological Type, 16*, 3–12.

Hai, D. M. (1983). Comparisons of personality dimensions in managers: Is there a management aptitude? *Akron Business and Economic Review, 14*(1), 31–36.

Hanewicz, W. (1978). Police personality: A Jungian perspective. *Crime and Delinquency, 24*(2), 152–172.

Harrison, D. F., & Lawrence, G. (1985). Psychological type and time orientations of middle school students: Do middle school students differ in projecting their personal futures? *Journal of Psychological Type, 9*, 10–15.

Henderson, J. C., & Nutt, P. C. (1980). The influence of decision style on decision making behavior. *Management Science, 26*, 371–386.

Hoy, F., & Hellriegel, S. (1982). The Kilmann and Herden model of organizational effectiveness criteria for small business managers. *Academy of Management Journal, 25*(2), 308–322.

Jacoby, P. F. (1981). Psychological types and career success in the accounting profession. *Journal of Psychological Type, 4*, 24–37.

Jaffe, J. M. (1980). The relationship of Jungian psychological predispositions to the implementation of management by objectives: A sociotechnical perspective (Doctoral dissertation, University of Southern California, 1980). *Dissertation Abstracts International, 4*(11), 4833A.

Jung, C. G. (1971). Psychological types. In H. G. Baynes (Trans.) and revised by R. F. C. Hull, *The collected works of C. G. Jung* (Vol. 6). Princeton, NJ: Princeton University Press. (Original work published 1921)

Kilmann, R. H., & Mitroff, I. I. (1976). Qualitative versus quantitative analysis for management science: Different forms for different psychological types. *Interfaces, 6*(2), 17–27.

Lewis, R., & Margerison, C. (1979). *Personal mapping-understanding personal preferences.* Cranfield, Bedford, England: Management and Development Research Centre, Cranfield School of Management.

Lueder, D. C. (1986a). Psychological types and leadership styles of the 100 top executive educators in North America. *Journal of Psychological Type, 12,* 8–12.

Lueder, D. C. (1986b). The "rising stars" in educational administration: A corollary to psychological type and leadership styles. *Journal of Psychological Type, 12,* 13–15.

Macdaid, G. P., McCaulley, M. H., & Kainz, R. I. (1987). *Myers-Briggs Type Indicator atlas of type tables.* Gainesville, FL: Center for Applications of Psychological Type.

McCaulley, M. H. (1975). How individual differences affect health care teams. *Health Team News, 1*(8). (Available from Center for Applications of Psychological Type)

McKenney, J. L., & Keen, P. G. W. (1974). How managers' minds work. *Harvard Business Review,* May–June, 79–90.

Mitchell, W. D. (1981). *A study of type and social climate in a large organization.* Unpublished manuscript.

Mitroff, I. I., & Kilmann, R. H. (1975). Stories managers tell: A new tool for organizational problem solving. *Management Review, 64*(7), 18–28.

Myers, I. B. (1974). *Type and teamwork.* Gainesville, FL: Center for Applications of Psychological Type.

Myers, I. B. (in press). *Contributions of type to executive success.* Unpublished manuscript, Gainesville, FL: Center for Applications of Psychological Type.

Myers, I. B., & McCaulley, M. H. (1985). *Manual: A guide to the development and use of the Myers-Briggs Type Indicator.* Palo Alto, CA: Consulting Psychologists Press.

Nightingale, J. A. (1973). The relationship of Jungian type to death concern and time perspective. *Dissertation Abstracts International, 33,* 3956B. (University Microfilms No. 73-3609).

Ohsawa, T. (1975, October). *The use of the MBTI in Japan.* Paper presented at the First National Conference on the Myers-Briggs Type Indicator, Gainesville, FL.

Ohsawa, T. (1981, June). *A profile of top executives in Japanese companies.* Paper presented at the Fourth Biennial Conference on the Myers-Briggs Type Indicator, Palo Alto, CA.

Otte, P. J. (1983). *Psychological typology of the local firm certified public accountant.* Unpublished doctoral dissertation, Western Michigan University, Kalamazoo.

Otte, P. J. (1984). Do CPAs have a unique personality: Are certain personality "types" found more frequently in our profession? *The Michigan CPA,* Spring, 29–36.

Peters, C. E. (1981). An investigation of the relationship between Jungian psychological type and preferred styles of inquiry (Doctoral dissertation, Ohio State University, 1981). *Dissertation Abstracts International, 44*(06), 1974B.

Rifkind, L. J. (1976). An analysis of the effects of personality type upon the risky shift in small group discussions. *Dissertation Abstracts International, 36*(12), 7734A. University Microfilms No. 76–13, 830)

Roach, B. (1986). Organizational decision-makers: Different types for different levels. *Journal of Psychological Type, 12,* 16–24.

Seiden, H. M. (1970). Time perspective and styles of consciousness. *Dissertation Abstracts International, 31,* 386B. (University Microfilms No. 70–11, 275).

Slocum, J. W., Jr. (1978). Does cognitive style affect diagnosis and intervention strategies of change agents? *Group and Organization Studies, 3*(2), 199–210.

von Fange, E. A. (1961). *Implications for school administration of the personality structure of education personnel.* Unpublished doctoral dissertation, University of Alberta, Alberta.

Wade, P. F. (1981). *Some factors affecting problem solving effectiveness in business: A study of management consultants.* Unpublished doctoral dissertation, McGill University, Montreal.

Yang, A. I. (1981). Psychological temporality: A study of temporal orientation, attitude, mood states, and personality type (Doctoral dissertation, University of Hawaii, 1981). *Dissertation Abstracts International, 42*(04), 1677B.

# Stars, Adversaries, Producers, and Phantoms at Work: A New Leadership Typology

Ira J.
Morrow
and
Mel Stern

Assessment centers are a widely accepted method for accomplishing several important human resources objectives. Pioneered by AT&T in the mid-1950s, assessment centers provide a detailed behavioral evaluation of prospective candidates for managerial or nonmanagerial positions either prior to entry into an organization or prior to consideration for, or promotion to, a higher level of responsibility (Bray, Campbell, & Grant, 1974). In addition, assessment centers have been used to facilitate further training and development both for managerial and nonmanagerial personnel.

Although a considerable body of assessment center research literature has emerged (Bray & Howard, 1983; Campbell & Van Velsor, 1985; Moses & Byham, 1977; Thornton & Byham, 1982), previous efforts have not determined the combination of intellectual and personality qualities associated with differential levels of performance in a management assessment program; nor have they integrated these qualities to construct discrete behavioral and personal profiles with broad implications for leadership effectiveness and development.

The present study examines the factors that distinguish individuals who perform at superior, average, and poor levels in a management assessment program (MAP). Specifically the paper considers:

The extent to which relative degrees of success in a MAP are quantitatively associated with scores on assessment exercises and assessment dimensions.

The relationship between MAP performance and various procedurally independent personality and mental ability measures.

How MAP participants performing at superior, average, and poor levels in the MAP are qualitatively described in terms of their strengths and weaknesses by executives and managers serving as observers in the MAP.

Given that management assessment is geared toward the evaluation of skills commonly associated with leadership, the questions explored here go beyond explaining the different levels of performance in an assessment program. Stated broadly, this paper discusses the qualities that present leaders of a major corporation seek in identifying the next generation of leaders.

The data presented here will, where possible, be synthesized into a detailed profile or composite sketch of individuals who are perceived by present managers and executives to have superior, average, or poor potential for management success. The paper concludes with a discussion of the implications for leadership effectiveness and development.

**Research Setting** Data for this research consists of scores and evaluations given to participants in IBM's Management Assessment Program (MAP) designed to evaluate management potential within the corporatewide Finance, Business Planning, Information Systems, and Administration functions. Over 2,200 individuals have been evaluated in this program since its inception in 1966.

**MAP Participants** MAP sessions are attended by 12 individuals. Participants in a given session are all at approximately the same job level but are sent from different divisions and locations around the country. They are, for the most part, nonmanagers in various professional/technical positions in the four functions served by the MAP: finance, information systems, administration, and planning.

In order to be sent to the program, participants must be consistently good performers in their positions, and, in the opinion of their local management, have potential for greater levels of responsibility in management positions. Participants are recommended by their managers to progressively higher levels of management up to their division level functional executive (e.g., division director of I/S, or division controller). This executive then submits names of nominees to one of four career development managers (one for each of the four functions served by the MAP) who assemble "class lists" for each scheduled MAP session.

**MAP Exercises** The MAP is designed to enable four IBM managers or executives to observe and evaluate participants in three individual and four group exercises over a two-and-a-half-day period. The individual exercises include:

*Job Environment Report and Interview*: Participants are asked to write about their jobs and careers. The written report serves as a springboard for a one-to-one interview with an observer.

*In-Basket and In-Basket Interview*: Participants assume the role of newly appointed managers and are asked to handle the mail that has been left by their predecessors. Their work is discussed in a one-to-one interview with an observer.

*Personnel Development Problem and Presentation*: Participants function in the role of consultants who have been asked to analyze and make recommendations to improve a fictitious company's personnel operation. A brief presentation is made to observers who play the role of the clients' senior management.

The group exercises consist of:

*Site Selection*: Participants are assigned roles in a fictitious corporation and asked to address a business problem and reach a group decision to recommend to their company president.

*Manufacturing*: Participants are asked to run a company and engage in buying, manufacturing, and selling without being assigned specific individual roles. There are many regulations to comply with and rapidly changing conditions to adjust to.

*Task Force*: Participants are again assigned roles in a fictitious corporation and asked to decide between a number of business opportunities to replace the loss of a major client.

*Leaderless*: Participants sponsor their own fictitious candidates for a promotion and are asked to provide a brief presentation about their candidate and then discuss all the candidates. The group is then asked to provide a rank-ordering of the candidates from the most to least qualified for the promotion.

**MAP Dimensions**  The participants' performance in the MAP exercises is rated along 11 behavioral dimensions deemed important for effective managerial performance at IBM. These dimensions, which are based on a job analysis conducted when the MAP was established, are listed in Table 1.

**Mental Ability Tests and Personality Questionnaire**  During the MAP, participants are offered the opportunity (voluntary) to take several mental ability and personality paper-and-pencil tests. These include:

The School and College Ability Test (SCAT) which measures verbal and quantitative abilities.

The Mental Alertness Test (MAT) which measures an individual's capacity for acquiring and utilizing new knowledge and skills. High scorers tend to learn more quickly, see complex relationships faster, and be more flexible and versatile in new situations.

The Ship Destination Test (SDT) which measures arithmetical reasoning and problem solving. This test contains minimal language or verbal content; therefore individuals with reading, language, or verbal comprehension deficiencies should not be at a disadvantage.

The personality questionnaire utilized in the MAP is the Gordon Personal Profile and Inventory. In all, eight personality dimensions are scored, including:

Ascendancy (ASC): High scorers tend to be active, to take the lead in group situations, and to be self-assured and assertive in relations with others; low scorers are relatively passive and inclined to be unassertive in groups. They are likely to listen rather than talk and to lack self-confidence.

Responsibility (RESP): High scorers are more likely to stick with assigned tasks until completion, even though the tasks may be relatively uninteresting. Low

# TABLE 1
## Assessment Evaluation Dimensions

1. ACTIVITY LEVEL: Sustains a level of work activity over time — including work speed, amount of work accomplished, endurance.

2. ADAPTABILITY: Performs under less-than-optimum conditions — unstructured problems, too little time and/or resources, limited information.

3. ADMINISTRATIVE CONTROLS: Tracks and records the progress of activity. Develops procedures for collection and evaluation of required information.

4. ANALYTICAL/INTEGRATIVE ABILITY: Identifies inconsistencies and subtle relationships in information. Relates facts from various and unconnected sources. Relates facts to yield new conclusions.

5. COMMUNICATION: Speaks and writes with an appropriate style and vocabulary. Adapts communication style to the audience. Is understood.

6. DECISION MAKING: Develops and evaluates the alternatives which exist for solving a problem. Ensures that realistic, practical constraints are addressed and that the full implications of a problem or situation are considered.

7. DIPLOMACY: Negotiates individual interests to create a result acceptable to all. Seeks decisions which cause no one to "lose face." Is tactful and considerate — not brusque or abrasive.

8. MANAGING INDIVIDUALS: Assists others to improve their performance. Requests input from others, listens, and acknowledges contribution. Delegates effectively.

9. ORGANIZATIONAL AWARENESS: Shows awareness of interests and objectives of other parts of the organization. Considers same in developing plans and actions.

10. PERSONAL IMPACT: Affects others — convinces those holding opposing or neutral positions, pushes forward own interests or ideas despite opposition.

11. PLANNING AND PLAN EXECUTION: Formulates plan to achieve objectives, revises plans as required. Planning considers needs for others to work together.

*In rating these dimensions, observers utilize a five-point scale with: 1=far above average, 2=above average, 3=average, 4=below average, and 5=far below average. In addition, the same scale is utilized to provide an overall rating of the participants' performance in each of the assessment exercises.*

scorers tend not to finish uninteresting tasks, are less persevering, and are more flighty and irresponsible.

Emotional Stability (ES): High scorers tend to be calm, with a high frustration tolerance. Low scorers are more nervous or tense, with a lower frustration tolerance.

Sociability (SOC): High-scoring individuals are more likely to be gregarious, while low scorers tend to feel more comfortable with limited social contact.

Cautiousness (CAUT): High scorers tend not to take chances and to carefully consider decisions, while low-scoring individuals are inclined to be more impulsive, to take greater risks, and to make snap decisions.

Original Thinking (OT): High scorers are more likely to enjoy working on difficult problems and playing with new ideas, while low scorers tend to be less interested in complicated problems or new knowledge.

Personal Relations (PR): High scorers are inclined to be more trusting, tolerant, and patient in dealing with others, while low scorers are generally more critical and easily irritated or annoyed.

Vigor: High-scoring individuals tend to have a generally higher energy level, move and work rapidly, and are more achievement oriented, while low scorers are more likely to tire easily, to have lower vitality, and to be less productive.

For all of the mental ability tests and the personality questionnaire, raw scores and percentiles (based on a norm group of approximately 1,500 past MAP participants) are calculated. These scores are never disclosed to the observers or to anybody aside from the assessment staff and the individual participant. Thus, although these tests are scheduled during the assessment program, they are meant to be used only by the individual participant for gaining additional self-insight and by the MAP professional staff for research purposes and for discussion with participants. Test scores have no influence on any aspect of the formal assessment process or program outcome.

On the day following completion of the last assessment exercise, the four observers and the MAP staff meet to conduct a wrap-up session. During the session, the exercise write-ups and dimension ratings of each participant on each exercise are reviewed and discussed. Participant summaries, which are filled out by each observer for each participant prior to the wrap-up session, are also read aloud. These summaries, which serve as the ultimate qualitative outcome of the MAP, ask observers for their general impression of the participant, perceived strengths and weaknesses, and recommendations for improvement, based upon the participant's performance in the entire MAP.

The Overall Assessment Rating (OAR) is generated for each participant during the wrap-up session. The OAR asks observers to rate the participant's likelihood of success in their next management-level position, with success defined as being an above average performer within 12 months of obtaining the new position.

The rating scale for the OAR is as follows:

1 = very high probability of success (91–100%)
2 = high probability of success (71–90%)

3 = moderate probability of success (31–70%)
4 = low probability of success (11–30%)
5 = very low probability of success (1–10%)

This prediction is generated by each observer for each participant, and each participant's average OAR is calculated. The OAR constitutes the ultimate quantitative outcome of the assessment process.

**The Research Sample** The three performance groups examined in this study were defined based on the OAR received by the participants. To establish discrete and extreme groupings participants were selected as follows:

Superior: OAR = 1.0
Average: OAR = 3.0
Poor: OAR = 4.3–5.0

This means that for the Superiors all four observers rated the participant as a 1. Similarly, all Averages received ratings of 3 from each observer. A range was chosen for the Poors to increase sample size, since relatively few 5.0 ratings are given.

Three types of data were analyzed—dimension and exercise scores, mental ability and personality test scores, and qualitative descriptions of performance. For the qualitative analysis, only ten participants were available for the Poor group, and we elected to equalize the other two groups by selecting only the ten most recent cases in each of these groups. Table 2 which follows shows the sample examined for each data analysis.

## Exercise and Dimension Results

The average exercise ratings for the three performance groups are shown in Figure 1, and the average dimension ratings are shown in Figure 2.

---

**TABLE 2**
**Sample Size**
**Superior, Average, and Poor MAP Performers**

**PERFORMANCE GROUPS**

|  | Superior | Average | Poor | Time Frame |
|---|---|---|---|---|
| Tests | 51 | 71 | 49 | 1978–84 |
| Exercises & Dimensions | 33 | 50 | 26 | 1982–84 |
| Qualitative Description | 10 | 10 | 10 | 1983–84 |

---

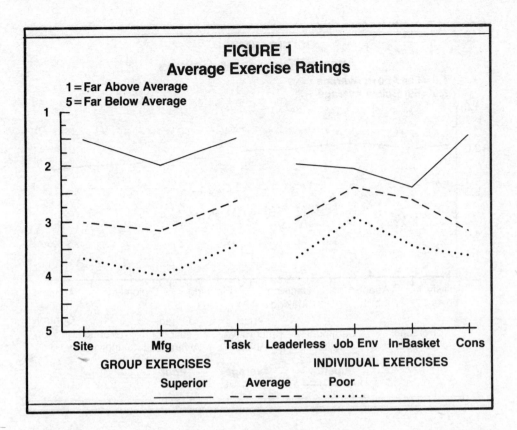

**FIGURE 1**
**Average Exercise Ratings**

1 = Far Above Average
5 = Far Below Average

GROUP EXERCISES: Site, Mfg, Task

INDIVIDUAL EXERCISES: Leaderless, Job Env, In-Basket, Cons

Superior — Average — — — Poor · · · · · ·

The results are striking both in the consistency of differences among groups (there is no group overlap on any dimension or exercise) and for the size of these differences (all differences are statistically significant). For all exercises and for all dimension averages, Superior performers are rated significantly higher than Average performers who, in turn, are rated significantly higher than Poor performers.

While the exercise and dimension results are powerful and striking, they are no stronger than we should expect them to be. In a very real sense, these results are a measure of the internal validity of the management assessment program. Observers, in arriving at their individual OARs, have available only their observations (and ratings) of exercise and dimension performance and some information regarding the educational and job experience of participants. Were the results to be less marked, there would be speculation that factors other than exercise performance were exerting an undue influence on program outcome, for example, assessor bias.

It is noteworthy that the differences between the three performance groups are larger in the four group exercises than in two of the three individual exercises. This is reasonable, considering that a wider range of comparative performance levels is obvious to observers in group exercises where six participants perform simultaneously, than in individual exercises where no interaction takes place. Stated differently, performance on group exercises where there are opportunities for social interaction between peers is a more powerful and dramatic discriminator between relative levels of MAP performance

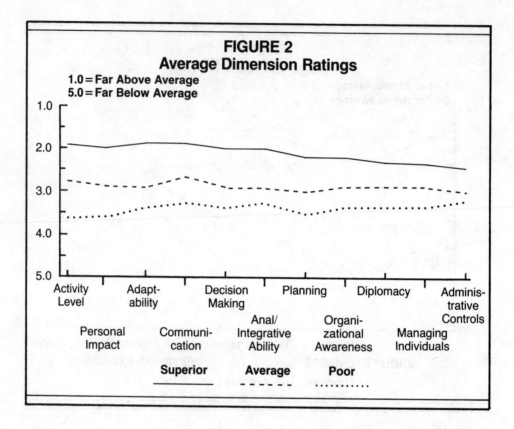

**FIGURE 2**
**Average Dimension Ratings**

1.0 = Far Above Average
5.0 = Far Below Average

Activity Level · Adaptability · Decision Making · Planning · Diplomacy · Administrative Controls

Personal Impact · Communication · Anal/Integrative Ability · Organizational Awareness · Managing Individuals

**Superior** —— **Average** - - - - - **Poor** ··········

than is performance on individual exercises. Hence, a fuller range of performance anchoring is utilized by observers.

The average dimension scores shown in Figure 2 are arranged in decreasing order of the mean difference between the Superior and Poor groups. This can be viewed (in a nonstatistical sense) as indicating that those dimensions on the left (i.e., Activity Level, Personal Impact, etc.) are more powerful in determining who will be seen as a Superior versus Poor performer than are the dimensions on the right (i.e., Administrative Controls, Managing Individuals, etc.). For five of the dimensions (Activity Level, Personal Impact, Analytic Ability, Organization Awareness, and Diplomacy) there is no overlap between the worst of the Superior performers and the best of the Poor performers. These five dimensions bear a substantial similarity to the terms used to differentially describe Superior and Poor performers as will be seen in the qualitative descriptions results section of this paper.

The small interdimension differences found within each group in contrast to the larger between-group differences for any dimension cannot be easily explained. It is possible that the Superiors are better in all respects than the Averages who, in turn, are better in all things than the Poors. The results to be presented for the test and the qualitative analyses seem in large part to support this contention. However, it is still likely that there is some halo in ratings of dimensions within exercises. The participant who is rated below average on Activity Level may also be rated below average on Decision Making

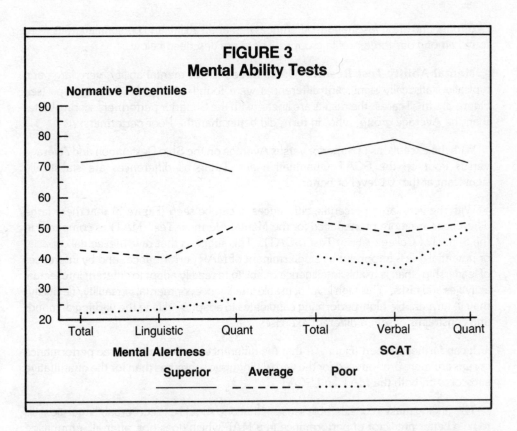

**FIGURE 3**
**Mental Ability Tests**

Normative Percentiles

or Diplomacy. Where an opportunity to demonstrate the latter two was called for and not acted upon, the rating would be valid. If the group or individual exercise flow was such that an opportunity did not present itself, such ratings would be in error. As MAP administrators, the authors believe that some such errors occur but that most are caught in the review/editing/wrap-up procedures.

## Test Results

For interpretive purposes, we can differentiate clearly between findings for the mental ability and personality paper-and-pencil tests and the exercise and dimension ratings. Although administered during the MAP, test results are not divulged to the assessors at any time. Performance by participants on these tests is totally independent of any assessor ratings or comments regarding participant program performance.

Test results, in percentile format, are presented in Figure 3 (mental ability) and Figure 4 (personality). The normative group in both cases is approximately 1,500 prior attendees, not including the current sample. For comparative purposes on the mental ability tests, test manual norms would indicate our population to be equivalent to "graduate degree engineers" on the Ship Destination Test and "business executives" on the Mental Alertness Test.

Strong, and often fascinating, differences in mental ability and personality traits were found among our three profile groups. These are described below.

**Mental Ability Test Results** On all three tests of mental ability, very large and typically statistically significant differences were found among the three groups (see Figure 3). In all cases, the results are linear, with the Superior performers scoring better than the Average group, who, in turn, did better than the Poor performers.

With the exceptions of Superior versus Average on the Ship Destination and Average versus Poor on the SCAT Quantitative and Total, all differences are statistically significant at the .01 level or better.

With the very large percentile differences, it can be seen (Figure 3) that these large differences are more pronounced for the Mental Alertness Test (MAT) as compared to the School of College Ability Test (SCAT). This suggests that raw intellectual capacity or potential is less important as a determinant of MAP performance, and by inference, of leadership, than is usable intelligence or ability to readily adapt to different intellectual activities and tasks. This high level of usable intelligence, or mental versatility/flexibility, may in turn enable high-performing candidates to adapt readily to the varying demands and constraints of seven different exercises.

It can further be seen (Figure 3) that the differences between the three performance groups are more pronounced for the verbal/linguistic subscores than for the quantitative subscores on both the MAT and SCAT.

This finding makes considerable sense in that one should expect verbal/linguistic skills to be a better predictor of performance in a MAP which does not, after all, emphasize but, in fact, purposely eschews technically oriented exercises. The emphasis is on, as it should be, nontechnical leadership potential. The technical abilities of MAP candidates are presumed to be sound; otherwise they probably could not be performing effectively in their current technical positions, primarily in the functions of finance and information systems, and thus would not be invited to attend the MAP. In this regard, it is useful to note that even the Poor performers score relatively high on the quantitative subscore of the SCAT which emphasizes the kinds of quantitative manipulations learned in formal education settings. However, these technical positions make fewer verbal/linguistic demands upon their incumbents. The emphasis would generally be quite different in managerial positions where one is presumably somewhat removed from technical demands and where there is a greater emphasis on the ability to lead, motivate, coordinate, and communicate—all of which require a higher degree of verbal/linguistic fluency.

In sum, then, we conclude:

MAP performance and, by inference, perceived leadership potential, is strongly related to general mental ability.

Mental versatility/flexibility is more important than the academic type of intelligence in the MAP. Leadership behaviors, by inference, seem to depend more on how rapidly one can put mental abilities to effective use in varying and rapidly changing situations than on the degree of one's general mental ability.

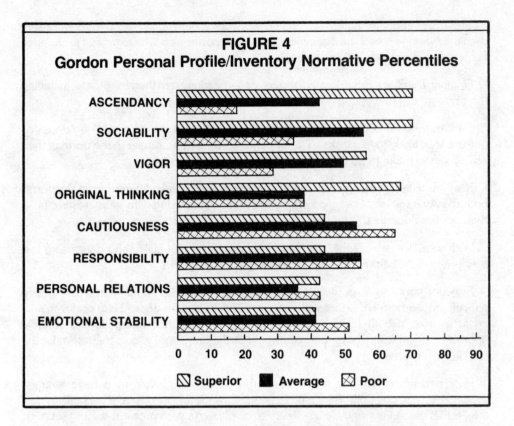

**FIGURE 4**
**Gordon Personal Profile/Inventory Normative Percentiles**

ASCENDANCY
SOCIABILITY
VIGOR
ORIGINAL THINKING
CAUTIOUSNESS
RESPONSIBILITY
PERSONAL RELATIONS
EMOTIONAL STABILITY

0  10  20  30  40  50  60  70  80  90

▨ Superior    ■ Average    ⊠ Poor

Verbal ability is more critical than quantitative ability for MAP success. As individuals rise from technical to managerial or leadership roles, verbal ability is an increasingly important determinant of success even in a highly technologically oriented organization like IBM.

**Personality Trait Scores** Results for the Gordon personality traits are shown in Figure 4. Most immediately noticeable are the strong linear relationships or trends displayed for most of the traits by the three profile groups. For six of the eight trait measures, significant differences are found between two or all three of the groups, the only exceptions being Emotional Stability (anxiety) and Personal Relations (trust in others).

In order of decreasing/statistical difference, the six traits that discriminate between Superior, Average, and Poor MAP performers include:

*Ascendancy:* Superior performers clearly differentiate themselves from the other two groups and the norm in describing themselves as adopting an active/leadership role in group settings. Poor performers describe themselves as passive and unassertive. Average performers, as is the case with most of the traits, are found in the middle groups, at the norm.

*Sociability:* Superior performers like to be with and work with people while Poor performers describe themselves as significantly less gregarious with somewhat-restricted social contacts.

*Vigor:* Superiors are energetic and like to work more rapidly, accomplishing more than the Average person, in distinction to the Poor performers who express a preference for setting a slow pace and tire more easily.

*Original Thinking:* Superior performers are more interested than the others, including the norm group, in working on difficult, thought-provoking problems.

*Cautiousness:* Poor performers consider matters carefully before making decisions and are least likely to take risks. The Superior group is more similar to the norm in their willingness to make rapid decisions and perhaps to take chances.

*Responsibility:* Although none of the groups is significantly different from the norm, both the Average and Poor performers are more persevering with uninteresting tasks than are the Superiors.

With some literary license, we may integrate the mental ability and personality test results and describe the three performance groups as follows:

Superior performers are very bright and alert individuals. They like working with difficult problems and new ideas and are very effective in this area. They prefer to take an active role in both social and business settings, and their energetic and sociable approach, along with their strong command of the language, allows them to take the lead in such groups.

Poor performers are the antithesis of the Superiors. While they have average academic intellectual skills, they tend to be significantly less flexible and versatile in new intellectual situations and have less desire to be placed in such problem-solving settings. In a similar vein, they prefer more limited social contacts. Although they tire more easily than the norm for assessment participants, they do have a heightened sense of responsibility which may allow them to see a task through to completion. As a result of the confluence of these characteristics, they tend to adopt a nonassertive, passive role in groups.

Average performers, as described by the tests, occupy the middle ground in both intellectual capacity and personality descriptors. The only instance where they fall outside the boundaries set by the other two groups (not significantly) is in Personal Relations where they display slightly less patience with or tolerance for other people.

## Qualitative Descriptions

The third type of data consists of the descriptive observations and impressions of the participants by the observers. After all seven exercises are concluded, each observer independently writes a summary for each participant containing three major sections: overall impression, strengths, weaknesses.

Content analyses of the strengths and weaknesses sections were conducted. Typically, single words or short phrases were used in these sections and the overall impressions were occasionally used for clarification (i.e., "aggressiveness" listed as a weakness might be shorthand for "overaggressive/undiplomatic" or "underaggressive/nonassertive" behavior described in the overall impression section).

Categories of comments were initially established by a review of nonsample Participant Summaries and were only slightly modified in analysis of the 30 performance summaries comprising the sample for the content analysis.

The major categories identified are described below:

- **Analytic Ability:**

   Strength—analytic and/or integrative skills, intelligent, bright, quick
   Weakness—incomplete/shallow/poor analysis

- **Diplomacy:**

   Strength—diplomatic, sensitive/responsive to others' needs, good interpersonal/listening/negotiation skills (active diplomacy)
   —pleasant, personable, easygoing, cooperative (passive diplomacy)
   Weakness—undiplomatic, insensitive, overly aggressive, instills fear, brusque, condescending

- **Communication:**

   Strength—good oral and/or written communication, articulate, persuasive
   Weakness—poor oral and/or written communication, inarticulate, too soft-spoken, hesitant/tentative speech

- **Activity:**

   Strength—hardworking, tenacious, intense, determined, energetic
   Weakness—low participation/activity/energy, unaggressive, passive

- **Leadership:**

   Strength—leadership as a stand-alone word or followed by a string of descriptors
   Weakness—rarely cited and then connected with comments on low participation

- **Decision Making:**

   Strength—decision maker, takes a position, establishes a course of action
   Weakness—not cited

Although a number of other descriptors were used for strengths and weaknesses, for example, maturity, businesslike appearance, negative attitude, self-confidence, and so forth, the above categories accounted for over 75 percent of the comments provided by the observers.

Two of the categories, Diplomacy and Activity, require further explanation. Diplomacy as a strength was coded into an Active or a Passive role. In the Active definition, the word *diplomacy* itself tends to be used and the participant is described as being active and accomplishing something while attending to the needs/input of others. An example of this type of statement is "very diplomatic and political—gets it done without being overbearing." Comments coded under the second definition, Passive, *never* used the word *diplomacy*, tended to be short such as "pleasant personality," "personable," and, quite often, damned with faint praise: for example, "never offensive to others."

There is little overlap in the two definitions: 22 participants are cited for diplomacy as a strength; only 3 are cited in both the Active and Passive role, for example, "personable and diplomatic." Most often in the Passive case, the comment coded as Diplomacy is listed as the only strength (never true with Active Diplomacy) and typically is tied in for that participant with a listed weakness of "passive" or "nonparticipative." The observers are clearly trying to be diplomatic themselves by ensuring that the strengths section is not left blank and that the participant has something positive to ingest.

The category Activity is also notable in that the strength and weakness definitions are not really opposites of each other. As a strength, what we found were statements of style, endurance at a task, and intensity of effort. The weakness comments, though, reflect low activity level, limited participation, and passivity. This opens the door in a number of instances for a participant to be cited for Activity as both a strength and weakness. In all these cases of dual citation, what the participant summaries indicated was little to no involvement in group process but a focus on a specific task or content issue such as calculating costs. This concern will be addressed further in our discussion of content analysis results for Poor performers.

To ascribe a particular strength or weakness to a participant, we chose a decision rule of citation of that characteristic by two or more observers. This seems a reasonable choice point between allowing a single observer's potentially erroneous citation to rule the day and being excessively conservative in requiring three or four disparate observers to agree on a quality.

The results of the content analysis of strengths and weaknesses cited for the three performance groups are indicated in Table 3.

The following "word pictures" of the three performance groups emerge from the content analysis: Superior performers are seen as diplomatic and sensitive leaders. They have sharp analytic skills and are able to determine a course of action and effectively communicate it to others. Superior performers may not be perfect people; however, as a group, they are seen as having no consistent weaknesses. Further, when a weakness is cited, it is almost always limited in scope: for example, "voice projection—low," or "frequency—at times," or "intensity—be a little more assertive."

Average performers are also seen as analytically astute, although not quite as consistently as Superiors. They are not perceived to be effective diplomats or politicians; rather, they are the reverse. Their brusque, sometimes overconfident and condescending approach is seen as having a negative effect on their co-workers, a reaction of which they are not always aware. Those who are more participative in groups receive comments such as "he is abrasive with his peers and frequently undermines his own influence by running roughshod over others." Less active individuals "cannot lead with limited participation and relative insensitivity to the feelings of others." Even those individuals not seen as overtly undiplomatic and destructive of group efforts (30%) were cited for "inexperience in groups," "limited negotiation skills," or "needs to learn to motivate people and create team effort." Essentially, Average performers are seen as having some desire and potential to be leaders but require group dynamics training/experience, as well as moderate to substantial movement from aggressive to assertive behavior.

## TABLE 3
## Content Analysis of Qualitative Description
## for Superior, Average, and Poor Performers

| | Superior | | Average | | Poor | |
|---|---|---|---|---|---|---|
| **STRENGTH** | DIPLOMACY (ACTIVE) | 90% | ANALYTIC ABILITY | 70% | ACTIVITY | 60% |
| | ANALYTIC ABILITY | 80% | COMMUNICATION | 40% | DIPLOMACY (PASSIVE) | 40% |
| | COMMUNICATION | 50% | DIPLOMACY (PASSIVE) | 20% | ANALYTIC ABILITY | 30% |
| | LEADERSHIP | 50% | | | COMMUNICATION | 20% |
| | DECISION MAKING | 40% | | | | |
| **WEAKNESS** | COMMUNICATION | 20% | DIPLOMACY (ACTIVE) | 70% | ACTIVITY (LEVEL) | 80% |
| | | | ACTIVITY (LEVEL) | 40% | ANALYTIC ABILITY | 20% |
| | | | ANALYTIC ABILITY | 30% | DIPLOMACY (ACTIVE) | 20% |
| | | | COMMUNICATION | 30% | | |

*% = Percentages of participants cited by two or more observers as displaying this strength or weakness.*

Poor performers are typically nonparticipative and passive and have very little impact on group performance. In one subcategory are participants who seem overwhelmed by the experience of assessment—they interact at truly minimal levels in group exercises and seem to have difficulty at one-on-one communications in individual exercises. These individuals have no impact on group activities and are essentially a nonpresence. As one assessor remarked to an author, "Who was that shadow?" A second grouping of Poor performers were those who did participate in a limited fashion in group activities. They performed tasks and analyses (often with intense determination) and occasionally provided their groups with information helpful in problem solution. What they never did was attempt leadership or focus on group process, that is, organizing the group, determining and assigning roles, or recommending decision rules. They tend to function in a support or staff role, rather than in a managerial or leadership capacity.

## Implications and Recommendations

Several common threads emerge from the various quantitative and qualitative analyses. There are a number of qualities or characteristics that uniquely define the performance groups and differentiate them from the others. These are, most notably, intellectual capacity/alertness and interpersonal/group dynamics skills. For the sake of convenient comparison, we provide in Table 4 descriptive profiles and, with some trepidation, the prototypical names of Star, Adversary, Producer, and Phantom.

**TABLE 4**
**Descriptive Types and Profiles for**
**Superior, Average, and Poor MAP Performance**

| TYPE | GROUP | PROFILE |
|---|---|---|
| THE STAR | Superior | Smart<br>Sensitive<br>Social<br>Self-Assured<br>Self-Starter<br>Sustained |
| THE ADVERSARY | Average | Able/Analytic<br>Argumentative/Adamant<br>Abrupt<br>Abrasive/Abusive |
| THE PRODUCER | Poor | Perform (Within Role)<br>Persevere<br>Painstaking |
| THE PHANTOM | Poor | Polite<br>Passive<br>Paucity<br>Perturbed/Paralyzed |

It is clear from this research that there is an exceptionally strong relationship between mental ability/versatility (both tested and "real world") and leadership effectiveness. Both the external and internal environments of most of today's organizations are characterized by incredible degrees of complexity, ambiguity, and turbulence—qualities that assessment mimics in microcosm. As far back as 1973, for example, Henry Mintzberg's research indicated that managers work at a fast and unrelenting pace, on numerous activities, and that they must react rapidly to the many problems they face (Mintzberg, 1973). The world has become even more complex, turbulent, deregulated, and globally competitive since Mintzberg's research, and it seems reasonable to assume that this trend will continue for the foreseeable future. An obvious conclusion, then, is that mental agility will become an even more vital determinant of managerial effectiveness in the years ahead.

This bodes ill for our Phantoms and Producers, based on the premise that mental agility is not mutable or readily improved in adults. While these groups are not unintelligent, they are clearly at a disadvantage when competing with a Star or an Adversary. Considering the highly selective nature of assessment, Phantoms and

Producers may perform better than their peers who do not get nominated for the program. They may be more intelligent, more diligent, or more expert than some other competitors for short-range promotional opportunities. As they rise through the corporate hierarchy, however, and the pyramid becomes narrower, they will increasingly find Stars and Adversaries as their competition for positions that are increasingly complex and fast-paced. Even the Producers who demonstrate a willingness to work hard and an often-intense focus on a task will be less able to effectively compete for leadership/executive positions with their intellectual superiors who are also more energetic and willing to lead. While developmental activities such as time-management courses, assertiveness training, and so forth, might be of value, we are not aware of any direct means to narrow the existing gap in intellectual power which, on a relative basis, will grow with upward mobility.

Another obvious lesson from this research is the importance of diplomacy as a leadership skill and, more specifically, the emergence of the Adversary prototype. A considerable body of research in the field has identified interpersonal skills, consideration, or social-emotional or employee-centered behaviors as a major component of effective leadership (Yukl, 1981). What we have seen in this study of potential leaders is a quantitatively linear, but a qualitatively nonlinear, distribution of "diplomacy" with all other noted components of leadership (e.g., intelligence, vigor, etc.) occurring in a linear fashion. Our Stars are seen by observers as being actively diplomatic; Adversaries are actively undiplomatic; and Producers and Phantoms are passively diplomatic. The Poor-performing groups are diplomatic by default. They do not participate or, if they do, they focus on narrow aspects of the task rather than on the process. They do not attempt leadership. They are seen by observers as personable and cooperative because they do not ruffle feathers or challenge other participants.

Stars manage their peers and interact with observers in an actively diplomatic fashion. They listen, encourage the less active to participate, are aware of how to deal with others' reactions to their assertions, and use proper social etiquette (i.e., "please" and "thank you"). In conversation with Stars, the authors have found that these behaviors for some are not perceived by them to be "natural" but are the specific result of conscious, practiced efforts. They realize that they are frustrated when working with slower thinkers and also that acting out that frustration would be counterproductive to goal attainment.

Adversaries may instill fear, but they are not necessarily malicious. Some of our Adversaries, like the Stars above, indicated in discussions with the authors that they had become aware that abrasive, aggressive behavior has a negative effect on people and were trying to correct this limitation. Obviously, however, diplomacy had not become habitual for them. However, most felt that in their natural habitat (daily job), when they were not being poked and prodded by investigators (observers and MAP staff), they were effective and efficient as well as respected, and not feared. We believe this may be true. In a known and stable environment with established rules and weaker competition, they are probably less likely to exhibit the aggressive and abrasive behavior seen by the observers. For our Adversaries, the time-constrained, new, and potentially stressful situations posed by the MAP may have encouraged the expression of these previously infrequent or unnoted dysfunctional behaviors. To the extent that Adversaries will find themselves in the future in naturally occurring stressful, ambiguous, or competitive environments, these latent tendencies may continue to have dysfunctional consequences for Adversaries. Others, namely Stars, will be sought out for leadership roles in these trying circumstances.

Post-MAP comments from Poor performers indicate a misperception of what is being sought in the MAP that relates to Adversary versus Star behavior. They often voice their belief that the MAP encourages and desires vicious, cutthroat behavior. This suggests a lack of appreciation of the difference between the aggressiveness of an Adversary, the assertiveness of a Star, and their own passivity. In terms of the "flight versus fight" syndrome, Phantoms respond by fleeing from the fray to become passive bystanders, and Producers respond by engaging in busywork. Adversaries do enter the fray and involve themselves with group process as well as task issues, but their fight behaviors actually detract from their perceived effectiveness. Stars are often above the fray, but when they do fight they are aware of words and behaviors and they have the necessary behavioral repertoire available to balance both task and social requirements.

Adversaries would benefit from improving their self/other awareness and their interpersonal and group dynamics skills. They have the intelligence and activist style to move ahead in management but, as these positions get more complex and fast-paced, they run the risk of damaging the people/departments they manage and, ultimately, their own career aspirations. They may always experience difficulty when competing with Stars because of the intellectual acuity difference but at least they will be better able to showcase their talents and not be their own enemy.

Producers and Phantoms also would benefit from training in assertiveness, negotiation skills, and group dynamics. While their relative lack of intellectual prowess will likely close out higher-level management positions for them, they may still find themselves involved in unstructured group activities such as task forces. In such settings, because of their technical job expertise or their choice, they may sometimes serve in a formal leadership role. Based on their apparent misunderstanding of aggression and assertion they might then behave like Adversaries and have a detrimental effect on their groups.

Without getting bogged down in discussions of whether leaders are "born" or "made," we believe that Adversaries, Producers, and even Phantoms can, within limits, increase their contribution to groups and reduce their real or potential damage to group process through training and experience (see Table 5). However, due to limitations of both organizational resources and the capacity of adults to radically alter their personality or augment their intelligence, these three types of individuals are at a multidimensional and, perhaps, insurmountable disadvantage compared to Stars. In complex organizational settings that include Stars—Adversaries, Producers, and Phantoms are not likely to emerge as "the leader."

# TABLE 5
## Prototype Descriptions and
## Developmental Recommendations

**TYPE**

**DESCRIPTION**

Exceptionally bright (especially verbally), intellectually alert and curious, energetic, social, adopts an
active/leadership role in groups, sensitive to group
dynamics and process, diplomatic, and effective in
dealing with others. Weaknesses are minor and
idiosyncratic.

**THE STAR**

**DEVELOPMENTAL RECOMMENDATIONS**

Need only fine-tuning or refinement of skills already
present. Promote rapidly to higher levels of management responsibility to encourage continued
growth and challenge.

**DESCRIPTION**

Bright but not nearly as strong in intellectual capacity as the Star, moderately active in groups but efforts to lead are counterproductive.
Aggressive/combative/insensitive behavior leads potential followers to ignore or actively reject them.
While not specifically destructive of group effort,
their lack of sensitivity to others and group process
makes them less effective as leaders.

**THE ADVERSARY**

**DEVELOPMENTAL RECOMMENDATIONS**

Require increased sensitivity to others and awareness of their impact. Training and practice in negotiations skills, group dynamics, team building, and
assertiveness are needed. Should actively seek
feedback from superiors, peers, and subordinates
regarding their reactions, especially in first few management positions.

*Continued on next page*

**TABLE 5**—*Continued*

**TYPE**

---

**DESCRIPTION**

Less intelligent than the other two performance groups, most notably in intellectual alertness/versatility. Limited activity level and then only in a staff or support role. Work effort is intense, determined, and focused on limited tasks with little awareness of group process/dynamics.

**THE PRODUCER**

**DEVELOPMENTAL RECOMMENDATIONS**

As above, should seek interactional skills training and feedback opportunities. Encourage making presentations and participating in or chairing groups, for example, task forces, committees. Likely to be more effective in supportive staff role than in high-level management position.

---

**DESCRIPTION**

Similar to Producers intellectually, but with lower activity levels to the point of being a nonpresence. Appear confused and overwhelmed by the total experience.

**THE PHANTOM**

**DEVELOPMENTAL RECOMMENDATIONS**

Training, practice, and feedback as above. Success in a management position is more likely in an established department in a stable organizational environment.

# References

Bray, D. W., Campbell, R. J., & Grant, D. L. (1974). *Formative years in business: A long-term AT&T study of managerial lives.* New York: Wiley.

Bray, D. W., & Howard, A. (1983). Personality and the assessment center methods. In C. S. Spielberger & J. N. Butcher (Eds.), *Advances in personality measurement* (Vol. 3). New York: Erlbaum Associates.

Campbell, D. P., & Van Velsor, E. (1985). *The use of personality measures in the Leadership Development Program.* Greensboro, NC: Center for Creative Leadership.

Mintzberg, H. (1973). *The nature of managerial work.* New York: Harper and Row.

Moses, J. L., & Byham, W. C. (Eds.). (1977). *Applying the assessment center methods.* New York: Pergamon.

Thornton, G. C., & Byham, W. C. (1982). *Assessment centers and managerial performance.* New York: Academic Press.

Yukl, Gary A. (1981). *Leadership in organizations.* Englewood Cliffs, NJ: Prentice-Hall.

# Some Personality Characteristics of Senior Military Officers

*Herbert F.
Barber*

During the first two weeks of the U.S. Army War College academic year, all students complete a series of psychological and physical assessments to assist them in self-reflection and goal setting as part of a personal development program. Among the psychological assessments included in the program are the Myers-Briggs Type Indicator, Element B, and the Rokeach Value Surveys. The students are currently the senior leaders of the military and will be involved in executive leadership in the future. By their selection, these students have been recognized as successful senior leaders. An examination of the results of these assessments and a comparison with the general population provide some additional insights into the psychological characteristics of leaders.

## Subjects

The 270 subjects were students at the U.S. Army War College (USAWC), Carlisle Barracks, Pennsylvania. The subjects were primarily lieutenant colonels and colonels in the U.S. Army with some representatives from other services, foreign countries, and civilian government organizations. Eleven of the students were female. The selection process for attendance to USAWC is highly competitive. To be selected, every student must have been a successful leader throughout their career and 90 percent of the group have commanded at the Battalion or higher level. The average age of the students is 43 years with 19 years length of service.

## Instruments

**Myers-Briggs Type Indicator (MBTI):** The MBTI yields four indices of personality: EXTRAVERSION(E) versus INTROVERSION(I)—whether one prefers the external world of people and things or the internal world of ideas; SENSING(S) versus INTUITION(N)—whether one pays more attention to realistic, practical data ("hard facts") or to one's imagination and the possibilities of a situation; THINKING(T) versus FEELING(F)—whether one values impersonal logic or personal values/emotions when processing information or making decisions; JUDGING(J) versus PERCEIVING(P)—whether one tends to analyze and categorize the external environment or to respond to it flexibly and spontaneously.

**Element B:** Element B measures a person's characteristic behaviors toward other people in the areas of inclusion, control, and openness. These three needs (needs satisfied through interaction with others) are operating to various degrees within each of us. INCLUSION refers to the desire to join, to be social, to be accepted by others. It deals with the extent to which we want to belong to the group. CONTROL involves the desire for structure, for clear lines of authority, and to have someone be in charge of the group. It has to do with making decisions, power or influence over others, and the acceptance of the authority of others. OPENNESS concerns the extent to which we desire to be emotionally close to others, to be trusted and/or are trusting of others. In any interaction, there are behaviors exhibited by others toward the respondent (what you get from others). The other side of that interaction deals with behavior the respondent exhibited toward others (what you do or give to others). Finally, the questionnaire also describes the way things actually are and the way the respondent would like them to be. This can be thought of as a measure of satisfaction or dissatisfaction with the current situation.

*Rokeach Values:* The Rokeach Terminal and Instrumental Values Surveys ask the respondent to compare and rank order alphabetically arranged values in terms of importance to them. Instrumental values are concerned with modes of conduct (e.g., being honest, being logical) and terminal values involve end states of existence (e.g., a world at peace, happiness). A few of the terms have been modified (e.g., capable was changed to competent and a sense of accomplishment was changed to a sense of service) by the Army Research Institute for use at the USAWC. A complete list of the instrumental and terminal values is presented in the appendix.

## Method

Each of the instruments was administered to the students over a one-week period early in the academic year. Class norms were computed and compared with normative data gathered on as close to "general population adult males" as possible. Since the subjects consisted of 96% males, it was felt that the most appropriate comparisons would be with adult males. The general population norms were obtained from the respective test authors' manuals or writings.

## Results

**MBTI** The MBTI Type Table shown in Table 1 displays the 16 possible combinations of the four preference pairs. The percentages of officers having each psychological type are presented. For comparison purposes, the percentages of 5,632 male college graduates (Myers & McCaulley, 1985) are also shown. Of the 16 possible types, 53.5% of the officers are ISTJ and ESTJ. In fact, 71.1% of the students are in the "four corners" (i.e., ISTJ, ESTJ, INTJ, and ENTJ). In contrast, only 31.5% of the compar-

## TABLE 1
## Myers-Briggs Type Indicator
## Percentage of the 16 Types

| ISTJ | ISFJ | INFJ | INTJ |
|---|---|---|---|
| «««« 32.2 | «««« 3.0 | «««« 1.9 | «««« 9.0 |
| »»»» 10.6 | »»»» 6.3 | »»»» 2.9 | »»»» 4.3 |
| **ISTP** | **ISFP** | **INFP** | **INTP** |
| «««« 5.6 | «««« 0.4 | «««« 1.1 | «««« 2.6 |
| »»»» 6.8 | »»»» 5.1 | »»»» 5.8 | »»»» 5.8 |
| **ESTP** | **ESFP** | **ENFP** | **ENTP** |
| «««« 3.4 | «««« 1.5 | «««« 1.9 | «««« 4.9 |
| »»»» 6.5 | »»»» 5.4 | »»»» 7.5 | »»»» 6.2 |
| **ESTJ** | **ESFJ** | **ENFJ** | **ENTJ** |
| «««« 21.3 | «««« 1.9 | «««« .7 | «««« 8.6 |
| »»»» 11.2 | »»»» 6.6 | »»»» 3.7 | »»»» 5.4 |

«««« *Senior Military Officers (270)*
»»»» *General Population Male College Graduates (5,632)*

ison group fall in those four categories. What the four corners have in common are the Thinking and Judging preferences. Myers and McCaulley (1985) describe TJs as "the logical decision makers" who are "tough-minded, executive, analytical, and instrumental leaders" (p. 36).

Table 2 focuses on the four preference pairs separately. As a group, the officers are slightly more introverted and more likely to be sensors than the general population group. Introverts focus inside themselves on concepts and ideas, are thoughtful and reflective, and enjoy independence and privacy. Sensors are down-to-earth and practical, focus on the here and now, and are good at dealing with details and specific facts. These results reinforce indications that these senior military officers are predominately thinkers and judgers especially in comparison with the general population group. Thinkers are concerned with making logical, objective, and firm decisions. They are impersonal in their judgments and emphasize justice, fairness, and cause and effect. Judgers are decisive and are looking for closure. They plan ahead, are well organized, work from schedules, and are punctual.

**Element B** The mean responses to the Element B questionnaire are presented in Table 3. The comparison data was obtained on 172 adult males presented in the Element B manual (Schutz, 1983). In addition to the mean ratings, a difference score was computed which measures the degree of satisfaction or dissatisfaction with the

## TABLE 2
## Myers-Briggs Type Indicator
## Percentage of Preference Pairs

| SENIOR MILITARY OFFICERS | | GENERAL POPULATION (MALE) | |
|---|---|---|---|
| E | 44.2 | E | 52.5 |
| I | 55.8 | I | 47.6 |
| S | 69.3 | S | 58.5 |
| N | 30.7 | N | 41.6 |
| T | 87.6 | T | 56.8 |
| F | 12.4 | F | 43.3 |
| J | 78.6 | J | 51.0 |
| P | 21.4 | P | 49.1 |

## TABLE 3
## Element B Mean Scores

| | THE WAY IT IS | THE WAY I WANT | DIFFERENCE (Satisfaction) |
|---|---|---|---|
| I INCLUDE PEOPLE | «««« 4.2 | «««« 5.4 | «««« − 1.2 |
| | »»»» 4.6 | »»»» 5.2 | »»»» − 0.6 |
| PEOPLE INCLUDE ME | «««« 3.5 | «««« 5.7 | «««« − 2.2 |
| | »»»» 3.5 | »»»» 5.0 | »»»» − 1.5 |
| I CONTROL PEOPLE | «««« 4.8 | «««« 6.5 | «««« − 1.7 |
| | »»»» 3.8 | »»»» 5.0 | »»»» − 1.2 |
| PEOPLE CONTROL ME | «««« 5.0 | «««« 4.3 | «««« 0.7 |
| | »»»» 4.2 | »»»» 3.2 | »»»» 1.0 |
| I AM OPEN WITH PEOPLE | «««« 2.6 | «««« 3.5 | «««« − 0.9 |
| | »»»» 3.2 | »»»» 3.9 | »»»» − 0.7 |
| PEOPLE ARE OPEN WITH ME | «««« 3.5 | «««« 4.7 | «««« − 1.2 |
| | »»»» 2.7 | »»»» 3.9 | »»»» − 1.2 |

«««« Senior Military Officers (270)
»»»» General Population − Male (172)

current situation (i.e., "The Way It Is" minus "The Way I Want"). With the exception of "People Control Me," the wanted scores are higher than the way things actually are. These difference scores indicate a general dissatisfaction with the current situation for both groups. In comparison with the general population group, the officers have a higher need to be in control during interaction with others. In addition, while the officers felt that people controlled them more than desired, they had higher acceptance that someone should be in control of a situation, even if the individual in control was someone else. While the officers were not as open with other people, they did want people to be open with them. In fact, they felt that people were more open with them than did the comparison group. In addition, there is a large difference (larger than the comparison group) between "I am open with people" and "I want people to be open with me" indicating they wanted openness from others but were not as willing to be as open themselves.

**Rokeach Values** Tables 4 and 5 list the top five and bottom five values for both the officer group and a national sample of 655 males presented by Rokeach (1973). The highest- and lowest-ranked Instrumental Values are presented in Table 4. The officers ranked being competent and logical as more important and being ambitious and courageous as less important than the national sample. In fact, the national sample ranked being logical towards the bottom of the list. Further, the officers felt that being forgiving, cheerful, and polite were less important than did the comparison group and being intellectual and imaginative were more important.

Table 5 presents the Terminal Values data. The officers ranked self-respect, a sense of service, and wisdom more important and a world at peace, a comfortable life, and happiness as less important than the comparison group. They ranked comfortable life as one of the least important values. In addition, the officers ranked equality as less important and mature love as more important than did the comparison group.

# TABLE 4
## Instrumental Values

| GENERAL MALE POPULATION (655) | SENIOR MILITARY OFFICERS (270) |
|:---:|:---:|

### "TOP FIVE" MOST VALUED

| GENERAL MALE POPULATION (655) | SENIOR MILITARY OFFICERS (270) |
|:---:|:---:|
| HONEST<br>(sincere, truthful) | HONEST<br>(sincere, truthful) |
| AMBITIOUS<br>(hardworking, aspiring) | RESPONSIBLE<br>(dependable, reliable) |
| RESPONSIBLE<br>(dependable, reliable) | COMPETENT<br>(capable, efficient) |
| BROAD-MINDED<br>(open-minded) | COURAGEOUS<br>(standing up for your beliefs) |
| COURAGEOUS<br>(standing up for your beliefs) | LOGICAL<br>(consistent, rational) |

### "BOTTOM FIVE" LEAST VALUED

| GENERAL MALE POPULATION (655) | SENIOR MILITARY OFFICERS (270) |
|:---:|:---:|
| LOVING<br>(affectionate, tender) | LOVING<br>(affectionate, tender) |
| INTELLECTUAL<br>(intelligent, reflective) | FORGIVING<br>(willing to pardon others) |
| LOGICAL<br>(consistent, rational) | OBEDIENT<br>(dutiful, respectful) |
| OBEDIENT<br>(dutiful, respectful) | CHEERFUL<br>(lighthearted, joyful) |
| IMAGINATIVE<br>(daring, creative) | POLITE<br>(courteous, well-mannered) |

# TABLE 5
## Terminal Values

| GENERAL MALE POPULATION (655) | SENIOR MILITARY OFFICERS (270) |
|---|---|

### "TOP FIVE" MOST VALUED

| GENERAL MALE POPULATION (655) | SENIOR MILITARY OFFICERS (270) |
|---|---|
| WORLD AT PEACE (free of war and conflict) | FAMILY SECURITY (taking care of loved ones) |
| FAMILY SECURITY (taking care of loved ones) | SELF-RESPECT (self-esteem) |
| FREEDOM (independence, free choice) | FREEDOM (independence, free choice) |
| COMFORTABLE LIFE (a prosperous life) | SENSE OF SERVICE (contribution to society) |
| HAPPINESS (contentedness) | WISDOM (a mature understanding of life) |

### "BOTTOM FIVE" LEAST VALUED

| GENERAL MALE POPULATION (655) | SENIOR MILITARY OFFICERS (270) |
|---|---|
| MATURE LOVE (sexual and spiritual intimacy) | COMFORTABLE LIFE (a prosperous life) |
| WORLD OF BEAUTY (beauty of nature and the arts) | EQUALITY (brotherhood/equal opportunity for all) |
| SOCIAL RECOGNITION (respect, admiration) | SOCIAL RECOGNITION (respect, admiration) |
| PLEASURE (enjoyable, leisurely life) | PLEASURE (an enjoyable, leisurely life) |
| EXCITING LIFE (a stimulating, active life) | WORLD OF BEAUTY (beauty of nature and the arts) |

# APPENDIX

| Terminal Values | Instrumental Values |
|---|---|
| A comfortable life | Ambitious |
| An exciting life | Broad-minded |
| Equality | Competent |
| Family Security | Cheerful |
| Freedom | Concerned |
| Happiness | Courageous |
| Inner Harmony | Forgiving |
| Mature Love | Helpful |
| National Security | Honest |
| Pleasure | Imaginative |
| Salvation | Independent |
| Self-Respect | Intellectual |
| Sense of Service | Logical |
| Social Recognition | Loving |
| True Friendship | Obedient |
| Wisdom | Polite |
| World at Peace | Responsible |
| World of Beauty | Self-control |

# References

Myers, I. B., & McCaulley, M. H. (1985). *Manual: A guide to the development and use of the Myers-Briggs Type Indicator*. Palo Alto, CA: Consulting Psychologists Press.

Rokeach, M. (1973). *The nature of human values*. New York: Free Press.

Schutz, W. (1983). *The Schutz measures: Elements of awareness* (research ed.). Palo Alto, CA: Consulting Psychologists Press.

# Leadership in Latin American Organizations: A Glimpse of Styles Through Personality Measures

T. Noel Osborn and Diana B. Osborn

Osborn and Osborn (1986) reported Myers-Briggs and FIRO-B data from a sample of 206 Latin American middle-level managers. These data were compared to those of a homologous group of 875 U.S. managers, with implications for style similarities and differences along these two popular test measures.

The results are reviewed in Tables 1 and 2. They suggest that U.S. managers may find their Latin American counterparts similar in some ways. After all, the Sensing, Thinking, Judging type is common to both groups. But the groups are different, too. U.S. managers may find themselves uncomfortable with the increased level of extraversion and of "outer" relationship behavior exhibited by Latins. They may also be put off by a less intuitive approach to decision making when an appreciation of the possibilities rather than the facts seems relevant to the problem at hand.

An important difference may arise concerning acceptance of the participative management model considered almost standard in current leadership literature. Such authors as Ouchi (1981), Peters and Waterman (1982), and Kanter (1983) all suggest a higher degree of employee participation in decision making. Reflecting his control scores, the Latin American manager may view leadership in a much more authoritarian way than the U S. manager. Even if he accepts the concept of participative management in principle, it may be considerably more difficult to get him to implement a particular technique such as quality circles, for example. A focus on the development of the subordinate to assume higher levels of authority may threaten the Latin manager, if it is perceived that his own authority may be diluted in the process. The U.S. executive must take into account the possibility of

# TABLE 1
## Myers-Briggs Type Indicator (MBTI)

### Latin American and U.S. Managers

| | Latin Americans n=206 | | U.S. n=875 | | chi$^2$ |
|---|---|---|---|---|---|
| | (n) | % | (n) | % | df = 1 |
| EXTRAVERTS | 119 | 58 | 438 | 50 | 3.97* |
| INTROVERTS | 87 | 42 | 437 | 50 | |
| SENSORS | 161 | 78 | 455 | 52 | 46.54** |
| INTUITIVES | 45 | 22 | 420 | 48 | |
| THINKERS | 189 | 92 | 717 | 82 | 11.81** |
| FEELERS | 17 | 8 | 158 | 18 | |
| JUDGERS | 179 | 87 | 604 | 70 | 26.65** |
| PERCEIVERS | 27 | 13 | 271 | 30 | |

### Mexican and U.S. Secretarial Level

| | Mexicans n=100 | | U.S. n=346 | | chi$^2$ |
|---|---|---|---|---|---|
| | (n) | % | (n) | % | df = 1 |
| EXTRAVERTS | 58 | 58 | 186 | 54 | 1.46 |
| INTROVERTS | 42 | 42 | 160 | 46 | |
| SENSORS | 89 | 89 | 256 | 74 | 15.46** |
| INTUITIVES | 11 | 11 | 90 | 26 | |
| THINKERS | 77 | 77 | 135 | 39 | 46.30** |
| FEELERS | 23 | 23 | 211 | 61 | |
| JUDGERS | 90 | 90 | 228 | 66 | 32.76** |
| PERCEIVERS | 10 | 10 | 118 | 34 | |

*$p \leq .05$
**$p \leq .001$

a practical refusal of his Latin colleague to work enthusiastically with the participative management model.

Tables 1 and 2 contain data concerning not only these executive comparisons, but also comparable new data covering clerical personnel. Our sample is 100 Mexican secretaries/administrative assistants who have taken the Center's "Support Your Boss" *(Seminario para Asistentes de Ejecutivos)* program in Spanish, compared to a corresponding sample of 375 U.S. secretarial level personnel who took the program in English at the Center for Creative Leadership.

In summary, the secretarial sample shows results similar to those presented for their "bosses": On the Myers-Briggs Type Indicator, Mexican secretaries are significantly

# TABLE 2
## Fundamental Interpersonal Relationship Orientation Behavior (FIRO-B)

### Latin American and U.S. Managers

**LATIN AMERICANS**
**n = 206**

|            | INCLUSION | CONTROL | AFFECTION |
|------------|-----------|---------|-----------|
| expressed  | 4.4***    | 5.3*    | 4.6***    |
| wanted     | 3.0       | 2.7**   | 5.2       |

**U.S.**
**n = 875**

|            | INCLUSION | CONTROL | AFFECTION |
|------------|-----------|---------|-----------|
| expressed  | 3.5       | 4.8     | 3.0       |
| wanted     | 2.9       | 3.1     | 4.8       |

*Note: All managers are from organizational Levels 3 and 4.*

### Mexican and U.S. Secretarial Level

**MEXICANS**
**n = 100**

|            | INCLUSION | CONTROL | AFFECTION |
|------------|-----------|---------|-----------|
| expressed  | 4.8*      | 2.9***  | 4.5***    |
| wanted     | 3.9       | 2.0**   | 5.5       |

**U.S.**
**n = 346**

|            | INCLUSION | CONTROL | AFFECTION |
|------------|-----------|---------|-----------|
| expressed  | 4.3       | 2.0     | 3.7       |
| wanted     | 3.4       | 3.4     | 5.3       |

   * *Statistically significantly higher than U.S. sample, p<.02*
  ** *Statistically significantly lower than U.S. sample, p<.01*
*** *Statistically significantly higher than U.S. sample, p<.001*

## TABLE 3
### Type of Distribution of
### Latin American Middle-Level Managers

N = 206    Mean age = 39    Date '82–'84    Sex 90% m

| ISTJ | ISFJ | INFJ | INTJ |
|------|------|------|------|
| n = 59 | n = 3 | n = 0 | n = 15 |
| (28.6%) | (1.4%) | (0%) | (7.3%) |
| ISTP | ISFP | INFP | INTP |
| n = 6 | n = 1 | n = 0 | n = 2 |
| (2.9%) | (.4%) | (0%) | (1%) |
| ESTP | ESFP | ENFP | ENTP |
| n = 9 | n = 1 | n = 3 | n = 4 |
| (4.3%) | (.4%) | (1.4%) | (1.9%) |
| ESTJ | ESFJ | ENFJ | ENTJ |
| n = 81 | n = 2 | n = 6 | n = 13 |
| (39.3%) | (1%) | (2.9%) | (6.3%) |

more STJ than their U.S. counterparts. On FIRO-B, they are also significantly more expressive of interrelationship behaviors, and the "authoritarian" model (higher expressed control, lower wanted control than U.S.) also fits their scores. It turns out that Latin secretaries in this sample are very similar to their bosses in many ways, and different from their U.S. counterparts in many of the same ways their bosses are. In this same vein, it also turns out that the Mexican secretaries in our sample are much more "Thinking"-oriented than their U.S. counterparts, in fact nearly the reverse: where many more U.S. secretaries are "feelers" than "thinkers," in our sample of Mexican secretaries the opposite is true.

Tables 3 through 6 present Myers-Briggs-type data for both the earlier sample of managers as well as the secretarial sample. It was interesting for us to compare these tables by cultural origin, that is, overlay the managers' table on the secretarial table for Latin groups and U.S. groups. Doing so reveals that the "Latin American firm," composed of managers and "their secretaries" in our samples, is considerably more predominant in STJ styles than "U.S. firms," where the overlay produces a better balance across the 16 types of the table. In fact, it would appear that the combination of Latin managers and secretaries in our samples produces a heavy loading on the left-hand column of the type table. This may mean, if such a broad hypothesis can be made to stand, that the culture of the typical Latin firm may be more solid and stable, but also more bureaucratic and resistant to change than that of the U.S. organization. The Latin firm may also lack the "feeling" component, mainly covered by the secretarial level in the U.S. sample. That is, attention to values and sentiments, important in implementation of decisions as people everywhere become more "knowledge workers," may be more difficult in the culture of the Latin organization.

## TABLE 4
## Type Distribution of Mexican
## Secretaries & Administrative Assistants

N = 100    Mean age = 35    Date '85–'86    Sex 100% f

| | | | |
|---|---|---|---|
| ISTJ<br>n = 31<br>(31%) | ISFJ<br>n = 4<br>(4%) | INFJ<br>n = 1<br>(1%) | INTJ<br>n = 1<br>(1%) |
| ISTP<br>n = 3<br>(3%) | ISFP<br>n = 0<br>(0%) | INFP<br>n = 1<br>(1%) | INTP<br>n = 1<br>(1%) |
| ESTP<br>n = 1<br>(1%) | ESFP<br>n = 3<br>(3%) | ENFP<br>n = 1<br>(1%) | ENTP<br>n = 0<br>(0%) |
| ESTJ<br>N = 35<br>(35%) | ESFJ<br>N = 12<br>(12%) | ENFJ<br>N = 1<br>(1%) | ENTJ<br>N = 5<br>(5%) |

## TABLE 5
## Type Distribution of
## U.S. Middle-Level Managers

N = 875    Mean age = 40    Date '79–'83    Sex 85% m

| | | | |
|---|---|---|---|
| ISTJ<br>n = 184<br>(21%) | ISFJ<br>n = 15<br>(1.7%) | INFJ<br>n = 17<br>(2%) | INTJ<br>n = 103<br>(11.7%) |
| ISTP<br>n = 36<br>(4.1%) | ISFP<br>n = 9<br>(1%) | INFP<br>n = 24<br>(2.7%) | INTP<br>n = 51<br>(5.8%) |
| ESTP<br>n = 31<br>(3.5%) | ESFP<br>n = 7<br>(.7%) | ENFP<br>n = 43<br>(4.9%) | ENTP<br>n = 70<br>(8%) |
| ESTJ<br>n = 147<br>(16.7%) | ESFJ<br>n = 26<br>(2.9%) | ENFJ<br>n = 17<br>(1.9%) | ENTJ<br>n = 97<br>(11%) |

## TABLE 6
## Type Distribution of
## U.S. Secretaries & Administrative Assistants

N = 346    Mean age = 35    Date '79–'83    Sex 99% f

| | | | |
|---|---|---|---|
| ISTJ | ISFJ | INFJ | INTJ |
| n = 34 | n = 43 | n = 0 | n = 6 |
| (10%) | (12%) | (0%) | (2%) |
| ISTP | ISFP | INFP | INTP |
| n = 11 | n = 24 | n = 41 | n = 10 |
| (3%) | (7%) | (12%) | (3%) |
| ESTP | ESFP | ENFP | ENTP |
| n = 9 | n = 20 | n = 18 | n = 8 |
| (3%) | (6%) | (5%) | (2%) |
| ESTJ | ESFJ | ENFJ | ENTJ |
| n = 46 | n = 53 | n = 14 | n = 9 |
| (13%) | (15%) | (4%) | (3%) |

At the moment, these conclusions are quite speculative and are presented in this paper only to indicate the possibilities for the kind of data we are generating. As leaders and managers extend their activities across cultural and national boundaries, data of this sort becomes increasingly important.

## References

Kanter, R. (1983). *The change masters*. New York: Simon & Schuster.

Osborn, T. N., & Osborn, D. B. (1986). Leadership training in a Latin context. *Issues and Observations, 6*(2). Center for Creative Leadership: Greensboro, NC.

Ouchi, W. (1981). *Theory Z: How American business can meet the Japanese challenge*. Reading, MA: Addison Wesley.

Peters, T., & Waterman, R. (1982). *In search of excellence*. New York: Harper & Row.

# SECTION G

**Intellectual Qualities
of Leaders**

# Intellectual Qualities
of Leaders

The American tradition is so strongly anti-elitist that we resist any evidence which indicates that leadership and authority belong more often to those who come from more privileged classes or who are born brighter. In fact, a substantial part of the psychological literature, reviewed succinctly by Most, supports the notion that excessive intelligence is a handicap to leadership. In this section, the authors deal with current concerns about the mental abilities required of leaders and how such abilities must be used if the organization is to benefit.

## Hypotheses About the Relationship Between Leadership and Intelligence
Robert Most

This paper is a review of various studies of the relationships found among measures of intelligence, personality, and leadership. The dominance scale on the California Psychological Inventory, Wechsler Intelligence Scale scores, and Gough's Leadership Index are among the measures used.

Robert Most, Vice President for Research and Development, Consulting Psychologists Press, Inc., 577 College Avenue, Post Office Box 60070, Palo Alto, California 94306. (415-852-1444). PhD, Wayne State University.

## Predicting Performance During the Apprenticeship
Earl H. Potter III and Robert R. Albright II

Graduates of the Coast Guard Academy are studied as they move into their first or apprenticeship assignment aboard ship, a period of uncertainty, time pressure, and heavy work loads. Under these circumstances, the dynamics of career progress and career transitions can be studied. The important variables in predicting performance during the apprenticeship include ability to deal with stress, intelligence, past performance under demanding conditions, and an officer's history of difficulty in figuring out and responding to the demands of his or her supervisor.

Earl H. Potter III, Associate Dean for Academics and Associate Professor of Management, Department of Economics and Management, U.S. Coast Guard Academy (db), New London, Connecticut 06320-4195. (203-444-8334). PhD, University of Washington. Past Yale Visiting Faculty Fellow, Mellon Foundation. Recipient of U.S. Coast Guard Commendation Medal. Author and coauthor of various articles and chapters.

Robert R. Albright II, Instructor of Economics and Management, Department of Economics and Management, U.S. Coast Guard Academy (db), New London, Connecticut 06320-4195. (203-444-8339). MBA, University of Pittsburgh. Recipient of Meritorious Service Medal and Coast Guard Jarvis Award. Past commanding officer, USCGC *CAPE SHOALWATER*. President, Board of Directors of Big Brothers/Big Sisters of southeastern Connecticut. Author of "Patrol Boat Law Enforcement Tactics," *Coast Guard Group Miami Operations Plan.* Coauthor of *The U.S. Coast Guard Academy Class of 1986: Biographical Predictors of Success.*

## Intellectual Styles
Robert J. Sternberg

Intellectual styles are not levels of intelligence, but ways of using intelligence—a propensity. Three different styles of mental self-government are postulated: executive, legislative, and judicial. This model leads to an assessment not so much of an individual's intelligence, but rather how that intelligence is directed or exploited. Factors influencing the development of different styles are discussed.

Robert J. Sternberg, IBM Professor of Psychology and Education, Yale University, Post Office Box 11A, Yale Station, New Haven, Connecticut 06520-7447. (203-432-4633). PhD, Stanford University. Author of *The Triarchic Mind* and *Beyond IQ.* Coeditor of *Practical Intelligence: Nature and Origins of Competence in the Everyday World.*

## Street Smarts
Richard K. Wagner and Robert J. Sternberg

Academic intelligence is not unimportant to leadership, but it must be complemented by a well-developed practical intelligence or "street smarts." Performance on this measure of tacit knowledge aims to produce a measure that differentiates experts from novices, relates to measures of success in career pursuits, and is not closely related to IQ. Preliminary results are reported.

Richard K. Wagner, Associate Professor, Department of Psychology, Florida State University, Tallahassee, Florida 32306. (904-644-1033). PhD, Yale University. Coeditor of *Practical Intelligence: Nature and Origins of Competence in the Everyday World.* Coauthor of The Tacit Knowledge Inventory for Managers (TKIM).

Robert J. Sternberg, IBM Professor of Psychology and Education, Yale University, Post Office Box 11A, Yale Station, New Haven, Connecticut 06520-7447. (203-432-4633). PhD, Stanford University. Author of *The Triarchic Mind* and *Beyond IQ.* Coeditor of *Practical Intelligence: Nature and Origins of Competence in the Everyday World.*

# Hypotheses About the Relationship Between Leadership and Intelligence

*Robert Most*

Edward Wenk in *Tradeoffs* (1987) makes a strong case for intelligence and foresightful thinking among leaders in both the public and private sectors. He provides a number of examples of how the lack of prior intelligent thinking by decision makers has led to catastrophes and political conflict.

In an interesting counterargument to Wenk's point, political scientists have hypothesized that less intelligent U.S. presidents have made better presidents. In recent times we have witnessed the very intelligent and involved Jimmy Carter, whose presidency was marked by inflation and instability, versus the less intelligent Ronald Reagan, whose presidency has been economically and socially stable.

Despite the importance of the question, leadership researchers have devoted comparatively little attention to the relationship between intelligence and leadership (Bass, 1981). Following are a few hypotheses that have been offered about the relationship:

1. Leaders are more intelligent than the group, on average, but not too much more.

2. Other qualities besides intelligence are needed for leadership.

3. Among mental abilities relating to intelligence, some will be more predictive of leadership abilities than others.

Although none of the above hypotheses have much research supporting them, I will present some evidence for each.

**Are Leaders More Intelligent?** Bass (1981, p. 47) lists 16 studies of the relationship between leadership and various characteristics such as IQ, grades (elementary school through college), age, height, and weight. The correlations between IQ and leadership range from -.14 to .90. The average coefficient was approximately .28 and only one study showed a negative correlation. Thirteen of the studies showed correlations above .10. Thus, it is reasonable to draw the conclusion that there is some relationship between intelligence and leadership.

Bass (1981) also reviews 33 studies of intelligence and leadership in children and students that were conducted prior to 1970. All but four of these studies indicated that child or student leaders surpass the average member of the group in intelligence. However, "in most of these studies there is considerable overlapping of intelligence test scores, indicating that superior intelligence is not an absolute requirement for leadership" (p. 50).

In studies after 1970, Bass found 25 studies that showed a positive relationship between intelligence and leadership.

**How Much More Intelligent Than the Group Is the Leader?** The strongest of Bass' findings is that leaders can be more intelligent than the group but not too much more intelligent. There seems to be a social relativity factor.

In Bass' review of 25 studies conducted after 1970 he found five studies that indicated that extreme differences between the intelligence of leaders and followers actually mitigate against the exercise of leadership.

In a study by Hollingworth (1926), children of average intelligence were found to choose leaders whose IQ was in the 115 to 130 range but never 160. Leaders of IQ 160 might lead a group of children with an average IQ of 130. The issue is one of communication. Children with an IQ in the average range cannot comprehend the vocabulary of children whose IQ is substantially higher than their own. There are differences as well in interests, goals, and activity patterns that are barriers to joint participation.

In college student organizations, McCuen (1929) found that there was "a tendency to select leaders with scores *slightly* above the average with respect to the group."

Ghiselli (1963) found a curvilinear relation between intelligence and managerial success. He writes, "The relationship between intelligence and managerial success is curvilinear with those individuals earning both low and very high scores being less likely to achieve success in management positions than those with scores at intermediate levels."

**Are Other Qualities Besides Intelligence Needed for Leadership?** In reviewing the studies before 1970, Bass (1981) notes that even when intelligence was found to be a factor in leadership, leaders were seen to exhibit other traits such as maturity and conscientiousness. He writes, "Thus, it appears that high intelligence may be associated with other characteristics which contribute toward a person's value as a leader."

On the California Psychological Inventory (CPI), the Dominance scale, which is an excellent predictor of leadership (Megargee & Carbonell, 1988), correlates with Wechsler Adult Intelligence Scale scores only .07 for men and .24 for women, showing no particular relationship (Gough, 1987). There was no relationship between high

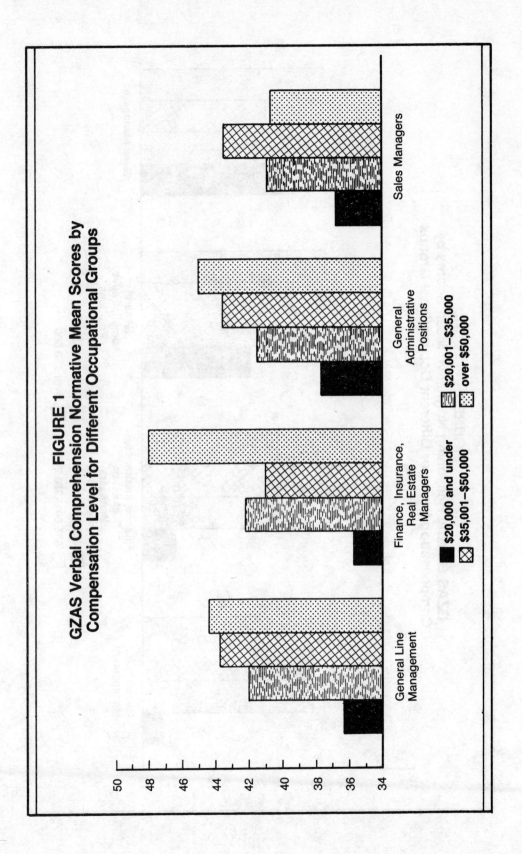

**FIGURE 1**

**GZAS Verbal Comprehension Normative Mean Scores by Compensation Level for Different Occupational Groups**

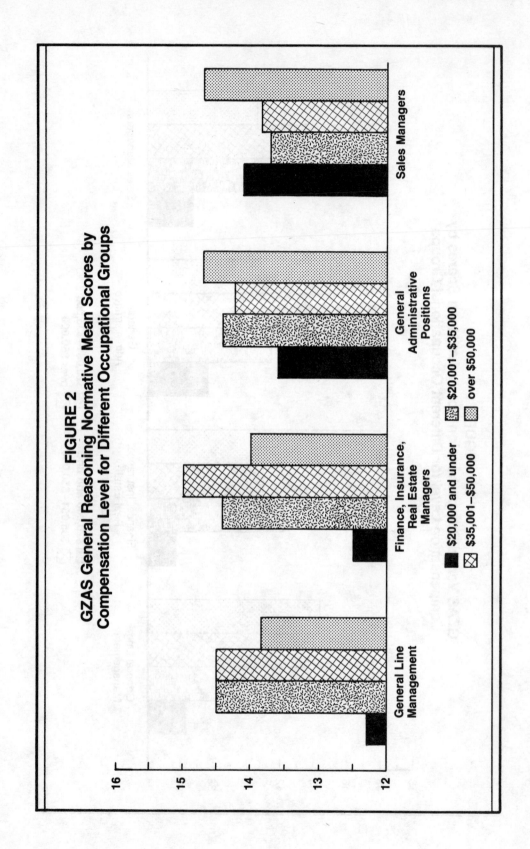

**FIGURE 2**
**GZAS General Reasoning Normative Mean Scores by Compensation Level for Different Occupational Groups**

school students nominated as leaders and scores on the Intellectual Efficiency scale (a scale that correlates well with IQ).

The CPI Leadership Index (Gough, 1969) does not contain the Intellectual Efficiency scale but it does contain the related Achievement via Independence scale. The scales contained in the Leadership Index could be considered evidence that it takes more than intelligence to make for leadership. The scales on the index are Dominance, Self-Acceptance, Well-Being, a negative loading on Good Impression, and Achievement via Independence.

**Are Some Mental Abilities More Predictive of Leadership Than Others?** If there is sufficient evidence that intelligence can be a factor in leadership, are there some types of intelligence that are more related to leadership than others? Figures 1 and 2 from Guilford-Zimmerman Aptitude Survey (Guilford & Zimmerman, 1981) scales provide some tentative evidence that Verbal Comprehension is more predictive of compensation level than is General Reasoning. Verbal Comprehension is essentially a measure of vocabulary or word knowledge, and General Reasoning is a measure of problem-solving skill. Of course, this evidence is indicative of leadership only to the extent that compensation is an index of leadership.

## Conclusion

A brief survey such as this is not sufficient to answer the question about the relationship between leadership and intelligence. The question is an important one, however, and research is needed to provide evidence of a relationship and to examine the nature of the relationship. Of the three hypotheses examined here, the most intriguing one was that leaders may be more intelligent than the group average but not too much more intelligent.

## References

Bass, B. M. (1981). *Stogdill's handbook of leadership*. New York: Free Press.

Ghiselli, E. E. (1963). The validity of management traits in relation to occupational level. *Personnel Psychology, 16,* 109–113.

Gough, H. G. (1969). A leadership index on the California Psychological Inventory. *Journal of Counseling Psychology, 16,* 283–289.

Gough, H. G. (1987). *California Psychological Inventory administrator's guide.* Palo Alto, CA: Consulting Psychologists Press.

Guilford, J. P., & Zimmerman, W. S. (1981). *The Guilford-Zimmerman Aptitude Survey: Manual of instructions and interpretations* (rev. ed.). Palo Alto, CA: Consulting Psychologists Press.

Hollingworth, L. S. (1926). *Gifted children.* New York: Macmillan.

McCuen, T. L. (1929). Leadership and intelligence. *Education, 50,* 89–95.

Megargee, E. I., & Carbonell, J. L. (1988). Evaluating leadership with the CPI. In C. D. Spielberger & J. N. Butcher (Eds.), *Advances in personality assessment* (Vol. 7). Hillsdale, NJ: Lawrence Erlbaum Associates.

Wenk, E. (1987). *Tradeoffs: Imperatives of choice in a high-tech world*. Baltimore, MD: Johns Hopkins University Press.

# Predicting Performance During the Apprenticeship

*Earl H.
Potter III
and
Robert R.
Albright II*

When industrial/organizational psychologists and managers get together to discuss the selection of applicants for a career in management, their different objectives do not always facilitate a common understanding of career development. The manager wants to select people who will make the greatest contribution to the bottom line. The classical industrial psychologist seeks to maximize the variance in "success" accounted for by an equation. Neither may be moved to attempt to understand the dynamics of success across the stages of a career. It is also unlikely that either will question the nature of the expectations which define career success at each level of the organization. As a result they may cut personnel costs and achieve high multiple R's but they do not develop a comprehensive grasp of career development. Without a complete picture of who succeeds at each level of the organization, and why, theorists and practitioners alike are limited in their ability to design organizations for the greatest effectiveness.

From our perspective it is just as important to be able to predict performance in the first assignment as it is to predict who will rise to the top levels of management. Common sense argues that different skills and attributes are required for success at different levels in organizations. In fact, recent writing on career stages (e.g., Dalton & Thompson, 1986) documents the difficulty of making successful transitions between stages. The greatest difficulty occurs when familiar behaviors must be abandoned in order to succeed at the next-higher level. Past success is only the best predictor of future success when the future requires the same behaviors that led to success in the past. Successful contributors at one level may fail at the next and the process of "natural selection" in the organization may eliminate people with skills and attributes which would later be valuable to the organization.

In order to understand success at each career stage it is essential first to identify discrete career stages and then to develop predictions specific for each level. Katz (1985) distinguishes the socialization processes which take place during the first year of employment as the first stage. During this time new employees (1) establish their role identity, (2) learn to deal with their boss and other employees, and (3) decipher the reward systems and situational norms. Dalton and Thompson (1986) call this period the apprenticeship. It is a time full of uncertainty requiring adaptive skills which facilitate information gathering and problem solving. It seems likely that the skills and attributes which lead to success at this stage will differ from the skills and attributes associated with success when employees have gained experience in the organization.

Research on management success, however, most often concentrates on the attributes which characterize those who have risen to the top of organizations. Prediction equations are, therefore, most often developed to select the sort of people who make it to the top. Even the longitudinal research of Howard and Bray (1988) looks at performance over fairly long periods of time without attention to the stages through which managers pass during that time.

The best example of this tendency in the study of military leadership is Campbell's 1987 study of General and Flag officers in the Department of Defense. In brief, Campbell describes officers who rise to this level as "dominant, competitive, action-oriented patriotic men who are drawn naturally to physically adventuresome, militaristic activities, and who are repulsed by artistic, literary, musical, and nurturing activities." When matched with a high degree of social responsibility and personal integrity, as these men were, the country is well served. With a different set of core values such men might become threats to stability. Campbell wonders aloud if the development and selection processes result in leaders who have the attributes necessary for leadership in the next decades. His speculation focuses on the right questions—his data focus on leadership at the top.

In order to understand the process which produces generals and admirals we need to begin at selection and trace the development of those officers through each stage of their careers. If we develop a thorough understanding of the factors which lead to career success at each stage of a career we will be better able to select those who will succeed. We will also be better able to design organizations which raise up the kind of people we want to succeed. This study began when the U.S. Coast Guard Academy class of 1986 entered the academy in the summer of 1982. At this time we have followed the graduates of that class through their apprenticeship—the first two years of their service as junior officers.

The Coast Guard Academy might be considered a four-year-long assessment center. Approximately one-half of the cadets who enter graduate. Those who do graduate will rise through a series of progressively finer screens. Along the way officers who do not fit the profile of the ideal officer at each successive grade will be dropped by the "up or out" promotion process. Those who reach the top will lead a service dominated by academy graduates. Only one of the admirals currently on active duty is not an academy graduate.

Education at the Coast Guard Academy is accomplished in a highly structured environment. Cadets are restricted to the confines of the academy grounds except for specifically defined "liberty" periods. The curriculum, which is highly technical, has little room for freedom; their dress is governed by a book of uniform regulations; and obedience is greatly valued. Cadets pursue a Bachelor of Science in one of seven majors while at the same time performing duties as members of the Cadet Regiment. Their performance of these duties is evaluated by classmates, cadets senior to them, and commissioned company officers. Especially during the first or "Swab" year the sum of academic and military duties is daunting. Cadets who graduate have mastered the skills needed to balance competing demands under great pressure. In appearance and bearing they have a common quality that is unmistakable. Yet, they are certainly not the same. In acceptance of the regulations and underlying values and in their degree of mastery there is wide variation. Our first interest was to examine the development that took place over these four years in order to define the characteristics that facilitate or inhibit later success.

Following graduation every new ensign is assigned to duty aboard a ship for two years. About one-third serve as student engineers learning propulsion, electric, water, and heating/cooling systems. Two-thirds will be assigned as deck officers responsible for maintenance, navigation, and operational planning. All will pursue qualification as officers of the deck (OOD's) who, as the captain's surrogate for four-hour "watches," are responsible for every aspect of the ship's mission. While the primary mission of vessels may differ, the duties of junior officers aboard ships have more in common than they differ. Since the Coast Guard officer, at least initially, is a generalist, the first two years of service can be considered a common apprenticeship.

While most of the tasks assigned to a junior officer are highly structured, complete with manuals, the primary task of fitting into a new role is highly unstructured. This task is a demanding one for all but is probably more difficult for some than others. One hypothesis is that officers who were more successful at the academy will have an easier time adapting to the new role. The primary task at the academy, however, is academic. Success at the academy may not be clearly related to success at acquiring the new role. Second, the apprenticeship is certainly a stressful period. Individual differences in tolerance for stress may also be related to success as a junior officer.

Finally, the task of developing a cognitive map (Louis, 1980) of the new environment is an intellectual challenge. Intelligence may lead to greater effectiveness. On the other hand, earlier work by Potter and Fiedler (1981) found that when stress was high the correlation between intelligence and the performance of Coast Guard staff officers was significant and negative. Follow-up work by Barnes, Potter, and Fiedler (1983) at the Coast Guard Academy found that the relationship between intelligence and performance for junior cadets at the academy was diminished by stress. On the contrary, for seniors the relationship between intelligence and performance was higher for those who reported a high level of stress in significant interpersonal relationships.

Barnes et al. argued that only cadets who were highly motivated still cared enough about their performance at the end of the final semester, when the study was conducted, to feel stress in their relationships with instructors and company officers. High motivation and four years of experience in the development of strategies for success allowed seniors to make the best of their intellectual assets—even under stressful conditions. If junior officers behave like entering cadets, the stress of the apprenticeship should decrease the contribution to performance made by intelligence. If they are able to transfer the skills developed in four years at the academy, intelligence should enhance performance. We will begin the study by discussing the development of cadets during the four years of academy education and training.

## Study I

**Method** *Subjects.* The class of 1986 numbered 250 when they entered the academy in July of 1982. Four years later 138 graduated of which 128 were U.S. nationals. In the summer of 1988 we asked each of the 128 U.S. graduates to participate in a follow-up study; 120 of these agreed to participate and to date we have obtained complete performance records for 100. The majority of the incomplete records are due to lags in the performance appraisal system which seem to have no systematic pattern that might bias the results of the study. Thirteen of the graduates were women. Ninety-four percent of the graduates were 21 or 22. Only five were minorities.

*Measures.* Cattell's 16PF (1968 edition) Form A was the primary measure of personality. The first administration took place during the summer training period preceding the fall semester of the cadets' freshman year. The same form was administered again two weeks before graduation in the spring of 1986. Scores were derived separately for men and women for both tests using the norms for high school students.

Research conducted routinely at the Coast Guard Academy since 1977 has assessed stress in significant relationships. For freshmen, relationships with peers and senior cadets are most important (Barnes, Potter, & Fiedler, 1983). For seniors their relationships with the commissioned officers who supervise companies of 150 cadets are the most significant. The seniors or First Class cadets—about 20 in each company—supervise cadets junior to themselves in the performance of their military duties. Each company has several administrative or maintenance responsibilities directed by the First Class cadets, for example, maintenance of the vans used for transport of the cadet corps or ordering and maintaining the stock of paper supplies needed to run the cadet regiment. First Class cadets are responsible to company officers for their own performance and the performance of the cadets whom they supervise. Stress in these relationships was assessed with a four-item, seven-point Likert scale which asked cadets, for example, to identify how much stress they felt in their relationship with their company officer as a result of that officer placing high demands for performance on the cadet without providing adequate direction or support. In other words, cadets who report high stress with their company officers are saying that they are having a hard time figuring out and meeting the demands of their supervisors. With a range of 4 to 28 the mean score on this scale was 14.3.

Potter and Fiedler (1981) found that experience seemed to moderate the impact of stress on the performance of officers. Potter (1982) translated those results to cadet experience, finding that as cadets increase in class they are better able to deal with stress. Research on cognition and stress (Lazarus & Folkman, 1984) suggested that experience might alter the cognitive appraisal of stressful situations including relationships with company officers. After numerous conversations with cadets Potter constructed a 23-item scale which described possible cognitive responses to the academic and military demands of the academy. A principal component factor analysis with varimax rotation of this scale for the class of 1986 resulted in eight factors with eigenvalues over 1.0 accounting for 67% of the variance. The first of these accounted for 17% of the variance and included eight items such as:

How important is it that your instructors approve of you?

When someone criticizes my performance, it doesn't take me long to figure out what to do in order to avoid being criticized for the same thing again.

It is worth the extra effort it takes to bring up your military grade.

This factor reflects a general concern for approval and is significantly related (-.55, p < .001) to Watson and Friend's (1969) scale which measures a fear of negative evaluation. With low scores reflecting a high concern for approval the range was 12 to 45 with a mean of 26.2.

The Coast Guard Academy curriculum is highly technical. All cadets take two semesters each of Physics, Chemistry, and Calculus as well as Electrical Engineering, Basic Naval Architecture, and Celestial Navigation. Half the graduates major in one of three Engineering disciplines.

We decided that the most appropriate measure of intelligence would be quantitative and chose the Scholastic Aptitude Mathematics test (SATM). The range on the SATM was from 500 to 750 with a mean of 645.

The measure of undergraduate performance was class rank which is determined by a composite of academic (75%) and military (25%) performance. While not pure, this criterion is much like the job performance criteria used in most selection studies. It is a mix of objective performance and style. One purpose of this study was to assess the relevance of class rank to performance after graduation.

**Results** Table 1 shows the correlations between 16PF scores in the freshman year and the senior year, short-term test-retest data reported by Cattell, Eber, and Tatsuoka (1970), and correlations reported by Nichols (cited in Cattell et al., 1970) for college students obtained four years apart. Over the short term dependabilities are fairly high with intelligence being the lowest. The academy data compare favorably with Nichols' data. The lowest correlations according to Cattell et al. represent lesser stability as a result of trait change due to maturation or learning. The only significant differences between the stability coefficients reported by Nichols and those for cadets are for shrewdness (p < .01) and apprehension (p < .01). This contrast suggests that the environment of the academy may have a greater impact on trait development in these dimensions than a typical college might.

Table 2 shows the differences in 16PF scores for cadets after four years at the academy. In general, they are more stable, self-assured, relaxed, and able to deal with stress. They are more concerned about their self-image and more sensitive to the group. They are more outgoing and imaginative and more trusting and forthright. They are also more prudent or sober and restrained. They differ from the average in that they are more intelligent and spontaneous, more dominant, more stable and able to deal with stress, more self-assured, and more forthright.

## TABLE 1
## Correlation between 16PF Score for:

### (a) Cadets in Freshman and Senior Years
### (b) Short-Term Retest of 146 Subjects and
### (c) Male and Female Students Before and After Four Years of College

| 16PF Score | (a) r (N=92) | (b) Short-Term Retest (N=146) | (c) Male (N=432) | (c) Female (N=204) |
|---|---|---|---|---|
| Cool – Warm | .53 | .81 | .49 | .62 |
| Concrete – Abstract | .16 | .58 | .28 | .23 |
| Affected by Feelings – Emotionally Stable | .38 | .78 | .45 | .48 |
| Submissive – Dominant | .54 | .80 | .47 | .52 |
| Sober – Enthusiastic | .38 | .79 | .48 | .52 |
| Expedient – Conscientious | .51 | .81 | .54 | .46 |
| Shy – Bold | .57 | .83 | .49 | .64 |
| Tough-minded – Tender-minded | .50 | .77 | .63 | .53 |
| Trusting – Suspicious | .41 | .75 | .40 | .42 |
| Practical – Imaginative | .36 | .70 | .43 | .49 |
| Forthright – Shrewd | .12 | .61 | .39 | .21 |
| Self-assured – Apprehensive | .29 | .79 | .57 | .52 |
| Conservative – Experimenting | .35 | .73 | .52 | .51 |
| Group-oriented – Self-sufficient | .43 | .73 | .46 | .50 |
| Undisciplined Self-conflict – Following Self-image | .49 | .62 | .41 | .41 |
| Relaxed – Tense | .51 | .81 | .56 | .51 |

They have, in a word, matured; but they have not become carbon copies of one another. In fact, as Table 3 shows, the variance in 13 of 16 scales has increased. There is significantly more variation in the degree to which they are outgoing, conscientious, and suspicious. In the high-pressure environment of the academy where the official norms are clear there are many ways of adapting. Some embrace the values of the academy and some feign them. For example, in interviews with 41 cadets just before graduation Potter asked, "Do you think that you will be a good officer because of or in spite of the academy?" Eleven answered "in spite of," five felt that it was a combination of both, and 25 answered "because of." Those who answered "in spite of" described life at the academy as a game that they had learned to play. Under these conditions it is not surprising that while 70% became more conscientious 30% became less so. Twenty-two percent became more suspicious and skeptical while 78% became more trusting, and 24% shifted towards reserve while 76% became more outgoing.

## TABLE 2
## Changes in 16PF Scores During Undergraduate Years at the U.S. Coast Guard Academy

| 16PF Score (Normalized for High School Students) | First Year Average | Graduation Year Average | Average Change |
|---|---|---|---|
| Cool—Warm[1] | 4.84 | 5.45 | .61** |
| Concrete—Abstract | 7.45 | 7.07 | − .38 |
| Affected by Feelings— Emotionally Stable | 5.63 | 6.73 | 1.10*** |
| Submissive—Dominant | 7.01 | 7.36 | .35 |
| Sober—Enthusiastic | 7.13 | 6.67 | − .46* |
| Expedient—Conscientious | 5.71 | 6.10 | .39 |
| Shy—Bold | 5.62 | 6.66 | 1.04*** |
| Tough-minded—Tender-minded | 5.22 | 5.26 | .04 |
| Trusting—Suspicious | 6.26 | 5.26 | − 1.00*** |
| Practical—Imaginative | 4.62 | 6.18 | 1.56*** |
| Forthright—Shrewd | 4.90 | 4.02 | − .88*** |
| Self-assured—Apprehensive | 5.38 | 4.08 | − 1.30*** |
| Conservative—Experimenting | 5.16 | 5.22 | .06 |
| Group-oriented—Self-sufficient | 6.11 | 5.66 | − .45* |
| Undisciplined Self-conflict— Following Self-image | 5.16 | 6.48 | 1.32*** |
| Relaxed—Tense | 6.52 | 4.99 | − 1.53*** |

[1]High scores are associated with the second term in the dyad.
 * $p < .05$
 ** $p < .01$
 *** $p < .001$

Stress with company officers was significantly related to specific aspects of personality. Cadets who as freshmen were more tender-minded and sensitive ($r = .21$, $p < .05$), more suspicious ($r = .23$, $p < .05$), and less shrewd and socially aware ($r = .25$, $p < .05$) reported more stress with company officers as seniors. In the senior year only boldness or the ability to take stress was significantly related to stress with company officers ($r = -.32$, $p < .01$). It seems that the relationships that we observe between freshman year personality variables and stress in the senior year tell us more about the source of stress in relationships with company officers. Other factors account for much more of the variance than the traits measured by the 16PF but the cadets more likely to experience stress with company officers are the ones who may have a harder time figuring out social cues. According to Cattell et al. (1970) they would tend to expect attention and affection and would characteristically report a lot of annoyances. Prone

## TABLE 3
## Difference in Variance for 16PF Scores
## of Cadets in Freshman and Senior Years

| 16PF Score | Frshmn Year Variance | Sr Year Variance | + Score |
|---|---|---|---|
| Cool – Warm | 2.91 | 4.21 | 2.57** |
| Concrete – Abstract | 2.28 | 2.50 | .45 |
| Affected by Feelings – Emotionally Stable | 3.03 | 3.98 | 1.65 |
| Submissive – Dominant | 3.53 | 3.84 | .59 |
| Sober – Enthusiastic | 3.02 | 3.98 | 1.67 |
| Expedient – Conscientious | 3.24 | 4.53 | 2.27* |
| Shy – Bold | 4.00 | 3.94 | .20 |
| Tough-minded – Tender-minded | 3.91 | 3.69 | .39 |
| Trusting – Suspicious | 3.18 | 5.80 | 3.76*** |
| Practical – Imaginative | 3.67 | 3.43 | .32 |
| Forthright – Shrewd | 3.63 | 3.67 | .06 |
| Self-assured – Apprehensive | 3.01 | 3.87 | 1.43 |
| Conservative – Experimenting | 4.27 | 4.28 | .01 |
| Group-oriented – Self-sufficient | 2.85 | 3.66 | 1.58 |
| Undisciplined Self-conflict – Following Self-image | 3.61 | 3.88 | .47 |
| Relaxed – Tense | 3.33 | 3.86 | 1.00 |

* $p < .05$
** $p < .01$
*** $p < .001$

to projection they would see fault in others when they were frustrated in meeting their interpersonal needs. The fact that there seems to be more substance in the relationships between freshman and senior years raises the question of how well the majority have learned to "play the game" by the end of their senior year. It is not possible to tell whether real change or self-presentation is the reason for the different profile we observe in freshman and senior personality scores of cadets who report high stress with company officers.

Concern for approval is unrelated to stress with company officers. Senior cadets who have a high concern for approval are more abstract-thinking ($r = .29$, $p < .05$), more tense ($r = .20$, $p < .05$), and more self-assured ($r = .22$, $p < .05$). As freshmen they were more traditional ($r = .22$, $p < .05$) and group-oriented ($r = .24$, $p < .05$). In other words, they are cadets who care—who want to do well. Neither concern for approval nor stress with company officers is related to class rank. Cadets who rank high in the class are more likely to be self-sufficient (r = .25, p < .01) and more cool or prone to stand by his or her own ideas (r = .23).

In order to examine the interaction between concern for approval and stress with company officers, each distribution was divided at the median and the correlation between intelligence and class rank computed for each quadrant of the two x two table. Table 4 shows that the only significant correlation between SAT scores and class rank is for cadets who report both a high degree of stress and high concern for approval. These findings echo those of Barnes et al. (1983). In the last semester these cadets are involved enough to be frustrated with difficulties. We would argue and the data suggest that they have developed skills for dealing with these difficulties such that they are able to focus their intellectual resources on the tasks at hand. Therefore, the higher their intelligence, the higher their class rank (since the highest rank is "1" the correlation is negative).

## Study II

**Method** *Performance*. The Coast Guard assesses the performance of junior officers every six months using a 23-item behaviorally anchored rating scale divided into six major areas: performance of duties, interpersonal relations, leadership skills, communication skills, personal qualities, and representing the Coast Guard. Each major area is followed by a narrative and the whole report is summarized in a comment on the officer's leadership and potential for positions of higher responsibility.

We reviewed the performance reports which each officer received during the two-year initial assignment. Four distinct patterns emerged. First, an officer might start out strong and continue to perform at a high level. These officers were either seen as natural leaders with great value to the service or seen as unique in the rater's experience and very special. Second, an officer might start slowly, making mistakes and demonstrating some weaknesses, but develop rapidly during the course of the two years finishing as a strong contributor to the effectiveness of the unit. Third, an officer might

---

**TABLE 4**
**SAT x Class Rank Correlations**
**for Cadets with High and Low Concern**
**for Approval and Stress with Company Officers**

|  |  | STRESS | |
| --- | --- | --- | --- |
|  |  | Hi | Lo |
|  | Hi | − .44<br>p = .043 | − .10<br>NS |
| CONCERN |  |  |  |
|  | Lo | + .33<br>NS | + .27<br>NS |

be a steady, dependable but unremarkable performer who was an asset but not the key to success. Fourth, an officer might demonstrate weakness that persisted over the two years. For some the evaluator's judgment might be that the officer needed further development or would be successful in a less demanding assignment. These were marginal performers. Others were judged to be too weak for promotion. These officers failed to be promoted from ensign to lieutenant (junior grade) at the end of the usual 18-month trial period.

We decided that the most appropriate performance measure for the apprenticeship would be a single rating which reflected performance over the entire period. The following scale summarizes overall performance during the apprenticeship:

5. (N = 8)  Comments include "the best I've ever seen," "a rising star," "innovations will benefit the entire service." Demonstrated strength from the start, no weaknesses noted.

4. (N = 26)  Strong from the start, excellent initiative and stamina, "maturity unusual for a junior officer," highly recommended for command, but not "the best ever."

3. (N = 29)  "Solid performer," may have minor difficulties at the start but excellent record overall by second year, may be recommended for command but without enthusiasm, reports are positive but lack superlatives and excitement.

2. (N = 16)  Persistent flaws that impair performance, significant command attention needed to get the officer's attention, comments include "slowly improving," "recommendation for command withheld pending further growth," "recommended for responsible positions ashore." Not recommended for command.

1. (N = 7)  Failed of selection for lieutenant (junior grade) or evaluator expresses serious doubts that this officer will "make it," comments clearly convey negative evaluation, for example, "this officer is lazy."

Commentating on the performance of high performers evaluators draw a vivid picture of the ideal junior officer during the apprenticeship. He or she is eager, responsive, and a fast learner. They listen well and become deeply involved in their work, routinely working long hours. Much of the work is highly structured. High performers are well focused, timely, and correct even under conditions characterized by multiple tasks, close deadlines, and unfamiliar routines. For example, junior officers manage the ship's classified documents. The Internal Revenue Service could take lessons in complexity and detail from the manuals written to govern this chore. High performers are meticulous and always on time with required reports. The less able make mistakes. The low performers don't do the reports without being hounded or lose documents. At sea shipboard work is a 24-hour affair. The ideal officer is highly skilled and able to keep a clear head going for days with as little as four hours sleep per night.

**Results**  Table 5 shows the relationships between 16PF scores in freshman and senior years and performance during the apprenticeship. Officers were divided into two groups, High Performers (levels 4 and 5) and Low Performers (levels 1 and 2). Officers who as freshmen were more tender-minded, suspicious, and tense perform less well.

## TABLE 5
## Differences in 16PF Scores for Officers
## with High and Low Performance Evaluations

| Freshman Year 16PF<br>Senior Year 16PF | High | Low | t |
|---|---|---|---|
| Hi Cool—Warm Low | 4.94 | 5.09 | .32 |
| | 6.03 | 5.61 | – .68 |
| Concrete—Abstract | 7.68 | 7.41 | – .69 |
| | 7.09 | 6.96 | – .30 |
| Affected Feelings—Emotionally Stable | 5.81 | 5.82 | .03 |
| | 6.69 | 6.52 | – .30 |
| Submissive—Dominant | 7.16 | 6.77 | – .70 |
| | 7.44 | 7.22 | – .43 |
| Sober—Enthusiastic | 7.03 | 7.50 | 1.03 |
| | 6.47 | 6.61 | .25 |
| Expedient—Conscientious | 6.16 | 5.50 | – 1.38 |
| | 6.44 | 5.70 | – 1.39 |
| Shy—Bold | 6.19 | 5.14 | – 1.83 |
| | 7.19 | 5.74 | – 2.63** |
| Tough-minded—Tender-minded | 4.55 | 6.14 | 3.01** |
| | 4.91 | 5.61 | 1.34 |
| Trusting—Suspicious | 5.84 | 6.82 | 2.00* |
| | 5.03 | 5.52 | .76 |
| Practical—Imaginative | 4.90 | 4.32 | – 1.24 |
| | 6.59 | 5.83 | – 1.46 |
| Forthright—Shrewd | 4.81 | 4.91 | .20 |
| | 3.28 | 4.48 | 2.13* |
| Self-assured—Apprehensive | 5.00 | 5.59 | 1.18 |
| | 3.88 | 4.43 | 1.02 |
| Conservative—Experimenting | 5.13 | 5.36 | .39 |
| | 5.25 | 5.35 | .17 |
| Group-oriented—Self-sufficient | 6.03 | 6.55 | 1.11 |
| | 5.69 | 5.91 | .45 |
| Undisciplined Self-conflict—<br>Following Self-image | 5.42 | 5.32 | – .20 |
| | 6.91 | 6.00 | – 1.68 |
| Relaxed—Tense | 5.87 | 7.32 | 3.13** |
| | 5.04 | 4.63 | .80 |

*p<.05   **p<.01

## TABLE 6
## One-Way Analysis of Variance
## with Levels of Performance

**a. Class Rank**

| | Low | | | | High |
|---|---|---|---|---|---|
| Performance Level | 1 | 2 | 3 | 4 | 5 |
| Mean Class Rank | 72 | 93 | 73 | 70 | 34 |

$F = 3.52, p < .01$

**b. SATM**

| | Low | | | | High |
|---|---|---|---|---|---|
| Performance Level | 1 | 2 | 3 | 4 | 5 |
| Mean SATM | 708 | 636 | 655 | 633 | 612 |

$F = 2.46, p < .05$

**c. Stress with Company Officer**

| | Low | | | | High |
|---|---|---|---|---|---|
| Performance Level | 1 | 2 | 3 | 4 | 5 |
| Mean Stress Score | 20.4 | 16.9 | 13.5 | 12.8 | 9.3 |

$F = 4.07, p < .01$

As seniors high performers were more bold or able to deal with stress and more forthright. In general, the ability to deal with stressful conditions seems critical to success in the apprenticeship. The ability to make sense out of the interpersonal environment is also important.

The freshman year is also an apprenticeship. When cadets responded to the 16PF in those circumstances, those who expected attention and affection and were more likely to feel annoyed with people exercising authority experienced more stress with their company officers. As officers, they do not perform as well. These findings suggest that this pattern is an enduring trait which is more accurately described by personality measures obtained in the freshman year than by measures obtained after four years of exposure to the expectations of the academy. Officers who in their apprenticeship as cadets would have had a more difficult time making sense out of their interpersonal environment do not perform well in the second apprenticeship when the most difficult task is to adopt a new role and define new relationships.

If this is the case, it is puzzling that officers who are less shrewd and socially aware perform better. One possible explanation lies in the nature of the ideal junior officer. The ideal junior officer is eager, attentive, and open. Coast Guard cadets seem unusual in the degree to which they are socially naive, natural, and genuine. The average Coast Guard Academy cadet at graduation (4.0) is more than two points below cadets at the Naval Academy (6.4) and Military Academy (6.1; Cattell et al., 1970). Forthrightness seems more suitable to the role of eager, attentive student than a polished, diplomatic nature. In combination with a high tolerance for stress, assertiveness, and self-confidence the picture is of a warm, earnestly involved, hard charger who fits the ideal desired by the mentors of junior officers. This may not be the style which leads to success at higher levels of the organization, but it works here.

Officers who were successful at the academy are more likely to be successful after graduation. Table 6a is a one-way analysis of variance for class rank by performance levels. For levels 2 through 5 the relationship is linear with the highest performers clearly the most successful at the academy. The lowest performers, however, are not the lowest in class rank. Table 6b is a one-way analysis of variance for SATM scores by performance levels. This analysis clearly shows that the lowest performers as a group are the brightest. The lowest SATM scores are for the highest performers; however, the mean score does not differ significantly from the mean SATM score of officers at levels 4, 3, and 2. Table 6c is a one-way analysis of variance for stress with company officers by performance levels. As cadets the lowest performers were those who had the highest degree of stress with their company officers.

These findings suggest officers who have difficulty in relationships with supervisors may be less able to apply their intellectual skills to the task during the apprenticeship. Table 7 repeats the analysis of the relationship between SATM scores and performance for officers who had reported high and low stress with company officers and expressed high and low degrees of concern for approval. In this case, the only significant relationship is a negative correlation between SATM scores and performance for officers who had both high stress and a high concern for approval. The higher the SATM score the lower the performance.

---

**TABLE 7**
**SATM x Performance Correlations for Officers**
**Who Had Reported High and Low Stress with Company**
**Officers and High or Low Concern for Approval**

|  |  | STRESS | |
|---|---|---|---|
|  |  | Hi | Lo |
|  | Hi | − .52 | − .23 |
|  |  | p = .025 | NS |
| CONCERN |  |  |  |
|  | Lo | − .28 | − .10 |
|  |  | NS | NS |

**TABLE 8**
**Stepwise Regression Equation Predicting**
**Performance During the Apprenticeship**

| Step # | Variable Entered | R | Multiple R |
|--------|------------------|-----|------------|
| 1. | SATM x Stress Interaction | .24 | .49 |
| 2. | Class Rank | .30 | .57 |
| 3. | Ability to Take Stress | .38 | .62 |

$f = 10.85, \; p < .001$

In summary, an officer's ability to deal with stress, intelligence, past performance under demanding conditions, and history of difficulty in figuring out and responding to the demands of his or her supervisor are all important factors in predicting performance during the apprenticeship. Table 8 summarizes the relationships between these variables and the performance of new officers during their first assignment in an equation determined by stepwise regression. The interaction between SATM scores and stress with company officers is the most significant factor, followed by class rank and boldness or the ability to take stress. Together these variables account for 38% of the variance in performance.

## Discussion

The apprenticeship of a Coast Guard officer is a period characterized by uncertainty, time pressure, and heavy work loads. The ideal officer in these circumstances is eager, learns quickly, and has a high tolerance for stress. Officers who performed well at the academy are more likely to perform well after graduation but some academically able cadets fail as officers. This situation may not be unique to the graduates of the Coast Guard Academy. Schein (1964) estimated that over 50% of college graduates leave their new organizations within four or five years for all reasons. Certainly a portion of these early departures leave for the same reasons as our young officers. When new officers do fail, they are more likely to have had difficulty in the past figuring out and responding to the demands of supervisors. Under stressful conditions the most vulnerable to failure are bright people who seem to lack essential adaptive responses. With time they may develop adaptive strategies but in the novel conditions associated with organizational entry, even after earlier success, they have difficulty developing the cognitive maps necessary for success. Studies such as this one document the first link in the chain that leads to the generals described by Campbell.

The Coast Guard has constructed an elaborate training and development system for officers which graduates some people ill suited for the environment which they will enter. It might be possible to decrease the stress of entry by improving mentoring relationships or gradually increasing the load as adaptive strategies are developed. With a pyramidal structure which assumes the failure of increasingly higher percentages at each promotion step, it seems unlikely that the Coast Guard is highly motivated to take such initiatives. The culture places the burden of success squarely on the shoulders of the individual. The profile of the kind of person who will succeed under such conditions is finely drawn. The apprenticeship screens out certain sorts of people; it remains to be seen what traits and skills are favored at succeeding levels in the organization. As we follow the class of 1986 through their careers our interest at each level will be in understanding the dynamics of career success in order to better inform training and development decisions.

## References

Barnes, V., Potter, E. H., & Fiedler, F. E. (1983). Effect of interpersonal stress on the prediction of academic performance. *Journal of Applied Psychology, 68,* 686–697.

Campbell, D. (1987, August 30). *The psychological test profiles of brigadier generals: Warmongers or decisive warriors?* Paper presented at the annual convention of the American Psychological Association, New York, NY.

Cattell, R. B., Eber, H. W., & Tatsuoka, M. M. (1970). *Handbook for the sixteen personality factor questionnaire (16PF).* Champaign, IL: Institute for Personality and Ability Testing.

Dalton, G. W., & Thompson, P. H. (1986). *Novations: Strategies of career management.* Glenview, IL: Scott, Foresman & Co.

Howard, A., & Bray, D. W. (1988). *Managerial lives in transition: Advancing age and changing times.* New York: Guilford Press.

Katz, R. (1985). Organizational stress and early socialization experiences. In T. A. Beehr & R. S. Bhagat (Eds.), *Human stress and cognition in organizations: An integrated perspective* (pp. 117–139). New York: Wiley & Sons.

Lazarus, R. S., & Folkman, S. (1984). *Stress, appraisal, and coping.* New York: Springer Publishing.

Louis, M. R. (1980). Surprise and sense making: What newcomers experience in entering unfamiliar organizational settings. *Administrative Science Quarterly, 25,* 226–251.

Potter, E. H. (1982). What experience teaches: Cognitive responses to a stressful environment. *Proceedings of the Eighth Psychology in the DOD Symposium,* 219–227.

Potter, E. H., & Fiedler, F. E. (1981). The utilization of staff member intelligence and experience under high and low stress. *Academy of Management Journal, 24,* 361–376.

Schein, E. H. (1964). How to break in the college graduate. *Harvard Business Review, 42,* 168–176.

Watson, D., & Friend, R. (1969). Measurement of social-evaluative anxiety. *Journal of Consulting and Clinical Psychology, 33,* 448–457.

# Intellectual Styles*

Robert J.
Sternberg

Throughout my four years in college, my two roommates and I remained together. The roommates—Alex, Bob, and Cyril (only one of these names is unchanged)—seemed remarkably similar intellectually when they entered college. All had high Scholastic Aptitude Test scores, excellent grades in high school, and similar intellectual strengths and weaknesses. For example, all three were more verbal than quantitative, all reasoned well, but all were rather weak spatially. Thus, in terms of standard theories of intelligence, the three roommates had similar intellectual abilities. Moreover, today, all three roommates are successful in their jobs and have achieved some national recognition for their work, showing that the three roommates were similar in motivational levels as well.

If one looks beyond the intellectual similarities of the three roommates, one cannot help but notice some salient differences that have profoundly affected their lives. Consider some of the differences between Alex, Bob, and Cyril.

Alex, a lawyer, is admittedly fairly conventional, rule-bound, and comfortable with details and structure. He does well what others tell him to do, as a lawyer must, and has commented to me that his idea of perfection would be a technically flawless legal document or contract whereby those who sign on the dotted line are bound to the terms of the contract without loopholes. In a nutshell, Alex is a follower of systems and follows them extremely well, as shown by the facts that he is a Rhodes scholar and is today a partner in a major national law firm. Alex can figure out a system and work excellently within it.

Bob, a university professor, is quite different stylistically from Alex. He is fairly unconventional and, unlike Alex, dislikes following or even dealing with other people's rules.

* Preparation of this article was supported by Contract MDA90385K0305 from the Army Research Institute. Requests for reprints should be sent to Robert J. Sternberg, Department of Psychology, Yale University, Box 11A Yale Station, New Haven, CT 06520.

481

Moreover, he has relatively few rules of his own. Although he has some basic principles that he views as inviolate, he tends not to take rules very seriously, viewing them as conveniences that are meant to be changed or even broken as the situation requires. Bob dislikes details and generally is comfortable working within a structure only if it is his own. He does certain things well, but usually only if they are the things he wants to do, rather than what someone else wants him to do. His idea of intellectual perfection would be the generation of a great idea and a compelling demonstration that the idea is correct or, at least, useful. In brief, Bob is a creator of systems and has designed some fairly well-known psychological theories that reflect his interest in system creation.

Cyril, a psychotherapist, is like Bob but not Alex in being fairly unconventional. Like Bob, he dislikes others' rules, but unlike Bob, he has a number of his own. He tends to be indifferent to details. He likes working within certain structures, which need not be his own, but the structures have to be ones he had adjudged to be correct and suitable. Cyril does well what he wants to do. His idea of perfection would be a difficult but correct psychological diagnosis, followed by an optimal psychotherapeutic intervention. In sum, Cyril is a judge of systems. His interest, perhaps passion, for judging was shown early in his career when, as a college student, he constructed a test (which we called the "Cyril Test") to give to others, and especially to dates, to judge the suitability of their values and standards. Cyril was also editor of the college course critique, a role in which he took responsibility for the judgment and evaluation of all undergraduate courses at the university.

Although Alex, Bob, and Cyril are all intellectually able and similarly competent, even these brief sketches serve to illustrate that they use their intelligence in different ways. Alex is a follower or executor; Bob, a creator or legislator; and Cyril, a judge of systems. They differ in terms of their intellectual style, or ways in which they direct their intelligence. A style, then, is not a level of intelligence but a way of using it—a propensity. When one is talking about styles rather than levels, one cannot talk simply about better or worse. Rather, one must speak in terms of better or worse "for what?"

# The Model of Intelligence As Mental Self-Government

I am proposing here a model of intelligence as mental self-government. The basic idea is that governmental structures may be external, societal manifestations of basic psychological processes that are internal and individual (see also Bronfenbrenner, 1977). Seeds of this notion can be found in the writings of political theorists, such as Hobbs, Locke, and Rousseau, whose political theories were based on psychological theories of what people are like. The difference here, perhaps, is that rather than attempting to understand governments in terms of the psychology of human beings, we try to understand the psychology of human beings in terms of governments. From this point of view, government in society is a large-scale, externalized mirror of the mind. People are systems, just like societies (Ford, 1986), and they need to govern themselves just as do societies. Mental incompetence results from a breakdown of self-regulating functions, and high levels of mental competence derive in part from superior self-regulation.

The view of intelligence as mental self-government focuses more on styles than on levels of intelligence. In standard theories of intelligence, including recent ones (Gardner, 1983; Sternberg, 1985), the emphasis is on levels of intelligence of one or more kinds. Measuring intelligence thus entails assessing how much of each ability the individual has. In contrast, the governmental model leads to assessment not of how much intelligence the individual has, but rather of how that intelligence is directed, or exploited. Two individuals of equal intelligence, by any of the existing theories of intelligence, might nevertheless be viewed by the theory as intellectually quite different because of the ways in which they organize and direct that intelligence. In the next part of the article, the implications of the mental self-government model as a basis for understanding intellectual styles are explored in some detail.

Governments have many aspects, such as function, form, level, scope, and leaning. Three major functions of government are the legislative, executive, and judicial. Four major forms of government are the monarchic, hierarchic, oligarchic, and anarchic. Two basic levels of government are the global and the local. Two domains in the scope of government are the internal (domestic affairs) and the external (foreign affairs), and two leanings are conservative and progressive. In this part of the article, the implications of each of these aspects for understanding intellectual styles are explored.

**Functions of Government** Governments may be viewed as having three primary functions: legislative, executive, and judicial.

The legislative style characterizes individuals who enjoy creating, formulating, and planning for problem solution. Such individuals, like Bob, the university professor described earlier, like to create their own rules, enjoy doing things their own way, prefer problems that are not prestructured or prefabricated, and like to build structure as well as content in deciding how to approach a problem. People with legislative tendencies prefer creative and constructive planning-based activities, such as writing papers, designing projects, and creating new business or educational systems. They tend to enter occupations that enable them to utilize their legislative style, such as creative writer, scientist, artist, sculptor, investment banker, policymaker, and architect.

Individuals with an executive style are implementers. Like Alex, the lawyer described earlier, they like to follow rules and work within existing systems, preferring pre-structured or prefabricated problems which allow them to fill in content within existing structures. They prefer predefined activities such as solving algebra word problems or engineering problems, giving talks or lessons based on others' ideas, and enforcing rules. Executive types gravitate toward occupations such as lawyer, policeman, builder (of others' designs), surgeon, soldier, proselytizer (of others' systems), and manager (lower echelon).

The judicial style involves judgmental activities, as shown by the psychotherapist, Cyril, described earlier. Judicial types like to analyze and criticize, preferring problems in which they evaluate the structure and content of existing things and ideas. They prefer activities that exercise the judicial function, such as writing critiques, giving opinions, judging people and their work, and evaluating programs. People with a primarily judicial style tend to gravitate toward occupations such as judge, critic, program evaluator, admissions officer, grant or contract monitor, systems analyst, and consultant.

People do not have one or another style exclusively; rather, they tend to specialize, some people more than others. For example, one individual might be strongly legislative and only weakly executive and judicial, whereas another individual might be approximately equally balanced among the three functions. Thus, people differ not only in their direction of specialization, but also in the degree to which they specialize. People will gravitate toward problems whose solutions require their preferred styles of functioning. They may also use certain styles in the service of other styles. A primarily legislative type, for example, may use judicial functions primarily to further legislative ends.

We need to distinguish the proclivity toward a style from people's abilities to implement that style. It seems likely that most people will prefer styles that capitalize upon their strengths. But there is no logical or psychological reason why preferences and abilities will always correspond. Some people may prefer styles that are not as well-suited to their abilities as are others. In measuring styles, it is important to measure both predilections toward styles and abilities to implement them, in order to determine how well an individual's predilections and abilities match.

An important implication of these differences is that although style is generally independent of level of intelligence, it probably is not independent of level of intelligence within a particular domain. The same individual who might be thought to be a brilliant science student because he is a legislative type might be thought to be somewhat duller in business courses which emphasize executive skills.

**Forms of Mental Self-Government** Governments come in different forms. Four of those forms are the monarchic, the hierarchic, the oligarchic, and the anarchic. Logically, any form may be paired with any function, although psychologically certain pairings are likely to be more common than others.

People who exhibit a predominantly monarchic style tend to be motivated by a single goal or need at a time. Single-minded and driven, they often believe that the ends justify the means and attempt to solve problems full-speed ahead—damn the obstacles. Monarchic types are relatively unself-aware, intolerant, and inflexible and have relatively little sense of priorities and alternatives. They tend to oversimplify problems, often being more decisive than the situation warrants. In a limited sense, they may be systematic; however, they may neglect variables not obviously pertinent to their goal.

Individuals preferring a hierarchic style tend to be motivated by a hierarchy of goals, with the recognition that not all goals can be fulfilled equally well and that some goals are more important than others. They take a balanced approach to problems, believing that ends do not justify means, and view competing goals as acceptable (although they may have trouble if the priorities come too close to allow for formation of a hierarchy). Hierarchic types seek complexity and tend to be self-aware, tolerant, and relatively flexible. They have good senses of priorities; are usually decisive, unless priority setting becomes a substitute for decision or action; and are systematic in problem solving and decision making.

Individuals preferring the oligarchic style tend to be motivated by multiple, often-competing goals of equal perceived importance. Plagued by multiple, possibly competing approaches to problems, they are often driven by goal conflict and tension arising out of their belief that satisfying the constraints is as important as solving the problem itself.

They usually believe that ends do not justify means and find that competing goals and needs tend to interfere with task completion, because each goal and need is seen as of roughly equal importance. Oligarchic types seek complexity (sometimes to the frustration point) and are self-aware, tolerant, and very flexible. They tend to have trouble setting priorities because everything seems equally important, and thus they are rather indecisive and multiply systematic, with the multiple systems competing with each other because of the need to satisfy multiple equally important goals.

Anarchic stylists tend to be motivated by a potpourri of needs and goals that are often difficult for themselves, as well as for others, to sort out. They tend to take a random approach to problems, driven by what seems to be a muddle of inexplicable forces. They may act as though ends justify means, for lack of other standards. Anarchic types are often unclear or unreflective on their goals, overly simplistic, unself-aware, intolerant, and too flexible. They may believe that anything goes and have trouble setting priorities because they have no firm set of rules upon which to base them. They tend to be extreme, being either too decisive or too indecisive, and are thoroughly asystematic.

Some general issues arise with regard to formal style of mental self-government. Monarchists will often be too single-minded for the likes of most teachers and even social acquaintances. But in later life, their single-minded zeal may render them among the most successful of entrepreneurs or goal-attainers. Often, their memories of school will not be fond, because they will believe that their talents went unrecognized. Monarchists can also be difficult to live with because of their single-mindedness.

Hierarchical types can probably solve the widest variety of problems in school life and beyond, because most problems are probably best conceived of hierarchically. They will generally achieve a good balance between thought and action, but they must remember that the existence of priorities does not guarantee that those priorities are right. When there is a serious bottom line, or pressing goal, hierarchists may get lost or sidetracked in their own hierarchies, whereas the monarchist may blitz through and attain the goal.

Oligarchists will often frustrate themselves and others, in school and in careers, because of their indecision and hesitation. Because they tend to assign equal weights to competing means and goals, they may appear to be "lost in thought" and unable to act. They can act, but they may need others to set their priorities for them.

Anarchists are at risk of becoming educational as well as social misfits, and their talents may actually lead them into anti- rather than prosocial paths. Properly nurtured, they may have the potential for truly creative contributions to the world, if their anarchic style is combined with the necessary intellectual talents for creative performance. But proper nurturance may be quite a challenge because of the anarchists' unwillingness to work within existing systems in order to go, eventually, beyond these systems. Rather than working within existing systems, anarchists may end up attempting to destroy them.

**Levels of Mental Self-Government** Globalists prefer to deal with relatively large and abstract issues. They tend to ignore or dislike detail, choosing instead to conceptualize and work in the world of ideas. Their weaknesses are that they may be diffuse thinkers who can get lost on cloud nine, and that they may see the forest but not always the trees within it.

In contrast, localists like concrete problems requiring detailed work and are often pragmatically oriented and down-to-earth. Their weakness, however, is that they may not see the forest for the trees.

In terms of the three individuals described earlier—Alex, Bob, and Cyril—Bob and Cyril tend to be globalists whereas Alex tends to be a localist. The local style is not, however, inextricably linked to the executive style Alex has shown. Some executive types may prefer only to work at a broader level, accomplishing the main tasks in a project while relegating the more local details to others. Similarly, a legislative or judicial type could be more local than either Bob or Cyril.

Although most people prefer to work either at a more global or a more local level, a key to successful problem solving in many situations is being able to traverse between levels. If a person is weak within a given level, it is often helpful to pair up with someone whose strengths are complementary. In particular, although we often value most people who are most like ourselves, we actually benefit most from people who are moderately unlike ourselves with respect to preferred level of processing. Too much overlap leads to some levels of functioning simply being ignored. Two globalists, for example, may do well in forming ideas but will need someone to take care of the details of implementing them. Two localists may help each other in implementation but need someone to set down the global issues that need to be dealt with. Too little overlap, however, can lead to a breakdown in communication. People who do not overlap at all in levels may not be able to understand each other well.

**Scope of Mental Self-Government** Governments need to deal both with internal, or domestic, affairs and with external, or foreign, ones. Similarly, mental self-governments need to deal with both internal and external issues.

Internalists tend to be introverted, task-oriented, aloof, socially less sensitive, and interpersonally less aware than externalists. They also like to work alone. Essentially, their preference is to apply their intelligence to things or ideas in isolation from other people.

Externalists tend to be extroverted, people-oriented, outgoing, socially more sensitive, and interpersonally more aware than internalists. They like to work with others and seek problems that either involve working with other people or are about others.

Among the three individuals described earlier, Alex and Bob tend more toward the internal scope of mental self-government whereas Cyril tends more toward the external. These proclivities fit with their jobs. Alex works primarily in corporate law, dealing with legal principles and documents and less with people; Bob works primarily with ideas and instantiating them through experiments. Cyril, as a psychotherapist, is constantly working with people. It should be realized that there is some degree of situation-specificity involved. Bob, for example, works actively with students and frequently gives lectures on his work. At the same time, he tends to shun parties and generally prefers to deal with people socially when there is at least some degree of task orientation. Moreover, he recognizes the importance of dealing with people on his job and makes sure that, whatever his preferred tendencies, the job gets done when interactions with people are required.

Some people prefer to be internalists whereas others prefer to be externalists. Again, most people are not strictly one or the other but alternate between them as a function of task, situation, and people involved. But it is important to realize in education and job placement that a bright individual who is forced to work in a mode that does not suit him or her may perform below his or her capabilities.

**Leanings of Mental Self-Government** Governments can have various leanings. For present purposes, two major "regions" of leanings will be distinguished, conservative and progressive.

Individuals with a predominantly conservative style like to adhere to existing rules and procedures, minimize change, and avoid ambiguous situations where possible, preferring familiarity in life and work.

Individuals with a progressive style like to go beyond existing rules and procedures, maximize change, seek or at least accept ambiguous situations, and prefer some degree of unfamiliarity in life and work.

Although individuals may, on the average, tend toward a more conservative or progressive leaning in their mental self-government, there is clearly some degree of domain-specificity involved. For example, an individual who is conservative politically will not necessarily be conservative in his or her personal life, and similarly for a progressive. Thus, in evaluating styles, and especially leanings, tendencies within particular domains must be taken into account. Moreover, leanings may well change over time as people feel more or less secure in their environments. Thus, an individual who is new to an environment may tend to adapt conservatively, whereas an individual who has been in that environment longer may feel more free progressively to attempt to shape the environment. This aspect of style may be among the most mercurial of the various aspects.

# Development of Intellectual Styles

Where do these various modes of intellectual functioning come from? It is possible that at least some portion of stylistic preference is inherited, but I doubt that it is a large part. Rather, styles seem to be partly socialized constructs, just as is intelligence (Sternberg & Suben, 1986). From early on, we perceive certain modes of interaction to be rewarded more than others, and we probably gravitate toward these modes, while being constrained by our built-in predispositions as to how much and how well we are able to adopt these rewarded styles.

Consider some of the variables that are likely to affect the development of intellectual styles:

A first variable is culture. Different cultures tend to reward different styles. For example, the North American emphasis on innovation ("making the better mousetrap") may lead to relatively greater reward for the legislative and progressive styles, at least among adults. National heroes in the United States, such as Edison as inventor, Einstein as scientist, Jefferson as political theorist, Steve Jobs as entrepreneur, and Hemingway as author, tend often to be heroes by virtue of their legislative contribution. Other societies, such as Japan, that tend to value conformity and the following of tradition, may be more likely to reward executive and conservative styles. A society that emphasizes conformity and tradition to too great a degree may stagnate because of the styles induced into its members.

A second variable is gender. Traditionally, a legislative style has been more acceptable in males than in females. Men were supposed to set the rules, and women to follow them. Although this tradition is changing, the behavior of many men and women does not fully reflect the new values.

A third variable is age. Legislation is generally encouraged in the preschool young, who are encouraged to develop their creative powers in the relatively unstructured and open environment of the preschool and some homes. Once the children start school, the period of legislative encouragement rapidly draws to a close. Children are now expected to be socialized into the largely conforming values of the school. The teacher now decides what the student should do, and the student does it, for the most part. Students who don't follow directions and the regimentation of the school are viewed as undersocialized and even as misfits. In adulthood, some jobs again encourage legislation, even though training for such jobs may not. For example, high school physics or history are usually largely executive, with students answering questions or solving problems that the teacher poses. But the physicist and historian are expected to be more legislative. Ironically, they may have forgotten how. We sometimes say that children lose their creativity in school. What they may really lose is the intellectual style that generates creative performance.

A fourth variable is parenting style. What the parent encourages and rewards is likely to be reflected in the style of the child. Does the parent encourage or discourage legislation, or judgment, on the part of the child? The parent him- or herself exhibits a certain style, which the child is likely to emulate. A monarchic parent, for example, is likely to reward a child who shows the same single-mindedness, whereas an anarchic parent would likely abhor a child beginning to show a monarchic style, and try to suppress it as unacceptable. Parents who mediate for the child in ways that point to larger rather than smaller issues underlying actions are more likely to encourage a global style, whereas parents who do not themselves generalize are more likely to encourage a more local style.

A last variable is kind of schooling and, ultimately, of occupation. Different schools and, especially, occupations reward different styles. An entrepreneur is likely to be rewarded for different styles from those for which an assembly-line worker is rewarded. As individuals respond to the reward system of their chosen life pursuit, various aspects of style are more likely to be either encouraged or suppressed.

Obviously, these variables are only a sampling rather than a complete listing of those variables that are likely to influence style. Moreover, any discussion such as this inevitably simplifies the complexities of development, if only because of the complex interactions that occur among variables. Moreover, styles interact with abilities. Occasionally one runs into legislative types who are uncreative, creative people who eschew legislation, hierarchists who set up misguided hierarchies, and so on. But for the most part, the interactions will be more synchronous in well-adjusted people. According to the triarchic theory of human intelligence (Sternberg, 1986), contextually intelligent people are ones who capitalize on their strengths and who either remediate or compensate for their weaknesses. A major part of capitalization and compensation would seem to be in finding harmony between one's abilities and one's preferred styles. People who cannot find such harmony are likely to be frustrated by the mismatch between how they want to perform and how they are able to perform.

If styles are indeed socialized, even in part, then they are almost certainly modifiable to at least some degree. Such modification may not be easy. We know little about how to modify intelligence, and we know even less about how to modify intellectual styles. Presumably, when we learn the mechanisms that might underlie such attempts at modification, we will pursue a path similar to that some educators and psychologists are using in teaching intelligence (e.g., Sternberg, 1986).

We need to teach students to make the best of their intellectual styles. Some remediation of weaknesses is probably possible. But to the extent that it is not, mechanisms of compensation can usually be worked out that help narrow the gap between weak and strong areas of performance. For example, groups of children can be formed that pair children with different preferred styles. Ultimately, we can hope that a theory of intellectual styles will serve not only as a basis for a test of such styles, but also as a basis for training that maximizes people's flexibility in dealing with their environment, society, and themselves.

Schools most reward executive types—children who work within existing rule systems and seek the rewards that the schools value. To some extent, the schools create executive types out of people who might have been otherwise. But whether the rewards will continue indefinitely for the executive types depends in part upon career path, which is why school grades are poor predictors of job success. One's ability to get high grades in science courses involving problem solving, for example, probably will not be highly predictive of one's success as a scientist, an occupation in which many of the rewards are for coming up with the ideas for the problems in the first place. Judicial types may be rewarded somewhat more in secondary and especially tertiary schooling, where at least some judgment activity is required, as in paper writing. Legislative types, if they are rewarded at all, may not be rewarded until graduate school, where there is a need to come up with one's own ideas in dissertation and other research. But some professors—those who want students who are clones or disciples—may not reward legislative types even in graduate school, preferring executive types who will carry out their research for them in an effective, diligent, and nonthreatening way.

The fit between student and teacher, as between principal and teacher, can be critical to the success of the teacher-student system, or of the principal-teacher system. A legislative student and an executive teacher, for example, may not get on well at all. A legislative student may not even get along with a legislative teacher if that teacher happens to be one who is intolerant of other people's legislations. During the course of my career, I have found that although I can work with a variety of students, I probably work best with students whom I now, in retrospect, would classify as legislative. I can work reasonably well with executive types also. I am probably weakest with judicial students, who to me seem more eager to criticize than to do research. The general point is that educators need to take into account their own styles in order to understand how they influence their perceptions of and interactions with others. Clearly, certain children benefit from certain styles. A gifted executive-type student might benefit more from acceleration, where the same material is presented at a more rapid pace. A gifted legislative-type student might benefit more from enrichment, where the opportunity to do creative projects would be consistent with the student's preferred style of working.

It is necessary that schools take into account not only fit between teacher and student (or principal and teacher) style, but also the fit between the way a subject is taught and the way a student thinks. A given course often can be taught in a way that is advantageous (or disadvantageous) to a particular style. Consider, for example, an introductory or low-level psychology course. This course might stress learning and using existing facts, principles, and procedures (an executive style of teaching), or it might stress designing a research project (a legislative style of teaching), or it might stress writing papers evaluating theories, experiments, and the like (a judicial style of teaching). Little wonder I received a grade of "C" in my introductory psychology course, taught in the executive style! And, in retrospect, little wonder that, in my own psychology courses, I have almost always made the final grade heavily dependent upon the design of a research project. My style of teaching was reflecting my own style of thinking, as it does for others. The general principle of teaching style as a reflection of the teacher's preference is not limited to psychology or even science. Writing, for example, might be taught in a way that emphasizes critical (judicial) papers, creative (legislative) papers, or expository (executive) papers.

Sometimes, there is a natural shift in the nature of subject matter over successive levels of advancement, just as there is in jobs. In mathematics and basic science, for example, lower levels are clearly more executive, requiring solution of restructured problems. Higher levels are clearly more legislative, requiring formulation of new ideas for proofs, theories, and experiments. Unfortunately, some of the students screened out in the earlier phases of education might have succeeded quite well in the later ones, whereas some students who readily pass the initial stages might be ill-suited to later demands.

Perhaps the most important point to be made is that we tend to confuse level with style of intelligence. For example, most current intelligence and achievement tests reward the executive style by far the most—they require solution of prestructured problems. One cannot create one's own problems, or judge the quality of the problems on the test (at least not at the time of the test!). Judicial types get some credit for analytical items, but legislative types hardly benefit at all from existing tests and may actually be harmed by them. Clearly, style will affect perceived competence; but as noted earlier, style is independent of intelligence, in general, although not within particular domains. Style ought to count as much as ability and motivation in recommending job placements, although probably not in making tracking decisions that deal with issues of ability rather than style.

The styles of intellect proposed here are not, of course, the only ones ever to have been proposed. Theories of intellectual styles abound, and although it is not possible to review them exhaustively here, I will cite some pertinent examples.

Myers (1980; see also Myers & McCaulley, 1985) has proposed a series of psychological types based upon Jung's (1923) theory of types. According to Myers, there are 16 types, resulting from all possible combinations of two ways of perceiving—sensing versus intuition; two ways of judging—thinking versus feeling; two ways of dealing with self and others—introversion versus extraversion; and two ways of dealing with the outer world—judgment versus perception. Gregorc (1985) has proposed four main types or styles, based upon all possible combinations of just two dimensions—concrete versus abstract and sequential versus random. Taking a more educationally oriented slant, Renzulli and Smith (1978) have suggested that individuals have various learning styles, with each style corresponding to a method of teaching: projects, drill and recitation, peer teaching, discussion, teaching games, independent study, programmed instruction, lecture, and simulation. Holland (1973) has taken a more job-related orientation and proposed six styles that are used as a basis for understanding job interests as revealed by the Strong-Campbell Interest Inventory (Strong, Campbell, & Hansen, 1985). Holland's typology includes six "types" of personality: realistic, investigative, artistic, social, enterprising, and conventional.

Intellectual styles represent an important link between intelligence and personality, because they probably represent a way in which personality is manifested in intelligent thought and action. Attempts to understand academic or job performance solely in terms of intelligence or personality probably have not succeeded as well as we had hoped because they neglect the issue of intellectual style—the effect of intelligence and personality on each other. Thus, styles may represent an important "missing link" between intelligence, personality, and real-world performance.

Can styles be measured? I believe they can be. We are currently validating an inventory designed to measure intellectual styles. The inventory consists of a series of statements which students rate on a one to nine scale, depending on the extent to which each statement is viewed as describing the rater. For example, legislatively minded students would be expected to give high ratings to statements such as "If I work on a project, I like to plan what to do and how to do it" and "I like tasks that allow me to do things my own way." Executive types would prefer statements such as "I like to follow instructions when solving a problem" and "I like projects that provide a series of steps to follow to get a solution." Judicial students would affirm statements such as "I like to study and analyze the behavior of others" and "I like projects that allow me to evaluate the work of others." Measuring styles is a first step toward understanding people's preferences for ways of using their intelligence. Ultimately, we hope to be able to teach students to use various styles flexibly, so as to optimize the extent to which they can apply their intelligence, both in and out of school.

# References

Bronfenbrenner, U. (1977). Toward an experimental ecology of human development. *American Psychologist, 7*, 513–531.

Ford, M. E. (1986). A living systems conceptualization of social intelligence: Outcomes, processes, and developmental change. In R. J. Sternberg (Ed.), *Advances in the psychology of human intelligence: Vol. 3* (pp. 119–171). Hillsdale, NJ: Erlbaum.

Gardner, H. (1983). *Frames of mind: The theory of multiple intelligences*. New York: Basic Books.

Gregorc, T. (1985). *Inside styles: Beyond the basics*. Maynard, MA: Gabriel Systems, Inc.

Holland, J. L. (1973). *Making vocational choices: A theory of careers*. Englewood Cliffs, NJ: Prentice-Hall.

Jung, C. (1923). *Psychological types*. New York: Harcourt, Brace.

Myers, I. B. (1980). *Gifts differing*. Palo Alto, CA: Consulting Psychologists Press.

Myers, I. B., & McCaulley, M. H. (1985). *Manual: A guide to the development and use of the Myers-Briggs Type Indicator*. Palo Alto, CA: Consulting Psychologists Press.

Renzulli, J. S., & Smith, L. H. (1978). *Learning styles inventory*. St. Louis, MO: Creative Learning Press.

Sternberg, R. J. (1985). *Beyond IQ: A triarchic theory of human intelligence*. New York: Cambridge University Press.

Sternberg, R. J. (1986). *Intelligence applied: Understanding and increasing your intellectual skills*. San Diego: Harcourt, Brace, Jovanovich.

Sternberg, R. J., & Suben, J. (1986). The socialization of intelligence. In M. Perlmutter (Ed.), *Perspectives on intellectual development: Vol. 19. Minnesota symposia on child psychology* (pp. 201–235). Hillsdale, NJ: Erlbaum.

Strong, E. K., Jr., Campbell, D. P., & Hansen, J. C. (1985). *Strong-Campbell Interest Inventory*. Palo Alto, CA: Consulting Psychologists Press.

# Street Smarts[*]

Richard K.
Wagner
and
Robert J.
Sternberg

With surprising frequency, individuals who were academic superstars in high school, college, and even business school, have dramatically less success in their managerial careers. Conversely, individuals who are superstars as managers and executives often have unremarkable academic records.

There is mounting evidence that some individuals who fly through school and flop in the office lack "street smarts," the practical knowledge and judgment that are required to succeed in the office (Wagner & Sternberg, 1986). What is street smarts? How can it be measured? How can it be trained? Our goal in this article is to answer these three questions.

## What Is Street Smarts?

Recent research on differences between the school and office environments supports what most of us realized from our second day on the job: the kinds of problems found in school (and on IQ tests and many employment tests) are different from those found in the office (Sternberg & Wagner, 1986).

## Two Kinds of Problems

*Academic problems* are the kind of problem that is found in school. An example is to identify the factors of the algebraic equation $a^2 - b^2$. Problems such as these have a number of

[*] *Support for the research described in this paper was provided by Contract MDA90385K0305 from the Army Research Institute. This research would not have been possible without the cooperation of the Center for Creative Leadership, Greensboro, North Carolina. We especially appreciate the help of David DeVries, Mary Ellen Kranz, William Sternbergh, and the managers and executives who participated in our study. We thank Carol Rashotte who analyzed our data. Address correspondence concerning this manuscript to Richard K. Wagner, Department of Psychology, Florida State University, Tallahassee, FL 32306-1051, or to Robert J. Sternberg, Department of Psychology, Yale University, Box 11A Yale Station, New Haven, CT 06520-7447.*

characteristics (Neisser, 1976; Wagner & Sternberg, 1985). First, they are well-defined. When a teacher gave you a problem, you may not have known what the answer was, but you probably were sure what the problem was. Second, they are formulated by others. The teacher made up the problems (or, more likely, copied them from the instructor's workbook that comes with the text); you tried to solve them. Third, they usually come with all information that is necessary for problem solution. Fourth, they have only one correct answer, and one method of obtaining it. Fifth, they are unrelated to everyday experience.

*Practical problems* are the kind of problem that is found in the office. An example of a practical problem is how to turn around a pronounced morale problem. Practical problems are different from academic problems in five ways:

1. *Practical problems are not well-defined*. In fact, deciding just what the problem is can be the most important step to a successful solution.

2. *Practical problems usually are not formulated by others*. You must recognize that a problem exists and then define it. Even when practical problems are formulated by others (e.g., when your immediate supervisor gives you a problem to solve), the formulations frequently are incomplete or erroneous.

3. *Practical problems rarely have all needed information available from the beginning*. Knowing what additional information you need and how to get it is crucial to solving practical problems.

4. *Practical problems rarely have a single correct solution, or if there is one, it may never be known*. Rather, there usually will be several solutions, each arising from a different approach to the problem, and each having liabilities as well as assets.

5. *Everyday experience can be used to solve practical problems*. If everyday experience were not helpful, it is hard to imagine how practical problems could ever be solved, given the characteristics just mentioned.

Of course, both academic and practical problems can be found in school and in the office, but the proportion of problems that are practical rather than academic increases dramatically when one moves out of the classroom and into the office.

## Two Kinds of Intelligence

Until recently, almost all of what was known about intelligence applied to the kind of intelligence that pays off in the classroom. This kind of intelligence, commonly referred to as *academic intelligence* or school smarts, is what is measured by traditional IQ tests and some employment tests. The hallmark of academic smarts is facile acquisition of academic knowledge in formal classroom situations. IQ is quite predictive of ability to learn to solve academic problems in a formal classroom setting, but it is less predictive of ability to learn to solve practical problems in the office.

Recent research has identified a second kind of intelligence, which we refer to as *practical intelligence* or street smarts (Wagner & Sternberg, 1986). Scores on research measures of street smarts are quite predictive of ability to learn to solve practical problems in the office, but they are less predictive of ability to learn to solve academic problems in formal classroom settings.

The hallmark of street smarts is facile acquisition of *tacit knowledge*: work-related practical know-how that is learned informally on the job (Wagner & Sternberg, 1986). There are a number of common expressions to describe this kind of learning, including "learning the ropes" and "getting one's feet wet." One executive described the process of acquiring tacit knowledge as learning "what goes without saying around here."

We have identified three kinds of tacit knowledge that are applied by successful managers (Wagner, 1987).

### Three Kinds of Tacit Knowledge

1. Tacit knowledge about *managing oneself* refers to knowledge about self-motivational and self-organizational aspects of managerial performance. An example of tacit knowledge about managing oneself is knowing how best to overcome the problem of procrastination.

2. Tacit knowledge about *managing others* refers to knowledge about managing one's subordinates, peers, and superiors. An example of tacit knowledge about managing others is knowing how to convince a skeptical superior of the worth of one's idea. The importance of tacit knowledge about managing others is suggested by the fact that inability to get along with others is a frequent reason for derailment of fast-track executives (McCall & Lombardo, 1983).

3. Tacit knowledge about *managing tasks* refers to knowledge about how to do specific managerial tasks well. An example of tacit knowledge about managing tasks is knowing how to get your main point across when making a presentation.

Although there are situations that primarily involve only one of the three kinds of tacit knowledge, many managerial situations involve all three kinds of tacit knowledge. For example, chairing a group assigned to revise company policy on alcohol abuse is a task that requires tacit knowledge about managing oneself, others, and one's tasks.

Having considered the question of what street smarts is, we turn to the question of how street smarts can be measured.

## How Can Street Smarts Be Measured?

To the extent that intellectual competence is assessed in selection procedures for managerial and executive positions, what is assessed is academic smarts rather than street smarts. Combining a measure of street smarts with traditional selection procedures should improve selection of managers and executives. In addition, because academic and street smarts are only modestly related, a measure of street smarts may help to identify individuals who would be missed by traditional selection procedures, yet who would make excellent managers and executives.

The Tacit Knowledge Inventory for Managers (TKIM; Wagner & Sternberg, in press) has been constructed to assess managerial street smarts. The test consists of a series of work-related situations. A sample work-related situation that measures tacit knowledge about managing others follows:

*An employee who reports to one of your subordinates has asked to talk with you about waste, poor management practices, and possible violations of company policy and the law on the part of your subordinate. You have been in your present position for only six months, but in that time you have had no indication of trouble about the subordinate in question. You do not have an open-door policy, and employees are expected to discuss their concerns with their immediate superiors before bringing the matter to the attention of anyone else. The employee who wants to meet with you has not discussed the matter with her superior because of its delicate nature.*

*Rate the quality of the following response alternatives:*
  a. *Refuse to meet with the subordinate until she discusses the matter with your subordinate.*
  b. *Meet with the employee.*
  c. *Meet with the employee but only with your subordinate present.*
  d. *Turn the matter over to an administrative assistant.*

Performance is scored by comparing an individual's responses to those of a group of experts.

Eight studies of tacit knowledge in real-world pursuits have been carried out. Some studies have involved giving the instrument to nationwide samples of managers and executives, to M.B.A. students, and, to provide a measure of baseline performance, to individuals with no managerial experience. Other studies have involved giving the instrument to individuals in several organizations for whom detailed performance measures were available.

There have been four major results:

1. Successful managers and executives perform better on the TKIM than do less successful managers and executives.

2. Not all managers and executives acquire tacit knowledge. It appears to be the case that it is not experience per se that matters, but what one learns from it. There may be some truth to the bit of managerial folk wisdom that after ten years, a successful manager will have had ten years of experience, whereas an unsuccessful manager will have had one year of experience, ten times. Understanding why some managers profit from their experience and others apparently do not will require a better understanding of individual differences in facility for acquiring tacit knowledge, and also a better understanding of the assignments and situations that offer important lessons to be learned (McCall, Lombardo, & Morrison, in press).

3. The most successful managers and executives have acquired each of the three kinds of tacit knowledge—managing oneself, managing others, and managing tasks.

4. The facility with which tacit knowledge is acquired is pretty much unrelated to IQ, at least for groups of relatively high-scoring individuals (IQs of 110+), as managers and executives tend to be. Thus, the TKIM is not just an IQ test in disguise.

We will describe a recent study of the tacit knowledge of participants in the Center for Creative Leadership's Leadership Development Program (LDP), and then consider how tacit knowledge might be trained.

## The LDP Participants Study

We used the opportunity of studying the tacit knowledge of LDP participants to address three questions about tacit knowledge. The first is what the relation is between individual differences in tacit knowledge and IQ for experienced managers and executives. In previous studies of college undergraduates, correlations between IQ and measures of tacit knowledge have not been reliably different from zero. However, college undergraduates are novices at management and have less tacit knowledge about management than experienced managers and executives. Perhaps individual differences in IQ and tacit knowledge are related, but only for experienced managers. The second question we addressed is what the relation is between individual differences in tacit knowledge and scores on common measures of personality characteristics. Perhaps measures of tacit knowledge are simply proxies for personality inventories. The third question we addressed is what relations are between individual differences in tacit knowledge and observable behavior. Individual differences in tacit knowledge have been related to distal criteria such as salary or prestige of the organization one works in, but can individuals with lots of tacit knowledge be distinguished from individuals with little by their behavior when performing managerial tasks?

### Method

*Subjects* We obtained data from 45 LDP participants. Their average age was 44 years, with a range from 32 to 58. There were 4 women and 41 men. Included were midlevel managers, upper midlevel managers, and upper-level executives.

*Materials* The tacit-knowledge inventory consisted of nine work-related scenarios, each with ten response items to be rated for their quality. A sample scenario was presented earlier. The IQ test was the Shipley, which includes synonyms and series completions problems. Other measures included the California Psychological Inventory, the Myers-Briggs Type Indicator, the Fundamental Interpersonal Relations Orientation-Behavior (FIRO-B), the Hidden Figures Test (a measure of field independence), the Kirton Adaptation Innovation Inventory (a measure of a preference for innovation), and the Managerial Job Satisfaction Questionnaire.

The criterion to be predicted was Behavioral Assessment Data (BAD) ratings of performance in two managerial simulations called Earth II and Energy International. The participants were observed in small groups (n = 5). Ratings on a 10-(low) to 50-(high) point scale were made for performance in eight categories: activity level, led the discussion, influenced others, problem analysis, task orientation, motivated others, verbal effectiveness, and interpersonal skills.

*Results* Tacit-knowledge scores were generated by scoring deviations of responses from an expert prototype of 15 additional LDP participants. The expert group was selected to maximize simultaneously the variables of salary (all $100,000 +$), amount of experience (all but 1 with 15 or more years of experience), and organizational level (all but 1 were upper-level executives, including 6 CEOs). Note that because tacit-knowledge scores reflect deviation from the expert prototype, lower scores (i.e., more like the expert prototype) indicate better performance.

The individual BAD ratings were not sufficiently reliable to serve as separate dependent variables. A BAD total score was created by getting an average rating over all categories, and then summing this rating over the two problems. The split-half reliability of this total score was .59, after correction using the Spearman-Brown formula.

The range in tacit-knowledge scores was from 112 to 376, with a mean of 189.9 and a standard deviation of 59.4. The range for IQ was from 107 to 134, with a mean of 120.0 and a standard deviation of 7.1. Our sample was very representative of typical LDP participants in IQ, given the correspondence between our data and LDP program participant norms of a mean of 118 and a standard deviation of 7.1. The range in BAD total score was from 31 to 61, with a mean of 48.1 and a standard deviation of 5.9.

The best single predictor of performance in the behavioral simulation was tacit knowledge, with IQ as the second-best predictor. The correlation between tacit knowledge and BAD total was -.61 (p < .001). The correlation between IQ and BAD total was .38 (p < .001). The correlation between tacit knowledge and IQ was a nonsignificant -.14 (p > .05). The correlations among the other measures, BAD total, IQ, and tacit knowledge, are presented in Table 1. We determined whether tacit knowledge would predict performance in the behavioral simulation independent of the other predictors by using a series of hierarchical regressions. In each case, one or more variables were first used as predictors, and then tacit knowledge was added to the prediction equation. If the variables that are first entered are measuring the same thing as tacit knowledge, or if tacit knowledge measures something different but what it measures is not important to performance in the behavioral simulation, then there will not be a reliable increase in variance accounted for (delta $R^2$). On the other hand, if tacit knowledge is measuring something different from the other variables, and if what it is measuring is important to performance in the behavioral simulation, then there will be a reliable increase in variance accounted for. We present the results of eight hierarchical regressions in Table 2. Variables listed as other measures refer to the variables that were used as first predictors before adding tacit knowledge to the prediction equation. The first hierarchical regression had IQ as a first predictor. The second through seventh hierarchical regressions had subtests from one of the tests and IQ as the first predictors. The eighth hierarchical regression had as first predictors subtests from any of the tests for which there was a significant simple correlation between the variable and the total score on the behavioral simulation. The values of delta $R^2$ are the increase in proportion of variance accounted for in the behavioral simulation when tacit knowledge is added to the prediction equation; the values of $R^2$ for the full model are the proportion of variance accounted for in the behavioral simulation by the other measures and tacit knowledge.

For each of the eight hierarchical regressions, there was a large, significant increase in variance accounted for when tacit knowledge was added to the prediction equation. Thus, tacit knowledge was related to performance in the behavioral simulation independent of IQ, personality variables, and job satisfaction. For most of the regressions, the total variance accounted for approached the reliability of the behavioral simulation total score. Thus, the combination of tacit knowledge, IQ, and selected personality variables was a potent predictor of performance in the simulation.

## TABLE 1
### Correlations of Test Measures with BAD Total Score, IQ, and Tacit Knowledge Score

| | BAD | IQ | TK |
|---|---|---|---|
| **California Psychological Inventory** | | | |
| Dominance | .13 | − .07 | − .01 |
| Capacity for Status | .09 | − .05 | − .01 |
| Sociability | .07 | − .06 | .14 |
| Social Presence | − .01 | .08 | .29* |
| Self-Acceptance | .17 | .23 | .10 |
| Sense of Well-Being | − .17 | − .08 | .17 |
| Responsibility | .01 | .00 | − .15 |
| Socialization | − .04 | − .09 | .12 |
| Self-Control | − .35** | − .30* | .19 |
| Tolerance | .09 | .07 | − .04 |
| Good Impression | − .30* | − .25 | .21 |
| Communality | − .10 | − .05 | .12 |
| Achievement via Conformity | − .06 | .12 | − .05 |
| Achievement via Independence | .27* | .26* | − .24 |
| Intellectual Efficiency | .20 | .19 | .04 |
| Psychological Mindedness | .06 | .40** | − .19 |
| Flexibility | − .05 | .12 | − .02 |
| **FIRO-B** | | | |
| Inclusion Expressed | .24 | .08 | − .03 |
| Inclusion Wanted | .14 | .16 | − .19 |
| Control Expressed | .38** | .17 | − .25* |
| Control Wanted | − .08 | .17 | − .12 |
| Affection Expressed | .23 | − .12 | − .08 |
| Affection Wanted | .11 | − .05 | − .03 |
| **Hidden Figures** | | | |
| Field Independence | .29* | .22 | − .25* |
| **Kirton Adaptation-Innovation** | | | |
| Innovation | .22 | .19 | .07 |
| **Myers-Briggs Type Indicator** | | | |
| Extraversion | − .07 | .23 | − .23 |
| Sensing | .20 | .10 | − .17 |
| Thinking | − .05 | − .26* | − .08 |
| Judging | − .05 | − .04 | .13 |
| **Managerial Job Satisfaction Questionnaire** | | | |
| Satisfied with Work | − .14 | − .10 | .17 |
| Satisfied with Superior | − .04 | − .16 | − .13 |
| Satisfied with Co-Workers | .10 | − .07 | .00 |
| Satisfied with Pay | .15 | .02 | .06 |
| Satisfied with Promotions | − .24 | − .08 | .08 |

## TABLE 2
### Hierarchical Regressions of BAD Total
### on Other Measures and Tacit Knowledge

| Other Measures | Delta $R^2$ for TK | $R^2$ for Full Model |
|---|---|---|
| 1. IQ | .32*** | .46*** |
| 2. CPI, IQ | .22** | .66* |
| 3. FIRO-B, IQ | .32*** | .65*** |
| 4. Field Independence, IQ | .28*** | .47*** |
| 5. Innovation, IQ | .33*** | .50*** |
| 6. Myers-Briggs, IQ | .35*** | .56*** |
| 7. Job Satisfaction, IQ | .32*** | .57*** |
| 8. All Predictors Reliably Correlated with DV (k=5) | .17* | .54*** |

Note:
 * $p < .05$
 ** $p < .01$
 *** $p < .001$

We turn next to the question of how to train street smarts.

## How Can Street Smarts Be Trained?

How might the acquisition of tacit knowledge be facilitated for executives and managers? Because the formal study of tacit knowledge is in its infancy, we do not yet know to what degree tacit knowledge can be trained. It is likely that some form of training will facilitate the acquisition of tacit knowledge for most individuals. However, it also is likely that some individuals simply are better than others at acquiring tacit knowledge, and these individual differences will not disappear with training. The best strategy would seem to be both to select individuals who appear to be most facile at acquiring tacit knowledge and to train individuals to help them reach their potential.

At present we are exploring two different approaches to training tacit knowledge: a direct approach and an indirect approach.

**Direct Instruction of Tacit Knowledge** Although tacit knowledge is not routinely taught, we think it is likely that some aspects of tacit knowledge can be taught. The problem is deciding what specifically to try to teach.

In an exploration of a method of determining what specifically to try to teach, we focused on the ability to persuade another of the worth of one's idea or product. We focused on this ability because previous research suggests that it is critical to executive and managerial success (Wagner & Sternberg, 1985), and because we could identify a naturally occurring group of individuals who are without a doubt experts in persuading others of the worth of a product: successful commission salespersons.

We examined the tacit knowledge of commission salespersons by studying the rules of thumb they used in sizing up sales situations and customers (Wagner, Rashotte, & Sternberg, 1987). A *rule of thumb* is a useful principle with wide application, not intended to be strictly accurate. An example of a rule of thumb employed by successful managers as well as salespersons is "think in terms of tasks accomplished rather than hours spent working." We have developed a method for validating rules of thumb that allows us to distinguish between rules that are used and rules that appear to be useful but are not actually used. We have identified a set of rules of thumb that are used by successful commission salespersons, and are identifying rules of thumb that are used by successful managers. We have incorporated rules of thumb in the latest tryout version of the Tacit Knowledge Inventory for Managers, as illustrated in the following example that concerns managing others:

*Recently, your company began allowing departments to switch to flextime scheduling. Flextime scheduling means the manager and employee agree on a working schedule that is not confined to 8 to 5. Over half of the departments have switched to flextime scheduling.*

*Your subordinates want to switch to flextime scheduling. However, you do not believe flextime scheduling will work for your department because your department must communicate frequently with outside organizations, and that must be done from 8 to 5. You have told your subordinates why you oppose flextime scheduling, but many are very angry with you. Some are almost rude. Morale has never been worse. You considered calling a meeting to resolve the issue. However, you believe neither you nor your subordinates will change positions.*

*WOULD YOU . . .*
  *a. Call a meeting to discuss flextime scheduling.*
*or*
  *b. Wait to see if morale improves; call a meeting if it does not.*

*You decide to meet with two subordinates who will serve as representatives for your other subordinates.*

*WOULD YOU . . .*
  *a. Ask for a list of their requests concerning flextime scheduling, promising only to try to think of a way of addressing them that also would address your concerns.*
*or*
  *b. Describe your concerns about flextime scheduling that your subordinates will have to find a way to address before you will try it out.*

*A group of your subordinates comes up with a creative solution to the problems you have about flextime scheduling. You remain skeptical, but agree to try flextime scheduling for one month provided there is a fair and binding evaluation.*

*WOULD YOU . . .*

    *a. Determine the evaluation criteria pretty much on your own, with a fair amount of consultation with your subordinates.*

*or*

    *b. Try to determine the evaluation criteria jointly with your subordinates.*

*After the trial, it is obvious that flextime scheduling has not worked, for the very reasons you thought it wouldn't.*

*WOULD YOU . . .*

    *a. Blame the failure on the unique role of your department in the company.*

*or*

    *b. Remind your subordinates, in a nice way, that you warned them but they chose not to listen to you.*

One member of each pair of answer options represents a rule of thumb; the other is a control item. The rules of thumb that are represented, respectively, are the following: tackle personnel problems immediately, never let them fester (i.e., call the meeting); frame problems in a way that gives others significant responsibility for coming up with a solution (i.e., make it the subordinates' responsibility to address your concerns rather than vice versa); get a consensus on evaluation procedures from those who are affected by them, so as to avoid later challenges (i.e., determine the evaluation criteria jointly); and let others save face (i.e., pass up the opportunity to say, "I told you so").

Our plan for direct training is to give managers a form of the Tacit Knowledge Inventory for Managers as a pretest. Next we will provide a training program, based on the rules of thumb, that includes (a) descriptions of the rules, (b) descriptions of the rules' triggering circumstances, (c) application examples, (d) having managers apply specific rules to situations they have faced in the past, and (e) having managers describe likely future opportunities to apply specific rules. Training would conclude with administration of a second form of the Tacit Knowledge Inventory for Managers as a posttest.

**Indirect Instruction of Tacit Knowledge** The goal of the indirect instruction approach is not to train tacit knowledge but rather to train strategies individuals can use to facilitate their acquisition of tacit knowledge. Why try to train acquisition strategies in addition to providing direct instruction of tacit knowledge? The reason is that at least some of the tacit knowledge that a manager or executive needs to acquire is probably specific to his or her company, department, and immediate co-workers.

One of our approaches to indirect training focuses on three processes that appear to be involved in the acquisition of tacit knowledge: selective encoding, selective comparison, and selective combination (Sternberg & Wagner, 1988). *Selective encoding* refers to determining what is relevant and what is not for one's purpose in learning. *Selective comparison* refers to relating the new information to the relevant aspects of what one already knows. *Selective combination* refers to combining the relevant information into a coherent package.

Consider how these processes operate in the example of a new entry-level manager in a chemical company. The new manager wants to determine what leads to promotion in this particular company. She engages in selectively encoding to determine what is promotion-relevant and what is not. Does the company only care about bottom line? What about getting along with others? Are dress and attendance at social functions important? The manager engages in selective comparison to draw on her past experience, if she has any, or perhaps on stereotypes or what she has read if she has no experience, for help in deciding what is likely to be relevant. Finally, the manager is likely to use selective combination to combine the information she has selectively encoded and compared into a summary description of what leads to promotion in this company.

A second approach to indirect training focuses on strategies for effectively generating and validating hypotheses about tacit knowledge. An example of hypothesis generation would be to ask yourself, upon completion of significant assignments, what, if anything, you believe you have learned from the assignment about your strengths, weaknesses, likes, and dislikes; about those of others; and about how to do important work-related tasks well. For example, you might generate the hypothesis that you are the "victim" of bootlicking; that is, your subordinates only say positive things about your ideas, thereby robbing you of a vital source of constructive criticism. Your next step would be to validate your hypothesis, perhaps by proposing an obviously bad idea and asking for feedback. If your hypothesis is confirmed, you can then begin to change anything in your own behavior that might be inhibiting constructive criticism, and to work "provides constructive criticism" into your subordinates' performance appraisal system.

## Conclusions

To summarize, we have attempted to answer three questions: What is street smarts? How can street smarts be measured? How can street smarts be trained? We have come up with the following answers.

1. The hallmark of the street smart executive or manager is facile acquisition and use of work-related tacit knowledge about managing oneself, others, and one's tasks.

2. Street smarts can be measured by assessing an individual's tacit knowledge. One method for doing so is to present individuals with work-related situations that require tacit knowledge to deal with effectively.

3. Two promising approaches to training are to teach rules of thumb that are employed by successful managers and executives as a means of conveying relatively general tacit knowledge, and to teach acquisition strategies useful in acquiring more specific tacit knowledge.

## References

McCall, M. W., & Lombardo, M. M. (1983). *Off the track: Why and how successful executives get derailed* (Tech. Rep. No. 21). Greensboro, NC: Center for Creative Leadership.

McCall, M. W., Lombardo, M. M., & Morrison, A. M. (in press). *The lessons of experience.* New York: Harper & Row.

Neisser, U. (1976). General, academic, and artificial intelligence. In L. Resnick (Ed.), *The nature of intelligence* (pp. 135–144). Hillsdale, NJ: Erlbaum.

Sternberg, R. J., & Wagner, R. K. (Eds.). (1986). *Practical intelligence: Nature and origins of competence in the everyday world*. New York: Cambridge University Press.

Sternberg, R. J., & Wagner, R. K. (1988). Individual differences in practical knowledge and its acquisition. In P. L. Ackerman, R. J. Sternberg, & R. Glaser (Eds.), *Learning and individual differences* (pp. 255–278). New York: W. H. Freeman.

Wagner, R. K. (1987). Tacit knowledge in everyday intelligent behavior. *Journal of Personality and Social Psychology, 52*, 1236–1247.

Wagner, R. K., Rashotte, C. A., & Sternberg, R. J. (1987). *Tacit knowledge in sales: Rules of thumb for selling anything to anyone*. Manuscript submitted for publication.

Wagner, R. K., & Sternberg, R. J. (1985). Practical intelligence in real-world pursuits: The role of tacit knowledge. *Journal of Personality and Social Psychology, 48*, 436–458.

Wagner, R. K., & Sternberg, R. J. (1986). Tacit knowledge and intelligence in the everyday world. In R. J. Sternberg & R. K. Wagner (Eds.), *Practical intelligence: Nature and origins of competence in the everyday world* (pp. 51–83). New York: Cambridge University Press.

Wagner, R. K., & Sternberg, R. J. (in press). *The Tacit Knowledge Inventory for Managers*. San Antonio, TX: The Psychological Corporation.

# SECTION H

## Development of Leadership

# Development of Leadership

Leaders do not suddenly emerge full-blown. For leaders, there is a life before and a long line of ancestors. How a society assures an adequate supply of leaders for the next generation is poorly understood. The articles in this section deal in various ways with this problem. Some insights are gained by studying certain traits among younger people. Another approach is to watch the developmental process throughout a career, while yet another is to develop measures to provide insight into landmark events in a career. While this volume primarily examines people in the work force, we fail to enhance the overall quality of leadership unless we expand our horizons to understand how leadership qualities are developed in members of the younger generation.

## Perceptual Accuracy of Self and Others and Leadership Status As Functions of Cognitive Complexity
Hal W. Hendrick

Undergraduate students in a leadership course viewed the first part of the film *Twelve Angry Men* and made predictions about the order in which each juror would change opinion. Students also ranked all members of the class on effectiveness in class and leadership exercises. Behavior prediction accuracy, accuracy of self-perception of leadership status, and rated leadership status are examined in relation to scores on the Abstract Orientation Scale, a measure of cognitive complexity. Implications of the findings are discussed.

Hal W. Hendrick, Professor of Human Factors and Dean, College of Systems Science, University of Denver, University Park, Denver, Colorado 80208. (303-871-3619). PhD, Purdue University. Secretary General, International Ergonomics Association.

## A Study of the Developmental Experiences of Managers
Anna Marie Valerio

The developmental experiences of managers in one organization (NYNEX) were studied as a basis for management development programs, using the classification of events and the interview questions used by Lombardo et al. (1983). Managers completed questionnaires and an in-depth interview about key events in their careers and about lessons learned. Learning and the events promoting learning are reported in detail. Greater emphasis on lateral movement for development, programs for female and minority managers, and the establishment of a core curriculum for generic management skills training were recommended on the basis of the study's findings.

Anna Marie Valerio, Associate Director, Selection Systems, NYNEX Corporation, 1113 Westchester Avenue, White Plains, New York 10604-3510. (914-644-6725). PhD, City University of New York.

## BENCHMARKS: An Instrument for Diagnosing Managerial Strengths and Weaknesses
Cynthia D. McCauley and Michael M. Lombardo

BENCHMARKS is a management feedback instrument constructed to identify managers' strengths and weaknesses. A manager does a self-rating and is rated by subordinates, peers, and superiors. Scale scores of successful managers in market-driven organizations are contrasted with scale scores of successful managers in "clannish organizations." Four validity analyses are reported using as criteria: assessment of promotability, performance evaluations, and a three-point measure—derailed/no change/promoted.

Cynthia D. McCauley, Director, Education and Nonprofit Sector Research Group, Center for Creative Leadership, 5000 Laurinda Drive, Post Office Box P-1, Greensboro, North Carolina 27402. (919-288-7210). PhD, University of Georgia. Author of *Developmental Experiences in Managerial Work* and *Dynamics of Derailment*. Coauthor of BENCHMARKS. Author of various articles in *Academy of Management Journal*, *Applied Psychological Measurement*, and *Journal of Management*.

Michael M. Lombardo, Director, Leadership Development Research Group, Center for Creative Leadership, 5000 Laurinda Drive, Post Office Box P-1, Greensboro, North Carolina 27402. (919-288-7210). EdD, University of North Carolina–Greensboro. Coauthor of *The Lessons of Experience*, *Looking Glass: An Organizational Simulation*, and BENCHMARKS. Author of various technical reports. Author of various articles in *Management Science* and *Journal of Management*.

## Assessing Opportunities for Leadership Development
Marian N. Ruderman, Patricia J. Ohlott, and Cynthia D. McCauley

The Job Challenge Profile (JCP) aims to assess the developmental potential of managerial jobs and to identify different types of developmental job elements. Twelve scales assess demands or challenges described by managers such as the context of the job, other people, the assignment goals, and the type of transition the job entails. Preliminary studies relate scale scores to general ratings of development and to specific lessons learned.

Marian N. Ruderman, Behavioral Scientist, Center for Creative Leadership, 5000 Laurinda Drive, Post Office Box P-1, Greensboro, North Carolina 27402. (919-288-7210). PhD, University of Michigan. Coauthor of "Explanations of Success and Derailment" in *Journal of Business and Psychology* and "The Role of Procedural and Distributive Justice in Organizational Behavior" in *Social Justice*.

Patricia J. Ohlott, Research Associate, Center for Creative Leadership, 5000 Laurinda Drive, Post Office Box P-1, Greensboro, North Carolina 27402. (919-288-7210). BA, Yale University; Doctoral Candidate, Duke University. Coauthor of "Multiple Assessment of Managerial Effectiveness: Interrater Agreement and Consensus in Effectiveness Models" in *Personnel*.

Cynthia D. McCauley, Director, Education and Nonprofit Sector Research Group, Center for Creative Leadership, 5000 Laurinda Drive, Post Office Box P-1, Greensboro, North Carolina 27402. (919-288-7210). PhD, University of Georgia. Author of *Developmental Experiences in Managerial Work* and *Dynamics of Derailment*. Coauthor of BENCHMARKS. Author of various articles in *Academy of Management Journal*, *Applied Psychological Measurement*, and *Journal of Management*.

## Leadership and Youth: A Commitment
Frances A. Karnes

The Center for Gifted Studies at the University of Southern Mississippi has developed a summer residential Leadership Studies Program that provides leadership instruction and measures outcomes with a Leadership Skills Inventory (LSI). The results of the analysis of those data and other research studies focusing on leadership and youth are reported.

Frances A. Karnes, Professor of Special Education and Director–Center for Gifted Studies, University of Southern Mississippi, Southern Station, Box 1, Hattiesburg, Mississippi 39401. (601-266-7101). PhD, University of Illinois, Champaign-Urbana. Author of leadership skills rating scales (diagnostic) and instructional materials and various journal articles and books.

# Perceptual Accuracy of Self and Others and Leadership Status As Functions of Cognitive Complexity

*Hal W. Hendrick*

Management, or its leadership influence aspect, has been defined historically as getting things done through others or by similar definitions (Bennis, 1959; Munson, 1921; Nash, 1929; Shartle, 1951; Stogdill, 1950; Tannenbaum, Weschler, & Massarik, 1961; Tead, 1935). Bass (1961) notes further that a manager's effort to change the behavior of others is attempted leadership; when others actually change, this creation of change in others is successful leadership. Implicit in this influence process is the importance of perceiving and interpreting accurately the behavior of others, especially how likely they are to respond to changes in their environment, including the manager's own behavior. This assessment skill has been described variously in the literature as social perceptiveness, social acuity, sensitivity, empathy, social intelligence, social insight, and person perception (Gough, 1976). Fundamental to this skill appears to be one's ability to perceive the behavioral cues of others (Harvey, 1966).

Although the ability to sense and interpret behavioral cues is accepted intuitively and theoretically as critical to the influence process, relatively little is reported about what and how personality factors contribute to, or inhibit, effective cue utilization, including behavioral cues. One line of cognitive-style personality research suggests that the degree of cognitive complexity or concreteness/abstractness may be an important higher-order personality determinant of cue utilization, including behavioral cues. Cognitive complexity is reported to have two major structural dimensions: differentiation and integration (Bariff & Lusk, 1977; Harvey, 1966; Harvey, Hunt, & Schroder, 1961; Schroder, 1971). Differentiation can operationally be defined as the number of dimensions extracted from a set of data and integration as the number of interconnections between rules for combining structured data (Bariff & Lusk, 1977).

A concrete or simple cognitive style is one in which relatively little differentiation is used in structuring concepts. Experiential data are categorized by the individual within relatively few conceptual dimensions; and within concepts, there exist relatively few categories or "shades of grey." In the extreme, a concept is divided into just two categories characteristic of either/or absolutist thinking. In addition, concrete thinkers are relatively poor at integrating conceptual data in assessing complex problems and developing creative or unique, insightful solutions. In contrast to concrete-functioning individuals, cognitively complex persons tend to demonstrate high differentiation and effective integration in their conceptualizing (Harvey, 1966; Harvey et al., 1961; Hendrick, 1979).

A number of researchers have studied cue utilization as a function of cognitive complexity in interpersonal judgment (Alcorn & Torney, 1982; Brannigan, 1978; Brounstein, 1975; Brown, 1975; Capurso & Blocher, 1985; Delia, Clark, & Switzer, 1974; Domangue, 1978; Durand, 1978; Ikegami, 1983; O'Keefe & Delia, 1978; Pettinelli, 1973; Scott, 1975). These studies showed positive relationships between cognitive complexity and various effectiveness measures of interpersonal judgment. Leonard (1974) found that cognitively complex employment interviewers showed greater discrimination in their interviewee rating than did cognitively simple interviewers. White (1977) studied predictions of 72 persons comprising a cognitively complex and a cognitively simple group. The cognitively complex group made predictions based on consideration of more relations in the social structure than did the cognitively simple group. Gast (1987) in a leadership study of 45 federal supervisors found that cognitively complex supervisors showed greater discrimination in their performance ratings of subordinates than did their more cognitively concrete counterparts; these data also suggested that the cognitively complex supervisors were better able to sustain high-quality relationships with their subordinates. In an information-processing study by Nydegger (1975), the results suggested that "abstract" designated leaders made better use of feedback cues than did more "concrete" leaders.

Additional studies have shown greater and more effective cue utilization among more cognitively complex persons in problem solving. Harvey (1966) has summarized several studies by himself and colleagues demonstrating that abstract persons have a greater sensitivity to minimal cues and a greater ability to use them appropriately and completely. Similar results were obtained by Lundberg (1972) for complex decision making in a management simulation study. Ceci and Liker (1986) found that cognitively complex avid racetrack males were more accurate in predicting post time odds than their cognitively concrete colleagues. Hendrick (1979) found that groups comprised of cognitively complex members not only completed a problem-solving task twice as fast as more concrete-functioning groups, but also the cognitively complex members demonstrated greater flexibility of set and more complete and effective cue utilization. These findings held true for both groups of undergraduate students and experienced managers.

The present study was designed to investigate further the relation of cognitive complexity to effective cue utilization in ways important to managers or to others in leadership positions. In comparison with more cognitively simple or concrete persons, cognitively complex or abstract persons were hypothesized to (a) make more effective use of available behavioral cues to predict the future behavior of others, (b) be more accurate in judging their own leadership effectiveness status within a work group of peers, and (c) hold higher leadership status within a work group of peers. It also hypothesized that these dependent variables of status, perception of one's own status, and prediction of behavior of others would be significantly related to one another.

## Method

**Subjects** The subjects were 117 senior and junior college undergraduates enrolled in eight sections of an elective leadership course in the Rocky Mountain region. All 117 students were male. Class section size varied from 12 to 18 students each, with a modal size of 13. Ages of the students ranged from 19 to 23, with a modal age of 21. On the day of the experimental task, four members of the class were absent and were deleted from the study, leaving 113 in the final sample. The four absent students were all from different class sections.

**Materials** The measure of cognitive complexity used in this study was the Abstract Orientation Scale (AOS) developed and validated by O'Connor (1972). O'Connor has presented data for 467 adults showing significant relationships in the theoretically expected direction (p < .001) for the AOS with Harvey's This I Believe (TIB) Test, the California F Scale (Adorno, Frankel-Brunswik, Levinson, & Sanford, 1950), Rokeach's (1960) Dogmatism Scale, seven Belief System Inventory (Kaats, 1969) scales, and eight scales from the Omnibus Personality Inventory (Heist & Young, 1961). Scott, Brown, and Kaats (1970, May) found the AOS to predict 16 of 20 measures assessing characteristics theoretically related to abstractness at beyond the .01 level and the other four at beyond the .05 level. These results were slightly better than for the TIB and notably better (p < .01) than for two other measures of cognitive complexity. Hendrick (1979) found that the AOS significantly related to problem-solving behavior in the theoretically expected direction on three separate criterion measures—completion time, pace, and cue utilization. Hendrick (in preparation for submission for publication) also found the AOS test-retest reliability to be .82 for 102 male military personnel and significantly related to their TIB scores (p < .001).

The AOS was utilized in this study in lieu of the more extensively validated TIB because of its shorter administration time, an important consideration for classroom use, and because it can be machine scored.[1] The AOS consists of 30 items, but only 18 are used in the scoring of the instrument. Individuals respond to item statements by marking their degree of agreement or disagreement using a six-point scale.

The task materials for this study consisted of the film *Twelve Angry Men* and a form which was given to each student for recording his judgments. These materials are further described in the procedure.

---

[1] *The TIB requires content analysis of each item for each person by trained judges. Because of this laborious scoring procedure, the TIB normally is used only when conceptual system determination (Harvey et al., 1961) is to be made in addition to level of cognitive complexity.*

**Procedure** During a prerequisite organizational behavior course, all of the students in the study sample were administered the AOS along with their classmates as part of another research project. This administration took place during the year prior to enrollment in the leadership course in which the present study was conducted.

For the first five weeks of the leadership course, the students participated in group discussions of case studies and reading materials and took part in various classroom exercises involving various dimensions of leadership behavior. These discussions and exercises during the first 12 one-hour class sessions provided opportunity for each section member to become aware of each other member, the resources he brought to the class section, and his method and pattern of participation. Although taught by three different instructors, considerable uniformity of course content and teaching methodology was maintained across all eight sections. This uniformity was maintained by close adherence to the same detailed course outline and by discussion of each lesson among the three instructors within several days of its being taught. During the next lesson, which occurred in the sixth week of the course, each student ranked all of the students in his section, including himself, in terms of the degree of leadership influence exercised in the classroom. The instructor collected a copy of each student's ranking. These, in turn, were summed for each participant to determine his composite ranking.

During the 14th session, the class viewed the first 38 minutes of the film *Twelve Angry Men* which depicts the deliberations of the jury at the end of a murder trial. The film is rich in its portrayal of group dynamics phenomena. Issues of leadership, conformity, and deviation are highly visible in the emerging patterns of interpersonal relationships of the jurors. Each juror exemplifies a distinct personality and his arguments and nuances of behavior easily suggest a degree of attitudinal and behavioral flexibility. The initial vote of the jury, after their discussion, is 11 to 1 guilty. The film was stopped at the point where the jury is preparing for its second vote. The class was then told that during the remainder of the film the jurors who had initially voted guilty changed their vote, one by one, resulting in a final vote of 12 to 0 for not guilty. Each class member then was given a form depicting the jury seating arrangement. On this form, each juror was identified as he was in the film, that is, by occupation or some distinguishing characteristic such as "old retired man." The class then was instructed to predict the order in which the jurors would change their votes from guilty to not guilty. This private prediction was prepared in duplicate. One copy was kept by the student for use in a group decision-making exercise, and the other copy was given to the instructor. Following the group exercise, the class was shown the remainder of the film.

The private decisions of each student were compared with the correct solution. The sum of the absolute differences between the correct order, as depicted in the film, and the student's own order constituted his "prediction error score." The composite ranking of each student within his class section, divided by section size, was designated as his group "leadership status." The absolute deviation of each student's own ranking of himself, divided by section size, from his leadership status score constituted his "self-perception score."

## TABLE 1
## Summary of Variable Intercorrelations and Results

| VARIABLE: | | A | B | C | MEAN | SD |
|---|---|---|---|---|---|---|
| AOS Score | (A) | | | | 75 | 11.0 |
| Behavioral Prediction Error | (B) | .44** | | | 19 | 7.5 |
| Self-Perception Error | (C) | .39** | .42** | | 20 | 15.7 |
| Leadership Status | (D) | .29* | .04 | .25* | 48 | 20.7 |

** p<.001
 * p<.01

## Results

Table 1 shows the means and standard deviations for the independent and three dependent variables. The AOS scores demonstrate good variability with no apparent restriction in range. The use of absolute deviations, rather than taking direction into account in determining the self-perception scores, resulted in a skewed distribution; the median for this distribution is 18, and the $Q = 8.9$.

Table 1 also depicts the matrix of product moment correlations for the four variables. Scatterplots of these bivariate distributions show them all to be essentially linear with good homoscedasticity. AOS scores were found to correlate with both the prediction error and self-perception error scores at the .001 level and with leadership status at the .01 level. In comparison with the more concrete-functioning students, the more cognitively complex students (a) were more accurate in their predictions of the behavior of the jurors in the experimental task, (b) were more accurate in assessing their own peer status, and (c) tended to hold a higher leadership status within their class sections. Accuracy of one's self-perception of status also was found to correlate with actual group leadership status ($p < .01$) and with the prediction error scores ($p < .001$).

## Discussion

The results of the present study are consistent with the findings from previous research cited earlier on cognitive complexity and cue utilization. As cognitive complexity increases, people's ability to more fully and effectively utilize available cues also increases. In the behavioral area, this theoretically should result in more accurate perception both of one's own status and of the likely behavioral responses of others. The present study offers confirmatory evidence that this is the case.

Prior research also consistently has shown that more cognitively complex individuals are more emphatic and people-oriented (Harvey, 1966; Harvey et al., 1961). Fiedler's (1967) leadership research suggests that those who are more people-oriented, that is, high scorers on his Least Preferred Co-Worker (LPC) instrument, should be more effective leaders in those situations which call for use of interpersonal leadership skills. Fiedler has identified those situations as the broad range of intermediate or "moderate" leadership favorableness situations, which tend to predominate in most organizational settings. Since the LPC basically is a differentiation task (Foa, Mitchell, & Fiedler, 1971; Mitchell, 1970) and differentiation is one of the two basic dimensions of cognitive complexity, it is not surprising that the high LPC scorers have been found to perform well in these intermediate leadership favorableness situations (Fiedler, 1967). Indeed, studies by Foa et al. (1971) and by Mitchell (1970) found LPC scores to be positively related to various measures of cognitive complexity. Evans and Dermer (1974) found low LPC scorers to consistently score low on measures of cognitive complexity although there was no consistent pattern for high LPC scorers. Recently, Hendrick (in preparation for submission for publication) found a significant relationship ($p < .01$) between LPC scores and both the AOS and TIB scores for a group of experienced managers. These findings suggest that cognitively complex leaders also will tend to be more effective leaders in moderate leadership favorableness situations. A significant relationship between leadership effectiveness status and cognitive complexity in the present study is consistent with, and offers additional support to, this suggestion.[2]

Because of the cognitive nature of the abstractness or cognitive complexity dimension, one might suspect that it is general intelligence that really is being measured. Prior research (Ceci & Liker, 1986; Harvey, 1966; Harvey et al., 1961; O'Connor, 1972) has shown consistently only low positive or no correlation between measures of general intelligence and cognitive complexity, including the AOS, when education level is held constant. To the extent that measures of cognitive complexity are related to leadership effectiveness, as is suggested by the findings of this study, they are likely to contribute unique variance to leadership predictor composites which are heavily weighted on aptitude measures. This would appear to be a potentially useful area for future leadership research in applied, as well as laboratory, settings.

Since accurate perception and insight into self and others, problem-solving behavior, greater flexibility, and empathy and interpersonal skill all appear to characterize the more cognitively complex persons, it is not surprising that these persons also would be perceived as the more effective leaders in task groups, as was the case in this study. Given the progressively increasing emphasis on participative management in our modern organizations, one could hypothesize that it is the cognitively complex leaders who will be the most successful and effective in the coming decades. The present study offers support for this hypothesis and suggests this as a fruitful area for follow-up research.

## References

Adorno, T. W., Frankel-Brunswik, E., Levinson, D. J., & Sanford, R. N. (1950). *The authoritarian personality*. New York: Harper and Row.

---

[2] *In the present study, although there were good leader-member relations and classroom exercises and discussions had a stated objective, the tasks were otherwise unstructured and position power was weak. Thus, the leadership favorableness situation was "moderate" based on Fiedler's (1967) classification.*

Alcorn, L. M., & Torney, D. J. (1982). Counselor cognitive complexity of self-reported emotional experience as a predictor of accurate understanding. *Journal of Counseling Psychology, 29*, 534–537.

Bariff, M. L., & Lusk, E. J. (1977). Cognitive and personality tests for the design of management information systems. *Management Science, 23*, 820–837.

Bass, B. M. (1961). Some aspects of attempted, successful, and effective leadership. *Journal of Applied Psychology, 45*, 120–122.

Bennis, W. G. (1959). Leadership theory and administrative behavior: The problems of authority. *Administrative Science Quarterly, 4*, 259–301.

Brannigan, M. B. (1978). Elementary principal's conceptual level and variables involved in teacher evaluation. *Dissertation Abstracts International, 39*, 3251A. (University Microfilms No. 78-23,545)

Brounstein, D. A. (1975) Cognitive concreteness-abstractness and social competence. *Dissertation Abstracts International, 36*, 490B. (University Microfilms No. 75-14,502)

Brown, D. L. (1975). Cognitive complexity and intelligence factors in judgmental processes. *Dissertation Abstracts International, 36*, 4127B. (University Microfilms No. 75-27,888)

Capurso, R. J., & Blocher, D. H. (1985). The effects of sex-role consistent and inconsistent information on social perception of complex, androgynous, and sex-typed women. *Journal of Vocational Behavior, 26*, 79–91.

Ceci, S. J., & Liker, J. K. (1986). A day at the races: A study of IQ, expertise, and cognitive complexity. *Journal of Experimental Psychology: General, 115*, 255–266.

Delia, J. G., Clark, R. A., & Switzer, D. E. (1974). Cognitive complexity and impression formation in informal social interaction. *Speech Monographs, 41*, 299–308.

Domangue, B. B. (1978). Decoding effects of cognitive complexity, tolerance for ambiguity, and verbal-nonverbal inconsistency. *Journal of Personality, 46*, 519–535.

Durand, R. M. (1978). Cognitive complexity and the perception of attitude objects: An examination of halo error. *Perceptual & Motor Skills, 46*, 1235–1239.

Evans, M. G., & Dermer, J. (1974). What does the least preferred co-worker scale really measure?: A cognitive interpretation. *Journal of Applied Psychology, 59*, 202–206.

Fiedler, F. E. (1967). *A theory of leadership effectiveness*. New York: McGraw-Hill.

Foa, U. G., Mitchell, T. R., & Fiedler, R. E. (1971). Differentiation matching. *Behavioral Science, 16*, 130–142.

Gast, I. F. (1987). Leader cognitive complexity and its effects on the quality of exchange relationships with subordinates (Doctoral dissertation, George Washington University, 1987). *Dissertation Abstracts International, 47,* 5082B.

Gough, H. (1976). Personality and personality assessment. In M. D. Dunnette (Ed.), *Handbook of industrial and organizational psychology* (pp. 571–607). Chicago: Rand McNally.

Harvey, O. J. (1966). System structure, flexibility, and creativity. In O. J. Harvey (Ed.), *Experience, structure, and adaptability* (pp. 39–65). New York: Springer.

Harvey, O. J., Hunt, D. E., & Schroder, H. M. (1961). *Conceptual systems and personality organization.* New York: Wiley.

Heist, P., & Young, G. (1961). *Omnibus Personality Inventory.* New York: Wiley.

Hendrick, H. W. (1979). Differences in group problem-solving behavior and effectiveness as a function of abstractness. *Journal of Applied Psychology, 64,* 518–525.

Hendrick, H. W. *Leadership behavior and effectiveness as a function of cognitive complexity.* Manuscript in preparation for submission for publication.

Ikegami, T. (1983). The process of information integration in impression judgment and its relation to the cognitive complexity-simplicity. *Japanese Journal of Psychology, 54,* 189–195.

Kaats, G. R. (1969). Belief systems and person perception: Analysis of a service academy environment. *Dissertation Abstracts International, 31,* 454A. (University Microfilms No. 70-05,804)

Leonard, R. L. (1974). The delineation of boundary conditions in the similarity-attraction paradigm: Cognitive complexity. *Personality and Social Psychology Bulletin, 1,* 86–87.

Lundberg, O. H. (1972). An empirical examination of relationships between cognitive style and complex decision making. *Dissertation Abstracts International, 33,* 19A. (University Microfilms No. 72-19,341)

Mitchell, T. R. (1970). Leader complexity and leadership style. *Journal of Personality and Social Psychology, 16,* 166–174.

Munson, E. L. (1921). *The management of men.* New York: Holt.

Nash, J. B. (1929). *Phi Delta Kappan, 12,* 24–25.

Nydegger, R. V. (1975). Information processing complexity and leadership status. *Journal of Experimental Social Psychology, 11,* 317–328.

O'Connor, J. (1972). Developmental changes in abstractness and moral reasoning. *Dissertation Abstracts International, 32,* 4109A. (University Microfilms No. 72-03,831)

O'Keefe, B. J., & Delia, D. G. (1978). Construct comprehensive and cognitive complexity. *Perceptual & Motor Skills, 46,* 548–550.

Pettinelli, J. D. (1973). Cognitive complexity in human judgment. *Dissertation Abstracts International, 34*, 2344B. (University Microfilms No. 73-26,363)

Rokeach, M. (1960). *The open and closed mind*. New York: Basic Books.

Schroder, H. M. (1971). Conceptual complexity and personality organization. In H. M. Schroder & P. Svedfeld (Eds.), *Personality theory and information processing*. New York: Ronald Press.

Scott, C. R. (1975). The effects of pyramidal construing and cognitive structure upon interpersonal prediction and construct organization. *Dissertation Abstracts International, 36*, 3070B. (University Microfilms No. 75-27,722)

Scott, J. E., Brown, D. E., & Kaats, G. R. (1970, May). *Interrelationships and validities of four measures of cognitive complexity*. Paper presented at the meeting of the Rocky Mountain Psychological Association, Salt Lake City, UT.

Shartle, C. L. (1951). Studies in naval leadership. In H. Guetzkow (Ed.), *Groups, leadership, and men: Research in human relations*. Pittsburgh, PA: Carnegie Press.

Stogdill, R. M. (1950). Leadership, membership and organization. *Psychological Bulletin, 47*, 1–14.

Tannenbaum, R., Weschler, I. R., & Massarik, F. (1961). *Leadership and organization*. New York: McGraw-Hill.

Tead, O. (1935). *The art of leadership*. New York: McGraw-Hill.

White, C. M. (1977). Cognitive complexity and completion of social structures. *Social Behavior and Personality, 5*, 305–310.

# A Study of the Developmental Experiences of Managers

*Anna Marie Valerio*

The telephone industry has been undergoing one of the largest transformations in the history of American business. In 1984, AT&T divested itself of its local telephone operating companies which resulted in the formation of seven regional companies, popularly termed the "Baby Bells." The breakup of AT&T has required that the emerging regional companies perform functions which were formerly handled by AT&T. Therefore, human resource functions such as personnel research, selection systems methodology, and training now reside within each regional company. Traditionally, the Bell System companies relied upon recruitment and selection to attract and advance talented individuals and to insure that the necessary management skills were available. Current demographic, technological, social, and economic concerns, however, have contributed to a present focus on training and development in American business. In adapting to a competitive, post-divestiture environment, the former Bell System companies may be particularly affected by these concerns. Training and development have always been highly valued within the Bell System. However, following divestiture, New York Telephone, a subsidiary of the regional company, NYNEX, set out to develop new human resource programs in management development. The present study was undertaken as part of this effort when it became apparent that effective program development required understanding the nature of how different types of job experiences within the context of employment at New York Telephone affected management skill and knowledge.

Empirical evidence for the importance of job experience on managerial development may be found in AT&T's Management Program Study (MPS) and Management Continuity Study (MCS; Bray & Howard, 1983). In particular, results on occupational involvement and job challenge provided information relevant to the design of the present study. In tracking managers from several Bell System operating companies for over 20 years, one of the factors found to be highly related to career success was occupational involvement. Managers at upper levels in the organizational hierarchy manifested greater occupational involvement at Year 19 of the study than did managers at lower levels. Thus, more successful managers remained more involved in their work than did their less successful counterparts, even when they were in their midforties.

Questionnaire results also indicated that career was rated as one of the most important things in their lives and that they worked more hours at home than did less successful managers. Bray and Howard (1983) also found that job challenge was an important factor in advancement; that is, only 30% of college recruits who were predicted to reach middle management actually attained it eight years later if they had experienced low job challenge. Of those who had been predicted to fail to reach middle management, 61% attained it if they had experienced high job challenge.

Job challenge may be important because it serves as a stimulus in the learning of adaptive managerial skills. In a study of more than 400 executives at seven Fortune 500 corporations, challenging job assignments have been shown to be very important for managerial development (Lombardo, McCall, Morrison, & White, 1983; McCall & McCauley, 1986; McCauley, 1986). Lombardo et al. (1983) identified critical types of assignments or "turning point jobs" such as projects and task forces, line-to-staff switches, and increases in job scope. Along with these key event assignments were identified the lessons learned from them.

The present study on the developmental experiences of managers was conducted in response to the organization's need for management development programs. While the AT&T Longitudinal Studies provided data from Bell System companies as an aggregate, a practically oriented study was needed to answer questions within the context of a particular company. Similarly, the research conducted by the Center for Creative Leadership aggregated information on managers across different companies and thereby served as a reference for comparison of results. The classification of event categories and the interview questions employed by Lombardo et al. (1983) also functioned as a useful methodology for a needs analysis.

## Procedures

**Pilot Study** A pilot study following the same methods described below was initially conducted with 14 managers for purposes of refining methodology. The same categories used by Lombardo et al. (1983) were employed in the present study with the following exceptions: "Breaking a Rut" was renamed "Self-Initiated Activities"; "Business Mistakes" and "Subordinate Performance Problems" were called "Learning from a Negative Experience." Four new key events were added: Rotation to AT&T, Staff Person to Vice President, Unique Positions, and Attendance at Advanced Management Potential Assessment (AMPA). The data on key events were analyzed independently by two researchers and interrater agreement was 88% on a total of 37 key events.

**Participants** The participants in the study were 41 managers (8 were female), ranging in age from 31 to 62 years. Their average age was 43. Three levels of

# TABLE 1
## Interview Questions

Having looked at key events, we'll now address some other situations which may have had a lasting effect on you. What happened? What did you learn from the experience?

1. What was your first managerial job? Was there anything special about it? About your first boss?

2. What was the biggest challenge you ever faced and how did you deal with it?

3. What event (or events) made you realize you were going to be successful as a manager?

4. At what point did you make a commitment to this company? How did this commitment express itself?

5. What was your darkest hour? How did you react to this situation?

6. Were you ever fed up but managed to restart? How did you restart?

7. Please describe the person who taught you the most during your career. Specifically, how and what did this person teach you?

8. Did you have an advocate? Several? At any time in your career did you have someone who spotted you and followed your growth and provided you with opportunities? In what way did this person provide you with these opportunities?

9. Most of us have worked for a person we couldn't tolerate for one reason or another. What did you learn from such an experience?

10. Overall, how have you changed, plus and minus, over your career? If you ran into someone who knew you well years ago, what differences would he or she notice?

11. What part have events in your personal life played in your growth as a manager?

12. What kinds of personal sacrifices have you had to make to get where you are today?

13. Do you see it as necessary for a manager to make these sacrifices in order to get ahead?

14. Can you tell me something about your career that would have been different if you were a man/woman?

15. What advice would you give to a younger manager about managing his or her career?

## TABLE 2
## Key Event Categories

|  | % of Participants |
|---|---|
| Promotion/Increase in Scope | 54 |
| Special Projects | 37 |
| Exposure to Role Model | 27 |
| Self-Initiated Activities | 22 |
| Learning from a Negative Experience | 22 |
| Start-Up Operation | 15 |
| Rotation to AT&T | 15 |
| Staff Person to Vice President | 15 |
| Unique Positions | 15 |
| Attendance at Advanced Management Potential Assessment (AMPA) | 15 |

management were represented: Salary Grades (S.G.) 30, 40, and 50 (also referred to as third, fourth, and fifth levels). The salaries of these executives ranged approximately from $60,000 to $125,000. The sample was selected from a group of managers considered to be highly successful as determined by their performance history at New York Telephone.

**Methodology** Two questionnaires were mailed to each participant:

"Key Events" questionnaire in which managers were asked to describe three events in their careers which changed the way in which they manage and the lessons learned from those events.

Competency Questionnaire in which managers were asked to briefly describe on-job and off-job tasks which contributed to the development of each of 13 assessment dimensions.

Following completion of the questionnaires, an in-depth interview was conducted which covered the following areas:

Key events in the career
Early managerial experiences
Challenges and "dark hours"
Gender
The influence of role models and advocates
Personal life
Advice for new managers

Interview questions are given in Table 1. A total of 143 key events was reported by participants. The data on key events were analyzed independently by two researchers into 19 key event categories; the interrater agreement was 95%.

# Results

**Key Events and Lessons Learned**  The ten most important key event categories and the percentages associated with each are listed in Table 2.

When the total number of key events (143) was analyzed by examining the frequency of key event categories, significant differences were found among key event categories ($X^2 = 93.64$, $p < .001$, 18df). The most important key events appear to be the first five listed in Table 2. When key events data were examined separately for participants in S.G. 30, 40, and 50, there were significant differences in the salary grades at which key events occur. For both S.G. 40s and 30s, it appears that key events are more likely to occur at S.G. 21 and 30. Interestingly, no significant differences were found in the key events reported by S.G. 50s. Examination of the data, however, suggested that when key events are reported as occurring at S.G. 50, most of them are Increases in Scope.

Although the specifics of the assignments varied, the key event definitions and lessons learned from them are as follows:

● **Promotion/Increase in Scope**

This involves an increase in responsibility which is both broader and different from anything experienced previously. Promotion/Scope events included massive increases in numbers of subordinates, budgets, and functions to manage. It was the dramatic increase in level of responsibility, however, which was considered key.

Lessons learned:

Management style and skills such as motivating, developing, and rewarding subordinates
A broader perspective on the company
How to delegate work and responsibility to subordinates
Decision making and decisiveness
Organizing/prioritizing skills

Promotion/Increase in Scope was most frequently reported as occurring at Salary Grade 30.

● **Special Projects**

These usually involved working alone or with a small staff, skip-level reporting, and brief durations of several months. The ideas for these projects did not originate with the managers; rather, the managers were asked to work on these by one or more bosses. The projects were usually focused on solving a problem important to a particular department or to the corporation.

Lessons learned:

A broad perspective on the company
Exposure to top management providing increased visibility for promotional opportunities

Special projects most frequently occurred at Salary Grade 30.

## • Exposure to Role Models

These were people from whom a manager learned business skills. Positive role models often took the time to coach these skills, but sometimes mere observation of them was sufficient. Some role models were also negative; that is, they taught a manager "what not to do."

Lessons learned:

> The importance of interpersonal skills in dealing with subordinates, peers, and supervisors
> How to delegate work and responsibility to subordinates while giving them freedom and autonomy
> How to use a participative management style

Exposure to role models was cited most often as occurring at Salary Grades 21, 30, and 40.

## • Self-Initiated Activities

These events were characterized by one factor: they were initiated directly by the manager and did not come from any other source. They included such things as job transfers, new procedures instituted in a department, and projects undertaken to resolve specific problems.

Lessons learned:

> To take the initiative with your own career: volunteer for projects, take responsibility for finding solutions to problems
> To take risks by being innovative and creative

Self-initiated activities most frequently occurred at Salary Grade 21.

## • Learning from Negative Experiences

These included such things as receiving incomplete information or resistance from subordinates, overlooking information in decision making, receiving negative feedback from subordinates, not receiving organization or supervisor support for a project, and working for a difficult boss. In all cases, the situations were perceived as very negative by the manager but were regarded as "learning experiences," nevertheless.

Lessons learned:

> The importance of effective interpersonal skills
> The necessity for good follow-up and monitoring of projects
> Patience and humility

Learning from negative experiences occurred most frequently at Salary Grade 30.

## • Rotation to AT&T

This key event was usually a temporary assignment lasting from one to several years. Its parallel may exist today in a rotation to NYNEX and Bell Communications Research (Bellcore).

Lessons learned:

A broader vision of the company and the entire system as a whole
How to work cooperatively with people from different operating companies
Long-range planning

Rotation to AT&T occurred most frequently at Salary Grade 30.

## ● Start-Up Operations

In these events, managers create a business venture from nothing or almost nothing. They are accountable for the success of a new function within the organization but from the outset may only be given a broad goal, a desk, and a telephone—the rest is up to them.

Lessons learned:

Effective interpersonal and negotiation skills
How to perform effectively in a stressful, unstructured, and often-chaotic situation
Time management

Start-up operations most frequently occurred at Salary Grade 30.

## ● Staff Person to Vice President

In this key event, the manager functioned as "the staff person" to an Assistant Vice President (AVP) or to a Vice President (VP). In most cases, the manager was at Salary Grade 30 and yet functioned as a Salary Grade 40 or 50. Responsibilities included preparing and delivering presentations, budget planning, and representing the supervisor at various meetings.

Lessons learned:

How the entire company operates
Interpersonal/negotiation skills

## ● Attendance at AMPA

In the Advanced Management Potential Assessment, potential for performance at Salary Grade 50 by managers currently at Salary Grade 30 is assessed. Both positive and negative feelings about AMPA were expressed by managers reporting this key event. While attendance was viewed as an opportunity for growth, managers were puzzled as to why such an important event in their careers was often not seen as an occasion for a career discussion by their AVP or VP. Managers felt that after AMPA's stressful and challenging four days, they were still "in the dark" with respect to the direction of their careers.

Lessons learned:

Areas of strengths and weakness
The need to change management style
Lack of correspondence between assessment performance and job performance
Concrete examples of areas in which improvement was necessary

**Early Managerial Experiences** Previous studies of leadership have found that the early years in a manager's career are crucial for development and the present results agree with this. In general, the first five years in the careers of the managers studied appear to have been critical to the understanding of how the business works and the fundamentals of acceptable interpersonal behaviors. How is this information transmitted? How does the new manager become socialized in this system? The greatest influence is exerted by the first or one of the first bosses to whom the manager reports.

A full 50% of the managers reported that when they were first-level managers, they were most influenced by their second-level bosses, and 26% reported that it was their third-level manager who had the greatest impact. Almost three-quarters of the responses described early bosses in positive terms. The most favorable perceptions were of bosses who provided emotional support by helping and encouraging subordinates (38%) and of bosses who were knowledgeable and shared that knowledge (35%). Over a quarter (28%) described bosses who had given them the freedom to try new things and make decisions, and the latitude to make mistakes.

Good bosses were described as having several of these traits. What emerges, then, is a picture of the characteristics of a manager as teacher:

> Has knowledge and imparts it
> Is supportive of subordinates
> Gives freedom to make decisions, try new things, make mistakes
> Gives subordinates large projects and responsibility
> Provides feedback on performance

Negative perceptions (30%) included views of bosses who provided no help, showed no interest, and either taught nothing or taught subordinates "what not to do."

At what point do managers make a commitment to the company? Almost half of all participants (48%) indicated that they had made a commitment within the first five years of employment; almost a quarter (24%) had actually done so at the point of entry or within the first year. Among the reasons cited for having made a commitment were promotions, challenging and enjoyable work, fair pay treatment, and company benefits.

How do managers change over the course of their careers? Half (51%) of all responses noted that the managers experienced an increased sense of confidence over the course of their careers. Almost half (49%) stated that their orientation toward people had also increased. In particular, they noted that they were more "outgoing," "tolerant," and "considerate of others" as well as "more politically aware." A few noted that their management style tended to be more participative. Almost half also noted an improvement in their problem-solving skills (better planning, decision making, organizing) and that they were delegating more and/or delegating better.

How do managers gauge their success? In accounting for events that led them to realize that they would be successful, managers most often cited experiences of accomplishment on the job. They attributed their sense of accomplishment to being able to meet the demands of a variety of jobs (job rotation) or to specific incidents such as successful supervision.

**Job Challenges and "Dark Hours"** Challenging assignments and dark hours test the mettle of managers and teach them many valuable lessons. Most of the managers' "dark hours" were caused by being blocked from a move or a promotion, having a difficult boss, and encountering a significant job crisis. How do managers respond to these types of situations? Many participants admitted to feelings of disappointment, discouragement, and frustration (36% of responses). Interestingly, the most common way of solving the problem was to work around it and attempt to find a creative solution (36% of responses). Other participants worked hard to remain self-motivated by keeping productive and "hanging in," or by relying on support from superiors, subordinates, and family (33% of responses). A few tried a more aggressive approach of defending themselves and their ideas in the face of adversity (13% of responses). Most interestingly for career development, a full third of participants said that their "darkest hour" was alleviated by a job change, either lateral or upward.

What makes managers "fed up" and how do they get restarted? Precipitating causes were most likely to be a difficult, unsupportive boss or a "slump," that is, a period when the manager felt that efforts were stalled or a project was winding down. Other less common causes were failure to be promoted, a poor performance review, a job crisis, and political pressures. Managers get themselves restarted in two ways: looking for strength internally (55% of responses) or attempting to impact the external environment (58% of responses).

When motivating themselves by looking internally, successful managers use phrases such as "inner work standards move me on," "I wasn't going to let it get me down," "I looked at the larger perspective," and "I see the positive—I celebrate the smallest success." When looking externally, successful managers use phrases such as "I self-start a new project," "I come up with a game plan," and "I get into the creative aspects of the job." In the case of about one-third of the managers, an element of change, a new project, a new boss, a new job, or a vacation was important in enabling them to restart.

What do managers consider to be their biggest challenges? Over three-quarters of the responses noted that the biggest challenge involved taking on assignments or projects in which managers experienced a significant increase in job scope or in which they had no background or experience.

**The Issue of Gender** How does gender influence career development? Eighty-five percent of all participants expressed the idea that there have been in the past and still continue to be extreme difficulties to be overcome by females in the advancement of their careers. When responses were examined separately for males and females, the trend was still the same: 87% of all male participants and 63% of all female participants were in agreement. Many males simply stated, "I wouldn't have gotten as far" (34% of responses).

**Role of Other People** Corporations work via the relationships between the people in them. So just how is information passed along from one individual to the next? What are the most common and effective pathways? What role do advocates or mentors play in the course of one's career? What do managers do when they encounter roadblocks such as difficult bosses?

Managers were asked to describe the persons who taught them the most during their careers. Overall, the most frequently mentioned teaching relationships in the company occurred between managers at Salary Grades 21 and 30 (second and third levels) and their immediate supervisors. Another important teaching relationship also seems to occur between a third-level manager and a fifth-level manager. A great deal may be learned from one's peers, as well, for managers reported that learning relationships also occur between peers at first and second levels.

What exactly do managers learn from each other? Most obviously, they learn about the company, its operations, technical aspects, union considerations, and the business in general. They also learn many less tangible lessons by observing others as role models or by specific intervention from a supervisor. These learning areas may be categorized generally into managerial skills, political skills, personal qualities, and coaching/developing skills.

It is commonly accepted that one of the most important relationships in a corporation is that between a manager and an advocate, that is, one who spots the manager at any point, follows the manager's growth, and provides opportunities. All of the participants in the study had advocates: only 12% cited only one advocate; the remainder had multiple advocates during their careers.

Are there patterns to be found in these relationships? Advocate relationships occur at all levels but most frequently when a manager is at third level with advocates at fourth, fifth, and sixth levels. Advocates tend to be two levels above the level of the manager, however.

Female managers had advocates at all levels, but an advocacy relationship with a manager two levels above or even higher was cited more frequently than it was for the males. Caution needs to be exercised in interpreting the results because of the small sample size. Overall, the relationship between a third-level female manager and a fifth-level advocate was cited as most important for career growth.

Advocates take a proactive role in working towards a manager's promotion, helping by creating openings, fighting for the promotion, speaking to others of the manager's potential, giving excellent appraisals, tracking the manager's progress, and requesting that the manager work for the advocate. Advocates also assist by inviting the manager to meetings with upper-level managers and assigning special projects and presentations.

For female managers, all of the above roles of an advocate were important. However, assigning special projects and presentations for exposure and increased job scope were cited more frequently. Although the numbers are small and only trends may be reported here, females generally cite promotion as an opportunity provided less frequently than males. It may be possible that an advocate must be more subtle in the promotion of a female manager by building a consensus among his colleagues in allowing them to observe her performance directly.

What do managers learn from difficult bosses? Most managers learned to tolerate the boss and do their best job (31% of responses). Many others (40% of responses) said that working around the situation was the best solution and either left the job or worked around the person.

**Personal Life** The theme of 60% of the responses was that marriage and family have a positive influence by contributing to stability, increasing interpersonal skills, and improving organizing skills. There was also some mention (25% of responses) of difficult life experiences such as divorce, illness, midlife crises, and so forth. While these events were experienced as stressful, managers frequently hastened to add that they learned many valuable lessons from these as well. In almost one-quarter of their responses, managers expressed an involvement in, and enjoyment of, community activities. Some of the responses (18%) also addressed the need for a constant juggling of work and personal life.

The most commonly mentioned personal sacrifices made to get ahead were long hours spent on the job and working evenings and weekends (78% of responses). Managers do see it as necessary in order to get ahead, however.

**Advice to Other Managers** Participants were asked what career advice they would give to younger managers coming up in the business. The major ones are: keep informed, develop a supportive network, take the initiative, be true to yourself, seek help from an advocate, and establish priorities for your own career. The highest frequency of responses (63%) was found in the theme "keep informed." This advice was focused on broadening one's perspective via lateral moves within a department followed by movement across departments. Managers specifically included moving across disciplines and companies within NYNEX. Managers stated that the optimal time to remain in most jobs was approximately two years. They also recommended obtaining both line and staff experience and jobs allowing for interactions outside the company to obtain a better perspective of how the company is viewed by others.

**Development of Generic Management Skills** Managers were also asked to complete a Competency Questionnaire in which they were asked to describe on-job and off-job experiences which contributed to the development of 13 generic management skills. The major findings are shown in Table 3.

At which salary grades are these competencies most likely to be developed? The vast majority were developed at the second and third levels ($X^2 = 72.00$, p < .001, 4df). In fact, the frequency of responses was higher at third level for all of the competencies except written communication and fact finding. Oral defense, planning, and autonomy may be developed somewhat later in the career, as the frequencies of responses at fourth and fifth levels suggest. This may be particularly true for planning.

## Discussion

Although comparisons across leadership studies need be drawn cautiously due to differences in methods and samples, we may speculate on some of the results of the present study and those of Bray and Howard (1983) and Lombardo et al. (1983).

The results of the present study regarding personal sacrifices made for the sake of career success seem to suggest that the present sample of New York Telephone managers shares the same propensity for occupational involvement as did the successful MPS managers. Working evenings and weekends was seen as necessary for advancement by New York Telephone managers and the more successful MPS managers reported that they worked more hours at home than their counterparts at lower levels. The successful managers in the MPS study occupied approximately the same managerial levels (Levels 4–6) as did the New York Telephone managers (Levels 3–5). In fact,

## TABLE 3
## Results of Competency Questionnaire

| COMPETENCY | EXPERIENCES | |
| | On-Job | Off-Job |
| --- | --- | --- |
| ORAL PRESENTATION | Making presentations. | Community activities: making presentations, having leadership role. |
| ORAL DEFENSE | Defended company/ program. | School activities: course work, debating team. Community activities: leadership role. |
| WRITTEN COMMUNICATIONS | Prepared written reports. | School activities: term papers. |
| IMPACT | Making presentations. Variety of job assignments. | Community activities: leadership role. |
| BEHAVIOR FLEXIBILITY | Responding to the needs of others (dealing with customers). Job transfers. | Community activities. Personal experiences: dealing with family, moving, psychotherapy. |
| AUTONOMY | Assuming responsibility for a major project. | Personal experiences. |
| LEADERSHIP | Supervision of others to accomplish a goal. | Community activities. |
| FINDING AND USING INFORMATION | Did research on special project. | School activities: research paper. |
| ORGANIZING | Variety of job assignments. Undertaking a major task. | Community activities: leadership role. Personal experiences: juggling work and home life, running a household. |
| PLANNING | Planning for a department/district. | Community activities: planning. |
| DECISION MAKING | Making decisions in daily operations and special projects. | Personal experiences: making decisions on marriage, family, and so forth. |
| DECISIVENESS | Making decisions in daily operations and critical situations. | Personal experiences: making decisions on marriage, family. Community activities. |
| SELF-OBJECTIVITY | Assessment Center feedback. Appraisals/feedback from supervisors. | Community activities. |

since the present study was completed, approximately 25% of the New York Telephone sample have been promoted to the next level of management, so that more of these managers now occupy levels 4–6.

The AT&T studies also illustrate the importance of job challenge in the early years, which is in agreement with the present results on early managerial experiences. Among the reasons cited by managers for their early commitment to the company were job challenges and promotions.

Support for the notion that more successful individuals reach out for more stimulation and challenge both on the job and in other areas (Bray & Howard, 1983) is provided by the results of the Competency Questionnaire. Historically, managers in New York Telephone have received support and encouragement for their participation in community activities. These activities have contributed to the development of generic management skills, particularly if the manager assumed a leadership role in the community organization or activity.

The key events, reported by Lombardo et al. (1983), which occurred more frequently were increase in scope, special projects, and role models; the same pattern was found in the present study. Start-up and Fix-it assignments appear to be less common in New York Telephone. Of course, historically these types of events have not generally been required in the day-to-day provision of local telephone service. The data collected by Lombardo et al. (1983) were based on managers from several companies, most of which were highly entrepreneurial. It may be interesting to see if data obtained on managers in the regional companies would contain a greater frequency of start-up events in the future.

The purpose of the present study was to gather information on the developmental experiences of successful managers at New York Telephone and to utilize it in the design of management development programs. A new program for middle managers, "The Development Partnership," was, in fact, introduced within the company. The features of this program include a greater emphasis on lateral movement for development, programs for females and minority managers, and the establishment of a core curriculum for generic management skills training, all of which were recommended in the study report. Results from the Competency Questionnaire were utilized in the preparation of a *Corporate Resource Guide* for managers which identified on-job and off-job activities for self-improvement.

## References

Bray, D. W., & Howard, A. (1983). The AT&T longitudinal studies of managers. In K. W. Schaiel (Ed.), *Longitudinal studies of adult psychological development* (pp. 266–312). New York: Guilford Press.

Lombardo, M., McCall, M., Morrison, A., & White, R. (1983, August). Key events and learnings in the lives of executives. In M. Lombardo (Chair), *Key events in the lives of executives*. Symposium conducted at the 43rd annual meeting of the Academy of Management, Dallas, TX.

McCall, M. W., Jr., & McCauley, C. D. (1986, August). Analyzing the developmental potential of jobs. In J. L. Moses (Chair), *Expanded potential for job analysis.* Symposium conducted at the meeting of the American Psychological Association, Washington, DC.

McCauley, C. (1986). *Developmental experiences in managerial work: A literature review* (Tech. Rep. No. 26). Greensboro, NC: Center for Creative Leadership.

# BENCHMARKS: An Instrument for Diagnosing Managerial Strengths and Weaknesses

*Cynthia D. McCauley*
*and*
*Michael M. Lombardo*

This paper describes the development of a new management feedback instrument, BENCHMARKS, and its implications for what is important to measure when diagnosing a manager's strengths and weaknesses. A manager rates himself or herself on the 154 BENCHMARKS items and is also rated by subordinates, peers, and superiors. A summary report presenting self-ratings and averaged ratings by others on a number of dimensions (and on the items making up those dimensions) is then provided to the manager.

BENCHMARKS was constructed by studying how managers develop. This focus on what was learned by studying managerial development has broadened the scope of the instrument to include managerial values and perspectives as well as skills. It also helps ensure that BENCHMARKS measures competencies that managers are not born with and do not automatically bring to the job—things that might be realistically developed (Lindsey, Homes, & McCall, 1987). An instrument that provides a measure of status on a broad range of skills and perspectives that managers think are important to develop and that they believe can be developed seems appropriate for systematic management development.

In addition to looking at how well the manager performs in areas seen as important for the manager to develop, BENCHMARKS also gives a measure of potential flaws in the manager. The assumption made here is that not demonstrating a strength differs from the presence of a flaw. Flaws represent potential blocks to development.

**Origins of BENCHMARKS** BENCHMARKS is based on findings from a series of research studies focused on how executives learn, change, and grow over their careers (Mc-

Call, Lombardo, & Morrison, 1988). The research found that managers indeed do develop over their careers and that this development was driven by the manager's experiences. The purpose of the project was to understand which experiences mattered the most and how they mattered (i.e., what sort of development emerged).

Content analysis of extensive interviews with executives and open-ended questionnaire responses resulted in 16 categories of critical developmental events (e.g., turning around an organization or unit in trouble, having a role model) and 34 categories of lessons learned from these events (e.g., how to direct and motivate subordinates, how to cope with situations beyond your control, management values) (see Lindsey et al., 1987).

In addition, 19 top executives at three corporations provided descriptions of two people they knew well—an executive who succeeded and one who had recently derailed (i.e., been demoted, fired, or plateaued below level of expected achievement). Ten reasons for derailment were derived from these interviews (McCall & Lombardo, 1983).

**Instrument Development** Items were written to tap categories of managerial development; these were derived from content analysis of data collected in the two interview studies of executive development. Items in the first section were drawn from the 34 categories of lessons executives reported learning from critical events in their careers; items in a second section were drawn from the ten categories of flaws responsible for a manager's derailment.

Item stems were descriptive phrases of a managerial skill, perspective, or quality. Sample items are:

> develops subordinates by providing challenge and opportunity,
> accepts conflicts as inevitable and does not shy away from them.

The rater was provided with a five-point scale to indicate the degree to which the manager displayed the quality.

Initial groupings of items in each section were derived from a factor analysis of ratings on 336 managers by their immediate bosses. Further item analysis and evaluation of conceptual overlap in the items led to refinement of the groupings. Descriptions of the current scales that make up the instrument are presented in Figure 1.

Indices of scale reliability were high for the scales in Section 1: average alpha = .88, average test-retest coefficient for self-ratings = .72, average test-retest coefficient for ratings by others = .85, average interrater agreement = .58. These indices were somewhat lower for the flaws scales but still within acceptable ranges: average alpha coefficient = .83, average test-retest coefficient for self-ratings = .55, average test-retest coefficient for ratings by others = .72, average interrater agreement = .43.

**Relationship of Scales to Managerial Success** The BENCHMARKS ratings obtained from bosses in the scale construction process were correlated with several criteria that reflect the manager's probable or actual continued success in the organization:
(1) an overall assessment by the boss of the manager's promotability on a six-point scale;

# FIGURE 1
## BENCHMARKS: Scale Names, Descriptions, and Sample Items

| Section 1 Scales | Descriptions of Scales | Sample Items |
|---|---|---|
| **1A. RESOURCE-FULNESS** | Can think strategically, engage in flexible problem-solving behavior, and work effectively with higher management. | • makes good decisions under pressure with incomplete information<br>• links his/her responsibilities with the mission of the whole organization |
| **1B. DOING WHAT-EVER IT TAKES** | Has perseverance and focus in the face of obstacles. | • faces difficult situations with guts and tenacity<br>• controls his/her own career; does not sit and wait for the company to plan a course to follow |
| **1C. BEING A QUICK STUDY** | Quickly masters new technical and business knowledge. | • learns a new skill quickly<br>• quickly masters new vocabulary and operating rules needed to understand how the business works |
| **2A. BUILDING AND MENDING RELATIONSHIPS** | Knows how to build and maintain working relationships with co-workers and external parties. | • when working with a group over whom he/she has no control, gets things done by finding common ground<br>• relates to all kinds of individuals tactfully, from shop floor to top executives |
| **2B. LEADING SUBORDINATES** | Delegates to subordinates effectively, broadens their opportunities, and acts with fairness towards them. | • is willing to delegate important tasks, not just things he/she doesn't want to do<br>• relies on persuasion or expertise first; uses the power of the position as a last resort |
| **2C. COMPASSION AND SENSITIVITY** | Shows genuine interest in others and sensitivity to subordinates' needs. | • is willing to help an employee with personal problems<br>• is sensitive to signs of overwork in others |
| **3. STRAIGHT-FORWARDNESS AND COMPOSURE** | Is honorable and steadfast. | • relies on style more than substance in dealings with top management<br>• becomes hostile or moody when things are not going his/her way |
| **4. SETTING A DEVELOPMENTAL CLIMATE** | Provides a challenging climate to encourage subordinates' development. | • is willing to pitch in and lead subordinates by example<br>• develops subordinates by providing challenge and opportunity |
| **5. CONFRONTING PROBLEM SUBORDINATES** | Acts decisively and with fairness when dealing with problem subordinates. | • is able to fire loyal but incompetent people without procrastinating<br>• can deal effectively with resistant subordinates |

*Continued on next page*

**FIGURE 1**—*Continued*

| Section 1 Scales | Descriptions of Scales | Sample Items |
|---|---|---|
| **6. TEAM ORIENTATION** | Accomplishes tasks through managing others. | • acts as if his/her managerial success is built by a team of strong subordinates |
| **7. BALANCE BE-TWEEN PERSONAL LIFE AND WORK** | Balances work priorities with personal life so that neither is neglected. | • acts as if there is more to life than just having a career<br>• lets job demands cause family problems |
| **8. DECISIVENESS** | Prefers quick and approximate actions to slow and precise ones in many management situations. | • displays a real bias for action, calculated risks, and quick decisions<br>• does not hesitate when making decisions |
| **9. SELF-AWARENESS** | Has an accurate picture of strengths and weaknesses and is willing to improve. | • sorts out his/her strengths and weaknesses fairly accurately. |
| **10. HIRING TALENTED STAFF** | Hires talented people for his/her team. | • hires people who are not afraid of responsibility or risks |
| **11. PUTTING PEOPLE AT EASE** | Displays warmth and a good sense of humor. | • has a warm personality that puts people at ease |
| **12. ACTING WITH FLEXIBILITY** | Can behave in ways that are often seen as opposites. | • is tough and at the same time compassionate<br>• can lead and let others lead |

**Section 2 Scales**

| | | |
|---|---|---|
| **1. PROBLEMS WITH INTERPERSONAL RELATIONSHIPS** | Difficulties in developing comfortable working relationships with others. | • adopts a bullying style under stress<br>• isolates him-/herself from others |
| **2. DIFFICULTY IN MOLDING A STAFF** | Difficulties in selecting and building a team. | • chooses an overly narrow subordinate group<br>• is not good at building a team |
| **3. DIFFICULTY IN MAKING STRATE-GIC TRANSITIONS** | Difficulties in moving from the technical/tactical level to the general/strategic level. | • cannot handle a job requiring the formulation of complex organizational strategies<br>• can't make the mental transition from technical manager to general manager |
| **4. LACK OF FOLLOW-THROUGH** | Difficulties in following up on promises, really completing a job, and attention to detail. | • makes a splash and moves on without really completing a job<br>• has left a trail of little problems |
| **5. OVERDE-PENDENCE** | Relies too much on a boss, powerful advocate, or one's own natural talent. | • has chosen to stay with the same boss too long<br>• might burn out, run out of steam |
| **6. STRATEGIC DIF-FERENCES WITH MANAGEMENT** | Disagrees with higher management about business strategy. | • disagrees with higher management about how the business shoud be run |

# TABLE 1
## Validity Coefficients: Correlations of BENCHMARKS Scale Scores with Criterion Measures

| Scales | Boss' Assessments of Promotability (n = 336) | Independent Criterion of Promotability (n = 64) | Performance Evaluations (n = 69) | Failed/No Change/ Promoted (n = 253) |
|---|---|---|---|---|
| **Section 1:** | | | | |
| 1A. Resourcefulness | .60** | .22 | .22 | .22** |
| 1B. Doing Whatever It Takes | .58** | .31* | .26* | .29** |
| 1C. Being a Quick Study | .49** | .31* | .34** | .23** |
| 2A. Building and Mending Relationships | .37** | .02 | .03 | .18** |
| 2B. Leading Subordinates | .47** | .26* | −.02 | .18** |
| 2C. Compassion and Sensitivity | .21** | −.06 | −.03 | .12 |
| 3. Straightforwardness and Composure | .31** | .04 | −.18 | .14* |
| 4. Setting A Developmental Climate | .43** | .37** | .21* | .17** |
| 5. Confronting Problem Subordinates | .42** | .39** | −.06 | .15* |
| 6. Team Orientation | .26** | .09 | −.10 | .10 |
| 7. Balance Between Personal Life and Work | −.01 | .05 | .02 | .03 |
| 8. Decisiveness | .23** | .30* | .34** | .22** |
| 9. Self-Awareness | .45** | .18 | .19 | .19** |
| 10. Hiring Talented Staff | .45** | .44** | .17 | .21** |
| 11. Putting People At Ease | .12* | .01 | .04 | .14* |
| 12. Acting with Flexibility | .44** | .02 | .08 | .25** |
| | | | | |
| **Section 2:** | | | | |
| 1. Problems with Interpersonal Relationships | −.17** | .25* | .22 | −.08 |
| 2. Difficulty in Molding a Staff | −.40** | −.41** | −.06 | −.27** |
| 3. Difficulty in Making Strategic Transitions | −.46** | −.13 | −.05 | −.22** |
| 4. Lack of Follow-Through | −.35** | −.08 | .06 | −.16* |
| 5. Overdependence | −.25** | .11 | −.03 | −.11 |
| 6. Strategic Differences with Management | .03 | −.03 | .03 | −.10 |
| | | | | |
| Multiple $R^2$ | .46** | | | .25** |
| Estimated cross-validated $R^2$ | .42 | | | .19 |

*p < .05.   **p < .01.

---

(2) for one organization, an independent rating by the corporate management committee at the time BENCHMARKS data were collected on whether the manager was performing below satisfactory (coded "1"); performing satisfactorily, but unlikely to be promoted (coded "2"); and promotable (coded "3");

(3) for two organizations, performance evaluation ratings on a five-point scale obtained approximately two years after the initial BENCHMARKS ratings;

(4) for six organizations, subsequent movement of the manager within the organization 24 to 30 months after the initial BENCHMARKS ratings. In this time period, managers either had failed, resulting in demotion or termination (coded "1"), had experienced no movement or only lateral movement (coded "2"), or had been promoted (coded "3").

Table 1 presents the results of these analyses.

**Organizational Differences** Establishing the construct validity of BENCHMARKS involved testing hypotheses about group differences on scale scores. One set of hypotheses focused on expected differences between managers in organizations with different cultures. Based on one of the author's work with the organizations in the scale construction sample, two of the organizations were clearly market-driven, tough, and uncaring while two others were distinctively clannish, polite, and almost smothering with expectations of dress and behavior (Kerr & Slocum, 1987). Successful managers in the market-driven organizations were expected to be more decisive, deal more effectively with problem subordinates, be more adept at hiring talented staff, and have more difficulty molding a staff and making strategic transitions. On the other hand, successful managers in clannish organizations were expected to show more straightforwardness and compassion, be better at building and mending relationships, have a stronger team orientation, and have problems with overdependence. The results presented in Table 2 indicate that all but one of the expected differences between the two groups were in the predicted direction; four of the differences were statistically significant.

**Relationship Between Scales and Personal Qualities** Average ratings on BENCHMARKS by co-workers (subordinates, peers, and superiors) for 111 managers were correlated with scores on the Myers-Briggs Type Indicator (MBTI), the Kirton Adaptation-Innovation Inventory (KAI), and the Shipley Institute of Living Scale (see Table 3).

## TABLE 2
## Differences in Means Between Promotable Managers in Clannish and Market-Driven Organizations

| Scales | Clannish (n=43) Mean | SD | Market-Driven (n=59) Mean | SD | t |
|---|---|---|---|---|---|
| **Market-driven hypothesized to be higher on:** | | | | | |
| Decisiveness | 3.23 | .85 | 3.75 | .80 | − 3.1* |
| Confronting Problem Subordinates | 3.64 | .61 | 3.45 | .63 | 1.5 |
| Hiring Talented Staff | 3.60 | .61 | 3.92 | .48 | − 2.8* |
| Difficulty in Molding a Staff | 2.36 | .78 | 2.59 | .71 | − 1.3 |
| Difficulty in Making Strategic Transitions | 2.29 | .93 | 2.84 | .67 | − 2.9* |
| **Clannish hypothesized to be higher on:** | | | | | |
| Straightforwardness and Composure | 4.29 | .57 | 4.00 | .65 | 2.3* |
| Compassion and Sensitivity | 3.47 | .67 | 3.36 | .53 | .9 |
| Building and Mending Relationships | 3.73 | .58 | 3.53 | .54 | 1.8 |
| Team Orientation | 3.70 | .75 | 3.42 | .74 | 1.9 |
| Overdependence | 2.56 | .91 | 2.34 | .72 | 1.1 |

* $p < .05$.

# TABLE 3
## Correlations of BENCHMARKS Scales with MBTI, KAI, and Shipley[a]

| | Extraversion–Introversion | Sensing–Intuition | Thinking–Feeling | Judgment–Perception | Adaptive–Innovative | Shipley |
|---|---|---|---|---|---|---|
| **Section 1:** | | | | | | |
| 1A. Resourcefulness | .00 | −.02 | .01 | −.08 | −.03 | −.12 |
| 1B. Doing Whatever It Takes | −.07 | .11 | −.02 | .00 | .20* | −.06 |
| 1C. Being a Quick Study | .03 | .06 | .04 | −.01 | .06 | −.10 |
| 2A. Building and Mending Relationships | −.19* | −.10 | .24** | .00 | −.17 | −.11 |
| 2B. Leading Subordinates | −.11 | −.10 | .12 | −.06 | −.11 | −.10 |
| 2C. Compassion and Sensitivity | −.18 | −.04 | .25** | −.10 | −.10 | −.07 |
| 3. Straightforwardness and Composure | .01 | −.10 | −.04 | −.10 | −.17 | .02 |
| 4. Setting a Developmental Climate | −.06 | .08 | .11 | .05 | .05 | −.01 |
| 5. Confronting Problem Subordinates | .00 | .01 | −.18 | −.08 | .09 | −.07 |
| 6. Team Orientation | −.07 | .08 | −.02 | −.02 | .00 | −.03 |
| 7. Balance Between Personal Life and Work | −.17 | −.08 | .22* | −.12 | −.15 | −.05 |
| 8. Decisiveness | −.30** | .13 | −.13 | .17 | .41** | .03 |
| 9. Self-Awareness | −.08 | −.14 | .26** | −.07 | −.24 | −.05 |
| 10. Hiring Talented Staff | −.18 | .05 | −.07 | .00 | .11 | −.04 |
| 11. Putting People At Ease | −.35** | −.08 | .31** | .04 | −.09 | −.04 |
| 12. Acting with Flexibility | −.11 | −.02 | .20* | −.02 | −.07 | −.08 |
| **Section 2:** | | | | | | |
| 1. Problems with Interpersonal Relationships | .14 | .08 | −.25** | −.04 | .24** | .02 |
| 2. Difficulty in Molding a Staff | .05 | −.09 | −.06 | −.07 | −.01 | .09 |
| 3. Difficulty in Making Strategic Transitions | .01 | .01 | −.03 | −.01 | −.07 | .14 |
| 4. Lack of Follow-Through | −.12 | .04 | −.03 | .09 | .16 | .08 |
| 5. Overdependence | −.05 | .01 | .00 | .01 | .04 | .10 |
| 6. Strategic Differences with Management | .01 | −.01 | −.07 | −.14 | .06 | .07 |

*NOTE: For interpreting direction of relationship, Extraversion, Sensing, Thinking, Judgment, and Adaptive represent the low end of their respective dimensions.*
[a]$N=111.$
* $p<.05.$   ** $p<.01.$

The MBTI provides scores on four bipolar dimensions: extraversion-introversion, sensing-intuition, thinking-feeling, and judging-perceiving. By providing a score on an adaptive versus innovative dimension, the KAI describes an individual's problem-solving orientation. The Shipley is a short test of mental ability covering vocabulary and abstract reasoning.

## Discussion

**A Refined Model** The original qualitative studies of executive development resulted in 34 developmental lessons and ten fatal flaws. The development of BENCHMARKS has allowed for the empirical clustering of these lessons and flaws, resulting in a refined model of dimensions that are important to assess for management development purposes. The scales in the major section of the instrument (Section 1) can be further conceptually grouped into three important clusters:

*Respect for Self and Others.* One aspect of developing as a manager involves learning to have compassion and sensitivity toward others, to treat them with honesty and straightforwardness, and to put them at ease. This includes the ability to build cooperative relationships and handle conflicts without bloodshed. Scales focusing on oneself also belong in this cluster: having a realistic view of one's strengths and weaknesses and trying to balance one's personal and work lives. As frequently acknowledged by practitioners in the mental health field, knowledge and appreciation of self are important prerequisites for dealing with others effectively. This personal knowledge is also important for the ultimate expression of personal balance—being able to behave in opposite ways, such as being both tough and compassionate, being able to lead and let others lead as well.

*Adaptability.* Also important to the manager is developing the resourcefulness needed to cope with the demands of the management job, the drive and attitudes necessary to do this, and the ability to learn and make decisions quickly. These management demands include solving problems, thinking strategically, working with upper management, building structure and control systems, acting with incomplete information, taking full responsibility for actions, facing adversity, and seizing opportunities.

*Molding a Team.* A final cluster focuses on behaviors directed toward the specific group of individuals for whom the manager is responsible. These include: setting a developmental climate for subordinates, sizing up potential employees, delegating and encouraging, developing shared expectations, confronting problem people, and developing a team. Accomplishing these tasks is related to the skills and perspectives inherent in the other two clusters, namely, interpersonal skills and adaptability. Yet this cluster adds unique components needed in the manager: team-focused and able to motivate others.

The flaws section of BENCHMARKS fits within this model of managerial dimensions while providing additional information about the traps managers can fall into in each cluster. Managers can undermine respect for others by failing to smooth the edges of an abrasive personality and can undermine perspectives on self by remaining over-dependent on a boss. They will lack the skills necessary to adapt to the demands of higher-level positions if they have problems with follow-through or are uncomfortable moving from tactical to strategic thinking. They will have trouble dealing with subordinates if they want to do everything themselves or be surrounded with subordinates just like themselves.

**Predicting Managerial Success** All of the scales on BENCHMARKS were not equally predictive of measures of managerial success. Most consistently predictive across criteria were those scales clustered under adaptability: Resourcefulness, Doing Whatever It Takes, Being a Quick Study, and Decisiveness. A close second to these scales were Hiring Talented Staff, Setting a Developmental Climate, and Difficulty in Molding a Staff—all of which involve dealing with subordinates.

Scales reflecting respect for self and others tended to be least predictive of the criterion measures. Some of the scales, such as Balance Between Personal Life and Work, and Compassion and Sensitivity, may never be predictive of promotability criteria in many current corporate climates. Some climates may even engender negative interpersonal qualities. For example, managers rated higher on Problems with Interpersonal Relationships were more likely to be seen as promotable in the one corporation for which there was an independent assessment of promotability. Although these scales are less predictive of promotability, they remain important from the standpoint of covering developmental lessons seen as critical by executives. Understanding why these dimensions are less predictive of success even though they were seen as important by successful executives is an important next step.

Some of the relationships of BENCHMARKS scales with other measures of personal qualities are consistent with these findings concerning prediction of success. Managers scoring more in the "Feeling" direction on the MBTI's Thinking-Feeling dimension tended to be rated higher on the scales that were least predictive of managerial success. The management population tends to be heavily composed of individuals scoring in the "Thinking" direction (Campbell & Van Velsor, 1985).

Also, the data base on the KAI indicates the distribution of scores for the management population on this instrument has a midpoint more toward the innovative end of the continuum. Innovators tended to be rated higher on several BENCHMARK dimensions that were most predictive of managerial success, Doing Whatever It Takes and Decisiveness in particular. However, some potential flaws were also more strongly associated with the innovator—Problems with Interpersonal Relationships and Lack of Follow-Through.

**Comparison to Other Feedback Instruments** How does what is measured by BENCHMARKS compare to what is measured by other feedback instruments which were based on job analyses or studies of what managers do? To look at this question, the scales from BENCHMARKS were compared to those of two instruments published in recent years for use in management development: The Management Skills Profile (Personnel Decisions, Inc., 1986) and the Management Practices Survey (Yukl, 1987).

All three instruments share some core concepts. Each one contains a number of scales focused on dealing with subordinates, which involves motivating, rewarding, delegating, and developing. Each also encompasses interpersonal skills and behaviors such as managing conflict, interfacing with others outside of the work group, and showing concern for others. Finally, all three also emphasize the problem-solving aspect of the manager's job.

The Management Skills Profile and the Management Practices Survey, however, have dimensions not emphasized on BENCHMARKS. These are primarily administrative skills, such as planning, organizing, and monitoring, and communication behaviors, such as keeping others informed and making oral presentations. On the Management Skills Profile managers are also rated on their occupational and technical knowledge. BENCHMARKS does not provide ratings of level of knowledge, but rather ratings of how quickly a manager can master new knowledge.

Unique to BENCHMARKS are scales that capture straightforwardness (e.g., honesty, admission of mistakes), the ability to balance opposite qualities (e.g., self-confidence balanced with humility, toughness balanced with sensitivity), the tendency to balance work and personal life, personal styles that can lead to interpersonal problems (e.g., arrogance, cynicism, aloofness), and overdependency. BENCHMARKS also has a stronger emphasis than the other instruments on confronting problem subordinates and hiring talented staff.

The initial research which drove item generation for BENCHMARKS can account for some of the differences found between it and the other two instruments. First, the initial research involved managers at the executive level. Administrative and communication skills were not frequently mentioned as lessons learned by this group. These skills may be "platform" skills that need to be mastered early in a manager's career and thus did not receive much emphasis in the interviews.

Also, the item source for BENCHMARKS was based on lessons that executives said they learned. Over their careers individuals learn more than the skills and behaviors that are generally noted when studying what managers do. They also learn values and new perspectives. This is why factors like straightforwardness and balancing work and personal life appear in BENCHMARKS. It may also explain why BENCHMARKS emphasizes confronting problem subordinates and hiring talented staff—these may represent areas that the manager deals with relatively infrequently when looking at his or her total job but are fairly difficult skills to master, thus comprising a larger portion of the manager's developmental needs.

In summary, BENCHMARKS can provide measures of managerial strengths and weaknesses, reflecting what managers have reported learning in their careers. BENCHMARKS includes dimensions not found on current management feedback instruments. Some of the dimensions appear to be more predictive of managerial success than others. Differences in what it takes to be successful in various organizations are reflected in average BENCHMARKS measures.

## References

Campbell, D., & Van Velsor, E. (1985). *The use of personality measures in the Leadership Development Program.* Greensboro, NC: Center for Creative Leadership.

Kerr, J., & Slocum, J. W. (1987). Managing corporate cultures through reward systems. *Academy of Management Executive, 1*, 99–107.

Lindsey, E. H., Homes, V., & McCall, M. W. (1987). *Key events in executives' lives* (Tech. Rep. No. 32). Greensboro, NC: Center for Creative Leadership.

McCall, M. W., & Lombardo, M. M. (1983, February). What makes a top executive? *Psychology Today*, pp. 26–31.

McCall, M. W., Lombardo, M. M., & Morrison, A. (1988). *The lessons of experience*. Lexington, MA: Lexington Books.

Personnel Decisions, Inc. (1986). *Management Skills Profile*. Minneapolis, MN: Author.

Yukl, G. (1987, August). *A new taxonomy for integrating diverse perspectives on managerial behavior*. Paper presented at the meeting of the American Psychological Association, New York, NY.

# Assessing Opportunities for Leadership Development

*Marian N.
Ruderman
Patricia J.
Ohlott
and
Cynthia D.
McCauley*

*A good executive is born when someone with
some natural endowment (intelligence, vigor, and
some capacity for interacting with his fellow men)
by dint of practice, learning, and experience, develops that endowment into a mature skill.*

(Simon, 1977, p. 44)

In many contemporary organizations, development of executive leadership skills is synonymous with formal classroom
teaching and training (Hall, 1986). In fact, most of the research on executive learning focuses on what is learned from
such programs (Kelleher, Finestone, & Lowy, 1986). There
is an increasing awareness, however, that management development is much more than classroom training (Brousseau, 1984; Burke & Day, 1986); most development occurs
informally outside the classroom. Recent research has shown
that managers learn the majority of important lessons about
leadership from experiences they have while on the job
(Lindsey, Homes, & McCall, 1987; McCall, Lombardo, &
Morrison, 1988) and not from formal programs. On-the-job
challenges may be important in developing a manager because they stimulate performance and force a person to learn
to cope with the stresses and problems they create (Mc-
Cauley, 1986). Therefore, one way organizations can ensure
the continuity of strong leadership at the top is to maximize
the power of on-the-job development.

Unfortunately, our knowledge about the learning and development processes of managers within the context of their
everyday work is scarce (Davies & Easterby-Smith, 1984).
In many organizations, jobs are not systematically used to
develop executive potential. Even in companies which try to
use assignments developmentally, often the particular skills
or personal attributes which would be developed by such
assignments are not really known. Although there may be a

feeling that a given experience would be "good" for the manager, the assignment is not clearly linked to specific learning objectives (Hall, 1986). Often programs of rotational training are thought to broaden managers' experiences, but even though companies invest a great deal in such programs, the effectiveness of rotational training is not known (Beatty, Schneier, & McEvoy, 1987).

Before on-the-job experiences can systematically be used for development purposes, we need to be able to identify potential sources of development by examining managerial and executive jobs in depth. Once we are able to assess the sources of development inherent in different assignments, we can begin to link the sources to the skills, abilities, and perspectives associated with executive success.

One possible way to examine managerial jobs thoroughly and identify sources of development is through the technique of job analysis. Job analysis is a systematic means of gathering, analyzing, and documenting information about the basic content, requirements, and context of a job (Bemis, 1983). Traditional job analyses of managerial jobs (Hemphill, 1960; Tornow & Pinto, 1976) are designed to enhance person-job fit through selection and placement activities. The basic role of the traditional job analysis is to discover what a particular job calls for so that someone with the requisite skills, abilities, and knowledge can be selected or placed into a given job.

This traditional approach to placement is different from a developmental approach. Placing a person into a job for which they are fully prepared maximizes person-job compatibility and is unlikely to develop the individual. Studies of managerial growth and learning (McCall et al., 1988) point out that growth and development are most likely to occur when the person-job match is less than perfect. Learning occurs when people are put into situations where they have not previously mastered the behaviors needed for effective performance. Therefore, in order to identify sources of on-the-job growth it is important to assess situations which promote development and push incumbents to learn new skills. Traditional approaches identify the skills or abilities needed for a particular job, but are incapable of determining which features of the job will stretch the individual.

The questionnaire discussed in this paper attempts to provide a means for identifying and classifying sources of on-the-job development so that this information can be used to systematically increase the opportunities for on-the-job development. The questionnaire is based on information about challenging job experiences identified in studies of the experiences which developed successful executives (McCall et al., 1988; McCall, 1988; Lindsey et al., 1987; Morrison, White, & Van Velsor, 1987). Analysis of the hundreds of developmental experiences described retrospectively by 191 successful executives from six major corporations surfaced eight key situations, or elements, associated with growth and learning (Lindsey et al., 1987). The elements dealt with the mission of the job (e.g., playing for high stakes, scope and scale of the job), the context of the assignment (e.g., overcoming incompetent or resistant subordinates, handling business adversity), and the type of transition it was for the individual (e.g., degree of change for the person, facing situations for which the person did not have the traditional background). Figure 1 contains a description of these elements. Several other studies reviewed in McCauley (1986) provided indirect evidence that these sorts of job elements are developmental.

## FIGURE 1
## Key Developmental Job Elements[1]

1. **Dealing with the Boss** — By observing and having to deal with a variety of bosses, both good and bad, over the course of his/her career, the manager is required to adapt to and cope with diverse people in authority.

2. **Dealing with the Staff** — Handling staff who had been a former boss or peers; or who are incompetent, resistant, or inexperienced; or who exhibit performance problems.

3. **Other Significant Relationships** — The manager must work with people he or she has never had to deal with before and must overcome significant obstacles in achieving cooperation among them.

4. **The Stakes** — Stakes are high in situations involving high visibility to the top for the manager, tight business deadlines, and financial risks. Pressure to perform, often when resources are scarce and the risks are great, requires taking effective action in the face of stress and tremendous consequences.

5. **Adverse Business Conditions** — The manager must take quick and innovative action when faced with business hardships, such as strikes, shortage of resources, problems with consumers or suppliers, or obstacles created by foreign governments or the social and cultural contexts of the business.

6. **Scope and Scale** — Increasing size, complexity, and responsibility for people, finances, and operations require dependence on others and "managing by remote control."

7. **Missing Trumps** — Personal challenges result when a manager enters a business situation at a disadvantage, lacking the background, knowledge, or experience thought to be needed to get the job done. The manager must establish personal credibility while learning the job.

8. **Starkness of Transitions** — The greater the degree of change in assignment, and the more different from what the manager has done before, the more challenge the job provides.

[1]*Qualitative research (McCall et al., 1988) identified these challenges which drive learning on-the-job experiences.*

The Job Challenge Profile (JCP) provides a possible method for identifying and classifying the different types of developmental job elements. A preliminary report by McCall and McCauley (1986) demonstrated the viability of this questionnaire as a means of assessing sources of on-the-job development. However, this early research was based on a small sample size; therefore, substantive conclusions could not be drawn. This paper describes recent research testing the JCP with a larger sample; it demonstrates the potential value of analyzing the developmental features of different jobs by describing our attempts to identify domains of job challenge empirically and to investigate the relationships of these domains to various criteria pertaining to development. Although the data reported here are promising, they too should be considered tentative until a revision of the Job Challenge Profile can be tested with a sample representing a greater variety of jobs and validated against external indicators of managerial growth.

## The Job Challenge Profile (JCP)

The JCP consists of five sections which measure various aspects of experience perceived to be developmental.

The largest section consists of 155 items describing developmental aspects of jobs. These items were based on executives' responses to interview questions about key experiences in their lives which helped them to grow as managers. The items reflect the various categories of developmental job elements identified in the analysis of these interview responses (Lindsey et al., 1987).

The primary purpose of these items is to describe developmental experiences. Respondents are asked to rate to what extent a particular sentence is descriptive of their job on a five-point scale ranging from "to no extent" to "to a very great extent." The research reported here deals primarily with this part of the questionnaire.

A second portion of the JCP asks broad overview questions about the mission of the current job, level in the hierarchy, and budget and scope of the operation. A third section looks at what is learned from the job. Respondents are asked to rate the degree to which they are learning certain lessons from experiences in the current position. The fourth section asks for global ratings of job developmental potential and "demandingness," and the final section asks for background and career history information.

**Data Collection Procedures and the Sample** The sample for this version of the JCP consists of 346 midlevel managers and executives from nine different Fortune 500 organizations. The data were collected in 1986 and 1987. Respondents in a variety of jobs were asked by a senior human resource professional in their organization to complete the questionnaire. Completion of the questionnaire was strictly voluntary and confidential.

Respondents had been in their current position for an average of 2.7 years. They represented a wide variety of functional backgrounds. On the average, the managers and executives had five direct reports and were responsible for total work forces ranging from 0 to 17,000 with an average of 326. The sizes of the budgets for which they were accountable ranged from $0 to $1,700,000,000 with an average annual budget of $34,721,300. Forty-eight percent of the respondents had line responsibilities, 40% had staff responsibilities, and 12% had jobs that were not clearly one or the other.

The sample was largely white (96.2%) and male (90.8%); their ages ranged from 27 to 64 with an average age of 42 years. The study participants were well educated with 45.5% having a graduate degree. On the average, they had 12.5 years tenure in their organization.

**Development of Scales Measuring Sources of Development** A major analytical goal was to reduce the 155 items describing developmental aspects of jobs into a series of scales so that these scales could be used to describe particular ways in which a job was developmental. The scale development was done in several steps.

1. All 155 items were examined to assure their relationship to an overall index of development. This index was a sum of responses to five items asking for global ratings of the job's developmental potential or level of challenge. These items are: (1) Relative to other jobs and assignments you've had, how much is your current assignment contributing to your growth as a manager? (2) Relative to other jobs and assignments you've had, how demanding is this one? (3) Where do you stand in terms of mastering all the skills and abilities needed to handle your current assignment? (reversed) (4) To what extent do you believe your current job will advance your career? and (5) To what extent is your current job different from the one you had just before it? (reversed).

The index had a normal distribution. Correlations were computed between this index and the 155 items describing developmental aspects of jobs. The bottom 25% of items in terms of their correlation with the overall index of development were dropped from the analysis; they had correlations with the overall index of less than .01.

2. Correlations among the remaining 103 items were subject to a series of principal axis factor analyses for purposes of developing scales. Squared multiple correlations were used as initial communality estimates. Three different criteria for determining the number of factors to retain were examined (parallel analysis, scree plots, and Kaiser's criterion). Two different solutions suggested by the three different criteria were subject to a varimax rotation, and the nine-factor solution, explaining 58.4% of the variance, proved to be the most interpretable.

The first factor obtained was very large and conceptually seemed to assess different dimensions of one larger concept. Since the JCP was designed to aid human resource deployment decisions, more specific feedback information on the constructs represented in this first factor was desired than would be afforded by developing one large scale representing the whole factor. Therefore the items which loaded on the first factor were refactored separately. Four interpretable subfactors were found from the factor analysis.

3. Scales were constructed from each factor (or subfactor) by averaging responses to items which had the highest loadings on the factor. Items which loaded on more than one factor were placed conceptually. A total of 12 scales were developed, eight representing original factors and four representing subfactors. Descriptions of the scales and sample items are in Figure 2.

4. The scaling was refined further by examining item-scale correlations. Items found to correlate more highly with scales other than the one on which they were placed were moved to that scale if they fit conceptually; otherwise, they were dropped. Items with low item-scale correlations relative to the other items on the scale were dropped unless a strong conceptual argument could be made for keeping the item.

# FIGURE 2
## Job Challenge Profile: Scale Names, Descriptions, and Sample Items

| | Description of Scale | Sample Items |
|---|---|---|
| **1. LACK OF TOP MANAGEMENT SUPPORT**[a] | Senior management is reluctant to provide support or resources for current work or new projects. | • You have to convince top management to reverse its position on a major proposal.<br>• Resources are tight—you have to "beg, borrow, and steal" to get the job done. |
| **2. SUPPORTIVE BOSS**[a] | Immediate boss is supportive and widely respected. | • Your boss gives you useful advice and support. |
| **3. LACK OF STRATEGIC DIRECTION**[a] | There has not been a coherent organizational strategy or a clear direction for the manager's part of the business. | • There is no well-thought-out direction or plan relating your part of the business to the overall corporate strategy. |
| **4. CONFLICT WITH BOSS**[a] | Manager experiences conflict with boss due to differences in style or opinion or due to boss's flaws. | • Your boss is unaware of his/her shortcomings.<br>• Your boss's management style is very different from your own. |
| **5. INTENSE PRESSURE** | The job puts the manager under constant pressure because of deadlines, long hours, tough decisions, high stakes, and the large scope of the job. | • You are responsible for decisive action in a highly charged environment.<br>• There are clear deadlines by which your key objectives must be accomplished.<br>• This job puts considerable stress on your personal life. |
| **6. DOWNSIZING/ REORGANIZATION** | Decisions about staff reduction or restructuring have to be made. | • You have to lay off a significant number of your people.<br>• You have to carry out a major reorganization. |
| **7. ACHIEVING GOALS THROUGH PERSONAL INFLUENCE** | Getting the job done requires influencing peers, higher management, external parties, or other key people over whom the manager has no direct authority. | • A great deal of lateral coordination is required.<br>• To succeed in this job, you must influence and work with executives higher than your immediate boss.<br>• Achieving your goals depends on how well you handle difficult internal politics. |
| **8. PROBLEM SUBORDINATES** | Subordinates lack adequate experience, are incompetent, or are resistant. | • Your direct reports are not talented enough to carry out your vision.<br>• Your subordinates resist your initiatives. |

*Continued on next page*

FIGURE 2—*Continued*

| | Description of Scale | Sample Items |
|---|---|---|
| 9. ESTABLISHING PERSONAL CREDIBILITY | Manager lacks experience or credentials for the position resulting in a need to establish credibility with subordinates. | ● You are unfamiliar with at least one major aspect of what you manage (a function, technology, etc.).<br>● You now supervise people who were your peers. |
| 10. REVITALIZING A UNIT | A unit that is performing poorly or facing adverse business conditions must be turned around. | ● Your unit has a long history of poor performance.<br>● Facilities are in disrepair and/or badly outdated. |
| 11. EXTERNAL PRESSURES | Factors outside the organization (e.g., regulatory agencies, foreign governments, technological changes) result in challenges for the manager. | ● You have to carry out formal negotiations with an outside body.<br>● You can't speak a needed foreign language.<br>● Technological changes in your business are rapid and almost unpredictable. |
| 12. INHERITED PROBLEMS | In taking the job, the manager has to undo problems the former incumbent had created or take over problem subordinates. | ● Taking this job required you to dismantle the strategy your predecessor had established.<br>● You inherited widespread personnel problems. |

[a]*These four scales are based on the refactoring of factor 1 of the main factor analysis.*

Internal consistencies, reported in Table 1, for the scales are quite high, with alphas ranging from .69 to .83. Scale intercorrelations are fairly low, ranging from .02 to .53, with the highest intercorrelations being, as expected, among the four subscales representing Factor 1.

**Relationship of Challenges to Development and Learning** In order for the JCP to be an effective way of judging the developmental potential of a job, the scales need to be related to general estimates of the overall developmental potential of a given job. To examine this, the relationships of each specific job demand scale to three global ratings of development were assessed. The global ratings consisted of three questions which asked respondents to rate how developmental and demanding their current jobs were, as well as where they felt they stood in terms of mastering all the skills and abilities necessary to handle their current assignments. The correlations of the scales and these ratings are in Table 2. Nine of the 12 scales were related to at least one of the global measures of development. Establishing personal credibility is perceived as being the most developmental and demanding experience. Having a supportive boss, having to deal with intense pressure, and having downsizing responsibilities were also perceived as highly developmental. Conflict with boss is perceived as negatively related to development. At first glance, the relationship of conflict with boss to development is counterintuitive since the qualitative research (Lindsey et al., 1987) found difficult

## TABLE 1
## Intercorrelation and Internal Consistency
## of Job Challenge Scales

| | Alpha | 2 | 3 | 4 | 5 | 6 | 7 | 8 | 9 | 10 | 11 | 12 |
|---|---|---|---|---|---|---|---|---|---|---|---|---|
| 1. Lack Support | .72 | −.35 | .53 | .50 | .34 | .15 | .48 | .35 | .16 | .41 | .29 | .24 |
| 2. Supportive Boss | .76 | — | −.29 | −.54 | .10 | .05 | −.17 | −.09 | .17 | −.06 | .03 | .02 |
| 3. Lack Direction | .70 | | — | .42 | .19 | .02 | .37 | .23 | .14 | .43 | .07 | .14 |
| 4. Conflict with Boss | .70 | | | — | .28 | .18 | .34 | .33 | .11 | .29 | .09 | .27 |
| 5. Pressure | .83 | | | | — | .31 | .46 | .36 | .26 | .44 | .44 | .32 |
| 6. Downsizing | .75 | | | | | — | .05 | .19 | .21 | .35 | .21 | .44 |
| 7. Personal Influence | .79 | | | | | | — | .31 | .17 | .36 | .29 | .15 |
| 8. Problem Subordinates | .77 | | | | | | | — | .32 | .40 | .15 | .38 |
| 9. Personal Credibility | .76 | | | | | | | | — | .28 | .19 | .24 |
| 10. Revitalizing a Unit | .76 | | | | | | | | | — | .23 | .43 |
| 11. External Pressure | .70 | | | | | | | | | | — | .18 |
| 12. Inherited Problems | .69 | | | | | | | | | | | — |

## TABLE 2
## Sources of Developmental Job Demands
## Correlated with Three Global Development Ratings

| | GLOBAL DEVELOPMENTAL RATINGS | | |
|---|---|---|---|
| Source of Development | Developmental[a] | Demanding[a] | Mastering |
| Lack of Top Management Support | .04 | .10 | −.15** |
| Supportive Boss | −.29** | −.30*** | .17** |
| Lack of Strategic Direction | .09 | .09 | .05 |
| Conflict with Boss | .13* | .10 | −.15** |
| Intense Pressure | −.15** | −.32*** | .06 |
| Downsizing/Reorganization | −.17** | −.09 | −.15* |
| Personal Influence | .04 | −.04 | .06 |
| Problem Subordinates | −.11 | −.12* | .05 |
| Personal Credibility | −.40*** | −.33*** | .44*** |
| Revitalizing a Unit | −.08 | −.13 | .11 |
| External Pressures | −.08 | −.09 | −.04 |
| Inherited Problems | −.13* | −.14* | −.10 |

\* $p < .05$
\*\* $p < .01$
\*\*\* $p < .001$

[a] The responses to the questions were scored in reverse manner to the Sources of Development. For the Developmental and Demanding rating questions, high levels of development and demandingness received a low number.

bosses to be a highly developmental situation. One explanation may be that, retrospectively, a difficult boss is seen as developmental, but when one is currently experiencing it, conflict with the boss is seen as anything but developmental (McCall & McCauley, 1986).

Global measures assess how developmental a job is perceived to be by the job incumbent; however, they do not help us understand what specifically it is that managers learn from a given job. For the scales of challenging job demands to be useful they need to be related to specific types of learning as well as to global assessments of developmental potential. The 12 scales measuring sources of development were correlated with each of 34 specific lessons. The statements measuring the lessons were drawn from what executives in the Lindsey et al. (1987) study said they had learned from specific developmental events. All sources of development are significantly ($p < .05$) correlated with at least five, and as many as 31, specific lessons. The highest correlations between the sources of development and specific lessons are reported in Table 3. The correlations suggest some lessons may be learned from more than one source of development. For example, learning how to be comfortable with ambiguous situations is learned from being in a situation where there is an absence of support or guidance, such as a lack of top management support or a lack of strategic direction. The correlational patterns generally make intuitive sense. Being in a certain situation teaches a manager how to handle it; the necessity of needing a skill is associated with reports of learning it. For example, people faced with problem subordinates learn lessons about personal integrity and handling problem subordinates.

## TABLE 3
### Highest Correlations Between Developmental Elements and Specific Lessons[a] ($p < .05$)

| Element | n | r | Lesson |
|---|---|---|---|
| Supportive Boss | 168 | .27 | That being in charge means taking full responsibility for the consequences of your actions, even when the risks are great. |
| | 154 | .22 | That you can't manage everything by yourself: even if you are brilliant and work 18 hours a day, you can't keep your arms around all the important pieces. You have no choice but to depend on others. |
| | 262 | .17 | What you really want to do–what it is about management and business that really excites you. |
| | **(and 7 others)** | | |

*Continued on next page*

**TABLE 3** — *Continued*

| Element | n | r | Lesson |
|---|---|---|---|
| **Lack of Top Management Support** | 255 | .26 | That most important management situations are characterized by ambiguity, uncertainty, and stress; you have to learn to be comfortable with it and act in spite of it. |
| | 213 | .26 | To trust your own instincts when handling tough, complex, or new situations. |
| | 229 | .25 | That working with executives requires developing some special skills in presentation and persuasion. |
| | | | **(and 15 others)** |
| **Lack of Strategic Direction** | 255 | .26 | That most important management situations are characterized by ambiguity, uncertainty, and stress; you have to learn to be comfortable with it and act in spite of it. |
| | 152 | .22 | That only one person is ultimately responsible for your career: you. |
| | 185 | .16 | That politics are very much a part of organizational life and must be taken into account if you are to get things done. |
| | | | **(and 2 others)** |
| **Conflict with Boss** | 185 | .19 | That politics are very much a part of organizational life and must be taken into account if you are to get things done. |
| | 210 | .19 | That it's one thing to concoct a plan or a strategy, but quite another to carry it out. |
| | 185 | .17 | That opportunities can pop up at any time and you have to be prepared to seize them when they come. |
| | | | **(and 3 others)** |
| **Intense Pressure** | 192 | .31 | That neither the subordinate nor the organization benefits if you procrastinate in directly confronting a problem subordinate. |
| | 204 | .30 | That decisions must be made for the sake of the business, even if they involve human cost and hurt you personally. You have to grit your teeth and do what must be done. |
| | 255 | .29 | That most important management situations are characterized by ambiguity, uncertainty, and stress; you have to learn to be comfortable with it and act in spite of it. |
| | | | **(and 23 others)** |

*Continued on next page*

**TABLE 3**—*Continued*

| Element | n | r | Lesson |
|---|---|---|---|
| Downsizing/ Reorganization | 204 | .27 | That decisions must be made for the sake of the business, even if they involve human cost and hurt you personally. You have to grit your teeth and do what must be done. |
| | 247 | .24 | That formal negotiation (for example, with unions, clients, governments, partners) is an art with its own strategy and tactics. |
| | 192 | .21 | That neither the subordinate nor the organization benefits if you procrastinate in directly confronting a problem subordinate. |
| | | | **(and 5 others)** |
| Achieving Goals Through Personal Influence | 255 | .30 | That most important management situations are characterized by ambiguity, uncertainty, and stress; you have to learn to be comfortable with it and act in spite of it. |
| | 227 | .27 | That achieving cooperation among people over whom you have no formal authority requires subtle skills and a great deal of patience. |
| | 147 | .27 | That executives are human, too, with all the foibles and preferences and personality quirks that other people have. |
| | | | **(and 11 others)** |
| Problem Subordinates | 192 | .32 | That neither the subordinate nor the organization benefits if you procrastinate in directly confronting a problem subordinate. |
| | 134 | .28 | That a manager loses everything if he compromises his integrity, loses the trust of his people, or takes actions that damage his credibility. |
| | 229 | .22 | That you have personal limits and blind spots. |
| | | | **(and 5 others)** |
| Establishing Personal Credibility | 213 | .48 | That managing people with more experience or who were your peers or a former boss is a difficult proposition. |
| | 255 | .36 | That most important management situations are characterized by ambiguity, uncertainty, and stress; you have to learn to be comfortable with it and act in spite of it. |
| | 229 | .33 | That you have personal limits and blind spots. |
| | | | **(and 25 others)** |
| Revitalizing a Unit | 255 | .25 | That most important management situations are characterized by ambiguity, uncertainty, and stress; you have to learn to be comfortable with it and act in spite of it. |

*Continued on next page*

**TABLE 3**—*Continued*

| Element | n | r | Lesson |
|---|---|---|---|
| Revitalizing a Unit (continued) | 204 | .24 | That decisions must be made for the sake of the business, even if they involve human cost and hurt you personally. You have to grit your teeth and do what must be done. |
| | 263 | .19 | What you really want to do–what it is about management and business that really excites you. |
| | | | **(and 9 others)** |
| External Pressures | 247 | .43 | That formal negotiation (for example, with unions, clients, governments, partners) is an art with its own strategy and tactics. |
| | 187 | .27 | That it's important to keep a reasonable balance between your work life and your personal life. |
| | 185 | .21 | That opportunities can pop up at any time and you have to be prepared to seize them when they come. |
| | | | **(and 8 others)** |
| Inherited Problems | 192 | .33 | That neither the subordinate nor the organization benefits if you procrastinate in directly confronting a problem subordinate. |
| | 213 | .25 | That managing people with more experience or who were your peers or a former boss is a difficult proposition. |
| | 134 | .22 | That a manager loses everything if he compromises his integrity, loses the trust of his people, or takes actions that damage his credibility. |
| | | | **(and 16 others)** |

[a] *Responses to questions about learning a particular lesson range from 1, not learning it, to 5, learning hand over fist. N's vary because those who said they had already learned a lesson were deleted.*

A further way of examining the utility of these dimensions is to examine whether or not the dimensions can distinguish between jobs with very different circumstances. For example, a useful assessment of developmental potential should be able to distinguish between jobs as plainly different as line and staff jobs. Differences on the JCP scales for line and staff jobs were investigated with a subsample who had jobs that were clearly one or the other (48% had line jobs, 40% had staff). Seven of the 12 scales had significant ($p < .05$) differences for the line/staff t-test comparisons (see Table 4). Line jobs were characterized by higher levels of Lack-of-Top-Management Support, Conflict With Boss, Intense Pressure, Downsizing/Reorganization, Problem Subordinates, Revitalizing a Unit, and Inherited Problems than were staff jobs, reflecting the demands of being in charge and being responsible for measurable results characteristic of line positions.

## TABLE 4
### Mean Differences Between Staff and Line Jobs

| | Staff | | Line | | |
|---|---|---|---|---|---|
| JCP Scales | M | SD | M | SD | t value |
| Lack of Top Management Support | 0.89 | .70 | 1.06 | .74 | −2.13* |
| Supportive Boss | 2.87 | .83 | 2.76 | .87 | .95 |
| Lack of Strategic Direction | 1.18 | .94 | 1.23 | .97 | −0.35 |
| Conflict with Boss | 1.26 | .87 | 1.53 | .85 | −2.28* |
| Intense Pressure | 1.96 | .63 | 2.41 | .70 | −4.96** |
| Downsizing/Reorganization | 0.68 | .60 | 0.96 | .82 | −2.83** |
| Achieving Goals Through Personal Influence | 2.09 | .72 | 2.02 | .72 | .76 |
| Problem Subordinates | 0.83 | .60 | 1.13 | .69 | −3.43** |
| Establishing Personal Credibility | 0.98 | .58 | 1.12 | .68 | −1.73 |
| Revitalizing a Unit | 0.93 | .63 | 1.27 | .77 | −3.66** |
| External Pressures | 0.80 | .59 | 0.84 | .71 | −0.41 |
| Inherited Problems | 1.05 | .83 | 1.45 | .90 | −3.39** |

*$p < .05$, two-tailed
**$p < .01$
N Staff Jobs = 98
N Line Jobs = 127
Note: Higher scores indicate greater levels of the developmental job elements.

In addition to distinguishing between jobs with different demands, useful measures of developmental potential should distinguish between different types of transitions. According to qualitative research on development, part of what makes a job developmental is the personal transition for the incumbent (McCall, 1988). For example, jobs which are lateral moves for the incumbent should be perceived as different from jobs which are the result of a promotion of two or more levels. To test this out a sample of jobs which were a lateral move for the incumbent (N = 88) was compared to a sample of jobs which were the result of promotions of two or more levels (N = 65). Table 5 indicates that four of the scales had statistically significant (p < .05) differences. Lateral moves are characterized by a greater perceived Lack of Strategic Direction than are promotions of two or more levels. Promotions of two or more levels are experienced as having greater levels of Supportive Boss, Downsizing/Reorganization, and Establishing Personal Credibility.

## TABLE 5
## Mean Differences Between Lateral Moves
## and Promotions of Two or More Levels

| | GROUP | | | | |
| | Lateral Moves | | Promotions of Two or More Levels | | |
| JCP Scales | M | SD | M | SD | t value |
|---|---|---|---|---|---|
| Lack of Top Management Support | 0.97 | .76 | 0.93 | .73 | .31 |
| Supportive Boss | 2.56 | .87 | 2.86 | .98 | −2.03* |
| Lack of Strategic Direction | 1.32 | .97 | 1.00 | .95 | 2.07* |
| Conflict with Boss | 1.51 | .95 | 1.45 | .88 | .39 |
| Intense Pressure | 2.09 | .70 | 2.27 | .67 | −1.59 |
| Downsizing/Reorganization | 0.72 | .75 | 1.09 | .93 | −2.73* |
| Achieving Goals Through Personal Influence | 2.04 | .68 | 1.96 | .62 | .77 |
| Problem Subordinates | 0.84 | .70 | 0.99 | .66 | −1.36 |
| Establishing Personal Credibility | 0.86 | .55 | 1.28 | .63 | −4.33** |
| Revitalizing a Unit | 0.98 | .70 | 1.17 | .76 | −1.63 |
| External Pressures | 0.82 | .65 | 0.81 | .55 | .07 |
| Inherited Problems | 1.12 | .99 | 1.25 | .95 | − .78 |

$* p < .05$, two-tailed
$** p < .01$
[N] Lateral Moves = 88
[N] Promotions of Two or More Levels = 65
Note: Higher scores indicate greater levels of the developmental job elements.

## Discussion

The evidence suggests that the Job Challenge Profile is a useful method for assessing the developmental potential of managerial jobs. It has 12 scales measuring different sources of on-the-job development. These sources of development are distinctly different from the types of job characteristics typically assessed by managerial job analyses. In most cases the sources are demands or challenges that the manager has to face. They have to do with the context (e.g., top management doesn't provide adequate support), other people (e.g., incompetent or resistant subordinates), the assignment goal (e.g., revitalizing a unit in trouble), and the type of transition the job is for the incumbent (e.g., do they have to gain considerable personal credibility in order to do their job). There is considerable similarity between these empirically derived dimensions and the qualitatively derived job elements they are based on.

The research described here shows that the scales assessing sources of development are related to both general ratings of development and to specific lessons learned in managerial settings. These relationships suggest that the JCP shows promise as a method for assessing the developmental potential of job assignments. Further support for continuing to examine the questionnaire is that it was able to detect differences between very different jobs.

Before the questionnaire can be used for human resource deployment purposes there are several research questions which need to be answered. We plan to investigate the relationship of job incumbent assessments of the sources of development to external estimates of how developmental a particular job is. In addition, research needs to be conducted to investigate whether or not people who are placed in jobs which would be considered highly developmental according to the JCP actually do develop and grow over time. An additional avenue for research is to use the JCP in research about learning styles. Kelleher et al. (1986) found that not all managers are predisposed to learning from experience. The JCP could be used to see if and how different people faced with similar situations learn. Perhaps knowledge of different learning styles would lead to a better understanding of how on-the-job learning can be encouraged.

The initial research reported here shows the JCP to be a promising tool for analyzing the developmental potential of a given job. If additional research is confirmatory there are many ways the JCP can be used to help organizations assure the continuity of strong leadership through development processes. The primary expected use of the questionnaire is as an organizational audit tool. Essentially, the questionnaire can help organizations identify the sources of development in different parts of the company. The identification of developmental jobs and the tying of the sources of development to specific learning goals will be helpful information to those executives and managers interested in leveraging the differences in assignments for developmental purposes.

A second way the questionnaire can be used is to help managers understand the learning potential of their own job. Managers at different levels will be able to fill out the questionnaire and get information on the different sources of development inherent in their jobs. This could be helpful in aiding managers to understand what is developmental about their own situations and open their eyes to the learning potential in their assignments. In addition, this feedback can be used to help decision makers learn to think about using assignments in a systematic way for development. The feedback provides a language and a common basis for talking about the developmental nuances of different jobs. The information can be used to make the point that the job is a classroom and thereby encourage decision makers to consider ways they can make their subordinates' jobs more developmental.

Helping leaders develop is a critical issue. Although most important lessons about leadership occur on the job (McCall et al., 1988), we have little knowledge about how to identify and use sources of on-the-job development. The JCP shows promise as a means of identifying sources of development which could lead to more strategic uses of the developmental aspects of managerial jobs.

# References

Beatty, R. W., Schneier, C. E., & McEvoy, G.M. (1987). Executive development and management succession. In K. M. Rowland & G. R. Ferris (Eds.), *Research in personnel and human resources management* (Vol. 5, pp. 289–322). Greenwich, CT: JAI Press.

Bemis, S. E. (1983). *Job analysis: An effective management tool.* Washington, DC: Bureau of National Affairs.

Brousseau, K. R. (1984). Job-person dynamics and career development. In K. M. Rowland & G. R. Ferris (Eds.), *Research in personnel and human resources management* (Vol. 2, pp. 125–154). Greenwich, CT: JAI Press.

Burke, M. J., & Day, R. R. (1986). A cumulative study of the effectiveness of managerial training. *Journal of Applied Psychology, 71*(2), 232–245.

Davies, J., & Easterby-Smith, M. (1984). Learning and developing from managerial work experiences. *Journal of Management Studies, 21*(2), 169–183.

Hall, D. T. (1986). Dilemmas in linking succession planning to individual executive learning. *Human Resource Management, 25*(2), 235–265.

Hemphill, J. K. (1960). *Dimensions of executive positions* (Research Monograph No. 89). Columbus: Ohio State University, Bureau of Business Research.

Kelleher, D., Finestone, P., & Lowy, A. (1986). Managerial learning: First notes from an unstudied frontier. *Group and Organization Studies, 11*(3), 169–202.

Lindsey, E., Homes, V., & McCall, M. W., Jr. (1987). *Key events in executive lives* (Tech. Rep. No. 32). Greensboro, NC: Center for Creative Leadership.

McCall, M. W., Jr. (1988). *Developing executives through work experience* (Tech. Rep. No. 33). Greensboro, NC: Center for Creative Leadership.

McCall, M. W., Jr., Lombardo, M. M., & Morrison, A. M. (1988). *The lessons of experience.* Lexington, MA: Lexington Books.

McCall, M. W., Jr., & McCauley, C. D. (1986, August). *Analyzing the developmental potential of jobs.* Paper presented at the annual meeting of the American Psychological Association, Washington, DC.

McCauley, C. D. (1986). *Developmental experiences in managerial work: A literature review* (Tech. Rep. No. 26). Greensboro, NC: Center for Creative Leadership.

Morrison, A. M., White, R. P., & Van Velsor, E. (1987). *Breaking the glass ceiling.* Reading, MA: Addison-Wesley.

Simon, H. A. (1977). *The new science of management decisions.* Englewood Cliffs, NJ: Prentice-Hall.

Tornow, W. W., & Pinto, P. R. (1976). The development of a managerial job taxonomy: A system for describing, classifying, and evaluating executive positions. *Journal of Applied Psychology, 61*(4), 410–418.

# Leadership and Youth: A Commitment

*Frances A. Karnes*

Leadership development is formulated, accepted, and implemented almost exclusively in the institutions, agencies, and establishments of the adult world. Universal recognition of the urgent and growing need for dynamic, creative, and effective leaders has prompted the military, business and industry, the church, and the government, as well as colleges and universities, to commit increasing proportions of time and resources to the education and training of personnel. This ongoing process of preparation helps to ensure that leadership development will keep pace with the demands placed upon leaders.

While the research and educational efforts have enhanced the leadership development of adults, little has been undertaken to ensure that leaders of the future are given the opportunity at an early age to begin to realize and develop their leadership potential. Extracurricular activities in elementary and junior and senior high schools provide some opportunities from which a few of the more energetic, outgoing, and aggressive students emerge as leaders. Stogdill (1974) observed that leadership in elementary, junior and senior high schools, and college was predictive of adult leadership in business and social activities. He found that leadership in extracurricular activities was more highly correlated with adult leadership than was academic achievement.

A national survey was conducted to determine the current status of instructional opportunities and a review of the research was completed. Both indicated that there was little attention being directed to youth and leadership. Of the few existing programs, most were provided in a community setting with group membership required. There was a void of research on any aspect of youth and leadership. A systematic program for the development of leadership skills for youth was initiated in 1980 at the Center for Gifted Studies at the University of Southern Mississippi. Through the Leadership Studies Program, a summer residential activity, instruction is provided for youth. The *Leadership Network Newsletter* serves as a vehicle for disseminating information at the national and international levels. Several research projects have been conducted, and more are in the planning stages.

## The Leadership Studies Program

After a thorough review of the research on adults and the materials for training them, the Leadership Skills Development Program was designed and field-tested (Karnes & Chauvin, 1985). This program includes the *Leadership Skill Inventory* (LSI), a self-rating, self-scoring assessment instrument to determine strengths and weaknesses in the concepts and skills necessary for leadership. The components of the inventory are: fundamentals of leadership, written communications, oral communications, values clarification, decision making, group dynamics, problem solving, personal development, and planning. Studies additional to those reported in the manual have been conducted on the concurrent validity (Karnes & D'Ilio, 1988a) and on the criterion-related validity of the LSI (Karnes & D'Ilio, 1988b).

In an accompanying manual of activities, instructional strategies are keyed to all items on the inventory (Karnes & Chauvin, 1985). The program is diagnostic/prescriptive and has been successfully implemented as the base of the Leadership Studies Program for the last five summers. The effectiveness of the program has been documented (Karnes, Meriweather, & D'Ilio, 1987). Significant gains (< .01) have been made in all nine areas of the LSI.

As the culminating activity in the instructional component, each student identifies a need for leadership in their school, community, or religious affiliation and writes a "plan for leadership." These have been completed successfully and provide experiences for the students necessary for leadership development. Currently, public, private, and parochial schools are using the model, as well as colleges and universities offering programs for youth.

## Initial Research

The *High School Personality Questionnaire* (Cattell & Cattell, 1975), a self-rating measure, yields scores on 14 bipolar personality factors in addition to a Leadership Potential Score. This is based on the summing of weighted factors which were determined in Cattell's study of leadership in adults (1972) using the *Sixteen Personality Factor Questionnaire* (16 PF).

A study by Chauvin and Karnes (1983) was undertaken to determine the leadership profile of 181 secondary gifted students with intelligence quotients of 130 and above. Characteristics of leadership were based on earlier findings for adult leaders who responded to the 16 PF (Stice & Cattell, 1960). The intellectually gifted students scored higher on Factor B—intelligence, Factor F—enthusiasm, and Q2—self-sufficiency, while scoring lower on Factor G—conscientiousness and Q3—self-control.

In other investigations, groups of high school students have been studied. One group consisted of 199 students, in grades nine through twelve, attending a self-contained high school for intellectually gifted in the Midwest (Karnes, Chauvin, & Trant, 1984a), while the other unique group of subjects consisted of 176 students attending a fine and performing arts high school in the South (Karnes, Chauvin, & Trant, 1985b). The Leadership Potential Score on the *High School Personality Questionnaire* (HSPQ) failed to differentiate, in both groups of students, those who held elected leadership positions and those who did not (Karnes, Chauvin, & Trant, 1985b).

The HSPQ was administered to determine the personality characteristics of 52 male and 53 female students with high potential and/or demonstrated leadership ability who were nominated by school personnel for the Leadership Studies Program, a summer residential program for those in grades six through eleven. Girls scored significantly higher ($p > .05$) than boys on the primary factor of Factor C—emotional stability, Factor E—dominance, and the secondary factor of Independence (Karnes & D'Ilio, 1989a).

Forty-nine boys and 48 girls in grades four through six, who were intellectually gifted students as determined by state eligibility criteria, were presented a list of 34 leadership positions and were asked to mark whether men, women, or either sex could hold each position. Analysis of the findings indicated that boys tend to have more traditional sex role stereotypes than do girls (Karnes & D'Ilio, 1989b).

Seventy-six students in grades six through eleven who were nominated by their schools and attending the Leadership Studies Program and their parents were administered the Family Environment Scale (FES; Moos & Moos, 1981). The study was designed to investigate the perceptions of both groups as to the family environment of student leaders. The mothers' scores were significantly higher ($p > .05$) than the students' on Expressiveness, Independence, Intellectual-Cultural Orientation, and Moral-Religious Emphasis, subscales of the FES. The fathers' scores were significantly higher ($p > .05$) than the students' on the Expressiveness and Intellectual-Cultural Orientation subscales. The mothers' and the fathers' scores did not differ significantly on any of the ten subscales (Karnes & D'Ilio, 1988c).

## Leadership Network Newsletter

The *Leadership Network Newsletter* (LNN) is published twice a year by the Center for Gifted Studies at the University of Southern Mississippi to disseminate information on leadership programs for elementary and secondary youth in public, private, and parochial schools. Programs conducted for youth on college and university campuses are also reviewed. Instructional materials, including books and films, are included. The newsletter is disseminated nationally and internationally on a complimentary basis.

## References

Cattell, R. B. (1972). *Manual for the 16 PF*. Champaign, IL: Institute for Personality and Ability Testing.

Cattell, R. B., & Cattell, M. D. (1975). *Handbook for the junior-senior high school personality questionnaire*. Champaign, IL: Institute for Personality and Ability Testing.

Chauvin, J. C., & Karnes, F. A. (1983). A leadership profile of secondary school students. *Psychological Reports, 53*, 1259–1262.

Karnes, F. A., & Chauvin, J. C. (1985). *Leadership skills development program*. East Aurora, NY: United D.O.K.

Karnes, F. A., Chauvin, J. C., & Trant, T. J. (1985a). Comparison of personality profiles for intellectually gifted students and students outstanding in the fine and performing arts attending self-contained secondary schools. *Psychology in the Schools, 22*(2), 122–126.

Karnes, F. A., Chauvin, J. C., & Trant, T. J. (1985b). Validity of the Leadership Potential Score of the High School Personality Questionnaire with talented students. *Perceptual Motor Skills, 61*, 163–166.

Karnes, F. A., & D'Ilio, V. R. (1988a). Assessment of the concurrent validity of the Leadership Skills Inventory with gifted students and their teachers. *Perceptual and Motor Skills, 66*, 59–62.

Karnes, F. A., & D'Ilio, V. R. (1988b). Assessment of the criterion-related validity of the Leadership Skills Inventory. *Psychological Reports, 62*, 263–267.

Karnes, F. A., & D'Ilio, V. R. (1988c). Comparison of gifted children and their parents' perceptions of the home environment. *Gifted Child Quarterly, 32*(2), 277–279.

Karnes, F. A., & D'Ilio, V. R. (1989a). Leadership positions and sex role stereotyping among gifted children. *Gifted Child Quarterly, 33*(2), 76–78.

Karnes, F. A., & D'Ilio, V. R. (1989b). Personality characteristics of student leaders. *Psychological Reports, 64*, 1125–1126.

Karnes, F. A., Meriweather, S., & D'Ilio, V. R. (1987). The effectiveness of the leadership studies program. *Roeper Review, 9*(4), 238–241.

Moos, R. H., & Moos, B. S. (1981). *Family Environment Scale Manual*. Palo Alto, CA: Consulting Psychologists Press, Inc.

Stice, G. F., & Cattell, R. B. (1960). *The dimensions of groups and their relations to the behavior of members*. Champaign, IL: Institute for Personality and Ability Testing.

Stogdill, R. M. (1974). *Handbook of leadership*. New York: Free Press.

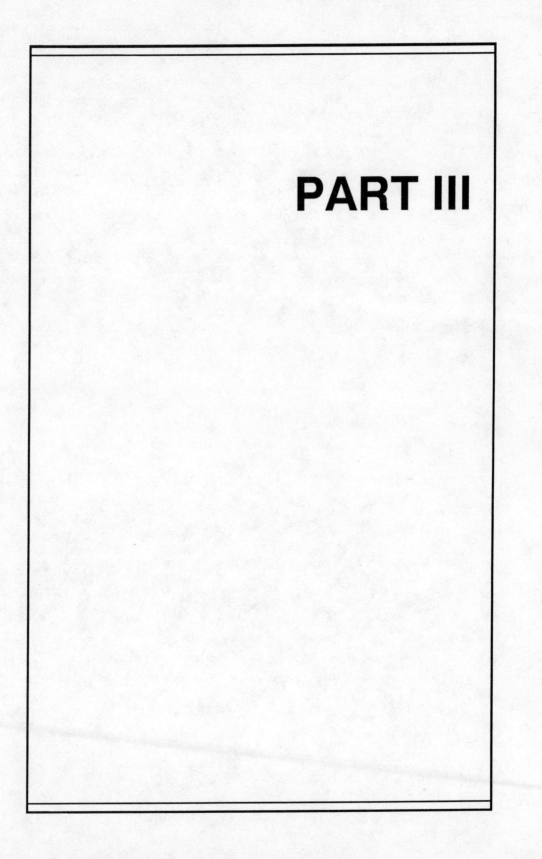

# PART III

# Proceedings of the San Antonio Conference on Psychological Measures and Leadership

*Miriam B.
Clark*

## Introduction

This is an account of what was experienced by 84 participants meeting at a conference, capturing some of what they said and some of what they wrote in their "diaries." Part II of this book documents what 51 of them presented in written, edited, and rewritten scholarly papers. Part I of the volume gives the reader a more general and coherent view of the field of leadership. But in Part III you will find formal and informal dialogues, credited and sometimes even uncredited quotations, questions, expostulations, criticism, challenges, and some monologues that are occasionally overlong and frequently convoluted. Discussions and animated conversations are frequently like that.

In an attempt to summarize discussions and include reactions interjected by speakers about previous interchanges, the text at times reads like a movie filmed with a hand-held camera. We apologize for disjointed form, but content—not form—was our goal. Formally transcribed tapes would have missed the mark in presenting creative thoughts and musings recorded in diaries long after original discussions took place.

The first draft of these proceedings was sent to participants to rework, and some later explication is included. Also, some text was taken from transcribed notes of live recorders, from conversations overheard at meals and in corridors, and from pertinent materials taped at sessions. When a small group decided to break off from a larger to speak more in depth about a subject, someone was sent hurriedly to the new location, if it could be found, to pick up retrospectively what had ensued. The participants used flip charts located in a main foyer to record their topic preferences and as sign-up sheets for those meetings which interested them. The problems of session scheduling and attendance choices were many and often impromptu, but the intent was to accommodate as many individual interests as possible.

Thus, the reader will find this account of the conference is a mix of minutes, descriptions of events, and the script of a play with countless acts. It must be said at the outset that each person at this conference was not only interested but also committed to learning as much as possible in two-and-a-half days about psychological measurement and leadership and each other's work. Feelings ran high and intellectual stimulation was palpable. Teachers became students and students became teachers. It is hoped that what is written here will stimulate the reader to capture the enthusiasm of the participants, to create the desire to return to Parts I and II for careful study, thereby clarifying and learning what is happening in this field.

## About the Conference

In San Antonio, Texas, on October 23, 1988, eighty-four persons met for two-and-a-half days to discuss Psychological Measures and Leadership. The decision to call this invitational conference was not made impulsively. Kenneth E. Clark had spent many months searching the literature and conversing with colleagues to discern the current status of measurement in leadership.

Many books were hitting the newsstands; hundreds of articles were being published in magazines and newspapers; new training programs and lecture series were being advertised and offered everywhere, most of them claiming to have found a new way—a perfectly paved road to successful leadership and management. But one prickly question remained to be answered: **Where were the data to substantiate these claims for providing wise advice and counsel?** This is not to say that a solid body of literature and research findings did not exist, but it certainly appeared that altogether too much of what was being offered up for public consumption was based on small samples of unrepresentative persons, conjecture, and singular experience. At the least, too few were backed up explicitly by hard data.

As a result, sponsorship by the Center for Creative Leadership in Greensboro, North Carolina, and The Psychological Corporation in San Antonio, Texas, was sought and secured, and the gestation period began in September 1987. A small committee was formed at the Center for Creative Leadership. A call for papers went out to all members of Division 5 (Evaluation, Measurement, and Assessment) and Division 14 (Industrial/Organizational Psychology) of the American Psychological Association. The announcement stated that the "conference [would be] comprised of those individuals best able to add to knowledge about the qualities of leaders and the ways in which these qualities develop. We are looking for persons who have data they are able to relate to significant effectiveness criteria, collected over a long period of time, with replicable means of data collection. Admissions will be limited in order to assure free interchange about data sources, the quality of data, and about most-needed improvements in our measures of leadership."

Kenneth E. Clark agreed to chair the conference, prepare the guidelines, manage communications, edit the papers, and write a report after the conference. It was also decided that no papers would be presented orally at prearranged sessions. Instead, papers were to be distributed prior to the conference, so that discussion could take off at once. It was also advertised to the invitees that the sessions would be informal and leaderless so that topics could focus on the expressed interests of participants.

Another letter was sent to a group of Fortune 500 companies familiar with the work of the Center for Creative Leadership inviting their corporate financial backing and the presence of two of their most concerned representatives. This letter stated, "We also invite organizations that are users or potential users of such measures to attend, and ask they be prepared to discuss their own need for better devices."

It was thought at first that the group would number 40 to 50 persons. Before long it became clear that the interest among scholars and corporate executives was greater than originally estimated. The decision was made to increase the number of attendees. Twenty-nine of those who submitted papers (solely or jointly) were advised that their work had been reviewed and approved, and that the papers would be copied and distributed to all participants prior to the meeting.

Nine corporations agreed to send representatives. These persons were identified as those in organizations who grappled daily with problems having to do with selecting, promoting, and utilizing managerial and leadership talent to maintain successful operation of the organization.

In addition, several persons were invited whose scholarly background in the field was recognized and respected. These persons were charged with the responsibility to act as observers, questioners, and critics. Also, based on their research interests or their conference responsibilities, staff persons from the Center for Creative Leadership and The Psychological Corporation were invited to attend.

The program of the conference was skeletal, but one item was spelled out. That was called Diary Time. A half hour, morning and afternoon, was set aside for writing up highlights, comments, reactions, and so forth, and a form for this purpose was distributed to the participants. These diaries have been excellent sources for writing these proceedings. The request for diaries was taken seriously; many sent addenda to the submitted forms after they had returned home and had reflected more about the conference. More than the allotted time was devoted to writing comments. The diaries ranged from critical statements about discussions to suggestions for needed studies, to new definitions, to recognition for personal change in direction of one's own research, and to next steps for the group, and so forth. They are tangible confirmation of the intellectual excitement and stimulation that pervaded this conference. Many of the direct quotes from participants came from this source.

On Sunday, October 23, the participants met for dinner and were placed alphabetically at tables, dispelling at once any ideas that cronyism was acceptable. They were called upon to introduce themselves, and this exercise was speedily accomplished and enjoyed by most. During the earlier registration period, brief abstracts of the papers, prepared by Clark, had been distributed (producing several audible sighs of relief by the few who had "not quite completed reading of the papers"); the assumption was that most persons were fully familiar with the content of the circulated papers. In any case, there were few who were unfamiliar with the scholarly accomplishments of those who had prepared these papers.

Even though everyone had been advised that there would be no formal structure to the conference (except for time slots and meal designations), and some persons had agreed to attend only if they didn't have to listen to long presentations of papers, this challenge "to get on with it" produced some befuddlement. This group experienced the sort of ambiguity that clouds the air of most organizations in transition when they are expected to act nontraditionally. These people were not novices in the field of leadership; they were persons with highly developed social skills, with intellectual and scholarly qualifications of extraordinary proportions, yet they felt the pressure and frustrations that occur at the outset when, without a "given" structure, persons meet to review their accomplishments, take stock of current assets, and plan for the future. It was a good beginning . . .

## The Proceedings

Monday a.m.:           **Opening Session**
Convenor:                 K. Clark

Thomas A. Williamson of The Psychological Corporation greeted the group as the president of one sponsoring organization; he was followed by Walter F. Ulmer of the Center for Creative Leadership as president of the other sponsoring organization. The former called for more emphasis on the education and development of leadership skills for children, young adults, and more mature managers. Ulmer challenged the group to develop a research agenda and to establish a research network, offering the Center for Creative Leadership as a facilitating center.

General discussion raised the following topics for further pursuit:
1. Cognitive complexity.
2. Transformational and transactional leadership.
3. Types—Psychological variables.
4. Gough's work on Realization of Life's Goals.
5. Training and development effects.
6. Personality issues—not tied to instruments. What it takes to be a great leader.
7. Emotional stability and strength.
8. What is known about the prediction and development of outstanding leaders.
9. Criteria of leadership.
10. Longitudinal studies.
11. Feedback from instruments—who gives it? quality of delivery? how development programs differ? outgrowth of transformational and transactional impacts?
12. Criterion variables—those things that make a difference.
13. Measurement instruments—differences—self-monitoring.
14. Power and empowerment—power-down.
15. Managing versus leading—definitions.
16. Various levels of organizations—shift from impact of person or group— carrying out of functions—how should the organization run?

17. Education and levels of intelligence.
18. Better comparative data would be helpful—use of existing data banks.

Monday, 10:30 a.m.:   **Cognitive Complexity**
Convenor:                Jacobs

This session was scheduled for Monday morning because Owen Jacobs was unable to remain at the conference longer than one day. Many believed that the concepts described required more time for adequate digestion than one session and consideration for one day. Jacobs asked for questions and issues that had arisen from his submitted paper. He described the Jaques model and then dealt with the group's questions. Hendrick, whose work is in the same field, also played a key role in responding to the questions.

Jacobs said that cognitive complexity can be developed. Each person has a fixed set of abilities in this regard, but the abilities can be developed so that an individual's full potential is achieved. Jacobs sees development enhanced through organizational experiences which require integration of multidimensional issues; usually these occur at the upper levels of the hierarchy.

Hendrick said the development of cognitive complexity has to do with experience in differentiating and integrating information. He described his work on cognitive complexity measures using the paragraph completion test, the abstract orientation test, and personality variables. He uses the Harvey, Hunt, and Schroder model which says that cognitive complexity is developable and that it has to do with child-rearing patterns. Studies show correlations of .5 and .6 between parental styles and the growth of cognitive complexity. Four patterns of child-rearing were described: (1) Punishing dominant parent, (2) Inconsistent punishing parents, (3) The participative parent who wants to feel liked, and (4) Both parents who treat child like young adult. It is the people reared by number 4 parents who have the highest levels of complexity.

Parental application of rules is a key factor in the development of cognitive complexity. (Hendrick and Jacobs did not agree or disagree on the parenting issue. Jacobs did agree that responses to rules were important.)

Yukl said that environment should play a bigger role than hierarchy in the model. Cognitive complexity is associated with what you do, not with the level. In a decentralized environment, jobs low in the hierarchy can be complex. To this, Jacobs responded that an organization does have to start at a level 4 or 5 (see the study in Part II). Ruderman, who is to be credited with most of the notes from this session, asked, "Does Jaques' theory confuse hierarchy and work level?"

Bentz said level distinction is very helpful. The jump from a level 6 to a level 7 is huge. Level 7 issues cannot be reduced because high levels of complexity and ambiguity must be dealt with. Williamson asked how to train cognitive complexity, to which Bentz replied that we don't know enough to train it. Moses added that being in situations with a rapid rate of change helps to develop it. Downsizing and restructuring create approaches for developing it. Sayles said that organizations often discourage their members from dealing with problems in a manner that reflects their "true" complexity. Single, "binary" analyses and answers are rewarded. People lower in the hierarchy are not rewarded for being able to work with complexity. Also, academia teaches linear thinking and sequentialism, not the handling of ambiguity. He went on to ask whether the model is too elitist, whether you need people in the bowels of the organization who can implement and fine-tune change. To this Jacobs responded, "The theory isn't elitist; it's observational."

Bray asked why it is so tied to managerial levels. Scientists also have complex jobs. Sashkin answered that there is more to it than level. Cognitive complexity is tied to function, not level. You cannot disconnect the organization from the issue. It is a necessary but not sufficient criterion for effectiveness. Jacobs said, "Yes, you need more than just the raw horsepower; you also need experience in developing cause-and-effect maps and the proclivity to do it." McCaulley added that intuition is associated with longer time perspectives. Lombardo noted in his diary that Jaques and Jacobs appear to disagree on the contribution of experience and how the capacity is predetermined. It may be that the notion might be construed as a set of demands that exist more or less independently of level at times.

Although asked how cognitive complexity could be measured, the question remained essentially unanswered. The problem of rapid change in organizations was not addressed. Lombardo asked a question in his notes, "How can we enhance/bring to fruition the capacity to grow through different levels of complexity? How can we affect proclivity to build dynamic models of learning from experience?"

Other issues surfaced, for example: the relationship to experiences that demand varying levels of complexity; what the models look like in the proclivity to build models from experience. If Jacobs says the career history carries most of the weight, how can one know that he is not making his prediction based solely on past performance and not on cognitive complexity? Is it possible to distinguish the measurement from the people who did it in this construct? Does the gap between levels 6 and 7 indicate disagreement with Jaques' level assumptions? At the session, Bray asked whether cognitive complexity is related to IQ. Hendrick said, "Not if you control for education." Whether there were differences in cognitive complexity in more "lateral" versus the more hierarchical military type of institution? Also, it was asked whether the ability to "see" complexity inhibits action and decision, or where does cognitive complexity become dysfunctional? In a nice professional, well-educated workplace, is complexity pushed further down into the organization?

Jacobs said that cognitive complexity means, in part, building cause-and-effect "maps"; broad versus narrow perspective. He also noted in response to an earlier question that Stamp used a clinical interviewing method based on three parts: (1) Brunner's card sort task, (2) phrase cards which reflect how you regard rules, and (3) a work history. For Jacobs, this is what carries the variance; he works looking at past levels of responsivity.

It was suggested that research needs to be done replicating Jaques' work, and the question about which experiences develop cognitive complexity needs further study. Also, the cognitive styles associated with transformational leadership should be explored, and the similarities of cognitive complexity, ambiguity, and uncertainty should be taken into account. This work should be compared with the work of Sparks and what is being done at the Center for Creative Leadership. Part of cognitive complexity should be: (1) empathy (understanding how other persons think), and (2) ability to see "ripple effect" in decisions (what Sayles would call second-order effect).

Rosenbach praised Jacobs for "guiding the discussion through where we've been and where we are now with cognitive complexity. The discussion was rich because a variety of methodologies, research questions, findings, and settings were discussed. I felt I had had a good understanding of the issues and was better prepared to look to the future."

Monday, 10:15 a.m.:  **Personality Issues**

This was a diverse session with many persons eager to indicate the validity of their different positions. One participant noted in a diary "missing was an overarching conceptual analysis or scheme into which we could fit the issues that were raised. . . . Perhaps one outcome of the discussion was that individual participants began to put together such an analysis for themselves."

The following questions were raised at the outset: Does leadership have to do with role-playing or role-taking? How does personality develop? Are personal (personality) characteristics teachable? What occurs in learning? Is leadership a way of being or an assumption of a set of behaviors? Can one develop a reasonable set of characteristics? How do leaders develop?

Gough listed some core attributes of leaders in all settings; for example, self-confidence and a tendency to respond to interpersonal demands. He said that to evolve a set of criteria for describing leaders, use whatever means are at hand to get nominations or ratings—for instance, ask peers, co-workers, supervisors, subordinates, or spouses for information. When commonality occurs, go on to the next step; find out what on the personality or individual side relates to these consensual appraisals from others. Be sure to carry out such inquiry in many settings across all regions of the life cycle and for all subgroups, including males and females. What we need, among other things, is a core list of attributes having true generality that can be rated and assessed in every study, so that each can be linked to all others.

Spence said that a core of concepts can be used, for example, self-esteem or self-confidence. Some personality traits are stable; some have dark sides (the negative characteristics of the positive), for example, self-esteem can become egotism, a sense of efficacy can become feelings of grandiosity.

Sternbergh asked Hogan, "Using intuitive discriminant analysis with figures, what variables or constellation of variables separates these figures?" Sparks said if it is labelled negative, we are putting a value judgment on it. Bass responded, "There is prosocial behavior versus self-concerned behavior," that is, the leader must have ethical integrity.

Mitchell urged care in not defining leadership in terms of behavior; rather, it is important to think in terms of output criteria such as effectiveness. Since those at the top of the company make the most money, the success criterion must be considered; is money the symbol of success? We must consider the accomplishments of the leader.

Wilson indicated that in cutting layers of an organization, promotion is often a matter of survival rather than leadership.

It was proposed that various criteria be used for rating leadership in different settings. It was noted that a global and international image should be emphasized, for example, the Japanese do not distinguish between management and leadership. However, in this case if leadership is seen as management effectiveness, then it could be seen as the same. Osborn referred to statements made by Bass and Morrow, indicating their importance because of their international orientation; what we define usually as leadership is specific to our culture. Bass said some languages don't have a word for leader; instead they look at the most enduring characteristics of the job. There are ethnicity items that actually identify ethnic groups, but if you just use a person's ethnicity you could make good predictions. Criteria should depend on what you are going to do with it. If you define leaders conceptually, you ask, "What are people influencing others to do? Where do goals come from? If leaders formulate goals, can they convince others?" Bass wants a theory about what produces theory, then use measures to substantiate it; if items identify ethnicity, then add education.

Clark Wilson wrote in his diary, "I am concerned that the heavy emphasis on personality obscures or ignores the more basic operational variables: (1) Personality variables to me are abstractions of observable behavior. (2) Most personality measures are self-assessments, but I have found over 15 years of using operational variables, self-assessments are seldom valid as tested against operational criteria, but ratings by relevant others—subordinates, peers, and so forth—are most valid. (3) Personality theory hardly exists. Variability of personality measures is questionable."

At varying times the following statements and questions were interjected: A leader takes the group in the direction it feels it is going; Manipulators are often most satisfying to bosses; In executive leadership, dominance "comes a cropper"; Is there a difference between manager and leader? Turning middle managers into leaders may be dysfunctional; We must be cautious about becoming too task-oriented; We must differentiate task analysis from job analysis; Can we identify ahead of time what we can recognize later?; What is the magnitude of the problem we are facing? Hogan was asked about the statement in his paper indicating that about 70% of workers do not like their bosses.

Hogan reminded the group that in the 1960s there was a shift from people effectiveness to group self-actualizations. It is easier to tell what a person is than tell what a situation is. It is necessary to set up defined limitations. If effectiveness is added, it may change data analysis.

Sparks said there were two keys: (1) effectiveness—must compare individuals at same level, and (2) success—times change, for example, keys were collapsed because over a 30-year time-span, recruiters started looking for those who were well-rounded.

## Monday, 2:00 p.m.: **Linking Training and Research**
Convenor:                                Wilson

Wilson spoke briefly, saying that the manager is responsible for the stated goals of the organization; leaders need to envision what ought to be done and have the guts to get it done. Self-assessment is useless, assessment by superiors is fair, but assessment by peers at the same level is best. Behavior can be changed. When feedback is followed by training, change is stabilized.

The group decided that further discussion is needed on the following: (1) In training and development, what is the implication of the data? What are the implications of what we know about leaders? Where have we come in the leadership area? (2) Are we training specialists or generalists? (3) Management styles are in a period of transition; how do we relate them to changing culture? (4) In feedback systems, who owns the data? How do we avoid anger and hostility? (5) What are special demands in training we give executives? (6) What is developable and what is not? (7) What can be done about skills and concepts at the precollege level to train students for the work force? (8) Is leadership trainable? (9) Are leaders born or made? (10) What are the cost benefits of training efforts? (11) How can we identify managerial problems sooner?

Clover said we can teach skills, but skills readiness is essential; otherwise opportunity for training is lost. It is essential to collect data and make people aware of needs (self-assessments are useless).

It was noted that organizations differ in development programs and three different approaches and philosophies were cited: (1) development for all as part of the value system, (2) development only for high potentials, and (3) pay for performance: if you enjoy your job, the company pays for the training. Rigorous selection of persons at the front end makes it possible to select a particular development program. However, all these variations are successful in the marketplace. Consistency within an organization is important. There is trouble when a company wants to engage in all three sorts of programs. Development is carried on for what is deemed important. It may affect recruiting practices and account for differences in what is valued. It was acknowledged that organizational development depends on a well laid-out plan. In one program at PDI (Personnel Decisions Inc.), development is based on individual coaching; this can change people if they are willing to accept feedback.

Concerning feedback, Wilson said that people react in different degrees. Ten percent generally use feedback positively, 10% do not, and 50–60% after evaluation by subordinates shows that change is possible. Goals should be clarified, and it should be determined how well people listen.

In a general discussion, the following points were made: (1) Leadership is trainable, (2) managerial problems are difficult to identify, and (3) the timing for communicating feedback from subordinates is crucial, and it should not be delayed; it should be done periodically and become part of the developmental process rather than attempting reclamation after a problem has happened. Derailment studies indicate that feedback may prevent derailment. The ownership of data was discussed, and it was noted that if feedback is kept private, it is benign. Whether it should be open to bosses is a highly sensitive issue. There is no question that shared feedback is most useful, and the effort should be made to share it.

Campbell asked the following: What do leaders have to know in terms of cultural climate? Different kinds of assignments may require different behavior. How does one manage in transition? How do you manage change since development takes place slowly, and change takes place quickly?

Wilson recommended reading William Bridge's *Transitions* to deal with change; one may have to clarify endings and prepare for the future and learn how people react to change.

Margolis warned that paternalism must be watched; for people to depend too much on employers is a mistake; to survive today in business and industry, emotional health is required. Another participant added that self-objectivity is essential through all levels of education and training.

Monday, 2:00 p.m.: **Studies of Actual Leaders**
Convenor: D. Campbell

Harrison Gough said of this session, "This was an excellent session. Several people gave brief synopses of their studies [e.g., Jon Bentz, Barry Posner, Frank Shipper, Hal Hendrick, Val Arnold, Doug Bray, Ann Howard]. The accounts were clear, succinct, informative, and interesting." Bray said there was some consideration for the stability of managerial characteristics over time by Bray/Howard. The point was made that experience alone doesn't teach managerial interpersonal skills.

Much of the description of this session is taken from the diary of Rich Hofmann, and he was impressed with the representation of an enormous amount of data that had been collected by many in the group. He said that "Posner discussed the development of some instrumentation. His approach was solid and followed the textbook methodology in a very precise fashion. I especially liked the fact that he summarized the qualitative similarities from his case studies. A leader is at his/her best when: (1) involved in a challenging process, (2) inspiring a shared vision, (3) enabling others to act, (4) serving as a role model that leads by example, and (5) acting as an 'encouraging heart.' Posner noted that they translated their findings into an instrument that accounted for 50–60% of effectiveness variation."

The role of intelligence was discussed. Mental ability was the best descriptor for AT&T; Gough said mental ability was not so important until arriving at top management level. Bentz said mental ability predicts effectiveness in lower-level executive positions. This prediction fades in studies with middle management but reappears in upper-level management studies. Mary McCaulley said that intuition is correlated with mental ability tests which focus on ability to deal with abstract, cognitive complexity. Practical sensing types don't score so high on most mental ability tests. Top management requires more broad-range, innovative solutions. She said that CCL data show more "intuitives" in top management than in middle management, so there may be a connection between tested mental ability, preference for intuition, and top management.

Potter said in his diary of his own research (Potter and Fiedler, AMJ, 1981 and a paper in progress) that stress due to ambiguity/overload interferes with the correlation with mental ability until the leader/manager develops strategies through experience to deal with stressful situations. Correlations also vary with the nature of tasks to be performed, some being more intellectually demanding. Potter believes that the pattern of Bentz's data probably cannot be taken as a general picture of the relationship between mental ability and career development.

Hofmann observed that the session reinforced what had struck him when reading the papers—that people are not considering the false negatives! He asked about those people we predict to be poor leaders who turn out to be good leaders. Are there such people? If there is talk about "young leaders" or "early managers," this data must exist.

If we do not have any false negatives, are the initial selection criteria too stringent or is there a nonlinear relationship between selection and effectiveness?

There is evidence that people in leadership positions evolve with the passage of time in their position and with leadership experience. Why hasn't someone done some cross-sectional studies (or have they?) to develop a developmental model that can be tested by some of the longitudinal studies?

Shipper said that frequency counts of "leaderly" acts are not related to quality of performance (this is the cause of a significant research problem for observational research and why critical incident methodology seems to work better). The problem with this method is the possibility for memory distortion. Use of common patterns and multimethod approaches help.

Potter said in his diary, "My concern is that those who play a role for the rewards will behave differently at some critical juncture down [up] stream. Otherwise, if they perform just like the people who have internalized the value system, who cares what they 'really feel or believe'? In other words, if it looks like a duck and quacks, isn't it a duck? Hendrick's data seems to point to the importance of internalizing the value system. Assessment centers do not distinguish between the two and in my experience a four-year screening at a military academy also misses the differences for many."

In general, the issue of values is left out of most discussions. How are they acquired in an organization? How does one select for a values match? What limits do values, implicit structures, and assumptions developed through experience place on the effectiveness, creativity, and flexibility of leaders?

Potter also noted that, in his work, personality traits predict response to stressful situations. Those responses shape the environment which in turn presses the person to change some behaviors reflected in certain personality measures, for example, equity/ambiguity leads to stress, leads to anger/frustration, leads to less trustfulness, which is reflected in the CPI.

The question was asked whether anyone has looked at the outliers in the Bray/Howard studies. The answer appeared to be no. Potter wonders if our methods do not foster a certain sameness among managers. Outliers are critical and may, in the overall organization, provide contrast, alternatives, and the low end of the scale. By taking a personal perspective and not a system perspective, we come to follow our successful predictions. Success is a result of a complex pattern of events which we do not fully understand. Outliers have compensatory strengths to make up for weaknesses among predictor variables. It is a very significant indictment that we do not look closely at these folks, as a rule.

Jon Bentz pointed out his research results with upper-level executives as parallel to those described by Owen Jacobs.

Bentz also noted that more research should focus on gender differences because he suspects that often, when we uncover no differences, what we are finding are the real, mature personality characteristics.

There are no real gender differences in terms of effective leadership. This has been said over and over, even to the point where Bentz made the profound statement that the "masculinity" scale that people use is probably a measure of "thick-skinnedness." Females with high masculinity scores are not lesbians; they have developed a thick skin. This is an important prerequisite for effective upper-level leadership. This might also be called an element of what is referred to as emotional strength.

Hofmann stated in his diary, "There is a lot of talk about mental ability, and a lot of confusion. I did not attend the session on Cognitive Complexity but have my suspicions that we are discussing the difference between two types of thinkers, both of whom may be intelligent by traditional IQ measures. From a Piagetian perspective we can think about three types of thinkers: (1) Concrete thinkers—people who cannot hypothesize well, cannot really conceptualize issues in any meaningful visions, and most likely cannot possibly be effective leaders. It is said that all adults are concrete thinkers 'once in a while.' (2) Formal thinkers—create knowledge! They are able to quickly conceptualize issues and manipulate them mentally. Such people can hypothesize solutions and strategies for solutions, even multiple solutions, and are effective at recognizing true cause and effect in the classic sense of the word. These people are visionaries, and with the right interpersonal skills have the potential to be our most effective leaders. (3) The third type of thinkers are those in-between who are formal thinkers some, but not all, of the time. What is important here is to realize that many intelligent people are formal thinkers in certain contexts, for example, math, philosophy, and so forth. I'm sure that in terms of leadership there are people who may be formal in this area but not in others. Furthermore, there may be leaders who are formal only in certain aspects of leadership. Thus, you may have leaders who are completely formal thinkers, and leaders who are contextually formal. Perhaps this is what is being called cognitive complexity."

Bentz said he would like to build a generic model of leadership based upon empirical analysis. Hofmann believes such a model is there, but in most statistical analyses the data are not powerful enough to identify the components of a general mode. It would be an excellent idea, continues Hofmann, to expose some of the participants to some of the more modern statistical models and analyses within the context of leadership data: (1) Most papers that use factor analysis use exploratory factor analysis techniques. It is possible to carry these techniques one step further by also using confirmatory factor analysis. Confirmatory factor analysis would tell the analyst "how well" an exploratory solution actually fits the data. It would also allow the analyst to generate a generic model that could be tested on different data sets and modified from different composites of variables. (2) A number of papers use repeated measures on individuals and then use univariate t-tests or "eyeballing" the means. These data and their associated research agendas really should be using linear discriminant function analysis.

Monday, 2:00 p.m.:  **Power and Empowerment**
Convenor:                   Hollander

Most of the initial portion of this session summary was taken from the diary of Cynthia McCauley, although the notes of others are interspersed. She indicated that the group focused first on definitional issues around the concept of power. Spence offered a clear distinction between the need for power (desire to dominate others for its own sake) and the need for influence (desire to effect outcomes). This distinction appealed to the group. Sashkin noted that this was similar to McClelland's distinction between personalized and socialized power. Another similar distinction was power over people versus power to accomplish things. If the recipient has no choice, it is power; if the recipient has a choice, it is leadership. People allow others to exercise power over them. Hollander noted there is power to assist others' power, and negative power that stops other people. Subordinates recognize the distinction between power and selfishness and power to effect good outcomes. Spence noted that it is easier to measure influence than power. One of her graduate students had developed two measures: (1) need for power, and (2) need for influence. It was agreed that effective leaders have a need for influence. Yukl urged that less time be spent on definitions and more time be spent on specifics of leadership behavior and processes, more time on the goodness of the leader and less on effectiveness.

Empowerment led to discussion of transformational leadership. Hollander said that transformational and transactional leadership are not dichotomous. Reservations about the concept were expressed as follows: Bass' model is too leader-centered; Are these leaders exploitive, asking for more from followers than they give in return? Current conceptualizations leave out the moral dimension that was important in Burns' book. There appears to be a paradoxical nature to transformational leadership. Examples can be given of leaders who created positive change (were very successful) but were disruptive and highly disliked.

Quotations from Steckler's notes include: "Sayles: Professionals are used to autonomy; they rationalize personal power, assume/argue it leads to good of society." "Spence: Power itself is a process, not negative." "Sergiovanni: Need to define the other side—who is 'led'; Pawns are manipulated; followers are compelled; subordinates are controlled." "Yukl: Leadership is goal bound, power is goal neutral . . . leadership [influence] to achieve goals that are agreed upon." "Cronin: Manipulation divorced from desirable ends does not equal leadership." "Sergiovanni: Hope we've addressed the moral question when we begin to train children."

Notes taken from other diaries include the following quotes: Gibbons: "Power is neutral. We individually, culturally, consensually decide when it is negative or positive, facilitative or coercive. . . ." There is a huge, largely unexplored topic concerning the relationship and dynamics of power, leadership, and nonhierarchical organizations/systems, socio-technical systems, and the general move toward flatter, more participative organizations. This is also a cultural issue, as well as an organizational design issue. It calls for new models of leadership which might be called "distributed leadership." Sashkin: "I think there is a real movement toward agreement on a generic 'exchange' model that incorporates both transactional *and* transformational leadership [Yammarino, Hollander, Sergiovanni]." Spence: "Excellent session. The group acted cooperatively to work out a conceptual model in which a working definition of power was developed, a distinction made between the need for power and need for influence, and techniques for achieving influence were identified. We also discussed *effective* techniques of leadership, including empowering followers. We began to discuss processes by which goals were identified [e.g., handed down from above versus generated by consensus] and the morality/ethics of goals. Unfortunately, time ran out. These issues deserved further consideration." Yammarino: "It seems that the notions of power, influence, authority, and leadership, in addition to the usual components, must explicitly include a focus on levels of analysis in their conceptualizations. For example, it may be that *power*, a characteristic of an individual, is a *person* level phenomenon; *influence*, a characteristic of a relationship, a *dyad-* or *group*-based phenomenon; *authority*, a characteristic of a position or role, a *collective* or *organizational* level phenomenon; and *leadership*, a process involving a person, a group, and their interaction in a situation, a *multiple-level* phenomenon."

Issues not fully clarified or directly addressed were: (1) Transformational leadership and empowerment as linked or overlapping concepts. (2) Resolving the tension between inspiring others to work toward the leader's vision and goals and empowering others to pursue their own goals. However, Spence asked at that point, "Where do the goals come from?" but the question was not answered. (3) Hollander tends to emphasize the follower's contribution to visions and goals whereas the transformational approach looks to the leader exclusively. (4) Does empowerment mean giving power over means or over ends? (5) Can I empower myself and merely enable others? (6) Why is so much time spent reexploring that power is not a zero-sum game? However, Hollander had noted at the outset that a primary determinant of how a leader uses or perceives power has to do with the zero-sum versus expanding concept of power. (7) Sayles asked about the situational factors that go beyond role and noted that there remains the dilemma and contradictions over use of power for one's own career and department versus broader organizational ends.

Monday, 3:00 p.m.: ## California Psychological Inventory–A Leadership Model
Convenor: Gough

Douglas Bray said, "Unlike the other sessions, this was a lecture with questions and answers rather than a discussion. It was, however, very well organized and engagingly presented." He added, "Gough made one eager to try out his typology, leading Bray [*sic*] to volunteer to have the CPIs given to the Management Continuity Study participants in 1977–1982 type-scored for correlation with a wide variety of assessment center measures."

Gough indicated, in his diary notes, his thanks to participants for scheduling and attending this session and said that about 50% of the material was from his preliminary paper for the conference. He noted, "The questions, comments, and so forth were astute and penetrating and will be helpful to me as I continue to develop the model and its implications."

VanVelsor said this session was a fairly detailed exploration by Gough of the three vectors, four types, and seven levels in his CPI model. She said it was what she wanted to hear because she wants to work with it. She left happy and ready to get to work.

Ruderman was impressed that Gough responded to the criticism that the CPI did not have an underlying factorial model. Gough's V3, a realization scale, is fascinating. It implies that everyone can grow, that each person has an optimal way of living for their particular style. It would be interesting to use V3 in studies of leadership development. What experiences promote greater realization? Do the Leadership Development Program and the Looking Glass program at CCL promote growth in V3? Do on-the-job experiences?

VanVelsor asked Gough whether one can move from one type to another. He responded, "No, not unless you are at the border. Certain extreme experiences like a lifetime prison sentence can influence your type."

Gough responded to a question about correlations with Holland types saying that V1 and V2 have some overlap with Holland. V3 is not found there. It would be interesting to see whether the person-environment bit as assessed according to Holland's model was correlated with V3. V3 relates to how you solve key issues dealing with others and to rules of life.

Ruderman and Hendrick asked Gough to describe further the Deltas (persons whose life-style is based on severe doubts about ordinary conventions and normative constraints, along with a detached, inwardly directed, private sense of personal experience). Deltas at high levels of ego integration can be visionary and creative but tend to avoid and shy away from any demand for leadership. Deltas seek a personal, even idiosyncratic, way of dealing with life's exigencies. At low levels on Vector 3, they may suffer from psychiatric disturbances such as depression, anxiety, and even psychosis.

Rule breaking and rule respecting are key notions in Gough's model and are assessed by scores on the second vector (V2). This vector is of particular pertinence to notions of cognitive complexity, creativity, and the desire for change.

Monday, 3:45 p.m.: **Instruments for Diagnosing Managerial Strengths and Weaknesses**

Convenor: Williamson

Some strengths noted were: an honest self-concept, ability to define problems: learning from one's mistakes, trust, consistency, balance, flexibility, creativity in having new ideas about changing environment—when to move and when to hold.

Some instruments were mentioned that can provide assessment: BENCHMARKS (feedback), tacit knowledge (identifies weaknesses and highlights the bootlicking problem), IBM form (based on feedback and subjective assessment), subjective techniques, AT&T forms, Survey of Management Practices, MMPI, CPI. It was noted in one diary that this portion of the discussion was fragmented, that it should have focused on skills rather than instruments.

A general discussion covered some of the following points: (1) Derailment often occurs because of failure to staff adequately or because of dishonesty. (2) Handling psychopaths in an organization is a heavy problem. They are alert and articulate, also impulsive and mean. (3) It might be useful to devise a new scale of narcissism, but there are other behavioral manifestations that should be considered as well. (4) Resentfulness specializes in betrayal; it is like having a time bomb in the organization. (5) Strong personalities will mask poor administrative skills; they are hard to pick up. (6) One overriding characteristic may be overaggressiveness and an inflated ego. When business is good these may be difficult to discern. (7) Six out of ten managers should not be managers, judging from responses of subordinates (other discussants indicated that it was more like 1/3). (8) Managers are not always appointed to do the popular thing and subordinates are seldom satisfied. (9) Many who become first-line managers are not trained in leadership; they are just promoted and have to fall back on their own resources. (10) Some of the papers prepared for this conference show ways of getting at criterion measures; vague estimates are not useful.

Richard Campbell asked: Is there such a thing as an absolute measure of leader competence and effectiveness? How do you decide that leaders are effective? What bases do you look at?

Moses added: Mergers and acquisitions mean more change, thus the need for more flexibility. Many current models are built on no change. Ten years from now we will have to take on more problems. Do we build a new instrument before hiring and during management?

Richard Campbell mentioned in his diary that "it would be useful to develop a basic list of dimensions/constructs we believe to be important for development and performance, and then sort the available instruments into groupings by dimensions."

## Monday Evening

Following dinner, at a session intended to set up a schedule for the rest of the conference, some of the following comments were made and suggestions were noted as topics for further discussion:
1. Alternative ways to look at intelligence.
2. Discussion about cognitive complexity, especially in regard to rearing children (Hendrick).
3. The group, although to be commended for acting like ladies and gentlemen, should begin to challenge each other.
4. Must fight out the personality-versus-skills issue.
5. Hear from David Campbell about his real data.
6. More from Posner: how they measure, how they meet problems.
7. More from Bray: how they tidied up.
8. Group urged to listen to tape on Power.
9. What are the practical items that can be taken back?
10. Need for literature in the field so that graduate students can get on with their research.
11. Need for more predictive knowledge: cannot operate on random chance.

General discussion ensued about the attraction of the field to graduate students, the issue of leadership in the broader context, and the differing attitudes of various individuals and segments of society about leadership, corruption, and any pathology in one's own discipline. There was talk about the need to understand leadership as a subject and its development as a tool, the requirement to combine the conceptual framework with its applications, and the desire for a clear understanding of where we are.

Tuesday, 9:00 a.m.:  **Styles of Intelligence**
Convenor:          Sternberg

Sternberg explained the highlights of his theory of mental self-management—the executive, legislative, and judicial styles—and emphasized that they were styles and not abilities. He said, as quoted by Valerio, "We are not born with a style—we are socialized into it." Ruderman, in describing the session, said, "More so than in his paper, Sternberg stressed that his theory is one of person-environment compatibility [although he didn't use that term]."

Bunker found many linkages to managerial selection, placement, and promotional issues in this session. He wrote, "This work helps explain needs for developmental efforts and offers strategies and tools for conceptualizing the role of preferences and styles in determining success in changing situations." Also, in Sternberg's model of creativity (Six-Facet Model)—Intelligence, Styles, Knowledge, Personality, Motivation, and Context—one might be able to enhance predictability in ambiguous and uncertain situations. Bunker was attracted to Sternberg's notion of "Selective Comparison," the ability to see the relevance of past performance components in a new situation, and the suggestion that this ability can lead to problems, that is, making selective linkages may lead to maximum negative transfer due to confusion and intermittent reinforcement.

Lombardo noted some points about the session as follows: style and ability often don't match, don't correlate much with intelligence/ability measures; style and ability should often be matched with jobs; some people overcapitalize on past strengths and use past successful habits and can't make transitions; experts are more befuddled than novices by changes in deep structure (like making lowest cards win in bridge); it may be easier to perform well in totally new situations: where half of past behavior works (you know what to do) is the worst situation—it's hard to figure out which half works, and confirmation bias and intermittent reinforcement (since some works) convince some people that their preferred style is still working; successful people exploit strengths, compensate for weaknesses—"Smart people are stupid at many things"; styles shouldn't correlate with GPA.

According to Hofmann, as written in his diary, "This presentation went far beyond the prepared paper. Sternberg presented a cohesive model that accommodates intellectual styles within a leadership/management context." Hofmann is especially interested in leadership in education. He believes that Sternberg's intellectual styles provide a model for (1) conceptualizing leadership roles in education, (2) the development of an instrument to assess leadership styles in education, and (3) carrying out a "task analysis" within educational settings that will allow one to organize the tasks into a meaningful structure. Further, he said, "It should also be possible to develop some curriculum materials that could be used to provide 'leadership experiences' within each intellectual style. Such materials should be invaluable for teaching adolescents about leadership roles."

Hofmann expects to use the Sternberg model to develop some assessment procedures in education, specifically for administrators and teachers, and perhaps develop a course for school administrators based on the Sternberg model.

Hawkins said, "The work will be important to transfer and promotion policy in industry."

Sternberg noted that one question to ask is: "What kind of styles do people have which make them appropriate for different jobs?" It is important for hiring and placement to understand preferences. Ask: "Do abilities and styles match?" If not, people may never feel happy in a job. Those promoted through the academic system rely on memory and analytic abilities, and maybe more is required in different situations.

Wagner said that frequent mistakes occur when a success is hired to do the same thing in a new organization and sees similarity where it doesn't exist. People need to be able to "unpack" what they know. Successful behaviors not understood but developed through situation and specific reinforcement are much less transferable.

Potter said that the concept of what you are promoted for, not necessarily being the same as what you need at upper levels, is a well-known notion, but Sternberg's theory and forthcoming test of styles offer a useful handle on personality dimensions on this question. He added, "It is tough to select a person, as we must, for what they will do, not for what they have done."

Sternberg's paper deals with styles and generalized task structures; it deals less with specific skills. For example, Sternberg indicates that social skills are more important for some leadership roles than for others; even performance skills are related more to what people like and dislike.

Discussion ensued about group intelligence. It was said that the best predictor of performance of the group is using the most intelligent member as leader. The "eager beaver" who leaps to the fore is often not helpful. If creativity is needed in an organization, a creative person will rise; if not, the organization may fail.

From the comments of several persons who attended the session, it appears that there is some overlap with the Myers-Briggs. It was suggested that this overlap might make Sternberg's assessment procedures stronger and more generalizable. Potter said that what distinguishes Sternberg, Holland, MBTI, and others are the driving models behind the measurement device; there is some comfort in the common features we define given such different starting places. Ruderman said she would like to know more about discriminant validity with other models of person-environment fit. "The notion of maximum negative transfer is very exciting to me. I think this is what happens when people derail. The situation changes and they don't go with it. This is why it is important to study transitions. At times of change we learn a lot about the dynamics of person-environment fit." Mary McCaulley, in her diary notes, said, "MBTI assumes people differ on the priorities for mental functions by each type, but good type development means conscious direction of powers of perception and judgment." She described certain areas in which she saw similarities between Sternberg and MBTI, and these could be the subject for a study.

Other suggestions included: further exploration of the overlap in the various style models, since Sternberg feels they share some common core and have some unique features; pursuit of the concepts having to do with facility in changing styles and the degree of match between abilities and styles; study of other types of intelligence and how they are related to style preferences and performance in different types of job situations; research on how people can shift from one style to another in reference to work, for example, R & D organization (style conflict as a person shifts from research to management); some consideration to the question of whether the analogic government model within the paper is appropriate; the necessity to clarify the underlying theory; swifter report of research to guide action, since the environment is shifting rapidly, calling for different styles and abilities to lead. Since issues such as selection ratios, base rates of success, quality of performance appraisal, and so forth, are relevant but seldom discussed regarding what we think we know, consideration might be given at the initial placement of college hires, for example, to a match between a new hire and a department receiving the new hire. Research of this type would help to make this interesting theory more applicable to a real world setting. Additional suggestions included: further measures are needed on motivation and this work needs to be linked to performance measures to determine if preferences for styles and situations actually lead to enhanced outcome; further work is needed to discover whether Sternberg's Triarchic Intelligence Scales show differential relationships to the different Mental Self-Management Styles.

Some questions that arose at the session and in diaries are: In which jobs can it be demonstrated that certain styles lead to more effective performance? How do styles develop? If styles are socialized by the environment, does the organization develop what it needs? Since longitudinal work takes place within organizations, how are we to get a picture of development across boundaries and in many different environments?

Tuesday, 9:00 a.m.:          **Coherent Theory**
Convenor:                        Hogan

Using his "Big 5" personality dimensions, Hogan has found effective leaders to have the following profiles:
  1. Intellectance—high
  2. Adjustment—high
  3. Prudence—high
  4A. Ambition—high
  4B. Sociability—variable, not an important dimension for leadership
  5. Likability—very high

According to Cynthia McCauley, Hogan's approach to linking personality dimensions and effective leadership seems to have at least two aspects that differ from the other "personality" folks at the conference: (1) He is interested in personality from the perspective of the observer; that is, an individual's personal reputation from the perspective of the outsider, rather than the individual's perspective on how he/she really is. (2) He distinguishes between individuals who are able to gain high status (i.e., move up in the organization) and those who are effective leaders (i.e., those whose teams are most effective). This second distinction can be seen in Hogan's paper where he points out three types of people who can gain status successfully but are not good leaders.

One basic problem in personality research was noted by Spence: We may be measuring the same things but labeling them differently. For example, a high correlation between one person's DOMINANCE scale and another person's NARCISSISM scale may be due to a lot of overlap in the items on the two scales.

Questions remaining at the close of the session included: (1) How can one identify the three types of people noted by Hogan as harmful to have in leadership roles? The evidence to date about these types is anecdotal. (2) What about Clark Wilson's challenge at a previous session to understand the relationships between the kinds of variables measured by the "personality" types and the "skill" types (and which are more important for understanding leadership)? Although one diary suggested this might have been a good session to start thinking about how the two perspectives are linked, this did not materialize.

Sayles wrote: "Hogan presented an appealing, parsimonious 'theory of personality'. Actually the theory part was quite separable from the constructs by which he simplified or aggregated what I had been hearing about such constructs. It seemed to me that the traits he dealt with were those that had substantial applicability to managerial behavior. His emphasis on parsimony and simplicity was most functional."

Tuesday, 9:00 a.m.: **Transformational Leadership**
Convenor: Bass

Bass summarized his paper and noted that, in his work, descriptions by subordinates correlated more highly with outside criterion for transformational rather than for transactional leadership. He said that contingent reward has considerable payoff, but more payoff seems to occur from transformational leadership; passive management is contraindicated and laissez-faire management is negative. He proposed that the similarities and differences among Burns, Sashkin, Bass, Posner, Yukl, Clover, Rosenbach, and Gibbons should be considered. All but Burns were present at the session. Burns, in 1978, had said that most social scientists had been doing research on transactional leadership, but that did not explain the movers and shakers; he introduced the concept of transformational leadership. Transformational leadership increases awareness, raises people level (Maslow), and gets subordinates to transform self-interest to societal needs. Rosenbach indicated at a later time that his studies clearly show that truly effective leaders are strong on both transactional and transformational leadership behaviors. Steckler noted in her diary that there is an empirical disagreement between Burns and Bass. Leaders can be transactional, but are more effective if they are transformational. The factors involved are: (1) Charisma, (2) Inspiration (Clover said he had a great deal of data on both), (3) Intellectual stimulation (new solutions to old problems), (4) Individualized consideration (focus on equity, not equality [Zaleznik]), (5) Contingent reward (promise), (6) Management by exception, and (7) Laissez-faire.

Sashkin said he differed from Burns, not Bass. Sashkin agrees that transformational and transactional are separate, not dichotomous, dimensions. The theory, actually, can be traced back to Max Weber, there being economic and noneconomic bases. Charisma is connected to noneconomic factors. Sashkin differs from Bass in that Sashkin fits all aspects of transformational mode into 3 and 4, taking his behavioral categories out of Bennis. He described his scales as: (1) Focused Communication, (2) Basic Communication Skills, (3) Consistency and Trust, (4) Unconditional Positive Regard (Carl Rogers), and (5) Creating Risk Opportunities. Three scales Sashkin is working on currently are: (1) Need for Social Power, (2) Effectiveness, and (3) Time-span of Vision. None of the first five focuses on vision, but on articulation. He believes that charisma is a consequence, rather than a cause: Charisma is a report by others. Behaviors of five of the above that lead to effective response, he calls charisma. This is not a difference in measurement, but in concept.

Gough noted in his diary, concerning Sashkin's presentation, that "this integration of thoughts about personality attributes was of great interest because, by attending to them, one can identify *in advance* persons with a potentiality for transformational leadership."

Bass added that transformational leaders create cultures and transactional leaders live within cultures.

Posner presented the following thoughts: Perhaps some of the differences between Bass's framework and ours might be linked to the organizational settings in which we began. Bass began with military personnel and we began with Silicon Valley executives. The development of transformational leaders should be seen as the development of a skill known as leadership. Asking people to describe a time when they were at their personal best as a leader led us to develop a comprehensive framework of the actions of people when they are leading others. The five scales developed were: (1) Challenging the Process (leaders experiment, take risks, innovate, and learn from mistakes), (2) Inspiring a Shared Vision (leaders are possibility, not probability, thinkers; optimistic and personally enthusiastic about future opportunities and they establish links with their constituents' aspirations), (3) Enabling Others to Act (these are some of the classic team-building notions, involving building trust, cooperative goals, and empowering others so that commitment and ownership abound), (4) Modeling the Way (leaders are clear about their values/standards and set the example for others, bringing credibility to the vision; they also plan small wins), and (5) Encouraging the Heart (leaders foster courage so that others will persist, providing both individual recognition and promoting team celebrations, create a family feeling). While each of these practices demonstrates statistical independence, they are quite interconnected and dynamic in practice. Much of Kouzes' and Posner's data comes from middle- and senior-level managers. Posner also maintained that these five leadership behaviors can be taught, and an individual's leadership skills can be enhanced.

Apparently Bass, Sashkin, and Posner are in accord, but Posner states the need for courage and optimism. It was said that transformational leaders beget transformational leaders. Sashkin asked who in the audience had worked for transformational leaders—many raised their hands. Someone interjected that older, traditional companies reward transactional leaders but make discretionary opportunities available. Bray said that people who were promoted to leadership positions were predisposed to grow and, if they met a favorable environment, moved along. Bray continued, "Personnel departments propagate transactionals and thereby prevent moves into organizational transformation. Top-level people involved in culture are necessary to effect change." It was also noted that developmental experiences added into the mix. Sashkin added that in regard to behavior and development, people can learn from the dark side of charisma: They must look at power and examine value systems and the vision. Leaders must carve out a leadership role. People have more power than they give themselves credit for.

Colquitt, in his diary, said about this session: "Here are dimensions, or characteristics of effective leader/managers . . . what now? What do we do with this information? Posner is taking positive steps in the context of training; Bill Clover is using this for development purposes; what are others doing with this information? This is what we need more of."

Gibbons believes that transformational leaders are better developed, have had higher demands placed on them as children, are higher on self-esteem, possess a human relationship passion (they realize themselves best with others), can raise up followers, and take care of their own development. In her diary, she said, "There is considerable congruence among these positions/theories and where there appear to be differences, they are largely complementary and expansive rather than contradictory."

Hendrick questioned whether an underlying concept may have to do with cognitive complexity, whether those who operate at higher levels are transformational. Later in his diary, Hendrick said, "One of the most important things to come out of the discussion was that through the use of differing approaches there was a convergence of the findings of the various researchers at the conference on the nature of transformational leadership and the characteristics associated with it. A second major observation was the relation between the variables associated with transformational leadership and those associated with more cognitively complex functioning. There appeared to be general agreement that true transformational leadership probably requires at least an intermediate level of cognitive complexity in one's functioning. There is a need to do research on transformational leadership that looks directly at the complexity level of those who are identified as transformational leaders versus those who clearly are not. Based on the papers and discussions, I was particularly struck by the similarity between the variables the transformational leadership researchers have found to be important and the variables that consistently have been found to be related to more cognitively complex functioning. These dimensions are summarized in my paper. What I hope to do now is to work with some of the transformational leadership researchers to see if we can provide confirmatory evidence of the relationship between cognitive complexity and transformational leadership."

Gough noted that it appeared that the Bass scales for transformational leadership are most widely used and that David Campbell's new CWO scales are very promising to assess personal qualities as well as specifics of the organizational settings. He would also like to see CPI data on transformational versus transactional leaders. Among the hypotheses coming to mind are higher Empathy, Achievement via Independence, and Independence scores for Transformationals, with higher Socialization, Self-Control, and Achievement via Conformance scores for Transactionals. Leaders of both kinds should score high on the CPI for Dominance and Capacity for Status.

Yammarino's diary voiced the following observations: "In terms of the *variables* [factors, dimensions, etc.], there seems to be a great similarity between the works of Bass, Posner, and Sashkin. Each also seems to be aligned with Plato's basic qualities of the 'ideal man' who must balance the 'military man' [courage, inspiration, etc.], the 'rational man' [thinking, intellectually stimulating], and the 'religious man' [considerate, empathic, dealing with others]. Bass, Posner, and Sashkin all seem to consider these *emotional, intellectual, and people-based* phenomena in their work. The main difference in the works of Bass, Posner, and Sashkin seems to be their differing emphasis on *levels of analysis*. Bass seems to emphasize the leader and leadership—*person* level of analysis dominating. Posner seems to emphasize the followers and leadership—the *group* level of analysis dominating. Sashkin seems to emphasize the organization and leadership—the *collective/organization* level of analysis dominating."

Vice's diary notes included: "This session displayed three [at least] experts who were willing to objectively offer up their wisdom to the group in a selfless way. They were in search of understanding and elevation of the level of collective knowledge at, perhaps, their own expense as it relates to self-recognition."

Tuesday, 10:30 a.m.:     **Cognitive Complexity/**
                                      **Tacit Knowledge**
Convenors:                         Hendrick/Wagner

Hendrick gave a lecturette and responded to questions. Wagner spoke briefly and answered questions. According to recorders, the two presenters were not in agreement in their theories but did not discuss their differences.

Hendrick lectured on the Harvey/Hunt model of complexity, pointing out, according to one participant, that people learn through a diversity of experiences which help them to develop the differential categories of reasoning necessary for handling complex situations. Cognitive complexity is related to many different personality variables, such as flexibility, openness to change, values, and a low need for structure. Hendrick said that descriptions of highly cognitively complex people appear to be similar to descriptions of transformational leaders.

Sternberg said that Hendrick's theory is culture-bound, that it is similar to Kohlberg's work which has been shown to be quite culture-bound.

Wagner said that in his work in tacit knowledge, he distinguishes practical intelligence from academic intelligence. While practical intelligence has more to do with rules of thumb, practical intelligence deals more with ill-defined problems. Asked by Morrow whether his (Wagner's) model was as culture-bound as Hendrick's, Wagner replied, "Yes, to some extent it is culture-bound. It looks at differences between experts and novices in our culture." Wagner was asked about the differences between knowing and doing, indicating that Wagner's theory looks at knowing, not doing. Wagner said, "This is true. Some people may know what to do, but may not take the proper steps."

Asked by Bass whether the model is like the old model of social intelligence, Sternberg replied, "No, it's very different."

Some notes taken from diaries include: (1) Ruderman's interest in seeing work on the differences between practical intelligence and cognitive complexity. Since Wagner and Hendrick did not discuss their differences, how similar are Wagner's rules of thumb to Hendrick's ability to differentiate a variety of situations? Ruderman would also like to learn more about Wagner's and Sternberg's measures. Apparently they develop scoring procedures by looking at the degree of differentiation between novice and expert (manager) responses. How are the problem scenarios elicited? How close to real life are the problem scenarios, and how similar is what experts say they do to what they actually do? She would like to see evaluation of scenarios based on real situations. (2) Cynthia McCauley said that the following chart presented by Wagner as an overhead helped her think more clearly about tacit knowledge but also about why we are not doing a good job at developing leadership capacities in youth:

| Academic Problems | Practical Problems |
|---|---|
| 1. well-defined | 1. ill-defined |
| 2. formulated by others | 2. formulated by oneself |
| 3. all information given | 3. missing information |
| 4. single solution | 4. multiple solutions |
| 5. single method | 5. multiple methods |

Relative to academic problems, McCauley continued, "We aren't giving students an opportunity to practice leadership. We need to give students more opportunity to tackle practical problems. Why should they have to wait to enter the working world to start developing tacit knowledge about managing themselves and managing others?" (3) Hawkins questions whether one can train (across cultures?) for tacit knowledge. He also noted that there was little significance between IQ and tacit knowledge, but IQ and tacit knowledge are not measuring the same thing. He believes a training module would be helpful to the field, agreeing with the definition of tacit knowledge, and that there are interesting prospects for this work in industry. (4) Hofmann stated that Hendrick's model of cognitive complexity was insightful and conceptually valuable. Although there was some concern that Hendrick's model for cognitive complexity was just a rehash of Rokeach, Hofmann does not think so. Hendrick imposed a coherent developmental or hierarchical structure on his model that Hofmann does not remember Rokeach discussing. Certainly, following from Descartes, it is true that there is overlap with good theories. Hendrick's ideas simply represent an extension of an already good model. (5) Williamson asked not only whether tacit knowledge can be trained, but also whether it is company specific and whether it is domain specific.

| Tuesday, 10:45 a.m.: | **The CWO Scales** |
|---|---|
| Convenor: | D. Campbell |

Harrison Gough wrote in his diary notes: "This was a masterful and witty presentation of a very promising new set of measures. Beyond doubt, the CWO Scales are going to be widely used and will be playing an important part in *future* research on leadership."

Since Campbell's paper is included in Part II of this volume and describes the new measures, any summary of his report at the conference session that was devoted to its review is unlikely to do it justice.

| Tuesday, 11:00 a.m.: | **Longitudinal Studies** |
|---|---|
| Convenor: | Bray |

Valerio, in her diary notes, summarized the session as follows: Bray began with a brief history of classic longitudinal studies. Those in the room who have been involved in longitudinal studies presented outlines of their work and results. Howard provided information on the scope of the MPS and MCS studies at AT&T. Yammarino outlined the study he is doing with Bass on Predicting Transformational Leadership from past behaviors of officers at the U.S. Naval Academy. Potter spoke about the study conducted at the Coast Guard Academy. Wilson presented his survey of management practices. Sparks presented his study at Humble Oil. The Personnel Development Series battery included MAT, nonverbal reasoning measure, biodata, Guilford-Martin, and a proprietary test of judgment. The results here showed that biodata became more valid year by year. Mitchell presented the LIMRA Career Profile System which screened *14 million* applicants. He reported also that the most valid measure was biodata. Spence reported on a study with new PhDs who were awarded degrees from 1978 to 1981. Spence thought the best predictor was personality data. Some additional notes Valerio added were: Howard's statement that from early career through to the 20-year point, the best predictors were abilities and advancement motivation; Potter's statement that the Coast Guard data resembles Gough's Alpha 7s; Mitchell's statement that biodata testing needs to be done annually to maintain validities. Valerio seconded a suggestion that a volume of longitudinal studies should be published in which cross-comparisons are made and the information on what we *do* know is collected in one or two volumes.

This session was an opportunity to hear about the major organizational research projects, longitudinal studies of career development, executive success, personality profiles, and so forth. Since they are many and extensive, there appeared to be insufficient time to get deeply into the findings. Alan Colquitt said in his diary that it renewed his interest in the criterion problem, and he was sorry that Mitchell and Sparks did not succeed in getting an in-depth discussion going in this area. In addition, Colquitt said, "It absolutely fascinated me to hear [from Ann Howard] that one-third of their college sample changed in the predictions of how far they would make it [scary, too, emphasizing the importance of time of criterion measurement and the stability of our measures]. Two possibilities: (1) Their scores on the relevant abilities, and so forth, changed and therefore, there were predicted level changes. (2) What changes is not the scores (e.g., improvements, decrements) on the relevant abilities, but what abilities are relevant, and therefore, predicted level changes. Either is interesting, and potentially damaging to systems designed to predict success [selection or promotion]. The first suggests that scores change on our predictors over the years and, therefore, relationships between predictors and criteria may change. So when we collect predictor data is critical. The second one is perhaps the most troubling if the relevant and valid predictors change, so timing of criterion data and predictor data are only good within a particular time window. Beyond that, other relationships are more powerful and other things work better."

R. Campbell expressed his gratitude for gaining more specific information on the Exxon studies that he had not seen in print and for discovering several longitudinal studies of which he had been unaware. He said that it reinforced his feeling that peer and subordinate ratings of leaders should be used more in studies, fully recognizing they are but two slices or views (important ones) on the leader's behavior. Also, Campbell said we know little about how differences in organizations influence development, and this is a serious limitation at a time when organizations are changing rapidly.

Howard called the session one on predictive studies, noting that there were interesting descriptions of a number of studies but, due to time restraint, there was little time for research outcomes. She said, "For predictive studies, we need to integrate and contrast results with repeated collections of criteria; we need to explain conditions under which validity increases and decreases over time. For longitudinal studies with repeated predictor measurements, we need to research what causes growth and decay in managerial characteristics over time."

There was expressed interest in diaries to hear more about the following: (1) Shipper's comments about both breadth versus depth of skills. (2) Outliers and the people who were not predictable, for example, those predicted to succeed who did not and vice versa. Is it because of the unmeasured variable problem; the environment did not allow them to succeed; they did not have the luck, breaks, the developmental manager/bosses, the right assignments . . . ? (3) Potter noted that his work closely parallels Yammarino and Bass, that he has added in-depth interviews and used actual performance reports and has a cleaner undergraduate success measure. He believes it will be *very* valuable to have both perspectives. (4) Spence believes achievement motivation is a most significant predictor. Sternberg noted this is hardest to measure. Have Spence and Sternberg discussed her measure and his new model of creativity? (5) Potter questioned whether cross-organizational career development and predicted successful careers built diagonally might show evidence quite different from what is found in these studies all within an organization.

Following are some points noted by participants that may have been part of the general discussion or may have been generated by discussion at the session. In either case, they appeared in diaries without connectors to particular areas in the presentation or dialogue, but appeared worthy of note: (1) Desire to lead among young corporate hires is not very strong; (2) Managers who get to the highest levels demonstrate strong administrative skills; (3) Leaders need opportunity to celebrate; (4) Think in terms of leader effectiveness: leadership is what the leader accomplishes; (5) In defining leading and managing, the former pertains to explicit function and is well defined, the latter pertains to making the organization work; (6) Yammarino, in review of his work with Bass, accepted USNA definition of success which includes a factor for an engineering major (success) versus humanities major (failure). They may see this as a system problem in terms of success and failure, but there is no way that it should be counted as a personal failure to graduate in the humanities; (7) It was noted that not as much was done with culture differences between cohorts as there should be in the AT&T studies; (8) Networking ability seems to be an important feature of success.

Tuesday Noon

At Tuesday lunch the following participants met to discuss Leadership Education, with Cronin acting as facilitator: Rivera, Hofmann, M. Clark, Rosenbach, Sashkin, Karnes, Margolis. Rivera, who described the San Antonio Youth Literacy (Leadership) Program, is an upbeat, committed person who is doing an outstanding volunteer job working with Hispanic and Black youth to prepare them for leadership. The program acronym is SAYL. Karnes described her program for the talented and gifted.

Tuesday, 2:00 p.m.:    **More from Barry Posner**
Convenor:                      Posner

Posner gave a lucid description of the origins of his scheme and questionnaire. He described his workshop and Howard said she "especially liked to hear how he trains people to be more inspirational in his workshops." Potter quoted Posner as follows: "All leaders are born—at least given our current methodological constraints . . . . There are an unlimited number of places where a leader can play at a professional level."

Potter said he liked Posner's questions, for example, "Think of the time when you were at your best as a leader" and "What are the characteristics of the person you would want to work for, be willing to follow, and so forth?"

Posner described people as wanting honesty, competence, vision, and inspiration in their leaders. In their subordinates, they want honesty, compliance, dependability, and cooperation. He asked if, as executives, we really want leaders below us. One participant noted that this presents a number of real concerns concerning all the talk of empowerment, self-management, and leadership development.

Posner reviewed, out of his paper, the five practices of leaders being at their personal best:

*Challenging the Process*: actively searching out ways to innovate and improve; leaders experiment, take risks, learn from mistakes; "leaders and leadership connected with times of change" different from everyday experience; changing from way things are to way they could be.

*Inspiring a Shared Vision*: envision shared uplifting future hopeful, think in terms of possibilities not probabilities; didn't necessarily believe probabilities on their side, get beyond self-doubt; leadership equals self-development and self-confidence; leaders earn or acquire followers.

*Enabling Others to Act*: team building, making others into leaders (developmental-consciousness of what had been unconscious); creating win-win situation, building mutual trust and respect by:

*Modelling the Way*: lead by example; figure out a way to get started; commit self first.

*Encouraging the Heart*: courage; recognize individual contributions, classic reinforcement; celebrate team accomplishments, build sense of family and social network system.

Some other questions and comments that were recorded in diaries include: (1) It's difficult to believe that *everybody* has a vision. Maybe they can think up one if so required, but that doesn't mean it's been there all along. (2) Are these results method-bound à la Herzberg? (3) Where does transformational leadership fit in with the total scheme of running an effective organization? How much variance does it account for? How does it develop? (4) Potter asks, "To what degree do people learn roles that are easily shed [Bentz's upstream swimmers who wait out a misfit in expectation of later opportunity] and to what degree do we socialize people such that it is difficult to change [Wagner/Sternberg organization structure and tacit knowledge interfering with later effectiveness when we see similarity in dissimilar settings]?" (5) How about a lateral move or movement up the ladder that lessens power but increases experience opportunities—do we have any research on that? (6) Sashkin said that we need the ability to identify the person who can develop subordinate leadership and still maintain quality control; it takes more time and energy for the leader to attain the sharing of purpose, the internalization of the leader's vision by the subordinate, so there is confidence that the leader will continue to be supported. (7) Ulmer was quoted as saying that in a large organization, classical management skills are essential to create the kind of environment within which transformational leadership can happen. Vision only makes sense in an organization that functions well. You can "transform" portions of the organization beneath you when you are out of step with the whole organization. Your subordinates will see it; supervisors may not see it, or they may tolerate these styles because of the results. (8) Cronin said there is a paradox between wanting to develop other leaders versus wanting the organization to perform in their own likeness. Ulmer replied that to do so takes people with *inner confidence* more than mental health, tremendous inner resources. Pertinent to this issue, the article by Kouzes in the *New York Times*, "When Leadership Collides with Loyalty," was noted. (9) Cynthia McCauley said, "Although Posner was included among the 'transformational leadership' researchers in an earlier session on the topic, his approach seems different and more appealing for the following reasons: (A) His research base focused on effective leadership processes rather than on effective leaders—what happens when effective leadership is taking place, not what are effective leaders like. This seems to fit with reality better—individuals are not necessarily effective leaders all the time. By looking at each individual's best as a leader, one gains a better understanding of leadership at all levels. (B) He tries to address why the identified effective practices are indeed effective by looking at what impact they have on followers. When you study leadership, followers are an important part of the equation. When you study leaders, the followers seem to be ignored. (C) Concepts like 'vision' and 'inspiration' are grounded in actual behaviors in this approach. Because of this, leadership isn't raised to a mythological status. (D) The approach is developmentally focused. Posner uses his model in an effort to increase leadership behaviors in others . . . .. Posner gave me additional insights into why challenging jobs can be developmental learning opportunities. Not only do challenges motivate and stretch abilities, they also represent times when leadership is called forth and can be practiced most effectively."

Tuesday, 2:00 p.m.:    **From Research to Practice**
Convenor:                        Bray

This session was a small heterogeneous group which, because of its heterogeneity and the mixed expectations of both practitioners and researchers, was less enthusiastically received than it could have been had there been a carefully planned agenda and structure. Some participants recorded that they had heard some shrewd observations, but others, mainly practitioners, were disappointed in not having had the opportunity to express their own interests in practical applications of the research papers. One person said there was no theory, little content, and the emphasis was on procedure.

Some insightful points noted by Grabow were Bray having said: (1) AT&T did not find plateauing to be a big problem; people get enough cues before it happens to prepare themselves. (2) It is important to distinguish between performance appraisal and potential appraisal. (3) We waste a lot of time and money on career planning "because it's what we tend to do for the people who aren't promotable to try to keep them happy." "Utility isn't the answer. True managers don't believe utility analyses results—the numbers are too *big* and the input too blue sky. But we *do* need to show the impact of our programs—show that they reliably produce the effects we claim for them."

Tuesday, 2:00 p.m.:  **Dealing with Ambiguity**
Convenor:  R. Campbell

Moses talked about ambiguity, saying, "If one were dropped into a thoroughly unknown place, various behaviors could be expected. One might ask, 'How do I get back?' Another might realize, 'Even the office doesn't know where I am, so I might as well have fun.' Think about the confidence levels in these two, and the comfort level, and the ambiguity tolerance. What skills are necessary? What about interpersonal skills? How does one measure management effectiveness?"

There is a difference between complexity and ambiguity; complexity may exist in the situation and be dealt with by some, but ambiguity is different. If you understand a mission, it may be complex without being ambiguous. It is frustrating not to know goals; high-level managers may find new goals and rules in new situations. Also, what is ambiguous for one may not be for another. Ambiguity is like a slide getting out of focus. Many managers are maladaptive. Some make it through in times of flux, but can be dangerous (see Hogan's narcissism theory). In ambiguity, some use certain rules of thumb to act. Therefore, the concept is not the complexity, not the uncertainty; rather, it may be too much information, or the lack of information, or a change of rules.

Moses believes we must start to give leaders tools to cope with ambiguous situations and environments. A question arose about intervention. Possibilities include: change of job, training, organizational diagnosis; make the individual aware of self-style with feedback about ambiguity behavior. Moses uses a workshop (LGI Looking Glass Incorporated) that he has modified to fit his needs. For the second day of the simulation he has designed his own material, but he always selects an adaptive person according to his scale as an overall manager. He used checklist observations, had them identify what was ambiguous, used feedback, introduced ambiguity, used peer evaluation, and, within LGI, he had it acquire another company. He suggested that the simulation can be set up to merge with another company or to change some positions. He would now have it deal with rumors of acquisitions. He had administrators take charge of establishing roles. Moses said that in a company obsessed with data, those trying to reduce ambiguity or the necessity for decision making, attempts are made to increase competence in dealing with ambiguity. Managers look upward for problem identification, because not knowing problems causes ambiguity. It is necessary to break up things into components to solve problems. Also, in highly competitive businesses, customers must be pleased. Further, the kind of industry or organization is important in attempting to cause change. For example, in high-performing industry, rewards go to innovative teams.

R. Campbell suggested in his diary, "We know enough to make interventions; we should use them to develop our understanding as well."

When describing his assessment dimensions, Moses talked about the following: Tolerance of Uncertainty, Risk Taking, Problem Solving, SAT scores correlating with (1) Adaptives. (2) Stylized ones are competent but uncomfortable with uncertainty and risk taking. The third group is poor at problem solving, is not bright, and is (3) Unconcerned. The fourth group is (4) Overwhelmed, but they may be competent in unambiguous situations. The Stylized group is the easiest to change; they get rid of the problem and work harder. They are sensitive to feedback but don't ask for it. Stylized organizations like stylized managers. The Unconcerned group does not pay attention to feedback. Some statements made about Adaptives included: If they are sent out of the culture, they can bring back useful methods; they generally do not get rewarded at lower levels; they are successful in some environments but not in others; they are competent and of high intelligence and make good leaders. Only about 10% are Adaptives.

A question arose about how to get people to shift when huge discontinuities develop. It was said that most ambiguities exist in start-ups; for fix-it situations, stylized people are best.

R. Campbell asked the group to think about how they would go about preparing their organizations to deal with ambiguity. Organizations are becoming more and more ambiguous; it is impossible to design ambiguity out of a job. The right kinds of people must be selected for the position. Also, the educational system must be redesigned so people will fit into jobs. Ambiguity is not bad, but the educational system must be adjusted to build opportunities to learn coping strategies. In addition, we should be asking, "Did intervention make a difference in my life?"

Barber, in his diary, noted that there are two components to ambiguity: (1) being comfortable with ambiguous environments, and (2) being effective in ambiguous environments. Also, he said there is a pressing need to work on measures.

Wednesday a.m.: **Final Morning of Conference**
Convenor: K. Clark

K. Clark stated that the following topics had been noted on sign-up sheets, but groups had not met: (1) Criterion, (2) Changing culture (Latin America), (3) Existence beyond this meeting (to handle topics beyond what were discussed here), and (4) Change of viewpoint and insights.

K. Clark said there will be a published volume to reflect, with the help of the participants, what occurred at this meeting, and he would be responsible for editing. It is important to have discussed the state of the art with regard to leadership and measurement and the variety of conceptual orientations. He added that each person will be responsible for release of copyrighted materials. The abstracts will not be part of the publication. The report and this conference could turn out well enough to bear repetition.

Ulmer said, "The resources of the Center will be available to facilitate a group like this. It will serve as a data repository for common research projects and information exchange." Bentz noted there was such diversity of points of view that threads should be pulled together, and the cutting edge issues in areas of leadership needed to be emphasized. Morrow suggested subgrouping the various areas with an overview. The papers included for publication in the volume can be as long as necessary to cover the topic, but those that go beyond scope will be pruned. Sashkin advised using blue pencil heavily.

K. Clark continued, saying that the forthcoming book is intended to move the world, not merely the field, ahead. Each participant at the conference will receive a free copy.

The intent is to be sure that what has been written for this conference and discussed by the participants becomes known by a large audience. It needs excellent technical quality.

There was a lengthy discussion concerning international issues in this session. Afterwards, Noel Osborn wrote in his diary, "I think it interesting, and only partially appreciated at this conference—Bass and Morrow seem acutely aware—of the influence that *culture* has on the concept and valuation of leadership. Of course, across international boundaries, the cultural set will be broadly variant. But even in the United States, there are considerable cultural differences. For example, in an Atlanta Black ghetto, maybe a 'street smart' kind of leadership intelligence is the key predictor of effective leadership. In the kind of 'culture' or environment we are surrounded by at this conference, the hotel/restaurant business, maybe the principal leadership requirement is an overwhelming supply of extroversion, or self-control, so as not to overeat or overdrink with all that is available in such a milieu. Even our measurement methodology is affected by the cultural milieu: for example, if you ask me to predict who will be the presidential candidate in 1999 in Mexico, I might best use biodata, not personality measures to arrive at a set of possible candidates [e.g., both parents Mexican, alumnus of National U., postgraduate work abroad, son of current political figure, etc.]. In general, I think we in the United States are not sufficiently aware of cultural influence on leadership issues. In an earlier session, Bass pointed out that the word for leadership is difficult to translate into different languages. But even the concept of leadership is handled differently: In the U.S. culture, *leadership* is the ideal so we worry considerably about it and anxiously want to predict it. In other cultures, *membership* may be the ideal and its prediction may be handled quite differently."

During this session, Noel Osborn spoke briefly about cultural change and shifting demographics in the United States and the need for educated responses in this area. In the 1980s, the United States is experiencing a larger inflow of migrants than at any other time since the 19-teens (which was the largest in-migration period in our history). Today, nearly 40% of U.S. population growth is coming from *outside* the United States. In the 19-teens, most migrants came from Europe (Italy, Hungary, Russia, Britain). In recent years, they have been arriving from Mexico, the Philippines, Korea, and Cuba. Counting undocumented migrants, estimates are that as many as 1.8 million enter this country every year. This new phenomenon is being called the "Browning of America," and precious few U.S. leaders seem aware of it.

Current trends will make for new cross-cultural demands for leadership: By as early as 1990, Hispanics will replace Blacks as the largest U.S. minority; in less than 20 years in California, Hispanics will be 30% of the population, Asians 12%, and *White Anglos will be in the minority*; this year in the California schools Whites *are* in the minority in the California public school system. In the next generation, it will be as hard to imagine the United States without Hispanics and Asians as today it would be to imagine it without Italians and Irish. Osborn believes we must prepare our leaders and managers to be more effective in organizations whose workers *and* customers are largely of different cultural backgrounds than suburban middle-class Anglos.

Bass cited a chapter in his Handbook, noting the decline of literature on the management of diversity. He said the supervising of ethnics should be studied. It should be emphasized that diversity is more than a synonym for affirmative action: It is a condition of the environment that requires different actions on the part of organizational members. Much has been said about women, but there is a decline in publications about them. There is no literature about Asians except those in high-tech fields. There is almost nothing studied and written about Native Americans, except for the Eskimos.

Williamson added we must take into account that large segments of U.S. industry are being taken over, for example, Japanese manufacturing in this country. Foreign ownership of U.S. firms and multinational organizations all present different challenges to leaders. Wilson noted another aspect of this issue, namely the mix of management from one country based in a plant in another country and the question of teamwork with other cultures. Morrow said that researchers from other countries should be identified.

Moss stated we should be concerned with ethics in leadership. There is obligation to and by organizations to study the ethics of leadership in business, industry, education, and government.

Potter, in his diary, said, "Our research has done little with values and beliefs of leaders. We see the challenge posed by new combinations of people as a new challenge. I think it is an old one we mostly ignored before."

Rivera warned that, concerning Hispanics, we should draw minorities into consensus rather than allow polarization to occur. Education is essential; we must bring leaders into the mainstream. How early must we begin to focus on education and training for young people?

Sparks added that in selection and validation studies of intermixed industries and businesses, an item such as "knows when to get help" is important. Selection tests may need revamping or replacement, considering language differences; how can organizations be managed when they don't speak the same language?

Bass stated we must develop unity in diversity, rethink the leader-subordinate relationship; what will be seen as good by diverse groups can move us toward a unified concept, but diversity must be taken into account.

Bentz reminded the group about federal guidelines concerning tests and their validity with minorities, of the papers done on fairness, saying that unless ways are found to bring the polarity together, we face revolution. We are no longer a western civilization only.

Bray said, "There are conflicting intellectual theories, but in the test fairness issue, what Bentz says is a dead issue." Others in the audience disagreed and held that the social fairness issue, as it relates to minority selection, placement, and promotion, will be enduring professional and societal concern.

Concerning foreign research, the following points were made: Sashkin said that cultures that characterize issues by nationalities should be studied (see Hofstede). The need exists for application of what they learn in other cultures (see Schein). A reference was made to David Campbell's Peruvian study on risk taking. Bass said there are I.O. psychologists all around the world, and we must realize that the cross-cultural concern waxes and wanes. At some times there are less people managing abroad. There seems to be general decline of interest in that area currently. It should also be asked whether Americans select for common values and whether self-selection occurs. We must remember that socialization occurs.

Wednesday Morning:          **Closing Session**

At the closing session on Wednesday morning there was discussion on the following: (1) Multiculturalism on both ends. It was suggested that research on the Myers-Briggs Type Indicator, which is used internationally, can be a bridge; (2) Impact of American testing (technological aspects of theories); (3) Academic conceptualizers and those who put ideas into action should collaborate. Call in some line managers; ask industry what is needed. Are we keeping up with problems?; (4) Change is accelerating in society, and the application of theory is not keeping pace. What are the implications for business?; (5) There is an academic and corporate split and are, therefore, different points of view. How can we bridge the gap?; (6) The corporate side wants help especially with ethnic problems; (7) Practitioners who are not researchers do not wait on research; there is a lessening in industry of people who do both. Industry is a perfect laboratory. Those who must respond to client problems often apply good research; (8) The relevance of research must be stressed; (9) Fifty to sixty percent of research is not updated; (10) Concerning scales and selection processes, we must be careful to put organizational performance measures into context and have a better understanding of what is being measured; (11) We really have many overlapping areas of work here— understanding, prediction, and development. These different contexts for thinking about leadership bring us to very different assumptions, trade-offs, time lines, needs, compromises, and so forth; (12) How do we identify what we need for the future?; (13) How do we achieve understanding of our own differences?

Some questions remaining are: Do current methods select for values, awarenesses that will lead to success in diverse organizations? How do we structure managers to best develop their cognitive capacities for the future? Relating to business, practices and processes need interpretation; should we be looking at customer needs? How does the transformational leader get inspiration from potential customers? When the customer is the leader, does the leader become a follower? To what degree are leaders the followers of their subordinates? (From Donald Kennedy, President of Stanford, "The leader's job is to energetically mirror back to the institution how it best thinks of itself.") What sorts of studies are needed? What kind of interpretation is required? What purpose is served? Must we step out of the academic orientation? What are the real problems in leadership now? Is the research keeping up with what's happening? Are the instruments current? What is the electronic mail effect, especially a single leader with a dispersed unit? From a training point of view, what are the applicable skills? (Perhaps we should use trainers as bridgers; academic hypotheses as a model does not complete the circle, abstractions must be shown, applications taught, trained, and tested; academics are stopping too soon.)

Called upon for a final statement, Williamson said, "We must make what is found available to youth. Look ahead 20 years. What is the world going to be like? What works? Validity is not a dead issue. Confrontation is almost upon us. Is what we are doing useful to line managers, here in the United States and internationally?"

Ulmer said in his concluding remarks that the conference represents what the Center for Creative Leadership is about, that is, bridging the gap. What should we learn and do for the next century? We need to conceptualize and create productively for leadership. We have ten years to solve the problem of enormous cultural diversity. We have to get together on lifelong learning and retrain our work force. We have to redress remedial inefficiencies—they are inexcusable today; we must share information. We are mature and capable, and we must get rid of compartmentalization.

In closing, Kenneth Clark said that for a long time he was restive because there was so much folklore and so little data in the leadership field. He has worried about false beliefs about leadership and has been disturbed about the unavailability of literature. All this was the reason for the conference where "everybody was a student and everybody was a teacher and everybody knew they didn't know enough."

Concerning our orientation toward the future, he continued: Demographics should not overwhelm us. Literature in the early 1930s indicated that a dreadful change in the United States was coming because of immigration. Instead, today we have a post-Wilkie vision of "One world." We live with problems, and a healthy society solves problems. Challenges must be faced, and we are up to it. People don't change much, but behaviors can change. Environments change. Our view of ourselves tends to be unchanging. Instead we should be studying change and understanding other people's internal beliefs.

Some diary comments and quotations about the final session and the conference include: "On the last day the people from industry appeared to be setting themselves apart; they probably sat outside the circle, because they felt outside the circle. Roles should be clarified. The role of those from industry is to tell the academics where they [the academics] are off-base and where ideas are practical. Of course, we need to realize that the quid pro quo is that we consciously pay attention to their agenda . . . [give me something to use when I get back home]."

"I would like to see more on the relationship between pathology or weak ego functioning and leadership, and I would also like to see more on why good people do not step forward to lead. Related to this is the question of the process that makes for leaders. Do we have the right processes to get the best people or do the 'best and the brightest' hang back? It would be fascinating to poll the motivation of our leaders. What do they get out of being there and what made them decide to put themselves forward?"

"I think a good comprehensive integration of the field so we can see who is calling the same process by different names would help a lot."

"Real progress in this field can come from integration of the different methodologies and beliefs represented here: (1) The quantitative data from traditional industrial psychologists versus the more qualitative data from more sociologically oriented folks. (2) The bias toward selection versus development; nature versus nurture. (3) The different management levels and different ends of the effectiveness continuum we're studying."

"Methodology discussions interested me. For example, Bentz' stress on not oversimplifying complex problems was good. Sparks' example of the criterion problem where grievances assumed to be bad were actually an indicator of something good. I have always been interested in the difference between what we name things and what they actually signify. Wilson was helpful here when he said we need to hypothesize, test, and refine. I think we need a more explicit relationship with industry where they are the laboratory for ideas, and we both look at them rigorously and look at papers to see which described equal-partners academic-applied models."

"The topic [leadership] is absolutely crucial—the future of America literally depends on it. So, Bravo!"

"I hadn't realized how, in preparing for the Conference, I had forgotten to see leadership in a lifelong, societywide framework."

"As I look back, the Conference clearly was a catalyst for important new understandings and accomplished more than we rationally could have expected. It set the foundation, and defined the issues more clearly. It brought us together in a way that facilitated interaction. And it has never happened before. A wonderful first!"

## Extended Remarks

The format of the conference and the opportunity to write diaries encouraged some participants to write short essays or long thoughts on topics that intrigued them. Some of these have been selected for recording here, to give an added flavor to the interchange of opinions that the report of the proceedings provides. The notes were all written independently and have not been assembled in any special order, save to make sure that Morrow's essay concludes the Proceedings section, and this book.

**Spence:** If the study of leadership is viewed in the light of the full range of research on abilities and human development, then leadership may be considered as a subset of achievement-oriented behavior, which has been studied intensively. Achievement motivation is related to two sets of characteristics: (1) self-esteem and efficacy, and (2) personal agency—somewhat related to dominance. The latter set can have a "dark side," but the dark side can be mitigated by a sense of concern for others.

**Steckler:** My own belief is that valuable products are created primarily out of personal passion and are done because it excited the individual doing it; collective ends can be agreed upon and achieved when personal goals and organizational goals overlap, and people get some personal needs met through organized collective action.

**Morrow:** Cognitive complexity and tacit knowledge were discussed by Hal Hendrick and Richard Wagner respectively. Cognitive complexity was dismissed by many as old hat (as the authoritarian personality revisited, but today with some new formulations), while tacit knowledge was received more favorably as an original approach. This surprised me. Isn't all of experiential learning, which has been an intrinsic part of business education, training, and development for perhaps 20 years or more, based on the premise that classroom smarts is not the same thing as being able to apply successfully concepts in the real world? Haven't we used case studies in business education to enhance students' abilities to be "street smart"?

The work on tacit knowledge, albeit in its infancy, also appears to be based on a number of simplifications. A major point was made by Wagner of the distinction between performance in school and performance in the work world and the nature of academic versus practical problems, but these distinctions seemed too forced and too clean. For example, not all academic problems are well-defined. Is a college student's problem of how to write a sound term paper and get it in on time much different from a manager's problem of how to write and submit a persuasive and timely report? I think not. Likewise, are all practical problems really ill-defined? Isn't much of what takes place in organizations indeed well defined by procedures, guidelines, policies, rules, schedules, budgetary constraints, past practices, and so forth? On the other hand, I also think it may be misguided to establish the norms for judging tacit knowledge by establishing experts' "rules of thumb." If we accept the notion that we are in an area of turbulent change and intense environmental complexity, the only useful rule of thumb for a street smart manager may be not to trust any rules of thumb at all!

**Osborn, D.**: During these discussions I began to recognize similar threads of thought appearing over and over again. That is, that strategic use of differences is essential to effective leadership, be it "inter"personal differences or "intra"personal differences.

It means that in the complex range of abilities, personality characteristics, and types of intelligence that one possesses, an effective leader is able to use strategically those qualities that are appropriate to the situation and the people involved (i.e., Myers-Briggs integration, or Sternberg's "Mental Management").

At the same time, one will manifest external responses in a given situation—be it decision-making style, leadership style, feedback approach, or problem-solving style—which also must be appropriate to the situation and people involved.

In order to have this range of internal and external flexibility, a leader needs tremendous inner and outer awareness, and development of self. If the awareness or self-development is not there, then we find CCL's "derailment" syndrome or Hogan's shallow "Charismatics." When those qualities do exist, then we find Bass' Transformational Leaders or Gough's higher-level Alpha, Beta, Gamma, or Delta leaders.

**Morrow**: During our discussions, I was continuously troubled by a feeling that all or most of our work on leadership is culturally specific and ethnocentric. I would like to believe that at the very least our theoretical concepts have some application and relevance in other western countries, but I wonder if perhaps too much of our work is exclusively USA-bound. Future conferences sponsored by the Center for Creative Leadership should make a special effort to have a more international focus.

**Arnold**: We must pay attention to effectiveness, over and above success, because definition of success may vary depending on company bottom line, and is thus too value-laden a criterion.

**Steckler**: The discussions I found most effective were laying out basic ground rules: mapping out areas of agreement, differences of opinion, deciding which issues were most central, looking at relationships between concepts, finding areas of overlapping passion. Asking, could collaboration follow? (As Tom Sergiovanni said to me as we were leaving the power session: "Even if all we did was hash out some definitions, we usually do that alone in our offices and it felt good to do that with 15 others who are interested in similar questions.")

**Morrow**: I conclude that the leadership field is at an exciting and frustrating point of development. We appear to be peeling a very complex onion, with each layer revealing yet another facet of leadership without necessarily enhancing our grasp of the phenomenon. Some of these layers seem to capture the imagination of the people in the field and serve as a rallying point. Clearly, the concept of transformational leadership has this quality of allure and popularity. At times, however, I fear that we keep applying new terms to the same old concepts. For example, putting all the jargon aside for the moment, isn't transactional leadership essentially the same thing as management, and is transformational leadership really any different from leadership per se?

**Hofmann**: All of the analyses that have been presented have a weakness because they have not studied the negative cases. What are leaders like who do not follow the usual pattern? What are those persons like, and what are their accomplishments? What can we say about those who have the measured qualities of leaders, but who have not sought or attained leadership status?

The nature of the conference directed attention to leadership with a focus on new research. Many participants viewed the problem in a much broader perspective, as can be discovered by reading the report of the proceedings. Issues of the development of successful leadership in the next generations troubled many persons. We see fewer members of the baby-boom generation interested in leadership than their predecessors. They are less interested in service to society, more interested in making money. Alexander Astin's annual survey of freshmen attitudes and aspirations is discouraging. Howard and Bray's findings on reduced motivation for advancement is alarming. At what age do we attack the problem? And how?

**Steckler:** We have a problem. There is a moral imperative to create knowledge about the training and education of children in leadership and more generally for collective action to address problems of our society.

Where do we start? What training should we be providing for parents? What programs should we develop for primary schools, secondary schools, colleges? If we cannot even manage to teach all of our public school students to read, how can we be effective in leadership development? How much of this problem is related to problems of reduced productivity in industry, and lowered competitiveness on the worldwide scene?

These questions are as critical to our survival as a nation dedicated to freedom as is national military preparedness. Where shall we begin, what resources must we marshal, what groups must we enlist to aid in the task? These are the next questions we must address, just as we plan expanded research programs to build on today's newly acquired knowledge.

**Morrow:** I couldn't help but take note of the fact that this conference on leadership took place in San Antonio, the location of one of the most heroic acts in U.S. history—the defense of the Alamo. I'm troubled by the fact that no one, including myself, speaks of qualities such as the willingness to work hard, self-sacrifice, dedication, personal integrity, optimism—and yes, perhaps even heroism—when we write about and talk about leadership. Without these qualities, where will our leaders be taking us? The closest we came to these notions is Barry Posner's dimension of "Modeling the Way," for which he should be commended. One aspect of "modeling the way" seems to entail the leader's willingness to take a personal risk. This goes beyond Burns' transformational leadership quality of being able to get subordinates to transcend their self-interest (what about the leader's being able to transcend his/her own self-interest?), and Sashkin's transformational leadership quality of creating risk opportunities for others.

Continuing with the Alamo metaphor, when it became obvious that General Santa Anna's army was going to vanquish the Alamo, legend has it that William Travis drew his fateful line of commitment in the dirt and said, "Those prepared to give their lives in freedom's cause, come over to me." In other words, he was already over the line and serving as a role model and inspiration. Are there any leaders out there today who demonstrate qualities of self-sacrifice and heroism? How are these qualities manifest in large, bureaucratic organizations and in smaller, entrepreneurial organizations? Who are our leadership heroes and what can we learn from them of relevance to today's organizations? How do we inspire people, or create vision, if the corporate or bureaucratic goals are rather mundane—such as to capture another 5% of market share, or to improve the efficiency of a work team or a military squadron by x%? I don't know the answers, but when it comes to future leadership research and conferences, let's all try to "Remember the Alamo!"

Pat Alexander
Center for Creative Leadership
5000 Laurinda Drive
Post Office Box P-1
Greensboro, NC 27402
919-288-7210

Val Arnold
Personnel Decisions, Inc.
2000 Plaza VII Tower
45 South 7th Street
Minneapolis, MN 55402-1608
612-339-0927

Herbert F. Barber
Department of Command,
    Leadership and Management
U.S. Army War College
Carlisle Barracks, PA 17013
717-245-4014

Bernard M. Bass
Center for Leadership Studies and
    School of Management
State University of New York at
    Binghamton
Binghamton, NY 13901
607-777-4028

V. Jon Bentz
201 Willow Road
Elmhurst, IL 60126
312-833-7149

Billy Bowen
Vice President
Training & Development
USAA Building
9800 Fredericksburg Road
San Antonio, TX 78288
512-498-1654

Douglas W. Bray
Development Dimensions
    International
21 Knoll Road
Tenafly, NJ 07670
201-894-5289

Kerry Bunker
Center for Creative Leadership
5000 Laurinda Drive
Post Office Box P-1
Greensboro, NC 27402
919-288-7210

David P. Campbell
Center for Creative Leadership
Post Office Box 1559
Colorado Springs, CO 80901
719-633-3891

Richard Campbell
New York University
Department of Psychology
6 Washington Place
New York, NY 10003
212-998-7811

Kenneth E. Clark
Center for Creative Leadership
5000 Laurinda Drive
Post Office Box P-1
Greensboro, NC 27402
919-288-7210

Miriam B. Clark
Center for Creative Leadership
5000 Laurinda Drive
Post Office Box P-1
Greensboro, NC 27402
919-288-7210

William H. Clover
Director of Executive Education
  and Leadership Development
TRW, Inc.
Cleveland, OH 44124
216-291-7000

Alan Colquitt
Personnel Research Consultant
Procter & Gamble
2 Procter & Gamble Plaza
Cincinnati, OH 45202
513-983-5798

Thomas Cronin
1425 La Mesa Street
Colorado Springs, CO 80904
719-475-1900

David L. DeVries
Executive Vice President
Center for Creative Leadership
5000 Laurinda Drive
Post Office Box P-1
Greensboro, NC 27402
919-288-7210

John R. Dilworth
President
The Psychological Corporation
555 Academic Court
San Antonio, TX 78204-2498
512-270-0350

Tracy Gibbons
Organization Development
  Consultant
Digital Equipment Corp.
2352 Main Street
Concord, MA 01742-3880
508-496-3016

Harrison G. Gough
Department of Psychology
University of California, Berkeley
Berkeley, CA 94720
415-642-5050

Karen Grabow
Director, Personnel Planning
  Training and Development
Target Stores
Post Office Box 1392
Minneapolis, MN 55440-1392
612-370-5723

Peter Gratzinger
Human Factors Advanced
  Technology Group
4340 Redwood Highway, Suite 26
San Rafael, CA 94903
415-492-9190

Keith Halperin
Personnel Decisions, Inc.
2000 Plaza VII Tower
45 South 7th Street
Minneapolis, MN 55402-1608
612-339-0927

Garry Hannah
Manager, HR Development
Pillsbury
200 South Sixth Street
Minneapolis, MN 55402
612-330-4197

R. Ray Hawkins
Industrial Psychologist
Eli Lilly & Co.
Lilly Corporate Center
Indianapolis, IN  46285
317-276-3872

Ray Hedberg
AVP, Personnel
Norfolk-Southern Corp.
185 Spring Street S.E.
Atlanta, GA 30303
404-529-2300

Hal W. Hendrick
Dean, College of Systems Science
University of Denver
University Park
Denver, CO 80208
303-871-3619

Rich Hofmann
Department of Educational Leadership
Miami University
350 McGuffey Hall
Oxford, OH 45056
513-529-6640

Robert Hogan
Tulsa Psychiatric Center
University of Tulsa
1620 12th Street
Tulsa, OK  74120
918-584-5992

Edwin P. Hollander
CUNY I/O Psychology
Doctoral Program
Baruch College and University
  Graduate Center
Box 512
17 Lexington Avenue
New York, NY 10010
212-725-3201

Eileene Homan
Harcourt Brace Jovanovich, Inc.
6277 Sea Harbor Drive
Orlando, FL 32887

Ann Howard
Leadership Research Institute
21 Knoll Road
Tenafly, NJ 07670
201-894-5289

Martha Hughes
Center for Creative Leadership
5000 Laurinda Drive
Post Office Box P-1
Greensboro, NC 27402
919-288-7210

T. Owen Jacobs
Chief, Executive Development
  Research Group
U.S. Army Research Institute
(PERI-RO)
5001 Eisenhower Avenue
Alexandria, VA 22333-5600
202-274-9045

Nancy Jagmin
Project Director
HBJ Leadership Group
The Psychological Corporation
555 Academic Court
San Antonio, TX 78204-2498
512-270-0450

Frances A. Karnes
Department of Special Education
  and Director, Center for Gifted
  Studies
University of Southern Mississippi
Southern Station Box 1
Hattiesburg, MS 39401
601-266-7101

John M. Keene
Director, Applied Research
The Psychological Corporation
555 Academic Court
San Antonio, TX 78204
512-270-0450

Patricia Knoff
Director, HR Development
Pillsbury
200 South Sixth Street
Minneapolis, MN 55402
612-330-7218

Michael M. Lombardo
Center for Creative Leadership
5000 Laurinda Drive
Post Office Box P-1
Greensboro, NC 27402
919-288-7210

Bernard Lubin
Department of Psychology
University of Missouri at Kansas
  City
Kansas City, MO 64110
816-276-1072

Jan Margolis
Vice President, Human Resources
Banker's Trust Company
280 Park Avenue 20 West
New York, NY 10015
212-850-4779

James McBride
Director, Personnel and Career
  Assessment Group
The Psychological Corporation
1250 Sixth Avenue
San Diego, CA 92101
619-699-6812

Cynthia D. McCauley
Center for Creative Leadership
5000 Laurinda Drive
Post Office Box P-1
Greensboro, NC 27402
919-288-7210

Mary H. McCaulley
Center for Applications of
  Psychological Type
2720 N.W. 6th Street
Gainesville, FL 32609
904-375-0160

Angela McDermott
Procter & Gamble
2 Procter & Gamble Plaza
Cincinnati, OH 45202
513-983-5798

Terry Mitchell
The Psychological Corporation
555 Academic Court
San Antonio, TX 78204-2498
512-270-0450

Ira J. Morrow
The Lubin Graduate School
  of Business
Pace University
1 Pace Plaza
New York, NY 10038-1502
212-488-1846

Joseph L. Moses
Manager of Research
AT&T
Room 3225
550 Madison Avenue
New York, NY 10022
212-605-7624

Jerome Moss, Jr.
University of Minnesota
425 Vocational and
  Technical Building
1954 Buford Avenue
St. Paul, MN 55108
612-624-0718

Robert Most
Vice President for Research
  and Development
Consulting Psychologists Press,
  Inc.
577 College Avenue
Post Office Box 60070
Palo Alto, CA 94306
415-852-1444

Diana B. Osborn
TEAM
14206 Arbor Oak
San Antonio, TX 78249
512-493-1452

T. Noel Osborn
TEAM
14206 Arbor Oak
San Antonio, TX 78249
512-493-1452

Randy Overton
Research Department
State Farm Insurance Co.
1 State Farm Plaza
Bloomington, IL 61710
309-766-3659

Margery Pabst
Vice President
HBJ Leadership Group
780 Summit Avenue
St. Paul, MN 55105
612-290-0205

Barry Z. Posner
Leavey School of Business
  and Administration
Santa Clara University
Santa Clara, CA 95053
408-554-4500

Rick Poss
National Computer Systems
11000 Prairie Lakes Drive
Eden Prairie, MN 55344
612-829-3055

Earl H. Potter III
Department of Economics and
  Management
U.S. Coast Guard Academy
New London, CT 06320-4195
203-444-8334

Antonio T. Rivera
Executive Director, USAA
Human Resources Support
USAA Building
San Antonio, TX 78288
512-498-1446

William E. Rosenbach
Department of Management
Gettysburg College
Box 395
Gettysburg, PA 17325
717-337-6648

Marian N. Ruderman
Center for Creative Leadership
5000 Laurinda Drive
Post Office Box P-1
Greensboro, NC 27402
919-288-7210

Marshall Sashkin
U.S. Department of Education
Office of the Assistant Secretary
   for Educational Research and
   Development
Washington, DC 20208-5644
202-357-6120

Leonard Sayles
Center for Creative Leadership
Post Office Box P-1
Greensboro, NC 27402
919-288-7210

Thomas J. Sergiovanni
Trinity College
c/o The Psychological Corporation
555 Academic Court
San Antonio, TX 78204-2498
512-270-0450

Frank Shipper
College of Business
Arizona State University
Tempe, AZ 85287
602-965-9011

Jim Slaughter
National Computer Systems, Inc.
PAS Division
5605 Green Circle Drive
Minnetonka, MN 55343
612-933-2800

Greg Spalding
State Farm Insurance Co.
1 State Farm Plaza
Bloomington, IL 61710
309-766-3453

C. Paul Sparks
Serendipity Unlimited
Post Office Box 810024
Houston, TX 77281
713-774-1668

Janet Spence
Department of Psychology
University of Texas
Meezes Hall #330
Austin, TX 78712-7789
512-471-4308

Nicole A. Steckler
2482 N.W. Marshall
Portland, OR 97210
206-253-6051

Robert J. Sternberg
Yale University
Department of Psychology
Post Office Box 11A, Yale
   Station
New Haven, CT 06520-7447
203-432-4633

Mostafa Torki
Department of Psychology
Post Office Box 23558
Kuwait University
Kuwait 13097

Doug Tripp
National Computer Systems,
   Inc.
PAS Division
5605 Green Circle Drive
Minnetonka, MN 55343
612-933-2800

Walter F. Ulmer
President
Center for Creative Leadership
5000 Laurinda Drive
Post Office Box P-1
Greensboro, NC 27402
919-288-7210

Anna Marie Valerio
NYNEX Corporation
1113 Westchester Avenue
White Plains, NY 10604-3510
914-644-6725

Ellen Van Velsor
Center for Creative Leadership
5000 Laurinda Drive
Post Office Box P-1
Greensboro, NC 27402
919-288-7210

Michael Vescuso
President, HBJ Leadership Group
Union Square
10101 Reunion Place
Suite 200
San Antonio, TX 78216
512-344-0800

John H. Vice
Manager, Management
   Development
Eli Lilly & Co.
Lilly Corporate Center
Indianapolis, IN 46285
317-276-2028

Richard K. Wagner
Department of Psychology
Florida State University
Tallahassee, FL 32306
904-644-1033

Thomas A. Williamson
Director of HBJ/HRW Elementary
   Publishing Group
Harcourt Brace Jovanovich, Inc.
6277 Sea Harbor Drive
Orlando, FL 32887
407-345-3636

Clark L. Wilson
Clark Wilson Publishing Company
Box 471-129 Woodridge Drive
New Canaan, CT 06840-0471
800-537-7249

Francis J. Yammarino
Center for Leadership Studies and
   School of Management
State University of New York at
   Binghamton
Binghamton, NY 13901
607-777-3007

Gary Yukl
Management Department
School of Business
State University of New York at
   Albany
1400 Washington Avenue
Albany, NY 12222
518-442-4932

Robert A. Zachary
Director, Psychological Measurement
The Psychological Corporation
555 Academic Court
San Antonio, TX 78204-2498
512-270-0450

The following corporations provided financial assistance for the San Antonio Conference on Psychological Measures and Leadership:

Bankers Trust Company

Eli Lilly and Company

National Computer Systems, Inc.

Norfolk Southern Corporation

Pillsbury Co.

Proctor & Gamble Co.

State Farm Mutual Automobile
   Insurance Co.

TRW, Inc.

USAA

# Kenneth E. Clark

Kenneth E. Clark, Smith Richardson Senior Scientist at the Center for Creative Leadership, Greensboro, North Carolina, has served the Center as a member and chairman of the Board of Governors and President from 1981 to 1985. He was a faculty member at Minnesota for 20 years, and for 20 years was an Arts College dean, first at the University of Colorado, then at the University of Rochester. During World War II he served in the Navy's enlisted classification program as a commissioned officer, after civilian service with the Army Air Forces and the Army.

Earning a PhD degree in Psychology from Ohio State University in 1940, he joined the faculty in psychology at the University of Minnesota, serving as chairman from 1957 to 1960, and briefly as Associate Dean of the Graduate School. He studied the vocational interests of nonprofessional men and the educational backgrounds and careers of American psychologists. At Minnesota he won a collegewide award for outstanding teaching and four awards for contributions to student life.

He was Dean of the College of Arts and Science both at the University of Colorado, 1961–1963, and the University of Rochester, 1963–1980. He was a member of the President's National Medal of Science Committee, president of the American Board of Examiners in Professional Psychology, president of the American Psychological Foundation, member of the Army Science Board, chairman of the Association for the Advancement of Psychology, and chairman of the American Conference of Academic Deans. He authored *America's Psychologists* and *The Vocational Interests of Nonprofessional Men*; coauthored *The Graduate Student as Teacher*; and edited ten volume years of the *Journal of Applied Psychology*.

He chaired several boards of the American Psychological Association: Education and Training, Policy and Planning, Scientific Affairs, Council of Editors, and Publications and Communications. Also, he chaired a blue-ribbon committee on Professional and Scientific Aims of Psychology, the advisory panel on Scientific Information Exchange in Psychology, and cochaired the Commission on Organization of APA. He has been a consultant to the White House, the Office of Science and Technology, the Central Intelligence Agency, the Secret Service, the National Science Foundation, the National Institutes of Health, the Veterans Administration, the Navy, and the Army.

His awards include the Ohio State University's Centennial Achievement Award, membership in Phi Beta Kappa, the American Personnel and Guidance Association award for research excellence, and the E. K. Strong, Jr., Gold Medal. He also received the Gold Medal Award of the American Psychological Foundation, in August 1986, for a lifetime of exceptional contribution to psychological service in psychology.

# Miriam B. Clark

Miriam B. Clark was educated (1938–1940 and 1955–1960) at the University of Rochester, Rochester, New York. She earned a B.S. degree and election to Phi Beta Kappa and did graduate work in English and Education.

From 1964 to 1981, she served first as a Technical Associate, then Assistant to the Dean, then Assistant Dean and then Associate Dean in the College of Arts and Science, programs for undergraduates and all prog...

Upon retirement in 1981, she became a consultant for leaders... Center for Creative Leadership in Greensboro, North Carolina.

She has edited, with associates, a 1985 and a 1987 edition of *Leadership Ed... A Source Book*, a resource guide for those planning programs and teaching course... leadership in higher education. A 1989 edition is in process. She published, with Nowlis and Clark, *The Graduate Student as Teacher* in 1968. She also wrote the proceedings of a meeting of educators at the Center for Creative Leadership titled *Leadership Education Conference 1987* and is coeditor with Kenneth E. Clark of *Measures of Leadership*.

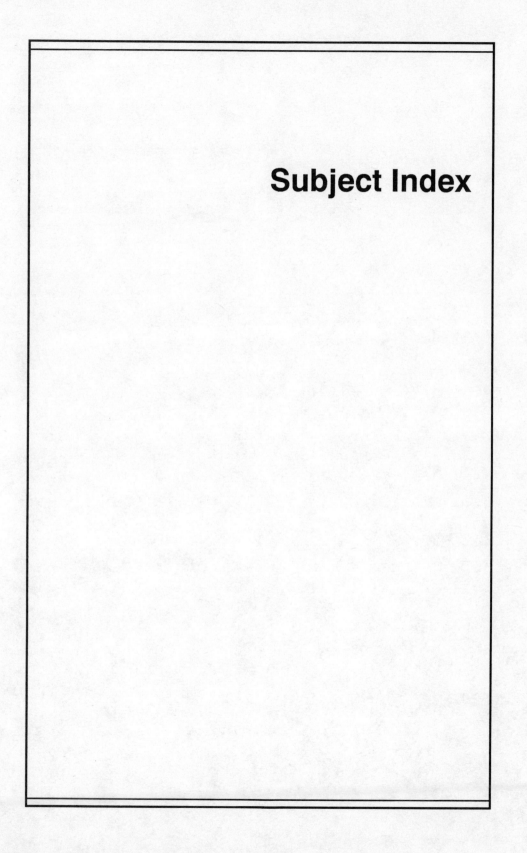

# Subject Index

# Subject Index

## A

Ability tests, 356
Absenteeism, 21
Accident rates, 21
Action plans, 72–75
Adaptation: during apprenticeship, 466, 470, 478; and task cycles, 189, 192
Administration, 297–98
Advancement, 64, 74–75; factors influencing, 21. *See also* Promotion(s)
Advertising, 328
Aging, 122–23
Air Force Academy, 8, 44, 171–84
Air Force maintenance supervisors, 220
Albright, Robert R., II, 457–58, 465–80
Altruism, 413
Alutto, J.A., 155, 168
Ambiguity, 43; and coping styles, 329–35; definition of, 328f; and managerial performance, 26, 51, 75, 327–36; patterning of, 283; role, 86; and top-level leadership, 277, 278–79, 282f
Ambiguity Research Study, 328–36
American Constitution, 12
American Telephone and Telegraph (AT&T). *See* AT&T (American Telephone and Telegraph)
ANOVA (Analysis of Variance), 368–78 *passim*
Anxiety, 75
Apprenticeship, 457–58, 465–79
Army, U.S., 8, 17, 61–62, 153; officers, and charisma, 154; Professional Development of Officers Study (PDOS), 290–92; Research Institute, 284, 286–94, 442; Reserve, 236; Senior Executive Service, 286; War College, 341, 441–43. *See also* Military leadership
Arrogance, 182
Assertiveness, 305
Assessment Center Technology, 134
Assurance, 139
AT&T (American Telephone and Telegraph): Advanced Management Potential Assessment (AMPA), 51, 331–35, 522, 527; and the Ambiguity Research Study, 328–36; divestiture of, 51, 278, 328, 521
Attentiveness, 307, 311
Austin, N., 4
Australia, 38, 208; Australian Police College, 394
Authoritarianism, 124

Authority, 76, 87; and charisma, 172; and control, 442; and the dominance scale, 51; Hollander and Offermann on, 18–19. *See also* Power
Autocratic leaders, 15, 86, 88–89
Autonomy, 64

## B

Baker, Paul C., 104
Banking, managers in, 63, 148, 199–203; and ambiguity, 328
Barber, Herbert F., 50, 341, 441–54
Barnes, V., 467–68, 473
Barr, L., 411f
Barr, N., 411f
Bass, Bernard, 5–7, 32–38 *passim*, 172, 188, 300; Multifactor Leadership Questionnaire (MLQ), 301; on studies of intelligence and leadership, 460; on transformational and transactional leaders, distinction between, 301
—and Yammarino, 32, 38, 44, 73–74, 88f, 147; on modeling and charisma, 173; and the Multifactor Officer Questionnaire, 63; and the paradigm shift in how leadership is conceptualized, 298, 315
Behavior, leadership: in ambiguous environments, 327–36; and behavioral cues, 511–19; future and past, 327, 457; relationship-centered, 298–99; "socio-emotional relationship," in Bales, 298–99
Belief(s): systems, 282, 306; and transformational leadership, 301ff, 306–7. *See also* Values
Bell Communications Research, 526
Bennis, W.G., 4, 88; Active vs. Reactive distinction in, 303; on exceptional executives, 307ff, 311; on leaders as "social architects," 314; and the paradigm shift in how leadership is conceptualized, 298, 315
Bentz, V.J., 8, 36–37, 60, 72–73, 102, 131–43, 344, 347
Bias, 47, 64, 131, 212; social desirability response, 209
Blake, R.R., 4, 299
Blanchard, K.H., 4, 103, 172, 314
Blaylock, B.K., 409, 410
Bolles, R.C., 189
Booth, Daniel, 196
"Bootstrapping," 31
Bottom-line leadership, 187, 315

Bray, Douglas, 6, 8, 36f, 39, 113–30; on opportunities for growth, 74; on personality differences, 53f; on promotion and success, 61, 72–73, 466, 522, 531, 533

Briggs, Katharine Cook, 383

British intelligence, 348

Brunel Institute of Social Studies, 284–86

Bruner, Jerome, 284

Bureaucracy, 38, 88

Burke, W. Warner, 6, 38, 45, 278, 297–325

Burnham, D.H., 300, 305–20

Burns, James M., 4, 38, 88, 297, 355; on transactional and transformational leadership, 154–55, 172, 206, 300f; and the paradigm shift in how leadership is conceptualized, 298

# C

Campbell, David, 8, 45–46, 220, 249–74, 466, 478. See also Strong-Campbell Interest Inventory (measure)

Campbell, J.P., 4, 104, 344f

Campbell, Richard, 76

Canada, 391, 394, 412

Carbonell, J.L., 364, 368

Card-sorting tasks, 284, 285

Career Assessment Inventory, 250

Carrier, H., 233

Carson, G.L., 364

Carter, Jimmy, 459

Cattell, R.B., 469, 564. See also Cattell's 16PF Form A (measure)

Causal maps, 282, 283, 293

Cause-and-effect relations, 283

Cayer, Maurice, 233–34

Ceci, S.J., 512

Center for Applications of Psychological Type (CAPT), 384–85, 388, 391, 394, 401

Center for Creative Leadership (CCL), 7f, 341, 388, 390f, 401, 411, 450, 522; data on extraversion, 407; Leadership Development Program (LDP), 391, 497–99

Center for Gifted Studies, Leadership Studies Program at, 509, 563–64, 565

CEOs (chief executive officers), 20, 32, 199–200, 497; exceptional, Bennis on, 307; hospital, turnover among, 347, 352; as thinking types, predominance of, 408; and SBU heads, comparison of, 287

Chain of command, 287–88

Chaining, 39, 190

Change: agents, 410; perception of self –, 173; and successful leadership, 511

Charisma, 44; and authority, 172, 300; dark side of, 50–51, 88f, 339–40, 343–54; House on, 298; and modeling, Bass on, 173; and transformational leadership, 88, 90, 153ff, 173; Weber on, 300. See also Charismatic leadership

Charismatic leadership: and Alphas, as defined in CPI, 358f; in crisis situations, 282; power need of, 300. See also Charisma

Chauvin, J.C., 564

Child abuse, 183

Childhood, developmental theories, 183

Churchill, Winston, 33, 49

Clark, Carol, 397

Cloud, Barbara, 397

Clover, William H., 39–40, 44, 73, 148, 171–84

Coaching, 153, 190

Coast Guard Academy, U.S., 8, 457, 466–79

Cognitive complexity, 507, 511–19; required for very top leaders, 284, 292–94

Cognitive learning paradigm, 189

Cognitive maps, 287, 294, 467

Cognitive sciences, 284

Cohen, Dennis, 200

Coherence, scale, 308

College students, 13, 41, 277, 457, 466–79, 493; grades earned by, prediction of, 58–59; in MBTI studies, 397ff, 407; rated by peers as leaders, 36, 52, 361–69 passim, 373

Colquitt, Alan, 39

Communications leadership, 187

Competence, 87–88

Competition, 65, 71, 73; global, 290, 327

Competitive leadership syndrome, 141

Complexity, and higher organizational roles, 277, 313; patterning of, 282, 283; resolution of, 287; stratification of organizations in terms of, 306

Complexity, cognitive, 507, 511–19; required for very top leaders, 284, 292–94

Computer services, 328

Concept-formation tasks, 284

Confidence, 39, 153, 154

Congressional Medal of Honor, 30 *

Consensus building, 36, 282, 287

Consideration, of employees and their feelings, 299

Consistency, 307

Constitution, U.S., 12

Consulting Psychologists Press, 383

Context, 71, 102, 131–43

Contingency models, 85–86

Contingency theories, 172

Cooke, R.A., 39, 54, 220, 239–48

Coping styles, and performance as managers, 329–35

Cornell County Cooperative Extension Associations, 235

Correlation coefficient, 66; interpretation of, between tests and criterion, 58–59

Cowley, W.H., 85

Cranfield School of Management, 388

Creativity, 12, 20, 488, 529, 563; adaptive managers and, 333f; factor, in the Campbell Work Orientations Survey, 249f; and intellectual styles, 54; and intuition, 408; and transformational leadership, 302

Criminals, 245

Criterion problem, 32, 58, 65f, 131, 134–36

Cronbach alpha, 310

Customer/client demands, 313

# D

Dalton, G.W., 466

Danforth Associates, 394

Dansereau, F., 155, 168

Deal, T.E., 88

Decision discretion, 36, 277, 281–82, 283, 284–86

Decision making, 12, 48, 55, 134, 333, 514, 564; analytical, 6; and the dominance scale, 51; and intelligence, 459; and MBTI measures, 340, 407f, 409–10, 413ff; military leaders and, 293, 408; model, in Vroom and Yetton, 85–86; and promotions, 33, 525; stress and, 26; and risk taking, 409–10; unshared, 378. *See also* Decision discretion

Decisiveness, 139, 333

Defense, U.S. Department of, 466

Democratic leadership, 12–14

Dependency, 85

Dermer, J., 516

Destiny, sense of, 303

Devanna, M.A., 173

Dienesch, R.M., 89

Dietl, J.A., 385

Diplomacy, 289, 346

Disciplinary threats, 152

Doering, R.D., 410

Dunnette, M.D., 4, 104

Durkheim, E., 308

# E

Early Identification of Management Potential (EIMP), 101, 103–12

Eastern Europe, 290

Eastman Kodak Company, 33

Eber, H.W., 469

Edison, Thomas, 487

Education, 11–15, 328, 391, 393–94, 487, 547; and academic problems, 493–94; at the Coast Guard Academy, 466–67; and creativity, 488; as a factor in the selection process, 57; and intellectual styles, 54, 488–90, 491; levels of, in the CPA, 285; levels, and measures of cognitive complexity, 516

Educational Testing Service, 383

Effectance, question of, 301, 309

Effectiveness, leader, 64; data about, gathering of, 18, 26; definition of, 65; personality dimensions of, 50–51, 62; and power, 91; and power sharing, 85; "soft" criteria of, 29, 235–36; traits of, 84

Effectiveness, managerial, 101, 210–13; research on, and behavior concepts, 223–25. *See also* Managerial Practices Survey (measure)

Ego integration, 52

Einstein, Albert, 487

Elections, 11; and "the criterion problem," 32; and followers and leaders, identification between, 87; presidential, 35

Elementary schools, 234–35, 254

Engineers, 158, 165

England, 208, 387f, 412

Envisioning/Anticipating, 62

Equal Employment Opportunity (EEO) requirements, 109

Equality, principle of, 12, 15

Erikson, Erik, 183

Error, 64

Espionage, 348–49

Ethics, 91, 378

Ethnic differences, 14, 109

Etzioni, A., 172

Evans, L.N., 85

Evans, M.G., 516

Evered, R.D., 409f

Excellence, 310; ideas of, 88; culture, organizational, 314–15

Executive, use of the term, 90

*Executive Educator*, 394

Exxon Corporation, Sparks' study at, 6, 8, 19, 36–37, 60–61, 72–73, 101, 103–12, 344

# F

Factor analysis, 26

Failure, 71; by elected leaders, 87; and leadership development, 41; responsibility for, 87

Family life, 54f. *See also* Life themes

Fange, Erich von, 394

Farragut, David, 103

Fazzini, Dan, 339–40, 343–54

Feedback, 307, 311, 330, 410, 512, 561; and good management, 528. *See also* BENCHMARKS (measure)

Fiedler, F.E., 4, 84, 91, 172, 467f; LPC model of, 85–86, 299f, 515–16

Fleishman, E.A., 4

Fleiss, J.L., 232

Foa, U.G., 516

Folk concepts, definition of, 356

Followers, 11–15, 55, 69, 83–91; distrust of, 378; empowerment of, 89, 308. *See also* Power; individual attention to, 88; relations with, study of, 19; and subordinates, contrast between, 34

Foremen, 299, 305

Fortune 500 companies, 522

Frames of reference, 287, 293. *See also* Time frames

Frazier-Koontz, Peter J., 388
Freedom, 12f, 15
Freud, Sigmund, 49, 85
Friend, R., 469
Fryer, Douglas, 104
Fulmer, R.M., 305

# G

Gagne, R.M., 190
Gains, 91
Galton, F., 84
Gandhi, M., 33, 300, 339
Garcia, J.E., 84
Garden, A.M., 410
Gardner, John, 4, 34, 36, 179
Gardner, W.L., 234
Gast, I.F., 512
Gaster, W.D., 385
Gender, 109f, 171, 355, 391; and career development, 524, 529f; and coping styles, 333; as a factor in the CPI, 365, 367; and HSPQ scores, 565; and legislative style, 488; and MBTI type differences, 407f, 414
Germany, 208
Ghiselli, E.E., 4, 343–44, 460
Ginn, C.W., 385
Goals, 90f, 139, 411, 415; achievement of, Hersey and Blanchard on, 103; achievement of, and leadership definition, 281; assignment of, in the JCP, 508; attainment of, as one of Parsons' four organizational functions, 306, 307–8, 310, 313; broad, and start-up operations, 527; and forms of mental self-government, 484–85; and task cycle theory, 186f, 189–90; team, achievement of, and type differences, 410; and transformational leadership, 151, 301
Godwin, K., 315
Gordon Personal Profile/Inventory, 51, 421
Gough, Harrison, 6, 8, 36, 37, 340, 355–79. See also California Psychological Inventory (measure)
Government model, of intelligence, 482–91
Governors, 18, 20
Graen, G., 86, 87, 89, 90
Gratzinger, Peter D., 39, 54, 220, 239–48
"Great Man Theory," 84
Gregorc, T., 491
Growth curves, in the CPA, 284–85, 286, 293
Guilford, J.P., 4, 115

# H

Hadwin, Alice, 397
Hai, D.M., 408
Hanewicz, Wayne, 394
Hardships, and leadership development, 41
Harris, P., 287
Harris, R., 349–50

Harrison, D.F., 409
Harvard University, 298
Harvey, O.J., 512, 513
Hater, J., 154, 164
Headhunters, 3, 50
Headship, 85
Health care organizations, 63, 148, 195–99
Heider, F., 87
Hellriegel, S., 385
Hemingway, Ernest, 487
Hemphill, J.K., 4
Henderson, J.C., 410
Hendrick, Hal W., 507
Hendrick, H.R., 84
Henry, E.R., 104
Heroes, 20, 30
Hersey, P., 4, 103, 172
Herzberg, F., 4, 50, 339; on worker motivation and hygiene factors, 346
Heterogeneity, 124–26
High schools, department heads in, 235, 315
High school students, 41, 493, 564–65; rated on leadership abilities, by principals, 36, 52, 340, 360f, 364, 367f, 370; MBTI study of, 397, 408
Hilgard, E.R., 189
Hindman, Don, 235
Hitler, Adolf, 339
Hobbs, Thomas, 482
Hogan, Joyce, 364
Hogan, R., 50–51, 339–40, 343–54; on criminals, 345; Empathy scale (1969), 363; on flawed managers, 348; Inventory of Personal Motives (IPM), 350–51. See also Hogan Personality Inventory (measure)
Holland, 208
Holland, J.L., 491
Hollander, Edwin, 8–19, 76–91, 172
Hollingworth, L.S., 460
Home economics, 63, 235
Hospital Weighted Equivalent Work Units (WEWUs), 192–95
House, R.J., 85, 86, 88, 172; on charisma, 298, 300; on transformational leaders, 298, 300f, 305
Howard, Ann, 6, 8, 36, 37, 39, 113–30; on opportunities for growth, 74; on personality differences, 53, 54; on promotion and success, 61, 72–73, 466, 522, 531, 533
Howell, J.M., 305
Hoy, F., 385
Hughes, Richard, 175n
Hull, Clark L., 189
Humble Oil & Refining Company, 107, 109
Hunt, J.G., 282
Husbands and wives, rated as leaders, 36, 37, 52
Hutchens, Nancy, 391
Hypocrisy, 307

Hypothesis testing, 27, 28

# I

IBM, 341; Management Assessment Program, 51, 419–39
Idiosyncrasy credit model, 87
Implicit leadership theories (ILTs), 84, 90
Individual Background Survey, 104
Industrial leaders, 152
Influence, 147–84; strong sense of, among effective leaders, 305
Influence process, 46, 185–205, 282, 511. *See also* Task cycle theory
Information: exchange of, about what ought to be done, leadership as, 282; exchange processes, 282, 284, 512; gathering, 287, 466
Initiating structure, 299
Insider trading, 91
Inspiration: leadership as, 147–84; and transformational leadership, 153
Institute of Government (University of North Carolina), 388, 394
Institute of Personality Assessment and Research (IPAR), 360f, 373
Integrity, 182, 378, 466, 555
Intellective functioning, 53–54, 73, 457–566
Intellectual: stimulation, 88, 153–54; styles, 458, 481–92
Internal consistency, of scales, 229–30
Internal Revenue Service (IRS), 474
Interpolation, 297
Intuition, 330, 408–9

# J

Jacobs, Owen, 6, 35–36, 38, 61, 62, 90; on military executive leadership, 277, 281–95
Jacobsen, Charlotte, 397
Jacoby, P.F., 385
Japan, 383, 387f, 411f, 487–88
Jaques, Elliott, 6, 35–36, 38, 61f, 90; on military executive leadership, 277–78, 281–95; theory of adult cognitive development, 305f, 310; time span capability in, 305–6, 313
Jauch, L.R., 282
Jefferson, Thomas, 487
Jersey Standard, 104, 107, 110
Job challenge, 522, 529
Jobs, Steve, 487
Joint/Unified Relationships, 61–62
Jones, W.H., 345, 347; Inventory of Personality Disorders (IPD), 349, 350; Inventory of Personal Motives (IPM), 350–51
Judgment, interpersonal, 512
Jung, C.G., 381–83, 384, 490

# K

Kahn, R.L., 86, 87, 302; interpolation and administration in, 297; on skill categories, 283
Kanter, R., 449
Kanuk, L., 233
Karnes, Frances A., 509, 563–66
Katz, D., 4, 86f, 302, 466; interpolation and administration in, 297; on skill categories, 283
Katz, R., 446
Keen, P.G.W., 409
Kelleher, D., 561
Kennedy, A.A., 88
Kilmann, R.H., 88, 411
Kipnis, D., 85
Knowledge, tacit, 495–503
Kotter, J., 4
Kouzes, James M., 38, 44, 62, 73–74, 149, 188, 205–15, 315; on role modeling, 173, 179, 181
Kuder Preference Record, 250
Kuhn, T., 315

# L

Laissez-faire leaders, 152, 154f
Latin America, 50, 53, 341–42, 387f, 391, 449–54
Laurent, Harry, 104
Lawler, E.E., 4, 104
Lawrence, G., 409
Leader Member Exchange Model (LMX), 86–87, 89, 90
Leadership: autocratic, 15, 86, 88–89; bottomline, 187, 315; charismatic, 282, 300, 358f. *See also* Charisma; and a common philosophy, definition of, 306–7, 308; communications, 187; democratic, 12–14; "Great Man" or "Great Person" theory of, 298; "highhigh," 299; laissez-faire leaders, 152, 154f; religious, 314, 383, 563; theory, visionary, 307–8, 309, 311–13
—behavior: in ambiguous environments, 327–36; and behavioral cues, 511–19; future and past, 327, 457; "socio-emotional relationship," and task-centered, in Bales, 298–99; relationship-centered, 298–99.
—definition of, 19–21, 30–34, 40–41, 65; historical, 511; in Jacobs and Jaques, 281–82
—effectiveness of, 64; data about, gathering of, 18, 26; definition of, 65; personality dimensions of, 50–51, 62; and power, 91; and power sharing, 85; "soft" criteria of, 29, 235–36; traits of, 84. *See also* Managerial Practices Survey (measure)
—and management, distinction between, 19–21, 70, 90, 206; Burke and Sashkin on, 303–4; Clover on, 172; and executives vs. midlevel managers, 297–98, 304; Sparks on, 103. *See also* CEOs (chief executive officers); Military leadership; Organizational leadership; Political leadership; Top-level

leadership; Transactional leadership; Transformational leadership

Leader-subordinate dyadic perspective, 155

Legitimacy, 87

Leister, A., 84

Leonard, R.L., 512

Lepsinger, Richard, 27, 43–44, 74, 219, 223–37, 281

Levinson, H., 4, 297

Lewin, Kurt, 306, 316

Liden, R.C., 87, 89

Life stages, intimacy and identity, 183

Life themes, 120–21

Lifetime earnings, 64

Liker, J.K., 512

Likert, R., 88

Lincoln, Abraham, 33

Lindsey, E., 555

Lingoes, J., 349–50

Listening skills, 307, 311

Literacy, 12

Locke, John, 482

Logic, 330, 341, 382f, 413, 415

Lombardo, Michael, 5, 25, 36–37, 41, 53, 74–75, 182, 347, 508, 531, 533; on turning point jobs, 522. See also BENCHMARKS (measure)

Lou Harris poll, 346

Love, 89, 176, 341, 445

Lueder, Donald, 394

Lundberg, O.H., 512

Lynch, Ron, 388, 394

Lyness, Karen S., 278–79, 327–36

# M

McCall, Morgan, Jr., 25, 36–37, 41, 74, 182, 183

McCauley, Cynthia D., 5, 26, 36, 53, 74–75, 347, 547–62. See also BENCHMARKS (measure)

McCaulley, Mary, 6, 8, 37, 52, 74–75, 188, 340, 381–418

McClelland, D.C., 300, 305, 308, 312–13

McCloy, T.M., 172

McCuen, T.L., 460

Macdaid, Gerald, 397

Machiavelli, N., 11

McKenny, J.L., 409

Major, K.D., 315

Management Assessment Program (IBM), 51, 419–39; Overall Assessment Rating, 423–24, 425

Managers, 25–30, 36–41, 277; adaptive, 329–30, 333f; flawed, 50–51, 54, 339, 346–52; mid- and lower level, and top-level leadership, comparison of, 297–98, 304; overwhelmed, 330f, 334; and street smarts, 493–504; stylized, 330, 333; unconcerned, 330, 333f

—and leaders, distinction between, 19–21, 70, 90, 206; Burke and Sashkin on, 303–4; Clover on, 172; and executives vs. midlevel managers, 297–98, 304; Sparks on, 103. See also Transactional leadership

Mann, R.D., 84

Mann-Whitney U Test, 179

Manufacturing, 328

Manus Associates, 229, 236

Marketing, 287

Marshall, George (general), 103

Martin, H.J., 282

Martinko, M.J., 234

Marx, Karl, 308

Mayo, E., 308

MBA programs, 308–9, 496

Means-ends analysis, 306

Megargee, E.I., 364, 368

Mental abilities, 6, 40–41, 50, 84, 139; ability to think and function over periods of at least a decade, 45; practical, 85; and promotion, 39, 72; thinking styles, 53–54, 84–85, 154. See also Cognitive complexity

Mental health, 120, 139

Mentoring, 153

Meyer, Edward C., 62

Michigan Four-Factor Theory of Leadership, 309

Miles, Sue, 235

Military leadership, 3, 19, 20, 21, 233, 254, 563; and decision making, 293, 408; and discretion in action, 277; efforts to improve the performance of, 61–63, 75, 286; excellence in, and time frames, 90, 283, 287, 289–92; executive, 277, 281–95, 341; and narcissism, 350; personality characteristics of, 341, 350, 441–48; training for, 13, 19; transformational leadership and, 147–48, 151–84. See also Army, U.S.

Miller Analogies Test, 104f

Mills, Douglas, 391, 401

Minorities, 12

Mintzberg, Henry, 4, 283, 434

Mission, 153f, 160; and consensus building, 289; and task cycle theory, 186, 187; and transformational leadership, 302f. See also Goals

Mitchell, T.R., 516

Mitchell, W.D., 411

Mitroff, I.I., 411

Modern Healthcare, 347, 352

Morale, 88, 182, 344, 347, 494

Morality, 172, 303

Morris, W.C., 307–8

Morrison, Ann, 25, 36–37, 41, 74

Morrow, Ira J., 341, 419–39

Morton, Gene, 195

Moses, Joseph L., 51, 278–79, 327–36

Most, Robert, 457, 459–64

Motivation, 55, 87, 175, 339; changes in, and maturity, 39, 122–24; effect on performance, 37, 467–68; effect on success, 6; and hygiene factors, 346; in the MPS study, 119–20; pattern, LPC-based, 299; screening for, 72; task, 299; and transformational leadership, 153–54; worker, 21, 38

Mouton, J.S., 4, 299

Multinational banks, 195–99

Multiple regression, 66

Munger, A.M., 104

Murray, H.A., 308, 312–13

Myers, Isabel Briggs, 383f, 411–12, 490–91

## N

Nanus, B., 4, 88; Active vs. Reactive distinction, 303; on leaders as "social architects," 314; and the paradigm shift in how leadership is conceptualized, 298, 315

Napoléon Bonaparte, 339

Narcissism, 88, 349–52

NATO (North Atlantic Treaty Organization), 290

Naval Academy, U.S., 5, 6, 151–69; selection devices of, 155. See also Naval officers

Naval officers, 5, 6, 20, 32, 63, 85, 147, 151–69

Naval Personnel Research and Development Center (NPRDC), 157

Naval War College, 160, 168

Nemeroff, W., 223

Newsweek, 346

New York City Human Resources Planners Association, 391

New York Times, 346

Nichols, Robert, 469

Nightingale, J.A., 409

Nippon Recruit Center, 383, 388

Nixon, Richard, 184

Normative skepticism, 52

Novacek, J., 349–50

NT (iNtuitive-Thinking) individual, 294

Nuclear power plants, 63, 148, 196–99

Nutt, P.C., 410

Nydegger, R.V., 512

NYNEX Corporation, 508, 521–34

## O

O'Connor, J., 513

Offermann, Lynn R., 8–9, 18–19, 76–91

Office of Naval Research, 17

Office of Strategic Services (OSS), 17

O'Hare, Donal, 5, 7, 36, 38, 73–74, 148; on leadership as one of several roles, 46, 185; studies of change, 63; task cycle theory, 39, 46, 185–205

Ohio State University, leadership study at, 19, 85, 298f

Ohlott, Patricia J., 26, 74–75, 508–9, 547–62

Ohsawa, Takeshi, 388

Open systems approach, 306

Organizational leadership, 88, 297–325; behavior corresponding to, 306–7; and belief systems, 306; effect on organizational functioning and culture, 305f, 307–8, 309, 313–14, 315; effective and ineffective, characteristics that differentiate, 45; personal characteristics of, 298, 300f, 305–6, 308–10; relational features of, 83–91, 298–300, 307–8; study of, beginnings of, 300–301; and time spans, 305–6, 309, 313

Organizational structure, Jacob and Jaques on, 282–83, 286–87

Osborn, Diana B., 50, 53, 341, 388, 391, 449–54

Osborn, R.N., 282

Osborn, T. Noel, 50, 53, 341, 388, 391, 449–54

Otte, P.J., 385

Ouchi, W., 449

## P

Parker, C.A., 364

Parker, T., 104

Parsons, T., 306, 307–8, 310, 313

Path-goal theory, 85, 86, 88, 172

Penalties, 152–53

People-orientation, 19, 39, 54, 71, 173, 239

Perceptual accuracy, 507, 511

Performance, 102; appraisal systems, 21, 33–34, 38–39; concern with, and the trait theory, 84; evaluation (CPE), 160, 164, 167; exceptional, study of, 88; of leaders with flawed personalities, 50, 54; limits indicators, bottom-line, 306; and predictors, 38, 465–79

Personal History Record, 104–5

Personality, 39, 339–454; description of, and folk concepts, 356; development, 54–55, 437f; dimension, "Big 5," 50–51, 348; factor, in the MPS study, 119–20; flamboyant, 64; flaws in, 50–51, 88. See also Managers, flawed; and the "Great Man" theory of leadership, 298; and managerial competence, 343–54; of managers in Latin American countries, vs. in the U.S., 50, 53, 341–42, 387f, 391, 449–54; measures, 49–55, 72, 339. See also specific measures; passive-aggressive, 339, 349; of senior military officers, 50, 341, 441–48; and task cycles, 46; and the trait theory of leadership, 36, 40, 84–85. See also Charisma; Motivation

Personnel Development Series (PDS), 107, 110

Peters, C.E., 414

Peters, T.J., 4, 88, 449

Philby, Kim, 348–49

Philosophy, common, definition of, 306–7, 308

Phrase cards, 284

Picture Technique, 104, 105

Pluralism, 14

Political leadership, 3, 12, 18f; and narcissism, 350; and power need imagery, 301. See also Presidents

Positive reinforcement, 153
Posner, Barry Z., 5, 35–39, 44, 62, 73–74, 149, 188, 205–15, 315; on role modeling, 173, 179, 181f
Post, J.M., 88
Potter, Earl H., III, 457–58, 465–80
Power, 139, 299; abuse of, 91; attitudes towards, in the U.S., 12; and charisma, 88, 300; episodic model of, 91; Hollander and Offermann on, 18–19, 89; Kipnis on, 85; sharing, and effective leadership, 85; used to empower others, 45, 278, 301, 305, 307f
— need for, psychological, 49, 54, 88, 181; and the Empowering Leadership scale, 312–13; and Murray's Thematic Apperception Test, 308, 312–13; and power need imagery, 301; and transformational leadership, 301, 305. See also Authority
Prediction, 38, 52, 58–65 passim, 74, 543; of college grades, 58–59; and the Dominance Scale, 6, 356; of high-level executive effectiveness, 137–42; of performance, during apprenticeship, 465–79; studies, long-term, 100–84
Presidents, 18f, 20, 29; election of, 35; House on, 300; Wenk on, 459. See also specific presidents
Privacy, need for, 49
Problem-solving ability, 6, 37, 329, 430, 564; and apprenticeship, 466; and cognitive complexity, 512f, 516; and coping styles, 331, 333; and managerial development, 528; and the Ship Destination Test (SDT), 421; and street smarts, 494f
Proclivity, 284, 294
Productivity, 18, 21, 38, 63, 69, 314, 347; changes in, and task cycle theory, 196–99; and charismatic leaders, 88
Professional Development of Officers Study (PDOS), 290–92
Profitability, 5, 28, 34, 73
Profits, 21, 63
Promotability, 20, 508, 543
Promotion(s), 3, 153, 502–3, 525; action plans and, 72–75; in the BENCHMARKS study, 536, 543; changes independent of, 122; in the Coast Guard, 466, 474; as criteria for managerial success, 61, 115, 117; decisions about, factors influencing, 64; increase in demands after, 41; and leadership potential, 31–32, 33f, 71; rates, 30–31, 33, 37; recommendation for early (CEP), 160, 164f, 167
Public school systems, 12, 14

## Q

Quality-of-work-life perceptions, 314f

## R

Racial differences, 109f
Raskin, Robert, 339–40, 343–54

Rational leadership, vs. emotional leadership, 172
Ray, B., 314–15
RBH Non-Verbal Reasoning Test, 104
Reagan, Ronald, 459
Regard, unconditional positive, 311
Regression equation, 59
Relevance, assessment of, 228
Reliability, 307, 349; of measures, 208–9, 210f, 231–32; of scales, 308, 310f
Religious leadership, 314, 383, 563
Renzulli, J.S., 491
Representation theory, 284
Resourcing, 287
Respect, 21, 45, 153, 182; and conflicts between sensing types and intuitives, resolution of, 408; and organizational leadership, 307, 311
Responsiveness, 85
Restructuring, corporate, 327f
Retailing, 328
Rewards, 152, 154, 466
Richardson, Bellows, Henry, & Company (RBH), 104
Rifkind, L.J., 409
Rigby, C., 287
Rights, individual, 12, 15
Risk taking, 307, 333, 409–10, 414
Roach, B., 385
Robertson, David, 394
Rogers, Carl, 311
Rokeach Values, 341, 441f, 445–47
Role: identity, during apprenticeship, 466f; models, 173, 179–82, 524, 526, 529–30
Roosevelt, Franklin D., 300
Rosenbach, William, 5ff, 38
Ross, Paul F., 104
Rousseau, Jean-Jacques, 482
Royalty, 11ff, 20, 289
Ruderman, Marian N., 26, 74–75, 347, 508–9, 547–62
Rupart, Randall, 391

## S

Salary, as a factor in EIMP studies, 105, 107
San Antonio Conference, 7f, 50, 62, 76
Sanford, F., 83
Sashkin, Marshall, 6, 35–36, 38, 45; on top-level executive leadership, 278, 297–325
Scandals, 91
Scheffe's Test of Differences, 333
Schein, E.H., 88, 306, 310, 314, 478; on visionary leaders, 307
Schutz "Element B," 341
Seiden, H.M., 409
Selection process, 43–48, 460; and leadership behavior, past and future, 327; of successful leaders, 466; and superstition, 23; validity of, 32, 57–67; variables used in, 23–34

Self, 311; —acceptance, 346; —confidence, 305, 330, 346, 350ff, 356, 431; —respect, 307, 341

Self-Performance Report, 104f

Sex differences, 109f, 171, 355, 391; and career development, 524, 529f; and coping styles, 333; as a factor in the CPI, 365, 367; and HSPQ scores, 565; and legislative style, 488; and MBTI type differences, 407f, 414

Sexton, D.L., 385

Shartle, C.L., 4, 85

Shipper, Frank, 5, 7, 36, 38, 73–74, 148; on leadership as one of several roles, 46, 185; studies of change, 63; task cycle theory, 39, 46, 185–205

Shrout, J.L., 232

Simon, H.A., 4, 282

Simonton, D.K., 355

Skinner, B.F., 189f

Slocum, J.W., Jr., 410

Smith, L.H., 491

Social: desirability response bias, 209, 311; —exchange model, 172; identity, 345–46; learning theory, 183; norms, 52

Socialization, 332, 466

Soviet Union, 290, 348

Sparks, Paul, 6, 8, 19, 36–37, 60–61, 72–73, 101–12 passim, 344

Spearman-Brown formula, 498

Spies, 348

Stability, 230–31

Stamina, 139

Stamp, G., 35–36, 38, 61, 284–86, 293

Standard Oil Company of New Jersey, 344

Stanford-Binet test, 356

Steelcase, 346

Stern, Mel, 341, 419–39

Sternberg, Robert J., 50, 85, 458, 481–504

Stewart, R., 83

Stogdill, R.M., 4, 84, 305, 355, 563; on the "Great Man" theory of leadership, 298

Stoner-Zemel, M.J., 310, 314, 315

Strategic Business Unit (SBU), 286–87, 288

Strategic Defense Initiative (SDI), 290

Strategic Management Group (SMG), 200

"Street smarts," 85, 493–504

Stress, 26, 50–51, 527; and ambiguity, 329; and apprenticeship, 457–76 passim; and change, 75; and flawed managers, 339–40, 346–47; treatment of, 410

Structure, and consideration, as two dimensions of leadership, 39

Styles, leadership, 220; instruction and, 38; and organizational culture, 88–89; task-oriented and relationship-oriented, 86, 239–40, 309; and thinking styles, 53–54, 84–85, 154

Success, 528, 540; assurances of, impossibility of, 70; and career progress, 6, 465–80; index, use of, in EIMP, 101, 105–7, 110; index, predictor scores vs., 60–61; mange-

rial, longitudinal studies of, 37, 113–30, 205; predictions of, 102, 113–30, 543; promotion as the criterion for, 61; and scales, relationship of, 536, 539; and street smarts, 493–504; and task cycle theory, 190

Succession-planning programs, 103–4

Superstition, 23

Survey of Peer Relations, 189

Survey of Sales Relations, 189

# T

Task cycle theory, 39, 46, 148, 185–205

Tatsuoka, M.M., 469

Teamwork, 38; effects of transformational leadership on, 148, 183; and team building, 175–76, 413; and type differences, 410

Temperament, 294

Test battery, 72

Thompson, P.H., 466

Thorndike, Edward Lee, 4

Tichy, N., 173

Time: frames, 90f, 283, 287, 289–92; horizons, executive, 283, 287, 289–92, 309; intervals, cause-and-effect, 283; orientation to, type differences in, 409; span capability, in Jaques, 305–6, 313; span of planning, 305–6, 309, 313

Tolman, E.C., 189–90

Top-level leadership, 277–336; and ambiguity, 277, 278–79, 282, 283; coping styles of, 329–35; and decision discretion, 277, 281–82, 283, 284–86; and the Leader Behavior Questionnaire (LBQ), 301, 308–21; vs. midlevel managers, 297–98, 304; military, 277, 281–95; and time horizons, 283, 287, 289–92, 309; and time spans of planning, 305–6, 309, 313; and type differences, 411

Trait theory, of leadership, 36, 40, 84–85

Transactional leadership, 6, 38, 85–88, 164, 166, 183, 187; as contingent reinforcement, 152, 154; effectiveness of, 6; as laissez-faire leadership, 152, 154, 155; as management-by-exception, 152, 154f; measures for, 44–45, 152–53. See also specific measures; and subordinates, 152–53; training programs to develop, 38; and transformational leadership, distinction between, 154–55, 278, 300–304

Transformational leadership, 6, 20, 73–74, 88, 187; Bass and Yammarino on, 147, 151–69, 188; Burns on, 38, 88; and charisma, 88, 90, 153ff; Clover on, 148; judgement of, 7; identification of, 301; and individualized consideration, 153ff; and intellectual stimulation, 153–54, 155; long-term forecasting of, 147; measures for, 44–45; and non-transformational leaders, 181–83; and power need, 301; Sashkin and Burke on, 278, 298, 300–325; three aspects of, 278; and transactional leaders, distinction between, 154–55, 278, 300–304; and visionary leadership, 307–8, 309. *See also* specific measures

Trauma, 41

Trawick, McE., 104

Trust, 12, 15, 40, 45, 187; in management, 21, 87; and openness, 442; and organizational leadership, 307; and transformational leaders, 153, 182

Truth, 307

Turlington, J.E., 293

Turnover, 88

*Twelve Angry Men*, 513f

# U

Uncertainty, 26; during apprenticeship, 466; and higher organizational roles, 277, 282, 283; patterning of, 283; reduction, 283; resolution of, 282, 287

United States Military Academy (West Point, New York), 52, 360f, 368–69, 376ff

Upward mobility, 292ff

# V

Vaill, P.B., 88

Valerio, Anna Marie, 39, 508, 521–34

Validation, 47, 57–67; on the LBQ, 314–15; long-term, planning of, 72; of the Managerial Practices Survey, 223–37

Validities: EIMP, 104–10; predictive, in the CPA, 285, 294. *See also* Validity

Validity, 192–95, 286, 508, 564; coefficients, 58–60; content, 227–28; criterion-related, 233–38; definition of, 67; generalization, 27; of selection procedures, 32; of tests, 27f, 38. *See also* Validities

Valley, C.A., 314

Value(s), 72, 408, 470; formation and clarification, 172, 564; and the MBTI measure, 340; organizational, leaders as transmitters and upholders of, 91, 306–7, 310; Rokeach, 341, 441f, 445–47; and transformational leaders, 153, 183

Van Fleet, David, 231, 233

Van Velsor, Ellen, 391

Variability, definition of, 67

Variables, 47–48, 58–59, 192

Variance, 59, 243, 245; analysis of, definition of, 66; definition of, 67; error, 33

Verification process, 190–99

Vertical integration, 287

Veterans Administration, 5, 63, 148, 192–95; Medical Center Study (VAMC), 196–99

Vision, organizational, 151, 153f

Visionary leadership theory, 307–8, 309, 311–13

Vries, Kets de, 297

Vroom, V.H., 4, 85–86, 172

# W

Wade, P.F., 391

Wagner, Richard K., 85, 458, 493–504

WAIS test, 356

Waldman, D.A., 155

Wall, S., 27, 43–44, 74, 219, 223–37, 281

Warren, R.A., 39, 54, 220, 239–48

Washington, George, 31–32

Waterman, R.H., Jr., 4, 88, 449

Watson, D., 469

Weber, Max, 88, 297; on charisma, 300; means-ends analysis of, 306

Weick, K.E., Jr., 4, 104

Wenk, Edward, 459

White, C.M., 512

Wiggins, J.S., 350

"Will," and "can," distinction between, 87

Wilson, Clark, 5, 7, 36, 38, 73–74, 148; on leadership as one of several roles, 46, 185; studies of change, 63; task cycle theory, 39, 46, 185–205

Wives and husbands, rated as leaders, 36f, 52

Wofford, Joan, 397

Women, 12, 36f, 52. *See also* Sex differences

Work groups, size of, 196

Work histories, and the CPA, 284, 285

Work units, effectiveness of, 34, 73

World War I, 17, 49

World War II, 17, 81, 104

# Y

Yammarino, Francis, 5ff, 32, 38, 44, 73–74, 88f, 147; on modeling and charisma, 173; and the Multifactor Officer Questionnaire, 63; and the paradigm shift in how leadership is conceptualized, 298, 315

Yang, A.I., 409

Yarborough, Glen, 176

Yetton, P.W., 4, 85–86, 172

Yukl, Gary, 27, 43–44, 74, 219, 223–37; on definitions of leadership, 281. *See also* Managerial Practices Survey (measure)

# Z

Zaleznik, A., 4, 172, 297

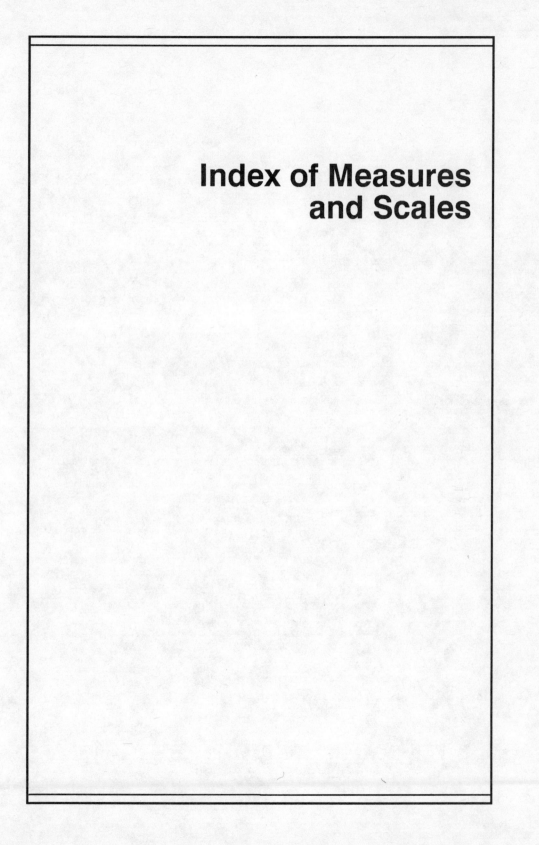

# Index of Measures
# and Scales

# Index of
# Measures and Scales

## A

Abasement, 129, 365, 373

Ability, 278

Ability to build and maintain the momentum for action, 381

Ability to Delay Gratification, 128

Abstract Orientation Scale, 507, 513–16

Academic Performance (measure), 158, 164–67, 175

Accurate assessment of existing situations, 381

ACE Psychol Test – Language, 141

ACE Psychol Test – Quantitative, 141

ACE Psychol Test – Quickness of Learning, 141

Achievement, 129, 240–44, 365

Achievement/Advancement, 129

Achievement motivation, 52, 124

Achievement via Conformance, 340, 366, 499

Achievement via Independence, 364, 366, 406, 463, 499

Achievement within the System, 411

Achieving Goals through Personal Influence, 552–61 passim

Acquiring the necessary resources, 45

Acting with Flexibility, 538–42

Active, 263, 362

Active Management-by-Exception, 44, 159, 161–64, 166, 188

Active versus Reactive, 45, 303

Activity Level, 422, 426, 431ff

ACUMEN scales, 240–46

Adaptability, 422, 426, 542

Adaptable, 362

Adapted Child, 365

Adaptive, 51, 278

Adjustment, 51, 350

Administrative Ability, 118

Administrative Controls, 422, 426

Administrative effectiveness, 134

Administrative Skills, 117, 127

Adult, 365

Advancement, 129

Advancement Motivation, 117, 122

Aesthetic Motives, 351

Aesthetic Values, 142

Affability, 119

Affected by Feelings–Emotionally Stable, 469–73, 475

Affection, 267, 451–52, 499

Affiliation, 122, 129, 240, 241–44, 365

Affiliative, 240–44

Affiliative Motives, 351

Aggression, 122, 129, 365, 367f, 373

Aggressive, 362

Aggressiveness, 430

Agreeableness, 141

A Leader, 266

Alertness in perceiving changes, 381

Allport-Vernon-Lindsay Scale of Values, 54–55

Allport-Vernon Scale of Values, 136

Altruistic Motives, 351

Ambition, 51, 119, 267, 348, 350

Ambitious, 446, 448

Ambitiousness, 46

American Council on Education Psychological Test (measure), 135

Analytical/Integrative Ability, 422, 426, 431–33

Anxious, 266–67

Approachability, 46, 194–95, 198

Approval, 240–44

Aptitude for Service (AFS) ratings, 368

Arousing, vs. clarifying, 45, 302f

Artistic interests, 142

Ascendance, 120, 129

Ascendancy, 51, 421, 429–30

Assertive, 361

Assessment Dimensions (measure), 8

Autonomy, 122, 129, 365, 532

Avoidance, 240

Awkward, 361f

## B

Balance between Personal Life and Work, 538–42, 543

Barron-Welsh Art Scale, 367

Bass/California F Scale, 115

Bass transformational leadership scales, 173–75

Baucom Femininity, 366

Baucom Masculinity, 366

Becoming an expert, 54

Behavior flexibility, 128, 334, 532
Behavioral Assessment Data (BAD), 497–500
Behavioral Prediction Error, 514f
Being a Quick Study, 537, 539–42, 543
Belief System Inventory scales, 513
Bell System Value Orientation, 128
BENCHMARKS (measure), 25–26, 36–37, 74–75, 508, 535–45
Bottom-Line Leadership, 309, 312, 318–21
Broad-minded, 446, 448
Brooding, 263, 266–67
Building and Mending Relationships, 537, 539–42
Building Trust, 46, 193–95, 197, 198
Business Game Forcefulness, 128
Business Game Overall, 128
Business Sociability, 411

# C

California Psychological Inventory (measure), 8, 25, 51–52, 340, 413; Adjective Check List (ACL), 360–62, 364–67, 373–75; Aptitude for Service variable, 360; categorization of people into four quadrants, 187–88, 357–60, 368–78; folk scales, definition of, 356; and Leaderless Group Discussions (LGD), 340, 360f, 364–67, 373, 377–78; and leadership and intelligence, relationship of, 457, 460–63; and NPI, comparison of, 349; Type/Level Model for interpreting, 340; use of, in the Center for Creative Leadership's LDP program, 497, 499–500; and West Point ratings on Aptitude for Service, 340. *See also* specific scales
Campbell Work Orientations Surveys (measure), 8, 25, 45–46, 220, 249–74
Capable, 361, 362
Capacity for Status, 52, 340, 349, 364f, 367, 401, 406, 499
Career Retention (measure), 158, 165, 167
Caring, 46, 200–201
Cattell's 16PF Form A (measure), 468, 469–73, 474f, 476, 564
Cautiousness, 51, 423, 429–30
Challenge, 411
Challenging the Process, 44, 188, 207, 208–12
Change, 129, 365
Charisma, 44, 46, 159–64 *passim*, 166, 174–81 *passim*, 200–202; Bass on, 188; in the LBQ, 309
Charismatic, 266
Cheerful, 446, 448
Clarification of Goals, 193–95, 197
Clarifying, 29, 43, 62, 152, 227–34
Clarifying Goals, 46, 197
Clarifying Roles and Objectives, 226
Clarity in conceptualizing the issues, 381
Clarity in weighing values, 381
Clear-thinking, 362

Clerical Interests, 142
Clever, 362
Coaching, 45
Cognitive ability, 118
Cognitive capacity, 277, 286
Cognitive time span, 305
College Grade Point Average (measure), 367
Comfort levels, 278, 284; and ambiguity, 329f, 333
Comfortable Life, 442, 445, 447f
Commercial Motives, 351
Commonplace, 362
Communality, 365, 366, 401, 406, 499
Communication, 422, 431–33
Communication Leadership, 310f, 318–21
Compassion and Sensitivity, 537, 539–42, 543
Competence, 46, 200–201, 240–44
Competent, 446, 448
Competitive, 240
Competitive Group Leadership, 128
Competitive Group Oral, 128
Competitive Group Oral Comm., 128
Competitive Group Overall, 128
Composure, 139
Computational Interests, 142
Concrete-Abstract, 469–73, 475, 511–12
Confident, 46, 362
Conflict Management & Team Building, 29, 44, 63, 227–34
Conflict with Boss, 552–61 *passim*
Confronting Problem Subordinates, 537, 539–42
Connections with Influential People, 202
Conscientiousness, 564
Consensus Building/Networking, 288–89
Conservative-Experimenting, 469–73, 475
Consulting & Delegating, 29, 43, 63, 225, 229–32, 234
Contemporary Affairs Test, 115, 118
Contingent promises, 44, 159, 161–64, 188
Contingent rewards, 44, 159, 161–64, 188
Control, 442, 444–45, 451–52, 499
Control of details, 46, 193–95, 197
Control of Incentives/Pay, 202
Conventional, 240–44
Cool-Warm, 469–73, 475
Cooperative tolerance, 141
Counseling Readiness, 365
Courageous, 362, 446, 448
CPA (measure), 25, 277, 284–86, 294
Creating, vs. Conserving, 45, 302f
Creative, 263
Creative Personality, 365
Creativity, 46, 128, 200–201, 274, 333f
Critical Parent, 365
Critical thinking, 115, 118, 129
Cultivating leadership talents, 45
Cultural Leadership, 310, 314, 318–21

**D**

Decision making, 46, 422, 426, 431–33, 532
Decisiveness, 333f, 532, 538–42, 543
Decisiveness in reaching good judgments, 381
Deference, 129, 365, 373
Delegating authority, 45
Delegation, 45, 193, 194–95, 198, 225
Denial of Social Anxiety, 350
Dependency, 129
Dependent, 240–44, 362
Depressed, 266–67
Derail/no change/promoted (measure), 508
Detachment, 363, 366ff
Determined, 362
Developing, 29, 43, 63; a long-range plan, 45
Difficulty in Making Strategic Transitions, 538–42
Difficulty in Molding a Staff, 538–42, 543
Diplomacy, 422, 426f, 431–33, 435
Discretion in action, 277
Dogmatism Scale, 513
Doing Whatever It Takes, 537, 539–42, 543
Dominance, 6, 51f, 119, 129, 187–89, 340, 349, 356f, 363ff, 367f, 377, 406, 460–63, 499, 564
Downsizing/Reorganization, 552–61 passim
Drug & Alcohol Info Survey, 367
Dynamic, 46, 266

**E**

Early Promotion (measure), 160, 164, 165, 167
Economic Values, 142
Edwards Personal Preference Scales, 8
Edwards Personal Preference Schedule, 115
Effectiveness (measure), 159, 161–64
Effectiveness/Outcomes, 200, 202
Ego-Functional life theme, 120, 121
Ego Inflation, 350
Element B (measure), 441f, 443–44
Emotional Control, 141
Emotional Stability, 129, 423, 429–30, 564
Empathy, 52, 187ff, 340, 356f, 364, 366f, 377, 511
Empathy scale, Hogan's, 363
Empowered Leadership, 309, 312–13, 318–21
Empowering Through Excitement, 302
Enabling others to act, 44, 207, 208–12
Encouraging the Heart, 44, 188, 207, 208–12
Endurance, 129, 365
Energetic, 362
Energy, 117, 128, 141
Engineering Science (measure), 158, 165
Enterprising, 362
Enthusiastic, 266, 564
Envisioning/anticipating, 277
Equality, 447f
Establishing Personal Credibility, 553–61 passim

Excellence, 46
Exciting Life, 447f
Executive Battery of Psychological Tests (measure), 135, 141–42
Exhibition, 129, 365, 367f, 373
Expectations, 46
Expectations Inventory (measure), 115
Expectations of Excellence, 200–202
Expedient-Conscientious, 469–73, 475
Experienced, 46
Expertise, 46, 193–95, 197
Expressiveness, 564
External Pressures, 553–61 passim
Extra Effort (measure), 159, 161–63
Extracurricular Activities (measure), 158, 165–67
Extraversion, 366, 499
Extraversion (E) or Introversion (I), 382–83, 398–402, 407–15 passim, 441ff, 449–54 passim, 490–91
Extraversive-Introversive, 187–88
Extraverted, 53
Exxon interview, 105

**F**

Facilitation, 46
Family Environment Scale, 565
Family Security, 447f
Farsighted, 46
Fearful, 362
Feedback, 46, 193–95, 197
Feeling, 52, 53, 366
Femininity, 365f, 377
Field Independence, 499
Financial-Acquisitive life theme, 120
Financial Analysis, 411
Finding and Using Information, 532
Flexibility, 356, 366, 377, 401, 406, 499
Flexibility in handling work assignment, 132
Focused Leadership, 310, 311, 318–21
Folk measures, 356
Foresighted, 362
Forgiving, 446, 448
Forthright-Shrewd, 469–73, 475
Forward striving, 119, 129
Free Child, 365
Freedom, 442, 445, 447f
Freedom, from depression, 141
Fundamental Interpersonal Relations Orientation-Behavior (FIRO-B) scores, 341, 449, 451–52, 497, 499–500

**G**

GAMIN (measure), 28, 120
General Activity, 129, 138, 139
General Adjustment, 120, 130
General effectiveness factor, 127

General mental ability, 128
General Reasoning, 462f
Goal flexibility, 118
Goal Pressure, 46, 194–97
Good Impression, 364, 366, 463, 499
Gordon Personal Profile (measure), 28, 429
Gottschaldt Figures Test (measure), 367
Group-oriented–Self-sufficient, 469–73, 475
Guilford-Martin Inventory (measure), 115, 135
Guilford-Zimmerman Temperament Survey (measure), 104f, 461ff

## H

Happiness, 442, 445, 447f
Happy family life, 55
Harmonious Work Climate, 411
Hedonistic Motives, 351
Helpfulness, 267
Helping others, 54
Heterosexuality, 129, 365
Hidden Figures Test, 497, 499–500
High Origence/High Intellectence, 365
High Origence/Low Intellectence, 365
High School Class Rank (measure), 158, 162, 165ff
High School Grade Point Average (measure), 367
Hiring Talented Staff, 538–42, 543
Hogan Personality Inventory (measure), 348, 350–51
Honest, 446, 448
Hotheaded, 266
Humanistic-Helpful, 240–44
Humble's "Success Index," 107

## I

Ideal Self, 365
Imaginative, 446, 448
Immature, 362
Impact, 532
Impact belief, 305
Impulsivity, 119
In-basket decision making, 128
In-basket organization and planning, 128
In-basket overall, 128
In-Basket Test, 128
Inclusion, 442, 444–45, 451–52, 499
Independence, 52, 117f, 187–88, 340, 356f, 362f, 366ff, 564
Individual Background Survey, 104
Individualized consideration, 44, 159, 161–64, 174, 176, 180–81; in Bass, 188
Informing, 29, 43, 225, 227–34
Inherited Problems, 553–61 passim
Initiative, 362
Inner work standards, 117, 119, 124, 128, 130
Inspirational leadership, 44, 159–66 passim, 174, 176, 180–81, 188

Inspiring, 266
Inspiring a Shared Vision, 44, 188, 207, 208–12
Instrumental Values Survey (measure), 341
Integrity, 46, 200–202
Intellectence, 350
Intellective function, 52
Intellectual, 446, 448
Intellectual Ability, 117, 127
Intellectual-Cultural Orientation, 564
Intellectual Efficiency, 340, 366, 463, 499
Intellectual Leadership, 188
Intellectual Motives, 351
Intellectual Stimulation, 44, 159, 161–64, 174, 176, 180–81
Intelligence, 564
Intense Pressure, 552–61 passim
Interest in Subordinate Growth, 46, 194, 198
Interests narrow, 362
Internality, 363, 367
Interpersonal ability, 52, 118f
Interpersonal skills, 52, 117, 127
Interview oral communication, 128
Intraception, 122, 129
Intraceptive, 365
Introversion, 366
Intuiting, 366
Inventory of Personality Disorders (measure), 349–51
IQ tests, 286, 459–60, 493f, 497f, 500

## J

Jersey Standard "Success Index," 106, 107
Job Challenge Profile (measure), 26, 28, 75, 508–9, 550–62
Job Security, 269
Job Title, 200ff
Joint/unified relationships, concern with, 277, 287–88
Judging, 53, 367
Judgment (J) or Perception (P), 52, 340, 382–83, 398–401, 405, 408–15 passim, 442f, 449–54 passim, 499

## K

Kirton Adaptation-Innovation Inventory (measure), 497, 499–500, 540ff
Kuder Preference Inventory (measure), 136

## L

Lack of Follow-Through, 538–42, 543
Lack of inferiority feelings, 120
Lack of nervous anxiety, 141
Lack of Strategic Direction, 552–61 passim
Lack of Top Management Support, 552–61 passim
Laissez-faire, 44, 159–66 passim

Leader Behavior Description Questionnaire (measure), 44, 85
Leader Behavior Questionnaire (measure), 44f, 278, 301, 308–21
Leadership, 201f, 267, 431–33, 532
Leadership motivation, 119
Leadership potential, 46
Leadership Potential Index (measure), 44
Leadership Practices Inventory (measure), 44, 62, 149, 207–15
Leadership Practices Survey (measure), 44
Leadership Report (measure), 43
Leadership role, 129
Leadership skills, 128
Leadership Skills Inventory (measure), 509, 564
Leadership Status, 514f
Leading other people, 45
Leading Subordinates, 537, 539–42
Least Preferred Co-worker (measure), 86, 299f, 515–16
Leventhal Anxiety scale, 363, 366
Life Styles Inventory (measure), 52, 54, 240–47
Likeability, 51, 348, 350
Like-Indifferent-Dislike, 250
Likert scale, 207, 210, 468
Literary interests, 142
Locale-residential life theme, 120
Locus-of-Control scale (measure), 367
Logical, 446, 448
Logical analysis of causes and effects, 381
Long-Term Leadership, 309, 313, 318–21
Loving, 446, 448
Low Origence/High Intellectence, 365
Low Origence/Low Intellectence, 365

## M

Making money, 54
Making things happen, 54
Management Continuity Study, 521–22
Management Incomplete Sentences Test, 115
Management Judgment Test, 104, 105
Management Progress Study (measure), 6, 102, 113–30, 521–22, 531–33
Management Skills Profile (measure), 543f
Managerial Competence, 202
Managerial Job Satisfaction, 497, 499–500
Managerial Potential, 366
Managerial Practices Survey (measure), 8, 27–30, 62–63, 219, 223–37, 543f
Managerial Task Cycle (measure), 8, 148, 187, 193, 195f
Managing Conflict, 226
Managing Individuals, 422, 426
Marital-familial life theme, 120
Marlowe-Crowne Personal Reaction Inventory (measure), 209
Masculinity, 129, 141, 365f, 377
Math Aptitude, 157–58, 166, 167

Mature Love, 447f
Mechanical interests, 142
Meek, 362
Mental ability, 138, 139
Mental Alertness Test (measure), 421, 427f
Mental versatility/flexibility, 428f
Mentoring, 46, 200–202, 227–34
Mild, 361f
Military Leadership, 365
Military Performance (measure), 158, 164–67
Miller Analogies Test, 104
Minnesota Multiphasic Personality Inventory (measure), 50, 350, 356, 366f
Modeling, 46, 200–202
Modeling the Way, 44, 207, 208–12
Molding a Team, 542
Money, 129
Monitoring, 29, 43, 63, 227–34
Monitoring Operations and Environment, 226
Moral-Religious Emphasis, 564
Motivating, 29, 43, 62f, 226, 227–34
Motivation for advancement, 119
Multifactor Leadership Questionnaire (measure), 301
Multifactor Officer Questionnaire (measure), 6, 63, 158
Multinational concern, 277, 287, 288
Music interests, 142
Myers-Briggs Type Indicator (measure), 6, 8, 37, 52–53, 188, 195, 340f, 366–67, 381–418, 540ff; data, on Latin American managers, 449–54; development of, 381; and Jung's theory of psychological type, 381–83, 384; and measures of proclivity, 294; use of, in the Center for Creative Leadership's LDP program, 497, 499–500; use of, at the U.S. Army War College, 341, 441–43. *See also* specific scales

## N

Narcissistic Personality Inventory (measure), 349–50
Need achievement, 122, 124
Need for advancement, 117, 119, 128, 130
Need for peer approval, 128
Need for security, 128, 130
Need for superior approval, 118, 128
Networking, 226
Networking/Interfacing, 29, 43, 63, 227–34
Norm-Accepting–Norm-Questioning, 187–88
Norm-favoring, 366
Number Checked, 365
Number Favorable, 365
Number Unfavorable, 365
Nurturance, 129, 365
Nurturing Parent, 365

## O

Obedient, 446, 448
Objectivity, 139; in judging, 141
Occupational Life Theme (measure), 53, 120f
Omnibus Personality Inventory (measure), 413, 513
Openness, 442, 444–45
Oppositional, 240–44
Optimism, 129, 139
Oral communication skills, 117, 119, 128
Oral defense, 532
Oral presentation, 532
Order, 129, 365
Orderly planning, 46
Orderly Work Planning, 193–95, 197
Organization and planning, 128
Organizational Awareness, 422, 426
Organizational Beliefs Questionnaire (measure), 315
Organizational Leadership, 310, 313–14, 318–21
Organizational Sensitivity, 202
Organizing, 532
Original thinking, 51, 423, 429–30
Outgoing, 361, 362
Outgoing Affiliation, 411
Outgoing Friendliness, 141
Outspoken, 362
Overdependence, 538–42
Overwhelmed, 51

## P

Parental-familial life theme, 120
Participation, 193
Passive, 46
Passive Management-by-Exception, 44, 159, 161–64, 188
Passivity, 267
People/Security orientation, 54, 220, 240–44
Perceiving, 367
Perception, 398ff
Perception of social cues, 128
Performance Evaluation (measure), 160, 164, 167
Performance summary (measure), 159–60
Persistence, 200–202
Person Perception, 511
Personal Adjustment, 365
Personal Awareness, 200–202
Personal history record, 104
Personal Impact, 128, 422, 426
Personal organization, 134
Personal Relations, 423, 429–30
Persuasion, 46
Persuasive interests, 138, 139, 142
Persuasiveness, 200–202
Pessimistic, 362

Picture Technique, 104
Planning, 532
Planning & Organizing, 29, 43, 63, 225, 227–34
Planning and Plan Execution, 422, 426
Pleasure, 447f
Polished, 362
Polite, 446, 448
Political and Economic values, 138f
Political values, 142
Poor Morale, 350
Position, 200f
Positiveness, 119f
Power, 240–44
Power and authority, 54
Power Motives, 351
Power need, 305, 309
Power use/empowerment, 302
Practical-Imaginative, 469–73, 475
Pressure on Subordinates, 202
Primacy of work, 119, 124, 128f
Problem solving, 29, 43, 63, 226, 227–34, 334
Problem Subordinates, 552–61 *passim*
Problems with Interpersonal Relationships, 538–42, 543
Professional Competency Exam, 175
Promotion Recommendation (measure), 160, 164f, 167
Prudence, 51, 350
Psychological-Mindedness, 377, 499
Pushing-pressure, 46, 200–202
Putting People at Ease, 538–42

## Q

Quantitative mental ability, 139
Quitting, 362

## R

Range of interests, 128
RBH Non-Verbal Reasoning Test (measure), 104
Realism of expectations, 128
Realization, 366
Recognition, 46, 193–94, 198, 200–202
Recognition Motives, 351
Recognizing & Rewarding, 29, 43, 63, 225–27, 229–32, 234
Recommendations (measure), 158, 160, 165, 167
Recreational-social life theme, 120
Reflective awareness, 141
Reinforcement, 193, 200–202
Relaxed-Tense, 469–73, 475
Religious Motives, 351
Religious values, 142
Religious-humanism life theme, 120
Representing, 29, 44, 63, 227–34
Resentment, 349

Resistance to stress, 118, 128
Resourceful, 362, 537, 539–42, 543
Resourcefulness, 46, 200–201
Respect for Self and Others, 542
Respectful Leadership, 310, 311–12, 318–21
Responsibility, 366, 421–22, 499
Responsibility through Tolerance, 340, 377
Responsible, 446, 448
Retiring, 362
Revised Art Scale, 367
Revitalizing Unit, 553–61 *passim*
Risk Leadership, 310, 312, 318–21
Risk Taking, 46, 200–202, 333f
Rotter Incomplete Sentences Test, 115

# S

Sarnoff Survey of Attitudes Toward Life (measure), 115, 122, 129
SAT (measure), 58–59, 158, 367, 377, 469, 473, 476ff, 481
Satisfaction (measure), 159, 161–66
Satisfaction orientation, 54, 220, 240–44
Satisfied with Co-Workers, 499
Satisfied with Pay, 499
Satisfied with Promotions, 499
Satisfied with Superior, 499
Satisfied with Work, 499
School and College Ability Test (measure), 115, 118, 128f, 421, 428
Scientific Interests, 142
Security Motives, 351
Self-Acceptance, 52, 340, 363ff, 367f, 401, 406, 463, 499
Self-Actualized, 240–44
Self-assured–Apprehensive, 469–73, 475
Self-Awareness, 538–42
Self-Confidence, 46, 129, 138f, 141, 200–201, 361f, 365, 367
Self-Control, 356, 365, 366ff, 373, 406, 499, 564
Self-Esteem, 119, 120
Self-Objectivity, 128, 532
Self-Perception Error, 514f
Self-Performance Report, 104
Self-Respect, 442, 445, 447f
Sense of Service, 442, 445, 447f
Sense of Well-Being, 356, 406, 499
Sensing (S) or Intuitive perception (N), 52f, 382–83, 398–415 *passim*, 441ff, 449–54 *passim*, 490–91, 499
Sensitivity, 511
Serious vs. carefree, 138, 139
Service life theme, 120, 121
Serving as an officer, 45
Setting a Developmental Climate, 537, 539–42, 543
Sexual Knowledge Questionnaire (measure), 367
Sharp-witted, 362

Sheltered, 46
Ship Destination Test (measure), 421, 427f
Shipley Institute of Living Scale, 540f
Shy, 362
Shy-Bold, 469–73, 475
Silent, 362
Simple, 362
Skills Survey Leadership Scale, 45–46
Sober-Enthusiastic, 469–73, 475
Sociability, 51f, 138f, 141, 340, 349f, 356f, 363, 365, 401, 406, 429–30, 499
Sociable, 362
Social acuity, 511
Social Ascendancy, 138f, 141
Social Imperturbability, 350
Social Insight, 511
Social Intelligence, 511
Socialization, 366, 499
Social Maladjustment, 350
Social objectivity, 128
Social Perceptiveness, 511
Social Presence, 52, 340, 349, 365, 401, 406, 499
Social Recognition, 447f
Social service interests, 142
Social values, 142
Sophisticated, 362
Spontaneity, 141
Stability, 139
Stability of performance, 117f, 127
Straightforwardness and Composure, 537, 539–42
Strategic Differences with Management, 538–42
Stress Management, 202
Strong, 361f
Strong-Campbell Interest Inventory (measure), 8, 158, 250, 492
Strongly Dislike, 250
Strongly Like, 250
Stylized, 51
Subjective Depression, 350
Submissive-Dominant, 469–73, 475
Subordinate Growth, 193–94
Subordinate role, 130
Succorance, 129, 365
Supporting, 29, 43, 63, 227–34
Supporting and Mentoring, 225–27, 229–32, 234
Supportive Boss, 552–61 *passim*
Survey of Leadership Practices (measure), 46, 188, 192, 199–200
Survey of Management Attitudes (measure), 104
Survey of Management Practices (measure), 46, 148, 188, 192, 195–96

## T

Tacit Knowledge Inventory for Managers (measure), 495–96, 501f
Task/security orientation, 54, 220, 240–44
Teaching others, 54
Team Building, 46, 53, 193–94, 198, 226
Teaming with Other Executives, 200ff
Team Orientation, 538–42
Technical Competence, 200ff
Technical knowledge and information, 133
Temperamental, 266
Thematic Apperception Test (measure), 115, 308, 312–13
Theoretical values, 142
Thinking, 366
Thinking (T) or Feeling (F), 52, 340, 382–83, 398–401, 404, 408–15 *passim*, 442f, 449–54 *passim*, 490–91, 499, 543
This I Believe (TIB) Test (measure), 513, 516
Thorough, 362
Time emphasis, 46, 193–95, 197
Time span, 309
Timid, 362
Tolerance, 366, 499
Tolerance of Uncertainty, 53, 118, 124, 128
Total Sarnoff, 129
Tough-minded–Tender-minded, 469–73, 475
Trusting-Suspicious, 469–73, 475
Trust Leadership, 310f, 318–21
Trustworthy, 46

## U

Unambitious, 362
Uncertainty, tolerance of, 334
Unconcerned, 51
Undisciplined Self-conflict–Following Self-image, 469–73, 475
Upward Communications, 193ff, 197

## V

Values Compatible with Mine, 202
Variety, 411
Verbal Aptitude (measure), 157–58, 166f
Verbal Comprehension, 461, 463
Vigor, 51, 423, 429–30
Vision, 46, 200–201
Vision/Imagination, 200, 202
Vision of new possibilities, 381

## W

Weak, 361f
Wechsler Intelligence Scale, 457, 460–63
Well-Being, 364, 366, 463
Wise, 362
Withdrawn, 362
Work Conditions Survey, 115, 121

Work Facilitation, 194–95, 197
Working Conditions, 269
Work involvement, 117, 127
Work orientation, 124, 129, 366
World at Peace, 442, 445, 447f
World of Beauty, 447f
Worrying, 361f
Written communication skills, 128, 532